Summer's Crown

Stephen Chalke

Summer's Crown

The Story of Cricket's County Championship

Stephen Chalke

FAIRFIELD BOOKS

Fairfield Books
17 George's Road, Bath BA1 6EY
tel: 01225-335813
www.fairfieldbooks.org.uk

First published 2015

ISBN: 978 0 9568511 5 4

Jacket design by Robert Taylor
Page layout by Stephen Chalke

Printed and bound in Great Britain by
CPI Group, Croydon, Surrey

CONTENTS

Statistics

I am most grateful to Peter Griffiths of the CricketArchive website for generating the statistics I have used in this book.

This is not primarily a statistical book, but I have included some facts and figures where they have been of interest or thrown light on a topic. In the Appendix I have analysed the way the game has changed, and Peter's help in creating the spreadsheets on which these pages are based was essential.

Sometimes, in writing about a player, I have referred to records that relate exclusively to county championship cricket; sometimes I have referred to all first-class cricket. I hope that, where necessary, I have made the distinction clear. I have not, however, wanted to clutter the book with excessive references to statistics.

If you are in doubt, visit the CricketArchive website. It is remarkably comprehensive.

Illustrations

I am especially grateful to Roger Mann for his help in finding so many historical photographs for this book. Images from his collection appear on the following pages:

35, 52a, 61, 67, 73a, 73b, 75, 77, 86a, 87c, 89, 90, 91, 92a, 92b, 92c, 92d, 95a, 104a, 104b, 105b, 105c, 106, 108a, 108b, 111a, 111b, 113a, 113d, 124, 125, 127, 128, 131a, 131b, 131c, 133a, 133c, 133d, 133e, 139, 142a, 142b, 143b, 144, 148, 151a, 151b, 153c, 161a, 161c, 167b, 170, 179b, 179c, 205a, 211a, 331b

I am also especially grateful to the photographer Graham Morris and his wife Diana who have worked hard to provide me with photographs taken by Graham. His images appear on the following pages:

19, 25, 29, 39, 41, 43, 45, 49, 51, 244a, 244b, 245a, 249, 263, 264a, 264b, 265a, 265c, 268, 284a, 284b, 285b, 285c, 290, 291, 303a, 306a, 313b, 332b, 332c and Mushtaq on the front cover

My thanks are due to many others who have been so helpful in providing photographs and particularly to Matt Buxton of MB Media Solutions for his assistance in sourcing some of them.
They appear by kind permission as follows:

Getty Images: 13a, 21, 37, 52b, 140, 146, 180, 183a, 191, 200b, 201b, 201c, 212d, 221, 222a, 222b, 223a, 223c, 226a, 226b, 231a, 231b, 231c, 231d, 232, 245b, 245c, 247, 251, 252, 257, 265b, 269a, 269b, 271, 273a, 277a, 277b, 277c, 283, 285a, 287, 293a, 293b, 297a, 297b, 297c, 303b, 306b, 307a, 307b, 309a, 309b, 309c, 311, 312a, 312b, 313a, 313c, 315, 326 and the main image on the front cover

PA Photos: 23, 31, 164a, 165b, 184, 189a, 199, 211b, 243, 266, 289, 295, 310a, 310b

Christopher Saunders: 149, 167c, 178a, 192c, 192d, 235a, 331a

Essex CCC: 182a, 182b, 182c, 182d   Hampshire Cricket Archive: 13b, 208, 286
Michael Down: 178b, 179a, 189b, 193b   Nottinghamshire CCC: 167d, 192a, 192b, 255
Patrick Eagar: 27, 200a, 224, 248a   Ken Taylor: 185a, 185b, 185c;

Sarah Ansell: 305a; BBC: 288; Neville Chadwick: 33, 275; Vernon East: 235b; Mary Evans Library: 147; Geraint Jones: 305b; Mirrorpix: 205b; Rex Features: 214; Don Shepherd: 223b; Micky Stewart: 204; Surrey CCC: 164b; The Times: 227; David Wilkinson: 193c, 332a; Worthing Cricket Club: 207.

The line drawings on page 72 are from the magazine *Cricket Field* in 1893.

Fairfield Books has tried to find out the owners of all the photographs still within copyright and, if any photographic source believes that we have omitted one that is theirs, they should contact us to rectify the matter.

About this book

This book is the story of cricket's county championship. It is a competition that emerged out of Victorian England's desire for organised sport; it has stumbled through repeated crises of finance and structure, and it is still with us, still at the heart of English cricket in the 21st century.

The book is arranged in self-contained double-page spreads so that it can be opened wherever the reader fancies. It is also set out chronologically so that readers, if they so wish, may travel sequentially through the years.

The book begins with a spread on each county; they are, if you like, the dramatis personae. Then the body of the book is given to the history, which is presented in decades and which spotlights special players and teams, entertaining stories, fascinating images and some broader themes. Finally there is an appendix, a mixture of fact, analysis, ancillary information and quirky stories. The quirky things always appeal to me, and I have tried to find space for them through the book.

With 18 counties and 125 years to cover, it is not possible to be comprehensive in 350 pages. In making choices about what is and is not included, I have tried to retain some objectivity, but inevitably there are stories and characters included because they are of particular appeal to me.

The county championship has not stayed still for long. It has been repeatedly adapted, sometimes at a dizzying pace, to meet the challenges of each age. Cricket remains cricket throughout, however, and my intention is always to celebrate a competition that has given great pleasure down the years.

It is not entirely clear at what date the county championship began its formal existence. A consensus seems to have emerged around the year 1890 so this book, coming out in 2015, can be seen as marking the competition's 125th anniversary.

Will the championship survive for a 150th anniversary, even a 200th? If it does, and if somebody writes a fresh history, I am certain there will be as many new characters and stories to celebrate as can be found here. Cricket is a wonderful game for testing and revealing character and for generating stories. It is the best of games.

Stephen Chalke

England and Wales Cricket Board

I would like to thank the England and Wales Cricket Board for its generous support with the cost of producing this book. Without that help, the book would not have been possible in this form. However, if there is anything in the book that is not right, that is entirely my responsibility.

Introduction

The county championship has struggled repeatedly to find a satisfactory format, and it has for most of its history been financially unviable. Yet somehow, from Victorian times through to the 21st century, it has kept going – and without the loss of a single county along the way. It is a remarkable tale of survival against the odds, a survival which reflects the affection the competitition has inspired.

It took shape in the last quarter of the 19th century, in the years in which there emerged so many of our great sporting contests: the Football League, the All-England Tennis Championships, the Rugby Union Home Internationals, the modern Olympic Games. The first international cricket was played, with privately raised teams visiting Australia, who in turn sent sides to England, playing matches that would come to be called Tests. They drew large crowds but not on the scale of the big county matches. By the late 1880s the bank-holiday contests between Surrey and Nottinghamshire, the two leading sides, were generating an excitement as great as cricket had ever known.

The newspapers and sporting annuals took to printing a league table and to crowning a champion county. Yet for some years this was only an informal title, with publications reaching contradictory conclusions, at times not even agreeing which counties were participating in the contest. Then Kent's Lord Harris, the great power in English cricket at that time, created a Cricket Council, who devised a set of regulations. In 1890, for the first time, the counties began the summer with an agreed system for deciding the champions.

There were eight counties in 1890: the Big Six of Surrey, Middlesex and Kent in the south, Yorkshire, Lancashire and Nottinghamshire in the north, together with Sussex, the oldest of the county clubs, and WG Grace's Gloucestershire. Such was the immediate success of the championship that by 1899 their number had swollen to 15.

With the expansion of the competition, it was not possible to stage an all-plays-all, home-and-away league as Association Football did. In 1900 Lancashire, Yorkshire and Surrey had enough professionals to play a full 28 inter-county matches, but Somerset, largely amateur, were at full stretch with 16.

There was a minimum number of games that had to be played and, to gain admission, a county had to persuade enough of the existing counties to give them home and away fixtures. In 1905, a year in which the Australians were touring, the required number was set at only six, and

Northamptonshire, who had won the Minor Counties Championship in the previous two years, found six counties prepared to play home and away against them. They had a membership of only 600, they were £1,000 in debt, and they had to make substantial improvements to the facilities at their ground. But, full of optimism, they launched a fund-raising appeal, and they became the 16th county.

Did it make sense that they were admitted when Durham and Staffordshire remained among the minor counties? Almost certainly not. But that was the County Championship. Rather like the British Constitution, it emerged in its own haphazard way, and it survived and adapted to the consequences. Indeed, it was not long before influential voices were complaining that there were too many counties and that the whole edifice had become unwieldy.

If it had not been for the First World War, it is likely that the number of counties would have diminished. In August 1914, at a point of no return financially, both Gloucestershire and Worcestershire called members' meetings with a view to withdrawing from the championship for 1915.

War took its toll, with almost a third of the cricketers of 1914 not playing in the championship again, but ironically war helped the balance sheets of the counties. With no cricket, their expenditure was minimal, but many members continued loyally to pay their subscriptions.

Worcestershire sat out the 1919 season, when crowds flocked back to cricket after the hiatus, but in 1920 they returned, bringing the championship up once more to 16 teams. The next year it rose to 17 when Glamorgan, only a middling team in the Minor Counties, charmed nine of the county clubs into granting them a pair of fixtures.

For the first nine years after the war, up till the start of 1928, there were only three Test-playing countries: England, Australia and South Africa. Australia toured in 1921 and 1926, South Africa in 1924. In the other six summers there was only county cricket, and it was capable of drawing great crowds. On August Bank Holiday Monday in 1926 a record 46,000 people crammed into Old Trafford for the Roses match, with many more turned away.

That was a holiday-time fixture, a local rivalry between the two outstanding counties of the age. There was a great gulf between the strongest and the weakest counties, however, and among the strugglers the picture was different. Glamorgan and Worcestershire were two that were always close to bankruptcy, often searching for players. In 1925 Worcestershire made up their side with a 57-year-old vicar whose most recent first-class appearance had been for a Liverpool and District XI in 1893.

Some counties in the south employed few professionals. At one point in the 1920s Somerset had only two on their staff. Partly that was born of financial necessity but also, for most of those who sat on the committees of the southern clubs, it was seen as a desirable state of affairs. Cricket was a gentleman's game; its special ethos would best be upheld if it were not dominated by those who were paid to play.

In club cricket in the south of England there were no leagues till the late 1960s. Indeed, it was a rule of the influential Club Cricket Conference that its member clubs did not participate in competitions. By contrast, in the north and parts of the midlands, the leagues and knock-out cups had started in the 19th century, and they produced cricketers with a harder approach to the game than those playing for Kent and Sussex. The difference led at times to conflict, with Middlesex threatening to withdraw from fixtures against a Yorkshire team whom they found over-aggressive. But mostly, with the county teams reflecting the cricket played within their boundaries, the differences in tradition added to the richness and the variety of the competition.

The system for deciding the champion county went through many changes, not made easier by the wide variation in the number of matches each county arranged. In 1919 Yorkshire played 26 while their nearest rivals Kent played 14. In theory a county could win the championship by not playing the tougher fixtures, but this was not what happened. The stronger teams generated the biggest crowds; they were the ones everybody wanted to play. By contrast, it was the 1930s before Middlesex agreed to fixtures against Glamorgan and Northamptonshire.

In the early informal years of inter-county cricket many publications awarded the title of champion to the county which had lost fewest matches. As pitches and batting techniques improved, this led to some high-scoring draws, particularly as there was no procedure for declaring an innings. So 'wins minus losses' became the agreed system but, with uneven numbers of fixtures, this had to be divided by matches: but should the draws be included in that calculation or not? The system changed back and forth, never wholly satisfactory.

In 1920 the counties introduced points for first-innings lead in drawn games, but this had its drawbacks. If the reward for first-innings lead was too great, it encouraged teams to settle for that and not push for victory, a policy Lancashire adopted successfully, becoming champions in 1930 when they won five fewer games than Gloucestershire.

Time and again the points system was changed to correct the unforeseen consequence of the previous change. The simple truth was that three-day cricket did not lend itself as easily to a league system as a 90-minute football match.

In 1928, for the first time since 1894, the counties agreed to arrange the same number of fixtures – though not all against all, that would have been an impossible 32 games. This helped the logic of the competition, but in the midst of a severe economic depression it put too much strain on the lesser counties. After four years it was scrapped.

In the 1930s Leicestershire discussed an amalgamation with Lincolnshire, while the fortunes of Northamptonshire sank to rock bottom. After winning the first game of 1935 they went four years without victory. When war was declared at the end of the 1939 season, as at the end of 1914, the majority of counties were in a bad way financially.

Between 1922 and 1939 the championship was won every year by one of the four most northerly counties: Yorkshire, Lancashire, Derbyshire and Nottinghamshire. Further south, there was a more leisurely quality to the cricket, less sense that the winning was the be-all and end-all of it. For many of the spectators the matches were primarily social occasions, none more so than the festivals: Kent at Canterbury and Tonbridge, Sussex at Eastbourne, Gloucestershire at Cheltenham, Somerset at Bath. Cricket was part of the social calendar of the well-to-do.

With the exception of Leicestershire for one season in 1935, all the counties were captained by amateurs, some of whom did not warrant a place in the eleven. They came from the public schools, were of the officer class and were expected to uphold the social and moral values of the game. Early in his career with Surrey the great fast bowler Alf Gover, after a frustrating bowling spell, snatched his sweater and cap from the umpire. He realised his discourtesy, apologising immediately, but that was not enough for his captain Percy Fender. At close of play Gover was summoned to the captain's room and told that, if there were ever a repetition of the incident, he would never play for the county again. "You must learn to control yourself. You're a Surrey cricketer. You should be proud of that."

Such high-minded amateur captaincy has been swept away now, consigned to the dustbin along with much of the snobbery that accompanied it. Now we have an all-professional game, one in which winning is paramount, and in 2014 Yorkshire's captain Andrew Gale was banned for ill-discipline from the season's last two matches and from receiving the trophy on the day it was won.

Sometimes the amateur captain's idea of looking after the game went beyond matters of good conduct as Charlie Parker, the slow-left-arm bowler, discovered before the First War when he was leg-glanced repeatedly by Ranjitsinhji. "Excuse me, sir," he said to his Gloucestershire captain. "Do you think you could move second slip to the leg side, to stop that shot?" The captain looked at him with withering contempt: "Good God, man, are you trying to spoil the game?"

Attitudes moved on between the wars, but not that much. "Now listen to me," Surrey's Douglas Jardine once admonished a young, public-school-educated leg-spinner. "You and I are amateurs. It is only professionals who ask to have their field shifted when they're hit for four."

Geoffrey Howard, the distinguished post-war Secretary at Old Trafford and the Oval, played three games for Middlesex in 1930. He had taken a fortnight's leave from his position at Martin's Bank, and on the first day at Lord's he found himself batting in mid-afternoon against Charlie Parker. After a while Bev Lyon, the Gloucestershire captain, turned to Walter Hammond at slip. "Take over for half an hour, will you, Wally? I'm going for a haircut."

Dennis Brookes started his long professional career with Northamptonshire in the 1930s. "At the Oval," he recalled, "you could have as many drinks at lunch as you wanted, and they used to have Pimm's Number One. I can remember some of our senior players, they used to be a bit high by the time they went out. After the war they stopped that. It was just a pint of beer or its equivalent. In the pre-war days, it was very carefree, very enjoyable."

When county cricket resumed in 1946, the people, starved of entertainment, flocked to the games, just as they had done in 1919, and for some years 'Ground Full' signs were a common sight on Saturdays. In the golden summer of 1947, when the sun shone gloriously on the stirring deeds of Denis Compton and Bill Edrich, cricket did much to lift a people worn down by war and rationing. But Brian Castor, the Surrey Secretary, was right when one day, surveying the great crowd at the Oval, he turned to his assistant Geoffrey Howard: "It won't always be like this, you know," he said.

Castor was a traditionalist, a High Tory who had suffered as a prisoner of the Japanese and who longed to return Britain to the way it had been in the 1930s. Howard, grandson of the pioneer of garden cities, was a Fabian reformer, and he was looking to move cricket forward to cope with the changed realities of post-war Britain. They argued constantly in a good-natured way: "He called me a Communist," Howard recalled. "Anybody who wasn't a Tory was a Communist. We worked in the same office, and one day he got irritated with me to the extent that he swept his glasses off and threw them at me. It was near the end of the day, and before long we were both on our hands and knees in the half-light, searching for the glasses and laughing at ourselves."

The difference in their outlook went to the heart of the matter for English cricket – and for English society. In the 1950s, with the Conservative Party in power, the old traditions prevailed. County cricket, still benefiting from the tail-end of its post-war boom, had a rare decade of stability, its format remaining unaltered, and the England cricket team went seven years without losing a series.

Yet, beneath that tranquil surface, all was not well. The crowds were thinning, partly as a result of several wet summers and partly because other attractions were opening up with the rise of the motor car, the television set and the foreign holiday.

By the start of the 1960s county cricket was once more in a financial mess. Some counties, mainly in the midlands, had supporters' associations which raised money through football-pool schemes, a venture which brought unaccustomed wealth to Warwickshire but which the grander, prouder counties, such as Surrey and Yorkshire, rejected as vulgar.

Reflecting the spirit of the age, county cricket shook off its conservatism and embarked on a period of radical change. From the summer of 1963, well ahead of all other sports (except table tennis), cricket abolished the distinction between amateurs and professionals, a distinction that in the post-war years had only been maintained by a great deal of humbug and sleight of hand. And in the same summer it launched a knock-out cup, based on one-day games in which each team batted for a maximum of 65 overs.

In 1966, in several championship matches, cricket took on the powerful Lord's Day Observance Society, becoming the first sport to venture into Sunday play. In 1968 each county was allowed to recruit one overseas player without any period of residential qualification. Then in 1969, recognising the great success of the knock-out cup, a 40-over Sunday League was established. Amid all this there were countless experimental changes in the regulations, all designed to make the game more attractive. Contrary to the popular caricature, cricket was the sport quickest to embrace change.

The pace of life in England was becoming faster. People were entertained nightly by television, and they expected more excitement from their cricket than they had in earlier years. Furthermore, amid the technological advances, attention spans were growing shorter. The old, slow-moving world of the three-day county championship was out of kilter with the age.

Many regretted the changes, none more than Tom Cartwright, the great Warwickshire all-rounder of the 1960s. Brought up amid the car factories of Coventry, he was a lifelong socialist, but he mourned the passing of many aspects of the world in which he had grown up.

"There was much more of a rhythm of life then. A rhythm of going to work and coming home at the same time each day, a rhythm of learning a trade and progressing with it, a rhythm even in people's leisure pursuits, and it gave people good manners and a consideration for others. People had settled lives. They did things which were within their reach – going out into the country, doing the garden, spending a day at cricket. Now people are striving for things they can't attain, the structures break down and the natural rhythm is lost."

Could county cricket have stayed true to its old self, defiantly upheld its traditional image with its high ideals of sportsmanship? Or would that have led to its slow death, suffering the same fate as the once-thriving music halls and English seaside resorts? The Victorian Britain in which the championship had sprung to life was not the Britain of the mini-car, the Beatles and the package holiday in Benidorm. Even the stately homes were staging pop concerts to survive.

The 1970s were years of revival for county cricket. The first wave of overseas players brought fresh glamour, and there was great success in attracting commercial sponsorship. By 1972 there were three one-day tournaments sharing the summer with the championship, and that in time gave all 17 counties the experience of winning a trophy. It was an age of greater equality, with the championship won by nine different counties in the nine years from 1968.

The winning of trophies was important now as it had not been for most counties in earlier times, and this was reinforced when prize money was introduced into the championship in 1973. At that time 1973 was considered to be the competition's centenary and, to mark this, the Lord's Taverners charity presented a trophy. They arranged that it would be presented by their Patron, the Duke of Edinburgh, at Buckingham Palace, an annual ceremony that still survives.

Though the balance sheets were healthier in the 1970s, the county championship did not stand still for long. In most summers since the war, the counties had all played 28 matches, and the rise of one-day cricket saw a reduction to 24, then to 20. Then, concerned that the England players were not appearing often enough, it rose back to 22, then 24.

Bonus points were introduced, adding to the complexity of the point-scoring system, but the greatest change came in 1981 when the counties opted for the full covering of pitches whenever it rained. Then in 1988 the programme included some four-day matches, with the full switch to that format coming five years later. At that point, with Durham having become the 18th county, the programme was reduced to 17 games, each county playing each other once. It was a symmetry that had last existed in 1894.

'The County Championship is the true Grand National of cricket,' the Sussex captain John Barclay wrote in his book about the summer of 1981. 'It is a complete examination of skills and techniques, run over a course that takes in widely varying conditions and surfaces, and littered with testing obstacles, where the unexpected is never far away. It stretches every nerve and sinew of the body and brain and, above all else, is a great test of stamina.'

That was its traditional charm. Woven into the fabric of the English summer, it surfaced on grounds all over England, a pattern of matches whose scores each day on the sports pages captured the imagination of millions. For the players, it was six days a week for four months, often with demanding rail or road journeys between matches. It was a course for stayers, not thoroughbreds.

In its own way, it was part of that rhythm of life that Tom Cartwright so loved. Rooted in counties not cities, it reeked of an older world; its sense of tradition was part of its appeal.

Yet that was not enough by the 1990s. Britain had undergone an economic revolution, a stripping out of so many old attitudes in the name of improved efficiency and greater international competitiveness. Success was everything now; there was no room for those who simply muddled along.

The England cricket team had been overtaken by countries it had once beaten easily. Late in the 1990s it lay at the foot of the Test-playing rankings, below even Zimbabwe, and the England and Wales Cricket Board turned for fresh thinking to a former chairman of the supermarket chain Tesco, one of the great success stories of the economic revolution. His starting point was clear: a strong England team was the number one priority; everything below that should be working towards that goal.

Once more the county championship submitted itself to a radical overhaul. From 2000, in search of an extra competitive edge, two divisions were created, with promotion and relegation, a proposal that WG Grace had argued for a century earlier. Also the England cricketers were given central contracts, only appearing for their counties when England so wished.

There were so many developments. Concern about the quality of pitches had led to the importation of standard loams throughout the country which, with the decline in out-grounds and the covering of pitches, led in turn to a reduction in the variety of the surfaces used on the circuit. This, coupled with the impact of the limited-overs game, hastened a decline in spin bowling. In 1950, 56 per cent of all wickets in the championship were taken by slow bowlers; in 2014, it was 19 per cent.

The first wave of specially registered overseas players stayed with their counties for many years, but by the 1990s the top Test cricketers were much better paid, they had a more demanding schedule, and in most cases their appearances in county cricket were less substantial. They were less loyal to one county.

In their place came a second string of overseas cricketers who, by the rulings of the courts, often managed to avoid the restrictions on imported players. There was also a much greater movement of players between counties, movement that increased significantly after the creation of two divisions, so that the county sides changed their personnel much faster than in former times – and fewer players had roots within the counties they represented. As with the standardising of pitches, this created a homogeneity that removed some of the earlier character of county cricket.

The world is now a smaller place. No longer could a young Gloucestershire supporter look at a visiting Yorkshire team as John Light, now the county's President, did in the 1950s: "To us Cotswolds lads," he recalls, "they were like a visiting Test team from a distant Northern kingdom."

The teams may be less distinct from each other, less representative of their areas, but the creation of two divisions has increased the gap between the strong and the weak counties, back perhaps to where it was in the 1930s. As with the nation's economy, the emphasis on success has been accompanied by a widening gulf between rich and poor. So at the close of 2014, with the debts of some counties running into many millions, it is possible to imagine, as it was in the 1930s, that the championship might lose a member or two.

Yet, 125 years on from 1890, it has not yet done so. It is still with us, with all its failings, and it is still the competition that the players themselves value most. Nottinghamshire's Alex Hales speaks for many: "I enjoy playing Twenty20 more," he says, "but I'd rather win the championship."

"County championship cricket is our English breeding ground for Test matches," Geoffrey Boycott says. "It's not just about the techniques of the batsman and bowler. It breeds character, it breeds courage, all the things which you cannot get out of one-day cricket. One-day cricket is fun cricket. I enjoy it, and there is some skill, but it's fun cricket."

He would return to uncovered pitches: three longer days, with the bowlers forced to bowl more overs an hour. He would also like to see the championship back as the centrepiece of the county schedule, not wedged into spring and autumn to allow the limited-overs tournaments pride of place in high summer. "If county championship cricket is our breeding ground, which all the chairmen and chief executives say, then why do they relegate it to what they do?"

If history is any guide, the county championship will undergo further change soon enough. Its format has never seemed wholly satisfactory for long, and it has seldom stood on its own feet financially. From aristocratic benefactors through football-pool schemes and commercial sponsors to Sky television money, it has forever survived on handouts.

Yet survive it has – and, if the will is there, it will continue to survive. It does not hold centre stage in our sporting summer as it did in 1947. But no one who was present at Hove in 2003, when Sussex finally joined the list of champions, or at Taunton in 2011, when Lancashire won again after 61 years, or at Trent Bridge in 2014, when a Yorkshire eleven with nine home-grown players revived their proud tradition, could believe that the championship no longer matters.

At the close of 2014 George Dobell, writing on *Cricinfo*, reflected on the success of the young England players who had emerged that summer from the county game:

> Like the NHS, a reliable car and the health of your parents, county cricket will probably never be fully appreciated until it's gone ... It is too easy to point out the empty seats in the stands, the overdrafts at the bank and the fact that one or two teams always appear to be on the brink of ruin. And it's too easy to conclude that it doesn't matter and that few people care about it ... Yet the roots of almost everything good in English cricket can still be found in the county game. And if all involved just believed in it a little more, it could produce an even richer harvest.

Amen to that.

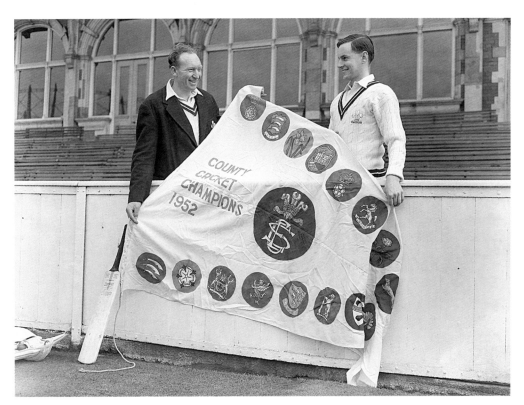

1952: The first year of the championship pennant

Stuart Surridge and Peter May display it outside the Oval pavilion

1973: The first year of the Lord's Taverners Trophy, presented always at Buckingham Palace

Richard Gilliat of Hampshire holds the cup while Prince Philip jokes with Peter Sainsbury

The Counties

Counties by population and area			
	Area *(sq miles)* 1891	**Population** *(000s)* 1891	1961
Derbyshire	872	432	877
Durham	1,195	1,024	1,516
Essex	1,414	761	2,288
Glamorgan	900	693	1,230
Gloucestershire	1,123	549	1,002
Hampshire	1,636	666	1,337
Kent	1,515	806	1,702
Lancashire	2,041	3,958	5,129
Leicestershire	862	379	683
Middlesex	279	575	2,235
Northamptonshire	1,003	308	398
Nottinghamshire	963	505	903
Somerset	1,659	510	599
Surrey	707	572	1,731
Sussex	1,480	555	1,078
Warwickshire	972	802	2,025
Worcestershire	690	442	570
Yorkshire	5,820	3,219	4,726

County boundaries have changed greatly since 1961 –
particularly in the case of Middlesex, which no longer exists.

For this reason it is difficult to establish
comparable figures for their current populations.

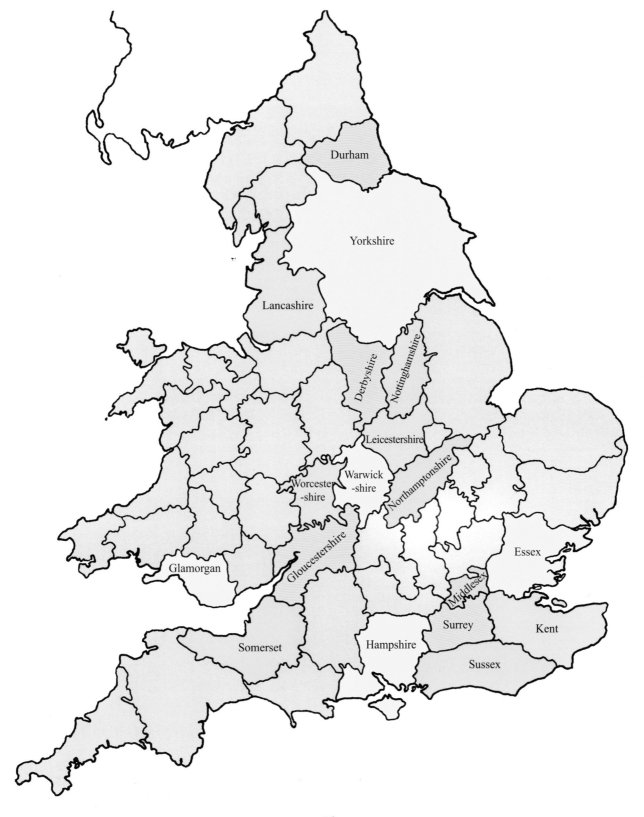

Derbyshire

Present county club formed: 1870
Joined county championship: 1895
Number of championships: 1

The county club was formed with great enthusiasm in the Grand Jury Room of the Town Hall, Derby, in November 1870. "The physique of Derbyshire men bears comparison with that of men in any other county," one speaker said, and so at first it proved. They beat Lancashire in their inaugural game, and for many years *Wisden* listed them as champion county for 1874 – on the basis that in their only four matches, against Kent and Lancashire, they had remained unbeaten.

Life became tougher in the 1880s. They lost badly in every game in 1886 and, as a result, suffered the unique fate of being stripped of their first-class status. Worse was to follow when their assistant secretary – Sam Richardson, captain in their famous first victory – absconded to Spain with £1,000 of club funds. There, under an assumed name, he lived till 1938, becoming the king's personal tailor.

Derbyshire regained first-class status in 1894, joined the championship in 1895 and, after a promising start, bumped along in the foothills of the competition for thirty years. Their record in 1920 – played 18, lost 17, one abandoned without a ball bowled – remains the worst by any county.

Then came the glory years when Arthur Richardson moulded a team of mostly local men, several from the pits, and they crowned a run of good seasons with the 1936 championship.

They were a strong team again in the 1950s when, led by Donald Carr, they had in Les Jackson and Cliff Gladwin as good a pair of opening bowlers as any in England. The two thrived on the county's green pitches, maintaining a tradition of seam bowling that continued with Harold Rhodes, Alan Ward and Mike Hendrick. They also had a superb keeper in Bob Taylor, the fifth and finest in a line of stumpers that stretched across almost every Derbyshire summer from 1890 to 1984.

Recent years have been hard. There was one golden summer in 1996, when the Australian Dean Jones flew in and lifted them to the verge of a second championship, but it all imploded midway through the next year with multiple resignations.

The coal mines have largely gone, and the membership is the smallest of the first-class counties. But in 2012, with no stars and against all predictions, they won the second division. Though there was barely a Derbyshire man among them, their spirit would have made that man in the Grand Jury Room proud.

> As I look back, a certain damp greyness seems to pervade all. The score at tea is likely to be 180 for eight as batsmen struggle for survival and all is aggressive hostility and combative drama. The folk heroes are bowlers; they reign supreme ... Derbyshire cricket is more functional and dramatic than ornate and artistic, just as are the bleak hills, stone walls and grey villages of this small county.
> *Guy Willatt, 1970*

COUNTY CHAMPIONSHIP PLACINGS YEAR BY YEAR

1890	91	92	93	94	95	96	97	98	99	1900	01	02	03	04	05	06	07	08	09	10	11	12	13	14		19	20	21	22	23	24	25	26
-	-	-	-	-	5	7	14	9	15	13	15	10	12	10	14	16	16	14	15	15	14	12	13	12		9	16	12	11	10	17	14	11

27	28	29	30	31	32	33	34	35	36	37	38	39		46	47	48	49	50	51	52	53	54	55	56	57	58	59	60	61	62	63	64	65
5	10	7	9	7	10	6	3	2	1	3	5	9		15	5	6	15	5	11	4	6	3	8	12	4	5	7	5	7	7	17	12	9

66	67	68	69	70	71	72	73	74	75	76	77	78	79	80	81	82	83	84	85	86	87	88	89	90	91	92	93	94	95	96	97	98	99
9	6	8	16	7	17	17	16	17	15	15	7	14	16	9	12	11	9	12	13	11	6	14	6	12	3	5	15	17	14	2	16	10	9

2000	01	02	03	04	05	06	07	08	09	10	11	12	13	14
D1	D2	D2	D2	D2	D2	D2	D2	D2	D2	D2	D2	D2	D1	D2
9	9	6	9	8	9	5	6	6	6	9	5	1	8	4

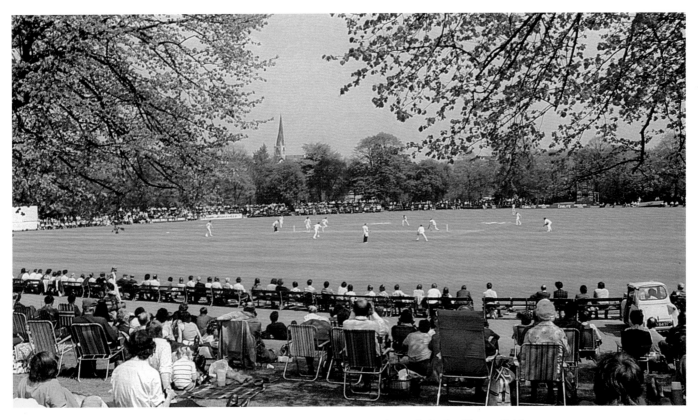

Queen's Park, Chesterfield

Set in a Victorian park, overlooked by the famous crooked spire, the ground has long been one of county cricket's delights. The crowds are knowledgeable, and the matches have thrown up many special moments: from the 554-run partnership of Yorkshire's Brown and Tunnicliffe in 1898 to the 163 hit by the Essex number eleven Peter Smith in 1947. Derbyshire dropped the ground after 1998, but they were back by 2006. Queen's Park was too special to lose.

County championship matches (1895-2014)		
Most runs	Kim Barnett	22,948
	Denis Smith	19,575
Most wickets	Les Jackson	1,578
	Cliff Gladwin	1,490
Most appearances	Derek Morgan	506

Post-war only (1946-2014)		
Most runs	Kim Barnett	22,948
	Derek Morgan	16,810
Most wickets	Les Jackson	1,578
	Cliff Gladwin	1,490
Most appearances	Derek Morgan	506

Last 25 years (1990-2014)		
Most runs	Kim Barnett	11,039
	Chris Adams	7,189
Most wickets	Dominic Cork	492
	Devon Malcolm	379
Most appearances	Karl Krikken	194

Championship grounds			
	First	*Last*	*Matches*
Derby – County Ground	1895	2014	621
Chesterfield – Queen's Park	1898	2014	374
Glossop – North Road	1899	1910	14
Blackwell – Miners Welfare Ground	1909	1913	7
Burton-on-Trent – Town Ground	1914	1937	13
Ilkeston – Rutland Recreation Ground	1925	1994	89
Buxton – The Park	1930	1986	41
Burton-on-Trent – Ind Coope Ground	1938	1980	35
Sheffield – Abbeydale Park	1946	1947	2
Heanor – Town Ground	1987	1987	1

Durham

Present county club formed: 1882
Joined county championship: 1992
Number of championships: 3

Perhaps, if they had not been so far north, Durham would have joined the county championship much sooner. They were joint winners of the first Minor Counties Championship in 1895, yet the next summer they could persuade only two counties, Northants and neighbouring Northumberland, to visit them.

With their best players migrating south, Durham remained in the minor ranks, leaving the cricketing passion of the north-east to find its outlet in local leagues, notably the Durham Senior League which, according to one writer in 1952, 'as a cricket nursery must rival any other league in the country ... with average gates around the three thousand mark.'

For many years Durham played an annual fixture against the summer's tourists, the only minor county to do so. Against the 1959 Indians, a roly-poly 17-year-old grammar-school boy from Burnopfield, Colin Milburn, hit a sparkling century and was promptly signed by Northamptonshire.

The Gillette Cup gave the minor counties a chance to take on their betters, and in 1973, against Yorkshire at Harrogate, Durham were the first to upset the form book. Twelve years later they repeated their success against a Derbyshire side that included Michael Holding. Between those triumphs they went five years unbeaten in the Minor Counties Championship.

It had long seemed illogical that the north-east had no first-class county, and in 1988, tired of "churning out youngsters for other counties", they set about changing that. Led by Don Robson, Labour leader of the county council, they tapped into a great groundswell of support, raising one million pounds – "People were ringing me up offering to help, rather than me ringing them" – and winning over the Test and County Cricket Board with their ambitious enthusiasm.

Geoff Cook, their first Director of Cricket, was a pivotal figure, returning to the north-east from Northampton. In the early years, with the best young talent already having left, he assembled a team of seasoned professionals, with Ian Botham the talismanic signing. Then gradually the home-grown players emerged, among them Steve Harmison, who opened the bowling for England when Test cricket came to Chester-le-Street in 2003. Five years later he took the wicket that brought the county its first championship. Durham might be a long way north, but it was no longer off the map of English cricket.

> To the sports fanatics of the north-east mere participation in the county championship is a revelation and, though the end results were disappointing, they were not disheartened. At the conclusion of the last match, many came onto the field to shake each player personally by the hand. "Eet's been a canny first season," they said, "and we canner wait for the next."
>
> *Simon Hughes, 1992*

COUNTY CHAMPIONSHIP PLACINGS YEAR BY YEAR

1890	91	92	93	94	95	96	97	98	99	1900	01	02	03	04	05	06	07	08	09	10	11	12	13	14		19	20	21	22	23	24	25	26
-	-	-	-	-	-	-	-	-	-	-	-	-	-	-	-	-	-	-	-	-	-	-	-	-		-	-	-	-	-	-	-	-

27	28	29	30	31	32	33	34	35	36	37	38	39		46	47	48	49	50	51	52	53	54	55	56	57	58	59	60	61	62	63	64	65
-	-	-	-	-	-	-	-	-	-	-	-	-		-	-	-	-	-	-	-	-	-	-	-	-	-	-	-	-	-	-	-	-

66	67	68	69	70	71	72	73	74	75	76	77	78	79	80	81	82	83	84	85	86	87	88	89	90	91	92	93	94	95	96	97	98	99
-	-	-	-	-	-	-	-	-	-	-	-	-	-	-	-	-	-	-	-	-	-	-	-	-	-	18	18	16	17	18	17	14	8

			2000	01	02	03	04	05	06	07	08	09	10	11	12	13	14
			D1	D2	D2	D2	D2	D2	D1	D1	D1	D1	D1	D1	D1	D1
			8	8	9	6	9	2	7	2	1	1	5	3	6	1	5

The Racecourse, Durham

The large, open field beside the River Wear was one of five grounds used by Durham before their Riverside development at Chester-le-Street became ready.

The county fared badly in championship games there – six defeats and a rain-ruined draw – but the ground was the scene of many special moments: Sachin Tendulkar's only hundred for Yorkshire, Ian Botham's last first-class match when the Australian tourists were forced to follow on and, above all, the first fixtures of Durham's first summer: the Sunday League victory over Lancashire, watched by a full house of 6,000, and the historic first championship game against Leicestershire.

The horse racing had long gone, banished in 1887 by university landlords disturbed by their students' gambling.

County championship matches (1992-2014)		
Most runs	Dale Benkenstein	8,734
	Paul Collingwood	8,511
Most wickets	Simon Brown	472
	Steve Harmison	445
Most appearances	Phil Mustard	166

Championship grounds			
	First	*Last*	*Matches*
Durham – The Racecourse	1992	1994	7
Stockton-on-Tees – Grangefield Road	1992	2006	12
Darlington – Feethams	1992	2002	10
Hartlepool – Park Drive	1992	1997	8
Gateshead – Eastwood Gardens	1992	1994	4
Chester-le-Street – Riverside	1995	2014	147

Essex

Present county club formed: 1876

Joined county championship: 1895

Number of championships: 6

Essex County Cricket Club started life in 1876, playing in the small town of Brentwood, an old coaching stop on the road between London and Colchester. Ambitious for bigger crowds, they upset many of their early patrons by moving into East London in 1885. There they set up home in the fast-expanding suburb of Leyton; they built a grand pavilion and had visions of rivalling Middlesex and Surrey.

They made rapid progress, entering the championship in 1895. Then one Saturday in August 1897, in front of a wildly cheering crowd of 15,000, they beat Lancashire to go to the top of the table. Around the grounds of England, reported *The Times*, 'Essex cricket is the thing chiefly talked of.' Within a week, alas, they lost heavily to Surrey, and the dream was over.

It would be 81 years before they would again head the table in August, and during those years financial crisis was rarely far away. They sold their Leyton ground to the Army Sports Council in 1922, and eleven years later they moved out completely, beginning a life on the road that each summer saw them play a series of cricket weeks at settings that took in the full variety of the county: urban, rural and seaside.

The nomadic Essex developed an intimate connection with their local clubs. It was, as the writer Robertson-Glasgow put it, 'Community Cricket, a share-out of hopes and disappointments, of triumph and reverse. All of which makes for the best kind of entertainment. For entertainment is the healthy child of skill and laughter.'

In the 1950s, with Doug Insole as captain, there was plenty of entertainment. For two years the *News Chronicle* ran a Brighter Cricket Trophy, and both times Essex won it easily.

The finances, however, grew worse and worse, till the playing staff was down to twelve. The breakthrough came in the late 1960s when an interest-free loan from the Warwickshire Supporters' Association allowed them to buy a home ground at Chelmsford and to build a pavilion.

Through the long years of wandering they had never lost their sense of fun, and in the 1970s their great team spirit was a vital factor in their rise to success. It had taken them a long time to fulfil the dream of August 1897, but the Essex teams that Keith Fletcher and Graham Gooch captained made up for the wait, winning six championships in 14 years from 1979.

> Essex were, and still are, a great county to play for. I cannot think of any club where the players have gained more enjoyment from their cricket. Although they have played the game seriously and keenly, there has always been an abundance of laughter and humour. This is something to be proud of, because cricket which is not enjoyed is not worth playing.
>
> *Trevor Bailey, 1982*

COUNTY CHAMPIONSHIP PLACINGS YEAR BY YEAR

1890	91	92	93	94	95	96	97	98	99	1900	01	02	03	04	05	06	07	08	09	10	11	12	13	14		19	20	21	22	23	24	25	26
-	-	-	-	-	9	5	3	5	6	10	10	13	8	14	12	7	7	11	14	11	6	15	15	8		14	9	15	8	13	15	7	9

27	28	29	30	31	32	33	34	35	36	37	38	39		46	47	48	49	50	51	52	53	54	55	56	57	58	59	60	61	62	63	64	65
8	16	12	6	10	14	4	8	9	9	6	6	4		8	11	13	9	17	8	10	12	15	14	11	5	6	9	6	6	9	12	10	15

66	67	68	69	70	71	72	73	74	75	76	77	78	79	80	81	82	83	84	85	86	87	88	89	90	91	92	93	94	95	96	97	98	99
16	15	14	6	12	10	5	8	12	7	6	6	2	1	8	5	7	1	1	4	1	12	3	2	2	1	1	11	6	5	5	8	18	12

2000	01	02	03	04	05	06	07	08	09	10	11	12	13	14
D2	D1	D2	D1	D2	D2	D2	D2	D2	D2	D1	D2	D2	D2	D2
2	9	1	7	5	5	3	4	5	2	9	7	5	3	3

Castle Park, Colchester

The most attractive of Essex's many out-grounds, Castle Park is now the last survivor. The county came first in 1914, when a military band played in the intervals and a ball was held at the Officers' Club. A hundred years on, they play a different music at the 'T20 Blast'.

County championship matches (1895-2014)

Most runs	Percy Perrin	27,703
	Graham Gooch	27,571
Most wickets	Morris Nichols	1,518
	Peter Smith	1,512
Most appearances	Keith Fletcher	529

Post-war only (1946-2014)

Most runs	Graham Gooch	27,571
	Keith Fletcher	27,123
Most wickets	Trevor Bailey	1,449
	John Lever	1,380
Most appearances	Keith Fletcher	529

Last 25 years (1990-2014)

Most runs	Ronnie Irani	12,060
	Paul Prichard	10,385
Most wickets	Peter Such	506
	Mark Ilott	502
Most appearances	James Foster	205

Championship grounds

	First	Last	Matches
Leyton – County Ground	1895	1977	374
Southend-on-Sea – Southchurch Park	1906	2004	112
Colchester – Castle Park	1914	2014	116
Colchester – Garrison Ground	1924	1972	21
Ilford – Valentine's Park	1924	2002	108
Chelmsford – County Ground	1926	2014	293
Clacton-on-Sea – Vista Road	1931	1966	59
Brentwood – Old County Ground	1934	1969	51
Westcliff-on-Sea – Chalkwell Park	1934	1976	65
Romford – Gidea Park	1950	1968	32
Chelmsford – Hoffman's Social Club	1959	1961	2
Harlow – Sports Centre	1970	1970	1
Southend-on-Sea – Garon Park	2005	2011	7

Glamorgan

Present county club formed: 1888
Joined county championship: 1921
Number of championships: 3

The Glamorgan club, not formed till 1888, is the youngest of the 18 first-class county clubs. At that time cricket in Wales was mostly played by gentlemen. 'It was a game alien to the mercurial nature of the Welshman,' Wilf Wooller, a later captain, suggested. 'It was too slow in tempo.'

The early years were difficult. In 1893, heavily in debt and unable to afford any professionals, they considered folding up. In 1905, in an ambitious move, they failed narrowly to persuade MCC to allocate Cardiff a Test against Australia, but after the First War they talked themselves into the county championship. In the first three years they won only five out of 64 games, and their debts rose from £350 to more than £6,000. They were still struggling in 1929, a summer in which they used six captains and five wicket-keepers.

Their fortunes changed when Maurice Turnbull, a gifted all-round sportsman, became captain and Secretary in 1930. A martinet with the professionals, he led the county forward on and off the field, overseeing an amalgamation with Monmouthshire and spreading out from Cardiff and Swansea to play at six grounds, two outside the county.

In the autumn of 1932 the committee, overwhelmed by the club's debts, had to be persuaded by Turnbull to keep Glamorgan going, but in 1937, for the first time, they won more matches than they lost. Their off-spinner Johnnie Clay, captain in the mid-'20s, made himself available for the whole season and took a record 170 wickets.

In 1948, never before higher than fifth, Glamorgan were champions, a triumph for Wilf Wooller in his second summer as captain and for Johnnie Clay, now 50 years old and returning to take vital wickets in the final matches. It was a one-off success, though, as it was in 1997 when Matthew Maynard's team clinched the title.

The county's best years were in the 1960s, culminating in the championship in 1969. Captained by Tony Lewis from Neath, they were a predominantly Welsh team, as they have always been at their best, and in both 1964 and 1968, amid scenes of great joy, they beat the touring Australians.

The mercurial Welsh might still prefer their rugby, but the passion engendered by those two victories told of a nation much more in love with cricket than it had been in the 1880s.

> The crowd response in matches against the tourists was amazing. They came onto the banks and sang the Welsh national anthem. Then, when we won the championship, we had telegrams from Welshmen all over the world. We had one from an RAF sergeant who had been listening in Singapore; he said he didn't normally drink, but he was writing this from underneath the piano.
>
> *Don Shepherd*

COUNTY CHAMPIONSHIP PLACINGS YEAR BY YEAR

1890	91	92	93	94	95	96	97	98	99	1900	01	02	03	04	05	06	07	08	09	10	11	12	13	14		19	20	21	22	23	24	25	26
-	-	-	-	-	-	-	-	-	-	-	-	-	-	-	-	-	-	-	-	-	-	-	-	-		-	-	17	16	16	13	17	8

27	28	29	30	31	32	33	34	35	36	37	38	39		46	47	48	49	50	51	52	53	54	55	56	57	58	59	60	61	62	63	64	65
15	15	17	11	15	15	16	13	13	16	7	16	13		6	9	1	8	11	5	7	10	4	16	13	9	15	6	11	14	14	2	11	3

66	67	68	69	70	71	72	73	74	75	76	77	78	79	80	81	82	83	84	85	86	87	88	89	90	91	92	93	94	95	96	97	98	99
14	14	3	1	2	16	13	11	16	9	17	14	13	17	13	14	16	15	13	12	17	13	17	17	8	12	14	3	18	16	10	1	12	14

2000	01	02	03	04	05	06	07	08	09	10	11	12	13	14
D2	D1	D2	D2	D2	D1	D2	D2	D2	D2	D2	D2	D2	D2	D2
3	8	5	5	3	9	8	9	8	5	3	6	6	8	7

Penrhyn Avenue, Colwyn Bay

No county has ever gone farther afield for a home game. Once, when the previous match was at Swansea, the team flew rather than face an overnight drive of 190 miles.

In 2000 Steve James treated the seaside crowd to Glamorgan's only triple century while in 1969 Tony Cordle came on fifth change and took nine wickets.

County championship matches (1921-2014)		
Most runs	Alan Jones	30,703
	Emrys Davies	24,831
Most wickets	Don Shepherd	2,012
	Jack Mercer	1,341
Most appearances	Don Shepherd	590

Post-war only (1946-2014)		
Most runs	Alan Jones	30,703
	Gilbert Parkhouse	21,006
Most wickets	Don Shepherd	2,012
	Robert Croft	976
Most appearances	Don Shepherd	590

Last 25 years (1990-2014)		
Most runs	Matthew Maynard	16,067
	Steve James	11,910
Most wickets	Robert Croft	975
	Steve Watkin	685
Most appearances	Robert Croft	327

Championship grounds			
	First	*Last*	*Matches*
Cardiff – Arms Park	1921	1966	205
Swansea – St Helen's	1921	2014	342
Pontypridd – Ynysangharad Park	1926	1990	36
Cowbridge – Broad Shoard	1931	1932	4
Llanelli – Stradey Park	1933	1965	23
Neath – The Gnoll	1934	1992	39
Newport – Rodney Parade	1935	1965	25
Ebbw Vale – Eugene Cross Park	1946	1983	24
Margam – Steel Company of Wales	1960	1962	3
Colwyn Bay – Penrhyn Avenue	1966	2014	28
Cardiff – Sophia Gardens	1967	2014	259
Abergavenny – Avenue Road	1983	1997	14

Gloucestershire

Present county club formed: 1871

Joined county championship: 1890

Number of championships: 0

Is there a county with a better All-Time Eleven? The batting genius of Grace, Jessop, Hammond and Graveney; the spin mastery of Goddard and Parker; the inspired keeping of Jack Russell; the best and most loyal of overseas stars in Procter, Zaheer and Walsh. Throw in the dashing strokeplay of Charlie Barnett or the brilliance of the young Charles Townsend, and it is as strong and as entertaining as any county's eleven.

Yet Gloucestershire have never won the championship, at least not since the spoilsports took away their unofficial triumphs in the 1870s. Several times they have come close, but always the yearning in the Cotswolds has remained unfulfilled.

They have never been a wealthy club. At times, as now, in an age of two divisions and easy transfers, that has been their handicap. In the 1870s their all-amateur elevens could beat professional teams from Surrey and Nottinghamshire, but that was because they had WG Grace. By the championship proper of the 1890s their professional staff was too small for them to compete consistently across 18 or 20 games. And the situation got worse. They only survived after the First War by selling their Bristol ground.

They should have been champions in 1930. But a quirk of the point-scoring system put their 15 wins below Lancashire's ten. Their free-thinking captain Bev Lyon, a man before his time, so hated draws that he upset the traditionalists with freak declarations. And he had great match-winners in Charlie Parker and Tom Goddard and, most of all, in Walter Hammond.

All they lacked was a top-class fast bowler. They never had one till Mike Procter arrived. Instead, with their Bristol pitch a slow bowler's heaven, they had a long line of spinners, so many in the 1950s that David Allen, a future England star, spent five years in the second eleven, waiting for his chance.

The big city of Bristol has produced its cricketers, none giving greater service than Arthur Milton, but the heartbeat of the county has always been further north, represented by men such as the inelegant opener Alf Dipper, a farmer from Apperley, and the steady slow-left-armer Sam Cook, a Tetbury plumber; the effervescent Jack Russell from the Stroud valley and the wholehearted 'Syd' Lawrence from Gloucester.

They tasted glory in 1999 and 2000 when, as kings of one-day cricket under Mark Alleyne, they won all four Lord's finals.

> Is there another county of such beauty? The stone-built cottages snuggling in the Cotswold hills. The magical villages, hidden in the ancient Forest of Dean. The mighty River Severn with its elvers. The town of Cheltenham – 'poor, pretty and proud', as my dad used to say. And my own beloved Gloucester, with its majestic cathedral and its throbbing industrial heart.
>
> *Bryan 'Bomber' Wells*

COUNTY CHAMPIONSHIP PLACINGS YEAR BY YEAR

1890	91	92	93	94	95	96	97	98	99	1900	01	02	03	04	05	06	07	08	09	10	11	12	13	14		19	20	21	22	23	24	25	26
6	9	7	9	9	4	10	5	3	9	7	14	14	13	9	8	9	10	10	16	12	12	11	9	16		8	8	7	13	11	6	10	15

27	28	29	30	31	32	33	34	35	36	37	38	39		46	47	48	49	50	51	52	53	54	55	56	57	58	59	60	61	62	63	64	65
12	5	4	2	2	13	10	7	15	4	4	10	3		5	2	8	7	7	12	9	6	13	12	3	12	14	2	8	5	4	8	17	10

66	67	68	69	70	71	72	73	74	75	76	77	78	79	80	81	82	83	84	85	86	87	88	89	90	91	92	93	94	95	96	97	98	99
15	17	16	2	17	8	3	5	14	16	3	3	10	10	7	13	15	12	17	3	2	10	9	13	13	10	17	12	6	13	7	4	18

2000	01	02	03	04	05	06	07	08	09	10	11	12	13	14
D2	D2	D2	D2	D1	D1	D2	D2	D2	D2	D2	D2	D2	D2	D2
4	4	8	3	6	8	7	7	9	4	5	4	9	6	8

County championship matches (1890-2014)		
Most runs	Wally Hammond	31,344
	Arthur Milton	27,528
Most wickets	Charlie Parker	3,022
	Tom Goddard	2,678
Most appearances	Charlie Parker	571

Post-war only (1946-2014)		
Most runs	Arthur Milton	27,528
	Ron Nicholls	21,096
Most wickets	Sam Cook	1,609
	John Mortimore	1,522
Most appearances	John Mortimore	541

Last 25 years (1990-2014)		
Most runs	Mark Alleyne	11,214
	Alex Gidman	10,641
Most wickets	Jon Lewis	746
	Mike Smith	511
Most appearances	Mark Alleyne	231

College Ground, Cheltenham

Even the Victorian chapel, with its tall, arched windows, is younger than the county cricket at Cheltenham. It started in 1872 with a single match, in which a young, slim WG bowled out Surrey twice in a day, and now it spans a fortnight, drawing cricket lovers from far and wide. If there is one place where time has stood still and county cricket is still in its old glory, it is here at the College Ground.

Championship grounds			
	First	*Last*	*Matches*
Gloucester – Spa	1890	1923	45
Clifton – College Close	1890	1932	33
Bristol – County Ground	1890	2014	705
Cheltenham – College Ground	1890	2014	273
Moreton-in-Marsh – Batsford Road	1914	1914	1
Bristol – Greenbank	1922	1928	18
Cheltenham – Victoria Ground	1923	1937	17
Gloucester – Wagon Works	1923	1992	151
Stroud – Erinoid	1956	1963	12
Lydney – Recreational Trust Ground	1963	1969	7
Gloucester – Archdeacon Meadow	1993	2008	14

Hampshire

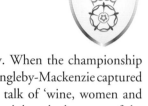

Present county club formed: 1863
Joined county championship: 1895
Number of championships: 2

It was fitting that Hampshire, home of the great Hambledon Club of the 18th century, should be admitted to the first-class ranks in the 1890s. In those years, with the army at Aldershot and the navy at Portsmouth, the county team drew heavily on a large cast of officers who popped in for the occasional game. Indeed, it was no coincidence that in 1900, when they were all in South Africa fighting the Boers, Hampshire had the worst summer in its history, failing to win a game.

By the 1920s the military men had faded away, but the team still contained the civilian equivalent of carefree officers and toiling infantrymen: Lord Tennyson, the fast-living Old Etonian, alongside Phil Mead, the ungainly left-hander who shuffled and pushed his way to the largest tally of runs the championship has ever known, and Alec Kennedy, a tough Scotsman who bowled more than 22,000 overs for the county. They say the footprints of his run-up never varied.

The dashing and the dour. It was much the same in the 1950s with Colin Ingleby-Mackenzie, 'Head of Pop' at Eton and every bit as cavalier as Tennyson, and Derek Shackleton, the steady Yorkshireman who for 20 summers bowled his metronomic medium-pace all day. When the championship was won so unexpectedly in 1961, Ingleby-Mackenzie captured the popular imagination with his talk of 'wine, women and song' and 'being in bed by breakfast', but the batsmen of the other counties thought only of the long hours they had spent trying to score runs off the parsimonious Shackleton.

A second championship followed 12 years later, a title that owed much to all-round team work and to the batting of Barry Richards and Gordon Greenidge, as fine an opening pair as county cricket has known.

Hampshire has never been a fashionable county with the selectors. Between 1923 and 1983 England played 455 Tests, awarding 5,005 caps, and Hampshire players received just 12 of them, a dismal record that was only improved by the South African-born Smith brothers, Chris and Robin.

Over the years the county has attracted some great players: Roy and Malcolm Marshall, David Gower and more recently Shane Warne, who came so close to captaining the county to a third championship in 2005. He was no Old Etonian, but he played his cricket with plenty of Tennyson's dash.

> Hampshire is the most polyglot of counties. Naval Portsmouth, big ship Southampton, holiday trade Bournemouth, army Aldershot, air experimental Farnborough, overspill Basingstoke and Andover, railway Eastleigh, cathedral and college Winchester, New Forest and Surrey-edge stockbroker belt, it has no common factor.
>
> *John Arlott*

COUNTY CHAMPIONSHIP PLACINGS YEAR BY YEAR

1890	91	92	93	94	95	96	97	98	99	1900	01	02	03	04	05	06	07	08	09	10	11	12	13	14		19	20	21	22	23	24	25	26
-	-	-	-	-	10	8	9	12	10	15	7	15	14	15	16	8	12	9	8	6	11	6	10	5		7	11	6	6	7	12	9	7

27	28	29	30	31	32	33	34	35	36	37	38	39		46	47	48	49	50	51	52	53	54	55	56	57	58	59	60	61	62	63	64	65
13	12	11	13	12	8	14	14	16	10	14	14	15		10	16	9	16	12	9	12	14	14	3	6	13	2	8	12	1	10	10	12	12

66	67	68	69	70	71	72	73	74	75	76	77	78	79	80	81	82	83	84	85	86	87	88	89	90	91	92	93	94	95	96	97	98	99
11	12	5	5	10	9	9	1	2	3	12	11	8	12	17	7	3	3	15	2	6	5	15	6	3	9	15	13	13	13	14	14	6	7

2000	01	02	03	04	05	06	07	08	09	10	11	12	13	14
D1	D2	D1	D2	D2	D1	D1	D1	D1	D1	D1	D1	D2	D2	D2
7	2	7	8	2	2	3	5	3	6	7	9	4	4	1

County championship matches (1895-2014)		
Most runs	Phil Mead	46,268
	Roy Marshall	27,095
Most wickets	Derek Shackleton	2,542
	Alec Kennedy	2,418
Most appearances	Phil Mead	668

Post-war only (1946-2014)		
Most runs	Roy Marshall	27,095
	Jimmy Gray	20,527
Most wickets	Derek Shackleton	2,542
	Peter Sainsbury	1,173
Most appearances	Derek Shackleton	553

Last 25 years (1990-2014)		
Most runs	Robin Smith	11,503
	Jimmy Adams	9,913
Most wickets	Shaun Udal	631
	Dimitri Mascarenhas	435
Most appearances	Shaun Udal	227

Dean Park, Bournemouth

The end-of-August Bournemouth week, with the ground filled with holiday-makers, was for many years a highlight of the summer. Both Kent and Glamorgan won their first titles here as, joyously, did Hampshire in 1961. Their other championship was won at Dean Park as well.

Tucked among prosperous Victorian houses, encircled by trees, it was the most attractive of the county's grounds – and the pitches took spin, too. When accountants called time on it in 1992, a spectator placed a rose on the square, with a card that asked, 'Will Ye No Come Back Again?'

Championship grounds			
	First	*Last*	*Matches*
Portsmouth – United Services	1895	2000	308
Southampton – Northlands Road	1895	2000	478
Bournemouth – Dean Park	1898	1992	314
Aldershot – Officers Club	1905	1910	3
Basingstoke – May's Bounty	1906	2010	44
Newport – Victoria Recreation	1938	1939	2
Cowes – J Samuel White's Ground	1956	1962	3
Southampton – The Rose Bowl	2001	2014	109

Kent

Present county club formed: 1870
Joined county championship: 1890
Number of championships: 6 + 1 shared

The greatest era of Kent cricket, when they took on and regularly beat All-England elevens, was back in the early Victorian years, long before the formation of the current club.

By 1890, when the championship proper began, Kent were no longer a power in the land. Indeed, when the competition was extended from nine to 14 counties in 1895, they finished in last place. Their cricket had a leisurely elegance, in keeping with their many atractive grounds and their fashionable cricket weeks. While other counties were becoming increasingly professional, their spirit remained steadfastly amateur.

They moved forward when they created a nursery at Tonbridge, an imaginative scheme that developed promising young cricketers, among them Colin Blythe, the gifted slow-left-armer, and Frank Woolley, the greatest player in the county's history. With this influx of professional talent, they won the championship four times between 1906 and 1913.

Blythe and Woolley had humble roots, but it is hard to imagine two professionals better suited to the ambience of Kent cricket: Blythe the sensitive violin-player who lost his life in the war and Woolley whose graceful batting lifted many a heart through the '20s and '30s. Though Kent won nothing in those decades, they were always a good team to watch.

The years after the Second War were hard ones. At one point the club asked the veteran Les Ames to take on the captaincy, but he was not prepared to give up his professional status and that proved a bridge too far for the committee.

After his playing days Ames returned as Secretary/Manager, the brains at the heart of a renaissance in the county's fortunes. They had in Colin Cowdrey a captain who played with a Kent smile and whose infectious enthusiasm created a happy environment for the new talents who were emerging, notably Derek Underwood, a slow-left-arm bowler of rare skill, and Alan Knott, a keeper in the great Kent tradition of Les Ames and Godfrey Evans.

Blessed with the best of overseas players in John Shepherd and Asif Iqbal, they became the team of the 1970s, winning three championships and seven one-day trophies.

The 1840s ... the years before the First War ... the 1970s: the three golden ages of Kent cricket are well spaced out. Will they wait as long for a fourth?

> I like to think that Kent cricket has been known for the fun and good humour engendered. Over the years, countless cricketers have said to me how lucky we are to play on so many lovely grounds, amid such pleasant countryside. Unsophisticated grounds too, but not primitive; most importantly, we have been able to play more amongst trees than concrete stands and soulless terraces. *Colin Cowdrey*

COUNTY CHAMPIONSHIP PLACINGS YEAR BY YEAR

1890	91	92	93	94	95	96	97	98	99	1900	01	02	03	04	05	06	07	08	09	10	11	12	13	14		19	20	21	22	23	24	25	26
3	5	7	4	4	14	9	12	7	8	3	7	7	8	3	6	1	8	2	1	1	2	3	1	3		2	5	4	4	5	5	5	3

27	28	29	30	31	32	33	34	35	36	37	38	39		46	47	48	49	50	51	52	53	54	55	56	57	58	59	60	61	62	63	64	65
4	2	8	5	3	3	3	5	10	8	12	9	5		6	4	15	13	9	16	15	16	11	13	16	14	8	13	10	11	11	13	7	5

66	67	68	69	70	71	72	73	74	75	76	77	78	79	80	81	82	83	84	85	86	87	88	89	90	91	92	93	94	95	96	97	98	99
4	2	2	10	1	4	2	4	10	5	14	1	1	5	16	9	13	7	5	9	8	14	2	15	16	6	2	8	9	18	4	2	11	5

2000	01	02	03	04	05	06	07	08	09	10	11	12	13	14
D1	D1	D1	D1	D1	D1	D1	D1	D1	D2	D1	D2	D2	D2	D2
6	3	3	4	2	5	5	7	8	1	8	8	3	7	6

County championship matches (1890-2014)

Most runs	Frank Woolley	43,703
	Wally Hardinge	30,774
Most wickets	'Tich' Freeman	3,151
	Colin Blythe	2,032
Most appearances	Frank Woolley	707

Post-war only (1946-2014)

Most runs	Colin Cowdrey	21,270
	Bob Wilson	18,509
Most wickets	Derek Underwood	1,873
	Doug Wright	1,182
Most appearances	Derek Underwood	490

Last 25 years (1990-2014)

Most runs	Robert Key	15,291
	David Fulton	10,783
Most wickets	Min Patel	537
	Martin McCague	379
Most appearances	Robert Key	239

Nevill Ground, Tunbridge Wells

The tree-lined ground, with its mauve rhododendrons coming into bloom in June, is one of county cricket's most peaceful settings. Yet here in 1913 the original pavilion was burnt down, probably by suffragettes.

Championship grounds

	First	Last	Matches
Town Malling – Old County Ground	1890	1890	1
Beckenham – Foxgrove Road	1890	1905	8
Tonbridge – Angel	1890	1939	99
Gravesend – Bat and Ball	1890	1970	102
Maidstone – Mote Park	1890	2005	175
Canterbury – St Lawrence	1890	2014	394
Catford – Private Banks	1892	1921	31
Blackheath – Rectory Field	1892	1971	81
Tunbridge Wells – Nevill Ground	1901	2014	184
Dover – Crabble	1907	1976	106
Chatham – Garrison Ground	1926	1927	3
Folkestone – Cheriton Road	1927	1991	75
Gillingham – Garrison Ground	1937	1968	27
Beckenham – Kent CC Ground	1954	2009	3
Dartford – Hesketh Park	1956	1990	32

Lancashire

Present county club formed: 1864

Joined county championship: 1890

Number of championships: 8 + 1 shared

The inaugural meeting in 1864 voted to create a county-wide club, with no 'fixed ground', but soon the dominant Manchester Club took control, playing most of the matches at Old Trafford and merging in 1880 to form the Lancashire County and Manchester Cricket Club, a name that survived till 1957. Liverpool was visited twice a summer, but it was not at the heart of the club. Apart from one year, it never has been.

Manchester was the fastest growing city in England, its mills and factories generating great wealth, but cricket had not yet taken hold among the workers. So Lancashire began life as a team of well-to-do gentlemen. When they hired professionals, they came from farther afield, and they were kept in place, being allocated a 'cow shed' in which to change and eat their own packed lunches.

By the 1890s, when the championship proper began, the team were mostly professionals. Led by Albert Hornby, a strict disciplinarian from a mill-owning family in Blackburn, they won the championship for the first time in 1897. With a large membership and big crowds, the club was in rude financial health, buying its ground and building a new pavilion.

A great rivalry with Yorkshire developed, huge crowds gathering for hard-fought contests that often ended in draws.

Lancashire dominated the championship in the late 1920s. Many found their approach too dour and functional – 'If cricket was always of this type,' the *Cricketer* magazine wrote, 'it would not long remain the national game' – but they won four titles in five years, two of them without losing a match.

By contrast, the two post-war Lancashire teams to achieve repeated success did so in the more dynamic arena of one-day cricket. Inspired by the signings of Clive Lloyd and Farokh Engineer and led with Methodist decency by Jack Bond, the county put years of internal division behind them with five trophies in four years from 1969. Then in the 1990s, with Wasim Akram, they were again one-day stars.

These successes proved a distraction in the championship, however, and the famously wet Manchester climate did not help. They went 60 long years without winning before in 2011 they were champions once more. Was it coincidence that that was the summer when, with Old Trafford out of action, they played around the county, mostly at Liverpool?

> We finished runners-up four times during my spell at the club, but we never really committed ourselves to the championship. Mostly we were regarded, by others and ourselves, as a one-day team. We were showmen, preferring the adulation and adoration of the crowds to the kind of clinical, professional performance required to beat Northants at an empty Wantage Road in May.
>
> *Mike Atherton*

COUNTY CHAMPIONSHIP PLACINGS YEAR BY YEAR

1890	91	92	93	94	95	96	97	98	99	1900	01	02	03	04	05	06	07	08	09	10	11	12	13	14		19	20	21	22	23	24	25	26
2	2	4	2	4	2	2	1	6	4	2	3	5	4	1	2	4	6	7	2	4	4	4	8	11		5	2	5	5	3	4	3	1

27	28	29	30	31	32	33	34	35	36	37	38	39		46	47	48	49	50	51	52	53	54	55	56	57	58	59	60	61	62	63	64	65
1	1	2	1	6	6	5	1	4	11	9	4	6		3	3	5	11	1	3	3	3	10	9	2	6	7	5	2	13	16	15	14	13

66	67	68	69	70	71	72	73	74	75	76	77	78	79	80	81	82	83	84	85	86	87	88	89	90	91	92	93	94	95	96	97	98	99
12	11	6	15	3	3	15	12	8	4	16	16	12	13	15	16	12	12	16	14	15	2	9	4	6	8	12	13	10	4	15	11	2	2

2000	01	02	03	04	05	06	07	08	09	10	11	12	13	14
D1	D1	D1	D1	D1	D2	D1	D1	D1	D1	D1	D1	D1	D2	D1
2	6	4	2	8	1	2	3	5	4	4	1	8	1	8

County championship matches (1890-2014)		
Most runs	Ernest Tyldesley	31,903
	Johnnie Tyldesley	30,865
Most wickets	Brian Statham	1,683
	Arthur Mold	1,300
Most appearances	Ernest Tyldesley	527

Post-war only (1946-2014)		
Most runs	Neil Fairbrother	18,483
	Ken Grieves	17,408
Most wickets	Brian Statham	1,683
	Roy Tattersall	1,056
Most appearances	Jack Simmons	402

Last 25 years (1990-2014)		
Most runs	Neil Fairbrother	10,687
	John Crawley	9,719
Most wickets	Glen Chapple	920
	Gary Keedy	622
Most appearances	Glen Chapple	293

Aigburth, Liverpool

When it opened in 1881, Aigburth had a more impressive pavilion than Old Trafford. But the ground's fortunes took a knock when the county's first visit ended in defeat by Cambridge University. As a result the scheduled fixture against Yorkshire was taken back to Manchester.

In 2011 Liverpool finally got to stage a championship match against Yorkshire. Chasing 121 in 15 overs, Lancashire won with four balls to spare, a crucial victory in their title-winning year.

Championship grounds			
	First	*Last*	*Matches*
Manchester– Old Trafford	1890	2014	1,062
Liverpool – Aigburth	1892	2014	150
Blackpool – Stanley Park	1906	2011	78
Lancaster – Lune Road	1914	1914	1
Nelson – Seedhill	1925	1938	9
Blackburn – Alexandra Meadows	1932	1935	4
Preston – West Cliff	1936	1952	4
Southport – Trafalgar Road	1959	2013	40
Lytham St Annes – Church Road	1985	1998	10

Leicestershire

Present county club formed: 1879
Joined county championship: 1895
Number of championships: 3

Always having to work hard to pay their way, Leicestershire have often been at the forefront of change. Before the First War they saw advantage in making Saturday the first, not the last, day of a match. In 1935 and again in 1946, they broke the mould by appointing a professional captain. And in 1962 they pioneered the Midland Knock-Out Competition, the success of which was the trigger for the rise of one-day cricket.

Of the 15 counties which made up the championship at the end of the 19th century none drew on a smaller population. But they had ambition, and in 1877 a private company developed a ground and hotel at Grace Road where in 1888 they beat the Australians. Seven years later the championship admitted them, and in their first game they triumphed over the champions, Surrey. They were heady days.

It was always a struggle, though. Grace Road was too far from the town centre, served only by horse trams, so in 1901 they moved to Aylestone Road, a well-appointed ground owned by the Electricity Board but one where 'clouds of fine ash crept into clothes and food; sandwiches were egg, tomato and grit, and it was impossible to keep fresh and clean.'

After the Second War the county returned to Grace Road, but its owners, the local education department, limited their use of it in term time. No county has played championship cricket on as many home grounds as Leicestershire.

On the field they had great stalwarts – Sam Coe, John King and Cecil Wood in the early years, Ewart Astill and George Geary between the wars – but championship success only came when they imported outstanding captains. Worcestershire's Charles Palmer took them to third place in 1953, Surrey's Tony Lock to second in 1967 and finally, in 1975, the Yorkshireman Ray Illingworth brought them their first championship title.

Masterminding these last two signings was Mike Turner, the Secretary/Manager who took the county forward in these years: buying and improving the ground, developing sponsorship and creating a happy and successful team. Appointed in 1960 at the age of 25, he was the epitome of the club's ambition, stepping down as the county entered its greatest years in the 1990s.

It has been downhill since then, on and off the field. But now, with the pioneering Wasim Khan appointed Chief Executive, there is hope that their progressive spirit will revive.

> The plain homeliness of the Midlands is expressed by Leicestershire cricket: it has no airs and graces, no excessive refinements. See an innings by Coe, and you ought not to be long guessing from the smack of rotund nature about it that he has spent the main portion of his days in the sun on a field with rustic benches running intimately round.
> *Neville Cardus, 1924*

COUNTY CHAMPIONSHIP PLACINGS YEAR BY YEAR

1890	91	92	93	94	95	96	97	98	99	1900	01	02	03	04	05	06	07	08	09	10	11	12	13	14		19	20	21	22	23	24	25	26
-	-	-	-	-	12	13	13	13	13	14	12	11	14	7	5	15	11	13	13	10	15	13	14	13		9	13	11	14	14	11	12	13

27	28	29	30	31	32	33	34	35	36	37	38	39		46	47	48	49	50	51	52	53	54	55	56	57	58	59	60	61	62	63	64	65
7	9	9	12	16	12	17	12	6	15	16	15	17		11	14	11	17	16	15	6	3	16	6	17	17	12	16	17	9	17	16	16	14

66	67	68	69	70	71	72	73	74	75	76	77	78	79	80	81	82	83	84	85	86	87	88	89	90	91	92	93	94	95	96	97	98	99
8	2	9	14	15	5	6	9	4	1	4	5	6	6	10	8	2	4	4	16	7	3	8	13	7	16	8	9	2	7	1	10	1	3

2000	01	02	03	04	05	06	07	08	09	10	11	12	13	14
D1	D1	D1	D1	D2	D2	D2	D2	D2	D2	D2	D2	D2	D2	D2
4	5	5	9	6	7	4	8	7	9	4	9	7	9	9

County championship matches (1895-2014)

Most runs	Les Berry	27,942
	Maurice Hallam	21,922
Most wickets	Ewart Astill	2,030
	George Geary	1,669
Most appearances	Ewart Astill	591

Post-war only (1946-2014)

Most runs	Maurice Hallam	21,922
	Nigel Briers	17,056
Most wickets	Terry Spencer	1,244
	Jack Walsh	1,014
Most appearances	Maurice Hallam	460

Last 25 years (1990-2014)

Most runs	Paul Nixon	11,274
	Darren Maddy	8,409
Most wickets	David Millns	438
	Alan Mullally	376
Most appearances	Paul Nixon	267

Oakham School

Leicestershire returned to the county of Rutland in 2000, after an absence of 62 years. The thatched pavilion had long gone, but the the setting was still a delight and the pitch a belter. Surrey's Ali Brown hit 295 on it.

Championship grounds

	First	Last	Matches
Leicester – Grace Road	1895	2014	716
Leicester – Aylestone Road	1901	1957	361
Hinckley – Ashby Road	1911	1937	19
Ashby-de-la-Zouch – Bath Grounds	1912	1964	42
Coalville – Fox and Goose	1913	1914	2
Loughborough – Park Road	1913	1952	15
Loughborough – College	1928	1929	2
Oakham School	1935	2007	9
Barwell – Kirkby Road	1946	1947	3
Melton Mowbray – Egerton Park	1946	1948	3
Coalville – Town Ground	1950	1950	1
Hinckley – Coventry Road	1951	1964	17
Loughborough – Brush Ground	1953	1965	15
Coalville – Snibston Colliery	1957	1982	8
Hinckley – Leicester Road	1981	1991	11

Middlesex

Present county club formed: 1864
Joined county championship: 1890
Number of championships: 10 + 2 shared

The county of Middlesex disappeared fifty years ago, its name surviving only in postal addresses and in county cricket. And the county cricket club almost did not make it beyond 1871. With substantial debts, few paid-up members and no proper ground, they called a general meeting where, by seven votes to six, they decided to soldier on.

With MCC at Lord's and Surrey at the Oval, many thought that Middlesex was one club too many for the capital, a view supported by the state of their fixture list in 1870: two games, both at the Oval against Surrey. They developed a field at West Brompton, but it was 'utterly unfit for a first-class match'. Then they had four years at a ground near the fast-growing Harrods store, their last game there ending abruptly when the groundsman, after changing the score on the board, dropped down dead. Eventually, in 1877, they overcame their reservations and accepted MCC's invitation to play at Lord's.

With Surrey fielding largely professional teams, Middlesex could call on the many gentleman cricketers who lived in London. On a good day this made them a strong and attractive side, but these amateurs had other commitments so they were not a consistent eleven – nor were they in a position to take on an extensive fixture list. Yet, playing most of their games with only two professionals, they surprised everybody by winning the championship in 1903.

They won again in 1920 under the captaincy of Pelham Warner, one of several amateurs who, playing at Lord's, were able to move with ease into the corridors of power. At the heart of the national game, Middlesex has provided England with more captains than any other county.

It was from the professional ranks that the great entertainers sprang: the ever-cheerful Patsy Hendren, the most prolific of run-scorers between the wars; then the glamorous Denis Compton who, with Bill Edrich, banished the cares of austerity to make the summer of 1947 the greatest in Middlesex's history.

The county's most prolonged period of success began in 1976 when in an all-professional era Mike Brearley, a man with new ideas, forged a winning side. Under him and his successor Mike Gatting, they were champions seven times in 18 years.

Middlesex are yet to repeat that success in the 21st century, but they remain strong contenders – still firmly on the map.

While the names of all other counties conjure up images of dales and downs and country pubs and softling-rustling fields of wheat, the name of Middlesex produces in the mind's eye only an endless vista of Tescos. Nobody could possibly feel any sentimental attachment to Middlesex the geographical area, were it not for the fact that it does have Lord's and Lord's houses the Middlesex cricket team.   *Barry Norman*

COUNTY CHAMPIONSHIP PLACINGS YEAR BY YEAR

1890	91	92	93	94	95	96	97	98	99	1900	01	02	03	04	05	06	07	08	09	10	11	12	13	14		19	20	21	22	23	24	25	26
7	3	5	3	3	6	3	8	2	2	7	2	12	1	4	11	11	5	4	6	3	3	5	6	2		13	1	1	7	8	2	6	6

27	28	29	30	31	32	33	34	35	36	37	38	39		46	47	48	49	50	51	52	53	54	55	56	57	58	59	60	61	62	63	64	65
9	8	6	16	11	10	12	10	3	2	2	2	2		2	1	3	1	14	7	5	5	7	5	5	7	10	10	3	3	13	6	6	6

66	67	68	69	70	71	72	73	74	75	76	77	78	79	80	81	82	83	84	85	86	87	88	89	90	91	92	93	94	95	96	97	98	99
12	7	10	11	16	6	8	13	6	11	1	1	3	14	1	4	1	2	3	1	12	16	7	3	1	15	11	1	4	2	9	4	17	16

2000	01	02	03	04	05	06	07	08	09	10	11	12	13	14
D2	D2	D2	D1	D1	D1	D1	D2	D2	D2	D2	D2	D1	D1	D1
8	5	2	6	4	6	9	3	3	8	8	1	3	5	7

County championship matches (1890-2014)		
Most runs	Patsy Hendren	37,418
	Jack (JW) Hearne	25,819
Most wickets	Fred Titmus	2,170
	Jack (JT) Hearne	2,032
Most appearances	Fred Titmus	597

Post-war only (1946-2014)		
Most runs	Mike Gatting	25,680
	Jack Robertson	22,572
Most wickets	Fred Titmus	2,170
	John Emburey	1,140
Most appearances	Fred Titmus	597

Last 25 years (1990-2014)		
Most runs	Mark Ramprakash	12,726
	Owais Shah	12,676
Most wickets	Phil Tufnell	688
	Tim Murtagh	456
Most appearances	Paul Weekes	210

Tivoli Road, Hornsey

Middlesex came once to Hornsey, in 1959, their only home match away from Lord's between 1877 and 1977.

Across the three days there were 3,404 paying spectators, a good crowd in the small club ground but disappointing to Middlesex who made a loss of £275. The game was played in a heatwave, Hampshire winning by two wickets off the third ball of the last over. The ground, below Alexandra Palace, was next door to the local swimming pool from where the shrieks of children could be heard all day.

Championship grounds			
	First	*Last*	*Matches*
Lord's	1890	2014	1,166
Hornsey – Tivoli Road	1959	1959	1
Uxbridge Cricket Club	1980	2014	43
Southgate – Walker's Ground	1998	2009	19

In 1977 Middlesex played Somerset at Chelmsford.

In 2014 Middlesex were due to play at Merchant Taylor's School in Northwood, but the match was abandoned without a ball being bowled.

Northamptonshire

Present county club formed: 1878
Joined county championship: 1905
Number of championships: 0

It could be argued that Northamptonshire owe their status as a first-class county to a girl called Charlotte from the village of Cogenhoe. She was the sweetheart of George Thompson who, as a young man, regularly walked with his dog the six miles from Northampton to see her. If it had not been for Charlotte, it is said, he would have gone to play for Kent, and Northamptonshire would not have dominated Minor Counties cricket in the early years of the 20th century. It was a domination that led to them joining the championship in 1905.

There were some tough times in the early years, none more humiliating than the day they were all out for 12 at Gloucester, but by 1912, with Thompson in his prime, they were playing good enough cricket to finish second in the table.

Such glory was fleeting. With the smallest population of the first-class counties, they finished every summer between the wars in the lower reaches of the table, at one stage going four years without a victory. It came to seem an anomaly that they, not Durham or Staffordshire, were in the first-class ranks. Even the homely Wantage Road ground, with its outfield recovering each spring from the Town's footballers, seemed second class.

In 1949, when Sussex allocated their Northants fixture to Worthing, the Town Clerk protested, only to receive the reply: 'Somebody must have them.' 'It did not seem in the best of taste,' wrote a former Northants Secretary, 'for one county to refer to another in much the same way as a smallpox epidemic.'

That year Northants recruited a new captain, the Surrey amateur Freddie Brown. He galvanised them, and with a rich irony they won by 147 runs at Worthing.

Better times lay ahead. In the 1950s and '60s, with the money from a thriving football pool scheme, their long-serving Secretary Ken Turner developed a strategy of recruiting players from the minor counties, notably Durham and Staffordshire. For more than twenty years they punched above their weight, three times finishing as runners-up.

Increasingly the recruits have come from farther afield, and none has settled and given greater value than the South African, turned Englishman, Allan Lamb. For seven years, from 1989 to 1995, he captained the county, developing a brand of dynamic cricket that made them once more a force in the land.

It remains to be seen whether they can be that force again.

> They have never relied to any great extent on local talent. I remember Brian Reynolds being introduced to me as 'our one native', as though he were some kind of Man Friday. There is something, however, about Northamptonshire, a mysterious spirit which takes a stranger, be he Australian, West Indian or even Yorkshireman, and stamps him as a permanent and local man.
>
> *A.A. Thomson, 1969*

COUNTY CHAMPIONSHIP PLACINGS YEAR BY YEAR

1890	91	92	93	94	95	96	97	98	99	1900	01	02	03	04	05	06	07	08	09	10	11	12	13	14		19	20	21	22	23	24	25	26
-	-	-	-	-	-	-	-	-	-	-	-	-	-	-	13	11	15	15	7	9	10	2	4	9		12	14	13	15	17	16	11	16

27	28	29	30	31	32	33	34	35	36	37	38	39		46	47	48	49	50	51	52	53	54	55	56	57	58	59	60	61	62	63	64	65
16	13	13	17	17	16	13	17	17	17	17	17	16		16	17	17	6	10	13	8	11	7	7	4	2	4	11	9	16	8	7	3	2

66	67	68	69	70	71	72	73	74	75	76	77	78	79	80	81	82	83	84	85	86	87	88	89	90	91	92	93	94	95	96	97	98	99
5	9	13	9	14	14	4	3	3	8	2	9	17	11	12	15	9	6	11	10	9	7	12	5	11	10	3	4	5	3	16	15	15	13

2000	01	02	03	04	05	06	07	08	09	10	11	12	13	14
D2	D1	D2	D2	D1	D2	D2	D2	D2	D2	D2	D2	D2	D2	D1
1	7	7	2	9	4	6	5	4	3	6	3	8	2	9

County championship matches (1905-2014)		
Most runs	Dennis Brookes	26,627
	Geoff Cook	19,526
Most wickets	Nobby (EW) Clark	1,048
	George Thompson	1,029
Most appearances	Dennis Brookes	464

Post-war only (1946-2014)		
Most runs	Dennis Brookes	22,370
	Geoff Cook	19,526
Most wickets	George Tribe	970
	Brian Crump	759
Most appearances	Brian Reynolds	399

Last 25 years (1990-2014)		
Most runs	David Sales	13,201
	Rob Bailey	11,099
Most wickets	Paul Taylor	513
	Jason Brown	392
Most appearances	David Sales	227

Town Ground, Kettering

Though not a large ground, Kettering was not known for high-scoring games. As one writer put it, 'Matches usually finish in good time for the next journey.' They certainly did in the 1930s for Yorkshire, who in two visits bowled out Northants four times for a total of 209 runs. In one of the matches the fast bowler Bill Bowes took the cheapest 16 wickets in first-class cricket – for 35 runs.

By 1971 the hiss of the steam trains from the railway embankment behind the poplars had given way to the klaxon hoots of the new diesels, and with a similar belief in progress the county said its farewell to Kettering.

Championship grounds			
	First	*Last*	*Matches*
Northampton – County Ground	1905	2014	925
Peterborough – Town Ground	1906	1966	43
Kettering – Town Ground	1923	1971	62
Rushden – Town Ground	1936	1963	21
Wellingborough School	1946	1991	43
Peterborough – Baker Perkins Ground	1967	1969	3
Luton – Wardown Park	1986	1997	11

Nottinghamshire

Present county club formed: 1841
Joined county championship: 1890
Number of championships: 6

Though Nottingham was only a medium-sized, lace-making town in the mid-19th century, it was pivotal in the development of professional cricket in the English provinces.

The All-England XI, who travelled around the country spreading the game's popularity, was the creation of William Clarke, a publican who had married the landlady of the Trent Bridge Inn and created Nottinghamshire's ground. The equally enterprising George Parr took over the All-England side, leading the first overseas tour to America and developing the county team. Then came Alfred Shaw and Arthur Shrewsbury, outstanding cricketers with the business acumen to organise early tours to Australia, and Billy Gunn, a double international in cricket and football, who set up the sports equipment firm Gunn & Moore and became the first professional to serve on the Notts committee.

In 1881 Shrewsbury and Shaw led a strike to establish the rights of the professionals, and as a result Notts became a well-run, prosperous club. Through much of the 1870s and '80s, they were the strongest county side, producing so many players that several had to migrate to other counties.

Other teams had passed them by the time the championship proper began in 1890, but they continued to be a good team, made up of local players. In 1907 they won the championship with 15 victories and no defeats in their 20 games, still the best season's results by a county, and they won again in 1929 when their five bowlers – Larwood, Voce, Barratt and the Staples brothers – were all recruited from mining communities.

The home-grown talent grew thinner after the Second War, and they were often to be found near the foot of the table. Their periodic revivals owed much to their ability to afford first-rate overseas players: Australian Bruce Dooland in 1953, West Indian Garry Sobers in 1968 and the pair that brought them two championship titles in the 1980s: South African Clive Rice and New Zealander Richard Hadlee.

In recent years, guided by the shrewd coach Mick Newell, Nottinghamshire have specialised in recruiting players from other counties, winning the championship in 2005 with a wholly imported eleven. It is very different from 100 years ago, yet in their readiness to adapt to the demands of the age they remain true to the enterprising spirit of their founding fathers.

> Coming from Bristol, the Trent Bridge pavilion seemed like a palace. All round the changing room there were easy chairs, not a hard bench anywhere and no splintery floorboards. There were showers and baths a'plenty, where all we had at Bristol was a thing like a horse trough. And a pile of luxury towels, hand and bath; no need to scrum for the best one. When I got my first month's pay, I went to see the Secretary. I thought they'd paid me two months by mistake.   *Bryan 'Bomber' Wells*

COUNTY CHAMPIONSHIP PLACINGS YEAR BY YEAR

1890	91	92	93	94	95	96	97	98	99	1900	01	02	03	04	05	06	07	08	09	10	11	12	13	14		19	20	21	22	23	24	25	26
5	4	2	6	7	12	6	10	8	10	5	9	3	5	5	10	5	1	8	10	5	8	8	5	10		3	7	8	2	2	6	4	4

27	28	29	30	31	32	33	34	35	36	37	38	39		46	47	48	49	50	51	52	53	54	55	56	57	58	59	60	61	62	63	64	65
2	3	1	4	5	4	8	9	5	5	10	12	12		13	11	14	11	15	17	16	8	5	11	8	15	17	17	16	17	15	9	15	17

66	67	68	69	70	71	72	73	74	75	76	77	78	79	80	81	82	83	84	85	86	87	88	89	90	91	92	93	94	95	96	97	98	99
17	15	4	8	11	12	14	17	15	13	13	17	7	9	3	1	4	14	2	8	4	1	5	11	13	4	4	7	3	11	17	13	16	17

2000	01	02	03	04	05	06	07	08	09	10	11	12	13	14
D2	D2	D2	D1	D2	D1	D1	D2	D1	D1	D1	D1	D1	D1	D1
7	7	3	8	1	1	8	2	2	2	1	6	5	7	4

County championship matches (1890-2014)		
Most runs	George Gunn	29,522
	Tim Robinson	22,893
Most wickets	Tommy Wass	1,517
	Bill Voce	1,218
Most appearances	George Gunn	543

Post-war only (1946-2014)		
Most runs	Tim Robinson	22,893
	Reg Simpson	21,708
Most wickets	Arthur Jepson	938
	Eddie Hemmings	799
Most appearances	Derek Randall	368

Last 25 years (1990-2014)		
Most runs	Paul Johnson	12,217
	Chris Read	12,102
Most wickets	Paul Franks	459
	Andre Adams	344
Most appearances	Chris Read	250

Trent Bridge, Nottingham

No county has played fewer home matches away from its main ground than Nottinghamshire. But then no county has looked after its main ground with greater care and developed it more sympathetically.

In some eras the pitches have been feather-beds, made for batting; at other times, in search of 'result cricket', they have been spiced up for the bowlers.

Always, though, the Nottingham club has known how to welcome its visitors. "There is a marvellous feeling of friendliness when you come to the ground," Tom Graveney says. "From the gateman to the President, you are made to feel at home."

Championship grounds			
	First	*Last*	*Matches*
Nottingham – Trent Bridge	1890	2014	1,209
Welbeck Abbey	1901	1904	2
Worksop – Town Ground	1921	1998	47
Shireoaks – Steetley Company Ground	1961	1961	1
Newark-on-Trent – Elm Avenue	1966	1978	11
Cleethorpes – Sports Ground	1980	1981	2

Somerset

Present county club formed: 1875
Joined county championship: 1891
Number of championships: 0

No county in the early years of the championship was as unpredictable as Somerset. Four times they lost inside a day, yet twice they beat Yorkshire in years when no one else did.

They started life in 1875, the brainchild of a group of gentlemen playing an ad hoc game at Sidmouth, and their first resolution was to be a wandering club without the bother of a home ground. In 1882 they were accepted into the first-class ranks, but that did not last long. 'Certain counties are trying to force their way to the front, notably Somersetshire,' wrote the *Lillywhite's Annual*, 'but professionals not being indigenous to the area it is feared that their advance is only temporary.' And so it proved. At the end of 1885, a dismal season during which they had played at Southampton with only nine men, they returned to the minor ranks.

Then came Henry Murray-Anderdon, a wealthy vicar's son who took on the position of Secretary and drove the club forward. The finances were sorted out, a ground in Taunton was bought, and new players appeared, notably Sammy Woods, a young Australian who was living in Bridgwater. Unbeaten in 1890, they were admitted to the championship.

The first years were not without days of glory, but their determination to remain a largely amateur side soon started to count against them. Their professionals, only two at one stage in the 1920s, changed in the groundsman's quarters, among the mowers, and observed the master/servant ways of Somerset's cheerful rural world.

An upturn in fortune came in the 1950s when the professional Maurice Tremlett was appointed captain. But the great change of culture came with the arrival in 1971 of the fiercely competitive Brian Close, a Yorkshireman accustomed to success. "He taught them how to really play cricket," one former player said. "Before that, I think they were playing at it."

With Coventry-born Tom Cartwright, county coach, at his side, they nurtured a group of young players – Botham, Richards, Marks, Roebuck – who would turn Somerset into the most exciting county side in the country, winning five one-day trophies in five years. But the old unpredictability was still there, and they failed to win the championship.

They still have not won it but, benefiting from Millfield School's output of talent, they have come agonisingly close.

> Somerset had a great appeal to me. The cricket was closer to the community than it had become at Edgbaston. And Somerset people are fairly down to earth. They're not over-impressed by flannel. They were country people; they all had glowing, ruddy faces that stood out at away matches in early season, when most people had a pallor.
>
> *Tom Cartwright, on coming from Warwickshire in 1970*

COUNTY CHAMPIONSHIP PLACINGS YEAR BY YEAR

1890	91	92	93	94	95	96	97	98	99	1900	01	02	03	04	05	06	07	08	09	10	11	12	13	14		19	20	21	22	23	24	25	26
-	5	3	8	6	8	11	11	13	13	11	12	7	10	12	15	11	14	16	11	16	16	14	16	15		5	10	10	10	9	8	15	14

27	28	29	30	31	32	33	34	35	36	37	38	39		46	47	48	49	50	51	52	53	54	55	56	57	58	59	60	61	62	63	64	65
14	14	15	13	13	7	11	15	14	7	13	7	14		4	11	12	9	7	14	17	17	17	17	15	8	3	12	14	10	6	3	8	7

66	67	68	69	70	71	72	73	74	75	76	77	78	79	80	81	82	83	84	85	86	87	88	89	90	91	92	93	94	95	96	97	98	99
3	8	12	17	13	7	11	10	5	12	7	4	5	8	5	3	6	10	7	17	16	11	11	14	15	17	9	5	11	9	11	12	9	4

2000	01	02	03	04	05	06	07	08	09	10	11	12	13	14
D1	D1	D1	D2	D2	D2	D2	D2	D1	D1	D1	D1	D1	D1	D1
5	2	8	7	4	8	9	1	4	3	2	4	2	6	6

The Recreation Ground, Bath

It was one of county cricket's premier festivals but the little-used municipal pitch became unreliable, at one stage being tended in his spare time by an AA patrolman.

The glorious setting and the good crowd kept the festival going into the 21st century, but the accountants were not keen nor, by the end, were the Somerset players. They complained that it felt like an extra away game.

County championship matches (1891-2014)		
Most runs	Harold Gimblett	19,966
	Peter Wight	15,964
Most wickets	Jack White	2,080
	Arthur Wellard	1,415
Most appearances	Brian Langford	479

Post-war only (1946-2014)		
Most runs	Peter Wight	15,964
	Bill Alley	15,584
Most wickets	Brian Langford	1,346
	Andrew Caddick	840
Most appearances	Brian Langford	479

Last 25 years (1990-2014)		
Most runs	Marcus Trescothick	15,051
	James Hildreth	10,186
Most wickets	Andrew Caddick	840
	Graham Rose	428
Most appearances	Marcus Trescothick	219

Championship grounds			
	First	*Last*	*Matches*
Taunton – County Ground	1891	2014	731
Bath – Recreation Ground	1898	2006	234
Weston-super-Mare – Clarence Park	1914	1996	188
Bristol – Broad Walk, Knowle	1926	1928	3
Frome – Agricultural Showgrounds	1932	1961	18
Wells – Rowdens Road	1935	1951	11
Stratton-on-the-Fosse – Downside School	1934	1934	1
Yeovil – West Hendford	1935	1939	5
Yeovil – Johnson Park	1951	1967	12
Glastonbury – Morlands	1952	1973	18
Bristol – Imperial Ground	1959	1966	8
Street – Millfield School	1961	1961	1

Surrey

Present county club formed: 1845
Joined county championship: 1890
Number of championships: 18 + 1 shared

Surrey were the first great team of the county championship proper, winning six titles in the 1890s. A prosperous club drawing fervent support from the crowded streets of South London, they had a large professional staff and, more than the other southern counties, set considerable store by winning.

There was disquiet in some quarters at their approach, and in 1899 Richard Webster, the Attorney-General and Surrey President, soon to be Lord Alverstone, summoned the county's Match Committee to his rooms in the House of Commons. He demanded that there be more amateurs in the team and that the amateurs show less familiarity with the professionals. Furthermore, he did not want the winning of the county championship to be the only object of their cricket. He is even reported as saying that he 'would be sorry if the championship remained for a long series of years with Surrey.'

His wish was granted as only once in the next fifty years were Surrey crowned champions. The great bowlers of the 1890s were all in decline by the turn of the century, and the Oval pitches became too flat for their successors. Instead, the county got to be known for the quality of its batting,

with three men – Tom Hayward, Jack Hobbs and Andrew Sandham – all scoring 100 hundreds.

A second golden age arrived in the 1950s. By good fortune Surrey found themselves with a quartet of world-class bowlers, all with different styles – Alec Bedser, Jim Laker, Tony Lock and Peter Loader – supported by brilliant close catchers and a square that was now decidedly helpful. In Peter May they had the outstanding batsman of the age and, above all, in Stuart Surridge, they had a captain who shook away the last cobwebs of Lord Alverstone's edict. He mixed happily with his men, and he was fiercely determined to win. A record seven years in a row, under Surridge and May, they won the championship.

The 1950s players, like their predecessors of the 1890s, were drawn almost entirely from the clubs and schools of Surrey, and so it would be when in 1999, under Adam Hollioake, they were once again the dominant side in county cricket. The Surrey strut, so unpopular and so feared by other counties, was back.

Good governance has made them in recent years a wealthy county. Defying their history, however, they have spent heavily on imported players, so far with little success.

> The essential character of the Oval is of bricks and mortar, and dust and noise. It is a part of London's busy-ness and bustle rather than a relief from these things. At heart it is a Cockney playground; its adherents may properly sit in shirt-sleeves and braces, and express opinions with all the noise and wit at their command. The Oval atmosphere condones, almost commands it. *J.M. Kilburn, 1952*

COUNTY CHAMPIONSHIP PLACINGS YEAR BY YEAR

1890	91	92	93	94	95	96	97	98	99	1900	01	02	03	04	05	06	07	08	09	10	11	12	13	14		19	20	21	22	23	24	25	26
1	1	1	5	1	1	4	2	4	1	7	6	4	11	11	4	3	4	3	5	2	5	7	3	1		4	3	2	3	4	3	2	5

27	28	29	30	31	32	33	34	35	36	37	38	39		46	47	48	49	50	51	52	53	54	55	56	57	58	59	60	61	62	63	64	65
6	6	10	8	8	5	9	11	11	6	8	3	8		11	6	2	5	1	6	1	1	1	1	1	1	1	3	7	15	5	11	4	8

66	67	68	69	70	71	72	73	74	75	76	77	78	79	80	81	82	83	84	85	86	87	88	89	90	91	92	93	94	95	96	97	98	99
7	4	15	3	5	1	12	2	7	6	9	14	16	3	2	6	5	8	8	6	3	4	4	12	9	5	13	6	7	12	3	8	5	1

2000	01	02	03	04	05	06	07	08	09	10	11	12	13	14
D1	D1	D1	D1	D1	D1	D2	D1	D1	D2	D2	D2	D1	D1	D2
1	4	1	3	3	7	1	4	9	7	7	2	7	9	5

County championship matches (1890-2014)		
Most runs	Jack Hobbs	38,737
	Tom Hayward	30,967
Most wickets	Tom Richardson	1,533
	Percy Fender	1,479
Most appearances	Jack Hobbs	538

Post-war only (1946-2014)		
Most runs	John Edrich	25,740
	Micky Stewart	20,905
Most wickets	Tony Lock	1,458
	Pat Pocock	1,297
Most appearances	Pat Pocock	450

Last 25 years (1990-2014)		
Most runs	Mark Ramprakash	15,331
	Alistair Brown	14,418
Most wickets	Martin Bicknell	830
	Saqlain Mushtaq	418
Most appearances	Alistair Brown	237

Whitgift School, Croydon

Surrey first came to Whitgift for a one-day game in August 2000. Part of the school's 400th anniversary celebrations, the match drew a Wednesday crowd of more than 3,000.

Three years later the ground was awarded a championship fixture. With a large audience soaking up the sunshine in the tranquil, picturesque setting, and with Mark Ramprakash hitting an imperious 279, the second out-ground in Surrey's long history made the most glorious of starts. Only the well-beaten Nottinghamshire team, changing in portakabins where the showers were visible to spectators and the toilet doors did not shut, had cause to grumble.

Problems with the arrangements brought an end to the venue in 2011, though there is still hope of a return.

Championship grounds			
	First	*Last*	*Matches*
Kennington Oval	1890	2014	1,257
Guildford – Woodbridge Road	1938	2014	73
Croydon – Whitgift School	2003	2011	9

Sussex

Present county club formed: 1839
Joined county championship: 1890
Number of championships: 3

Sussex may have been the oldest of the county clubs when the championship proper began in 1890, but the standard of their cricket was winning them little respect. There was even talk of the county losing first-class status. 'The best remedy is to import some young professionals from Nottinghamshire or Yorkshire,' *Wisden* thought. 'Otherwise they will gradually sink to the level of their neighbours Hampshire.'

The imports arrived but not as *Wisden* recommended. First came Charles Fry, a brilliant all-round sportsman from Oxford University, then his friend Kumar Shri Ranjitsinhji. Together with style they transformed the county into championship contenders – and they were great entertainers, too. 'I have never watched Sussex with my eyes on the scoreboard,' wrote Neville Cardus.

There was a strong sense of continuity about Sussex cricket through much of the 20th century, a stability rooted in several long-serving families, all born out of the soil of the county: the brothers Harry and Jim Parks and Jim's son, the younger Jim; George Cox senior and junior, father and son; the brothers Jim and John Langridge and Jim's son Richard; Fred Tate and his son

Maurice. Between 1890 and 1972 the men of the four families made more than 4,000 appearances in the championship.

There have been other brothers, too – Relf, Gilligan, Oakes, Buss, Greig, Wells – and other sons: Mike Griffith, Neil Lenham and now Luke Wells, son of Alan.

In among the faithful families there has been more than a dash of glamour: the princely Fry, the imperious strokeplay of 'Lord Ted' Dexter, the handsome charm of the South African Tony Greig and, above all, the men from the east: Ranji and his nephew Duleep, the Nawab of Pataudi and Imran Khan.

Seven times in the 20th century Sussex were runners-up in the championship, always under charismatic captains: from Ranji and Duleep to the young David Sheppard, in his only year in charge, and John Barclay, coming closest of all in 1981.

In 2003, amid great joy, they were finally crowned champions. Once more they had an eastern star in the leg-spinner Mushtaq Ahmed, but their inspirational captain, Chris Adams, was not in the old tradition of Sussex. He was a fiercely competitive northerner, down from Derbyshire.

Perhaps *Wisden* had been right all along.

> We do not make a fetish of the county championship. If we can win that honour without losing our characteristic free-and-easy style, we are very happy to do so. But if the effort to attain such distinction means games which are boring to the spectators, irritating to the players and contrary to the true spirit of what we call cricket, then we just as soon remain among the obscure.   *Maurice Tate, 1925*

COUNTY CHAMPIONSHIP PLACINGS YEAR BY YEAR

1890	91	92	93	94	95	96	97	98	99	1900	01	02	03	04	05	06	07	08	09	10	11	12	13	14		19	20	21	22	23	24	25	26
8	7	9	7	8	11	14	6	9	5	3	4	2	2	6	3	10	13	5	4	7	13	10	7	6		11	6	9	9	6	10	13	10

27	28	29	30	31	32	33	34	35	36	37	38	39		46	47	48	49	50	51	52	53	54	55	56	57	58	59	60	61	62	63	64	65
10	7	4	7	4	2	2	2	7	14	5	8	10		17	9	16	13	13	10	13	2	9	4	9	9	13	15	4	8	12	4	9	16

66	67	68	69	70	71	72	73	74	75	76	77	78	79	80	81	82	83	84	85	86	87	88	89	90	91	92	93	94	95	96	97	98	99
10	13	17	7	9	11	16	15	13	17	10	8	9	4	4	2	8	11	6	7	14	17	16	10	17	11	7	10	8	15	12	18	7	11

2000	01	02	03	04	05	06	07	08	09	10	11	12	13	14
D2	D2	D1	D1	D1	D1	D1	D1	D1	D1	D2	D1	D1	D1	D1
9	1	6	1	5	3	1	1	6	8	1	5	4	3	3

County championship matches (1890-2014)

Most runs	John Langridge	30,338
	Jim Parks, jnr	27,233
Most wickets	Maurice Tate	2,014
	George Cox, snr	1,645
Most appearances	James Langridge	561

Post-war only (1946-2014)

Most runs	Jim Parks, jnr	27,233
	Ken Suttle	26,588
Most wickets	Ian Thomson	1,431
	Tony Buss	886
Most appearances	Ken Suttle	546

Last 25 years (1990-2014)

Most runs	Murray Goodwin	14,135
	Chris Adams	10,560
Most wickets	Jason Lewry	584
	James Kirtley	516
Most appearances	Murray Goodwin	187

Castle Cricket Ground, Arundel

Has county cricket ever been played on a ground with a fixture list more varied than that of Arundel?

With its old wooden pavilion nestling peacefully among trees beneath the grand castle, it is a natural home for games such as Harlequins versus Quidnuncs, even Private Eye against BBC Radio News. But the ground also stages women's and under-19 internationals, matches for the deaf, the disabled and the blind, as well as hosting a summer-long programme of activity days for children with special needs and from inner-city London.

The Sussex fixture always draws a good crowd.

Championship grounds

	First	Last	Matches
Hove – County Ground	1890	2014	905
Hastings – Central Recreation Ground	1895	1989	134
Eastbourne – The Saffrons	1897	2000	149
Chichester – Priory Park	1906	1950	10
Horsham – Cricket Field	1908	2014	94
Worthing – Manor Sports	1937	1964	36
Arundel – Castle Cricket Ground	1990	2014	24

Warwickshire

Present county club formed: 1882
Joined county championship: 1895
Number of championships: 7

Up to 1881 Warwickshire County Cricket Club was no more than an occasional team of like-minded amateurs from the towns of Warwick, Leamington and Rugby. But in 1882, driven by the vision of William Ansell, a Surrey-born schoolmaster, it was re-formed to include the thriving city of Birmingham, the proud 'workshop of England' whose population was now greater than all the rest of the county.

The new Warwickshire, though still run by gentlemen, fielded elevens that were predominantly professional, in keeping with the spirit of 'free trade' Birmingham. Always, though, the captain was an amateur – even to the point where a newcomer, an Old Malvernian, arrived for his first game only to be told that he had to lead the side.

In 1911 the county appointed as captain the 22-year-old Frank Foster, a flamboyant character who played attacking cricket all summer and led them to their first title. But his brilliance soon burned out, and for many years the county were to be found in the lower reaches of the table.

It was only after the Second War that their fortunes revived, when they regained the progressive spirit that had infused their formation. They gave the captaincy to a professional, Tom Dollery, and, without an amateur in his side, he led them to a second championship title in 1951.

Two years later, putting aside the reservations that inhibited the grander counties, they set up a football pool scheme, collecting money weekly from the local streets and factories, and they became the wealthiest of the county clubs, developing a modern stadium that returned Test cricket to the city.

Birmingham had always had its share of incomers, as had 'boom-town' Coventry between the wars, and Warwickshire cricket reflected this. Their 1951 side contained three New Zealanders and three from the north-east; their title-winning side of 1972 had four West Indians and a Pakistani.

Success is now part of the expectations at Warwickshire. No other county has won the championship and two one-day trophies in a year, as they did in 1994; no other county has won four titles in the era of four-day cricket. Though the city of Birmingham struggles to maintain its municipal pride in a post-industrial age, the county cricket club still retains the provincial confidence of its founder William Ansell.

> Warwickshire is not a natural cricketing county. The village greens and commons of Sussex and Kent are comparatively unknown, and our public parks canot compare with those of other towns. But the population is large; it only needs energetic action and enthusiasm on the part of the rulers of the game, and Warwickshire should be in the forefront of the counties.
>
> *William Ansell, 1910*

COUNTY CHAMPIONSHIP PLACINGS YEAR BY YEAR

1890	91	92	93	94	95	96	97	98	99	1900	01	02	03	04	05	06	07	08	09	10	11	12	13	14		19	20	21	22	23	24	25	26
-	-	-	-	-	-	6	12	7	9	7	6	5	6	7	7	7	6	9	12	12	14	1	9	11	7		15	12	16	12	12	9	8	12

27	28	29	30	31	32	33	34	35	36	37	38	39		46	47	48	49	50	51	52	53	54	55	56	57	58	59	60	61	62	63	64	65
11	11	14	15	9	9	7	4	8	13	11	13	11		14	15	7	4	4	1	10	9	6	9	14	11	16	4	15	12	3	4	2	11

66	67	68	69	70	71	72	73	74	75	76	77	78	79	80	81	82	83	84	85	86	87	88	89	90	91	92	93	94	95	96	97	98	99
6	10	11	4	7	2	1	7	9	14	5	10	11	15	14	17	17	5	9	15	12	15	6	8	5	2	6	16	1	1	8	4	8	10

2000	01	02	03	04	05	06	07	08	09	10	11	12	13	14
D2	D2	D1	D1	D1	D1	D1	D1	D2	D1	D1	D1	D1	D1	D1
6	3	2	5	1	4	4	8	1	5	6	2	1	4	2

County championship matches (1895-2014)		
Most runs	Dennis Amiss	31,617
	Willie Quaife	31,467
Most wickets	Eric Hollies	2,105
	Syd Santall	1,126
Most appearances	Willie Quaife	611

Post-war only (1946-2014)		
Most runs	Dennis Amiss	31,617
	Mike Smith	24,393
Most wickets	Eric Hollies	1,423
	Jack Bannister	1,084
Most appearances	Dennis Amiss	491

Last 25 years (1990-2014)		
Most runs	Nick Knight	11,018
	Dominic Ostler	9,859
Most wickets	Dougie Brown	485
	Tim Munton	453
Most appearances	Dominic Ostler	185

Courtaulds, Coventry

The victorious Warwickshire side of 1951 had only two county-born players, Birmingham's Charlie Grove and Coventry's Fred Gardner, so it was fitting that the title was secured with a century on his home patch by local hero Gardner, who also played football for the City.

The crowds were great, swelled in the evening by men spilling out of the car factories and standing several deep between the pavilion and the Courtaulds works.

Championship grounds			
	First	*Last*	*Matches*
Birmingham – Edgbaston	1895	2014	1,107
Leamington Spa – Arlington Avenue	1905	1910	4
Coventry – Bull's Head	1905	1992	13
Nuneaton – Weddington Road	1912	1914	3
Coventry – Butts Ground	1925	1930	10
Nuneaton – Griff and Coton	1930	1989	25
Coventry – Morris Motors	1931	1932	2
Birmingham – Mitchell and Butler	1931	1938	8
Coventry – Courtaulds	1946	1982	55
Stratford-upon-Avon – Swans Nest Lane	2004	2005	2

Worcestershire

Present county club formed: 1865
Joined county championship: 1899
Number of championships: 5

So much of what is special about Worcestershire was put in place by Paul Foley, the county's Secretary in the 1890s. It was he who saw the potential of the farm fields beside the cathedral, he who pioneered the Second-Class Championship from which the county rose to first-class status, and he who actively recruited lady members, thus creating Worcestershire's distinctive family atmosphere. Tea in the Ladies' Enclosure, he proudly told the cathedral's Dean, "is quite the thing".

On the field Worcestershire owed much in the early years to the immensely talented Foster family of Malvern, seven brothers of whom three captained the county. But the finances, over-stretched from the beginning, were never sound, and the county came close to winding up on either side of the First War. In 1919 they did not enter the championship, the only county ever to miss a season.

Through the 1920s they never rose far above the foot of the table, relying on come-and-go amateurs who treated the county's fixtures much as they did those of the Gentlemen of Worcestershire. One prep school headmaster, unable to play, sent in his place one of his staff.

The Secretary appointed after the Second War, Brigadier Green, found himself taken to a city-centre office, thick with dust which he had to clear himself, and told that his staff would be one typist. He set up a Supporters' Association; they created county cricket's first fund-raising football pool, and gradually the facilities at the ground were improved.

Captained by Don Kenyon, they were champions in 1964 and 1965, the first of the counties outside the 'Big Six' to win the title two years running. Always a welcoming club, they provided a home for the South African Basil D'Oliveira, and he repaid them with long years of service as player and coach, service that his son Damian also gave. Another who came from Africa and stayed faithfully was Graeme Hick, whose runs helped to bring two more championships in the 1980s.

The trees have grown in front of the cathedral, and the ground has been built up, with vital income now coming from concerts, weddings and conferences. But the essence of the place is much as it has long been: a ground as attractive as any, a welcome as friendly as ever – and, of course, there are still those ladies' teas.

> The thing about Worcester is, it's a parochial ground. I'd walk into town with the wife, and somebody would say, "Hallo, Bob." "Who's that?" she'd say. "I haven't a clue, but he sits in a deckchair four places from the chestnut tree." "And who's that?" "I don't know. He works nights at Archdales, he rides an A7 motorbike, and he parks it in front of the pavilion." You know all these people.
>
> *Bob Carter*

COUNTY CHAMPIONSHIP PLACINGS YEAR BY YEAR

1890	91	92	93	94	95	96	97	98	99	1900	01	02	03	04	05	06	07	08	09	10	11	12	13	14		19	20	21	22	23	24	25	26
-	-	-	-	-	-	-	-	-	-	12	12	11	9	6	13	8	14	2	6	8	13	9	16	12		-	15	14	17	15	14	16	17

27	28	29	30	31	32	33	34	35	36	37	38	39		46	47	48	49	50	51	52	53	54	55	56	57	58	59	60	61	62	63	64	65
17	17	16	10	14	17	15	16	12	12	15	11	7		8	7	10	3	6	4	14	15	11	15	9	16	9	14	13	4	2	14	1	1

66	67	68	69	70	71	72	73	74	75	76	77	78	79	80	81	82	83	84	85	86	87	88	89	90	91	92	93	94	95	96	97	98	99
2	5	7	12	6	15	7	6	1	10	11	13	15	2	11	11	14	16	10	5	5	9	1	1	4	6	17	2	15	10	7	3	13	15

2000	01	02	03	04	05	06	07	08	09	10	11	12	13	14
D2	D2	D2	D2	D1	D2	D2	D1	D2	D1	D2	D1	D1	D2	D2
5	6	4	1	7	6	2	9	2	9	2	7	9	5	2

New Road, Worcester

Converted from farmland in 1898, the New Road ground was for many years considered the best in the country, with a beautiful batting strip and an outfield so smooth it staged bowls matches. Fred Hunt, its first groundsman, stayed in post till the end of the Second War, resolutely refusing a motorised roller. He got up each morning at five to feed and water the horse, and such was his care that he never had to pay out the pound he offered to anyone who found a dandelion. He also farmed the adjoining land and, with the county often looking for players, appeared in 53 matches.

County championship matches (1899-2014)		
Most runs	Don Kenyon	31,375
	Graeme Hick	28,776
Most wickets	Reg Perks	2,009
	Norman Gifford	1,485
Most appearances	Don Kenyon	538

Post-war only (1946-2014)		
Most runs	Don Kenyon	31,375
	Graeme Hick	28,776
Most wickets	Norman Gifford	1,485
	Jack Flavell	1,397
Most appearances	Don Kenyon	538

Last 25 years (1990-2014)		
Most runs	Graeme Hick	20,190
	Vikram Solanki	13,874
Most wickets	Stuart Lampitt	511
	Phil Newport	443
Most appearances	Graeme Hick	255

Championship grounds			
	First	*Last*	*Matches*
Worcester – New Road	1899	2014	977
Amblecote – War Memorial Ground	1905	1981	61
Bournville Cricket Ground	1910	1911	2
Dudley – Tipton Road	1911	1971	87
Kidderminster – Chester Road North	1921	2008	66
Evesham – Sports Club	1951	1951	1
Stourport-on-Severn – Chain Wire Club	1980	1980	1
Hereford – Racecourse Ground	1981	1983	3

Yorkshire

Present county club formed: 1863

Joined county championship: 1890

Number of championships: 31 + 1 shared

Not without reason is Yorkshire split into three ridings, for it spans an area greater than Middlesex, Surrey, Kent, Sussex and Hampshire combined. When the county cricket club was formed in 1863, it was based in Sheffield, the southernmost tip of the county, and its committee were all Sheffield men. With the county extending one hundred miles to the north, there were attempts to form rival Yorkshire clubs.

The discontent rumbled on, not helped by a team that sank to such a low point in 1891 that some queried whether the county any longer merited first-class status. Out of that crisis, however, came progress. The committee was restructured, the captain Lord Hawke acquired greater power, and in 1893 the championship was won for the first time.

The old Yorkshire eleven had been a little too fond of a drink, but now a new team emerged with a greater pride in its performance, a team that turned the county's cricket into something special and distinctive. In the words of JM Kilburn, 'It was the cricket of a close community, cricket expressed in terms of high self-confidence, cricket of technical excellence moulded and devoted to a team purpose.'

Fiercely committed to picking only those born in the county (though a blind eye was turned to Lord Hawke's Lincolnshire origins), they played the game hard and without frills. Such was their dominance in the first three years of the 20th century that they won 59 of their 80 matches and lost only twice.

Between the wars they remained the supreme team, winning 12 titles in 21 years, but they never grew complacent. They demanded the highest of standards, as the young Hedley Verity discovered after taking seven for 26. "It owt to 'a bin seven for 22," he was told back in the hotel. "Ah nivver saw such bowling. Whativver wa' t'doing to gie Judd that fower?"

After Surrey's domination of the 1950s, they were again supreme in the 1960s and still playing with the same spirit. "They were always arguing," one opponent recalled, "but, when you tried to argue against them, you came up against a brick wall. They were one clan, Yorkshire for Yorkshiremen."

Their refusal to employ overseas players, coupled with bitter internal divisions, brought long, painful years of failure, but that is behind them now. When they won the title in 2014, they had nine Yorkshire-born men in their eleven.

> Life in the north in the 1930s was a grim fight for survival. The cricket I grew up in was played fair, played tough and without any kid-glove approach. But it was *cricket*. The sort of cricket that produced Herbert Sutcliffe and Len Hutton. The sort of cricket I was to encounter when I played against Australians and West Indians, where you give nothing away and you play to win.
> *Brian Close*

COUNTY CHAMPIONSHIP PLACINGS YEAR BY YEAR

1890	91	92	93	94	95	96	97	98	99	1900	01	02	03	04	05	06	07	08	09	10	11	12	13	14		19	20	21	22	23	24	25	26
3	8	6	1	2	3	1	4	1	3	1	1	1	3	2	1	2	2	1	3	8	7	1	2	4		1	4	3	1	1	1	1	2

27	28	29	30	31	32	33	34	35	36	37	38	39		46	47	48	49	50	51	52	53	54	55	56	57	58	59	60	61	62	63	64	65
3	4	2	3	1	1	1	1	5	1	3	1	1		1	7	4	1	3	2	2	12	2	2	7	3	11	1	1	2	1	1	5	4

66	67	68	69	70	71	72	73	74	75	76	77	78	79	80	81	82	83	84	85	86	87	88	89	90	91	92	93	94	95	96	97	98	99
1	1	1	13	4	13	10	14	11	2	8	12	4	7	6	10	10	17	14	11	10	8	13	16	10	14	16	12	13	8	6	6	3	6

2000	01	02	03	04	05	06	07	08	09	10	11	12	13	14
D1	D1	D1	D2	D2	D2	D1	D1	D1	D1	D1	D1	D2	D1	D1
3	1	9	4	7	3	6	6	7	7	3	8	2	2	1

County championship matches (1890-2014)		
Most runs	Herbert Sutcliffe	32,814
	Geoff Boycott	29,485
Most wickets	Wilfred Rhodes	3,112
	George Hirst	2,095
Most appearances	Wilfred Rhodes	762

Post-war only (1946-2014)		
Most runs	Geoff Boycott	29,485
	John Hampshire	19,555
Most wickets	Fred Trueman	1,488
	Johnny Wardle	1,280
Most appearances	Brian Close	448

Last 25 years (1990-2014)		
Most runs	Anthony McGrath	13,575
	David Byas	11,270
Most wickets	Chris Silverwood	418
	Darren Gough	412
Most appearances	Richard Blakey	238

North Marine Road, Scarborough

In 2001 the seaside ground was the scene of one of Yorkshire's most emotional moments. Their captain David Byas, a farmer who had played for the Scarborough club, hit a century and took the winning catch to bring the championship to the county for the first time for 33 years. "It's like a fairy tale," he said from the pavilion balcony.

Championship grounds			
	First	*Last*	*Matches*
York – Wigginton Road	1890	1890	1
Dewsbury – Savile Town	1890	1933	39
Huddersfield – Fartown	1890	1955	48
Sheffield – Bramall Lane	1890	1973	244
Bradford – Park Avenue	1890	1996	256
Leeds – Headingley	1891	2014	407
Harrogate – St George's Road	1895	1996	78
Scarborough – North Marine Road	1896	2014	138
Halifax – Thrum Hall	1897	1897	1
Hull – The Circle	1899	1974	81
Middlesbrough – Acklam Park	1956	1996	42
Sheffield – Abbeydale Park	1974	1996	39

The History

from Surrey, champions in 1890, to Yorkshire, champions in 2014

1860s	Cricketing annuals start to compare the counties, with the first use of the word 'champions'.
1887	A Cricket Council is set up, to create the rules for a formal championship.
1890	The county championship is established, with eight counties participating: Gloucestershire, Kent, Lancashire, Middlesex, Nottinghamshire, Surrey, Sussex and Yorkshire.
1891	Somerset enters as the ninth county.
1895	Five more counties are admitted to the championship: Derbyshire, Essex, Hampshire, Leicestershire and Warwickshire.
1899	Worcestershire enters.
1905	Northamptonshire becomes the sixteenth county.
1919	For one summer only, the matches are all of two days' duration. In the first summer after war Worcestershire does not enter the competition.
1921	Glamorgan are admitted, bringing the number of counties to seventeen.
1952	A championship pennant is created, to be flown by the reigning champions.
1968	Overseas players are allowed to play for counties without any period of qualification.
1969	The championship is reduced to accommodate a 40-over Sunday League.
1973	A trophy is donated by the Lord's Taverners. Prize money is introduced.
1977	Cadbury-Schweppes becomes the championship's first sponsor.
1988	Some matches are extended to four days.
1992	Durham becomes the eighteenth county.
1993	All matches become four days in length.
2000	The championship is split into two divisions.

To begin at the beginning ... but when was that?

When did the county championship begin? Cricket historians still argue about it. Even *Wisden*, that definitive bible of cricket records, has changed its mind several times.

Did it start in 1873, the year when the counties agreed the rules of qualification for players? That is the year that *Wisden* always used to give, and it is the year chosen by Roy Webber in his 1957 book *The County Cricket Championship*.

Or was it in 1864, the year to which *Wisden* switched in its hundredth edition in 1963? This revision came about as a result of extensive research by Major Rowland Bowen, the eccentric and irascible cricket historian who is reputed to have tried to saw off one of his own legs and to have offered guns to Peter Hain's anti-apartheid 'Stop The 70 Tour' campaign. Bowen had actually argued for either 1865, on the grounds that that was the first year in which he had found a reference (in an annual, *Lillywhite's Companion*) to a county being 'better than any other', or 1869, when in the same annual the word 'champions' was first used. *Wisden*, however, with a touch of self-importance, opted for the earlier date of 1864, thus harmonising the births of its own almanack and of the county championship.

Perhaps we should opt for 1888, what Roy Webber called the beginning of the Second Phase. That was the first summer in which the Cricket Council, under the chairmanship of Lord Harris of Kent, had the power to decide the rules for county cricket. The championship of 1888 was also the first one for which *Wisden* published a table, though it was not the same as the one which had appeared in the newspapers.

There is a case for starting in 1895, when the number of participating counties rose from nine to 14. That, it could be argued, was the birth of the modern era. It was also the point at which the competition was recognised formally by MCC.

At present the consensus seems to be in favour of 1890, the first summer in which the counties agreed in advance what system would be used to establish the final order of the table. That is the date taken by Robert Brooke in his 1991 book on the championship. It is also the date which *Wisden* now uses, having decided during the 1990s to downgrade the earlier championships: first by labelling them as unofficial, then by removing them altogether from the main list and finally by discounting them in the tally of most championships won. Supporters of Gloucestershire who in 1994 could pick up their *Wisden* and discover proudly that their county had won

three outright championships now find themselves reading with melancholy that 'Gloucestershire, Northamptonshire and Somerset have never won.'

It is a messy business, but it was ever thus. In the 1950s a contestant on an ITV quiz show, *The 64,000 Question*, was asked to name the counties which had never won the championship and he failed to include Sussex, thus forfeiting his chance of winning £1,600 (64,000 sixpenny bits). According to *Wisden* Sussex had indeed not won, but this was not the view of Roy Webber whose recent book argued that they had shared the title with Lancashire and Nottinghamshire in 1875. As the *Playfair Annual's* statistician Webber proceeded to alter that publication's list of champion counties, a deviation from *Wisden* that survived for twenty years and delighted supporters of Sussex. Webber, however, failed to track down the quiz show contestant; the young lad may well have remained oblivious to the rumpus he had created in the cricket world.

The reality of it is that there was no single start date, no magical point at which the championship was created. In a very English way it emerged organically over many years.

County cricket clubs formed, they started playing one another and in time people began to make comparisons between them and to suggest which one of them was the best that year. Sometimes the word 'champions' was used. Newspapers, magazines and annuals then created tables, though initially their methods of ordering the counties varied. By the 1880s the idea of a champion county had captured the public's imagination, and in 1887 the counties recognised this by setting up a Cricket Council. Their intention was to agree a formal system for the championship, which they duly did in December 1889. The summer of 1890 was the first to be played under that agreed system.

Back in 1873 MCC had made a previous attempt to create a formal competition between the counties in the form of a knock-out tournament, called the Champion Cup, to be played at Lord's. In the event most of the counties pulled out, and only one match was played. In a low-scoring contest on a rough pitch, with several batsmen receiving unpleasant blows, Kent beat Sussex by 52 runs, and the idea died. Not everybody in Victorian England, it has to be said, wanted cricket to go down the path of competitions and trophies.

During those evolutionary years there were three crucial issues that had to be resolved:

1. Who was eligible to play for a county side?
2. Which counties were part of the championship?
3. How was the champion county to be decided?

The question of who could play for a county was resolved in 1873. At that point it was established that no cricketer could play for more than one county during the same season and that he may play for one of the following: the county of his birth, the county in which he had resided for the previous two years or 'the county in which his family home is, so long as it remains open to him as an occasional residence'.

This was a major step for the counties, suggesting that the competition between them was becoming more serious. No longer would the round-arm bowler James Southerton be able to fill his cricketing diary with matches for Sussex, Surrey and even Hampshire. In 1869, by spreading his favours, he contrived to play in all but seven of the 22 first-class inter-county matches. In 1872, playing for Surrey then Sussex, he dismissed Grace three times in five days. He was everywhere.

But which counties were part of the championship?

Since the competition had no formal existence, this was not always clear. In theory, it was based on the matches played between the first-class counties. But which counties were first-class? WG Grace, in his 1891 book *Cricket*, listed seven such in 1864: Surrey, Middlesex, Sussex, Cambridgeshire, Nottinghamshire, Yorkshire and Kent. But his table of results also includes their matches against Hampshire and Buckinghamshire.

By 1871 things had become a little clearer. Derbyshire, Gloucestershire and Lancashire had been added, while Cambridgeshire had faded away. Yet, well into the 1880s Hampshire and even Somerset were playing first-class matches, though not appearing in most championship tables. Then in 1888, when Derbyshire dropped back to second-class status, they appeared till early August in the table of the magazine *Cricket*. Only with the decisions of the Cricket Council in December 1889 did the possibility of such anomalies cease.

The greatest bugbear of all, however, was how it was decided which county should be awarded the title of champions.

Some years it was straightforward. In 1884, for instance, Nottinghamshire, playing ten matches, won nine and drew the other, while all the other counties lost at least three times.

But two years later it was not so clear. Were Nottinghamshire (played 14: won 7, drawn 7) champions on the generally accepted ground that they were unbeaten? Or was their record inferior to Surrey (played 16: won 12, drawn 1, lost 3)? The newspapers settled a little reluctantly for Nottinghamshire, but the magazine *Cricket* argued for Surrey, adding that Surrey had twice beaten the Australians. In future, it said, touring teams should be included in the county championship.

The following year the newspapers adopted a points system: one for a win, half for a draw. But the problem with this, as with the 'fewest matches lost' method, was that the counties played very different numbers of games. There was no central authority setting up a fixture list; the counties arranged what matches they chose. The smaller counties could not afford to play too many games, and sometimes there was a falling out, as when in the 1880s Middlesex and Nottinghamshire refused to play Lancashire in protest against the action of their fast bowler Crossland.

In 1874 most reckoned Gloucestershire to be the champion county, but *Wisden* has opted for Derbyshire on the basis that they did not lose any of their four matches (playing only Kent and Lancashire). By that reckoning Cambridgeshire should have been declared champions in 1864, as they won all their three games. In 1883 there was also disagreement when some gave the title to Nottinghamshire, some to Yorkshire and one publication awarded it jointly.

It was all a bit of a muddle, reflecting the fact that in no formal sense did the county championship actually exist before 1890, but it has kept cricket's historians busy, none more than the cantankerous Rowland Bowen. In the 1960s he established a subscriber-only periodical *Cricket Quarterly*, and such was his determination to impose his version of history that he stood for no opposition, even striking dissenters off his mailing list. One poor man, innocently applying for a copy, had his cheque returned with an angry reply, accusing him of being a banned subscriber returning under a false name.

This book hopes to be less controversial. It chooses to start in earnest with the summer of 1890, when for the first time the counties entered the season agreed on all the main issues.

There was no sense in 1890 that something new had been created. It was the same old championship as in 1889, but it had taken one more step on its evolutionary journey – a crucial step, one that finally eliminated so much of the previous confusion. Henceforth there would be no differences of opinion about which counties were taking part in the championship or which of them was the winner.

1880 England beat the touring Australians by five wickets at the Oval, the first such match played in England. County cricket, according to WG Grace, is 'in no way affected by the Australian visit; for, if anything, the interest displayed during the season was greater than in any previous year.' Nottinghamshire are the champions.

1881 Seven Nottinghamshire professionals go on strike for much of the summer. Their demands are for a summer-long contract, a benefit after ten years and the right to play in a privately arranged match against Yorkshire. Lancashire are champions, their only defeat of the summer when their full first team loses to Cambridge University.

At a meeting of county secretaries a proposal to reduce the residential qualification from two years to one is defeated.

1882 Australian tourists play one 'great match' against England – at the Oval in late August. Their seven-run victory prompts a mock obituary in the *Sporting Times*, with its legendary reference to the 'ashes' of English cricket.

Most publications award the title of champions jointly to Lancashire and Nottinghamshire.

1883 Opinions differ whether Nottinghamshire or Yorkshire (or both jointly) are champions.

Surrey and Nottinghamshire begin the tradition (which lasts till 1966) of playing each other on the bank holidays: Whitsun at Trent Bridge, August at the Oval. This is the first of the bank-holiday fixtures to be established.

1884 MCC adopts a revised Code of the Laws. The new version no longer contains any reference to the settling of bets.

Australian tourists play three 'great matches' against England: at Old Trafford, Lord's and the Oval.

Nottinghamshire are undisputed champions.

1885 Nottinghamshire are again champions.

Grace comments on the rise of the professional batsmen, who are now outnumbering the amateurs in the averages.

1886 England win all the three 'representative matches' against the Australian tourists.

Nottinghamshire are named as the champion county except in the magazine *Cricket*, which chooses Surrey. Its editor, Charles Alcock, is Secretary at the Oval.

1887 A point-scoring system – one for a win, half for a draw – starts to emerge. Surrey are the champion county.

On 12 July, at Lord's, delegates from the counties, under the chairmanship of Kent's Lord Harris, set up a Cricket Council to decide on the regulations for county cricket. Representatives are present from the nine first-class counties plus eleven others: Cheshire, Durham, Essex, Hampshire, Hertfordshire, Leicestershire, Norfolk, Northamptonshire, Somersetshire, Staffordshire and Warwickshire.

There are calls to speed up play by increasing the over to five balls. Teams are generally bowling about 36 four-ball overs an hour, though at Bradford Lancashire bowl 340½ overs in 7 hours 55 minutes: an hourly rate of 43, the equivalent of almost 29 six-ball overs (and with more changing of ends).

1888 Derbyshire drop out of the championship. The remaining eight counties play home-and-away against each other, with the exception of Middlesex and Sussex who have not met since 1868. Surrey are again the champion county.

Australian tourists visit England, once again playing at Lord's, the Oval and Old Trafford.

1889 Lancashire, Nottinghamshire and Surrey are considered to be joint champions.

Law changes include the switch to a five-ball over and a provision for teams to declare on the third day.

The captaincy of Nottinghamshire passes from the professional Mordecai Sherwin to the amateur John Dixon. It will be 1935 (Ewart Astill at Leicestershire, for just one summer) before a professional again captains a county side.

In September the foundation stone is laid of a new Lord's pavilion, to be completed for the following May.

In December the counties at the Cricket Council agree to create an official point-scoring system for the championship. Their intention is to introduce promotion and relegation between first- and second-class counties.

Unofficial champions 1864-1889

1864-1872

There are four main sources for the years from 1864 to 1872.
1. The list compiled by Rowland Bowen and printed in *Wisden* from 1963.
2. The list compiled for the 1903 edition of WG Grace's book *Cricket*.
3. *Bailey's Magazine*, published at the time.
4. John Lillywhite's *Cricketers' Companion*, also published at the time.

	Wisden 1963	Grace 1903	Bailey's	Lillywhite
1864	Surrey	Surrey		
1865	Nottinghamshire	Nottinghamshire		Nottinghamshire
1866	Middlesex	Middlesex		Middlesex
1867	Yorkshire	Yorkshire		Yorkshire
1868	Nottinghamshire	Yorkshire	Nottinghamshire	
1869	Notts/ Yorkshire	Nottinghamshire	Notts/ Yorkshire	Notts/ Yorkshire
1870	Yorkshire	Yorkshire	Notts/ Yorkshire	Yorkshire
1871	Nottinghamshire	Nottinghamshire	Notts/ Yorkshire	Nottinghamshire
1872	Nottinghamshire	Surrey	Notts/ Yorkshire	Nottinghamshire

1873-1889

The following are six of the best-known sources for the years from 1873 to 1889.
1. The list compiled by Rev RS Holmes and printed in *Wisden* up to 1962.
2. The list compiled by Rowland Bowen and printed in *Wisden* from 1963.
3. The list compiled for the 1903 edition of WG Grace's book *Cricket*.
4. The magazine *Cricket*, published at the time.
5. James Lillywhite's *Cricketers' Annual*, also published at the time.
   (John Lillywhite's *Cricketers' Companion* also appeared during most of these years, but its champions
   are the same in each year except 1873 when it awarded the title outright to Gloucestershire.)
6. The list compiled by Roy Webber for his 1957 book *The County Cricket Championship* and used
   in the *Playfair Cricket Annual* up to 1978.

	Wisden 1962	Wisden 1963	Grace 1903	Cricket	Lillywhite	Webber 1957
1873	Glos/ Notts	Glos/ Notts	Glos/ Notts		Glos/ Notts	Glos/ Notts
1874	Derbyshire	Gloucestershire	Gloucestershire		Gloucestershire	Derbyshire
1875	Nottinghamshire	Nottinghamshire	Nottinghamshire		Nottinghamshire	Notts/Lancs/Sussex
1876	Gloucestershire	Gloucestershire	Gloucestershire		Gloucestershire	Gloucestershire
1877	Gloucestershire	Gloucestershire	Gloucestershire		Gloucestershire	Gloucestershire
1878	Middlesex	*Undecided*	Nottinghamshire			Middlesex
1879	Notts/ Lancs	Notts/ Lancs	Notts/ Lancs		Notts/ Lancs	Notts// Lancs
1880	Nottinghamshire	Nottinghamshire	Nottinghamshire		Nottinghamshire	Notts/ Glos
1881	Lancashire	Lancashire	Lancashire		Lancashire	Lancashire
1882	Notts/ Lancs	Notts/ Lancs	Notts/ Lancs	Lancashire	Notts/ Lancs	Notts/ Lancs
1883	Nottinghamshire	Nottinghamshire	Yorkshire	Notts/ Yorks	Nottinghamshire	Nottinghamshire
1884	Nottinghamshire	Nottinghamshire	Nottinghamshire	Nottinghamshire	Nottinghamshire	Nottinghamshire
1885	Nottinghamshire	Nottinghamshire	Nottinghamshire	Nottinghamshire	Nottinghamshire	Nottinghamshire
1886	Nottinghamshire	Nottinghamshire	Nottinghamshire	Surrey	Nottinghamshire	Nottinghamshire
1887	Surrey	Surrey	Surrey	Surrey	Surrey	Surrey
1888	Surrey	Surrey	Surrey	Surrey	Surrey	Surrey
1889	Surrey/Lancs/Notts	Surrey/Lancs/Notts	Surrey/Lancs/Notts	Surrey/Lancs/Notts	Surrey/Lancs/Notts	Surrey/Lancs/Notts

The glorious summer of 1887

It was the summer of Queen Victoria's Golden Jubilee, a glorious summer with warm sunshine and barely a drop of rain between late May and mid-August. The farmers were in despair as their soil grew parched while in cricket the batsmen enjoyed a rich harvest. In the whole 19th century there was no drier year – and only one, 1921, since then.

With no touring team from Australia, it was left to county cricket to capture the imagination of the sporting public, and capture it, it did, with crowds greater than ever filling the grounds. On August Bank Holiday Monday, at the Oval, 27,000 people watched the first day of the crucial encounter between Surrey and Nottinghamshire, more than twice as many as had been there for any day of the England-Australia game the previous year.

From early morning they queued, and at the end of the luncheon interval it took some time for the police, aided by a few club officials, to push them all off the field of play. They were rowdy, engaging in 'noisy horseplay', and at one stage those on the grass began to skirmish with those behind, throwing sods of earth, ginger beer bottles and even stones. They reserved all their applause for the Surrey players – not clapping but roaring – and, in the evening, when Notts took the field, they encroached so far onto the grass that parts of the boundary were reduced by as much as twenty yards.

There was no official championship, no agreed method for deciding the champions, but these holiday-makers understood the significance of the contest. Nottinghamshire were the great team of the age – only two defeats in the previous four summers – but Surrey, if they could beat them here as they had done in the Whitsun match at Trent Bridge, would in all probability take the crown from them. The scenes around the ground may have disturbed many, but one thing was made crystal clear by the crowd. The county championship mattered.

The earlier game at Trent Bridge had not been without controversy. Cricket had not yet adapted its laws for an age in which its batsmen were often in the ascendant, and there was no provision for the declaration of an innings. The convention was for a team to bat and bat until it was all out, which, in the years when the county championship was decided by fewest losses, made sense. There were even games, three-day games, when the first team would bat for a full two days.

The summer of 1887 was different. This year there was to be a points system that placed a greater weight on victory; that required a new approach. Surrey's captain, John Shuter,

John Shuter

Surrey captain
1880 – 1893

The son of a timber merchant, educated at Winchester College, he brought an enterprising spirit to the Surrey side, lifting them from the doldrums to years of greatness

was quick to grasp the point. At one o'clock on the final day at Trent Bridge his Surrey side had reached 264 for three in their second innings, with a lead of 290. Was there nothing left to do but to make more runs? In a move that caused some friction, Shuter sent out his men to throw away their wickets, which they duly did: one was bowled, two caught, two charged down the pitch to be stumped and two hit down their wickets. Then his bowlers set to work, dismissing Notts with fifteen minutes to spare. It was highly unorthodox, 'not cricket' in the eyes of many, but it gave the southern county an early edge in the battle to be champions.

Nottinghamshire's captain was their professional wicket-keeper Mordecai Sherwin, a large and jovial man of 17 stone who kept goal for Notts County and ran a local pub, the Belvoir Inn. By the end of the summer he too was throwing away wickets in pursuit of victory, though opponents were now growing wise to the tactic. Against Sussex, according to the *Manchester Guardian*, 'Sherwin was evidently anxious to finish off the innings. He twice got out of his ground, but Mr Dudney would not stump him, so he hit his wicket.' It was farcical. By the start of 1889 the laws had been amended.

Nottinghamshire, unaccustomed to defeat, were involved in further controversy on the last afternoon of their match at Bramall Lane, Sheffield. For Yorkshire, with their headquarters in the south of the county, this was the game that mattered most in their summer, more important to them than the contest with Lancashire, and they found themselves on the last afternoon with the tough but tantalising task of scoring 119 runs in 85 minutes for victory. Lord Hawke, ever game for a challenge, promoted his hitters to the top of the order, and Billy Bates responded by attacking the bowling with great vigour. Less than an hour later, when he was out, Yorkshire needed only 28 runs in 28 minutes. With six wickets in hand, a memorable triumph was within their grasp.

The dour Fred Lee, reluctant to embrace risk, slowed their progress. 'He would not play the game for our side,' Lord Hawke wrote later, 'but stuck in without forcing.' The large crowd, especially those in Bramall Lane's Pit, grew restive at Lee's efforts: "Give it some wood ... There's plenty more after thee." With few of them carrying watches, they peered anxiously at the clock of St Mary's Church as the minute hand moved ever upward towards the hour.

Lee finally got the message and was stumped, as in quick succession were Bobby Peel and David Hunter, both of them after sprinting out to the middle. It was a clatter of wickets so fast that the next man, the ageing Tom Emmett, had no time to don his flannels, running out in grey trousers, braces and tie, with no spiked boots or leg guards. He pushed a single, leaving Saul Wade to score three runs off two balls. Wade could not get the first away; to the second he jumped out of his crease and was stumped by Sherwin. And that was it. In the words of one spectator, 'The clock struck six, the bell rang, stumps and the match were drawn, and Nottingham saved the most exciting match that was ever played on Bramall Lane or any other ground.'

Next day the *Manchester Guardian* castigated the spectators for their unsportsmanlike jeering of the fielding side: 'Notts had nothing to play for but a draw, and they certainly stuck pluckily to their work right up to the end without wasting time.' Yet within days the same newspaper was painting a quite different picture, one of the reigning champions saving the game by 'extremely deliberate manoeuvring in the last half hour ... It is not usual for a fielder who has been to the boundary to walk back to the wicket and carefully place the ball in the bowler's hands. Nor is it usual for fielders to walk with extreme slowness when "changing wickets" or for the bowler to study the opposite wicket with laborious scrutiny, and to take counsel as to the best method of attack.'

One letter-writer to the *Sheffield Telegraph* said the time-wasting 'would be a disgrace to any factory team'; another ventured that 'if Yorkshire had been playing at Trent Bridge and had acted in such a manner, the Nottingham roughs would not have kept their tempers, but would have resorted to something more expressive of their disgust than mere hissing.' More significantly, an anonymous member of the Yorkshire team told the *Sheffield Independent* that 'Yorkshire would have lost the match rather than adopt the same tactics.' He was 'disgusted with the way in which the time was dawdled away'.

It was evident that Notts would not give up lightly their status as champions, but in the vital bank-holiday match at the Oval their intensity of purpose was their undoing. On Tuesday the atmosphere, without the one-day holiday-makers, was more subdued, yet there were almost 17,000 paying spectators. They watched eagerly as Surrey's batsmen profited from an uncommon number of missed catches. The *Times* correspondent thought 'the extreme keenness and anxiety which animated both elevens had a bad effect upon the fielding, and chances were lost and opportunities thrown away which in an ordinary game would have been readily seized.'

Across the three days, in addition to the Surrey members, 51,607 spectators paid sixpence each to watch the game – some reckoned it set a new record for attendance at a cricket match in England – and on Wednesday afternoon they witnessed a thrilling four-wicket victory by Surrey. 'When all was over, the excitement of the crowd found vent and there was a demonstration in front of the Pavilion which must have lasted quite a quarter of an hour.'

It was the decisive contest of the summer. Though there were further twists and turns, at the end of August it was agreed by all that Surrey were the champions.

In the *Field* magazine a correspondent noted how attractive the matches between the leading counties had become: 'The desire to win, which inspires every true cricketer, is far stronger in these matches than most others.' He acknowledged that some saw only evil in this heightened competitiveness: 'There is no doubt that the struggle between Surrey and Nottinghamshire this year caused on one occasion the introduction of practices which no one would care to see common in the cricket field, and produced some ill-feeling between the two counties.'

Yet the rivalries, he continued, gave 'a vast amount of pleasure to the public' and needed converting into a more formal structure. 'Cricket elevens do not want to carry off challenge cups, or even medals, like Association football players. Still, they cannot help being at least as much interested as the general public in the result of their season's matches.'

The championship had no formal existence but, as the *London Standard* put it, it was 'nevertheless a reality and, as a thing, eagerly sought after as if it were much more than a phrase'.

Charles Alcock the pioneer

Charles Alcock was that most rare of characters, a man of vision with a close attention to detail and a driving energy that never let up. In the years from the mid-1860s to the early 1890s, when the playing and organising of sport in Britain was growing and changing at a rapid pace, he was in the thick of much of it.

For 35 years, from 1872 till his death in 1907, he was Secretary of Surrey County Cricket Club. For 25 years, from 1870, he was Secretary of the Football Association. And, if the joint holding of those two posts is hard for a modern mind to grasp, he was also for the last 40 years of his life an active and pioneering journalist and publisher. In 1868 he launched a *Football Annual*, recording scores for the winter game as *Wisden* did for cricket. He edited for many years *James Lillywhite's Cricketers' Annual*, and in 1882 he began *Cricket*, a well-written and informative magazine which he was still editing and publishing when he died. As one cricket writer of the time succintly put it, 'He was a worker.'

He was born in 1842 in Sunderland, his family moving when he was young to Essex. He was sent to Harrow School, with the expectation that when he left he would join the family shipbroking business. He did for a while in a half-hearted way, but he was soon gaining work reporting on sport for a number of publications. He was also playing sport – cricket for the Gentlemen of Essex, football for the Wanderers, a club mainly of Old Harrovians which he founded in 1863.

Was he a good cricketer? An entry in Haygarth's *Scores and Biographies* calls him 'a steady bat, a fair change fast bowler and an excellent long stop or long field', adding that 'he is a great lover of the game'. Surviving scorecards show no notable achievements, though once in the 1860s, in a match in Hamburg, he played under a pseudonym for France against Germany. In later life he told an interviewer that he had made the highest score and won the prize of a bat.

His footballing achievements were considerably greater. A tall man by the standards of the time, and well built, he was a goal-scoring forward who could hold his own when the game got physical.

In those days of the 1860s, when the first organised football clubs were still forming and no national rules had been agreed, Alcock played in March 1866 in what is considered to be the first representative match, between a London side and a Sheffield side, played under 'London rules'. In November 1867 he appeared in the first county football match, for Middlesex against Surrey and Kent, a game that took place in what *Field* magazine called 'the wilds of Battersea Park'.

Then in 1870, in his new role as FA Secretary, he organised international matches between England and Scotland, captaining the England team himself. There were five such matches, all played at the Oval, but they are not now treated as proper internationals on the grounds that the English FA was selecting both sides. He was injured when the first official international took place in November 1872, but he did play and captain England against Scotland at the Oval in March 1875. For much of the first half England were handicapped by the late arrival of their goalkeeper, who had missed his train from Sheffield. But Alcock scored his side's second goal, which he 'breasted' into the net, in a 2-2 draw.

As well as pioneering international football, he was the driving force in the creation of a knock-out tournament that came to be known as the FA Cup. Based on an inter-house tournament he had played at Harrow, it began life in the winter of 1871/72.

His own Wanderers, of which he was captain, were one of 15 clubs to enter, curiously reaching the final after four rounds in which they only won one game. Their first opponents, Harrow Chequers, could not raise a side; Clapham Rovers were beaten 3-1; and the 0-0 draw with Crystal Palace resulted in both clubs progressing to the semi-finals at the Oval. There the Wanderers drew 0-0 with Queen's Park from Glasgow, winning the replay when the Scots were unable to afford another long train journey south.

The final was also held at the Oval. The entrance fee, one shilling, was considered excessive, and only 2,000 spectators attended. The Royal Engineers were pioneers of a new-style passing game, quite different from the Wanderers' conventional dribbling, but they suffered a setback after ten minutes when a 'melée' resulted in Lieutenant Cresswell of the Engineers breaking his collar-bone. He refused to leave the field but his injury rendered him useless, and Alcock's Wanderers won the first FA Cup Final 1-0. Their goal-scorer, Morton Betts, was a Harrow Chequers footballer who appeared mysteriously under the pseudonym 'A.H. Chequer'.

It was the only time Alcock played in the final, though he was the referee in 1875 and 1879, by which time the competition was growing rapidly. In 1884 there were 100 teams taking part, and the final at the Oval was watched by 12,000 spectators.

There was a further development, however, one that would test Alcock's FA. Some clubs in the north were paying their players, and there were strong moves to throw them out.

Alcock argued that professionalism in sport was not a problem – 'Veiled professionalism is the evil to be repressed' – and eventually won the day.

It was a fast-changing world. In March 1889, before 27,000 spectators at the Oval, Preston North End beat West Bromwich Albion 3-0. That same winter Preston were also the winners of the first Football League.

The developments were as great in cricket. It was Alcock who was always at the centre of the arrangements made for Australian touring teams, and in September 1880 he was responsible for a late reorganisation of the visitors' schedule. Instead of a match against Sussex at Hove, he substituted a game against an England XI, captained by Lord Harris, at the Oval. Three such matches had taken place in Australia when private parties had toured there, but this was the first Test match in England. Great crowds made it a financial success, watching WG Grace hit 152 in a five-wicket England victory.

His first task when he became Surrey Secretary was to regularise the payments to the professionals, a move that was benevolently meant though it did not go down too well with one of them, Henry Jupp: "Last year, Mister Burrup, 'e paid me three times for the Lancashire match."

In the 1870s Surrey County Cricket Club was at a low ebb. On the field results were poor; off it, membership had declined. Alcock, still a young man, set to work with purpose. He generated income by bringing other sports to the ground, not just football but rugby, athletics, lacrosse and even cycling. From this the club was able to build up a larger pool of professional players so that, unlike the other southern counties, it could sustain a full summer-long fixture card. By the late 1880s they had become the premier county in the land.

Alcock spotted an opportunity when the local river was piped underground, arranging for the resulting spoil to be used to create the base of embankments round the field. Then in the 1890s, with a new ground lease agreed with the Duchy of Cornwall, the old, ramshackle pavilion was demolished, to be replaced by an elegant, twin-turreted one, designed by the same architect as at Old Trafford. Alcock was at all times a hands-on Secretary, literally so during the turmoil at the 1887 bank-holiday match against Notts when he lifted one unruly spectator off his feet and threw him back into the crowd. He was not sure, he admitted later, he had got the right man, but it did help to calm things down.

As the county championship moved from informal beginnings to an agreed structure, Alcock had great influence, both as Secretary of a leading club and as editor of his *Cricket* magazine.

In many ways Charles Alcock was an ideal figure for the time: an Old Harrovian patrician at ease with cricket's ruling class at Lord's and a practical man of business who commanded the respect and loyalty of the professionals. When several of them went on strike before the 1896 Oval Test, demanding a higher match fee, it was Alcock who firmly but sympathetically averted the crisis.

He had played his own sport as an amateur and upheld those values, but he also respected the need for working men to earn a living. Above all, he realised that the whole edifice required money and that that money would come more easily if there were structured competitions in place.

While others in the world of Victorian sport – the administrators of hockey and rugby union, for instance – held onto their strict amateur codes, refusing to sully their sports with 'ignoble pot-hunting', Alcock took football and cricket down a different path.

For football, that meant the FA Cup and international matches. For cricket, it was Test matches and the county championship.

1890 – 1899

An official championship
Eight counties in 1890, rising to fifteen in 1899
Surrey six times champions

It is remarkable that so much important cricket can be crowded into the brief English summer, and that a public should be found with so much time to give up to the game. Cricket has never been more popular than it is now, and for much of this popularity the skilled county teams in their keen competition for the championship are responsible.

A dozen years ago the visit of an Australian eleven had something like a monopoly of general interest. But times have changed. County cricket is the thing and no extraneous element can endanger its position.

The Times, April 1896

If either the Press or the counties have strength and courage enough to give up the championship competition, so much the better for sport. The present state of things makes for unmitigated professionalism, since it is only counties able to dispense with the assistance of gentlemen that can stand the strain of a full "first-class" campaign. And even from a spectacular point of view this is a consummation not to be desired. Wherefore it may be once more deduced that the championship and the classification of counties along with it were better abolished.

Cricket Field, 1893

Dressing and taking lunch in tents was considered no hardship in the sixties and seventies, though we should regard it differently now. I sometimes think that the modern conditions of cricket are too luxurious.

WG Grace, 1899

1890
The county championship begins its formal existence. There are eight counties: Gloucestershire, Kent, Lancashire, Middlesex, Nottinghamshire, Surrey, Sussex and Yorkshire. All counties play each other twice, with the exception of Middlesex and Sussex. With +1 for a win and -1 for a loss, the champions are the county with most points. Surrey are the champion county.

In August a meeting of the Cricket Council agrees to create three divisions, with promotion and relegation decided by play-off matches between top and bottom sides. The proposed divisions are:

1. Gloucestershire, Kent, Lancashire, Middlesex, Nottinghamshire, Surrey, Sussex, Yorkshire
2. Cheshire, Derbyshire, Essex, Hampshire, Leicestershire, Somersetshire, Staffordshire, Warwickshire
3. Devonshire, Durham, Glamorganshire, Hertfordshire, Lincolnshire, Norfolk, Northamptonshire, Northumberland

Amid considerable controversy a further meeting is held in December, attended also by many of the minor counties, and after a heated discussion a motion to suspend the Cricket Council 'sine die' is carried on the casting vote of the chairman. It will never be reconvened. Responsibilty for the county championship passes to MCC.

The London Underground introduces its first electric-powered section, running from Monument to Stockwell.

1891
Somerset joins the championship, which remains one division.

An Elementary Education Act introduces free education for the poor.

1892
All counties play each other twice, home and away. This arrangement, which lasts for three years, does not return till the creation of two divisions in 2000.

Keir Hardie is elected to the House of Commons as an Independent Labour MP.

1893
Yorkshire win the championship for the first time.

George Cadbury, the chocolate manufacturer, starts work on the building of a model village.

1894
The follow-on, compulsory at this time, is now enforced when the deficit is 120, not 80 runs.

The first Lyons tea shop is opened at 123 Piccadilly.

1895
Five new counties join the championship: Derbyshire, Essex, Hampshire, Leicestershire and Warwickshire. All counties are required to play home-and-away games against eight other counties for a minimum of 16 matches, though Surrey and Yorkshire play the full 26. Results among the established counties would have given Lancashire the title, but Surrey, by playing and beating more of the newcomers, finish in first place.

In a move against the strict amateur code of the Rugby Union 21 northern clubs form a breakaway Rugby League.

1896
With the Australians touring, counties are required to play only 12 games in the championship. The champions are the county with the highest percentage of points from finished games (excluding draws).

The Daily Mail, 'brash and breezy' and on sale for a halfpenny, is launched.
The speed limit for motor vehicles is raised from 16 to 20 mph.
The first Olympic Games of the modern age are held in Athens. Two-thirds of the competitors are Greek.

1897
Lancashire become the third county to win the championship.

Queen Victoria celebrates her Diamond Jubilee, awarding city status to Nottingham and Hull.

1898
WG Grace receives no support for his proposal that all counties play the same number of matches.

A moving staircase, the first in the UK, is installed at Harrods.

1899
The Australians play five Tests, with matches for the first time at Headingley and Trent Bridge. As in 1896 the requirement for participation in the championship is reduced to 12 games. Worcestershire, heavily in debt and with a half-built pavilion, persuade six counties to play them home and away and become the 15th county in the championship. Yorkshire, meanwhile, play the full 28 games.

War breaks out between the British and the Boers in South Africa.

Championship – top three

Leading batsmen

Leading bowlers

Leading wkt-keeper
Leading fielder *Victims*

1890

	P	W	L	D	Pts		Runs		Wickets		Victims
Surrey	14	9	3	2	6	A. Shrewsbury (Notts)	1,082	G.A. Lohmann (Surrey)	113	M. Sherwin (Notts)	39
Lancashire	14	7	3	4	4	W.G. Grace (Glos)	832	J.W. Sharpe (Surrey)	102		
Kent *(3=)*	14	6	3	5	3	J. Cranston (Glos)	798	R. Peel (Yorks)	90	G.A. Lohmann (Surrey)	26
Yorkshire *(3=)*	14	6	3	5	3						

1891

	P	W	L	D	Pts		Runs		Wickets		Victims
Surrey	16	12	2	2	10	R. Abel (Surrey)	916	G.A. Lohmann (Surrey)	132	D. Hunter (Yorks)	38
Lancashire	16	8	4	4	4	A. Shrewsbury (Notts)	794	J.T. Hearne (Middx)	118		
Middlesex	16	8	5	3	3	W. Gunn (Notts)	780	A.W. Mold (Lancs)	112	R. Abel (Surrey)	28

1892

	P	W	L	D	Pts		Runs		Wickets		Victims
Surrey	16	13	2	1	11	H.T. Hewett (Som)	1,047	W.H. Lockwood (Surrey)	114	M. Sherwin (Notts)	42
Notts	16	10	2	4	8	A. Shrewsbury (Notts)	920	A.W. Mold (Lancs)	104		
Somerset	16	8	5	3	3	W.W. Read (Surrey)	896	G.A. Lohmann (Surrey)	102	R. Abel (Surrey)	23

1893

	P	W	L	D	Pts		Runs		Wickets		Victims
Yorkshire	16	12	3	1	9	W. Gunn (Notts)	1,223	J.T. Hearne (Middx)	137	H.R. Butt (Sussex)	45
Lancashire	16	9	5	2	4	A.E. Stoddart (Middx)	1,178	W.A. Humphreys (Sussex)	122		
Middlesex	16	9	6	1	3	A. Ward (Lancs)	1,035	A.W. Mold (Lancs)	117	J. Tunnicliffe (Yorks)	31

1894

	P	W	L	D	Pts		Runs		Wickets		Victims
Surrey	16	13	2	0	11	W. Gunn (Notts)	851	A.W. Mold (Lancs)	144	D. Hunter (Yorks)	47
Yorkshire	16	12	2	2	10	W. Brockwell (Surrey)	754	T. Richardson (Surrey)	120		
Middlesex	16	8	5	3	3	A. Ward (Lancs)	751	J.T. Hearne (Middx)	119	R. Abel (Surrey)	26

Surrey also tied one match

1895

	P	W	L	D	Pts		Runs		Wickets		Victims
Surrey	26	17	4	5	13	R. Abel (Surrey)	1,787	T. Richardson (Surrey)	239	J.H. Board (Glos)	75
Lancashire	22	14	4	4	10	A. Ward (Lancs)	1,446	A.W. Mold (Lancs)	182		
Yorkshire	26	14	7	5	7	W.G. Grace (Glos)	1,424	R. Peel (Yorks)	136	J. Tunnicliffe (Yorks)	54

1896

	P	W	L	D	Pts	%		Runs		Wickets		Victims
Yorkshire	26	16	3	7	13	68.4	K.S. Ranjitsinhji (Sussex)	1,698	T. Richardson (Surrey)	191	H. Wood (Surrey)	62
Lancashire	22	11	4	7	7	46.7	W.G. Grace (Glos)	1,565	A.W. Mold (Lancs)	130		
Middlesex	16	8	3	5	5	45.4	J.T. Brown (Yorks)	1,556	J. Briggs (Lancs)	122	J. Tunnicliffe (Yorks)	51

1897

	P	W	L	D	Pts	%		Runs		Wickets		Victims
Lancashire	26	16	3	7	13	68.4	R. Abel (Surrey)	1,833	T. Richardson (Surrey)	238	C. Smith (Lancs)	65
Surrey	26	17	4	5	13	61.9	J.T. Brown (Yorks)	1,431	J. Briggs (Lancs)	140		
Essex	16	7	2	7	5	55.6	E. Wainwright (Yorks)	1,372	F.G. Bull (Essex)	109	J. Tunnicliffe (Yorks)	37

1898

	P	W	L	D	Pts	%		Runs		Wickets		Victims
Yorkshire	26	16	3	7	13	68.4	R. Abel (Surrey)	1,832	C.L. Townsend (Glos)	130	T.M. Russell (Essex)	62
Middlesex	18	10	3	5	7	53.8	J.T. Tyldesley (Lancs)	1,801	T. Richardson (Surrey)	126		
Gloucestershire	20	9	3	8	6	50.0	C.B. Fry (Sussex)	1,604	W. Rhodes (Yorks)	126	J. Tunnicliffe (Yorks)	28

1899

	P	W	L	D	Pts	%		Runs		Wickets		Victims
Surrey	26	10	2	14	8	66.7	K.S. Ranjitsinhji (Sussex)	2,285	A.E. Trott (Middx)	146	F.H. Huish (Kent)	70
Middlesex	18	11	3	4	8	57.1	R. Abel (Surrey)	2,134	W. Rhodes (Yorks)	129		
Yorkshire	28	14	4	10	10	55.6	T.W. Hayward (Surrey)	1,798	A.J. Paish (Glos)	125	J. Tunnicliffe (Yorks)	30

1890-1899

Leading counties

	P	W	L	D	T	%W
Surrey	206	126	38	41	1	61.2
Yorkshire	210	113	45	52	-	53.8
Lancashire	200	100	47	52	1	50.0
Middlesex	162	73	49	40	-	45.1

Leading batsmen

R. Abel (Surrey)	12,424
A. Ward (Lancs)	9,786
W. Gunn (Notts)	9,121
W.G. Grace (Glos)	8,669

Leading bowlers

A.W. Mold (Lancs)	1,150
T. Richardson (Surrey)	1,118
J.T. Hearne (Middx)	1,027
J. Briggs (Lancs)	950

Leading keepers & fielder

D. Hunter (Yorks)	439
H. Wood (Surrey)	410
J.Tunnicliffe (Yorks)	274

Overall statistics

Runs per wicket	22.1
Runs per 100 balls	45.7
% of matches drawn	29.4

Miscellany

Bobby Abel, opening for Surrey against Somerset at the Oval in 1899, scored 357* out of a total of 811. No batsman in first-class cricket has been at the wicket while more runs have been added to his team's score. Somerset were described by *The Times* as having 'fallen upon evil cricket days'.

*

At Old Trafford in 1897 Lancashire's slow-left-armer Johnny Briggs bowled 66 five-ball overs in Sussex's first innings of 476. In reply Lancashire batted till shortly before lunch on the final day, making 420. Then, with the game drifting to a draw, Briggs bowled unchanged through the rest of the day: 60 overs, all but one of them after lunch. The 14,000-strong Saturday crowd grew restive, cheering ironically each time he stepped up for a fresh over and barracking the Lancashire captain Archie MacLaren who remained 'as impervious as a stone wall'.

In all, Briggs bowled 630 balls, the most ever in a championship match, finishing with four wickets for 306 runs.

*

Walter Mead of Essex took 17 wickets for 119 runs against Hampshire at Southampton in 1895, the first of eleven instances of a bowler taking 17 wickets in a championship match. On the other ten occasions the bowler finished on the winning side; Mead's Essex lost by 171 runs.

At Hove in 1891 Kent, needing 139 to win, went to lunch on the final day on 33 for five. Their last hope rested with the amateur Charles Fox who had just gone in to bat. But, when play resumed, he was nowhere to be found and was ruled to be 'retired, out'.

By the time Fox returned to the ground, Sussex had bowled Kent out for 54. Asked to explain his absence, he replied: "I was having lunch with a widow."

*

At Taunton in 1895 Somerset's slow-left-armer Ted Tyler was hit for 427 runs in two consecutive innings as Essex made 692, then Lancashire 801. Somerset lost by an innings and 317 to Essex and an innings and 452 to Lancashire.

The matches were the first played for Somerset by the 17-year-old off-spinner Herbert Gamlin. He was out for a duck in all his four innings – caught, stumped, hit wicket and run out – and took two wickets for 182 runs. The first of his two victims was Lancashire's Archie MacLaren, caught on the long-off boundary for 424.

Later that summer, against Surrey at Taunton, Tyler took all ten wickets for 49 runs, but there was no such happy sequel for Gamlin, who had only one further game for the county – though he did play 15 times for England at rugby.

The championship in the 1890s

The championship of 1890, with an official status at last, involved eight counties: Gloucestershire, Kent, Lancashire, Middlesex, Nottinghamshire, Surrey, Sussex and Yorkshire. Except for Sussex and Middlesex who had not met since 1868, they all played each other twice. The format had been agreed by all the counties: one point for a victory, minus one for a defeat; the team with the most points would be champions.

The first match, on Monday 12 May, was at Ashley Down, Gloucestershire's one-year-old ground situated in open fields to the north of Bristol. At 12.15, from the newly-built pavilion into bright sunshine emerged Doctor WG Grace and his older brother EM, the Coroner. Historians may regard this as the start proper of the championship, but there was no such sense of history among the disappointingly small gathering of spectators as they watched Yorkshire's slow left-armer Bobby Peel running in from the pavilion end. His first over to WG was a maiden.

From the far end, where a grey-stone orphanage stood beyond the open field, the strongly-built William Whitwell of Saltburn took the second over, charging in with all the energetic enthusiasm of a newcomer in the Yorkshire team. The Coroner drove his first ball along the ground to mid-off, then skied the second to mid-on where the Yorkshire captain Lord Hawke held the catch. It was the first wicket to fall in the newly official championship, and a few moments later Goldney Radcliffe, 'a gentleman in a position to devote his whole time to the game', hit the first runs, a cut for four.

Later in the day Jimmy Cranston, a left-handed amateur with a sound defence and powerful drive, completed the championship's first century, but it was not enough to prevent the visitors from winning two days later by six wickets. In July, when the two teams met again, at Dewsbury during the town's Feast Week, Cranston again scored a century, he and WG turning almost certain defeat into a famous victory.

Cranston's two hundreds against Yorkshire led in August to his playing for England against Australia at the Oval, where he scored useful runs in a low-scoring, two-wicket victory. He was overweight and rather immobile in the field, but many now regarded him as the best left-handed batsman in England.

Alas, the story of the county championship's first centurion has no more moments of triumph. At Ashley Down in June the following year, when Gloucestershire next played Yorkshire, he was at the wicket in the match's closing stages, batting with great care on a wet pitch made devilish by a hot sun. Yorkshire were pressing for victory, needing three wickets in the final 15

minutes, when Cranston's partner Frank Townsend mis-hit a ball from Peel into the air. As John Tunnicliffe ran to make the catch, the two batsmen crossed. Townsend departed and, as he did so, Cranston – with no previous medical history – had an epileptic *grand mal* and dropped to the ground where he lay motionless. The crowd, already in a state of high excitement, watched with alarm as the Grace brothers hurried out to attend to him. Slowly he revived, then they carried him back to the pavilion. And, with four minutes remaining on the clock, the game resumed. Together the last two men came out to bat, and immediately one of them was caught at slip.

The champion county in 1890 was Surrey. Given the role of their Secretary Charles Alcock in formalising the competition, it was a fitting result. Matches at the Oval attracted great crowds, full of noise and bustle that was in marked contrast to the refinement on display at Lord's. As a result the county club was prosperous, able and willing to employ more professional cricketers than any of the other southern counties.

For six summers, from 1887 to 1892, Surrey were the strongest team in the land. They had riches in batting, most notably their little opener Bobby Abel, they had an astute captain in John Shuter and, above all, they had the best bowler in England, George Lohmann.

No professional in those years gave more to the game than Lohmann. With his blond hair, good looks and awareness of the crowd, he was a great favourite, throwing himself whole-heartedly into everything he did. He bowled medium-pace cutters with great skill, he batted with enterprise and he was sharp and athletic in the slips. In 1890, in a relentless schedule of 37 three-day matches, he took 245 wickets, scored 1,014 runs and held 60 catches.

By the end of 1892, only 27 years old, Lohmann was burnt out. He had contracted tuberculosis, and Surrey, the best of employers, sent him away to the warmer air of South Africa. He played intermittently thereafter, but he never regained his youthful zest, dying in 1901 at the age of 36.

Soon enough another great bowler emerged at the Oval: Tom Richardson, an out-and-out quick from gypsy stock in Mitcham. He is the only fast bowler ever to have taken 200 wickets in a championship season – with 239 in 1895 and 238 in 1897 – and his efforts, along with his fast-bowling partner Bill Lockwood, did much to bring the championship to Surrey in 1894, 1895 and 1899. With six titles in the decade, they were the county championship's first great team.

For all the devastating success of Lohmann and Richardson, the 1890s was a decade in which batsmen came into their own as never before, setting new records for individual and team scores that generated for the first time a popular interest in cricket statistics. In 1889 the *Wisden Almanack* introduced a two-page feature called 'Some Cricket Records'; by 1911 it had grown to 31 pages.

Prior to the 1890s WG Grace was the only man to score a triple century in an inter-county match, 318 against Yorkshire in 1876, and he also held the record for the highest score in all first-class cricket, 344 for MCC against Kent in the same year. He was still going strong in 1896 when, in his late forties, he hit 301 against Sussex, but the previous July his records were emphatically broken by Lancashire's young captain Archie MacLaren. That summer the Old Harrovian had upset his county by unexpectedly absenting himself for several weeks, to fulfil his duties as a prep school master in Harrow, even missing a further game to watch the Eton-Harrow match at Lord's. But his return at Taunton could hardly have been more spectacular. Batting as always with an immensely high backlift, he cut and drove a ragged Somerset bowling attack without mercy. Not only did he break all records with his score of 424, but he hit the runs in under eight hours, allowing plenty of time for his bowlers to dismiss Somerset twice.

Lancashire's total of 801 was also a world record, though it lasted less than a year, broken at Edgbaston the following May when Yorkshire, batting for a full two days, amassed 887 against Warwickshire. Two years later, in August 1898, Yorkshire's openers John Tunnicliffe and Jack Brown put on a mammoth 554 against Derbyshire, exceeding the record for any wicket by 156 runs. Tunnicliffe had spent the previous night in a Leeds inn where his bed was so damp he sat up in a chair. He missed breakfast, had a quick biscuit before play and, with the large crowd at Chesterfield creating chaos in the tents, he only managed to get a twopenny sandwich for lunch.

Yorkshire had begun the decade in poor shape. Too many of their best players lacked self-discipline, particularly when there was alcohol on offer. During 1891, when they spent much of the summer at the foot of the table, there were even mutterings to the effect that they should forfeit their first-class status.

Change came rapidly. The county, embracing a new committee structure, broadened out from its Sheffield base, players of firmer character came to the fore, and Lord Hawke finally moulded the team spirit he had long sought. In 1893 they won the championship for the first time, and they won again in 1896 and 1898. The other great northern county, Lancashire, won in 1897.

Archie MacLaren

Surrey, Yorkshire and Lancashire were the great clubs of the 1890s. Each could field a predominantly professional eleven and, as the championship expanded from eight teams in 1890 to 15 in 1899, they were the only counties capable of playing a full programme. In 1896 Yorkshire and Surrey played 26 matches, while Essex undertook 12 and Leicestershire 14. In this largely informal schedule, no county looked to improve its results by avoiding the stronger sides. Rather, the opposite. The best counties were the ones everybody wanted to play; they brought in bigger crowds and more money.

It was a decade in which the championship moved forward rapidly: from 54 fixtures in 1890 to 150 in 1899. At various times there was talk of creating two, even three divisions, with promotion and relegation, but by the turn of the century the first-class counties were happy with the status quo.

The county championship had come of age.

Some players of the 1890s

Bobby Abel of Surrey

Who that ever saw it could forget that curious little figure, surmounted by a somewhat faded and shrunken chocolate cap, the slow half-waddling gait that marked its progress to the wicket, and then the mastery of technique that could reduce all but the very greatest bowlers to frustration?   *Harry Altham*

Bobby Abel was the great favourite of the Surrey folk. The son of a lamplighter from the back streets of Rotherhithe he was one of the Oval's very own. Born in 1857, he learned his game without formal guidance on the rough pitches of Southwark Park, and he only got his chance with the Surrey Colts by telling them he was 20 when he was already 22.

Some purists said his bat came down crooked, that he was vulnerable against high pace, that at just 5'4" he was too short. But for twenty years he answered them in the only way he could – with runs. Not dashing or flamboyant but patient, reliable runs, scored with a quiet, unassuming air: 357 of them in one innings against Somerset in 1899, a record 12 centuries in 1900, then in the summer of 1901, at the age of 43, a record 3,309 first-class runs. In the words of CB Fry, he gathered runs like blackberries everywhere he went.

He was a dedicated professional, early to bed and sensible with money. Poorly paid, he invested what he could in a sports equipment business that became his life when failing eyesight ended his career at the age of 46. Soon enough Hayward and Hobbs were breaking all his records, but at the Oval he was remembered with great affection as 'The Guv'nor'.

The Guv'nor
The championship's leading run-scorer 1891, 1895, 1897, 1898 and 1902

A great career with a sad ending
1,300 championship wickets between 1890 and 1901

Arthur Mold of Lancashire

Mold was a beautiful bowler to watch. Three or four steps up to the wicket, a beautiful body swing, and the ball was propelled at great pace. His off break used to nip off the ground at lightning speed, and woe betide the man who received one on the knee, or on the inside of the right thigh.   *Pelham Warner*

Arthur Mold was a genial soul, an uneducated village boy from Northamptonshire who enjoyed a practical joke and a flutter on the horses. However, with a ball in his hand he created fear. He was fast enough in his prime to send a bail flying more than 63 yards – and all off the shortest of run-ups. A big-boned man, 5'10½" tall, he kept his weight under 13 stone by living carefully. As a result he could bowl all innings and all day and sometimes did, usually in tandem with slow left-armer Johnny Briggs. In 16 games for Lancashire in 1894 he took 144 championship wickets. In 21 games in 1895 he took 182. In June that year, against Yorkshire and Kent, he took 27 wickets in a week, 17 of them bowled.

All of these achievements were overshadowed one day in 1901 when a visiting Australian umpire no-balled him 18 times for throwing. Mold, by now 38 years old and broader of girth, was disconsolate, feeling that all the credit of his performances had been taken away. "I wish they'd told me before I started," he said sadly. He played only three more times for Lancashire.

In truth, there had been mutterings over the years, but opinions varied. Pelham Warner thought it 'difficult to say he actually threw' while Grace called him 'the fairest of bowlers'.

He deserves better from cricket history. Throughout the 1890s he was a great fast bowler.

W.G. Grace of Gloucestershire

> His stamina was extraordinary. No day was too long for him, and he was always merry and bright from Monday morning to Saturday night.
> *Sammy Woods*

> He was so keen, almost perhaps too keen, but he had a heart of pure gold, and was in consequence a very lovable person.
> *Cyril Foley*

By the 1890s Grace was past his prime, carrying so much weight it was hard to think he had once been a champion hurdler. Yet even in his late 40s he was a supreme competitor. In 1895, between May 9 and 30, he scored 1,016 runs, including his 100th first-class hundred. The following year the poor Sussex bowlers, Fred Tate and all, were hit for 243* at Hove and 301 at Bristol.

He could still bowl, too, as the people of Leyton discovered in 1898 when Gloucestershire played Essex for the first time. The great man, eleven days from his 50th birthday, took seven wickets in the morning, then hit a free-scoring 128. On the field and off he lived life to the full. His 100th hundred, on a cold spring day at Bristol, was an innings of 288, and in the evening he celebrated it in style with food and drink. Then he sat up till the small hours playing cards.

The old man of cricket
Born in 1848, still scoring 100s for Gloucestershire in 1898

Tom Richardson of Surrey

Always bright and cheerful

1895
25 matches
239 wickets

1897
26 matches
238 wickets

> He has a lion heart and an ever-cheerful temperament. Many and many a match has he won for Surrey.
> *CB Fry*

Tom Richardson was the most popular of cricketers. He ran in to bowl like 'a human express train in full career', and he had a dark glamour that came from his roots in a Romany community beside Mitcham Common. All his life he liked to wash in rain water.

No out-and-out fast bowler has ever stuck to his work with more enthusiasm than Tom Richardson, yet in his youth he could not join the army or police on account of an abnormality of the heart. Undoubtedly he was over-bowled at times but, no matter how long or hot the day, he never complained, never lost his humour, never let up. Then in the evening he thought nothing of walking the seven miles home from the Oval to Mitcham.

A natural bowler, with a high arm and a leap in his delivery, he bowled full of length, fast and straight. He died mysteriously at the age of 41, while out walking in France. Some have suggested suicide, but the likely explanation is that his overworked heart finally failed him.

John Tunnicliffe of Yorkshire

> "Long John of Pudsey" was my right-hand man, the most loyal of all my loyal men. ...
> He was more thoughtful, wiser than the rest.
> *Lord Hawke*

John Tunnicliffe was not the greatest or the most eye-catching of the Yorkshire team which won the championship five times in seven years at the turn of the century, but he was pivotal to its success, a devout Methodist who brought much-needed steadiness and sobriety to their endeavours. An impetuous batsman in his youth, he turned himself into an opener of great reliability, never better than at Chesterfield in 1897 when he and Jack Brown put on a record 554 for the first wicket.

A tall man, he was for many years the best short slip in the country, sometimes called the Octopus for the way he seemed to have hands everywhere. His 70 first-class catches in 1901 were a record till Wally Hammond, another great slip fielder, held 78 in 1928.

After cricket Tunnicliffe coached at Clifton College, Bristol, where Hammond, at the age of 17, was sent to work with him. Long John was 'a generous and tireless tutor', though the young man was not always keen to absorb the Yorkshireman's Wesleyan gospel of discipline and restraint.

Long John
Most championship catches each year 1895 to 1902

Stories of the 1890s

94 wickets in a month

Charles Townsend in August 1895

The gentlemen cricketers of Victorian times were mostly batsmen. With a few great exceptions, notably Arthur Shrewsbury of Notts and Bobby Abel of Surrey, the batting averages were dominated each year by amateurs. It was a quite different story, however, when it came to the hard work of bowling. In the newly expanded championship of 1895, there were 25 bowlers who sent down 600 or more overs – and 24 of them were professionals.

The 25th was Charles Townsend of Gloucestershire, an 18-year-old leg-break bowler so thin and frail-looking that his team-mate Gilbert Jessop reckoned 'it were well to provide the umpires with baskets to pick up the pieces in the event of his breaking in two.' He had so little body that, as he ambled to the bowling crease, all the batsmen seemed to see was a bewildering whirl of arms and legs. Then down came a succession of deliveries, fast leg-breaks that pitched with unerring accuracy. Some turned sharply away from the bat; others went straight on.

He was the son of Frank Townsend, a schoolmaster who had played for many years for Gloucestershire. He learned to bowl in a net, with a cocoa-nut mat, in his back garden. Then at Clifton College he had such success that in August 1893, still only 16, he was invited to play for Gloucestershire whose captain, WG Grace, was his godfather. Grace's own son, two years his senior, also made his debut, but it was Townsend who impressed the Doctor – so much so that in the Middlesex first innings he had the young stripling bowl 70 overs. In the next match, against Somerset at Cheltenham, Townsend took a unique hat-trick of stumpings, following that two days later with five wickets against the touring Australians.

By 1895, though barely ten stone, he had grown to a height of almost six foot. Now training to be a solicitor, he played one game in May, in which he hit 95, batting with his godfather when, to great acclaim, the old man completed his 100th first-class hundred. He returned in late July, and for the rest of the summer he took wickets every time he bowled: 28 in three matches in July, including 16 at Trent Bridge, then 94 in eight matches in August. No bowler in the history of the game has taken so many wickets in one calendar month.

No batsman seemed to have an answer to him. At Bristol, when rain reduced the game against Sussex to little more than a day, the visitors batted for the second time with only 90 minutes remaining, and he spun his way through the best of them – Fry, Ranjitsinhji and Murdoch – taking seven for 28 and bowling them out for 60 for a last-minute victory. 'One batsman of world-wide reputation,' ran one

report, 'was reduced to a state of extreme sadness by his total inability to cope with the young bowler.'

Was he over-bowled by Grace? Probably. He developed a form of tennis elbow and, though he took wickets aplenty in the next years, he was never quite the same force again. Instead, he became a superb left-handed batsman, good enough in the summer of 1899, at the age of 22, to score 2,440 runs, with nine centuries. Twice that year he played for England against Australia.

At the end of the following summer he gave up regular cricket for the law, becoming the Official Receiver for Middlesbrough, Stockton and Northallerton. In the next 22 years he found time for just 40 first-class matches. In 1906 against Worcestershire he hit 214; in 1909 against the Australians he hit 129. By then, though, his bowling greatness was only a memory.

His son David, an Oxford University blue, played three Tests in the 1930s. He was the last man to play for England without ever representing a first-class county.

The most curious of dismissals

Middlesex v Sussex, Lord's, Thursday 6 July 1893

It was soon after lunch on a hot summer's day. Many of the 10,000-strong crowd had made their way to St John's Wood after lining the streets of central London to cheer the Duke of York, the future King George V, as he rode in procession to his wedding at the Chapel Royal.

Guttridge of Sussex, a fast bowler, sent down a ball that came within a whisker of bowling the Middlesex batsman Cyril Foley. It struck the keeper on the pads and rebounded onto the stumps. Foley had not left his crease so with no ado the keeper started to replace the bails. He picked up the first, and Foley, an Old Etonian whose father had been Governor of Guernsey, bent down and picked up the other. The bowler – possibly he was unsure what had happened – let out an appeal.

To his astonishment, as he prepared to receive Guttridge's next ball, Foley saw the umpire – Henty, a Kent professional of the 1870s – with his finger raised. "You're out," he said.

"What for?" ... "For handling the bail."

Foley was too astonished to speak further. He departed, in his own words later, 'like a man in a dream'.

Outside the pavilion he was met by the former Middlesex batsman 'Buns' Thornton, a fellow Etonian who, on hearing the story, was appalled. "Go back," he instructed. "The umpire can't make rules." But Foley, still in a dream, climbed the steps to the dressing room where quietly he removed his pads.

The Times reported that Billy Murdoch, Sussex's Australian captain, followed Foley to the pavilion and, in the spirit of good sportsmanship, 'courteously invited' him to return, which he did, adding a further 30 runs to his score.

The report in the *London Daily News* was a little more graphic, saying that the large crowd started to hiss and that a knot of spectators gathered at the foot of the pavilion steps where Ford, the next batsman, lingered for some time.

The dressing room was at the back of the pavilion so Foley himself saw nothing of this. However, in his 1935 autobiography *Autumn Foliage*, he wrote what he was told: that the crowd had invaded the ground and that there was 'a devil of a row'. He thought he was in the dressing room for a quarter of an hour before Murdoch appeared.

Later that summer Henty, who earned a part-living as a billiard-hall manager, was suspended from umpiring, not officiating till the middle of the following year, then disappearing forever from the first-class circuit. 'Why he gave such a decision,' Foley wrote, 'no one has been able to discover.'

Enter Worcestershire

Worcestershire v Yorkshire, Worcester, Thursday 4 May 1899

So keen were Worcestershire to join the county championship that their Secretary, Paul Foley, spent much of 1898 persuading enough counties to grant them a fixture. Hampshire were the sixth and last, allowing them to reach the necessary threshold of 12 matches.

The county had a rental agreement with the cathedral on a farm field beside the River Severn, and they set about making it fit for first-class cricket. They borrowed money to build a pavilion and recruited the Kent groundsman who relaid much of the turf. Arrangements were made for the parking of carriages behind the pavilion while the entrance gates were, in the words of the *Worcestershire Chronicle*, 'removed farther from the obnoxious pigstyes'.

A side building, with two dressing rooms, was still being erected when Yorkshire, the reigning champions, arrived for the first match in May 1899. Legend has it that before play that day the Secretary, proudly wearing his brown bowler hat and boots, could be spotted applying the last coat of white paint to a sight screen. Then, as the pressmen were settling into their little box, the heavy roller broke loose and started running down the slope towards them. Fortunately it stopped just short of demolishing their hut, leaving Old Ebor of the *Yorkshire Evening Post* free to describe his surroundings: 'A highly-flavoured piggery near the press-box enabled town visitors to appreciate the charms of country life.'

During the afternoon, at the end of choral evensong at the cathedral, the congregation gathered on the steps under the west window, enjoying an excellent view of play free of charge. Interest had undoubtedly been aroused, the arrival of first-class cricket lifting membership of the county club from 286 to 700.

The match itself was almost a fairy tale for the newcomers. On top throughout the first two days, they reached 85 for two on the final morning, needing just 49 more runs for victory. At the wicket was the 21-year-old RE 'Tip' Foster, one of seven brothers who would play for Worcestershire in the early years, the only man to captain England at both football and cricket. He was in dominant mood, hitting freely, till he was bowled. Then, when the Yorkshire keeper David Hunter split a finger, Foster came out to field as substitute, immediately catching a team-mate. In quick time Worcestershire were bowled out for 122, losing by 11 runs, but for their tireless Secretary the greater victory lay in their new first-class status.

Images of the 1890s

Trouble at Tonbridge

Tonbridge Week was not only a pair of cricket matches at the Angel Ground, attended by the ordinary folk of the town. It was also a grand social gathering, with every evening offering festivities: shows, balls and concerts that attracted to the town a great influx of visitors, many of them not especially conversant with the finer points of cricket.

The fourth Tonbridge Week was held at the end of June 1893, a dry month that unfortunately turned wet at the start of the week. Lancashire were the first visitors and, though the pitch was damp and the light bad, they managed a full day's play on the Monday.

On Tuesday morning a steady drizzle cleared, to be followed by scudding showers, and it was decided to take lunch early and to hope for play at 2.30. All the while, a large audience built up and, though there was still rain in the air, they became angry when nothing happened at 2.30.

They gathered in front of the pavilion calling for the players and, when that produced no result, they 'invaded the wickets and not only trampled all over the pitch but pulled the stumps out'. With too few police to control the disturbance, the protest went on for twenty minutes before a heavy burst of rain sent them all running for cover.

The magazine *Cricket Field* was appalled:

> They seemed to think that a county cricket match had been arranged for their benefit only and that play should have taken place wet or fine. Unfortunately they did not limit their misbehaviour to the usual cheap witticisms at the expense of the players but, led on by one or two turbulent spirits, wrecked the wicket. This crass stupidity on the part of the mob was almost equalled by the inane remarks of the ladies and gentlemen in the subscribers' tents, many of whom had apparently come down on a wet afternoon to see cricket because there was nothing else to do.

There was talk of preparing a new pitch for the final day, but so much rain had fallen that next morning they were able to roll out the damage.

Carpenter and Thoms, the two umpires

One of the private tents

72

The penny rhymester

A familiar figure in the 1890s, patrolling the boundaries in the south-east, was the rhymester Albert Craig. A Yorkshireman by birth, he wrote and printed poems, selling copies of them at a penny each. The Oval was his favourite haunt, but he also liked to venture down to Kent and Sussex.

He was at Hove for the Whitsun holiday match of 1893 when WG Grace's Gloucestershire were set 200 to win on the final afternoon. At 127 for two they were heading for victory, but they were ambushed by Walter Humphreys, Sussex's veteran lob bowler, and collapsed to 196 all out. Humphreys was carried shoulder-high back to the pavilion. The last of the great under-arm bowlers, he took 122 wickets in 16 championship matches that summer. It was a perfect story for one of Craig's rhymes, and his 22-line effort began with gusto:

> With pleasure the heart of each Sussex man throbs
> To see Walter Humphreys come off with his "lobs".
> The contest was keen, but the Sussex lads won it,
> It isn't the first time good Humphreys has done it.
> The joy and excitement could not be kept under,
> They carried him right off the field – and no wonder;
> His past noble records he manfully broke,
> Seven wickets for thirty is no idle joke.

Albert Craig

Amateurs and professionals

In the 1890s at many of the counties there was little off-field contact between amateurs and professionals. They changed in different rooms, travelled in different class compartments on the railway and took the field of play from different gates. At Kent there was even this annual amateurs-only photograph.

One who especially resented all this was Teddy Diver, who played as an amateur at Surrey till the school at which he taught went bankrupt. Against his father's wishes he turned professional and played for Warwickshire. Conscious of his lowered status, he engaged in several protests, the most memorable occurring during the Australians' visit to Edgbaston in 1893. Unusually the professionals were invited into the pavilion for lunch but, when they found themselves given meat pies at a side table while the amateurs ate salmon, Diver led a walkout.

The Kent amateurs, 1897
standing: *Mr G.J. Mordaunt, Mr A.C. Norman, Mr H.C. Stewart*
seated: *Mr M.C. Kemp, Mr G. Marsham, Mr F. Marchant, Mr J.R. Mason,*
Mr J.N. Tonge, Mr E.B. Shine   in front: *Mr R.O. Livesay*

1891: Somerset – 'first-class ... at least until the end of the season'

Somerset v Surrey, Taunton, 13-15 August, 1891

There were sceptics aplenty when in 1891 Somerset – or Somersetshire, as they were called – gained admission to the county championship. Yes, they had beaten all opposition in 1890, but how good were Leicestershire and Devon, Glamorgan and Staffordshire? It would be a different matter, said the doubters, when the West Countrymen came up against Surrey and Lancashire.

So it proved in the early fixtures. On the first of June the newcomers arrived at the Oval with a weakened side and spent a long, hot day in the field, dropping several catches as the Surrey batsmen piled up 449 runs with such rapidity that they had time to take two Somerset wickets before the close. Heavy overnight storms left the pitch difficult the next morning, and the match was all over before lunch: Somerset, 37 all out in each innings.

It was a humiliation that proved the sceptics right, as the *Taunton Courier* was quick to appreciate: 'People will say that we have received a well merited sitting on; that we were "stuck-up", "over-ambitious" and that having last summer had such success the county thought herself much better than she really was, and deserves her drubbing. Cricketers in second-class shires will gloat over the defeat, and all manner of unkind and unfair things will be said.' The *Sportsman* made a point of describing Somerset as 'first-class in classification ... at least until the end of the season'.

There was little improvement the next week when Lancashire came to Taunton and won inside two days, their fast bowler Mold taking 15 wickets. In the northern visitors' view, their hosts were only first class in the hospitality they provided.

The Somerset team themselves were not downhearted. They were young, all but two of them public-school amateurs who played their cricket with a dash, and soon enough they were tasting success – against Kent, Gloucestershire and Yorkshire. By the time Surrey came down to Taunton in August, they knew they were good enough for first-class cricket.

But were they good enough to compete with the champion county? Unofficially or officially Surrey had worn that crown each year since 1887, and they arrived in Taunton once more at the head of the table, with eleven wins and a draw in their 12 matches.

Thursday 13 August. It was a big day in the life of the market town, with the Horticultural Society staging its annual flower show so that the outlying villagers could enjoy pelargoniums and cover drives all on the one day. Nearly four thousand made it to the County Ground, and they watched with alert excitement as the great men of Surrey emerged onto the field, men about whom most of them had only read. A correspondent to the *Exeter Gazette* overheard their talk.

First came the amateurs through the main pavilion gate:

"That's WW Read, the bigger of the two with the black moustache; the smaller one's Shuter."

"But who's the 13-stunner, with the fair moustache?"

"That must be KJ Key. There are only three amateurs."

Then came the professionals from the side gate:

"The little man leading must be Abel."

"That dark little man with the snake-like head and neck is Sharpe," piped up a schoolboy. "I've seen his photo."

The tall Maurice Read, the keeper Wood with his pads, the young Lockwood, they were all identified. Then an argument which was Brockwell, which Henderson. And finally the great George Lohmann – "that tall one with the fair moustache."

They settled to watch Lohmann bowl the first over, with the most extraordinary field: just one man on the leg side, Key at close mid-on. The farming folk of Somersetshire had never seen the like of it before.

On a placid pitch Herbie Hewett, their young Harrovian captain, struck a sparkling 55, but the innings fell away to a total of only 194. The general view was that it was far too few, but the best of the day came in the evening when their three bowlers – the two professionals, Ted Tyler and George Nichols, and the ever-exuberant young Australian Sammy Woods – sent back six Surrey batsmen for just 71 runs. What a surprise it was, and how the crowd cheered!

On Friday morning Surrey were all out for 154, and Somerset's batsmen fared better second time round. By Saturday afternoon, however, the game was heading for a draw. Surrey had been set 372 to win in four hours 10 minutes and, keen to end their championship programme undefeated, they were playing out time without undue alarm. 'The Surrey score went up,' reported the *Western Daily Press*, 'while the spirits of the Somerset partisans went down.' At five o'clock, with half an hour remaining, the scoreboard read 236 for five.

Sammy Woods, at home now in his adopted county with its country pursuits, did not give up. He 'found his way to Lockwood's wicket', and in the next over Ted Tyler ran down the pitch to take a return catch off Key's bat. The spectators 'yelled with delight' and, when next ball Brockwell was caught

Somerset 1891

(back row)
Ted Tyler, Gerald Fowler,
Archie Wickham, Richard Palairet,
John Challen (sitting on pavilion rail)

(middle row)
Sammy Woods, Lionel Palairet,
Vernon Hill, Crescens Robinson

(front, sitting)
Henry Murray-Anderdon (Secretary),
William Roe, Herbie Hewett (capt),
Arthur Newton, George Nichols

at mid-on, they 'positively lost their heads'. Amidst the excitement, and against all expectation, Maurice Read, who had batted calmly for three hours for 94, was 'clean bowled' by Woods. 'Around the ground hundreds of persons were standing on tiptoe with watches in their hands, counting the seconds and the balls.'

There were just eight minutes left when Sharpe, Surrey's last man, joined the diminutive keeper Wood in the middle, and they survived three five-ball overs. So keen were the Somerset fielders that twice, while the last ball of an over was being fielded, the remaining men began the dash to their new positions.

The umpires repeatedly consulted their watches and, with one and a half minutes remaining, the final over began: Sammy Woods bowling it to Sharpe, the steadfast number eleven. 'The first ball was a very wild one,' reported the *Western Daily Press*, 'and went over the batsman's head. The second was little better.' Then, according to Woods, the non-striker Wood turned to the bowler. "Keeps his end up well for a man with one eye, eh?" he said cheerfully.

"One eye? Which one?"

On receiving the reply Woods instantly hatched a plan to exploit the batsman's blind spot. 'I bowled the first round-arm ball of my life,' he wrote, 'and it hit his off stump.' It was middle stump in the *Western Daily Press*, leg stump in the *Morning Post*, but who cared? 'There

followed such a scene as would defy description – hats flying, old men running, people tripping over one another in their eagerness to get to the pavilion and cheer the victors.'

Percy Graves, ancestor of the poet Robert, even wrote a 133-line poem to celebrate the occasion:
And one oald gent his hat sent into tha' river saailin',
Another like a coalt he jomps all vours across tha' paailin',
And a fat old bloke went nigh to choake tell his buttons I undunned,
And then a blubbered like a babe vor joy that we'd a-wunned.

According to the *Western Daily Press* the joy spread far and wide: 'It was surprising the number of Somerset people one met with. Nearly every other person claimed connection with the county. Having passed through the chief towns on a railway journey might have furnished the only reason in some cases.'

Well, o'course we cheered vor Zummerzet as long as we could cheer,
And we hed out zplendid Zammy, our bowler wi'out peer,
And our clever Cap'm Hewett and our clinkin' pair of pro.'s,
Not forgettin' a good ringin' cheer vor our gallant Zurrey voes.

'This game made Somerset cricket,' Sammy Woods wrote 34 years later. 'Our spectators went balmy, flung their hats in the air and hit each other about. And they varmers do talk about it to this day, and lots of them still think I bowled Sharpe with a full pitch. 'Twas a long hop! "Don't ee tell 'em so!"'

The following summer Somerset finished in third place, and it was true, the farmers never did forget Sammy Woods, their very own Australian. It would be 66 years before the county would reach such heights again.

Lord Hawke: the man who made Yorkshire cricket

Yorkshire cricket was at its lowest ebb in 1889. Only victory in the final match, a rain-affected affair at Hove, lifted them from the ignominy of last place in the championship table. After seven years as captain of the county Lord Hawke realised that he had to make changes. He had to take more control.

Hawke was born in Lincolnshire, only qualifying to play for Yorkshire because his family rented a country estate near Tadcaster. The baronetcy had come indirectly to his father, a country parson, without any fortune. Nevertheless Hawke, with some help, lived as a country gentleman. In winters he undertook profit-making cricket tours to the colonies; in summers he captained Yorkshire. A deeply religious man, he believed cricket to be a great force for good, transcending boundaries of class, race and nationality.

At first his captaincy was part-time. In the early years he only played outside the term times at Cambridge, and he always had other interests: his duties as a captain in the West Yorkshire Militia and his love of shooting. In 1885 he did not play in even one inter-county match. Perhaps, as a result, he was inclined to leave things be. The professionals were talented men, and he loved them all. 'The boys of my old brigade,' he called them in later years. But their way of life, especially in relation to alcohol, was never going to bring the success that he craved for Yorkshire. So after the summer of 1889, when the team had won two and lost ten, he dispensed with four of them.

It was not a case of becoming more amateur. Rather the contrary. In August 1890 Hawke turned up for a match at Bradford, expecting George Harrison, a professional bowler, to be joining the team. The committee, however, had cancelled Harrison's invitation, replacing him with the Honourable Stanley Jackson, a promising Cambridge undergraduate. Jackson, it transpired, had written to them to say that he had a spare week or two before some I Zingari matches and would like to play.

Hawke was furious. He resigned the captaincy and was only persuaded to take the field because they would be ten without him. More than a week passed, with two matches played, before the matter was resolved and Hawke played again. Jackson, it was agreed, would only be selected if he committed himself properly, not giving priority to what one newspaper called 'the Zingari or other swell clubs' and, most importantly, the committee would not over-ride Hawke. When the storm had passed, the team went down to the Oval, without Stanley Jackson, and they beat that year's champions, Surrey. Harrison, in his first first-class outing of the summer, took ten wickets and, after further successes, ended the season at the top of the national bowling averages.

Martin Bladen Hawke, 7th Baron Hawke (1860-1938)

Yorkshire Captain 1883-1910

Yorkshire President 1898-1938

MCC President 1914

MCC Treasurer 1932-37

With each passing year Hawke's power increased. The Sheffield domination of the club was ended, and the team acquired new players that changed its character: Tunnicliffe, Hunter, Hirst, Brown, Haigh, Denton. Hawke was their father-figure, persuading the committee to pay them two pounds a week in winter and instituting a system of five-shilling rewards for good play. Never a lover of averages, he measured achievement always in the context of the match.

Hawke was still 'His Lordship', but now he had his own men. He cared for them, and in return they were loyal. In 1893, while the new team was taking shape, they won the championship for the first time. Then, in his years of glory from 1896 to 1908, he led them to a further seven titles. After that he played little, though he retained the formal office of captain for two more years. He became a major figure at Lord's, where like a true Yorkshireman he never missed an opportunity to promote his county's interests.

In later life he could sound like a reactionary old buffer but, in the years that mattered, he was in his own way a visionary. He raised the lot of the professional cricketer, and he created the culture that turned Yorkshire into the best team in the land. His legacy lasted for many, many years.

Lord Hawke's toughest decision

Yorkshire v Middlesex, Sheffield, Wednesday 18 August 1897

Bobby Peel was a great slow-left-arm bowler, a useful batsman and popular with the crowd. But by the summer of 1897, when he was 40, he was the last survivor of the team of the early 1880s, the last man with the habits of the bad old days.

After missing a month with a hand injury, he returned to the team in August, for the Middlesex match at Bramall Lane. On Monday, batting at seven, he hit a brisk 40; on Tuesday, bowling with his usual guile, he took five wickets. Then on Wednesday he played his last day's cricket for Yorkshire.

The accounts of what happened vary wildly, but some facts are clear. He did not bat during the morning when he should have done. Then after lunch, at the start of the Middlesex second innings, he bowled seven untidy and inaccurate overs for 15 runs and, after a while, left the field.

He had been drinking. He admitted that to a newspaper reporter the next day, though he said it was only 'two small glasses of gin and water' before going to the ground, nothing at lunch. The occasions when he 'slipped over' were nothing to do with the drink; three spikes had come out of his left shoe. Angered by the reports in the morning papers, he showed the reporter the shoe. In slipping, he said, he had hurt his knee and retired to the pavilion. Nobody had said a word to him. Then, at the end of the day, he went to collect his money and was told his services were not required for the rest of the season. "You have had a glass too many," the secretary said.

George Hirst, in later life, said Peel was in a bad way from his drinking the previous evening. The kindly Hirst advised him to stay at the hotel; he would tell Lord Hawke that Peel had been 'taken queer in the night'. But Peel turned up at the ground and, when he bowled, according to one report, 'It was manifestly impossible for him to do himself anything like justice.'

The journalists did not pry. 'It is hardly likely,' one wrote, 'that Lord Hawke, than whom there is no more tolerant captain, or one who has greater care for the professionals under him, would have taken the steps he did without sufficient reason.'

'Nothing ever gave me so much pain,' Hawke later wrote. 'Bobby was a real good fellow, but it had to be done for the sake of discipline and for the good of cricket.'

Peel then pre-empted any reconciliation by signing to play the next summer for Accrington, and Yorkshire began the search for his replacement. In May they settled on a 20-year-old from Kirkheaton, a lad who had been turned away by Warwickshire. His name was Wilfred Rhodes.

The highest championship total ever

Yorkshire v Warwickshire, Edgbaston, 7 & 8 May 1896

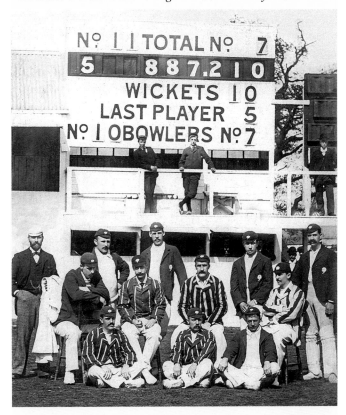

It was supposed to be a special match for Warwickshire, laying on a dinner on the second night to celebrate the opening of their pavilion extension at Edgbaston. Yet by then their team was exhausted, having spent two whole days in the field while Yorkshire, the laws preventing a declaration before the final day, compiled a total of 887. For the first time in cricket four batsmen scored centuries in the same innings, including Lord Hawke at number nine who hit a career-best 166.

Records galore were broken: Yorkshire's best of 590, Lancashire's 801 at Taunton, the Australians' 843 against Oxford & Cambridge Universities Past & Present. In all cricket only one larger total had ever been posted: 921 by Orleans CC against Rickling Green in Hertfordshire.

Lord Hawke's men earned £13 under his bonus scheme while Warwickshire, putting on a brave face, 'drew comfort in the excellence of their wicket'. On the third day, however, even that pride looked a little misplaced. When the board was reconstructed at lunchtime for this Yorkshire team photograph, the score taken down was 82 for six.

1899: On holiday with Hampshire

The amateur cricketers came and went at Hampshire, playing as and when they could fit in a game. In 1898 the captain Teddy Wynyard, an officer in the Welsh Regiment stationed at Aldershot, could be spared from military duties for only three games – or so he said. On at least two occasions eyebrows were raised when it was discovered he was playing cricket elsewhere.

It was the same pattern at several southern counties. A core of professionals was supplemented by a large, shifting cast of public school men, taking time off from the army or the church, from farming, banking or the law. Somerset had a number of vicars; Hampshire had more than its share of military men.

Professionals			
Average number in each county eleven in 1899			
Warwickshire	8.9		
Nottinghamshire	8.4	Sussex	5.8
Lancashire	8.2	Essex	5.1
Derbyshire	8.0	Hampshire	4.6
Yorkshire	7.9	Gloucestershire	4.5
Leicestershire	7.8	Somerset	4.4
Surrey	7.3	Middlesex	4.0
Worcestershire	5.8	Kent	3.3

These were the high days of the British Empire. Some of Hampshire's soldier-cricketers had been born or served in India, and by the winter of 1899 several, including Christopher Heseltine, Master of the New Forest Foxhounds, would be in South Africa, fighting the Boers. Evelyn Bradford spent the summer of 1898 with Kitchener in battle with the Mahdists in Sudan, James Spens had fought in Afghanistan in 1879, while Wynyard had been awarded a DSO in the Anglo-Burmese War of 1885. Cricket was not their profession; it was something to enjoy when time allowed.

Major 'Bertie' Poore of the 7th Hussars was another. After a modest cricketing youth in England, he had been posted to India where he taught himself the finer points of the game by reading the *Badminton Book of Cricket*, 'studying it as he would study for an examination'. He became a prolific run-scorer.

For three years he was ADC to Lord Harris, the former Kent captain who was now the Governor of Bombay. In 1895 the regiment was sent to South Africa where Poore scored two centuries in a week against an English touring team led by Lord Hawke. He was called 'the Grace of the Army', the Surrey fast bowler George Lohmann saying that he was "far and away the best batsman we have encountered".

Three matches had been arranged between the tourists and a representative South African eleven, and it was uncertain for a while for which side Poore would play. To the displeasure of some locals – he had only been in the country nine months – he finished up in the home team, a decision that led some years later to his being listed as a South African Test cricketer.

Within weeks of the the third game's conclusion he was heading north to Rhodesia where, serving with Robert Baden-Powell, he saw bloody action in Matabele and Mashonaland. He led a raid that killed 40 rebels, and on other occasion they chased them into caves which they dynamited. At one stage, too long away from base, they were reduced to eating some of their horses. Amidst all this he won the Matabeleland Lawn Tennis Championship, helped to build the cricket ground at Bulawayo and, though without flannels, scored some more hundreds.

In 1898 his regiment returned to England, where in June he won the Best Man at Arms title in the officers' section of the Royal Military Tournament. Among the disciplines were Heads and Posts (Turk's Head) and Lemon Cutting, fast horseback exercises requiring precision of swordsmanship.

He had some games of cricket with Hampshire, meeting up with Christopher Heseltine, who had been with Lord Hawke in South Africa, and Edward Sprot from his days in India. At first he found it difficult to adapt from matting to grass wickets, but there was no question of his being dropped – it did not work quite like that – and in the closing weeks of his leave he hit two hundreds and a 95.

Then came the fairy tale of his ten-week leave in 1899. In June, at the Royal Agricultural Hall in Islington, he was again the Best Man at Arms. Two days later at the Hurlingham Club, in the final of the Inter-Regimental Polo Cup, with two minutes to play and the score 1-1, he broke out of defence with a dashing run and scored the winning goal. Two days after that he was at the United Services Ground at Portsmouth, joining the Hampshire team for their game against Somerset. 'In delightful weather and before a small company' he made a scratchy start, 'once or twice snicking the ball', but he went on to score 104 and 119 not out, sharing a century partnership each time with Colonel Spens, now a 46-year-old instructor at Sandhurst. Later in the week at Southampton, against Mold and Briggs of Lancashire, he hit 111 and 40.

There was no cricket for Hampshire the following week, but Poore joined them again at the end of June, making only 11 against Essex at Southampton, then returning to Portsmouth to play Surrey who, with 11 wins and a draw, were top of the table on +100%. Hampshire, despite Poore's runs, were on -100%.

Poore was six foot four inches tall. CB Fry described him as 'long-limbed, sinewy and powerful. When waiting for the ball he draws himself up to his full height as WG does, and lifts his bat high in front, pointing towards point, with the face turned upwards. He is not a hitter in the ordinary sense of the term, yet at the same time he does hit, and very hard too.' Playing whenever possible off the front foot, he could 'smother' balls to which shorter men had to play back, and he specialised in drives through the covers and mid-off. His most unconventional stroke, one not in the *Badminton Book of Cricket*, reminded Fry of his performances in the Military Tournament: 'He has a peculiar slicing manner of cutting, treating the ball as if it were a lemon or a Turk's head; an accurate and commanding stroke, which travels fast and fine.'

Against Surrey Poore scored a chanceless 175. Then on the Saturday, when frequent showers threatened to ruin the finish, he made a quickfire 39, hitting the winning run with only five minutes to spare. In their fifth year in the championship Hampshire had finally beaten one of the great counties.

Poore was the talk of English cricket, and he was summoned to London to play for the Gentlemen against the Players, first at the Oval, then at Lord's. England were 1-0 down after three of the five Tests against Australia, and the country now wanted the dashing Major to come to the rescue. Alas, his fairy-tale summer did not extend beyond his games for Hampshire. At the Oval, where the pavilion was full of his army friends, he 'failed to do himself justice' with scores of 1 and 24; at Lord's he 'played very commonplace cricket' in an hour-long 27.

Back with Hampshire the runs continued to flow from his bat: a record-breaking 304 at Taunton, 122 at Worcester, a 'capital' 71 of 'brilliant hitting' against the Australians at Southampton and 79 and 53 not out at Derby. In the streets and country lanes of Hampshire, whenever they asked about the latest game, it was always the same question: "What did Major Poore do?"

Then on Saturday 12 August, at the end of a match at Leicester in which he had hit 157, he said his farewells and returned to his regiment. In nine championship matches he had scored seven centuries and averaged a remarkable 116.58.

That, though, was just by way of relaxation. Within months he would be in the thick of the fighting in South Africa, mentioned three times in despatches and winning the DSO. There was little time for cricket, though records survive of three hundreds he scored before the war was over.

Hampshire won four times in 1899. In 1900, with Poore and others away at war, they failed to win a single game.

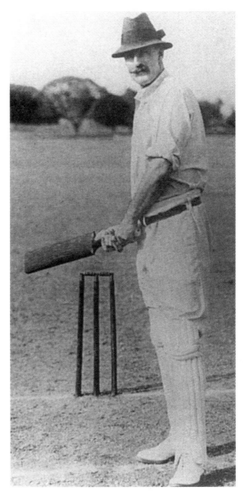

Major R.M. Poore
Seven centuries, including a triple,
in nine matches.

Average of 100 in championship season

Qualification: 1000 runs

	Year	Runs	Ave
W.R. Hammond	1934	2020	126.25
R.M. Poore	1899	1399	116.58
G. Boycott	1979	1160	116.00
G. Boycott	1971	2197	109.85
W.R. Hammond	1946	1404	108.00
M.R. Ramprakash	2006	2211	105.28
M.R. Ramprakash	2007	2026	101.30
I.T. Botham	1985	1211	100.91

1900 – 1909

Yorkshire five times champions
Northamptonshire the 16th county
An influx of colonial cricketers

Let us look at the various cricket grounds in England, at the new pavilions that have been erected, the new stands and embankments that can be seen on almost all county grounds, the large scoring boards, the covered accommodation, the manner in which the grounds are kept in order. All these things do not point to a dying game, but rather to a flourishing condition of things. We hear of county clubs losing so much per annum year after year, but somehow they flourish and grow.

WG Quaife of Warwickshire, 1906

County cricket is important and valuable because of the importance and value which it derives from the word county. The county stands for something that is particularly old and particularly English, and in everyday life a man derives advantage or importance merely because his connexion with his county dates back a large number of years. County support is extended to cricket on this principle, and it will surely be withdrawn in proportion as latter-day manipulators toy with or disregard that principle in their desire to overreach the county next door.

The one object of the county championship competition is to see which county can produce the best cricketers, and not which can purchase the best cricketers. Under the present system a millionaire with a hobby for cricket could make Rutland the champion county in about four years' time, and there need not be a Rutland man in the winning eleven.

The Times, 1906

1900
There are several changes in the laws of cricket: (i) the over increases from five to six balls; (ii) the declaration, previously restricted to the final day, can take place from lunchtime on the second day; (iii) the follow-on is no longer compulsory, with the required deficit raised from 120 to 150 runs.

The decade begins with 15 counties in the championship. The point system remains as introduced in 1896: +1 for a win, -1 for a loss, the champions have the highest percentage of points from games won or lost.

Yorkshire are the first county to win the championship without losing a game.

Women competitors are admitted to the second Olympic Games in Paris.

The Devon and Somerset Wanderers cricket team, on tour in France, find their 12-a-side, two-day game at the Velodrome de Vincennes is advertised on billboards as 'France contre Angleterre'. Years later, the Olympic Committee will deem it to have been an event in the 1900 Games, and the Wanderers will discover they are Olympic champions.

1901
A proposal to change the lbw law, removing the need for the ball to pitch in line, fails to secure a two-thirds majority.

In a demonstration, organised by Guglielmo Marconi, a signal sent from Cornwall is received in Newfoundland.

1902
The Australian tourists play five Tests, the third of them the only Test ever played at Bramall Lane, Sheffield.

Thomas Edison invents an electric battery.

1903
Middlesex win the championship for the first time. Their eight wins out of 18, with one defeat, is calculated to be superior to Yorkshire's 13 wins out of 26, with five defeats.

The Ford Motor Company is formed in Detroit.

1904
CB Fry proposes a knock-out tournament for the counties, but scheduling problems prevent the idea from taking off.

At the All-England Lawn Tennis Championship at Wimbledon Frank Riseley wins the right to play the defending champion at the end of a marathon 'semi-final' in which the players retire exhausted at two sets all and toss a coin.

At the Olympic Games in St Louis, Missouri, the first marathon runner home is disqualified for getting a 14-mile lift in a lorry. The gold medal goes instead to Tom Hicks, an American brass worker who is kept going towards the end with doses of strychnine and brandy. In 90° heat his winning time is just under 3 hours 29 minutes. The Cuban in fourth place, having not eaten for 40 hours, suffers from severe stomach cramps after diverting into an orchard and eating rotten apples.

1905
Northamptonshire become the 16th county in the championship.

Albert Einstein publishes his Special Theory of Relativity.

1906
Kent win the championship for the first time. Yorkshire, playing 28 games, would have been champions if they had not lost to Nottinghamshire, one of four counties whom Kent do not play.

The counties reject by eight votes to seven a proposal to increase the two-year qualification for overseas players. Those in favour are Yorkshire, Essex, Kent, Leicestershire, Worcestershire, Nottinghamshire and Minor Counties.

The Liberal Party wins a landslide victory in the General Election. Labour increases its MPs from two to 27.

1907
For the first time South Africa play Tests in England. In a three-match series they lose 1-0.

Nottinghamshire win the championship for the first time since the unofficial years of the 1880s.

Frank Tarrant, Middlesex's Australian, plays for Victoria during the winter. To prevent any repetition of this, MCC changes the rules of qualification: 'A British colony, dependency and state shall be regarded as a county.'

Sir Robert Baden-Powell runs his first scout camp, recruiting boys from Eton, Harrow and the East End of London.

1908
Yorkshire win the championship for the eighth time in 16 years.

London hosts the fourth modern Olympic Games at the newly built White City Stadium.

Jack Johnson, from Texas, is the first black man to become World Heavyweight Boxing Champion.

1909
The Imperial Cricket Conference is founded, with three members: England, Australia and South Africa.

Frenchman Louis Bleriot, in a monoplane, wins a £1,000 prize from the Daily Mail by flying across the Channel.

The Workman's Compensation Act is successfully used by an injured Crystal Palace footballer.

Championship – top three | Leading batsmen | Leading bowlers | Leading wkt-keeper / Leading fielder

1900

	P	W	L	D	Pts	%	Leading batsmen	Runs	Leading bowlers	Wickets	Leading wkt-keeper / Leading fielder	Victims
Yorkshire	28	16	0	12	16	100.0	K.S. Ranjitsinhji (Sussex)	2,563	W. Rhodes (Yorks)	206	H.R. Butt (Sussex)	61
Lancashire	28	15	2	11	13	76.5	R. Abel (Surrey)	1,880	A.E. Trott (Middx)	154	D. Hunter (Yorks)	61
Kent (3=)	22	8	4	10	4	33.3	T.W. Hayward (Surrey)	1,850	S. Haigh (Yorks)	145	J. Tunnicliffe (Yorks)	46
Sussex (3=)	24	4	2	18	2	33.3						

1901

	P	W	L	D	Pts	%	Leading batsmen	Runs	Leading bowlers	Wickets	Leading wkt-keeper / Leading fielder	Victims
Yorkshire	28	20	1	7	19	90.5	J.T. Tyldesley (Lancs)	2,605	W. Rhodes (Yorks)	196	F. Stedman (Surrey)	71
Middlesex	18	6	2	10	4	50.0	C.B. Fry (Sussex)	2,382	G.H. Hirst (Yorks)	135		
Lancashire	28	11	5	12	6	37.5	R. Abel (Surrey)	2,264	F.W. Tate (Sussex)	126	J. Tunnicliffe (Yorks)	62

1902

	P	W	L	D	Pts	%	Leading batsmen	Runs	Leading bowlers	Wickets	Leading wkt-keeper / Leading fielder	Victims
Yorkshire	26	13	1	12	12	85.7	R. Abel (Surrey)	1,570	F.W. Tate (Sussex)	153	J.H. Board (Glos)	55
Sussex	24	7	3	14	4	40.0	C.J. Burnup (Kent)	1,349	W. Rhodes (Yorks)	140		
Notts	20	6	3	11	3	33.3	J.T. Tyldesley (Lancs)	1,291	T.G. Wass (Notts)	138	J. Tunnicliffe (Yorks)	32

1903

	P	W	L	D	Pts	%	Leading batsmen	Runs	Leading bowlers	Wickets	Leading wkt-keeper / Leading fielder	Victims
Middlesex	18	8	1	9	7	77.8	C.B. Fry (Sussex)	2,413	W. Rhodes (Yorks)	143	H. Strudwick (Surrey)	72
Sussex	24	7	2	15	5	55.6	J.T. Tyldesley (Lancs)	1,618	C. Blythe (Kent)	137		
Yorkshire	26	13	5	8	8	44.4	A.C. MacLaren (Lancs)	1,565	S.F. Barnes (Lancs)	131	A.C. MacLaren (Lancs)	39

1904

	P	W	L	D	Pts	%	Leading batsmen	Runs	Leading bowlers	Wickets	Leading wkt-keeper / Leading fielder	Victims
Lancashire	26	16	0	10	16	100.0	C.B. Fry (Sussex)	2,376	E.G. Dennett (Glos)	123	D. Hunter (Yorks)	60
Yorkshire	28	9	2	17	7	63.6	J.T. Tyldesley (Lancs)	2,237	C. Blythe (Kent)	121		
Kent	22	10	4	8	6	42.9	T.W. Hayward (Surrey)	2,074	G.R. Cox (Sussex)	112	J. Tunnicliffe (Yorks)	57

1905

	P	W	L	D	Pts	%	Leading batsmen	Runs	Leading bowlers	Wickets	Leading wkt-keeper / Leading fielder	Victims
Yorkshire	28	18	3	7	15	71.4	D. Denton (Yorks)	1,963	W.S. Lees (Surrey)	169	H.R. Butt (Sussex)	81
Lancashire	25	12	3	10	9	60.0	C.B. Fry (Sussex)	1,912	G.R. Cox (Sussex)	154		
Sussex	28	13	4	11	9	52.9	W.G. Quaife (Warwicks)	1,785	E.G. Dennett (Glos)	131	T.S. Fishwick (Warwicks)	38

1906

	P	W	L	D	Pts	%	Leading batsmen	Runs	Leading bowlers	Wickets	Leading wkt-keeper / Leading fielder	Victims
Kent	22	16	2	4	14	77.8	T.W. Hayward (Surrey)	2,814	G.H. Hirst (Yorks)	182	J. Humphries (Derbys)	67
Yorkshire	28	17	3	8	14	70.0	J.T. Tyldesley (Lancs)	1,873	E.G. Dennett (Glos)	160	H. Strudwick (Surrey)	67
Surrey	28	18	4	6	14	63.6	G.H. Hirst (Yorks)	1,771	A. Fielder (Kent)	158	E.G. Hayes (Surrey)	46

1907

	P	W	L	D	Pts	%	Leading batsmen	Runs	Leading bowlers	Wickets	Leading wkt-keeper / Leading fielder	Victims
Notts	20	15	0	5	15	100.0	E.G. Hayes (Surrey)	1,721	E.G. Dennett (Glos)	184	F.H. Huish (Kent)	72
Worcs (2=)	18	8	2	8	6	60.0	J.B. Hobbs (Surrey)	1,717	A.W. Hallam (Notts)	153		
Yorkshire (2=)	28	12	3	13	9	60.0	J.T. Tyldesley (Lancs)	1,597	A. Fielder (Kent)	151	J. Seymour (Kent)	41

1908

	P	W	L	D	Pts	%	Leading batsmen	Runs	Leading bowlers	Wickets	Leading wkt-keeper / Leading fielder	Victims
Yorkshire	28	16	0	12	16	100.0	T.W. Hayward (Surrey)	1,874	C. Blythe (Kent)	167	F.H. Huish (Kent)	75
Kent	26	17	3	6	14	70.0	A. Marshal (Surrey)	1,655	G.H. Hirst (Yorks)	156	E.G. Hayes (Surrey)	39
Surrey	30	13	4	13	9	52.9	G.L. Jessop (Glos)	1,646	E.G. Dennett (Glos)	149	H. Whitehead (Leics)	39

1909

	P	W	L	D	Pts	%	Leading batsmen	Runs	Leading bowlers	Wickets	Leading wkt-keeper / Leading fielder	Victims
Kent	26	16	2	8	14	77.8	E.G. Hayes (Surrey)	1,844	C. Blythe (Kent)	178	H. Strudwick (Surrey)	66
Lancashire	24	14	4	6	10	55.6	J.B. Hobbs (Surrey)	1,771	E.G. Dennett (Glos)	135		
Yorkshire	26	12	4	10	16	50.0	D. Denton (Yorks)	1,544	W.S. Lees (Surrey)	120	J. Seymour (Kent)	35

1900-1909

Leading counties

	P	W	L	D	T	%W
Yorkshire	274	146	22	106	-	53.3
Kent	232	111	52	68	1	47.8
Lancashire	259	121	46	92	-	46.7
Surrey	283	110	66	106	1	38.9

Leading batsmen

T.W. Hayward (Surrey)	17,097
J.T. Tyldesley (Lancs)	16,543
G.H. Hirst (Yorks)	13,868
C.B. Fry (Sussex & Hants)	14,506

Leading bowlers

W. Rhodes (Yorks)	1,332
C. Blythe (Kent)	1,270
G.H. Hirst (Yorks)	1,110
S. Haigh (Yorks)	982

Leading keepers & fielder

H.R. Butt (Sussex)	576
F.H. Huish (Kent)	545
E.G. Hayes (Surrey)	317

Overall statistics

Runs per wicket	24.1
Runs per 100 balls	49.1
% of matches drawn	37.1

Miscellany

Archibald Fargus, making his debut for Gloucestershire against Middlesex at Lord's in 1900, had match bowling figures of 12 wickets for 87, the best ever in the championship by a debutant. The son of a popular novelist, he never came remotely close to repeating his triumph, taking only 21 wickets in a further 14 county matches before going into the church.

His *Wisden* obituary in 1915 described him as 'a good hammer and tongs bowler', reporting that he had gone down with *HMS Monmouth* on which he had been the chaplain. In fact, he had missed his train and was not on the ship. *Wisden* did correct its error but, when he finally died in 1963, it took the almanack 30 years to report his death.

*

At Hove in 1901 Sussex were asked by Nottinghamshire to follow on before lunch on the final day. Joe Vine was not out at the end of Sussex's first innings, having batted four hours for 55, and he was immediately sent back out to play for the draw, which he duly did, setting a championship record by not scoring his first run for 75 minutes.

*

In the week beginning Monday 4 June 1906 Tom Hayward of Surrey scored a record four centuries in six days: 144* and 100 at Trent Bridge, then 143 and 125 at Leicester.

At Leicester in 1902 the 20-year Reggie Crawford, a stylish batsman with a clubfoot, was so keen to reach his first hundred that, on 98 and 99, he ran out his last two partners. With his singing career limiting his appearances, he never did reach 100, one of only four men with a highest championship score of 99 not out. The other three all played for Somerset.

*

On 6 May 1909, in five hours 20 minutes of play at the Oval, Surrey hit Hampshire's bowlers for a mammoth 645 for four, the highest number of runs ever scored by one side in a championship day. By late afternoon the visitors had become so demoralised that they gave a bowl to their keeper, Jimmy Stone, who off the last ball before tea had Jack Hobbs caught in the covers for 205, the only wicket of his 306-match career.

Hobbs was using a bat pressed on him by a stranger with an offer of "five pounds for a hundred", and he won himself ten pounds. Ernie Hayes, making 274 at the other end, was left to regret that he had declined the same offer.

It was CB Fry's first match as a Hampshire cricketer, after 15 years with Sussex, and he must have wondered what the future held as his new side went down by an innings and 468 runs, the largest margin of defeat ever suffered in a championship match.

The championship in the 1900s

The championship enjoyed a rare decade of relative stability in the 1900s. The point-scoring system remained unaltered and, apart from the promotion of Northamptonshire, the number of fixtures in 1909 was much as in 1900.

At the start of the decade Yorkshire were indisputably the strongest county. These summers bore the rich fruits of Lord Hawke's long dedication to the cause, with their success built upon a core of reliable and highly talented professionals: the batsmen John Tunnicliffe, Jack Brown and David Denton, the keeper David Hunter and, above all, three of the best bowlers in the land in Wilfred Rhodes, George Hirst and Schofield Haigh, all of whom could bat.

As if these were not riches enough, there was also a trio of outstanding amateurs who appeared when opportunity allowed: Tom Taylor, a good enough batsman to be one of *Wisden's* five cricketers of 1900; Frank Mitchell who came back from the Boer War to be Yorkshire's leading run-scorer in 1901; and, above all, the Honourable Stanley Jackson, a supreme embodiment of that age's amateur ideal. He ended the summer of 1899 with a century, went off to fight in South Africa, whence he returned to hit a century in his only game of 1900; then, after missing the whole of 1901, he completed a hat-trick of hundreds in the first game of 1902. An Old Harrovian for whom Winston Churchill had fagged, he would hold office in the Conservative government of the 1920s and become Governor of Bengal.

In three summers from 1900 to 1902 Yorkshire's record was Won 49, Lost 2, and strangely the two defeats were both at the hands of the weak but always unpredictable Somerset, both of them on Yorkshire soil, too. In July 1901 at Headingley, in one of the biggest upsets in the history of the championship, Somerset began their second innings on the second morning with a deficit of 238 runs. "When we go down, we shall go down with a wollop," one of the Yorkshire team had told a reporter during their long, unbeaten run – and, my goodness, what a 'wollop' it was! Somerset scored 630, the highest score ever made against Yorkshire in a three-day game, then bowled their hosts out for 113.

The Headingley crowd took it well, massing in front of the pavilion and cheering the visitors heartily. The reception was different the following June when, on a wet wicket at Bramall Lane in Sheffield, Yorkshire, needing only 119 to win, were bowled out for 84. On that occasion, 'The crowd saw the wickets drop with a sullen bitterness.'

Yorkshire's next defeat, early in 1903, was also to Somerset, this time at Taunton in a game in which three serious injuries reduced them at one stage to eight men. But such giant-killing feats were not common during the decade. There was still a strong sense of old and new among the counties. Only once in the ten years did a lesser side – Worcestershire in 1907 – finish in the top four of the championship table.

Leicestershire were typical of the newer entrants. They were not the worst of sides – they finished fifth in 1905 – but only four of their 36 victories during the decade came in matches against the nine counties who had joined the championship before them. Their lack of grandeur, however, did make them open to new ideas. They raised money to create a new ground at Aylestone Road in Leicester, moving out of the rented Grace Road, and they experimented with an occasional Saturday start to their fixtures.

The elevation of Northamptonshire in 1905 came as a result of two years of runaway success in the Minor Counties Championship. To become the 16th first-class county they needed six teams to give them home-and-away fixtures, and eventually, when Derbyshire found space for them, they achieved this. Then they discovered the chasm they had crossed, as innings victories over Wiltshire and Northumberland gave way to innings defeats by Sussex and Surrey.

In 1903, the wettest summer of the century, Middlesex were the champions. With a small professional staff and Lord's often in use, they arranged fewer matches than the other old-established counties, and that year they won the title with just eight victories. Yorkshire, with a fuller programme, won 13, leading some to observe that the point-scoring system was placing too much importance on not losing. With standards of batting and of pitch preparation improving by the year, the proportion of games ending as draws was causing concern.

The title returned north in four of the next five years: to Archie MacLaren's Lancashire in 1904, to Yorkshire again in 1905 and 1908 and to Nottinghamshire in 1907. The success of the last of these was built largely on a pair of medium-fast bowlers, Albert Hallam and Tommy Wass, who could bowl all innings – and often did. Wass was one of the great county bowlers of the age, a wholehearted trier who lasted into his late thirties. He remains Nottinghamshire's highest wicket-taker of all time, yet he never got close to playing for England. A plain-speaking man, it is said that he rather 'frightened' the selectors at Lord's.

Tom Hayward of Surrey

2,814 championship runs in 1906

A quiet and unhurried craftsman, he knew that his livelihood depended on the runs he scored. 'I doubt if any professional has been more careful in his living or more painstaking in his methods to attain success,' Archie MacLaren wrote of him.

Tommy Wass of Notts

145 wickets at 13.57 in 1907

In his youth he would often walk 20 miles in a day. "The cricketers now," he said in 1949, "make too much use of their motor cars. How can they expect to be fit, when they hardly ever think of walking?"

Surrey, champions six times in the 1890s, did not win in the 1900s. Their great bowlers – Lohmann, Lockwood and Richardson – departed, and they became more of a batting team. The phlegmatic Tom Hayward scored big runs every year, never more than in 1906 when he set new records for runs and centuries in a season, and from 1905 he opened the Surrey innings with the young Jack Hobbs, also from Cambridge. Hayward, Hobbs and Ernie Hayes at three, Yorkshire could not boast a top order of that quality, but then Yorkshire had Haigh, Hirst and Rhodes to bowl teams out.

Kent had slow-left-arm Colin Blythe and fast bowler Arthur Fielder, and they won the championship in 1906 and 1909. The summer of 1906 brought much warm weather, and the race for the title was especially exciting. For most of the season it was Yorkshire's to lose, and lose it they did in the cruellest way – by one run at Bristol.

With the last pair together, Hubert Myers, the more capable batsman, mistakenly ran two off the last ball of an over, leaving the hapless Billy Ringrose on strike with one run wanted for the tie. The first ball from Gilbert Jessop, the Gloucestershire captain, flew down leg and might have gone for four byes but for 'an almost superhuman effort' by the keeper Jack Board; the next hit Ringrose's pad, brought a 'beseeching appeal' from Jessop and was given not out. The third hit the pad again and, as the batsmen set off for a leg bye, the umpire's finger went up.

A crowd of thousands gathered outside the pavilion, and Jessop made a speech. The papers talked about the need to brighten cricket, he said, but it needed no brightening when there were games such as this. Then he headed off to a sports day at the Bristol Rovers ground, where news of the victory had already spread. His arrival was greeted with such excitement that it was 'some little while before the interest of the spectators was again awakened in the sports'.

Telegrams of congratulation flooded in, many of them sent from Kent who were now on top of the table with only two matches to play. They won both games convincingly, finishing on 77.7%, ahead of Yorkshire on 70.0%. Such was the importance of not losing, and the complexity of the arithmetic, that one more run at Bristol would have taken Yorkshire up to 78.9% and to another championship.

When in autumn the Yorkshire team made its annual visit to Lord Hawke's Wighill Park, Hawke's sister turned to Ringrose: "Tell me, who was the wretched man who got out?" And Ringrose had to reply, "It was me, ma'am."

The championship really did matter.

Some players of the 1900s

Gilbert Jessop of Gloucestershire

> Gilbert Jessop was always a law unto himself as a hitter. When he was in the vein he would have scored if forty-four men were in the field. *Lord Hawke*
>
> The better I bowl, the harder he hits them. *George Hirst*

The son of a Cheltenham doctor, Gilbert Jessop was the most exciting cricketer of the Edwardian age. A shortish man, he crouched with knees bent as the bowler ran in, his hands apart as he clasped and unclasped his fingers around the handle of his heavy bat; then suddenly he was at the ball. If it was up to him, he stood still and drove. If it was short, no matter what the pace he danced towards it – or feinted to do so, then jumped back and cut. 'At his best,' CB Fry wrote, 'he can hit any ball bowled, no matter how good.'

His statistics are astonishing. In the list of 100s scored within an hour, his name appears 14 times, his nearest rival Ian Botham on three. He has four of the nine fastest 200s, all scored in the years when a six had to be hit right out of the ground. Only ten times did he bat for more than two hours, yet he scored 53 first-class 100s, 16 of them over 150.

It was not slogging. He was quick on his feet, had a sharp eye and was strong. Above all, he had a method, and he backed himself. At Bradford, in July 1900, Wilfred Rhodes was in the form of his life, and Jessop hit him out of the ground seven times in an hour. 'Runs are but playthings to him,' wrote a local reporter, 'and the best bowlers merely children.'

He could also bowl and field. Twice he took 100 wickets in a season, while in the covers he swooped and threw in the ball so fast the opposing batsmen never took quick singles.

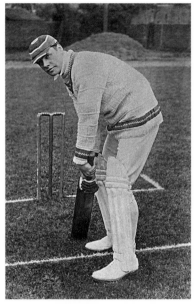

The Croucher

Across his 21-year first-class career he scored his runs at 80 an hour

Schofield Haigh of Yorkshire

> Schofie Haigh was probably the most popular professional in the world – and a grand cricketer. His laugh and his good nature combined with his unfailing cheerfulness could not be resisted. *Frank Mitchell*

Few bowlers in county cricket have achieved success as great and as sustained as Schofield Haigh. Yet such was the strength of Yorkshire in the 1900s that historians often leave him standing in the shadows of Hirst and Rhodes, no more than the county's third man from Huddersfield way. As a bowler and as a man he was much, much more than that.

Haigh did not come to the attention of Yorkshire till 1895, when he was already 24. At that point he was a fast bowler, rushing up on an over-long run, but by the turn of the century he had reduced his pace. There was still a jaunty spring in his run-up and a great stride at delivery, but he had learned the value of variation, cultivating a lethal slow yorker and an off-break that on a responsive surface was close to unplayable, pitching outside off and hitting leg stump. Even alongside Hirst and Rhodes he topped the Yorkshire bowling averages seven times in eight years from 1905. Five times he topped the national averages.

He was a good team man, too. Old Ebor of the *Yorkshire Post* called him 'the sunshine of the Yorkshire eleven', wearing 'a perennial smile' and 'bubbling over with humorous chuckles'. He was, CB Fry said, 'a thorough tryer', and he could bat, hitting four centuries, one before lunch at Trent Bridge, and once completing the 'double'. Eight times in his career Yorkshire were the champion county, and always his contribution was crucial.

Pivotal in Yorkshire's success

Top of the championship bowling averages five times in the 1900s

C.B. Fry of Sussex and Hampshire

> He was born for the highest work with men of the highest ability ... but he had ambitions rather than ambition. He was too various for the single aim; he lacked the ruthlessness that is ever present, however deftly disguised, in the careerist.
> *RC Robertson-Glasgow*

Charles Fry was a true Edwardian amateur: a sportsman who held the national long jump record and played football for England; an Oxford scholar who wrote a range of books, almost became a Liberal MP and ran a pioneering training ship for youngsters; a man with a fine figure and a regal bearing who represented India at the League of Nations and was offered the throne of Albania. When in old age he talked of taking up horse racing, he was asked: "What as, Charles? Trainer, jockey or horse?"

Yet he was not a dilettante. Rather, he studied cricket with analytical rigour. He lacked the flair of his great friend and Sussex team-mate Ranjitsinhji, but he had great powers of concentration and he created for himself a technique, based around straight and on-drives, that in 1901 brought him 3,147 runs, with 13 centuries. No batsman in these years scored runs with greater consistency. Nine times in 13 summers he finished first or second in the national averages.

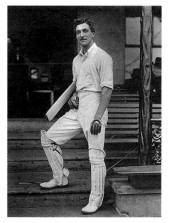

Charles Burgess Fry
Six hundreds in a row in 1901

Wilfred Rhodes of Yorkshire

Master of flight

Leading wicket-taker in 1900, 1901, 1903 – and still bowling in 1930

> There's more to bowling than just turning your arm over; there is such a thing as observation.
> *Wilfred Rhodes*

From his first appearance in the championship in 1898, when as an innocent 20-year-old he took 13 wickets for 45 runs at Bath, to his last as a canny veteran of 52, Rhodes was the supreme exponent of slow-left-arm bowling, allying a natural command of flight with a great cricketing brain. No bowler has ever studied his intended victims more astutely.

A great perfectionist, placing his fielders with geometric rigour, he was not given to idle pleasantries. As a bowler, he was always in control of himself and his emotions, in control of the ball too and, so it often seemed, the batsman. Patient on a true wicket, deadly on a sticky one, he took 100 first-class wickets in a season an unrivalled 23 times.

Yet it was batting he enjoyed most. Starting in the tail, he improved himself so much that he scored 1,000 runs in 20 consecutive seasons, 2,000 once, and became Jack Hobbs' opening partner for England. Twelve times during his career Yorkshire won the championship.

Johnny Tyldesley of Lancashire

> I have done my share of whirling buxom Lancashire lasses round a room, and that helps to keep a man light and quick on his feet.
> *Johnny Tyldesley*

Johnny Tyldesley was, in the eyes of many, the most gifted professional batsman of his generation. He allied his workmanlike skills and solid defence with a dashing spirit of enterprise that looked to dominate the bowlers. A short man, his speciality was the cut, which with lightness of foot he would play sometimes to middle-stump balls. Thirteeen times he passed 200, though his finest hour was at Old Trafford in 1905 when his dazzling 134 brought Lancashire its only Roses victory of the decade. Time and again he cut away Hirst and Rhodes, crisp strokes that lasted long in the red-rose memory.

He was at his happiest playing his shots, but he was no cavalier. Rather, he was a studious man, preferring to read on train journeys while the others played cards. He was still in his prime in August 1914, hitting four hundreds in six matches before war stopped play. Returning at the age of 45 in 1919, he was good enough to hit four more hundreds, including 272 against Derbyshire. A brilliant fielder, he was county coach when in the 1920s Lancashire won the championship three years in a row.

Johnny Tyldesley
2,605 championship runs in 1901

Stories of the 1900s

The man who walked out of county cricket

For many Sydney Barnes is the greatest English bowler of all time. In only 27 Tests, between 1901 and 1914, he took 189 wickets: 34 in the Ashes-winning series in Australia in 1911/12, a record 49 in South Africa two years later. A tall man with large hands and a high arm action, he was not fast through the air but he had supreme control, devilish variety, a great cricketing brain and total self-belief.

Yet, in the years of his glory, he was not playing county cricket. He had played just six times in nine summers, for Warwickshire and Lancashire, when in August 1901, to universal surprise, he was invited by the England captain Archie MacLaren to tour Australia. There, in the first two Tests, before he twisted his knee, he took 19 wickets.

MacLaren persuaded him to play regularly for Lancashire, which he did somewhat reluctantly for two summers. The money was not what he had been earning in the leagues, and his demands for a winter job and a special benefit were not well received. Certainly he was an 'obstinate cuss', but he had no intention of ending his days like so many old professionals who, as he put it, 'returned to the mine or factory, or took a fourth-rate beerhouse, trading as best they could upon their faded glories'.

So while he was setting records in Test cricket, he was playing in the Saturday leagues and turning out for Staffordshire. He had a good clerical job and, without the relentless round of county cricket, he stayed fit. He was 55 in 1928 when the West Indians thought him the best bowler they faced all summer. The next year, playing for Minor Counties against the South Africans, he bowled unchanged for 32 overs and took eight for 41.

Sydney Barnes

'Fostershire'

It is said that the Reverend Henry Foster, a good cricketer, gave up the game because, as a student at Cambridge in the 1860s, he could not afford the Clare College eleven's match fees. He was ordained into the church, took a teaching post at Malvern and fathered ten children, seven of them boys whose cricketing skills he developed assiduously in the nets. His wife Sophia assisted, bowling underarm lobs at them from an early age.

All seven boys played for Worcestershire, their careers spanning from 1890 to 1934. Harry, the eldest, captained the county for eleven of its first twelve championship years, his reign only broken by 'Tip', the third born. Maurice, the sixth, was captain for three years in the 1920s.

'Tip' was the most talented, but his stockbroking business kept him from regular cricket after 1901. Nevertheless he found time to tour Australia in 1903/04 where his 287 at Sydney remains the highest score ever made on Test debut. Back home he did not play in 1904 nor for much of 1905 but, when he did pick up a bat again, against Kent in late July, he set a new record score for the county with a brilliant 246.

In three further Tests, against South Africa in 1907, he became the only man to captain England at cricket and football.

In 1899, against Hampshire, 'Tip' and second-born Wilfrid each scored a hundred in both innings, a unique occurrence in county cricket. Wilfrid, a soldier, went off to fight the Boer War and played only intermittently thereafter — though he did play at Taunton in 1905, alongside 'Tip', Henry and Geoffrey, the only time four brothers have appeared together in a county championship match. Not without reason were Worcestershire known in those years as 'Fostershire'.

They were elegant and powerful off-sided batsmen, who between them scored 42,526 first-class runs, with 77 centuries, and they all played rackets, giving them strong wrists.

Basil, the fourth born, played football with 'Tip' in the victorious Old Malvernians team in the Amateur Cup Final of 1902, but his county cricket was limited after he became an actor. Living in London in 1912, however, he fitted in several games for Middlesex — between winning the English Amateur Rackets Championship and appearing in a musical comedy *The Sunshine Girl*.

The youngest, Neville, spent most of his adult life in business in Malaya, where he captained the national side.

Their three sisters played golf, Cicely for England.

Northants take on the big boys

Gloucestershire v Northamptonshire, Gloucester, 10-12 June 1907

Northamptonshire, new entrants to the championship in 1905, were nothing if not optimistic. In that first summer they played the minimum 12 games, mostly against the lesser counties, and they won twice. The next year they played 16 and won four. So in 1907 they bravely went up to 20, adding more of the bigger fish, notably Kent, Lancashire and Gloucestershire.

Optimism was fine, but it did not score them runs against these stronger sides, as they soon discovered. They played Kent twice in succession in May, making 73 and 86 in an innings defeat at Catford, then 60 and 39 back at Northampton – and the 60 might have been a great deal worse. At one stage they were 4 for seven, still nine runs short of the lowest inter-county total ever, the 13 for which Yorkshire had bowled out Notts six years earlier. The *Sheffield Daily Telegraph* had triumphantly called that 13 'a record that will probably stand for all time'. Little did they know; it did not even last the decade.

Colin Blythe, Kent's slow-left-arm genius, was the destroyer at Northampton, taking 17 wickets including all ten in the first innings. So it was not at all what the doctor ordered when ten days later the Northants batsmen found themselves on the stickiest of wickets at the Spa ground in Gloucester, facing another top-quality slow-left-armer, George Dennett.

They had bowled out the home side for just 60, but the pitch was at its most treacherous when they went out to bat. They got to six without loss, then to 10 for one, but the ball was turning almost square for Dennett and they had no answer. An innings that started at 1.10 was all over at 1.50. Northants, 12 all out; Dennett, eight for 9. Back in Northampton some jokers in a corn merchants sent the Northants captain Edmund Crosse a telegram: 'BRING THE BOYS HOME AT ONCE – MOTHER.'

The pitch eased as Gloucestershire managed 88 in their second innings, leaving Northants 137 to win. With the sun no longer burning down on the pitch, it was not a hopeless task – or would not have been if the nerves of the batsmen had not been so shredded. Dennett duly took a hat-trick; but for a dropped catch he would have had four in four, and soon enough the visitors were 33 for seven, all seven falling to the slow-left-armer. With ten minutes to go, George Thompson, the one bright star in the Northants team, and Sidney King, a 21-year-old amateur making his debut, were 'playing keeps', hoping for better fortune in the morning. Gilbert Jessop, the Gloucestershire captain, urged his Northants counterpart to play an extra half hour, 'but Mr Crosse could not see his way to accede.' At 40 for seven stumps were drawn. Dennett's day's work of 21 overs had yielded him 15 wickets for 21 runs.

The next day the rain was back, storms appearing whenever there was a prospect of play, and 'the players whiled away the time with golf shots, tent cricket, etc.' Jessop set up a race in which his 40-year-old keeper Jack Board, with a five-yard start, took on young Sidney King, a noted track athlete. A seven-and-sixpenny silk tie was at stake, and Gloucestershire even won that, Board surprising everybody with a three-yard victory.

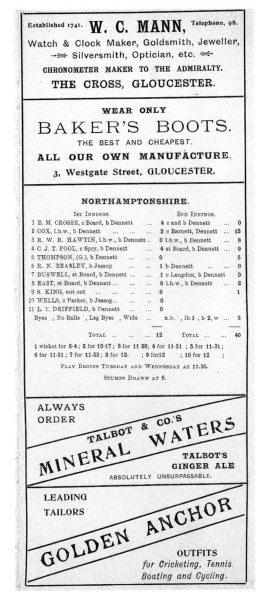

NORTHAMPTONSHIRE.

	1st Innings.		2nd Innings.
1 E. M. CROSSE, c Board, b Dennett	4	c and b Dennett	0
2 COX, l.b.w., b Dennett	2	c Barnett, b Dennett	12
3 R. W. R. HAWTIN, l.b.w., b Dennett	0	l.b.w., b Dennett	8
4 C. J. T. POOL, c Spry, b Dennett	4	st Board, b Dennett	9
5 THOMPSON, (G.), b Dennett	0		5
6 R. N. BEASLEY, b Jessop	0	b Dennett	1
7 BUSWELL, st Board, b Dennett	1	c Langdon, b Dennett	0
8 EAST, st Board, b Dennett	0	l.b.w., b Dennett	2
9 S. KING, not out	0		1
10 WELLS, c Parker, b Jessop	0		
11 L. T. DRIFFIELD, b Dennett	0		
Byes , No Balls , Leg Byes , Wide		n.b. , lb.1 , b 2, w	3
TOTAL	12	TOTAL	40

1 wicket for 6-4 ; 2 for 10-17 ; 3 for 11 26 ; 4 for 11-31 ; 5 for 11-31 ;
6 for 11-31 ; 7 for 11-33 ; 8 for 12- ; 9 for12 ; 10 for 12 ;

PLAY BEGINS TUESDAY AND WEDNESDAY AT 11.30.

STUMPS DRAWN AT 6.

Northants won their next two matches, against Hampshire and Derbyshire, but Dennett had not finished with them. In July at Northampton he took another 15 wickets.

Still optimistic, the Midlanders added Yorkshire to their fixture card the next year. In their first encounter, at Northampton, they were bowled out twice in less than three hours – for 27 and 15. Their match total of 42 runs remains, like their 12 at Gloucester, an all-time championship record.

Images of the 1900s

County cricket escapes to Blackpool

From 1906 to 1910 Lancashire played an annual match at Blackpool. The committee were persuaded that a great crowd would attend, and they did. But the ground did not prove ideal for county cricket. It had a pronounced slope, the wooden pavilion was primitive, and there was little shelter during rain. At the AGM one member, to a chorus of 'hear hear', called it 'by far the worst place where first-class cricket is played'.

This photograph of the crowd was taken on Thursday 9 July 1908, when the *Manchester Guardian* reported:

> One of the delights of the Blackpool ground is the complete escape it affords from the familiar conventions of county cricket. You have skylarks singing immediately above the pitch, and oxen gazing over fences at the strange sport; a card boy strolls casually across the sight-board just as the bowler is beginning his run, and another gets into the way of a racing fielder and is pitched among the spectators.

The ground itself is fairly good in point of quality, but it would be better if the boundaries were approximately on the same level, instead of one being a storey above the other, and if man or nature had pitched it somewhere in surroundings a little more pleasant to look upon; the accommodation, too, for distant visitors who make a day of the match, remains, in spite of the pointed protests of two years ago, of the crudest character.

Where else on a ground that has pretensions to county cricket could one see a group of reputable club members, including several gentlemen in Orders, patiently sitting for half an hour at an empty luncheon table, in the hope, as a waitress naïvely assures them, that, when the players and Committee have finished, there will probably be enough left to go round the public guests?

From the golden age of Neville Cardus's youth

If we think of the 1900s as a lost golden age of cricket, an era in which free-flowing amateur batsmen held sway – Ranjitsinhji, Jessop, MacLaren, Jackson – then almost certainly we have been influenced, directly or indirectly, by the romantic prose of Neville Cardus.

Cardus was born in Rusholme, Manchester in 1888, to a mother who was a part-time prostitute. He had a hard childhood, leaving his board school at 13, but he found other worlds through the books in his local library, through his discovery of classical music and through the cricketers at Old Trafford whom he watched from the cheap seats with awe.

Was it really a golden age, an age in which batsmanship was an art not a science, in which cricket was an expression of personality, played with an enterprise and a splendour that was lost for ever in the Flanders mud, or was Cardus a fanciful romantic aching with nostalgia for the scenes of his youth?

Whichever way, he became the greatest cricket writer of his generation, and that might not have happened if the Lancashire team he watched in his youth had not been such a great one.

In 1904, when the 16-year-old Cardus was working as an insurance clerk, Lancashire won the championship without losing a game. Their bowling – Hallows, Cuttell and Brearley – was strong, but it was the batting that stayed forever with Cardus: the brilliance of Johnny Tyldesley and, most especially, the panache of the two amateurs who opened the innings:

> Never again can I hope to see a Spooner. Did he actually exist, or did I dream of him while locked in at school on a summer's afternoon? I shall believe to my dying day that Spooner was the Herrick of cricketers, making a loveliness of batsmanship too gentle to last. I see him now, leaning forward, his bat all curves, rippling the off-side field until light seemed to play on it.

> MacLaren was the most majestic batsman I ever saw; his style belonged to a period when cricket was moving beyond its zenith. To see him at the wicket was like reading prose in Gibbon. The noblest Roman of them all, magnificent in his ambition and reckless in his sovereignty. Did I dream of him too?

Lancashire, 1904 champions

Standing: J Sharp, WR Cuttell, W Findlay, A Kermode, LOS Poidevon, J Hallows, JS Heap
Sitting: JT Tyldesley, AH Hornby, AC MacLaren, RH Spooner, HG Garnett

Cricketers from the colonies

KS Ranjitsinhji
India to Sussex

Albert Trott
Australia to Middlesex

Charlie Llewellyn
South Africa to Hampshire

Charles Ollivierre
West Indies to Derbyshire

The popularity of county cricket had grown to a new peak in the 1900s. The championship was contested with ever-increasing keenness, with many of the counties happy to look beyond their boundaries for fresh, match-winning talent. In some cases, to the alarm of traditionalists, they were even looking beyond the shores of Great Britain.

In those high days of Empire it was not uncommon for Englishmen to be born abroad. Lord Harris had started life in Trinidad, where his father was Governor; so, too, had Pelham Warner, the Middlesex captain. Teddie Wynyard, the Hampshire captain, was born in India, as was his team-mate Major Bertie Poore, who played for South Africa while stationed there. For such men it was sufficient qualification that they had some family connection with their county.

Kumar Shri Ranjitsinhji was in a different category. He was an Indian prince who came to England to study at Cambridge University, after which his friend Charles Fry persuaded him to play for Sussex. In some quarters Ranji's dark skin created problems; they say that was the reason why he did not make his debut for England at Lord's in 1896. He played the next Test at Old Trafford, however, and he was magnificent, hitting an unbeaten 154 while all around him were failing. The writer Home Gordon described the innings in glowing detail to a senior MCC man, only to be told that it was 'disgusting degeneracy to praise a black': 'If England could not win without resorting to the assistance of coloured men, it had better devote its skill to marbles.'

Ranji was simply too good a cricketer and too fine a man not to overcome such attitudes. In both 1899 and 1900 he passed 3,000 first-class runs, the first batsman to achieve the feat, and he did it in gloriously elegant and wristy style, even creating a new stroke, the leg glance. His was a magic that was at the very heart of that Edwardian Golden Age, and his style came with substance, too. Among those who have scored 10,000 championship runs, his career average of 62.04 reigns supreme.

Above all, he was an amateur, and he behaved as one. One day at Lord's, when he claimed to have fielded a ball inside the boundary, when the crowd protested and the umpire did not immediately accept his word as a gentleman, he was furious: "It seems to me, Barlow," he told the old pro, "that you have a great deal too much to say for yourself."

The problem for the traditionalists, those who wanted to preserve the identity of the county sides, lay not with the amateurs but with the growing number of men who were making their way from the colonies to earn a better living in the county game. Albert Trott was an early one. An Australian Test cricketer not picked for the 1896 tour of England, he came anyway, spent two years qualifying for Middlesex and set the world of cricket ablaze with his fast-medium bowling and big hitting. In his first summer of championship cricket he was the leading wicket-taker, and he also hit a ball over the roof of the Lord's pavilion, the only man ever to do so. Both that year and the next, in all first-class matches, he did the special 'double' of 1,000 runs and 200 wickets.

He was not blessed with great intelligence, nor did he take care of his health and money as he should have done, but for a while he burned brightly, inspiring several counties to look for overseas talent. Other Australians were John Cuffe at Worcestershire, Les Poidevon at Lancashire, Frank Tarrant at Middlesex and Alan Marshal at Surrey.

When it was discovered that the last of these, Marshal, was being paid a retainer while qualifying for Surrey, opposition came to a head. Essex proposed an increase of the residential qualification for overseas players to five years. Kent, who with Yorkshire were sticking firmly to county boundaries for their players, offered a more conciliatory motion, arguing only for an unspecified increase, but this was defeated by eight votes to seven, a result that might have been different if Gilbert Jessop from Gloucestershire had not missed his train.

Marshal had great success at Surrey, but it all went wrong in the middle of his third summer when some horseplay in the streets of Chesterfield, during which he gave a false name to the police, started a downward slide that led to his leaving the Oval early the following year. Worse for English cricket was that the circumstances surrounding his departure caused the resignation of Surrey's young captain Jack Crawford, the boy wonder who had played for England within months of leaving Repton School. Against the trend of these years Crawford took a job as a schoolmaster in Adelaide where in his first summer his runs and wickets did much to bring the Sheffield Shield to the unfancied South Australia.

Another economic migrant was Charlie Llewellyn from Pietermaritzburg, a South African Test cricketer who came to Hampshire on the recommendation of Bertie Poore. In his first season he did the 'double', and he was named next year in the England 14 for the First Test at Old Trafford, a selection which provoked the Australian Warwick Armstrong to exclaim: "I thought we were playing England, not South Africa."

Llewellyn had a dark complexion and was almost certainly of mixed race, but he seemed to pass for white, unlike Charles Ollivierre who toured with a West Indian team in 1900 and stayed to qualify for Derbyshire. It took him a while to adapt his batting to English conditions but in full flow, with his superb wrists, he was a delight to watch, holding his place in the county side for six years till poor eyesight forced his retirement. In later life he coached in Holland.

Ollivierre's finest hour

Derbyshire v Essex, Chesterfield, 18-20 July 1904

'There are some who are very fond of attempting to find new records,' wrote one paper on Thursday morning. 'Derbyshire's latest performance should find them congenial employment.'

The boundaries at the Chesterfield ground were short, the sun was burningly hot, and through Monday and the early part of Tuesday 'Peter' Perrin of Essex batted his way to 343 not out. A wealthy man whose family owned London pubs, he had a heavy build, standing in the crease and driving the ball mightily. He hit 68 boundary fours, a record that would stand for 90 years, till Brian Lara's 501. Essex were all out for 595.

It was a pitch made for batsmen, and Charles Ollivierre, far from his native Grenadine Islands, had the day of his life. Light of foot and flashing of blade, he scored a sparkling 229. 'There is no prettier player in first-class cricket,' one paper wrote. 'He imparts into his late cut an extraordinary amount of energy. Few men affect a more commanding pose at the wicket.' Derbyshire ended the day on 448 for four.

With a draw inevitable, the visitors celebrated in style that night. Perrin's triple-century was the first by an Essex man.

Wednesday was cooler, and Derbyshire batted till one o'clock, ending on 548. With the game so far producing 1,143 runs, there was talk of the match record being broken.

Then, with a hint of rain in the air, Essex were bowled out for 87. Was the pitch wearing? Were they the worse for their Bacchanalian night? And why did Frank Gillingham, their East End curate, not bat? Had he 'gone in the thigh' or was he, as rumour had it, 'declining to play with drunkards'?

Derbyshire needed 147 in two hours, and within 50 minutes Ollivierre had raced to his fifty. Could he complete that rare feat of 200 and 100? It looked likely, till Bill Storer started to hog the strike. Was Storer trying to get bonus money for a fifty, or was he – as Essex's Edward Sewell mischievously suggested – 'a man who believed in England for the English and was not enamoured of importations, especially those of ebony hue'?

The match was won, Storer ending on 48, Ollivierre on 92, and the 3,000-strong crowd streamed across the ground. In the pavilion, when Storer apologised, Ollivierre 'said he was only too pleased to see the runs got'. It was his 28th birthday and, 4,000 miles from home, he 'laughed cheerily'. It was his finest hour.

In Derby the news was 'greeted with absolute incredulity'. The *Daily Telegraph* called it 'the most astonishing victory in the history of cricket', while, for those seeking records, Perrin's 343 was, and still is, the highest score ever made in a losing cause.

1906: George Hirst's summer of plenty

George Herbert Hirst is the greatest county cricketer ever. That is what Geoffrey Boycott thinks. He may well be right.

Year after year, on the summer-long round of county matches, the sturdy all-rounder gave his all. He bowled long spells of left-arm pace, with a run-up that was far from easy on his body. 'Starting with a sort of hop,' wrote Leicestershire's Albert Knight, 'he bounces to the wicket almost as roundly as an india-rubber ball, a wearing, caring action which takes a great deal out of him.' He was a good fielder – 'agile, cheerful and brilliant,' his captain Lord Hawke called him – and he batted at four or five, where he was happy to subordinate himself to the needs of his team: to defend patiently on the difficult days or to take the attack to the bowler. A solid, strong man, he was quick on his feet and especially powerful square of the wicket, as his obituary in the *Guardian* testified: 'Hirst's pull,' it read, 'was surely the noisiest shot in cricket.'

Born in September 1871 in the village of Kirkheaton outside Huddersfield, he left school at ten years old, working first for a hand-loom weaver in the village, then in a dye-works on the other side of the valley. He played cricket whenever he could, first with the other village boys, then from 14 at the Kirkheaton club, and at 19 he made his Yorkshire debut.

In 1895 he took 100 wickets for the first of 15 times. In 1896 he also scored 1,000 runs, as he did 19 times. But his great breakthrough came at the turn of the century when he discovered the ability to 'swerve' the ball in the air. On what he liked to call his 'funny days', this swerve was extraordinary, something beyond the ken of even great batsmen such as Fry and MacLaren. 'When the ball leaves his arm,' one bewildered batsman wrote, 'it appears to be coming straight but, when it reaches the wicket, it is like a very good throw from cover point.' In 1901, in all first-class matches, Hirst took 183 wickets and scored 1,950 runs.

By the summer of 1906 George Hirst was approaching his 35th birthday. His nights were broken by a newborn baby, his third child, and he was carrying a bad knee that required strapping whenever he went out to bowl. But he was no complainer, far from it. 'Cricket is a game,' he used to say. 'And, when you're both a bowler and a batter, you're twice as happy. You enjoy yourself twice as much.'

'His smile used almost to meet at the back of his neck,' Lord Hawke said. Or, as Pelham Warner wrote, 'It does one good to see him laugh. In many ways he is the ideal cricketer, so straight, so strong, so honest.'

Between Monday 7 May and Saturday 1 September 1906 there were 17 weeks, and into them Yorkshire fitted 32 three-day matches, 28 of which were in the championship. George Hirst played all 32, batting 53 times and bowling 1,211 overs. Indeed, in one of his only two breaks, he should have played a 33rd game, for the Players against the Gentlemen in early July, but by then he 'felt obliged to save himself for Yorkshire', a decision that caused some ripples at Lord's.

On the last day of June, after just eight weeks of cricket, Hirst completed his season's double of 1,000 runs and 100 wickets. He had already bowled almost 640 overs: 80 a week.

As summer wore on and the heat rose, the muscles in his legs came to feel like iron. Night and morning he massaged them with Neats-foot Oil. One day he asked the doctor why he was having to do this. "Don't you realise, Mr Hirst," came the reply, "you've given your legs more use than five ordinary men in a lifetime. You're lucky if you can keep them in order with a drop of oil."

Every game was vital as the closest of championship races developed. Against rivals Kent he took 11 wickets and hit a match-winning century at Catford, then back at Sheffield saved the game with eight wickets and a hard-fought 93. He took 14 wickets against Notts at Dewsbury, and at Old Trafford he turned a Roses match on its head with a battling 85 on what *Wisden* called 'a more or less ruined wicket'. He hit six centuries during the summer, but for many this was his finest innings. 'It is a truism,' wrote the *Yorkshire Post*, 'that no batsman is more capable of forcing runs under difficult conditions than this great-hearted Yorkshireman.'

As the last week of August began, his season's tally was 1,837 runs and 184 wickets. All for Yorkshire, the great majority of them in championship games. It was a prodigious summer's work, but the best was still to come.

On Monday 27 August Yorkshire began their final championship match, against Somerset at Bath. The country was in the grip of a heatwave, and the hills around the city made the hot air at the Recreation Ground especially stifling. Hirst came to the wicket at 161 for three, and he hit a chanceless century. The next day he took six wickets, bowling unchanged for 26 overs. Somerset were all out for 125 and could have been asked to follow on. But Ernest Smith, the schoolmaster who was standing in as captain for Lord Hawke, did not want in such extreme heat to send his bowlers straight back out.

It was a sound theory, except in practice it did not work out like that. Wilfred Rhodes, who had just bowled 14 overs, opened the innings with John Tunnicliffe – and, when after an hour Tunnicliffe was caught, Ernest Smith told George Hirst to go in. He wanted to accelerate the scoring.

Hirst, as always, did what the game required. With 'hitting of the most invigorating kind', he raced to 50 in 35 minutes, 93 in an hour. At this point he hit the ball high into the 'long field' and watched as the fielder spilled the catch. The poor man also split a finger, and in the heat Somerset wilted. Lionel Palairet, their captain, took to bowling under-arm lobs, and even the wicket-keeper had two overs, during which Palairet kept without gloves. At the end of the day both Hirst and Rhodes came off with centuries.

The next day he sent down 15 overs – 'bowling at a great pace' – and took another five wickets. He remains the only man in the history of cricket to score two hundreds and take five or more wickets in both innings in a match. 'A weak leg handicapped him last season,' wrote the *Yorkshire Post*, 'and has several times threatened to do the same this year, but he has persevered with a pluck that is characteristic of the man.'

The Yorkshire team now had to travel to Scarborough, a rail journey of more than eight hours, and the next morning Hirst was in the field again, opening the bowling for Yorkshire against a strong MCC side. With his hundreds at Bath he had passed 2,000 runs, and all the talk now was whether he could take the five wickets he needed for 200. The temperature was climbing to the highest it had been for thirty years, and Hirst, a week short of his 35th birthday, bowled 33 overs in the day. At tea his wicket tally stood at 199. MacLaren, his first victim, called him 'the most untiring and enthusiastic cricketer who ever wore flannels'.

The tension was too much for two elderly ladies, the mothers of Hirst and Rhodes. They went for a walk in the streets outside the ground and, when the first ball after tea was bowled, they heard a great roar, followed by much cheering. He had done it. The 'double double'. 2,000 runs and 200 wickets. Never before or since has cricket seen its equal.

With three extra matches in September he finished with 2,385 first-class runs and 208 wickets. It was a summer-long feat of great skill, of great temperament and, above all, as such a relentless schedule required, of great stamina. He was asked if anybody would ever do it again, and he replied with a smile: "If they do, they'll be very tired."

Those were the facts, but the man was more than that, as became clear when in later life he became an inspirational coach both at Eton College and with Yorkshire. In the words of the writer Alfred Gibson, 'He belongs to the optimistic order that infect others with their good spirits.'

He retired in September 1921, playing his last day on his 50th birthday, at the end of which he stood on the balcony at Scarborough and addressed the crowd. "What can you have better," he asked, "than a nice green field, with the wickets set up, and to go out and to do the best for your side? I leave first-class cricket to those who have got to come. I hope they'll have the pleasure in it that I have had."

The rise of Kent

In the 1890s Kent were the most amateur of the county sides, often taking the field with an eleven that included only two or three professionals. They never challenged for the championship, but they played attractive cricket, especially in high summer when the best of the amateurs were available.

The expansion of the championship in 1895 gave them a jolt. Competing against counties of far inferior pedigree, they won only three times all season and finished in last place. The shock of it was expressed by *The Times*: 'That a county which has such a history and is so closely identified with cricket should be in such a position seems impossible.'

The following summer, in Lord Harris's tent at the Canterbury Festival, the committee made a decision that would, within only a few years, have a profound effect on their fortunes. They resolved to develop some young professionals from within the county's boundaries. The Tonbridge club agreed to host the scheme, and one hundred pounds were set aside. The club found local employers willing to offer winter work, and by spring the first group was reporting to the Angel ground. Among them was a tall 19-year-old lad called Arthur Fielder, a raw fast bowler from the nearby village of Plaxtol.

Later that summer came a quiet 18-year-old apprentice engineer from Deptford, Colin Blythe. He had gone along to watch Kent at Blackheath and, before play, had been roped into the nets to 'bowl a few' at one of the county's batsmen. He had played almost no serious cricket, but the ease of his slow-left-arm action immediately impressed the watching Captain William McCanlis, a former Kent amateur who was soon to take over the Tonbridge nursery scheme.

It was a stroke of luck. Deptford was a rough area, 'a place' – as McCanlis put it – 'one would hardly go to in search of cricketers'. But there was no luck about the way Blythe developed once he started at Tonbridge. The days were carefully managed, the coaching of the bowlers was simple, focusing first on length, and the lads were sent off to play for nearby clubs. By August of his second year there Blythe was making his debut for Kent, Fielder joining him the next July.

Others progressed from Tonbridge into the county side: Fairservice, Seymour, Humphreys, Hubble, Hardinge. By the summer of 1906 they were all playing alongside Blythe and Fielder. While other counties were spending money on overseas players, Kent had created a home-grown team.

Fielder developed into an outstanding fast bowler, good enough in Australia in 1907/08 to take 25 wickets in four Tests. A strong man with great stamina, he won many a match for Kent – though not as many as Colin Blythe.

While Fielder's bowling was an expression of muscular power, Blythe's was sensitive, artistic, almost gentle, as befitted a man who played the violin in his spare time. On a broken pitch his slow-left-arm spin was deadly, but he had sufficient variation and control to be a fine bowler on all surfaces. He did not give the ball as much air as his great Yorkshire contemporary Wilfred Rhodes but, in the view of many, including Ranjitsinhji and Pelham Warner, he was the harder of the two to face. In all Test cricket since 1900 only Sydney Barnes has taken 100 wickets at an average lower than Blythe's 18.63.

Colin Blythe

The very look on his face, the long, sensitive fingers, the elastic back sweep of the left arm before delivery, the short dancing approach, the long last stride and the final flick of the arm as it came over, all these spoke of a highly sensitive and nervous instrument, beautifully co-ordinated, directed by a subtle mind, and inspired by a natural love of his art.

Harry Altham

Inevitably Kent's fortunes improved in the first years of the century. They never finished above Yorkshire or Lancashire in the championship table, seldom above Sussex, but they won more games than they lost and they came to be seen once more as one of the stronger county sides.

Then came the summer of 1906. They started badly, losing to Yorkshire and only just escaping with a draw against Essex. Then they beat Sussex by an innings, their first victory over their neighbours for seven years. It was an impressive performance, with Fielder taking eleven wickets and Humphreys striking a bright century. Yet *The Times* sounded a note of caution: 'Kent often have caused the leading side of the year trouble, but the inability of the best amateurs to play regularly will always prevent them from winning the championship.'

It was not, however, a returning amateur that would provide the extra spark their team required but the emergence of another of Captain McCanlis's nursery lads, the 19-year-old son of a garage mechanic from the village of Leigh, five miles from Tonbridge. His name was Frank Woolley.

He was known to have promise, with both bat and ball, but at this stage he was principally a slow-left-arm bowler and Kent already had one of those. However, Blythe was injured in the Sussex match, dropping a sharp return catch, and had to miss three games. So in stepped the youngster. He travelled with the team on the long trip to Manchester where on the first day he twice dropped Johnny Tyldesley as the Lancastrian hit 295, and he took one wicket for 103 runs. On the second day he was bowled for nought.

On the final day, batting at eight, he top-scored with an elegant 64. The *Athletic News* called him 'a tall, thin split of a youth. Nothing better has been seen than his on-drives, fine, simple and unadulterated. We shall hear more of this man.'

A week later, at the Oval, he played a game that he never forgot. He bowled out three good batsmen as he and Fielder dismissed Surrey for 73, then he played an innings of 72 that lifted Kent from 61 for six to 200 all out. In the Surrey second innings he took five wickets, then – with Kent needing 128 – he guided them from 99 for eight to a one-wicket victory. A scene of mayhem ensued as Kent supporters rushed out to congratulate him. He got 'two proper whacks' from an umbrella, lost his bat, was shaken repeatedly by the hand, had two sovereigns pressed into his palm, and was so disoriented by the time he finally sank into the bath that he forgot to take off one of his boots.

Blythe was back for the next game at Tonbridge. Woolley, however, stayed in the team, and on his home ground he scored his first first-class hundred. It would be 32 years, at Tunbridge Wells, before he would score his last, his 145th.

At the halfway stage of that 1906 summer Kent had won five, drawn four and lost two, a typical Kent season. Then, with the weather settling to long weeks of sunshine, they won their last eleven matches, every one of them emphatically, and they pipped Yorkshire to the title.

Fielder and Blythe ran through side after side, sharing 153 wickets in those eleven games. Seymour and Humphreys scored important hundreds, but it was not all down to Captain McCanlis's professional protégés. At Canterbury there were as many as six amateurs in the eleven, and during the week four of them scored centuries.

The Times was not wrong; Kent still needed its amateurs. But they alone would never have won the championship. They needed the men from the Tonbridge nursery.

The Canterbury Festival
as described by Lieutenant-Colonel Newnham-Davis (1906)

Somebody has called Canterbury Week the Goodwood of Cricket, and the first-sight of the great half-hoop of tents, the flags, the carriages, and the moving crowd does suggest a racecourse.

To the right towers the Pavilion. Just before us on a gentle mound are lines of spectators on benches, and behind them are carriages and motors. A broad curve of canvas tents, in many places two deep, sweeps away to the left, a big tree roughly marking its centre. Beyond again are carriages and drags, a large stand, a band on a raised platform, more trees, another curve of seated spectators, and another stand.

Each little enclosure in front of the tents is as gay as a flower bed, with the summer dresses of the ladies. On the benches is by no means a mass of neutral colour, for the Kentish lassies of all degrees of life love to watch a cricket match, and the garrison has come down in full force, both Cavalry and the County regiment, The Buffs, to see the County Eleven play. As the band on the far side of the ground ceases to play, another band hidden from view by the tents sends out a burst of melody; we hear the sharp notes of the horn as a road coach from Margate drives into the ground; a passing train whistles – there is plenty of sound as well as plenty of colour in this assemblage.

1910 – 1919

The weaker counties in financial trouble

Four years lost to war

Two-day matches in 1919

Unfortunately, at the present moment there does not seem to be the same "county spirit" as there used to be. Perhaps it is owing to the fact that people have to work more strenuously than they had to 20 years ago. They are still keen to know how the cricket of the day is going, but they do not turn up in numbers, and numbers mean gate-money, and gate-money means everything to a county, stoutly though the authorities may deny it.

The Times, May 1914

Why not open a competition (with a prize) for the best guess at what will be the way of reckoning championship winners next season? Personally I like the method of counting two points for every man who scores 13, deducting one point for a score of over 100 and adding one for losing on the first innings if the match is finished.

Letter to the magazine Cricket, September 1911

The season of 1919 proved, beyond all question or dispute, that cricket had lost nothing of its attraction for the public. Indeed, one may go further than that. County matches drew far larger attendances than in ordinary seasons before the war. The faint-hearts, who had jumped to the conclusion that cricket would never again be its old self, were utterly confuted. Such being the pleasant state of affairs in the first year of peace, I trust we shall hear no more about the need for drastic alteration to the game.

Wisden Cricketers' Almanack 1920

1910 To reduce the increasing number of draws, the championship table is now calculated by percentage of wins in all matches, not just in those that are won or lost.

There are two changes to the laws: (i) To score a six it is no longer necessary to hit the ball out of the ground, only to clear the boundary; (ii) A declaration can take place at any time on the second day.

Dr Crippen, suspected of murdering his wife, is arrested at sea as a result of new radio communications.

1911 Warwickshire win the championship, the first of the counties promoted in the 1890s to do so.

A new points system is introduced: 5 for a win; 3 for a draw if ahead on first innings, 1 if behind.

King Edward VII dies in May. No county cricket takes place on the day of his funeral.

A maximum 60-hour week is introduced for shop workers.

The Norwegian Roald Amundsen becomes the first man to reach the South Pole.

1912 An experimental Triangular Tournament is played, between England, Australia and South Africa. There are nine Test matches, with the decider – in which England beat Australia – extended beyond the normal three days.

In March both crews sink during the University Boat Race.

In April the liner RMS Titanic goes down on its maiden voyage across the Atlantic, with the loss of 1,500 lives.

1913 Kent win a fourth championship title. Wisden regrets that they are 'so largely dependent on professional talent.' Northamptonshire propose a new structure for the championship: two-day games with seven-hour days, all playing all and the bottom two to apply for re-election as in the Football League. In an atmosphere of ill-will Lancashire call a secret meeting of the eleven best-supported counties and propose throwing out the others: Derbyshire, Essex, Somerset, Worcestershire and Northamptonshire. Peace is restored when both schemes are withdrawn.

A National Insurance scheme, to protect workers against sickness and unemployment, is introduced.

At the Derby suffragette Emily Davison dies after throwing herself in front of the King's horse.

1914 The final matches of the season are cancelled on account of the war, leaving Surrey at the head of the table.

WG Grace calls for there to be no champions, but Middlesex, Surrey's only remaining rival, concede the title.

On 28 June Archduke Ferdinand, heir to the Austro-Hungarian throne, and his wife are assassinated in Sarajevo.

On 4 August Germany invades Belgium, and Britain declares war against Germany.

Late in August the first British Expeditionary Force suffers heavy losses in the battle for the Belgian town of Mons.

1915 *A German submarine sinks the liner Lusitania off Ireland, with the loss of 128 American lives.*

Allied troops make no progress in the war.

1916 *The British army launches the Somme Offensive.*

For each of the six miles of ground gained during the 20-week engagement the Allied forces lose 88,000 men.

1917 *The United States of America enters the war.*

Bolshevik revolutionaries, under the leadership of Vladimir Lenin, seize power in Russia.

1918 *On 11 November an Armistice is signed to end the war.*

750,000 Britons, as well as 200,000 from the Empire, have died during the four years of fighting.

In the December General Election voting is extended for the first time to women – but only those over the age of 30.

1919 In the aftermath of war a reduced programme of county matches is arranged.

All county matches are played over two days: 11.30-7.30 on the first, 11-7.30 on the second.

The points system for the championship reverts to the one used in 1910: percentage of wins in matches played. Worcestershire, in financial difficulty, do not enter a side.

A world-wide epidemic of flu takes the lives of 250,000 people in Britain.

Championship – top three — Leading batsmen — Leading bowlers — Leading wkt-keeper / Leading fielder Victims

1910

	P	W	L	D	%W	Leading batsmen	Runs	Leading bowlers	Wickets	Leading wkt-keeper / fielder	Victims
Kent	25	19	3	3	76.0	J.T. Tyldesley (Lancs)	1,961	W.C. Smith (Surrey)	215	F.H. Huish (Kent)	70
Surrey	28	16	7	5	57.1	A. Hartley (Lancs)	1,511	J.A. Newman (Hants)	156		
Middlesex	22	11	5	6	50.0	E. Humphreys (Kent)	1,483	C. Blythe (Kent)	149	G.R. Cox (Sussex)	40

1911

	P	W	L	D	Pts	%	Leading batsmen	Runs	Leading bowlers	Wickets	Leading wkt-keeper / fielder	Victims
Warwickshire	20	13	4	3	74	74.0	T.W. Hayward (Surrey)	1,963	H. Dean (Lancs)	175	F.H. Huish (Kent)	91
Kent	26	17	4	5	96	73.8	J. Sharp (Lancs)	1,959	W.C. Smith (Surrey)	152		
Middlesex	22	14	5	3	79	71.8	D. Denton (Yorks)	1,744	C. Blythe (Kent)	125	K.G. MacLeod (Lancs)	40

1912

	P	W	L	D	Pts	%	Leading batsmen	Runs	Leading bowlers	Wickets	Leading wkt-keeper / fielder	Victims
Yorkshire	28	13	1	14	90	72.0	D. Denton (Yorks)	1,831	C. Blythe (Kent)	170	F.H. Huish (Kent)	63
Northants	18	10	1	7	60	70.6	E.G. Hayes (Surrey)	1,453	E.G. Dennett (Glos)	118		
Kent	26	14	5	7	82	65.6	R.R. Relf (Sussex)	1,397	A.S. Kennedy (Hants)	112	J. Seymour (Kent)	35

1913

	P	W	L	D	Pts	%	Leading batsmen	Runs	Leading bowlers	Wickets	Leading wkt-keeper / fielder	Victims
Kent	28	20	3	4	110	81.5	J.B. Hobbs (Surrey)	2,238	M.W. Booth (Yorks)	158	F.H. Huish (Kent)	84
Yorkshire	28	16	4	7	95	70.4	C.P. Mead (Hants)	2,146	J.W. Hitch (Surrey)	154		
Surrey	26	13	5	8	81	62.3	H.T.W. Hardinge (Kent)	1,949	E.G. Dennett (Glos)	153	J. Seymour (Kent)	43

1914

	P	W	L	D	Pts	%	Leading batsmen	Runs	Leading bowlers	Wickets	Leading wkt-keeper / fielder	Victims
Surrey	26	15	2	9	93	74.4	J.B. Hobbs (Surrey)	2,499	C. Blythe (Kent)	159	G.B. Street (Sussex)	69
Middlesex	20	11	2	7	70	70.0	C.P. Mead (Hants)	2,235	A.S. Kennedy (Hants)	148		
Kent	28	16	7	5	87	62.1	F.E. Woolley (Kent)	1,933	M.W. Booth (Yorks)	141	J. Seymour (Kent)	40

1915

1916

FIRST WORLD WAR

377 men played in the county championship in 1914.

40 died during the four years of the war.

81 more did not return to county cricket.

1917

I see them in foul dug-outs, gnawed by rats,
And in the ruined trenches, lashed by rain,
Dreaming of things they did with balls and bats,
And mocked by hopeless longing to regain
Bank-holidays, and picture shows, and spats,
And going to the office in the train.

Siegfried Sassoon

1918

1919

	P	W	L	D	%W	Leading batsmen	Runs	Leading bowlers	Wickets	Leading wkt-keeper / fielder	Victims
Yorkshire	26	12	11	3	46.2	J.W.H. Makepeace (Lancs)	1,747	W. Rhodes (Yorks)	142	A. Dolphin (Yorks)	67
Kent	14	6	7	1	42.9	G.E. Tyldesley (Lancs)	1,618	J.W. Hitch (Surrey)	103		
Notts	14	5	8	1	35.7	H. Sutcliffe (Yorks)	1,601	T. Rushby (Surrey)	99	P. Holmes (Yorks)	31

1910-1919

Leading counties

	P	W	L	D	%W
Kent	147	90	23	34	61.2
Yorkshire	165	79	27	59	47.9
Surrey	156	73	29	54	46.8
Middlesex	120	52	25	43	43.3

Leading batsmen

J.B. Hobbs (Surrey)	10,339
C.P. Mead (Hants)	9,877
J.T. Tyldesley (Lancs)	9,036
D. Denton (Yorks)	8,447

Leading bowlers

C. Blythe (Kent)	748
J.W. Hitch (Surrey)	655
H. Dean (Lancs)	633
E.G. Dennett (Glos)	611

Leading keepers & fielder

F.H. Huish (Kent)	373
H. Strudwick (Surrey)	347
J. Seymour (Kent)	189

Overall statistics

Runs per wicket	24.2
Runs per 100 balls	50.5
% of matches drawn	31.1

Miscellany

Against a full-strength Yorkshire attack at Bradford in 1911 Leicestershire's Cecil Wood became the first of only two men (Somerset's Jimmy Cook in 1989 the other) to carry his bat for a century in each innings of a match. Playing 'with wonderful patience', he hit 107* out of 309 and 117* out of 296.

Leicestershire were a poor side that summer, losing their first ten games, but the amateur Wood, a coal merchant, did his best to prevent humiliation, carrying his bat five times.

In his full career he carried his bat a record 17 times.

*

When Worcestershire's fast bowler Dick Burrows bowled Bill Huddleston at Old Trafford in 1911, one of the bails is said to have landed 67 yards and six inches behind the wicket, the longest recorded distance a bail has ever travelled.

*

Sussex's Harry Simms, an Old Malvernian born in South Australia, hit only one first-class century – at Hove in 1912. The game was drifting to a draw so he took on the slow-left-arm bowling of Notts' John Gunn, jumping out of the crease to drive him repeatedly. In a whirlwind innings of 126 he hit ten sixes and was dropped three times on the boundary.

With both their main slow bowlers injured, Gunn sent down 14 overs, at the end of which he had conceded 153 runs.

At the Oval in June 1914 Hampshire's Arthur Jaques, trying to staunch the flow of Surrey runs, was bowling with eight men on the leg-side and only CB Fry, at mid-off, on the off.

Andy Ducat was batting. On the football field, for Aston Villa and England, he was described as 'incredibly light on his feet, as if he's treading on air', and he brought the same quick energy to his cricket. "You'll be the death of me," Andrew Sandham would complain when they batted together.

Ducat late-cut a ball from Jaques. Fry hesitated, thinking it was going for four, but the ball stopped just short of the boundary. Though a fit man, Fry was now 42 years old and, by the time he got all the way down to third man, Ducat had run seven, equalling the most runs ever scored off a ball, without the aid of overthrows, in a championship match.

Before play started next morning, Ducat fitted in a trip to St Stephen's Church in Hounslow to get married. With Surrey off duty the next week, he honeymooned in Chelmsford.

The Oval field was vast in those days, twice previously yielding all-run sevens, and in 1929 it was the scene of an innings of 82 by Ducat, which featured seven all-run fours – and, helped by overthrows, a nine. No cricketer was fitter so it was a great shock when, at the age of 56, in a wartime match at Lord's, he collapsed and died while batting.

The championship in the 1910s

The 1910s proved a difficult decade for county cricket. There was a widespread feeling that the championship was an unsatisfactory competition, several county clubs fell into serious financial difficulty, then came four years of war in which many cricketers lost their lives.

Kent were the county with fewest worries at the start of the decade. Not only were they champions in 1909 and 1910, but they played around the county on attractive grounds, staging Cricket Weeks which were vibrant social occasions. Men watched in comfort from the seats of their brand new motor cars, women paraded the latest fashion, and in the evenings there were dinners, theatre performances and even film shows to attend. Consequently Kent were prosperous, unlike many of the county clubs. But, as *The Times* observed, 'such Weeks are possible only in certain counties.'

There was concern that too many county matches were being drawn, with the 'minus one for a defeat' leading to over-cautious play, so in 1910 a simpler system was adopted. The champion county would be the one with the highest proportion of victories. Kent, with 19 victories out of 25, were clearly the team of the year.

A more complicated system operated in 1911, with first-innings points awarded in drawn matches. Unfortunately the two counties in contention, Kent and Warwickshire, were playing different numbers of matches, 26 against 20, so the arithmetic became highly convoluted, bewildering even.

It was a glorious summer, hot and sunny for weeks on end. In July and early August Warwickshire, playing dynamic cricket under their new captain Frank Foster, won a string of matches that took them to second place in the table. Yet Kent, going for a hat-trick of championships, were not faltering – not, that is, till the rain came and they found themselves at the Oval, battling with Surrey on the stickiest of wickets. Frank Woolley, bowling slow-left-arm with unnerving accuracy, took seven wickets for nine runs, and the Kent keeper Fred Huish set a world record with nine stumpings in the match – but Kent were left to make 102 for victory and they did not make them. With ten runs wanted, their last man was caught in the slips, a diving, rolling catch that it took a while for the two umpires to adjudicate. When the finger went up, the arithmetic of the championship grew even more fiendish.

With one set of matches remaining, Kent were still in first place with a percentage of 72.8, Warwickshire on 69.0. But if they both won, Warwickshire, because they had played fewer

matches, would rise to 74.0 and Kent only to 73.84. And if they lost, depending on first-innings points, they could both finish below the 71.81 that Middlesex, if they won, could reach.

In the event all three counties won their last matches, and Warwickshire were crowned champions. Popular champions, too. They had played positive cricket all summer, and they had struck a blow for the newer counties. The only problem was that they had not played Kent or Middlesex.

It was not their fault. Prior to that summer they had been a moderate side, not known for attracting spectators home or away. Counties were free to arrange their own fixtures, and several chose not to invite Warwickshire.

Such anomalies were part of the on-going difficulty of the county championship. There were too many teams, many of them were not able to play a full set of matches, and every system of point-scoring seemed to generate problems. At least, the weather in 1911 had been magnificent. That was more than could be said for the wretched 1912. No summer in the whole 20th century had fewer dry days.

This time it was Northamptonshire's turn to catch the cricket world by surprise, winning ten of their 18 matches and coming within a whisker of the championship. In a summer

**Fred Huish
of Kent**

*Nine stumpings
in one match,
1,310 victims
in his career –
and they say that
in later life he
could remember
every one of them.*

in which England played six Tests in an experimental Triangular Tournament with Australia and South Africa, the East Midlanders escaped any call-ups, using only 12 men in their whole campaign. Their batting was unexceptional, not one man averaging 30, but they had a bowling attack, led as ever by George Thompson, that could make the most of the succession of damp pitches on which they played.

The discrepancy in matches played by the two main title contenders was even greater than in 1911: Northamptonshire playing 18 to Yorkshire's 28. The two games between the counties were both rain-affected draws, but in each case it was clear that Yorkshire were much the stronger side. At Bradford, on a truncated final day, Northants were bowled out for 74 and had to follow on. Then, with one batsman retiring ill, "too seedy to carry on", they hung on for the draw, battling through 39 overs to finish on 24 for seven.

Yet, despite all that, Northamptonshire would have been crowned champions if they had secured two more points: another ten runs for first-innings lead at Chesterfield, for instance, or one more rain-free hour at Leicester.

County cricket, so confident ten years earlier, was deep in the doldrums. The word was that several shire counties were on the verge of disappearing: Gloucester, Derby, Leicester, Worcester. Lancashire were having to make economies; even the champions Yorkshire were losing money. "Something has to be done," everybody agreed, and soon enough the reformers were offering solutions: two-day games, covered pitches, Saturday starts, two divisions.

The championship remained unchanged in 1913, when Kent won their fourth title in eight years, and again in 1914 when hope was running out for some counties. In August both Gloucestershire and Worcestershire called crisis meetings, tabling motions that would put their clubs into abeyance.

The declaration of war, on August 4, overtook such decisions. At first, with some uncertainty, the cricket carried on. Then, as the mood of the country changed, it was brought to a halt. Surrey led the table but, with their final two matches cancelled, there were some who thought it wrong in the circumstances to award the title. Middlesex, their only rivals, did not agree, conceding to Surrey.

For four years there was little cricket played, though many county members continued loyally to pay their subscriptions. In some cases the county clubs, with a much reduced expenditure, were better off. The Oval was requisitioned by the War Ministry while the pavilions at Trent Bridge and Old Trafford were turned into military hospitals.

Every county lost cricketers, Gloucestershire most of all with eight of their 1914 players killed. Many others were wounded or grew too old to return.

When the counties met in February 1919, they were unsure how to proceed. What public interest could they expect so soon after the war? How many of their players would be demobilised and available in May? They decided to play a reduced programme – 124 games only, where there had been 192 in 1914 – and to limit the games to two longer days. Worcestershire did not enter a team.

The two-day matches were not a success. Even with the extended playing hours too many of them were drawn, and the players all complained of the travel difficulties generated by the late finishes. With so little cricket played during the war, the standard had fallen significantly; especially there was a dearth of young fast bowlers. Yet the public did turn up to the games, in great numbers, and most counties came to regret not arranging more fixtures.

The championship was back to the simple proportion-of-wins system of 1910, and it turned into a thrilling contest between Yorkshire and Kent. Yorkshire's last game at Hove was a rain-ruined draw while Kent, needing to win at Lord's to overtake them, could not take the last two Middlesex wickets. Two crucial catches were dropped, and for almost an hour the amateur Frank Mann blocked resolutely, forsaking his normal aggression to deny the Kent bowlers. It was a performance that brought him considerable abuse from a section of the crowd, abuse that did not impress the *Times* correspondent: 'Mr Mann was playing a splendid game for his side and deserved all encouragement and applause for his fight. A better example of bad manners allied to appalling ignorance has seldom been seen anywhere at any time.'

The crowd was back, though, as it had been at the Oval in mid-August when the long-deferred benefit match of the immensely popular Jack Hobbs took place. On the second evening, with the light fading and drizzle in the air, Hobbs and Jack Crawford brought Surrey to a famous victory over Kent, hitting a stunning 95 runs in 32 minutes. Many of the 12,000-strong crowd raced onto the field, and they carried Hobbs aloft to the pavilion, depositing him with wild enthusiasm over the rails. His damp flannels were black from their constant thumps of praise, and the thumb was all that remained of one of his batting gloves. When he finally gathered himself up, he discovered a pound note in his hand.

The war was over. Cricket was back. County cricket at its best.

Some players of the 1910s

Jack Hobbs of Surrey

> Everything that Hobbs does as a batsman or fielder is without fuss and graceful. He has never departed from sound methods, but has kept his natural free game pure throughout his career.
> *Archie MacLaren*

> No sportsman ever more thoroughly deserved hero-worship and nobody ever bore unbounded popularity more modestly. You could never imagine him suffering from conceit.
> *HDG Leveson Gower*

Jack Hobbs was the complete batsman. There was no one special stroke; he played them all with a serenity and a dependability that made him not only the best batsman but the most popular cricketer in England. From humble origins, the son of a Cambridge college servant, he handled his fame with a humility that did much to raise respect for the professional cricketer.

In 1905 at his beloved Oval, in his first championship match, he went out with a borrowed bat and hit a sparkling 155 – against Essex, the county which had rejected him. In 1934 he travelled to Old Trafford for his friend George Duckworth's benefit match and, feeling his 51 years of age, hit a steady, classical 116, the last of his 197 centuries. As he approached the pavilion, the Lancashire members to a man stood up and sang a hearty 'Auld Lang Syne'.

He was 36 when play resumed after the First World War, and for each of the next 15 summers he averaged over 50 runs an innings, with 132 centuries. Yet he always said he was at his best in the last years before the war; like Woolley, he thought the standard of the game higher then. In 1914 his runs did much to bring the championship title back to the Oval.

The Master in his youth
*Leading run-scorer
in 1913 and 1914*

Pride of Kent
*Only Mead has scored
more championship runs*

Frank Woolley of Kent

> There was all summer in a stroke by Woolley, and he batted as it is sometimes shown in dreams.
> *RC Robertson-Glasgow*

> The best batsman there has ever been from the spectator's point of view.
> *Fred Root*

With his great height, perfect balance, exceptional eye and easy swing of the arms, the left-handed Frank Woolley scored runs by the hundred with a seemingly effortless grace. He was a professional, money-conscious and famously reluctant to pay for a drink, but, with a bat in his hand, there was never a streak of calculation or meanness. He batted for the team, and he batted for the joy, not for the average or the century. Thirty-two times he was out in the 90s, an all-time record, but it did not bother him. That was the way Kent taught him to play.

His gentle, almost lazy elegance found a perfect backdrop at the county's festival grounds. The amateurs would play to the crowd by giving the ball a big bang, yet none of them out-paced the languid, undemonstrative Woolley with his perfectly timed drives, cuts and pulls. Even in his last summer, when at the age of 51 he was asked to open the Kent innings, he could hit a hundred at faster than a run a minute, without ever resorting to brute force.

Long, long after he had gone, the people of Kent glowed with their memories of his stroke-play. And not just the people of Kent. "To see a hundred by Woolley," the Yorkshire bowler Bill Bowes said, "would keep you going for years."

He was also a fine slow-left-arm bowler, taking more than 500 wickets in the first three summers of the 1920s, and a brilliant slip fielder, with a record 1,018 first-class catches.

George Thompson of Northamptonshire

> But for his bowling it is quite safe to say that Northamptonshire would not in 1905 have been given a place among the first-class teams.
> *Wisden Cricketers' Almanack*

What was it that kept George Thompson at Northampton in the long years before they became first-class? No one took wickets like he did in minor counties cricket – nearly nine a game some years – and he was successful, too, when he played for MCC and festival sides. In June 1902 at Eastbourne he took eight for 88 against the Australians. Then that winter, hired by Pelham Warner for a tour of New Zealand, he played in 22 games against teams of various size and took 200 wickets.

He stayed proudly with his own home county, worked as Assistant Secretary and gave his all when in 1905 Northamptonshire became first-class. Day after day he bowled long, demanding spells of accurate, probing medium-pace – though not always uncomplainingly. "George bowled till he got tired," one team-mate said of him, "and when he got tired, he got bloody awkward."

Without doubt his bowling was the county's principal strength in its testing first years in the championship. He was a useful batsman, too, good enough to hit nine first-class centuries.

Northants legend
Their first England cricketer

Willie Quaife of Warwickshire

WG Quaife
Oldest man, at 56, to hit a first-class century

> Billy was at his best when the score was 13 for two and he had to pull the side round. He was the best defensive player I've seen. I used to love batting with him to watch his footwork.
> *'Tiger' Smith*

Willie Quaife may have been the shortest of men but, as he liked to say, "Good things are often found in small parcels." Playing straight, steady cricket and punishing the bad ball, he scored 1,000 runs in a season 24 times. He was also an effective slow bowler and an outstanding cover fielder. A teetotaller who kept himself supremely fit, he played county hockey into his 50s and thought nothing of a game of tennis after a long day's cricket.

A man of principle, he had several disputes with Warwickshire, becoming the first professional there to win a contract longer than one year. They finally retired him after the 1927 season, when at the age of 55 he had scored 835 runs and taken 50 wickets, but even then he forced them to allow him back for a farewell match. The next August he arrived with an injured foot, got out his bat once more and scored a patient, faultless 115.

Jack Hearne of Middlesex

> His batting, like his appearance, was trim and cool. So smooth and contained was his method that few spectators, with all respect to them and their shillings, could know how wonderful was the art presented to them.
> *RC Robertson-Glasgow*

As a young man Jack Hearne was the great hope of English cricket, a better prospect than his Middlesex contemporary Patsy Hendren. But where Hendren was a robust character, full of cheeky humour, Hearne was a shy, thoughtful man, immaculate in appearance but never with a trace of showiness. He scored a Test century in Melbourne when only 20, but after that his best days were with Middlesex.

He was a gifted, artistic batsman, wristy and with great powers of concentration, and his bowling took more than 1,800 wickets: leg-breaks before the war, off-breaks after. Three times he completed the rare season's 'double' of 2,000 runs and 100 wickets, a heavy workload for a slightly built man with a weak chest. 'Had he been stronger,' Pelham Warner said, 'he might well have been as great an all-rounder as anyone.' Nevertheless, with both bat and ball, he was at the heart of the Middlesex team well into the 1930s. For team-mate Harry Lee, 'Jack was my ideal of the complete cricketer.'

'Complete cricketer'
Only Woolley did the double of 2,000 runs and 100 wickets more times

Stories of the 1910s

The innings of a lifetime

Sussex v Nottinghamshire, Hove, Saturday 20 May 1911

It was a cold Saturday in May. The first game of Sussex's season. As lunch approached on that final day at Hove, the sparse, well-wrapped crowd would have expected to be packing up soon. Nottinghamshire had lost seven second innings wickets, and they were only nine runs to the good.

Out to the middle walked a tall, muscular, dark-haired man with unusually long arms. He was carrying a two-pound-three-ounce bat with an extra rubber grip on the handle, and he was flexing a right wrist that had been troubling him. Alletson was his name. Edwin Alletson. 'Ted'. A county cricketer of no great distinction. He had bowled just one of the 130 overs in the Sussex innings and was down to bat at number nine.

'The morning of the match,' he wrote 45 years later, 'I rose early and went and had a swim in the sea before breakfast. I had a sprained wrist. It did it a lot of good.'

The son of a wheelwright on the Duke of Portland's estate at Welbeck, he had joined the Notts staff as a promising bowler who could bat a bit. But his bowling had come to nothing much, and he was holding onto a place in the team on account of his reliable fielding and some occasional hard-hitting runs down the order. Indeed, here at Hove he might not have been playing if the fast bowler Tommy Wass had been fit.

In the 50 minutes before lunch he looked to play his shots, though no more so than he always did. On 25 he skied a ball into the covers that fell just short of a fielder, then on 42 he was dropped at slip. He came off with 47, but in the process he had lost two partners, the latter to the last ball of the morning. Nine wickets were down, and the lead was a mere 84 runs.

According to Alletson, before play resumed at 2.15 he spoke to his captain: "Mr Jones, does it matter what I do?" The answer was 'no' so he resolved to have some fun at the expense of Sussex's veteran slow-medium bowler Ernie Killick. "I'm not half going to give him some stick," he told his team-mates.

Alletson had little footwork, but he stood tall in the crease and, with his strong upper body and long arms, he could, as the *Manchester Guardian* put it, 'wield the bat with the swing of a windmill.' Mostly he hit the ball in the air, down the ground, though one of his sixes at Hove was a short-arm jab that went over point and smashed a window of the pavilion.

The Notts number eleven, Riley, was no batsman, but in the 40 minutes which the innings lasted after lunch he survived 19 balls, scoring 10 runs. At the other end, off 52 balls, Alletson took his score from 47 to 189. He hit Killick's second over for 22 (two 6s, two 4s and a 2), and he hit his fourth, which included two no-balls, for 34 (three

Ted Alletson
After lunch he faced 52 balls as follows:
.441242.16.42464.6344.2146.
43466.4446....4.4226144.W

106

6s and four 4s). It remained the world record till Garry Sobers, also batting for Notts, hit six 6s in 1968.

"I was out at long-off," Sussex's Bob Relf recalled, "and some of his drives were carrying as far as the hotel or over the stand to the skating rink. It was the sort of thing you sometimes see a tail-ender do for three or four balls, but this just went on, over after over."

After 90 minutes of batting – 50 before lunch, 40 after – he had reached a score of 189, just two big hits from what would still be, by more than 20 minutes, the fastest double-hundred in first-class cricket. He swung another ball down the ground, and on the boundary in front of the stand Charles Smith held the catch. In taking it, he had a foot behind the line and, as Alletson walked away, his team-mate George Gunn ran on to tell him he was not out. But Alletson was happy to leave. "It's all reet," he said. As Gunn later put it, 'He had had enough.'

Sussex, needing 237 to win, ended the day on 213 for eight.

Alletson's innings was the talk of the cricket world. 'A performance like this,' the *Manchester Guardian* declared, 'does more than all the deliberations of cricket councils to rehabilitate the national game in popular favour. Alletson henceforth will rank among the heroes of English cricket.'

His next innings came the following Thursday at Bristol. Promoted to number seven, he hit a whirlwind 60 in the last half hour of the day. At the weekend, affected by the euphoria, the selectors invited him to take part in their Test Trial.

His career did not progress, though his lusty hitting continued to enjoy its moments of triumph. At Dewsbury he struck the parsimonious Wilfred Rhodes for three successive sixes, and at Trent Bridge, when he overheard Derbyshire's slow-left-armer Fred Bracey telling his captain "I can get rid of this chap", he hit him for four sixes in two overs. One of the sixes is said to have landed on a house in Radcliffe Road, a carry of 160 yards.

As a bowler he developed through long practice a fast and highly effective leg-break, but there were doubts about his jerky action and he had to give it up. In 119 first-class matches he took just 33 wickets and had a batting average of 18. In the Great War he served in an artillery regiment, then spent 30 years at Manton Colliery near Worksop.

He was not in the first rank of county cricketers, barely in the second rank, but that only adds to the fairy-tale feel of his forty minutes of carefree glory at Hove. "It was the best innings I ever saw," wrote Sussex's captain Bertie Chaplin, "bar none. It was simply wonderful. And the man had an injured wrist too."

A wounded soldier goes out to bat

Somerset v Sussex, Thursday 22 May 1919

It was hard getting up teams at the start of 1919. So many men had not been demobilised. Somerset struggled for a captain. At one stage they even accepted an offer from the 52-year-old Sammy Woods to come back, though in the event he did not.

The first team to visit Taunton were Sussex, and they were in a worse state. Indeed, so short were they that they turned up with an opening batsman, Harold Heygate, who had last played for them as a fresh-faced lad, not long out of public school, in 1905. Scorecards exist of games he played in Canada in 1908 and 1909, but whether he had played since then is not clear. There had been so little cricket.

What is clear from reports of the Taunton game is that Heygate was not fit. Some described him as 'crippled by rheumatism', others 'suffering severely from a wound in the leg, received during the war', a wound that had him 'limping about' in the field in Somerset's first innings. Back in 1905 in his last championship match he had made 80 and 68 not out against a strong Kent side. But now, when it was the turn of Sussex to bat, he was not fit to open the innings. At the end of the day he went in at number eleven and was bowled for nought. The next day his place in the field was taken by a Taunton club cricketer. In his serge suit he watched from the pavilion as Somerset, batting badly, were all out for 103.

Sussex, needing 105 to win, were soon 48 for six, but they recovered to 103 for six, to the brink of victory. Then two wickets fell, a single was scored, and a third wicket fell. The scores were level, and Heygate was in no state to bat. The umpire, the old Surrey pro Bert Street, removed the bails.

In the pavilion somebody, probably the ever-sporting Sammy Woods, persuaded Heygate to go out, which after some delay he did. 'Adjusting his pads, he stepped limping onto the field in civilian dress.' Both captains wanted to play on but, as Heygate hobbled painfully towards the middle, Len Braund, the veteran Somerset all-rounder, turned to Bert Street: "He's taking an awfully long time, isn't he?" At that, 'Street, with the rules of cricket engraved on his mind, upset all calculations by pulling up the stumps.' The match was over. It was a tie.

It all caused quite a stir. It was Sussex's first match of peacetime, and a wounded soldier, a war veteran, had been prevented from batting by an over-officious umpire.

Anyway, what were they to put on the scorecard? He was not 'absent', and 'timed out' was not in the laws, not then. *The Times*, in disgust, opted for 'not allowed to bat'.

Images of the 1910s

 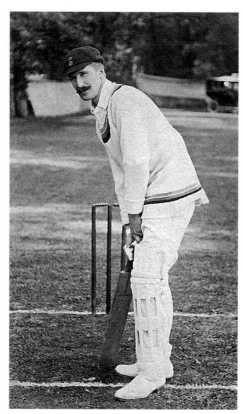

Arnold Warren (left), from the mining village of Codnor,
and his captain Jack Chapman, an Old Uppinghamian

Cricket's oldest batting record

When the Derbyshire captain Jack Chapman joined fast bowler Arnold Warren at the wicket on the morning of Tuesday 21 June 1910, the two of them cannot possibly have imagined that they were about to set a world record for a ninth-wicket partnership, still less that the record would be standing 104 years on, the oldest batting record in *Wisden*.

There was a good crowd at the Miners' Welfare Ground in Blackwell. The colliery owner, a Derbyshire committeeman, had been selling tickets at the pit, a shilling for the three days, and he had made it clear to off-duty miners that he expected them to support the coming of county cricket to their village.

Derbyshire were a poor side, without a win in eight games that summer. Following on 244 runs behind, they were 131 for eight when Chapman came out. Their Warwickshire opponents, not confident of the train service from this obscure outpost, were keen to wrap up the game and get back to Birmingham.

Warren and Chapman swung their bats, and in 40 minutes to lunch they scored 73 carefree runs. One Warwickshire player later suggested that his team, assuming an easy victory, had drunk too much the previous night: "If we had gone to bed early, the game would have been won."

In the afternoon their fielding grew ragged and they became frustrated. Frank Foster, a fast left-armer, resorted to bowling leg-theory, hitting Warren on the back of his knee. "If you don't stop that," the fiery Warren said, with his bat raised, "I'll knock your bloody head off." The calmer Chapman, meanwhile, was having the time of his life, one of his sixes landing in nearby allotments.

The follow-on was saved; records tumbled, and the miners of Blackwell cheered. By the time Warren was caught at slip for 123, his only century, the partnership had yielded 283 runs.

Warren wanted to bowl leg-theory back at them, but he was still hobbling and the game petered out uneventfully.

Recruiting for war

In 1915 the Gloucestershire and England cricketer Gilbert Jessop, now a captain in the Manchester Regiment, used his popularity to speak at a series of recruitment meetings. At the end of the rallies men would fall in behind a drum-and-bugle band and march away. A typical rally might enlist 150 men.

The following year Jessop, suffering from severe lumbago, was sent to a clinic in Bath. There he was placed inside a coffin-like box and subjected to extreme heat, being told that, if it became too uncomfortable, he should raise the lid. The attendant left the room, the catch fell and, when he was finally released, his heart had been badly damaged.

He lived till 1955, but he could never play cricket again.

Pavilion Hospital

In October 1914 the Old Trafford pavilion was converted into a military hospital run by the Red Cross. Wards were created throughout the building, with further beds in a large marquee on the green at the rear. Sheep grazed on the cricket field.

When the hospital closed in February 1919, it had provided care for more than 1,500 patients. Most of them were convalescing, and the atmosphere was generally cheerful, with many entertainments laid on.

Towards the end of the war, however, a boat from America arrived in Manchester docks, full of men from the southern states who had fallen victim to a flu epidemic on the voyage and were dying. Matron took in as many as she possibly could and, for two or three months, in the words of one worker there, 'the home of cricket was more like the home of death.'

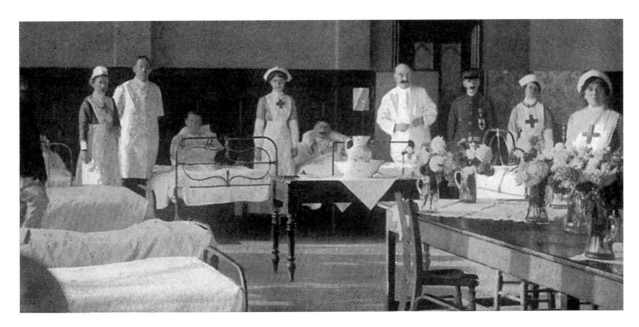

1911: Warwickshire transformed

Warwickshire has become a rollocking side of real cricketers; it has rid itself of its old humdrum ways as one shakes off a nightmare by the glories of daylight.

So wrote the *Observer* newspaper as the county season of 1911 reached its climax. It had been a magnificently hot summer – in the whole century only 1976 would rival it – and the championship was building to a breathtaking climax.

The general expectation was that Kent would win the title, as they had done in the previous two years. For most of that baking-hot summer they held first place in the table, but rain arrived in late August and with it came defeat by nine runs on a treacherously sticky Oval pitch. Suddenly the arithmetic had changed. Warwickshire only had to win at Northampton, and they would take the championship, the first of the counties promoted in the 1890s to do so.

Twelve months earlier the Midlanders had finished in 14th place after stumbling through their 20 fixtures with five different captains. The county side had developed a reputation for playing dull cricket; attendances were poor and the finances parlous. With a touch of desperation the committee turned to the 22-year-old Frank Rowbotham Foster to lead the side in 1911. From the family that owned the gents outfitters Foster Brothers, he was a high-spirited young man who lived life with a dash, a risk-taker who believed in positive cricket, though he was still a relative newcomer to the first-class game.

It was a gamble, and it looked a disastrous one when, as the first fixture of the summer approached, the club received a letter from him, saying that he had changed his mind. He had fallen in love and did not think he would bother with cricket during the summer. Without him Warwickshire lost by an innings at the Oval, a game which led one writer to wonder whether they justified any longer their first-class status.

Foster's father persuaded him to change his mind, and the following week, at the age of 22 years and three months, young Frank was in charge at Old Trafford for the second match. Most of his team were seasoned professionals – one of them, Dick Lilley, had played for Warwickshire before he was born – yet with the naïve optimism of his privileged youth Foster exhorted them to play positive cricket. Then, when it was his turn to bat, he was bowled for nought.

It could so easily have gone badly wrong. "All for one, and one for all," he told them. Yet when it came to travelling by train between matches he was relaxing in the first-class compartment while they were back in the third.

The professionals took to him, though. The team won at Old Trafford, their first victory over Lancashire for nine years, and they followed that with enterprising defeats of Leicestershire and Sussex. Foster was playing his part, too, unlike some of his predecessors as captain. He hit crucial, nerveless runs in the two-wicket victory over Sussex. Then against Yorkshire at Edgbaston he completed an extraordinary first-innings double: 105 runs and nine wickets. He also had a happy knack of winning the toss when it mattered.

He was a right-handed batsman, who always looked to score his runs quickly, and a left-arm bowler who loped in off a six-yard run, then with a high arm got surprising pace off the pitch. "He was a natural, uncomplicated cricketer," the team's young keeper 'Tiger' Smith remembered many years later. "I never saw him in the nets at Edgbaston. He'd just stroll onto the pitch and look a fine all-rounder and a good slip. His confidence was amazing."

He was a breath of fresh air, and the professionals accepted him – all, that is, except Dick Lilley, the veteran England keeper who, with the emergence of 'Tiger' Smith, was playing as a specialist batsman. He was 44 years old, he knew the county circuit as well as anybody, and he was not averse to adjusting the field if he felt Foster was missing a trick. At Harrogate, fielding at short leg, he did it once too often and rather too loudly. "I'll take your advice if you come to me," Foster rebuked him, "but don't make me look a fool," at which Lilley departed in high dudgeon to the outfield. In the professionals' room during lunch Lilley fumed about "the young kid" telling him off, suggesting that they should refuse to go back out under his captaincy. Foster's response was to hit a brilliant century and to tell the committee that he no longer wanted Lilley in the eleven. By that stage Foster was walking on water and, great servant though Lilley had been to the county, they agreed to the request.

In that golden summer three of the older professionals had the seasons of their lives. Runs flowed from strong, big-hitting Lancastrian Crowther Charlesworth, a rough diamond who could be 'a real handful' after a couple of pints, and from the gentler Sep Kinneir, who in the dressing room smoked his pipe and argued about current affairs with Syd Santall, a staunch Tory. "In those days," 'Tiger' Smith said, "pros weren't expected to talk about politics, least of all own up to being a socialist." Most crucial, though, was the success of their 36-year-old fast bowler Frank Field, a one-time farm labourer who, with Foster

(left) Frank Foster and (above) the team versus Lancashire at Edgbaston in August
back: Richards (trainer), Tiger Smith, Jack Parsons, Crowther Charlesworth, Sep Kinneir
middle: Syd Santall, Frank Stephens, Frank Foster, George Stephens, Frank Field
front: Willie Quaife, Charlie Baker

at the other end, took wickets as he had never done before. He was fast, he could get a ball to lift off a length, and, above all, he was a great-hearted trier. In the words of one opponent, 'He was one who, with a WG set at both ends, and Ranji, Fry, Hayward and Johnny Tyldesley to come, would still have bowled his ribs out on the "let 'em all come" principle.'

With Foster doing the double (1,383 runs and 116 wickets in 18 matches) and the 39-year-old Willie Quaife as fit and dedicated as ever, they won match after match through July and August till, to widespread amazement, the championship was theirs to lose. The unfashionable men from Birmingham, whom Middlesex, Kent and Nottinghamshire did not even condescend to play, were striking a blow for all the lesser counties. They only needed to win at Northampton.

On Saturday morning Foster went out to toss. The pitch was true, the sun was shining, but there was rain coming and Northants had in their Trinidadian slow-left-armer Syd Smith a fine wet-wicket bowler. Of all the tosses that summer this was the one he had to win. And he lost it.

"Lost it?" Field said. "What good are you!" Then he added, "Leave it to me. I'll bowl them out." And he and his captain did – for just 73. By close Warwickshire were 226 for six.

On Sunday, the rest day, rain fell incessantly. "We played poker, bridge, any old game," Foster said. "We laughed, talked, told every tale which came out of the ark. We enjoyed simply being alive, laughing in the face of fate."

Fate at the last was kind to them. They resumed play at three o'clock on Monday, completed the victory on Tuesday morning and caught the train back to Birmingham where they were greeted by streets lined with cheering supporters.

Foster, along with 'Tiger' Smith and the 40-year-old Sep Kinneir, spent the winter in Australia, winning back the Ashes by four Tests to one. Foster, bowling in tandem with Sydney Barnes, took 32 wickets in the series and scored 226 runs.

It is hard to think of another English cricketer who has achieved so much so young. Yet the glory faded fast.

The summer of 1912 was wet. Foster's adventurous batting was not suited to the damp pitches, Field struggled with a bad elbow, and Warwickshire returned to mid-table. Foster had a motorbike accident in 1915, and his life spiralled downwards, ending in an asylum. His was the saddest of stories.

Yet, for that one glorious summer of 1911, Frank Foster was the golden boy of English cricket – and Warwickshire, 'humdrum Warwickshire', were the toast of the land.

August 1914

Monday 3 August. A bank holiday. Large crowds gather at eight county matches around England while the newspapers talk of war. At the Oval Jack Hobbs, in the form of his life, scores 226 against Notts. At Edgbaston Percy Jeeves, the young Warwickshire fast bowler, takes seven wickets. At Old Trafford the Lancashire captain Albert Hornby is called away to advise the War Office. Amid great uncertainty the cricket carries on.

Tuesday 4 August. The army begins to mobilise its reservists. At the Oval Arthur Carr, the Notts captain, receives a telegram ordering him to report to the 5th Lancers in Dublin. "Well, I'll have my innings first," he says, and he makes a steady 30 before leaving. The Leicestershire amateur Aubrey Sharp departs from Northampton before his side's second innings; in his absence they lose by four runs. Pelham Warner, captain of Middlesex, and Sir Archibald White, captain of Yorkshire, also leave their teams. The situation is growing graver by the hour. At 11pm war is declared.

Wednesday 5 August. More reservists are called up. At Exeter Dorset arrive for their Minor Counties match against Devon with eight men. The game is abandoned, along with all Dorset's remaining fixtures. The Canterbury Week balls on Wednesday and Friday are cancelled, also the performance of the Old Stagers theatre group. The exuberant enthusiasm of the festival has drained away, but the cricket goes on. Colin Blythe, Kent's slow-left-armer, takes ten wickets in the match against Sussex.

Thursday 6 August. The Oval is requisitioned by the War Office, and Surrey's next match, against Kent on Monday, is rescheduled to Lord's. At Worcester Jack Hobbs hits a third successive century. MCC issues a statement: 'No good purpose can be served at the present moment by cancelling matches.'

Friday 7 August. The pavilion at Trent Bridge is to be a military hospital. The forthcoming cricket weeks at the ports of Dover and Portsmouth are cancelled, the matches moved to other grounds. Somerset cancel their game on Monday against Northamptonshire. Lord Kitchener, Secretary of State for War, calls for 100,000 men to volunteer for a Second Army to support the 165,000 regulars.

In the first week 40,000 men volunteer for service and begin training, but none are yet crossing the Channel. County cricket, with the exception of Somerset's cancelled fixture, carries on as best it can. The Surrey-Kent match at Lord's is for Jack Hobbs' benefit, and the takings are poor – so he accepts Surrey's offer to defer it to the next season. Will that be 1915? The talk is of the war being over by Christmas.

At Lord's Hobbs is lbw to Colin Blythe for 6, one of nine first-innings wickets for the slow-left-armer, but Surrey win the game. They stay at Lord's to beat Yorkshire by an innings, with Hobbs scoring 202. He has now hit 10 centuries during the summer, and the newspapers are asking, 'Can he equal the record of 13 by Fry and Hayward?' Surrey, with 13 wins and one defeat, are well clear at the head of the championship table.

But should they still be playing? On the whole, with no troops yet in action, the answer seems to be yes. The *Observer* expresses this view:

> It seems as well that the tension which naturally is affecting the public at the present time should be relieved as much as possible, and any sport or pastime which will enable them to temporarily relieve the mind will do more good than harm.

Monday 17 August. A British Expeditionary Force of 70,000 regular soldiers lands in Belgium, determined to reverse the advance of the German army. The week's county cricket matches do not attract large crowds. At Canterbury Colin Blythe, the country's leading wicker-taker, takes seven wickets for 20 runs against Worcestershire. At Leyton a young Cambridge undergraduate Geoffrey Davies hits an 81-minute maiden century for Essex. But the newspapers give these achievements little space.

The Second Army has its 100,000 recruits, but on Tuesday 25 August Lord Kitchener tells the House of Lords he may need an army of 600,000. He launches an appeal for a further 100,000 men to come forward. Meanwhile, county cricket stumbles on.

In Eastbourne the young Sussex all-rounder Maurice Tate umpires a match between his club side and a naval team whose fleet is stationed close by. Every few minutes a telegram arrives, calling one player after another away to army or navy service, till there are only three or four left on each side.

Thursday 28 August. Somerset play for the first time in Weston-super-Mare. The plan was to end their season with a festival week, and after much soul-searching they decide to go ahead with the matches 'to take the public mind off the war'. However, 'the festival character of the function will be reduced to a minimum.'

By now the Somerset team is severely depleted. Many cricketers have signed up for service, while war has 'so depleted JC White's farm of men and horses that he is unable to leave Stogumber'. Yorkshire are their first opponents, and heavy overnight rain leaves the Somerset batsmen on 'the most difficult wicket they have batted on for many a long day'. Alonzo Drake and Major Booth bowl unchanged through the innings, taking five wickets each, as Somerset are all out for 44. 'They are likely to bowl a good many years and not find another such wicket,' writes the *Western Daily Press*.

Drake and Booth. They are Yorkshire's future. They bowled unchanged at Bristol in the first half of the week, and they bowl unchanged again when Somerset are all out for 90 in the second innings. This time Drake takes all ten, the first Yorkshire bowler ever to do so.

Saturday 29 August. In Temple Gardens in London, Field Marshal Lord Roberts inspects a newly trained battalion of Royal Fusiliers, formed out of the first volunteers from the City of London. "You are the pick of the nation," he tells them. "I respect and honour you more than I can say. My feeling towards you is one of intense admiration. How different is your action to that of the men who can still go on with their cricket and football, as if the very existence of the country was not at stake! This is not the time to play games, wholesome as they are in days of piping peace!"

'NO TIME FOR GAMES' becomes the headline. The *Daily Mail* publishes a shaming photograph of a group of young men at a cricket match, and letters are widely printed, attacking those who are 'skulking at home, watching football or cricket'. Meanwhile printed handbills are distributed: 'To golfers, cricketers, footballers under 50, BE MEN. Drop your playthings; drill with rifles.' WG Grace, reflecting the changed mood, calls for an end to county cricket.

MCC, still in two minds, decides not to send teams to the Scarborough Festival, which is then cancelled. Its statement says that it is 'evident that the continuance of first-class cricket is hurtful to the feelings of a section of the public.'

Monday 31 August. The news from Belgium is alarming, with many casualties reported. County cricket decides to play one last round of matches, then close down.

Michael Green gets special dispensation from the Gloucestershire Regiment to play at the Oval but, even with him there, Gloucestershire can only muster ten men. Surrey beat them by an innings, with Jack Hobbs hitting his eleventh and last hundred of the summer, while at Weston-super-Mare Essex win by ten wickets, their victory owing much to another dashing hundred from the young Geoffrey Davies.

Surrey's victory leaves them top of the table with their last two games cancelled. Despite a call from WG Grace to annul the competition, MCC declare Surrey champions.

And that is it for county cricket – till May 1919.

By then Geoffrey Davies will have been killed in the Battle of Loos in 1915, Major Booth on the first day of the Somme Offensive in 1916, Percy Jeeves three weeks later, and Colin Blythe near Passchendaele in 1917. Alonzo Drake will have gone, too, dying of a heart attack in February 1919.

Second Lieutenant Major Booth
West Yorkshire Regiment

Private Percy Jeeves
Royal Warwickshire Regiment

Sergeant Colin Blythe
Kent Fortress Royal Engineers

Captain Geoffrey Davies
Essex Regiment

1920 – 1929

A post-war boom in popularity

Glamorgan the 17th county

Domination by the northern counties

There can be no question but that the county championship has grown too big, and that it would be a good thing for first-class cricket generally if the number of counties were reduced to twelve, each playing the other. There are many who think the time has arrived when it would be kind to be cruel, and to eliminate at least four counties.

Pelham Warner, September 1921

The championship ought to be cut down severely, and the sides banished that are obviously too weak. It is impossible for the strongest cricketer to get through the programme with his form at all keen. He gets stale before August is in, for there is not only the day-by-day labours in the field; there is an enormous amount of travelling, often by night.

Cec Parkin, 1923

The county cricket championship rather resembles the British Constitution in one way, for it has grown up more or less by haphazard, it contains some things hardly to be defended by exact laws or logic, and its origins cannot be easily traced.

There seems little prospect of a coherent championship such as obtains in league football and each system of 'marking' provides new ground for complaint. But the championship must be a pretty sound thing after all since it has survived its own deficiencies and has provided, as this year, some healthy excitement in its closing stages.

The Manchester Guardian, September 1927

1920 Worcestershire re-enter the championship. The points system is now 5 for a win, 2 for first-innings lead in a draw. After the unsuccessful experiment with two-day cricket in 1919, matches revert to three days. Unlike the pre-war Monday and Thursday starts, most matches are now scheduled to begin on Saturdays and Wednesdays. At Northampton Percy Fender of Surrey hits the fastest hundred of all time, in 35 minutes.

At the Olympic Games in Antwerp Great Britain's hockey team wins the gold medal. Only four countries enter. Denmark are beaten 6-1, Belgium 12-1 and the French so over-indulge themselves at a sumptuous dinner that they are unable to put their side into the field.

1921 Glamorgan become the 17th county in the championship.

Marie Stopes sets up a Mothers' Clinic in London, offering advice on birth control.
For the first time women serve on a jury hearing a divorce case.

1922 The minimum requirement for participation in the county championship is increased from nine to eleven 'home and away' fixtures, i.e. from 18 to 22 matches.

The British Broadcasting Company is formed, transmitting programmes from Marconi House in London.

1923 Yorkshire win the championship with a record 25 victories, 13 of them by an innings.

The FA Cup Final is held for the first time at the new Wembley Stadium, with a capacity of 100,000. With 126,000 tickets sold, the crowd spills onto the field. A lone policeman on a white horse eventually allows the match to go ahead.

1924 The championship reverts to the 1914 points system: 5 for a win; 3 for a draw if ahead on first innings, 1 if behind.

The first Labour Government is formed under the premiership of Ramsay MacDonald.

1925 With no overseas team touring during the summer, the counties are required to play a minimum of 24 matches. Yorkshire become the first county since 1890 to win the championship four years in a row.

To improve road safety, white lines are painted on some roads. Traffic lights are planned for London's Piccadilly Circus.

1926 India, New Zealand and West Indies are admitted to the Imperial Cricket Conference. At the Oval England win back the Ashes for the first time since the war.

A General Strike, in support of coal miners, lasts for nine days in May.
The Scottish inventor John Logie Baird sends the first moving pictures by wireless.

1927 The championship points change again. It is now 8 for a win; 5 for a draw if ahead on first innings, 3 if behind. The New Zealanders tour but do not play any Tests: the last English summer, outside wartime, without Test cricket. The circumference of a cricket ball is reduced by a quarter of an inch.

With hickory in short supply, golf club manufacturers in America experiment with the use of steel.
American Charles Lindbergh completes a non-stop solo flight across the Atlantic. The 3,600 miles take 33 hours 39 minutes.

1928 Lancashire complete a hat-trick of championship victories. West Indies tour England, playing three Tests. They become the fourth Test-playing side.

Alexander Fleming discovers a mould that kills bacteria. He calls it Penicillium Notatum.

1929 For the first time since 1894 all counties play the same number of matches: 28. As a result the championship is no longer decided on percentages. Gloucestershire win most matches, 15, but finish fourth. Nottinghamshire, the champions, win 14; Yorkshire, in third place, only 10. At the counties' November meeting Gloucestershire argue for an increase in the number of points awarded for a win, but the status quo is preserved for 1930. Two experimental changes are made to the laws: (i) an increase in the size of the wicket and (ii) batsmen to be given lbw when the bat has made only a slight contact with the ball.

Share prices crash on the New York Stock Exchange, triggering a major depression.
Telephone boxes are introduced onto the streets of London.

Championship – top three

1920

	P	W	L	D	Pts	%
Middlesex	20	15	2	3	77	77.0
Lancashire	28	19	5	4	97	74.6
Surrey	24	15	6	3	79	68.7

Leading batsmen (Runs)
- P. Holmes (Yorks) 2,029
- J.B. Hobbs (Surrey) 1,935
- G. Brown (Hants) 1,863

Leading bowlers (Wickets)
- A.S. Kennedy (Hants) 164
- F.E. Woolley (Kent) 164
- L.W. Cook (Lancs) 150

Leading wkt-keeper / Leading fielder (Victims)
- J.C. Hubble (Kent) 68
- F.E. Woolley (Kent) 36

1921

	P	W	L	D	Pts	%
Middlesex	20	15	2	3	75	78.9
Surrey	24	15	2	7	81	70.4
Yorkshire	26	16	3	7	88	70.4

Leading batsmen
- C.P. Mead (Hants) 2,270
- V.W.C. Jupp (Sussex) 1,934
- C.A.G. Russell (Essex) 1,930

Leading bowlers
- J.A. Newman (Hants) 172
- A.S. Kennedy (Hants) 168
- A.P. Freeman (Kent) 156
- C.W.L. Parker (Glos) 156

Leading wkt-keeper / Leading fielder
- W.H. Livsey (Hants) 76
- P.G.H. Fender (Surrey) 48

1922

	P	W	L	D	Pts	%
Yorkshire	30	19	2	9	107	73.8
Notts	28	17	5	6	93	71.5
Surrey	24	13	1	10	77	67.0

Leading batsmen
- C.P. Mead (Hants) 2,438
- H.T.W. Hardinge (Kent) 2,068
- C.A.G. Russell (Essex) 2,042

Leading bowlers
- C.W.L. Parker (Glos) 195
- A.P. Freeman (Kent) 194
- A.S. Kennedy (Hants) 177

Leading wkt-keeper / Leading fielder
- G.B. Street (Sussex) 77
- A. Waddington (Yorks) 38

1923

	P	W	L	D	Pts	%
Yorkshire	32	25	1	6	133	85.8
Notts	26	15	3	8	85	68.0
Lancashire	30	15	2	13	87	60.0

Leading batsmen
- C.P. Mead (Hants) 2,265
- E.H. Hendren (Middx) 2,263
- J.W.H. Makepeace (Lancs) 1,976

Leading bowlers
- C.H. Parkin (Lancs) 176
- M.W. Tate (Sussex) 174
- C.W.L. Parker (Glos) 167

Leading wkt-keeper / Leading fielder
- G.B. Street (Sussex) 80
- C.P. Mead (Hants) 41

1924

	P	W	L	D	Pts	%
Yorkshire	30	16	3	11	88	76.5
Middlesex	22	11	3	8	69	69.0
Surrey	24	9	1	14	67	67.0

Leading batsmen
- W.W. Whysall (Notts) 1,786
- G.E. Tyldesley (Lancs) 1,607
- A.E. Dipper (Glos) 1,558

Leading bowlers
- C.W.L. Parker (Glos) 184
- C.H. Parkin (Lancs) 169
- G.G. Macaulay (Yorks) 159

Leading wkt-keeper / Leading fielder
- J.C. Hubble (Kent) 62
- P.G.H. Fender (Surrey) 30
- E. Robinson (Yorks) 30

1925

	P	W	L	D	Pts	%
Yorkshire	32	21	0	11	117	86.7
Surrey	26	14	2	10	84	76.4
Lancashire	32	19	4	9	117	75.5

Leading batsmen
- P. Holmes (Yorks) 2,123
- J.B. Hobbs (Surrey) 2,084
- A. Sandham (Surrey) 2,056

Leading bowlers
- C.W.L. Parker (Glos) 200
- C.F. Root (Worcs) 196
- M.W. Tate (Sussex) 194

Leading wkt-keeper / Leading fielder
- W.L. Cornford (Sussex) 65
- W.R. Hammond (Glos) 55

1926

	P	W	L	D	Pts	%
Lancashire	32	17	2	13	106	75.5
Yorkshire	32	14	0	18	104	74.3
Kent	28	15	2	11	92	65.7

Leading batsmen
- G.E. Tyldesley (Lancs) 2,365
- C.P. Mead (Hants) 2,274
- H.T.W. Hardinge (Kent) 2,174

Leading bowlers
- C.W.L. Parker (Glos) 198
- A.P. Freeman (Kent) 163
- E.A. McDonald (Lancs) 163

Leading wkt-keeper / Leading fielder
- B. Lilley (Notts) 80
- S.J. Staples (Notts) 37

1927

	P	W	L	D	Pts	%
Lancashire	28	10	1	17	154	68.8
Notts	28	12	3	13	152	67.9
Yorkshire	28	10	3	15	135	62.5

Leading batsmen
- W.R. Hammond (Glos) 2,522
- C.P. Mead (Hants) 2,331
- A.E. Dipper (Glos) 1,972

Leading bowlers
- C.W.L. Parker (Glos) 183
- A.P. Freeman (Kent) 158
- C.F. Root (Worcs) 145

Leading wkt-keeper / Leading fielder
- H. Smith (Glos) 59
- W.R. Hammond (Glos) 38

1928

	P	W	L	D	Pts	%
Lancashire	30	15	0	15	186	77.5
Kent	30	15	5	10	167	69.6
Notts	32	13	3	16	168	68.0

Leading batsmen
- C.P. Mead (Hants) 2,843
- F.E. Woolley (Kent) 2,582
- W.R. Hammond (Glos) 2,474

Leading bowlers
- A.P. Freeman (Kent) 216
- E.A. McDonald (Lancs) 178
- C.W.L. Parker (Glos) 143

Leading wkt-keeper / Leading fielder
- L.E.G. Ames (Kent) 100
- W.R. Hammond (Glos) 58

1929

	P	W	L	D	Pts
Notts	28	14	2	12	158
Lancashire	28	12	3	13	148
Yorkshire	28	10	2	16	148

Leading batsmen
- A.E. Dipper (Glos) 2,079
- W.W. Whysall (Notts) 2,079
- A. Sandham (Surrey) 2,038

Leading bowlers
- A.P. Freeman (Kent) 199
- T.W.J. Goddard (Glos) 154
- J.C. White (Som) 149

Leading wkt-keeper / Leading fielder
- L.E.G. Ames (Kent) 102
- B.H. Lyon (Glos) 45

1920-1929

Leading counties

	P	W	L	D	%W
Yorkshire	294	154	20	120	52.4
Kent	278	144	57	67	51.8
Lancashire	296	148	30	118	50.0
Nottinghamshire	270	128	43	99	47.4

Leading batsmen

C.P. Mead (Hants)	20,920
E.H. Hendren (Middx)	17,879
A.E. Dipper (Glos)	17,475
F.E. Woolley (Kent)	17,255

Leading bowlers

C.W.L. Parker (Glos)	1,681
A.P. Freeman (Kent)	1,628
J.C. White (Som)	1,316
A.S. Kennedy (Hants)	1,310

Leading keepers & fielder

W.H. Livsey (Hants)	544
H. Sidwell (Leics)	469
P.G.H. Fender (Surrey)	304

Overall statistics

Runs per wicket	24.4
Runs per 100 balls	45.7
% of matches drawn	34.3

Miscellany

On Tuesday 10 June 1924, while the litter of the previous day's bank-holiday crowd was still being picked, Yorkshire's openers Holmes and Sutcliffe stepped out of the Headingley pavilion, followed comically by a trotting dog. The ground was damp from overnight rain, but the day would be short. They only needed to score 58 runs to beat their arch rivals Lancashire.

Yorkshire were reigning champions, top of the table once more, but then, in the words of Cardus, 'Out of the blue sky of complacence came the thunderbolts.' In 70 minutes, with the ball popping and Lancashire's spinners Tyldesley and Parkin unerringly accurate, the Leeds crowd watched stunned as their mighty Yorkshire eleven were bowled out for 33.

No county has ever chased a smaller target and lost.

*

George Gunn of Notts had an unusual batting technique. He moved down the wicket even to fast bowlers, knocking the ball into gaps with 'a demure impishness'. At Leyton in May 1924, scoring at an 'insolently fast' pace and achieving a feat unique in championship history, he brought up his hundred without a single boundary. 'He batted as if he had been playing with the children on the sands,' wrote *The Times*. 'In fact, when just before he was out, he allowed himself a commonplace four to the on, one felt that his innings was marred by a crudity.'

At the Oval in 1921 Leicestershire's Tom Sidwell was ruled 'out, absent' when he arrived too late to resume his overnight innings. He had taken the tube to Kensington, not Kennington.

*

Glamorgan were so short of players for their last match of 1922 that they fielded four debutants, among them Royston Gabe-Jones, a 15-year-old Blundell's schoolboy.

He was sent in at number seven, higher than he had batted in his school side, and he survived for an hour and a half, his plucky six not out helping to save the follow-on.

Never invited back for a second game, he remains the only 15-year-old ever to play in the county championship.

*

In six innings in a fortnight in June 1925 Patsy Hendren hit an extraordinary 869 runs. The crowning glory of the sequence came at Trent Bridge when Nottinghamshire set Middlesex 502 to win. Notts had the strongest of bowling attacks, including a young quick called Harold Larwood; they had bowled out Middlesex for 127 in the first innings.

At 231 for six Middlesex looked beaten but Hendren, with a near-flawless 206, led them to a victory that, he wrote later, 'will remain in my memory as long as memory lasts'.

No county has ever chased a larger target and won.

The championship in the 1920s

County cricket enjoyed a great surge of popularity after the First World War. Pelham Warner, the Middlesex captain, thought that interest was 'greater than at any other period in the history of the game'. He attributed this partly to the fact that during the war the army's training programme had included cricket, and 'as a consequence hundreds of thousands of men became imbued with its spirit and tradition.'

The crowds were certainly filling the grounds in 1920 when, for the first time since 1914, a full programme of three-day matches was played. The season's championship did not disappoint, either, remaining undecided till the last evening of the last day. Middlesex, Lancashire and Surrey were the three contenders and, when Middlesex beat Surrey at Lord's to claim the crown, the scenes that followed were as emotional as any in the history of the county game.

Middlesex's triumph, by the narrowest of margins, came as a result of winning all their last nine games, and they began the summer of 1921 by winning eight, creating a still unmatched record of 17 championship victories in a row. Such a start might have made them runaway winners, but again, as in 1920, they found themselves at Lord's at the end of August, playing Surrey for the title.

On the last day Middlesex were set 322 for victory, and they scored them for the loss of four wickets. Their heroes, both centurions, were typical of their mix at that time: the great Jack Hearne, the most dedicated of professionals, and the little known Dick Twining, a wealthy amateur who had made himself available for the last two games. When the crowd cheered with delight in front of the pavilion that night, *The Times* thought they barely recognised Twining. Almost certainly they would not have known how six years earlier, during the Gallipoli campaign, he had been badly wounded in the knee. It was two years before he could walk without crutches – and even now, though he had scored a championship-winning 135, he was a little lame. The war was over, but it was not easy to forget.

Throughout the decade the Big Six – Yorkshire, Lancashire and Notts in the north; Surrey, Middlesex and Kent in the south-east – dominated, but from 1922 the power within that elite group shifted north. Yorkshire became the team to beat, winning the championship four years in a row from 1922, then Lancashire won three. It would be the summer of 1947, after another war, before the title would return to the south.

Yorkshire were a team with strength in every department. More than most in those years they burned with the desire to win, and they hated losing, which they seldom did. In five years from 1922 they won 95 games and lost just six. Unfortunately their approach was at times at odds with the spirit in which cricket was played elsewhere, especially in the south, and for a while they became an unpopular side. In 1924, when several of the team were away at a Test trial, they lost at Lord's to Middlesex, their main rivals for the title, and the return game at Bramall Lane turned into a most acrimonious affair. Two of their bowlers, Abe Waddington and George Macaulay, delightful men off the field, became demonstratively aggressive towards both batsmen and umpires, and elements of the Sheffield crowd were quick to join in. Middlesex were appalled and for several weeks, till Lord Hawke got involved, it looked as if they would refuse to play Yorkshire the next year. Surrey were rumoured to be thinking the same way.

The Yorkshire captain was Geoffrey Wilson, whose early cricket at Harrow and Cambridge was no preparation for this. Despite leading the county to three championships in three years, he stepped down in favour of the 46-year-old Arthur Lupton, an army major who soon introduced a greater discipline. Under Lupton Yorkshire had their best year of all, winning the championship with 21 victories and no defeats.

They were undefeated in 1926 as well, but this time they were pipped to the title by Lancashire. It rankled with Yorkshire as they had the better of both Roses matches, winning by an innings at Bradford, but Lancashire were an outstanding team, too. In particular, they had the one thing Yorkshire lacked: a match-winning fast bowler, Ted McDonald, though even that caused grumbling across the Pennines, as McDonald was not a Lancastrian but an Australian Test cricketer who had qualified as a result of playing league cricket for Nelson.

McDonald was 35 years old at the start of 1926 but, for the next four years, he carried the Lancashire attack, sending down 1,200 overs a season. With his long, graceful run-up, silent and menacing, and his advancing years, he was undoubtedly overbowled, and it showed at times in his mood. At Dover, when the game was slipping away among the Kent festivities, the band on the edge of the grass playing the madrigal from 'The Mikado', he was bowling weary off-spinners. Then suddenly, with a fish sandwich and a glass of whisky inside him, he was back at full pace, turning the game with a hat-trick. The county's success was built on his wickets, and there would have been many more if he had had a Hammond or a Woolley in the slips to hold the flashing edges. Only

Dick Tyldesley, the jovial leg-spinner with the increasingly Fallstaffian girth, could win matches like McDonald did, and he needed pitches to help him.

The batting was, for the most part, utilitarian. Ernest Tyldesley lacked the flair of his much older brother Johnny before the war, but on the damper pitches of northern England his consistency was invaluable. In 1926, in a run of 11 innings for Lancashire, he hit seven 100s, three 50s and a 44 – and, amidst all that, he played two further innings: 131 for the Players against the Gentlemen and 81 for England against Australia. Much under-rated by history, the modest, dedicated Tyldesley hit 102 first-class hundreds.

Harry Makepeace was the rock of the innings. The one-time Everton and England wing-half, he was 45 years old in 1926, and his batting, never the most stylish, had become more stodgy with the passing of each year. Yet that summer he hit 2,100 championship runs, and in the last match, when it mattered most, he hit the Notts bowlers for a rapid 180, sending Neville Cardus into paroxysms of delight: 'It was the authentic Makepeace, seen as it were in "quick motion". The old warhorse forgot his years and scars; he was mettlesome, crying "Ha! Ha!" amongst the trumpets.'

It was a great triumph for Lancashire. They had not won the title since 1904, before even Makepeace's time, and they won again in 1927 and in 1928 when they were unbeaten in 30 matches and their opener Charlie Hallows scored 1,000 runs in May. Yorkshire were also unbeaten in 1928, as they had been in 1926, the only two occasions when a county has remained undefeated and not been crowned champions.

The arithmetic of the championship continued to cause problems. It was unsatisfactory that counties played different numbers of games, not least because that generated hard-to-fathom percentages. It was also proving hard to get the balance right on first-innings points. Five for a win, three for first-innings lead in a draw, did lead to situations where teams preferred to sit on their three points rather than risk them in search of the five. But conversely, when it was only two points for a draw, there were rain-affected games in which the leading counties blocked for a 'no result' rather than have their percentage reduced by gaining two points out of five. Once at Leicester Yorkshire refused the extra half hour when only one run short of their opponents' first-innings score.

This reached the point of farce in a minor-counties match, in which on the last afternoon Staffordshire, resolving not to chase Leicestershire 2nd XI's first-innings score of 124, took more than 60 overs to score 76. Sydney Barnes at his most

Ted McDonald
484 wickets in the championship, 1926 to 1928
To Cardus, he was 'a Lucifer of his craft,
a satanic bowler, menacing but princely'

stubborn was in the thick of it, blocking relentlessly, till the Leicester captain George Rudd, after speaking several times to the umpires, lost patience. His team conceded 49 wides and byes as a helpless Staffordshire were forced to take the lead.

In 1929 the counties all played 28 matches, which was one step forward. Nottinghamshire, with a new-ball attack of Harold Larwood and Bill Voce, were champions, but again the final table had an unsatisfactory look. Gloucestershire, a rising power with Wally Hammond in their ranks, were down in fourth place despite winning more matches than any other county – five more than Lancashire in third place. Not only did it seem wrong but it was encouraging what many were calling 'safety first' cricket.

County cricket retained its great popularity, but still it struggled to find an ideal format.

Some players of the 1920s

Philip Mead of Hampshire

> I'd rather have bowled at Hobbs or Hammond than Philip. With them there was at least
> a gleam of hope.
> *Maurice Tate*
>
> He may not have caught the eye, but the players in the middle knew just how good he was.
> *'Gubby' Allen*

He did not have the domineering power of Walter Hammond, the graceful elegance of Frank Woolley or the classical ease of Jack Hobbs, but in the county championship Philip Mead scored more runs than any of them: 1,000 in a season 26 times, 2,843 in 1928, 46,268 in his career, 132 centuries, they are all records for the championship.

A dock-worker's son from Battersea, he joined the ground staff at the Oval in 1902, a 15-year-old slow-left-arm bowler who could bat a bit. After two summers Surrey released him, then changed their minds, only to learn that he had found his way to Southampton. So the unfashionable Hampshire was the county he served, loyally and without fuss, till 1936. The rock of their batting, he would emerge from the pavilion with his rolling gait. Then before each ball he would perform the same elaborate ritual of shuffling his feet, tugging the top of his pad and touching his cap several times. With the best of defences he never gave his wicket away, often joking that the 50s and 100s paid for his bags of coal in winter – though they also paid for his cigarettes and bets on horses.

The Test selectors did not favour him, thinking him a poor fielder and a slow scorer. Yet, with his ability to memorise the field around him, he was the master of the well-placed single, and he averaged 40 runs an hour through his career. Hampshire folk certainly knew his worth.

The rock of Hampshire
The highest run-scorer in championship history

Charlie Parker of Gloucestershire

> On bad wickets, I do not know that I have ever seen a more dangerous attacker.
> His bowling it was that taught me so much about slip-fielding, for we worked together.
> *Wally Hammond*

With his cap tilted at a pronounced angle and his shirtsleeve dangling loosely as he came in to bowl, Charlie Parker was a distinctive figure in 1920s county cricket. He bowled slow-left-arm, with cunning flight, immaculate length and an ability to turn the ball both ways.

One of nine children born into a farm-labouring family north of Cheltenham, he had been to grammar school and developed a mind of his own, a trait that became more pronounced after the First World War. Previously a fast bowler, he insisted on bowling slow and did so till he retired at the age of 52 in 1935. Only when things were going badly, when his temper was fraying, his cap tilting further over his left eye, would he resort once more to sending down a fast ball. At all other times he preferred the subtler crafts of flight and guile.

He was inclined to let little things upset him, not least dropped catches – "If I had a fiver for each of them, I should never need to bowl another ball" – but that changed when Hammond appeared in the slips. In those golden years the slow-left-armer, now well into his 40s, harvested wickets by the bucketload. Once, tormenting Essex on a spiteful track in Gloucester, he took 17, six of them caught by Hammond. Yet he only played one Test for England. With his sharp tongue and his radical politics, he was thought to be 'an awkward customer', a verdict not softened when he told Pelham Warner some 'home truths' in a hotel lift.

He went his own way, independent to the end and appreciated by his fellow professionals. Knowledgeable about classical music and politics, brilliant at golf, he was always his own man.

A man with his own mind
The championship's leading wicket-taker five times in six years

Maurice Tate of Sussex

> His heart was as big as his boots, and his boots were enormous. *AA Thomson*
>
> I bang it down on the seam and hope for the best. *Maurice Tate*

Maurice Tate started out as a batsman who bowled off-spinners but in 1922, at the age of 27, he was turned into a quick bowler, soon becoming the best fast-medium bowler of his generation. In three successive summers, as well as scoring his customary 1,000 runs, he took 200 wickets.

'Chubby' Tate had strong shoulders and chest, and big hands, and, though his run-up was only eight strides, he could make the ball fizz alarmingly off the pitch. He bowled off-cutters and out-swingers, and he had the stamina – 'stanima', as he would have called it – to send down 1,500 overs a summer. A placid man with a countryman's humour, he was still going strong at the age of 40.

As a batsman he was good enough to open the innings for Sussex, but he was at his happiest striking big sixes over long-on and mid-wicket. His one Test century, at Lord's, took less than two hours.

He was a star of English cricket – he took 38 wickets in a Test series in Australia – but it never changed him. With one and all he was approachable, cheerful, down to earth – and very popular.

A natural bowler

2,019 championship wickets

Patsy Hendren of Middlesex

Elias Henry Hendren

Only Hobbs hit more than his 170 first-class centuries

> Add to all his merits a perennial cheerfulness and a zest in the field which even the hottest day could not quench, and you have the embodiment of all that is meant when a cricketer says, "He's the man for my side." *Harry Altham*

Patsy Hendren was a prolific run-scorer in the 1920s, scoring 2,000 in each of the ten summers. For such a jolly man he was a surprisingly nervous starter, perhaps reflecting his insecurity as the son of an Irish plasterer. Once he was in full flow, however, he was a joy to watch. He had a wonderful eye, ready to hook even the fastest bowlers, and for a stocky man he was exceptionally light on his feet. Against the spinners nobody danced down the pitch so often and so far. A professional football in winter, he was a bundle of energy at the crease and an outstanding fielder. The crowds loved him.

Though a shrewd man, he had an impish streak which, with his heavy face and his superb gift of timing, made him a natural comic, able to inject laughter into the tensest moment. He was the era's greatest entertainer – and one of its very finest cricketers.

Fred Root of Worcestershire

> Powerful and enduring in physique, endowed with contempt for adversity and all pettiness, he fought and toiled and joked through anything that batsman or climate could set against him. No other bowler could watch him without admiring him and catching something of his spirit.
>
> *RC Robertson-Glasgow*

Son of the Leicester groundsman, Fred Root played for Derbyshire before the war, but it was only with Worcestershire that he was allowed to develop his in-swing bowling. Packing the field with legside catchers and bowling long spells, he carried the struggling county's attack for ten years. The victories were rare, though they did beat Lancashire when he was 41 years old. After two days' play, Cardus in the *Guardian* compared him to 'a hen who has had her head cut off and runs on impetuously, under the beautiful but sad illusion that she is still alive'. Root's reply was to take a career-best nine for 23.

His book, *A Cricket Pro's Lot*, is full of delightful stories. In one, he is urged by a team-mate to run out a batsman lying injured in mid-pitch. Refusing to do so, he turns to the team-mate: "Here's the ball; you come and do it then," to which he gets the reply: "Oh, I'm an amateur. I can't do that."

Master of inswing

In 1925 he took over half of Worcestershire's wickets

Stories of the 1920s

Wally Hammond's wonder week

Cheltenham, August 1928

Gloucestershire cricket came first to the Cheltenham College ground in 1872, expanding to two games in 1879, then to a three-game festival in 1906. It was held in August, starting on the second Saturday when much of the harvesting on the surrounding farms had been done.

Charles Light, a young Cotswold forester, attended for the first time in 1926. "We cycled from Sheepscombe, through the harvested fields. Then at the ground there was a big yard where you could park your bike all day for twopence. Dennett, the old Gloucestershire spin bowler, was on the gate, collecting the money."

Wally Hammond, the rising star of the county's cricket, spent that summer of 1926 in a nursing home, battling against a life-threatening illness contracted in the Caribbean. Yet any fear that his great talent had been diminished was soon dispelled when on his return in May 1927 he scored 1,000 runs in just 22 days. However, even that was less remarkable than his week at Cheltenham in August 1928.

Returning from the Oval Test, he joined the Festival on Wednesday, against Surrey. It had rained the previous day, and the pitch, drying out under a hot sun, was 'on the difficult side'. Yet Hammond, brimming with intent, cut his first ball for four and 'sent the score along at a merry pace'. He was out early in the afternoon for 139.

The next day he held four slip catches, took the wicket of Jack Hobbs and, with the pitch still not easy, came off at close of play on 64 not out. On the final day he took his score to 143, then – as Charlie Parker spun his way through the Surrey batting – he held a further six catches, all in succession. In one match he had scored a century in each innings, taken the wicket of Hobbs and set a world record, still unequalled, of ten catches.

Worcestershire were Gloucestershire's next opponents. "The village cricketers all used to come on the Saturday," said Charles Light, "and the beer tent did good business. Flowers Bitter was the best. It was a penny more than Stroud or Ciren Beer, but it was worth it."

In the morning they saw Hammond take the new ball. The sun burned down on a heavy dew, the ball swung and came off the pitch at pace, and in barely an hour Worcestershire were all out for 35. Hammond took nine for 23, one of his wickets smashing a stump. The other wicket fell to Parker, caught by Hammond in the slips.

"The wicket was a bit tricky," was Hammond's explanation to the local paper – but not so tricky that, when he batted, he could not stay in for two hours and make 80 runs. 'He did not reveal his most attractive form,' *The Times* wrote, 'but he seldom wasted an opportunity to score by a cleverly placed stroke.'

Wally Hammond, aged 25, in 1928

In four days he had scored two centuries and an 80, held ten catches in a match and taken nine wickets in an innings. Yet such was his reputation – 'the young man of 25 on whom the mantle of WG Grace has fallen' – that not everybody that day was impressed.

"We only had the one day off work each week, you see," recalled Charles Light, who was not among the crowd. "If we came we had to miss our own match, and we were playing at Ampney Crucis. I remember getting back to North Cerney on the bus, and we met our secretary. He was an older man, he always came to the festival, and we asked him all about it. 'Oh,' he said, 'it was rather dull.' Those were his very words. He reckoned Hammond's 80 was slower than usual."

On Monday, as a gentle postscript, Worcestershire lost by an innings. Hammond, bowling fast-medium unchanged for 34 overs, took a further six wickets.

Of Glamorgan and Worcestershire

The summer of 1921 brought a 17th county into the fold, Glamorgan. Unlike Worcestershire and Northants, the two previous newcomers, they had not been dominant in the minor county game, but they did have charm and diplomatic skill and they used both to persuade nine of the first-class sides to offer them fixtures. It was not a universally popular development; there were many who were unhappy that an already over-subscribed championship was continuing to grow in this ad hoc way.

For their first match Glamorgan played Sussex at Cardiff. They opted for experience, fielding a team with an average age of 38, and under sunny skies, in front of 8,000 cheering Welshmen, they won by 22 runs. There were speeches from the balcony and great jubilation, but alas, it was not a portent for the summer. Their remaining 17 games produced one win and 14 defeats, and they finished in last place. *The Cricketer*, looking back to their first victory, called it 'a calamity': 'It fired the inflammable Celtic imagination and created an inflated idea of possibilities, destined to bitter disillusion.'

Their best amateurs were too old or too rarely available, they could not afford many professionals, and the challenging task of selection was entrusted unhelpfully to the full 18-strong committee. Yet they kept cheerful to the end, as Neville Cardus noted on the last day: 'Every man was on his toes, for all the world as though it were May, not September. The right spirit this; it will surely take Glamorgan quite a long way in time.'

Indeed it would, though not in the 1920s. Most years they could be found near the foot of the table, keeping company with Worcestershire and Northants. Worcestershire had returned to the fold in 1920. Always on the brink of bankruptcy, their ability to raise teams relied on the goodwill of a large cast of amateurs. In 1921 they offered a first game to that year's Cambridge captain, just appointed headmaster of a local prep school. Unable to spare the time, he sent one of his staff to take his place, and the man top-scored with 82.

In 1925 they called on 39 different players, including the Reverend Reginald Moss, whose county debut against Gloucestershire at the age of 57 years and 88 days makes him the oldest man ever to play in the championship. In his youth he had won a cricket blue at Oxford, but that was way back in 1889.

On the Sunday rest day Moss conducted the service at the little Cotswold church of Icomb where he was rector. Then on Tuesday evening, going in to bat at number eleven, with 15 runs needed for victory, he was – in the words of *The Times* – 'an easy victim to Hammond'. Bowled for nought.

The glorious uncertainty of cricket

Lancashire, champions in 1926, were favourites to win again as the summer of 1927 drew to a close. Unbeaten in their 26 matches, they were comfortably clear of Notts in second place, with only games at Eastbourne and Leicester left to play.

Against Sussex at Eastbourne they met with disaster, bowled out for 99 and 76 and defeated by an innings. There was no disgrace in losing their wickets to England's Maurice Tate, but the press had a field day with their other assassin: 'Tishy' Browne, a holidaying clergyman.

A fast inswing bowler, Reverend Francis Browne had what his captain Arthur Gilligan called 'the queerest action I have ever seen. He starts off rather like a carthorse breaking its traces and bolting; he then approaches the crease at a fearsome pace and delivers the ball off the wrong foot.' One professional, facing him for the first time, said he was not sure 'if the ball was going to come out of his right hand, his left hand or his ear-hole'. At Eastbourne Browne bowled 46.1 overs in the match and took eight wickets for 50 runs.

Lancashire only drew at Leicester, and Notts were suddenly in first place. All they had to do was to go down to Swansea and not lose to bottom-of-the-table Glamorgan. Already the civic authorities were setting in motion plans for a grand reception for the team. The once-great Nottinghamshire would be champions for only the second time since the 1880s.

Glamorgan, so full of hope back in 1921, were at rock bottom. They had not won a game all summer, and the wet weather had hit them hard financially. Their survival into 1928 now depended on a last-ditch appeal for donations.

Notts were full of confidence. A first-innings total of 233 was not what they expected, but it should have been enough – if only Lionel Kirk, their stand-in captain, had not dropped the Glamorgan opener Eddie Bates when he was on 36. He went on to hit 163, and on the final morning, batting on a drying wicket, Notts were all out for 61, beaten by an innings.

The Welsh crowd were jubilant. Yes, the heroes of their victory were casts-off from other counties – Sussex, Hampshire and two from Yorkshire – but what did it matter? A full hour after the conclusion, they were still there, full of hwyl. One man, in his excitement, fell down the terrace and broke an arm. Another, an 80-year-old Welshman from Pittsburgh, was seeing cricket for the first time and was so 'filled with pride' that he promptly made 'a handsome donation'.

Lancashire, meanwhile, were champions again – not by the front door but, as Cardus put it, 'by way of the fire escape.'

Images of the 1920s

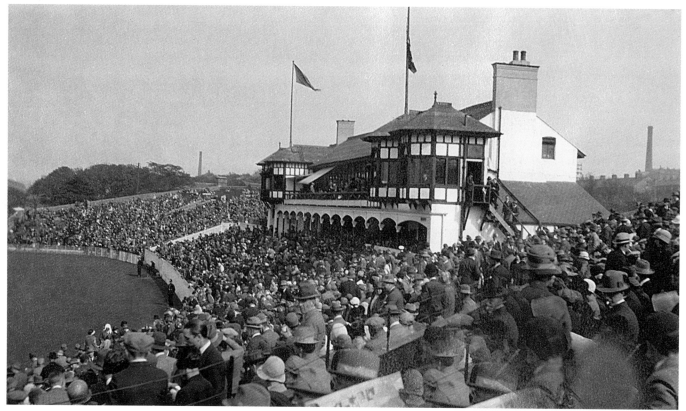

Yorkshire v Lancashire, Whit Bank Holiday 1926

Whit Monday at Bradford

The Park Avenue ground at Bradford added two new stands in 1926, bringing its capacity to 22,000, but it still came nowhere near to accommodating all those who arrived for the Bank Holiday Monday of the Roses match. By 11.30 all gates, but for a single one for members, were shut, with thousands outside on the street, including several 'charabanc parties from Lancashire and the East Riding'.

The General Strike had been over for less than a fortnight, but cricket was having no difficulty in returning to normal.

'The air was stirring with the proper Yorkshire temper when the match went on this morning,' Neville Cardus wrote. 'A great crowd sat in the sunshine and expectantly

stood on tip-toe.' As Lancastrian wickets fell, 'They roared out delight' with 'shouts of savage joy'.

This was the high peak of Roses matches. In the return game in August, at the much larger Old Trafford ground, the attendance on the Bank Holiday Monday was 46,000, the greatest number ever for a single day of a county match.

The sun shone and Cardus, at home amid his fellow northerners, was in heaven:

Who could be dull with all the crowd's splendid humanity around him? They sat and stood, rank on rank, happy as sandboys, happy in their applause, happy in their grumblings.

Victory at Blackheath

Each year in July the Surrey cricketers came to the Rectory Field at Blackheath, and each year they were beaten by Kent, usually by a great margin. At the end of another crushing defeat in 1922 the Surrey captain Percy Fender tried to cheer up his ageing keeper Herbert Strudwick by offering him a cigarette. "No, thank you, Mr Fender," Strudwick, a non-smoker, said wearily. "I'll have my first when we beat them here."

Back they all came in 1923. Another Saturday in July, another full ground. *The Times* reporter caught the mood:

> This is no ordinary county match. It is the match in which the cricket of Kent is annually vindicated by the humiliation of its neighbour. The Kent crowd do not come to Blackheath to see a match, but – like the French revolutionaries – to dance the *carmagnole* at an execution. Long before the time for starting, they were sitting three deep round the ground, licking greedy lips.

Surrey did not have a strong bowling attack, but they had a captain in Fender who was full of imaginative tricks, a man who loved to think beyond the orthodox. Many thought him the best captain England never had. Part Huguenot, part Scots, he was perhaps too much of an outsider, too clever for some and much too quick to ruffle establishment feathers.

Yet at Surrey they loved him. A fine all-round cricketer, he was the scorer of the fastest hundred of all time, in 35 minutes, and at Blackheath he hit two crucial and 'merry' fifties, capping them on the final day with four wickets and two catches as he masterminded a 222-run victory over Kent. The jinx of the Rectory Field was finally broken.

> The Surrey team made hurriedly for the pavilion, the silence of the crowd being broken by a few ecstatic yells from the Surrey supporters. Still silent, the crowd congregated outside the pavilion, and at last a voice shouted, "We want the best gentleman in England."

Fender made his victory speech. Then he went to give a cigarette to his keeper, only to find him already puffing away. "I decided not to wait for yours, Mr Fender," said Strudwick cheerily.

Surrey captain Percy Fender speaks to the crowd, Blackheath, July 1923

1920: A thrilling climax at Lord's

Pelham Warner's best days had long passed by the summer of 1920. He had captained England to Ashes triumph in Australia way back in 1903/04, and now he was 47 years of age, bald-headed and stiff in the limbs.

After losing four years to the war, he had come back in 1919, still hoping that at last he might captain Middlesex to the championship. But the tiring two-day matches left him 'a dead dog' by mid-July, and Middlesex, so strong before the war, finished 13th out of 15. He knew it was time to call it a day. Yet still he had that same boyish enthusiasm for it all, and he let himself be persuaded to carry on.

Through the first months of the 1920 summer the team showed improvement, but any chance of contesting the title seemed to be gone when at Leyton at the end of July, needing 118 for victory, they were bowled out for 113. Warner was last man out for a battling 46, *The Times* suggesting that he was more 'tired out' than 'bowled out'. His inability to run quick singles had cost them the match, the paper said, though others pointed to the Middlesex first innings when Warner, on 22 not out, had had to leave the game to attend a selection meeting at Lord's.

Before the next match Warner announced that he would be retiring at the end of the season. 'His decision is final,' reported *The Times*. 'He will not allow himself to be tempted back to the field.' His Middlesex team lay sixth in the table, a long way adrift of Kent, Surrey, Yorkshire and Lancashire.

Then came the month of August. The weather was warm and dry, the crowds were enormous – a record 66,500 paying spectators over the three days of Kent's visit to the Oval – and Middlesex won eight matches in a row.

At Canterbury they were up till the small hours on the second night, being wined, dined and entertained by the Old Stagers, whose show included a recitation by a glamorous lady:

> I think I could love you if like Hendren you could pull
> Or if like Greville Stevens you could bowl
>> With Jack Hearne and Lee in
>> Why, cricket's worth seein',
> And for Nigel Haig I'd gladly give my soul.
>> ... And I lurk round every corner
>> For a glimpse of 'Plum' Warner,
> Oh, I'm sure I could love him if I tried.

Kent, needing 123 to win, were 107 for six, and they lost by five runs, the crucial moment when the veteran 'Punter' Humphreys, in his last game for Kent, was called for a sharp single and Patsy Hendren swooped from the covers and threw down the wicket. When the last man was bowled, the ageing Warner 'bounded in the air like a young kangaroo'. "Still fighting," he said cheerfully to one reporter.

At Bradford the margin of victory was just four runs. Yorkshire's last pair looked to have stolen the game with a stand of 45, but Warner stuck with his 19-year-old leg-spinning amateur Grenville Stevens for the decisive over. 'Mr Stevens bowls a remarkable number of really bad balls,' one reporter wrote, 'but conversely he bowls, and not too infrequently, what must be very nearly the best ball in England.'

The noisy crowd fell silent as, without hurry, Stevens bowled four balls, each played firmly and confidently by the batsman Abe Waddington. A lone Yorkshire voice called out from the terraces: "You're beat, Plum" – and Stevens answered him with a perfect googly that pitched on off and hit middle-and-leg.

Middlesex had only five professionals in their squad, and for the most part they were the match-winners in this winning run. Patsy Hendren, Jack Hearne and Harry Lee the batsmen, Hearne and Jack Durston the bowlers, with the veteran Joe Murrell behind the stumps, the only one of the five to whom Warner would turn for advice.

To these professionals he was not 'Plum' but 'The General', a strict and at times distant figure in his Harlequin cap. On the good days they were 'Harry', 'Young Jack', 'Patsy' and 'Joe' but, when things were going badly and he was chewing his nails, they became 'Lee', 'Hearne', 'Hendren', 'Murrell'.

They knew, however, that he read the game better than anybody, that he was a brilliant tactician and that, when it mattered, he would always stick up for his men. 'For such a skipper,' Harry Lee wrote, 'any side will perform great deeds.'

Of the amateurs Warner himself, his successor Frank Mann and the young Nigel Haig played regularly. The rest appeared when they could: from Churchill Gunasekera, the Seneghalese doctor, to Clarence Bruce, the future Lord Aberdare.

Together they won eight games in a row, reaching the last round of matches in first place, closely followed by Lancashire and Surrey. Any of the three could be champions.

Saturday 28 August 1920. Middlesex versus Surrey at Lord's. It was the first day of the football season, with 50,000 at White Hart Lane as well as great crowds for the games in the new Division Three. Yet at Lord's the ground was full by mid-afternoon. 'Clergymen, city men and ladies in dainty summer frocks were glad enough to get a seat on the grass in

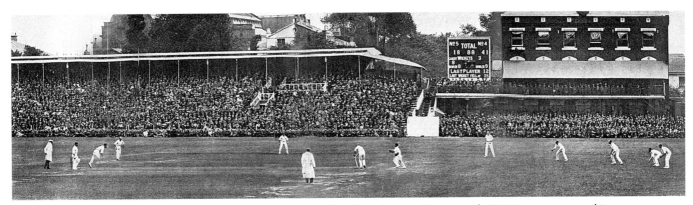

Middlesex v Surrey, Lord's, Saturday 28 August 1920: Hitch bowls to Warner with 25,000 spectators watching

front of the ropes.' In places they were 10 or 20 deep; there were even some, as never before, on the grass in front of the pavilion. 'A feeling of drama overlay the day.'

Middlesex batted first and were soon in trouble. Warner came out to a great ovation – 'An old man at cricket, there was almost a touch of sympathy for him' – and he steadied the innings, batting four and a half hours for an unbeaten 70. At the close Middlesex were 253 for eight. 'One's imagination runs riot,' wrote *The Times*, 'when one wonders what the state of the game would have been had it not been for Mr Warner.'

On Monday, in front of 20,000 spectators, Surrey's Andrew Sandham carried his bat for an imperturbable and beautifully crafted 167, giving his team a first-innings lead of 73. In the evening there was only time for Middlesex to reach 27 for no wicket. With Lancashire on the verge of victory at Old Trafford, it was hard to see how Warner's Middlesex side could now win the championship.

Tuesday morning's *Times* printed a letter, signed FAIR PLAY. It pointed out that, against the other title contenders, Lancashire had drawn two and lost four, with many of their wins coming against lesser counties, counties which Middlesex – with their shorter programme – had not played. It was an injustice, argued FAIR PLAY. MCC should exercise its authority and award the title to Middlesex.

Perhaps it was as well that only much later was it learned that the anonymous FAIR PLAY was, in fact, Warner himself.

In the morning Harry Lee and Challen Skeet took Middlesex to 199 for no wicket. Lee, who had played his first cricket up against a lamp post off Oxford Street, completed his fifth century of the summer while Skeet, dropping in on county cricket between Oxford University and a diplomatic posting to the Sudan, chose this, the most important day in Middlesex's history, to score his first and only hundred.

With some quick hitting after lunch, Warner was able to set Surrey to score 244 runs in three hours. By now word had travelled, and the terraces were filling up.

With Percy Fender as captain, Surrey were always going to give it a go, and at 120 for two, with Sandham again well set, they looked the likelier winners. Then Warner spotted Fender on the balcony signalling impatiently to the batsmen, and he despatched Hendren into the deep. The big-hitting Tom Shepherd immediately swiped at a ball from Stevens, sending it high towards the nursery end, and they all watched as Hendren ran yards and yards, from long-off to long-on, to hold what he later called 'the best catch of my career'. 'His arms were stretched almost out of their sockets,' Harry Lee said. 'Had he started smoking a year earlier and been a fraction of an inch shorter as a result, he would not have made it.'

Was it a last magnificent stroke of captaincy from the bald-headed man in the Harlequin cap, the man who all his life was happy to talk cricket all day? Or was it, as one newspaper wrote, 'fickle fortune smiling on the Middlesex captain'?

From that point on, batsmen perished regularly till at 6.22, with one last wicket to take, Stevens bowled his 'best ball in England' and it knocked back the stumps of Strudwick.

Middlesex had won by 55 runs, they were the county champions, and the great crowd surged forward. Warner was rugby-tackled, lifted off his feet and carried all the way to the pavilion. They called for speeches, and there were plenty.

Warner had scored a hundred for England, won the Ashes in Australia, but nothing compared with this, the winning of the championship at his beloved Lord's: 'I was very near to breaking down as I stood on the balcony of the pavilion and looked down on the thousands of cheering spectators. I have had many happy moments, but never a happier.'

1922: Two contrasting styles of cricket

The fun-loving gambler

Warwickshire v Hampshire, Edgbaston, 14-16 June 1922

Lionel Tennyson, captain of Hampshire, was a great optimist. Heir to the baronetcy created for his poet grandfather, he had survived three woundings during the war and lived to the limit a life of late-night parties, country sports and cricket. An inveterate gambler, he once had to sell his new Rolls Royce to pay for a bad evening at the card table.

On a damp morning at Edgbaston Tennyson asked Warwickshire to bat first, and they were all out for 223. By then the pitch was firm and true, and the Hampshire batsmen went out, expecting to take a first-innings lead.

Forty minutes later they were all out for 15, four of which were from a legside ball that went for byes. Some say the pace of the pitch surprised them; they were playing back when they should have been forward. Others thought they 'got into a funk', unnerved when their opener Alec Bowell was bowled by fast bowler Harry Howell for nought and returned to the pavilion carrying a shattered stump. Eight of them made ducks, and the team was in despair – but not Tennyson. Asked to follow on, he turned to his men: "Never mind, lads," he said. "We'll get 500 this time."

At close of play, when Hampshire were three down for 98, the Warwickshire captain Freddie Calthorpe suggested to Tennyson that the amateurs should go off and play golf when the game ended next day. This 'brought a flood of good Anglo-Saxon from Tennyson', a confident assertion that Hampshire would win and the placing of several long-odds bets.

Next morning Tennyson received an anonymous postcard, suggesting that his team might do better painting spots on rocking horses. Soon enough the dependable Phil Mead was bowled by an inswinging yorker, and Tennyson, after a few big hits, was caught in the slips. George Brown batted carefully but, when the sixth wicket fell, they were still 31 runs behind.

The Warwickshire Secretary, wanting the game to last a little longer, sent out a message, asking his captain not to take the new ball. Against various change bowlers Hampshire then took the lead, but they were only 66 ahead when their keeper Walter Livsey, at number ten, joined Brown. Livsey was employed by Tennyson as his valet, and somehow that day he stuck around while Brown batted 'with great guts'. The new ball was taken, the day grew long, and poor Billy Quaife, at the age of 50, finished up bowling 49 overs.

Brown made 172, Livsey completed his maiden century at the start of the final day, and Hampshire, after a first innings of 15, ended with a lead of 313. They then bowled out a demoralised Warwickshire for 158. To many it remains the most astonishing game in the championship's history.

Tennyson, having collected his winnings from the home dressing room, danced a Highland Fling in the showers, then uncorked the champagne. "I'd love to meet the chap who sent me the postcard," he said triumphantly.

What fun! It was always fun with the Honourable Lionel Tennyson.

Lionel Tennyson

A different atmosphere

Lancashire v Yorkshire, Old Trafford, Tuesday 8 August 1922

Failing to win the championship had become by the 1920s a grave matter in Yorkshire, but it was not as grave as when they lost to Lancashire. Twice a year the two counties met, at the Whit and August bank holidays, and their contests were fought out always in a grim, tense atmosphere, the great majority of the games ending in deadlock.

'There was a sternness about the games,' Yorkshire's Herbert Sutcliffe wrote, 'that was different from the atmosphere of other county games.' It was Sutcliffe's view that such contests provided 'the ideal preparation for Test cricket'.

Rain often played a part, especially in Manchester, and in August 1922 it was torrential on the Monday. Yet somehow, though 'the wicket was as dead as Queen Anne', they started the final day on time on Tuesday. Yorkshire, thanks to a snick through the slips, took a first-innings lead of four runs. Then, as the sun broke through and the pitch grew treacherous, they bowled out Lancashire for 135. It left them 132 for victory, and they had 2¾ hours to make them.

How the crowd loved it: the tension rising, wickets falling and all the time the batsmen content to nudge along at two runs an over. The bowlers appealed repeatedly, making evident to all their disbelief when the answer was 'not out'. When Abe Waddington was given run out, he stood for an age, convinced the bails were off when the ball broke the wicket. This was not cricket as it was played at Hove and Canterbury.

The run-out left Yorkshire on 108 for eight which was, in effect, nine as their captain Geoffrey Wilson was in bed in a Manchester nursing home, recovering from the removal of his appendix.

At 6.30, with half an hour remaining, all that stood between Lancashire and a rare Roses victory were the two old men of the Yorkshire team: the 44-year-old Wilfred Rhodes, a canny veteran of many such struggles, and the 43-year-old Winchester schoolmaster Rockley Wilson, playing his first game of the summer. They spoke not a word when Wilson reached the middle. They had no need to. They were both Yorkshiremen; they knew they had not to lose.

The rest of the team left to catch the train to Bristol, not wanting a repeat of their recent journey to Maidstone. On that occasion, playing at Harrogate, the Essex captain Johnny Douglas had refused to add time to the first two days, forcing the young Geoffrey Wilson, anxious about train times, to accept a shortened match. On the final afternoon play ended with Essex one wicket from an innings defeat, and so outraged were some of the older Yorkshire professionals that an argument ensued that went on so long that they all reached the railway station too late. With no option but to take a slow night train and walk in the small hours across London, they arrived at Maidstone the next morning at nine o'clock.

This time, with Rhodes and Wilson batting, they caught the Bristol train in time, speculating in the carriage about the game they had left behind. 'We reckoned the odds were something like a thousand to one on Lancashire winning,' Sutcliffe wrote. The departing professionals had no faith in their ageing Winchester schoolmaster's ability to survive for half an hour in such an atmosphere on so testing a pitch.

The off-spinner Cec Parkin, a master of such surfaces, was bowling to Wilson. Cardus was enraptured: 'He hurled a yorker at his middle stump and then came towards the base of his wicket a red-hot shooter. Wilson stopped them and could even smile at the devilry of them.'

With Wilfred Rhodes 'a Gibraltar of certitude', the score crept up. At the start of the last over it stood at 127. There were just five runs to be scored.

Parkin's first four balls were pushed back with a straight bat by Rhodes. The fifth, adding to the drama, was a no ball, and Rhodes pushed that back too, saying afterwards that he had heard the call too late. Now it was four to win. With two balls remaining, Yorkshire were one hit from glory.

The previous week Somerset's white-haired veteran Ernie Robson had captured the headlines, striking a six in the final over to win a thrilling two-wicket victory over Middlesex.

But that was Taunton; this was Old Trafford, a Roses match, with a tension around the ground that, according to Cardus, 'seemed to have a low throbbing sound'. The unflustered Rhodes blocked the fifth ball, pushed a single off the last, and walked off, content that he had done his job.

"Why take the risk and undo all the good work?" he said. After all, with the two points for first-innings lead, they were still top of the table. 'Against some other team,' one reporter speculated, 'Rhodes might have felt stirred to adventure all. But these Lancashire and Yorkshire matches are unique; here it is a point of muscular honour not to let go.'

On the night train to Bristol, Rhodes and Wilson, together with the scorer and a reporter, sat and talked cricket. They arrived at Temple Meads station at six the next morning.

Essex, Somerset and Leicestershire meander along

1920s

There were strong counties and weak counties in the 1920s, and the gap between them was wide. In the top places in the table each year could be found Yorkshire, Lancashire, Kent, Surrey, Notts and, more often than not, Middlesex. At the other end there were the perpetual also-rans: Worcestershire, Northamptonshire and the newcomers Glamorgan, counties which struggled to survive and which rarely rose above the last four or five places.

Among the rest there were counties who in a good year might finish fourth or fifth – Sussex and Gloucestershire were two – and counties who had no expectation that they would reach such heights. Among these were Essex, Somerset and Leicestershire. Always short of money, they lacked the playing staffs to compete with Yorkshire, Lancashire and Surrey.

In 1922 Essex, with their membership down below 1,000, sold their Leyton headquarters to the Army Sports Council and became tenants. Even this, however, did not give them the spare cash to improve facilities there, as the editor of the *Daily News Annual* made clear in 1927:

> The accommodation for the shilling patrons has long been inadequate, and I hope most devoutly that the old ammunition boxes, masquerading under the name of ring seats, will be cleared out, bag and baggage, never to return. In the past the charm of county cricket has served to counter many creature discomforts: today a public rocked to sleep in a luxurious cinema demand a reasonable return for open air investment.

Essex were at their lowest ebb in 1928. In the spring their long-serving groundsman 'Bung' Brewer, worried about the future, committed suicide. In the summer they won only two of their 28 matches. Then, as the year drew to a close, they created a furore by sacking their captain Johnny Douglas.

He had led the side through good times and bad since 1911. Learning the game at Felsted School, he was not a natural cricketer, owing his original appointment in 1911 to the fact that his father held part of the mortgage on the ground. But he was a tremendous trier – 'as great a cricketer as a man can make himself without that innate spark that is beyond acquiring,' wrote JM Kilburn – and, certainly in his younger days, a most engaging character. He toured Australia in 1911/12 when, after Pelham Warner fell ill early on, he led England to a 4-1 Ashes victory that turned him into a national hero. As a middleweight boxer he won Olympic gold in London in 1908, and he had a good war, rising to the rank of Lieutenant-Colonel.

By 1928, however, he was 46 years old and, with his powers declining, his great desire for men who gave their all had turned into a bullying intolerance of weakness. When two of his best professionals, Eastman and Nichols, were injured, he was wholly unsympathetic: "I don't care if you suffer the pangs of hell while you're unfit to turn out for the county."

'He had become difficult in the field,' wrote the young amateur Charles Bray, 'with a tendency to blame others for his own shortcomings. I recall one match just after he had delivered a lecture to us on fielding. He decided that he would shout the name of the fielder who was to take any high catch. The ball was duly skied, and he first shouted "O'Connor", then "Nichols" and finally "Bray", by which time the ball dropped within a couple of feet of himself, to our amusement and his extreme anger.'

That summer Essex were represented by 38 diffferent players, the great majority of them amateurs who came in for the occasional match. Some, such as Leonard Crawley and Claude Ashton, were outstanding cricketers, but many were not as good as the professionals whom they displaced. In the world of club cricket, men took to asking each other: "Have you had a game for Essex this year?"

In some respcts it was a good policy, keeping the county team in touch with the clubs, but it did not create a harmonious side. The decision not to reappoint Douglas, after so many years of service, was a hard one, and it was extremely badly received by Douglas himself. But it did allow the county to move forward to some happier and more successful years.

Somerset were the most amateur county of all. In 1923 they only employed two professionals, and they made a virtue of it. One committeeman called the county 'the last hope of amateurism' while another, at a dinner, declared, "Somerset play cricket as it should be played. They haven't won the championship, they never will, and I don't want them to, either."

Among it all they did have good players, none better in those years than the unhurried, ruddy-faced farmer Jack White, a slow-left-arm bowler who, in the words of Robertson-Glasgow, 'perplexed and imprisoned batsmen by an accuracy of length, a subtlety of flight and a pertinacity of spirit which can rarely have been combined in any other cricketer'. When the England selectors persuaded him to leave his cows and tour Australia in 1928/29, he helped to win the Ashes with 25 wickets in the series.

'Farmer' Jack White
Somerset's greatest wicket-taker, 1909-37

George Geary
Leicestershire stalwart, 1912-38

Johnny Douglas
Essex captain, 1911-28

The county, though most years making a loss, had five professionals by 1929, though they still drew their share of occasionals from the amateur ranks. That year, with Wally Luckes struggling with his health, they used nine keepers, one of whom, Michael Spurway, an Oxford undergraduate from a well-connected county family, had hardly played all summer. At the Bath Festival one evening the older Jack MacBryan plied him with whisky, and he woke with a fearful hangover. "I went to the thermal baths, hoping that the atmosphere there would make me feel better, but it didn't. I really played very badly. I dropped two catches, and one of the guys went on to a hundred."

The next year they gave five games to Seymour Clark, who was keeping wicket on a primitive recreation ground for a team of railwaymen in Weston-super-Mare. By all accounts he was a fine keeper, but he had only taken up the game three years earlier and he had no idea about batting. His highest score for his railway team was 3, and in nine innings for Somerset he failed to score a run. He even managed to be bowled when Essex's Peter Smith, taking pity, offered him a ball that bounced twice before reaching him.

Against Yorkshire's Wilfred Rhodes he survived four balls before spooning a catch to silly mid-off. "I'm glad I got you when I did," Rhodes told him with uncharacteristic humour. "You seemed to be getting on top of me." Clark, preferring the security of his job, returned to the railways, for whose team he never did reach double figures with the bat.

Leicestershire had more professionals. In 1920 they were an elderly team, their eight regulars having an average age of 41, and for several years they were short of reliable batting. In 1924 they were dismissed for under 100 fourteen times, with their batsmen only managing one century between them, yet somehow they won seven matches and finished 11th. The *Cricketer* magazine wrote of them in 1926 that they were 'engaged in floating complacently down the streams of Time'.

Like Essex and Somerset they played the best cricket they could for the entertainment of their members. Nobody expected them to be challenging for the title, but from time to time they produced a cricketer good enough to play for England. The greatest was George Geary, a fast-medium bowler and useful batsman from the shoe-making village of Barwell. One of 16 children in a two-up, two-down house, he often had to eat his meals on the stairs. Yet, in a hard-working, uncomplicated way, he gave his life to cricket, and he finished up coaching at Charterhouse, a great influence on the young Peter May.

One Thursday afternoon at Pontypridd in August 1929, he received a telegram, telling him to report to the Oval for the Test on Saturday. Then he went into the field and, inside two hours, took all ten Glamorgan wickets for 18 runs. It was a world record, and he went home to his wife in fine spirits.

"I've done well today, missis. Took all ten wickets. For 18."

She said nothing, then pointed to the kitchen hearth.

"I've left you the stove to black-lead."

1927: The revolution is cancelled

"Pray God no professional ever captain England," was Lord Hawke's outraged response to a newspaper article in which Cec Parkin, the Lancashire bowler, had wondered what was wrong with the idea of Jack Hobbs or Herbert Sutcliffe, both fine men, captaining their country.

That was in early 1925 when Hawke's Yorkshire had just appointed a new captain: the 46-year-old Major Arthur Lupton, who had played one game for the county back in 1908. At the same time Northamptonshire were turning to the Honourable Maurice Fitzroy, an Old Etonian who was the son of a local MP. He had never played a first-class match.

Both men did well in their first year. Yorkshire were champions again, while Northants enjoyed unaccustomed success, winning nine matches. Yet neither captain was a cricketer of first-class standard, especially not Lupton who did not bowl and with the bat contributed barely six runs a match.

Lupton was one more in a succession of men trying to fill Lord Hawke's great shoes. The first, Everard Radcliffe, was pitch-forked into the job at short notice, at a point when the team was in decline, and he soon realised his error:

> I was certainly not a good enough player and, with increasing bouts of ear trouble and giddiness, I had neither the fitness nor the health for the job. I completely failed, and I cannot say I enjoyed the experience!

Lupton was more robust, and even at the age of 49, after three years, he wanted to carry on. The Yorkshire committee, however, had other ideas. They were not happy that Lancashire, under the inspiring captaincy of Leonard Green, had won the title two years in succession. Green was a fine all-round sportsman, a Colonel in the Territorial Army who had won a Military Cross in the war and owned a textile company in Clitheroe. If only Yorkshire could find a man of that calibre!

There was no such person available so in November 1927 the Yorkshire committee took a decision that shook the world of English cricket. With Lord Hawke presiding, they decided by 13 votes to 11 to appoint the 32-year-old Herbert Sutcliffe, a professional cricketer, as captain for 1928. Then, in an even more shocking move, they voted by 19 votes to five that he need not become an amateur to do the job.

The prime mover was Alderman Richard Ingham, a self-made man with a worsted spinning business in Pudsey. Sutcliffe, a Pudsey boy, had been his protégé, and Ingham saw in him the same qualities that had led him to rise from humble roots to make a success of his life. He was not wrong in that. Of

Herbert Sutcliffe with Alderman Richard Ingham. Sutcliffe married Ingham's secretary Emmie.

all the professionals of that generation Sutcliffe, with his great self-discipline, his ambition and his supreme cricketing ability, was the best equipped to cope with such a ground-breaking role. Jack Hobbs would also have commanded the necessary respect but, as a more deferential character than Sutcliffe, he would not have wanted or enjoyed the responsibility.

First reactions to the news were overwhelmingly positive. Arthur Lupton, whose services had been discarded, called Sutcliffe "a gentleman and a sportsman to his fingertips". Jack Hobbs was glad they had avoided "the air of unreality" that would have come from Sutcliffe turning amateur. Bobby Abel, the great pre-war Surrey batsman, said: "It would have been a revolution in my day, but the war did much to level things up." The progressive CB Fry noted that Sutcliffe had served as an officer in the Sherwood Foresters: "It is an excellent thing for cricket. Surely if a man is good enough to hold an Army commission in the greatest war in history, he is good enough to lead a county team."

Then the problems started. It soon became clear that Lord Hawke was one of those who had voted against, and many joined him in lamenting the demise of the amateur captain. 'In the long run,' the *Yorkshire Evening Post* said, 'cricket will suffer a vital loss if amateurism, and the spirit of amateurism, is wiped out.' The *Sunday Post* put it more colourfully: 'Yorkshire are laying themselves open to the charge that their team is intended to be a victory-producing machine and nothing else.'

A second problem then arose. The 50-year-old Wilfred Rhodes was the senior professional, and he was not happy, telling a reporter that he thought "after playing so long, the committee would have given me the first chance of refusal of the captaincy." Furthermore, he was sorry Major Lupton was not being retained. He would rather have an amateur captain.

In no time everybody in Yorkshire had an opinion. Disgruntled members threatened to resign, and one – Sidney Grimshaw, a Leeds stockbroker who was a Rhodes supporter – organised a ballot of all seven thousand members.

YORKSHIRE COUNTY CRICKET CAPTAINCY.

(1) Are you in favour of the appointment of an Amateur or a Professional ?

_____

(2) If it is not possible to secure a suitable Amateur, whom are you in favour of—Wilfred Rhodes or Herbert Sutcliffe ?

_____

Signature_____

Address _____

Date_____

As it may not be possible to secure a suitable Amateur, will you please vote upon *both* propositions ?

While all this was going on, Sutcliffe was on tour in South Africa where his England captain was Ronald Stanyforth, an army captain whose only first-class cricket had been for MCC, the Army and the Combined Services.

Grimshaw received more than 3,000 ballot papers, with 83% voting for an amateur captain. The choice between the two professionals ran almost two to one in favour of Rhodes.

Sutcliffe, with great dignity, sent a telegram, declining the offer of captaincy, and the committee, reconvening, turned to an amateur, William Worsley, to lead the county in 1928.

In the whole history of the championship no captain has been appointed with less experience of good cricket than Worsley. The newspapers, keen to show their enthusiasm, made much of his innings of 42 for Eton against Harrow in 1909. They also noted that in 1924, at his own ground at Hovingham Hall, he had scored 135 for Major Walker's XI against the Yorkshire Gentlemen's XI. The *Yorkshire Post* was full of optimism:

> It is reasonable to expect that, when he becomes accustomed to what we may term the atmosphere of county cricket, Yorkshire's new captain will give dash and enterprise to the middle section of the batting.

He did not do that, scoring 235 runs in 28 matches, and his two years as captain did not bring the championship back to Yorkshire. The team was in transition, but he kept it going well enough as did his successor Alan Barber, a young schoolmaster. The title would be theirs seven times in the 1930s.

"I never counted the captain in the Yorkshire side," the professional Maurice Leyland once said, "but we won a few championships with the handicap of one."

So close to leading a social revolution in 1928, Yorkshire would not be captained by a professional till 1960.

Leonard Green
Lancashire captain, 1926-28

Maurice Fitzroy
Northants captain, 1925-27

Arthur Lupton
Yorkshire captain, 1925-27

William Worsley
Yorkshire captain, 1928-29

1930 – 1939

Yorkshire seven times champions

More financial problems for the lesser counties

War ends play in 1939

When things were good, counties launched out into all manner of expenses without being certain of the means to pay for them. Wages were doubled, huge stands were erected, nurseries set up, coaches retained – all to a degree that was never warranted.

The Cricketer, September 1931

Of recent times first-class cricket has had to face many difficulties. A series of wet summers brought some counties to the brink of bankruptcy; economic conditions make it harder than of old for amateurs to spare the time to appear frequently. Yet cricket still keeps up its end when the sun shines. The membership of most of the counties is far larger than in pre-war times; crowds are as big as ever on days of holiday when the weather is respectable; and the teams and their merits and demerits are discussed on all sides as if they stood among the most vital things of life.

The Observer, August, 1935

County cricket is in the same position as the voluntary hospitals, namely that it is subsisting on response to appeals.

Sir Home Gordon, April 1939

1930 As in 1929, all counties play 28 matches. It remains 8 for a win; 5 for a draw if ahead on first innings, 3 if behind. There is dissatisfaction that the system puts too much emphasis on first-innings points, leading to the championship being won by Lancashire, with 10 wins, ahead of Gloucestershire, with 15.
The summer's Tests against Australia are played over four days, rather than the traditional three.
Football's first World Cup is held in Uruguay in July. The hosts beat Argentina 4-2 in the final. Only 13 countries enter, and the refereeing generates much comment. In one match, with six minutes remaining, France are about to equalise against Argentina when the referee blows for time. In another the Bolivian coach is the referee, and he awards five penalties.

1931 The points system is changed. It is now 15 for a win; 5 for a draw if ahead on first innings, 3 if behind.
After two blank days at Sheffield the Yorkshire and Gloucestershire captains each declare their first innings after one ball. Despite expressions of disapproval, three other matches follow the same course later in the summer.
The wicket is increased in size: from 28 to 29 inches in height and from 8 to 9 inches in width.
New Zealand play a Test series in England for the first time.
Trolley buses are introduced in London.

1932 To eliminate the 'freak declarations' of the previous summer, one-day laws are introduced for games where there is no play on the first two days. The points awarded are 10 for a win, 3 for a defeat.
India play their first ever Test match, losing to England at Lord's.
One quarter of the British labour force is now out of work.

1933 After four years, the counties revert to playing different numbers of matches, with a minimum of 24.
The year begins with an international row over England's 'bodyline' bowling in the Ashes series in Australia.
In the FA Cup Final the players wear numbers on the backs of their shirts.

1934 Sir Walter Lawrence, a wealthy Hertfordshire builder, donates a trophy and £100 of credit at Harrods to the scorer of the fastest hundred of the summer. The 47-year-old Frank Woolley, in 63 minutes, is the first winner.
In an attempt to reduce the rising number of deaths on the roads, 30mph speed limits are imposed in urban areas, pedestrian crossings with blinking lights are introduced, and new motorists are required to take a test.

1935 An experimental lbw law is introduced, allowing a batsman to be out when the ball pitches outside the off stump.
Allen Lane publishes the first ten books in a revolutionary new series of sixpenny paperbacks called Penguins.

1936 Derbyshire win the championship. They are only the second county outside the Big Six to do so.
At the Radio Exhibition at Olympia television sets show the BBC's first talking pictures.
At the Winter Olympics in Bavaria Great Britain wins the ice hockey gold medal. Other countries are unhappy that nine of Great Britain's 13-man squad have grown up in Canada.

1937 An MCC commission reports on the dire financial state of county cricket. In an emergency, it says, only Kent, Middlesex and Yorkshire would not have to resort to appeals or borrowing. It recommends the establishment of a County Cricket Fund, 'to give help to necessitous first-class counties', and the reduction of the championship to 15 sides.
The Government launches a 'Fitter Britain' campaign. More playing fields, swimming pools and gymnasia are planned, specialist teachers will be trained at a new college, and a Propaganda Committee is set up 'to recommend means whereby the desire for physical well-being can be stimulated and maintained in all sections of the community'.

1938 The points system changes again: 12 for a win, 4 for first-innings lead in a draw, 8 for a win in a one-day match. Average points-per-match replaces the more complicated percentages.
The Lord's Test against Australia is televised.
Prime Minister Neville Chamberlain flies to Germany to negotiate a 'peace in our time' treaty.

1939 As a one-summer experiment eight-ball overs are introduced in England.
On 1 September German troops enter Poland. Two days later Britain declares war against Germany.

Championship – top three

1930

	P	W	L	D	Pts
Lancashire	28	10	0	18	155
Gloucestershire	28	15	4	9	152
Yorkshire	28	11	2	15	150

Leading batsmen (*Runs*)

- A. Sandham (Surrey) — 1,884
- W.W. Whysall (Notts) — 1,866
- F.E. Woolley (Kent) — 1,823

Leading bowlers (*Wickets*)

- A.P. Freeman (Kent) — 249
- C.W.L. Parker (Glos) — 162
- T.B. Mitchell (Derbys) — 134

Leading wkt-keeper / Leading fielder (*Victims*)

- L.E.G. Ames (Kent) — 82
- A.T. Barber (Yorks) — 31
- C.J. Barnett (Glos) — 31

1931

	P	W	L	D	Pts
Yorkshire	28	16	1	11	287
Gloucestershire	28	11	4	13	219
Kent	28	12	7	9	216

Leading batsmen

- E.H. Hendren (Middx) — 2,122
- H. Sutcliffe (Yorks) — 2,049
- K.S. Duleepsinhji (Sussex) — 1,857

Leading bowlers

- A.P. Freeman (Kent) — 241
- C.W.L. Parker (Glos) — 205
- H. Verity (Yorks) — 138

Leading wkt-keeper / fielder

- H. Elliott (Derbys) — 71
- W.R. Hammond (Glos) — 38

1932

	P	W	L	D	Pts
Yorkshire	28	19	2	7	315
Sussex	28	14	1	13	262
Kent	28	14	3	11	248

Leading batsmen

- H. Sutcliffe (Yorks) — 2,624
- W.R. Hammond (Glos) — 2,039
- G.E. Tyldesley (Lancs) — 1,962

Leading bowlers

- A.P. Freeman (Kent) — 209
- W.E. Bowes (Yorks) — 160
- T.W.J. Goddard (Glos) — 159

Leading wkt-keeper / fielder

- L.E.G. Ames (Kent) — 84
- W.R. Hammond (Glos) — 43

1933

	P	W	L	D	Pts	%
Yorkshire	30	19	3	8	315	70.0
Sussex	32	18	5	9	311	64.8
Kent	30	15	8	7	253	56.2

Leading batsmen

- W.R. Hammond (Glos) — 2,578
- E.H. Hendren (Middx) — 2,479
- C.P. Mead (Hants) — 2,478

Leading bowlers

- A.P. Freeman (Kent) — 252
- T.W.J. Goddard (Glos) — 170
- H. Verity (Yorks) — 153

Leading wkt-keeper / fielder

- H. Elliott (Derbys) — 81
- J.G. Langridge (Sussex) — 59

1934

	P	W	L	D	Pts	%
Lancashire	30	13	3	14	257	57.1
Sussex	30	12	2	16	243	54.0
Derbyshire	28	12	6	10	223	53.1

Leading batsmen

- H.H.I.H. Gibbons (Worcs) — 2,452
- F.E. Woolley (Kent) — 2,447
- J. Iddon (Lancs) — 2,261

Leading bowlers

- A.P. Freeman (Kent) — 187
- G.A.E. Pains (Warwicks) — 150
- C.I.J. Smith (Middx) — 139

Leading wkt-keeper / fielder

- G. Duckworth (Lancs) — 77
- J.G. Langridge (Sussex) — 44

1935

	P	W	L	D	Pts	%
Yorkshire	30	19	1	10	321	71.3
Derbyshire	28	16	6	6	266	63.3
Middlesex	24	11	5	8	202	56.1

Leading batsmen

- F.E. Woolley (Kent) — 2,187
- H. Sutcliffe (Yorks) — 1,966
- W.R. Hammond (Glos) — 1,803
- J.G. Langridge (Sussex) — 1,803

Leading bowlers

- A.P. Freeman (Kent) — 201
- T.W.J. Goddard (Glos) — 189
- H. Verity (Yorks) — 161

Leading wkt-keeper / fielder

- H. Elliott (Derbys) — 88
- J.G. Langridge (Sussex) — 41

1936

	P	W	L	D	Pts	%
Derbyshire	28	13	4	11	239	56.9
Middlesex	26	10	4	12	203	52.1
Yorkshire	30	10	2	18	230	51.1

Leading batsmen

- E.H. Hendren (Middx) — 1,963
- E. Paynter (Lancs) — 1,930
- C.J. Barnett (Glos) — 1,885

Leading bowlers

- A.R. Gover (Surrey) — 171
- H. Verity (Yorks) — 153
- R.A. Sinfield (Glos) — 146

Leading wkt-keeper / fielder

- E.W.J. Brooks (Surrey) — 72
- R.H. Moore (Hants) — 34

1937

	P	W	L	D	Pts	%
Yorkshire	28	18	2	8	302	71.9
Middlesex	24	15	4	5	246	68.3
Derbyshire	28	14	6	8	240	57.1

Leading batsmen

- J.H. Parks (Sussex) — 2,578
- W.R. Hammond (Glos) — 2,393
- J.G. Langridge (Sussex) — 2,364

Leading bowlers

- T.W.J. Goddard (Glos) — 215
- J.C. Clay (Glam) — 170
- H. Verity (Yorks) — 157

Leading wkt-keeper / fielder

- W.F.F. Price (Middx) — 78
- M.J. Turnbull (Glam) — 44

1938

	P	W	L	D	Pts	Ave
Yorkshire	28	20	2	6	256	9.1
Middlesex	22	15	5	2	184	8.4
Surrey	25	12	6	7	172	6.9

Leading batsmen

- J.G. Langridge (Sussex) — 2,302
- A.E. Fagg (Kent) — 2,297
- W.R. Hammond (Glos) — 2,180

Leading bowlers

- A.W. Wellard (Som) — 167
- M.S. Nichols (Essex) — 143
- R. Pollard (Lancs) — 139

Leading wkt-keeper / fielder

- W. Farrimond (Lancs) — 76
- B.O. Allen (Glos) — 40

1939

	P	W	L	D	Pts	Ave
Yorkshire	28	20	4	4	260	9.3
Middlesex	22	14	6	2	180	8.2
Gloucestershire	26	15	7	4	196	7.5

Leading batsmen

- L. Hutton (Yorks) — 2,167
- W.R. Hammond (Glos) — 2,121
- J.G. Langridge (Sussex) — 2,106

Leading bowlers

- T.W.J. Goddard (Glos) — 181
- H. Verity (Yorks) — 165
- R.T.D. Perks (Worcs) — 143

Leading wkt-keeper / fielder

- W.F.F. Price (Middx) — 73
- J.G. Langridge (Sussex) — 43
- A. Mitchell (Yorks) — 43

1930-1939

Leading counties

	P	W	L	D	%W
Yorkshire	288	164	26	98	56.9
Kent	283	114	90	79	40.3
Derbyshire	274	107	71	96	39.1
Sussex	298	112	67	119	37.6

Leading batsmen

W.R. Hammond (Glos)	19,123
H.H.I.H. Gibbons (Worcs)	16,103
H. Sutcliffe (Yorks)	15,990
J. O'Connor (Essex)	15,951

Leading bowlers

T.W.J. Goddard (Glos)	1,536
A.P. Freeman (Kent)	1,442
H. Verity (Yorks)	1,304
T.B. Mitchell (Derbys)	1,229

Leading keepers & fielder

H. Elliott (Derbys)	679
W.F.F. Price (Middx)	620
J.G. Langridge (Sussex)	320

Overall statistics

Runs per wicket	25.6
Runs per 100 balls	45.5
% of matches drawn	39.6

Miscellany

Cyril Perkins, a slow-left-arm bowler for Northants from 1934 to 1937, holds the unenviable record of playing most championship matches, 54, without ever being on the winning side. "We did get a bit despondent at times," he said, "but in the end you get so used to not winning that you just accept it."

He played for Suffolk till 1967 and was named in 2000 in the Minor Counties Team of the Century.

*

At Derby in 1937 Warwickshire captain Bob Wyatt had no hesitation in opting to bat first. The pitch 'looked full of runs', and at Edgbaston a fortnight earlier he had hit the Derbyshire bowlers for a career-best 232 in a total of 523 for seven.

Fast bowler Bill Copson was returning after three weeks out with a bad knee. Bowling fast and accurately, swinging the ball both ways, he struck four times as Wyatt's men slumped to 21 for six. Rolls Royce and LMS workers, on the first day of their annual holiday, cheered with pride, and they cheered even more when Copson finished the innings by hitting the stumps with four successive balls.

When in the evening the visitors batted again, his second ball also hit the stumps, making him the first bowler ever to take five wickets in six balls.

At Bristol in 1938 the unassuming Middlesex fast bowler 'Big Jim' Smith hit a fifty in 11 minutes, the fastest ever recorded off proper bowling in first-class cricket. It beat the previous record of 14 minutes, which he himself had equalled three years earlier at Maidstone.

Weighing 18 stone, he possessed only two real scoring shots. To anything of good length he plunged down his left foot and swung his bat ferociously in the direction of long-on. To anything short, he played a violent 'half-arm jolt'. Sometimes in the great whirl of his bat one hand came off the handle.

True always to his method, Smith hit 15 fifties, and a century at Canterbury in 1939, which the great crowd rose to a man to cheer. The Kent coach, the stylish former amateur Gerry Weigall, dismissed it as 'a prostitution of batting'.

*

Arthur Fagg, Kent's exciting young opener, broke into the England team in the summer of 1936, only to contract rheumatic fever that winter in Australia. Brought home on a stretcher, he missed the whole 1937 season.

He returned with a bang in 1938, hitting nine centuries. At Colchester against Essex he hit 244 in five hours in the first innings and 202* in under three hours in the second, the only man ever to hit two double-hundreds in the same match.

The championship in the 1930s

The champion counties of the 1930s were all from the north. Lancashire won in 1930 and '34, Derbyshire in '36 and Yorkshire in the other seven years. Southern counties challenged for the title each year, notably Gloucestershire, Sussex, Kent and Middlesex, but the character of their cricket had a stronger streak of amateurism, with a reluctance to put championship points above all else.

Northern counties drew their players from fiercely contested leagues while in the south, till the late 1960s, club cricket was a social game. Indeed, membership of the powerful Club Cricket Conference upheld the amateur ideal so fervently that it made it a condition of membership that a club did not play in 'any organised cricket league' and did not 'provide remuneration' for its players.

In 1930 the difference in approach was reflected at the top of the county table. With five points for a win and three for a draw with first-innings lead, Lancashire with just ten victories finished above Gloucestershire who, under the enterprising captaincy of Bev Lyon, won 15. That led inevitably to another change in the points system, the first of several in the decade.

The post-war boom in attendance had died away, there were some wet summers, and the smaller counties, burdened by having to play 28 fixtures, fell once more into financial difficulty. In 1934, to help them, the counties reverted to playing differing numbers of games.

Sussex enjoyed success. The summer of 1930 began with the opening of a modern scoreboard at Hove, donated by the sons of the late Sir Hildebrand Harmsworth, of the Northcliffe/Harmsworth newspaper family. And what a first day the board had! In 5½ hours of magical strokeplay Sussex's Duleepsinhji, 'scoring all round the wicket with delightful ease', hit 333 runs.

Kumar Shri Duleepsinhji

His 333 remained the most runs scored in a single day of county cricket till Brian Lara, going from 111 to 501, hit 390 in a day at Edgbaston in 1994.

In three successive seasons Sussex finished in second place. They might have won in 1932 if Duleep had not fallen ill, but their greatest disappointment came in 1934. They led the table through much of the summer and could still have won, had they beaten Lancashire at Eastbourne in late August. They lost the toss, however, and their northern visitors, having secured a first-innings lead, shut the game down. On a good pitch, in front of an increasingly disgruntled crowd, the Lancashire batsmen opted to play safe. That was the logic of the championship, as *The Times* observed:

> Championships may be a nuisance, but they exist and so long as they exist so must teams be expected to try to win them. It was hard on the crowd; it was all extremely uninteresting, but this is a world in which championships have their part.

Lancashire's star player that summer, symbolising their cricket, was the all-rounder Len Hopwood. He hit 1,583 runs as a patient right-handed opener with a minimal back-lift and took 110 wickets with orthodox left-arm spin. 'A utilitarian cricketer' is what his obituary in the 1986 *Wisden* called him. 'One cannot imagine any spectator looking back across 50 years and exclaiming nostalgically, "What fun he was to watch!"'

At the other end of the table Leicestershire were close to folding up. They approached Lincolnshire with a view to playing as a joint team, with some games at Skegness, but the minor county rejected them. They only stayed solvent thanks to the benevolence of Julien Cahn, a man who had made a fortune from selling furniture on hire purchase. When the county found themselves without a captain, he hired the New Zealander Stewie Dempster to manage one of his shops and, in the process, to qualify for the county so that he could captain them as an amateur in 1936.

With Dempster not yet eligible, the Secretary, Lieutenant-Commander Geoffrey Webb, stood in as captain for the first game of 1935, taking the team to Gravesend where they were beaten in two days. For the next game, at home to Sussex, the 47-year-old professional Ewart Astill was left in charge. In a major upset they beat a full-strength Sussex side by an innings, playing positive cricket, and it was decided to leave Astill to captain the whole summer. After thirty years

with the county, he was held in respect by the team, he knew the game inside out, and he had an outgoing, urbane manner that dealt well with social situations. He also had a pair of bowlers, Haydon Smith and George Geary, who could bowl sides out, particularly in that first summer of the new lbw law when batsmen could no longer pad away balls pitching outside off stump. When in the last match Smith and Geary bowled out Kent for 56, they set a new county record of 12 victories in a season, finishing in sixth place. The following year Astill returned to the ranks, and Leicestershire found themselves in familiar territory near the foot of the table. The time was not yet ripe for a professional captain.

Yorkshire were the county to beat. They had two of the finest bowlers of the era, the medium-quick Bill Bowes and the slow-left-armer Hedley Verity. They had great batsmen in the ever-reliable Herbert Sutcliffe, the powerful Maurice Leyland and the young Len Hutton. And among the lesser names there were seven who were good enough to represent England during those years. They played with a fierce, unyielding spirit, led from 1933 by Brian Sellers, whose iron discipline was mixed with sharp tactical acumen and infectious enthusiasm.

Sutcliffe played all 21 seasons between the wars, his batting crucial in the winning of 12 championships. He was methodical in everything he did, a self-made man who scored 2,000 runs in a record 14 consecutive summers and who instilled in the team's youngsters the standards of dress and behaviour expected of Yorkshire's professional cricketers.

But perhaps, in identifying the special greatness of the Yorkshire side of the 1930s, even Sutcliffe must take second place to Hedley Verity – as a match-winner and as a man. The son of a Leeds coal merchant and Methodist lay preacher, Verity stepped into the impossibly large shoes of Wilfred Rhodes, and such were his achievements that soon enough Yorkshire folk were arguing which of them was the greater.

In 1932, on a sticky wicket at Headingley, he took all ten Nottinghamshire wickets for ten runs, the best bowling figures in the history of the game, and at Lord's in 1934, in a Test against Australia, he took 14 wickets in a day. The latter performance brought out the best of Neville Cardus:

> Beautiful left-handed spin, there is nothing like it. The click of the finger, the spit of venom on the ground. The record-hunters will revel in his figures. And the gods of the game, who sit up aloft and watch, will remember the loveliness of it all, the style, the poise on light toes, the swing of the arm from noon to evening.

In a great Yorkshire side, Verity was a great, great bowler.

Some players of the 1930s

A true great of the game
36 double-centuries

Wally Hammond of Gloucestershire

> I cannot imagine that there was ever a more beautiful or majestic off-side stroke
> player, or one with more power, than Wally Hammond. *Les Ames*
> Walter Hammond was the finest player I ever saw on all types of wicket. He made
> batting appear ridiculously easy, and it never is that. *Len Hutton*

For many Hammond remains the greatest cricketer England has ever produced. On all the
surfaces of county cricket, he scored big runs and he scored them in a style that dominated
the bowlers, thrilled the crowds and won matches. He could be aloof and moody, leading
some to wonder how many runs he might have scored had he been always in the right frame
of mind. Nevertheless six seasons in a row he topped the national batting averages.

As a slip fielder he had no equal, taking a record 78 first-class catches in 1928. "My word!
Doesn't he see them quick!" Len Hutton exclaimed when he fielded next to him. He was also a
fine, if reluctant, medium-quick bowler who, one summer in his youth, took 84 wickets. Had
he bowled more, one team-mate reckoned, Gloucestershire would have won championships.

As a physical specimen Hammond was supreme, strong and graceful, with an aura from
the moment he stepped out of the pavilion. Robertson-Glasgow, one of many bowlers who
suffered at his hands, wrote of the intimidating effect of seeing him 'taking guard at 11.50
a.m., when lunch seemed far and the boundary near'.

He was a superman in county cricket, with all sorts of theories propounded about the
origins of his greatness. Someone even suggested that he blinked less than anybody else.

'Tich' Freeman of Kent

> Upon so many English batsmen Freeman imposed the belief that he could not be
> either played or hit, and he winnowed the faint-hearted like chaff. This was his
> greatness. No slow bowler within memory has cast such a spell on batsmen short
> of the highest class. *RC Robertson-Glasgow*

Alfred Percy Freeman was the quietest of men. Seeing him with his pack of cards playing
patience in the dressing room, hearing him turn down a drink for fear of displeasing his
wife Ethel, watching him trot his five paces to the bowling crease, it was hard to believe
that 'Tich', just 5'2" tall, was the greatest destroyer of batsmen county cricket has ever seen.

No one has come close to his 304 first-class wickets in the summer of 1928 – nor his 298 in
1933 when, at the age of 45, he bowled 2,039 overs. He took ten wickets in an innings three
times; 30 wickets in a week at Folkestone in 1932. Only starting his county career in earnest at
the age of 31, he took an extraordinary 2,222 first-class wickets after his 40th birthday.

There was a view, based on two indifferent tours of Australia, that his leg spin was
ineffective against the best batting. But, as one newspaper put it, 'If that were true, three-
fourths of the batsmen in county cricket are bad.' Many of them stayed rooted to the crease,
unable to tell leg-break from googly or to keep out his quicker top-spinner. Others, when
they advanced, found themselves stumped by Les Ames. In 1932 Ames made 64 stumpings.

Yes, he would have taken fewer wickets if Kent had had other bowlers of his class. And
yes, he was hit about at times but, as Ames wrote, 'Punishment never seemed to worry the
little wizard. His imperturbable mental outlook was one of his most valuable assets.'

When he finally retired, at the age of 48, he called his house Dunbowlin.

Most wickets in county cricket
*3,151 championship wickets
between 1914 and 1936*

Harold Larwood of Nottinghamshire

> Larwood has greater speed than anyone else; he has a control of length and direction that is simply marvellous, and he has the stamina to make the use of his speed when he is nursed correctly.
>
> *Herbert Sutcliffe*

A miner from Annesley Colliery, 'Lol' Larwood arrived at Trent Bridge in 1923 as a shy, pasty-faced 18-year-old with a strong neck, powerful shoulders and a raw fast-bowling talent. The coach Jim Iremonger created a classical action, the captain Arthur Carr built him up with beer, and he soon became the fastest and most-feared bowler in county cricket. With the tall left-armer Bill Voce at the other end, there was nowhere for a batsman to hide – as Leicestershire discovered in 1932 when the two men, unchanged, bowled them out twice inside three hours.

That winter, under Douglas Jardine, he helped to win back the Ashes, but the physical strain and the political fall-out took its toll on a quiet man who was happiest when tending his chrysanthemums or feeding the chickens on his smallholding. Stubborn to a fault he never played for England again, but for Notts he gave his all. In 1936, for the fifth time in his career, he topped the national averages.

The fastest
141 first-class wickets in 1932 – one every 29 balls

Alf Gover of Surrey

Great heart

The only out-and-out fast bowler since the 19th century to take 200 wickets in a season twice.

> A more hard-working fast bowler I have never known.
>
> *Errol Holmes*

The long, enthusiastic run-up of Alf Gover, all elbow and knees, was one of the great sights of the 1930s. Len Hutton called him 'one of cricket's greathearts', a bowler who never gave up, no matter how unresponsive the pitches at the Oval. Undoubtedly there were years when his captains overbowled him, but he was such a willing workhorse it was easy to do. Even in 1947, when at the age of 38 he bowled almost 1,000 overs, he refused the suggestion that he might shorten his run: "They pay to see me running in, old boy."

His most famous moment came in India when he rushed in on his long run and, with ball still in hand, ran through the crease, on towards the pavilion and straight into the toilets.

After his playing days he ran an influential cricket school in Wandsworth. He was the best coach in England, attracting all the great stars from Ray Lindwall to Viv Richards; he had an astute business brain; and, for all the ramshackle nature of the building, he knew how to create a magical environment and to inspire future generations of cricketers.

Arthur Wellard of Somerset

> His lusty, zestful spirit added tonic to the most listless game. He challenged fate blithely, even recklessly, and whether his gambles came off or not, the crowd loved him. *Bill Andrews*

Arthur Wellard may have been a Kentishman, but his easy-going, cheerful approach to life found a natural home in the West Country. He might have seemed a lazy man, a cricketer of natural gifts who never took a proper job in winter or learned to drive, who was at his happiest in a bar with a pint, a fag and an audience for his stories – or a gullible opponent for his ultra-sharp poker skills.

Yet on the field, however great the perspiration on his well-tanned face, however many catches went down in the slips, he would bowl and bowl, often switching to off-breaks when his role with the new ball was done. In 1938, at the age of 36, he bowled 1,233 overs and took 172 wickets.

The Somerset folk loved him for that, but they loved even more the seemingly nonchalant way he swung his bat. In 1935 his 1,232 runs included 66 sixes, most of them straight down the ground and out of it. Twice at Wells he hit five in an over. But he was no slogger and no simpleton. He was an observant, intelligent man whose aim in life was to enjoy himself. In so doing, he gave great pleasure.

"Watcher, cock"
Most wickets in3 1938

Stories of the 1930s

Death on the roads

The roads of England were as dangerous in the 1930s as they have ever been. In one week in July 1934, 180 people were killed, five times as many as are killed in a week now, and a further 6,000 were injured. Cars had few safety devices, roads were not well designed, and many drivers, with no organised system of instruction, raced along at inappropriate speeds.

The Times called for offenders to be 'justly punished'. In January 1935, within a month of this editorial, Vallance Jupp, former captain of Northamptonshire and a current player, was jailed for nine months for his part in an accident in which he had overtaken at speed on a hill, lost control of his car and killed the pillion passenger on an oncoming motorcycle.

The following year Northamptonshire, without a win all summer, played their last match at Chesterfield. Thanks to a brilliant 241 by their England opener Fred Bakewell, they came close to beating the new champions Derbyshire. Bakewell celebrated with 'four or five beers', then climbed into the passenger seat of the near-teetotal Reggie Northway's car. Their team-mate Jack Timms knew the route, and on dark, unfamiliar roads they followed behind him.

Bakewell fell into a deep sleep and, when he woke, he was in hospital. Had Northway fallen asleep at the wheel? Had he driven too fast over a hump-back bridge? All anybody knew was that Timms, wondering why they were no longer following him, had turned back and had found the car in a hedge, their two cricket bags thrown out and Northway lying dead in a ditch. Bakewell survived, but he was too badly injured ever to play cricket again.

Seven days later Gloucestershire played their last game, against a strong Nottinghamshire side at the Wagon Works ground in Gloucester. It was Tom Goddard's benefit match, and after the first day it looked possible that there would be no third-day takings for the off-spinner. "Don't you worry, Tom," Wally Hammond is reputed to have told Goddard on Saturday night, "I'll make sure it lasts" – and on Monday he hit an imperious 317. An innings victory followed on Tuesday afternoon when the jubilant crowd gathered in front of the little pavilion to hear a speech from their young captain Dallas Page whose first summer in charge had ended so well. "I am looking forward to next season with confidence," he told them. On his way home, a motorbike came out of a side road, Page swerved into a stone wall and, although he crawled out of his upturned car, he died that night of internal bleeding.

Charlie Bull   *Dallas Page*

Others to die on the road were Sussex's George Street, Essex's Dudley Pope and Lancashire's great bowler Ted McDonald, who was by then playing in the leagues.

In May 1939 Alex Snowden, another from Northants, was injured on the Saturday night of his team's game at Derby and was unable to resume his not-out innings on Monday.

A week later, tragedy struck at Chelmsford. On the Sunday of the bank-holiday match, several players went for a round of golf, eating in the evening at the Chase Roundhouse at Ingatestone. Worcestershire opener Charlie Bull and keeper Syd Buller were set to return to the hotel by taxi when they were offered a lift in a Morris two-seater. Bull perched on Buller's knee and, halfway up the hill at Margaretting, he screamed "Look out!" With no warning signal on the dark road, a lorry had stopped to repair its back light, the car hit the lorry, and Bull died almost instantly from a fractured skull.

Five years earlier, in the very same Whit fixture at Chelmsford, a Worcester batsman, Maurice Nichol, had been found dead in bed on the Monday morning, from a heart attack. As then, the cricketers decided to carry on.

In front of a 5,000 crowd and watched from the balcony of the adjoining hospital by the broken-ribbed Buller, the nine men of Worcester lined up for a two-minute silence, then tried their mournful best to play the game. Hugo Yarnold, their reserve keeper who had been scoring, took the gloves, and his duties in the box passed to the 19-year-old Margaret Platts, a doctor's daughter described in the local paper as 'a brunette and a popular young lady in Chelmsford'. It was the first time a woman had been the scorer in a county match.

As late as the 1960s, when the players of all the other counties were allowed to go by car, Worcestershire and Northants, haunted by these events, were still travelling in coaches.

A partnership of 555 – or was it 554?

At Leyton in June 1932 Percy Holmes and Herbert Sutcliffe of Yorkshire scored 555 runs for the first wicket against Essex, beating by one run the world record set by John Tunnicliffe and Jack Brown, also for Yorkshire, back in 1898.

At close of play on the first day the score stood at 423, and next morning the players were greeted by an expectant crowd: press photographers, film cameramen and excited Yorkshiremen, many of whom had escaped from their day's work. There was even a man who had made his way down from Hull.

Ever since 1919 the two of them had been a prolific opening pair for Yorkshire, a crucial part of the county's success. The 37-year-old Sutcliffe was one of the all-time greats of Test cricket, a batsman with immense powers of concentration and self-discipline, and he had found it hard to sleep after his effort on the first day. Holmes, a jauntier character, was less inclined to such mental exhaustion, but he was 45 years old and he was feeling his lumbago badly on the second morning. 'Bluntly,' Sutcliffe wrote later, 'I would not have given two pennies on our chance of putting another 25 on that score of 423.'

Yet somehow they stayed in, their early stiffness wore off, and, when at 522, Holmes played a loose shot and was almost caught in the slips, the magisterial Sutcliffe came down to admonish him. "Percy, do you, or do you not, want to go for this record?" Run by run the tension rose till, with the scoreboard showing 551, Sutcliffe pulled a ball to leg for four and the crowd roared with delight. 'I don't think I ever hit a ball with such joy,' he said.

The cheering died down eventually and, with his concentration broken, Sutcliffe swiped uncharacteristically at the next ball, edging it onto his foot, from where it ran back onto the stumps. The declaration was made, and the two of them left the field. They were ushered to the scoreboard where, amid a great cheering crowd, they shook hands before the score of 555.

Then it happened. As the cameras clicked, the scorers checked their books and the 555 behind Holmes and Sutcliffe suddenly became 554. What pandemonium ensued! Percy Holmes could see the funny side of it, calling it 'a rare to-do', but not Sutcliffe. He was outraged. Even forty years later, recalling the day, his voice would rise in 'a high-pitched crescendo of horror'.

Many are the accounts of what ensued. Some say the fault stemmed from the boys operating the board, that it really was 554 and that, amid all the hubbub, the Essex scorer ran into the pavilion to consult his captain Charles Bray, who told him to 'find a run' for them: "They deserve the record." As a result a no ball was added, appearing in different places in the two books. Some say it was the umpires who pointed out the missing no ball, others that it was a clergyman who had been keeping his own scorebook. Whatever the truth, the run was added. Holmes and Sutcliffe shook hands again, this time in front of 555.

The *Evening Standard*'s EW Swanton lost out in the rush for the ground's one telephone. His editor, furious that his paper had been scooped, punished Swanton by not sending him to Australia in the winter, thus leaving the young man with a lifelong regret that the 555 record had cost him the chance to witness the Bodyline series at first hand.

Images of the 1930s

1930s

William Whysall's coffin on its way to St Peter's Church, Mansfield, Friday 14 November 1930

The death of William Whysall

If anybody doubts the place of the county cricketer in people's hearts between the wars, they should reflect on the response to the death of William 'Dodge' Whysall.

The 43-year-old Nottinghamshire opener was no Test star, nor was he a stylish entertainer. Coming out of the Bullcroft Colliery team, he had a workmanlike approach to batting: a strong defence at the start of an innings and powerful shoulders when the time came to open up. He also had a great temperament: 'a marvellous man when the team was in a corner,' his captain Arthur Carr called him. In 1929, when they won the championship, he set a Notts record with 2,620 runs in all matches. Indeed, no one in county cricket scored more runs than Whysall across the four summers from 1927 to 1930.

In October 1930, two months after he had hit a career best 248 at Trent Bridge, he was on the dance floor, enjoying a Paul Jones. The music ended abruptly and he lost his balance, falling heavily. He laughed the accident off – "I dare not look at my elbow," he joked – and played golf the next day. The pain increased, however, and within a fortnight of the fall, despite a blood transfusion, he died of septicaemia.

The streets of Mansfield were lined several deep with mourners as his grief-stricken team-mates walked alongside the pall bearers. Two days later, on the Sunday, extra police were called to organise queues at the cemetery where more than ten thousand people came from far and wide, on foot and in motor cars, to pay their respects at the grave-side.

Cricket at Hastings

For the true lover of county cricket, played the southern way, there was no better fixture in the '20s and '30s than Sussex versus Kent, in early August each year at the Central Ground, Hastings. With the sun shining and a sea breeze, with the surrounding Regency terraces and the ruined Norman castle on the hill, it was a place of delight – and its cricket square, lovingly tended for nigh on fifty years by Alf Tutt, was fast and true, a paradise for a batsman when his eye was in.

In 1929, in a game which Sussex won at five o'clock on the final day, the two teams scored 1,451 runs. Kent had two leg-spinners, 'Tich' Freeman and 'Father' Marriott, and Sussex had Duleepsinhji, the most elegant batsman in England. On the first morning, with a mixture of quick-footed drives and wristy cuts, he hit 115 before lunch. Then on the second evening, 'gathering runs in the late sunshine like a bee gathers honey', he began a joyful innings of 246 that broke his uncle

Ranji's record on the ground. He danced down the wicket to Freeman, murdering his bowling as no one had ever done. "I've never seen a more wonderful display of batsmanship," the little man said as he hurried to congratulate Duleep. Such was the spirit of these neighbours' contests at Hastings.

In 1932, with Duleep now captain, Sussex were hard on the heels of Yorkshire in the championship, and across the three days, in brilliant sunshine, more than 20,000 paid for admission. In a high-scoring draw there were centuries from Harry Parks and John Langridge – but, alas, no runs for Duleep. He was ill, battling on against doctor's orders because his beloved uncle urged him to do so, for the sake of Sussex.

He played one more week, scoring 83 at Swansea and 90 at Taunton, then retired, exhausted and haemorrhaging, never to play cricket again. In his absence Sussex's season petered out. Like Ranji in 1902 and 1903, he had led them to second place.

A record crowd at the 1932 game between Sussex and Kent

The lovely fields and the glamour of Kent

Between the wars, though they never finished first in the championship, Kent won more matches than any other county except Yorkshire. If the simple system of 1919 had continued, when the title was awarded to the county with the highest percentage of wins, Kent would have been champions in 1926, 1927 and jointly in 1928. But, unlike the northern counties who dominated the '20s and '30s, Kent's victories were mixed with plenty of defeats. No county drew fewer matches.

They took their cricket all round the county of Kent. At one point in the 1920s they were playing on nine different grounds: from the Garrison ground near the Chatham dockyards to the Mote, beside the deer park, in Maidstone; from Blackheath in the metropolis to Tunbridge Wells, with its blooming rhododendrons, on the Sussex border; from the tiny Bat and Ball ground at Gravesend to the vast field at seaside Folkestone. In most cases the towns staged cricket weeks, the two three-day games accompanied by much social activity. Canterbury Week was famous throughout the upper reaches of society, and Tonbridge was not to be missed, either – with its dances on the Castle lawns, its firework displays and its Venetian fete on the Medway. Then there was Dover in August, where the wealthy, eating in style on the high-terraced hillside, looked down on the cricket and across to the hills that rose above the town. There were bands everywhere and marquees, rich with drink and laughter, from the exclusive Band of Brothers at Canterbury to the Cheerful Brotherhood of Sparrows at Folkestone.

'Kent cricket has about it a glamour,' Neville Cardus wrote in 1928. 'Sometimes I wonder whether this glamour is derived from Kent's actual cricket, or whether it is a sort of light reflected from the lovely fields of Kent. Would Kent be known today as a team that plays an animated game if it had been compelled to get through half of its engagements in the murky air of Sheffield, Leeds and Bradford?'

Kent's cricketers played with style and with a spirit of adventure. With the bat in 1928 they scored their runs at 3.23 an over where Lancashire, the champions, grafted at just 2.73. And their bowlers, bustling through their overs, none more so than the leg-spinner 'Tich' Freeman, conceded runs more freely, tempting the batsmen to play shots and get out.

There was a strong amateur tradition running through it all, upheld with a near-religious fervour by the all-powerful President, Lord Harris. 'Cricket,' he wrote to *The Times* on his 80th birthday in 1931. 'It is more free from anything sordid, anything dishonest, than any other game in the world. To play it keenly, honourably, generously, self-sacrificingly, is a moral lesson in itself, and the classroom is God's air and sunshine. Foster it, my brothers, so that it may attract all who can find time to play it; protect it from anything that would sully it, so that it may grow in favour with all men.'

Harris's idealism was mixed with a vigorous belief in the English class system, and through the 1920s, for all the spirit with which they played their cricket, there was a feudalism that separated professionals and amateurs. Frank Woolley, son of a car mechanic, batted with supreme elegance; 'Tich' Freeman, nephew of Essex's groundsman at Leyton, threw up his leg-breaks all day, and Les Ames, a grammar-school boy from Folkestone, kept wicket to him with stylish dependability. But they knew when not to speak. "One of our professionals," Ames said, "actually climbed down a drainpipe to get out of the Players' dressing-room rather than face His Lordship's wrath."

It was hardest for the lesser professionals, whose places in the team depended on the availability of the come-and-go amateurs.

Percy Chapman, 'Tich' Freeman and Frank Woolley

The summer of 1933 was not untypical: in May they played at Derby with ten professionals and one amateur, Godfrey Bryan, an army officer recruited to captain the side in his only championship game of the decade. But by late July, when the social round was in full swing, there were five, sometimes six, amateurs in the side.

Some of them were outstanding cricketers. 'Father' Marriott, a master at Dulwich College, would turn up in his school holidays and take 50 or 60 wickets, bowling his leg-breaks in tandem with Freeman. In 1933, at the age of 37, he was called up by England and, in his only Test, took eleven West Indian wickets.

Greatest of the amateurs, though, was Percy Chapman. Good-looking in his youth and debonair, a natural cricketer, he won the hearts of the nation when in his first Test as England captain, at the Oval in 1926, the Ashes were regained for the first time since the war.

Chapman, who worked for brewers in Hythe, lived life to the full, once in Brisbane eating 210 oysters in a session. With his 'hail fellow, well met' manner he was popular wherever he went, though soon enough the drink took its toll on his body. His weight increased, and he lost his quickness, at the crease and in the field.

When finally in 1931 he found time to captain Kent he was a breath of fresh air, sweeping away the stuffiness, the kind of pomposity that led 'Hopper' Levett, a farmer, to feel he was a lesser grade of amateur, "a bit rough and ready, not safe enough to put at the High Sherriff's table."

As a left-handed bat Chapman was not in Woolley's league – nobody was – but, like Woolley, he was at his best when playing his shots. At the Mote in 1927, on a drying pitch, he found himself at the wicket at 70 for five, facing Lancashire's fast Australian Ted McDonald, and in three hours of clean hitting, both powerful and wristy, he scored 260 runs. 'It is doubtful,' *Wisden* wrote, 'whether a finer innings has ever been seen.'

Cardus, in the *Manchester Guardian*, glowed with delight. He called the Mote 'the prettiest cricket field I have ever seen', Chapman's innings 'an exhilarating blend of power, flashiness, hazard, mastery and risk ... The crowd were in a heaven of delight ... So violent, so headlong was the cricket after tea that I could not drive my pen along fast enough to keep up with it ... No wonder the people down here love and worship their cricketers, even if they don't win the championship.'

Unheard-of scoring

Kent v Gloucestershire, Dover, Friday 20 August 1937

"Can we win?" the Kent skipper Gerry Chalk asked Les Ames as they left the field. "I doubt it," was the reply. "It all depends whether Frank can give us a start." "What do you think, Frank? Would you like to go in first?" Woolley was never a man to exude enthusiasm. He was 50 years old now; he had already scored 310 runs during the week and bowled 46 overs. With barely a word he put on his pads.

Kent were not the force they had been a few years earlier. 'Tich' Freeman had retired, Woolley was well past his prime, and the gifted amateurs were fewer. Yet there were still days when their optimistic spirit produced thrilling cricket, and this Friday at Dover, with a large crowd looking down from the banks of the amphitheatre, was one.

To beat Gloucestershire they needed to score 218 in 111 minutes, a tough target in those days of light bats, but Woolley, graceful even in his hard hitting, played 'exhilarating strokes all round the wicket'. His score was 44, the total 68, when after 25 minutes he was caught in front of the far sightscreen. Les Ames came next, more brutal than Woolley, and, even with fielders all round the boundary, he plundered the off-spinner Tom Goddard ruthlessly. With Bill Ashdown content to play second fiddle, the 150 was up in only 53 minutes. Among the pine trees at the bottom of the ground excited members spread out, ready to save precious moments by retrieving the ball quickly.

They need not have worried. After Ames fell to a catch in the deep, the big-hitting bowler Alan Watt appeared and in ten minutes, as the fielders descended from 'bewilderment' to 'utter demoralisation', he smacked 39 runs to bring Kent to victory with 40 minutes to spare. They had hit off the runs at a rate of nine an over, 185 an hour. It was, the *Guardian* said, 'unheard-of scoring'. *Wisden* agreed: 'History contains no mention of a faster scoring feat in first-class cricket.'

1935: Two fairy tales

Against all the odds

Yorkshire v Essex, Huddersfield, Wednesday 31 July 1935

"It was one of those days when everything goes right," the 88-year-old 'Hopper' Read, with typical modesty, reflected in the year 1998. "It was a very fast wicket, there was a bit of breeze, and we got two or three wickets rather quickly which is always a help."

It was the last day of July. Championship leaders Yorkshire, at full strength and unbeaten after 20 matches, were playing against the minnows of Essex at the Fartown ground in Huddersfield where they had not lost for more than a quarter of a century. The sun was shining, the groundsman said it was the best wicket he had prepared for years, and Brian Sellers, Yorkshire's captain, confidently opted to bat first.

Morris Nichols took the first over, 'galloping downhill, all elbows and feet, his hair gleaming as brightly as the pitch'. Hopper Read, 'even more angular in action, ran and bowled still faster at the other end'.

In less than half an hour they had the Yorkshire innings in ruins – at 9 for six. Read took the first four, including Maurice Leyland who played on to his first ball, while Nichols had Herbert Sutcliffe caught behind, then next ball bowled the young Len Hutton. In the words of the *Yorkshire Post*'s Jim Kilburn, 'The batsmen were routed, scattered, non-plussed and shockingly dismissed.'

Yorkshire rallied to 27 for six, lost three wickets on that score and, with the aid of a hit-and-hope four from number eleven Bill Bowes, were all out within the hour for 31. All the while, 'The spectators passed through the stages of wild alarm, distressed seriousness and bitter mirth.'

One Yorkshire member, arriving to see 27 for nine on the board and assuming Essex were batting, asked with excitement, "How many has Bowes got?", only to receive the answer, "Bowes? He's only just gone in." Another member, the solicitor cousin of ex-player Rockley Wilson, came in as the cricketers were leaving the field. "Why do we have to play second-class sides like Essex?" he exclaimed. "They're just not good enough."

Read, six for 11 in six overs, was in his second summer of county cricket. A young accountant, playing as an amateur, he had failed to make the Winchester XI and been rejected by Surrey, but at the age of 25 he was thought to be the quickest bowler in England. The *Cricketer* magazine called him 'the type of fast bowler England have been looking for. He has what may be termed a tearaway action, but he does bowl with tremendous zest and energy, and he is physically very strong.'

Essex took lunch at 39 for three and were soon 65 for five, but all-rounder Nichols put the pitch and day in context with a sparkling innings of 146. The young Oxford University amateur Brian Belle, in a ringed Harlequin cap, batted calmly and correctly for 63, and in the last over of the day Essex were all out with a lead of 303.

'Hopper' Read

Len Hutton recalled a diehard Yorkshireman arriving on the second morning and inspecting the pitch. "The pace has gone out of it," he reassured them. "You'll make 400." But they didn't. They were all out by one o'clock for 99. In the first over Nichols had Sutcliffe caught at slip for 1, Hutton again made 0, while Read broke Leyland's bat before bowling him for 2. Nichols, in the game of his life, took seven wickets, Read the other three.

'Time is a great healer,' wrote Jim Kilburn, 'and some time perhaps this nightmare will fade.'

A fortnight later 'Hopper' Read played for England at the Oval, taking six South African wickets. In the winter he toured Australia on an unofficial MCC trip designed to heal the wounds of Bodyline. He stood on the brink of cricketing greatness, but his employers saw things differently. In the spring of 1936 they made him choose between accountancy and cricket, and he chose accountancy.

The boy from Bicknoller

Somerset v Essex, Frome, Saturday 18 May 1935

The six Somerset professionals did not rate the young Harold Gimblett. He had been scoring runs aplenty for Watchet, the little harbour town on the north coast, but on trial in the Taunton nets they thought he was no more than a village hitter, lacking the craft to do well in county cricket.

"I'm afraid you're just not good enough," the Secretary John Daniell told him, sugaring the pill of rejection by paying him to stay till the end of the week. The 20-year-old farmer's boy acted as twelfth man in a game, helped on the ground and, on Friday afternoon, prepared to catch the bus home to Bicknoller in the Quantocks. However many runs he would score for Watchet in the years to come, it is unlikely that they would ever have a second look at him. A farmer, he was to be.

Then Fate struck. The amateur Laurie Hawkins had a bruised thumb and pulled out of the next day's game against Essex. With nobody else around, they turned to Gimblett: "Can you get to Frome tomorrow morning?" It was a cross-country journey of more than fifty miles, involving at least two buses. John Daniell, sensing the lad's difficulty, told him to be at Bridgwater by nine. "I'll ask Luckes to pick you up in his car."

At half past six in the morning, Gimblett was carrying his little bag across the farm field when, to his horror, he saw the early bus disappearing down the lane. There was not another one for two hours, and he walked on forlornly, saved only when a milk lorry picked him up. It was a bitterly cold day, and at the ground he was told that Somerset were batting first and he was at number eight.

At lunch Arthur Wellard, the well-seasoned pro from South London, saw Gimblett's patched-up bat. "You're not goin' out with that, are you, son? Go and 'ave a look in my bag. There's a bat in there."

Soon afterwards, with Somerset struggling on 107 for six, the boy from Bicknoller, making up numbers because nobody else had been around, joined Wellard in the middle. Wellard was one of the big hitters of county cricket – twice he hit five sixes in an over – but that day at Frome he was not the one who got the scoreboard rattling. In 25 minutes they added 69 runs, and the young Gimblett made 48 of them. Then, in a further 25 minutes with Wally Luckes, he raced from 48 to 88. And it was not slogging, as the reports made clear: 'His skill, grace, coolness and resource were little short of amazing.' ... 'He played his shots with care and on every occasion seemed to know where the ball was going.'

The scoreboard only gave the total, not the runs of the individual batsmen. So Gimblett will not have known, till the announcement, that he had completed a century – and in only 63 minutes, the fastest in England that summer. In all, he scored 123 in 80 minutes, and the folk of Frome, many of them farmers, applauded him with delight.

How English cricket celebrated! 'A fine, free bat and a wonderful nerve and eye. He treated all the bowling with the same cheerful

Harold Gimblett

contempt.' ... 'A natural cricketer, he batted like a master.' ... 'Is he the great boy cricketer England have been looking for?' ... 'Gimblett may even revolutionise cricket by reviving the half-lost arts of hard hitting and quick scoring.'

The fuss was not what he wanted. He disliked it when, working on the farm next day, pressmen arrived to interview him. Then on Monday 'he had to hide himself in the pavilion to escape the attentions of the autograph hunters.'

The next year he played for England. He became the greatest run-scorer in Somerset's history. But it never sat easily with him. For twenty years he opened the county's batting, always playing his shots, till the nervous pressure grew too great. He submitted to electro-convulsive therapy, then in May 1954, in mid-match, he walked away from it all. He took his own life in 1978.

Yet what joy he gave in those years, how Somerset supporters thrilled to his daring strokeplay. And to think they would never have seen him at all if Laurie Hawkins had not had a bruised thumb.

1936: Derbyshire reach the summit

Few counties have won the championship with less national fanfare than Derbyshire in 1936. The cricket writers applauded their triumph, but there was something slightly begrudging about their praise, as exemplified in the verdict of *The Times*:

> Paradoxical as it may appear, it is Derbyshire's relative weakness in batting which has contributed most to their success. Their scores have usually been low enough to give their bowlers a chance – and their bowlers have taken it.

The Cricketer devoted much of its congratulation to the question of whether Derbyshire had or had not won the title previously, back in 1874, while the *Observer*'s 'Watchman', summarising the championship season in four lengthy paragraphs, managed to comment on the fortunes of seven counties and not to mention Derbyshire at all.

Even on the day when they won the title, in the press coverage of their match at Wells, they took second place to Somerset's Arthur Wellard who, off five successive balls, hit five enormous straight sixes. In the most exciting of finishes Derbyshire lost by one wicket, but they were confirmed as champions when their rivals Yorkshire drew at Hove.

Derbyshire were unfashionable. They were a northern, industrial county, with a membership of just 2,220, half that of Lancashire, one-third of Yorkshire's. Their grounds were not among the most scenic in England, and their team lacked stars. Consequently the leading writers saw little of them.

Yet their success was no fluke. Rather, it was exactly what the championship should be all about: a county developing a home-grown side and playing positive, attacking cricket. The fact that they were such a small county, and that they had built themselves up after years of ignominious failure, made the achievement all the greater.

In 1920 they completed the worst set of results in the history of the championship. With money desperately short and a dearth of players, they lost 17 of their 18 fixtures – with the 18th, against Nottinghamshire, rained off without a ball bowled. They were still at rock bottom in 1924 when again they failed to win a match, but by then they had begun their search for talent among the collieries and local leagues.

Two of their best discoveries, fast bowler Bill Copson and leg-spinner Tommy Mitchell, owed their progress in cricket to the General Strike of 1926. Copson, an 18-year-old pitman at Morton Colliery, spent much of the nine-day strike 'mucking about' on the local recreation ground where, in makeshift cricket matches, his untutored ability to bowl fast and straight caught the eye. It was much the same story with the 23-year-old Mitchell, only his improvised games were twenty miles away, near the pithead of the Creswell Colliery, and he attracted attention with his prodigious spinning of the ball. But for the strike the pair of them might never have been cricketers at all, yet both went on to play for England.

In his early years in the Derbyshire team, the ginger-haired Copson had rather too frail a physique for a fast bowler – "He's had more dinner times than dinners," was the county coach's verdict – but he got married in November 1935, spent the winter training with Chesterfield football club and arrived for his summer's cricket bulkier and stronger. In the county's first home match, Surrey were 49 for two, needing only 45 more runs for victory, and Copson demolished them with a seven-over spell in which he took six wickets for eight runs. His wickets – 140 at an average of 12,80 – did much to win Derbyshire the championship, and they also won him a place on the boat to Australia that winter.

The bespectacled Tommy Mitchell was a different character. As an angelic nine-year-old he had sung 'Oh for the Wings of a Dove' in front of the King at Welbeck Abbey, but years in the pits had turned him into a complex character, sometimes full of infectious humour, other times bemoaning in blunt language the frustrations of his lot. An especial favourite of the crowd, he was a bundle of energy, quick to express the triumphs and disasters of his craft.

He had been on the Bodyline tour of Australia where, in a state match, he had bowled Bradman cheaply with his googly. But by 1936 his England career was over. Much as he spun the ball, he was thought to bowl too many bad deliveries for Test cricket, and he cannot have helped his cause when he told the England skipper Bob Wyatt, "You couldn't captain a box of bloody matches."

For Derbyshire he was a key element of the team's success, taking 100 wickets each year – often taking his wickets when others could not, never more so in 1936 than in the game at Chelmsford. On a good pitch Essex needed only 102 to win and were in control at 57 for three. Then Mitchell was brought on and, with his sleeves flapping as always, he bowled Jack O'Connor with a long hop and finished with a match-winning six wickets.

(left) Bill Copson   (right) the Derbyshire team
standing: Albert Alderman, Tommy Mitchell, Denis Smith, Alf Pope, George Pope, Stan Worthington, Elijah Carrington
sitting: Harry Storer, Harry Elliott, Arthur Richardson (captain), Harry Palmer (scorer), Leslie Townsend

The third key bowler in that summer of success was Alf Pope, whose brother George missed most of the campaign with a bad knee. The son of the Chesterfield groundsman, Alf had also spent time in the mines. At 6'4" he was among the tallest of bowlers in county cricket, able like his brother George to mix in-swing with deadly leg-cutters.

Another with a pit background was the wicket-keeper Harry Elliott. He had joined the club at its lowest point in 1920, and the years had turned him into the wise old man of the team, 40 years of age now – or so they all thought. In fact, in 1920, when had told them he was 24, he was 28, so he was already 44 – and would be 55 when he played for the last time.

All the county's 15 professionals were men of Derbyshire. Stan Worthington, whose batting that summer won him selection for Australia, had been an apprentice electrician at Bolsover Colliery. Denis Smith, the tall opener, came from the mining village of Somercotes and spent his winters in a foundry. His partner Albert Alderman, from Derby, worked in the office at Rolls Royce. Leslie Townsend came from a lace-making family in Long Eaton, Elijah Carrington from the Blackwell Colliery. Only Harry Storer was born outside the county, but he grew up in Ripley where he was an apprentice

fitter in the ironworks before becoming a footballer who played for England. By 1936 he was the manager of Coventry City FC where another of the Derbyshire team, Harry Elliott's nephew Charlie, played at right back.

They were captained by Arthur Richardson, whose family owned a tanning and leather business in Derby. Educated at Winchester, he was not worth a place in the team, averaging only 12 with the bat that summer, but the captain had to be an amateur and he was an astute captain, keen to play positive cricket and to win. As a result he was popular with his men, certainly more than the elderly army officer who stood in for him in an early game at Gravesend. It was the man's one and only appearance in championship cricket, and he did not endear himself to the team when, after calling for a risky single and being sent back, he advanced angrily on his partner. "When I say run," he barked, "you bloody well run."

They won the championship just that once, the crowning year of several when they were a formidable side. Theirs was a victory not of cricketing genius but, as TCF Prittie put it, 'of perseverance, determination and dependability … guts and keenness', the qualities in short of the hard-working, no-nonsense folk of industrial Derbyshire.

1939: The last summer before war

On Friday 26 May 1939, with the fateful news reaching Britain that Hitler and Mussolini had signed a military pact, a new Act passed into law, introducing six months of compulsory military training for selected 20- and 21-year-olds.

There followed a Whit holiday weekend in which the sun shone all over Britain. The people, anxious to forget their cares, went out in their millions: not just to the packed seaside resorts at Blackpool and Margate but to London Zoo to see the new panda, to scout camps in the Peaks, to motor racing at Brooklands – and more than 100,000 of them on the Monday to cricket.

At Old Trafford they watched Herbert Sutcliffe hit a faultless 165; at Cardiff they marvelled at the 'hurricane hitting' and electrifyingly fast bowling of the West Indian Learie Constantine; there was Hammond at Taunton, Compton at Lord's – and, most special of all for their long-suffering supporters, a Northamptonshire victory over Leicestershire.

Not since the first game of 1935 had the near-bankrupt Northamptonshire tasted success in the championship – a run of 99 matches, with 61 defeats and 38 draws, the worst in the history of the competition. Yet in brilliant sunshine on that Bank Holiday Monday, before an excited crowd of more than 6,000, they had Leicestershire batting a second time, needing 376 runs to avoid an innings defeat.

The pavilion had one telephone, and it was twelfth man Vince Broderick's duty to answer the incessant calls from members wanting to know the score: 60 for one, 100 for two, 121 for six. The extra half hour was taken and, as the last wicket fell, he looked out on a ground awash with spectators cheering wildly. "I always remember a lady running from the West Stand and making off with a stump."

An avenue was formed and three cheers 'heartily given'. Their young schoolmaster captain Robert Nelson stood on the balcony and made a speech: "Through all the rough times and trying circumstances," he told the beaming crowd, "the team have kept up their spirits wonderfully. We hope now that further victories are in store."

"Three cheers for Mister Nelson. Hip-hip-hooray."

'The bogey has been disposed of, the stigma removed,' the *Northampton Chronicle* declared triumphantly. 'Now further successes are confidently expected.'

Alas, it was their only victory of the summer, though it proved enough to keep them above Leicestershire in the final table. *Wisden* saw that as a 'definite advance'.

As summer progressed so the news from Europe grew more threatening. Yet county cricket carried on, living for the most part in its own bubble. "We didn't know a great deal about what was happening," Northamptonshire's Dennis Brookes recalled years later. "We read what Chamberlain was saying, but even then we didn't think there was going to be a war."

With each day of August there were fresh developments: German threats against the Polish city of Danzig, a treaty between Hitler and Stalin, an Emergency Powers Act passing through Parliament.

At Northampton, on the second day of their match, Lancashire's captain Lionel Lister, receiving a message from his Territorial Army unit, unbuckled his pads and departed. The West Indian tourists, anxious that they would be stranded, cancelled their remaining fixtures and sailed home. The Oval was taken over by the War Ministry, while at Lord's the treasures in the pavilion were packed up and driven away.

In this eerie atmosphere the last matches of August were played. The Yorkshire team were on their southern tour, playing at Dover, Bournemouth and Hove and winning the championship for the third year running. The 23-year-old Len Hutton was in the form of his life, hitting five centuries in the month, while Hedley Verity, taking wickets every time he bowled, was once more top of the national bowling averages, with his team-mate Bill Bowes in second place behind him.

Kent's season ended with a week at Dover, a memorable pair of games for their free-spirited captain Gerry Chalk. Against Yorkshire he opted with disastrous consequences to field first, only partly redeeming himself with a fighting century as they went down to an innings defeat. Then against Lancashire, needing 382 to win on the final day, he led the way with a hard-hitting 94 that brought them victory with an hour to spare. 'It was a day of high summer,' *The Times* reported from Dover on the first day. 'The bandsmen performed in their scarlet tunics, and outwardly all was peaceful and seemly on one of England's loveliest grounds.'

Elsewhere there were centuries for Middlesex's Bill Edrich and the Glamorgan captain Maurice Turnbull, and hat-tricks for Hampshire's 18-year-old newcomer Tommy Dean, and Essex's fast bowler Ken Farnes, a master at Worksop College who was fitting in some county cricket during his holidays.

There were also young men like Tommy Dean taking their first steps in the county game. At Dover, when Kent's regular keeper 'Hopper' Levett was called away to his Territorial unit, the gloves were given to a teenager called Godfrey Evans who, *Wisden* recorded, 'kept wicket specially well on the first day'.

For Surrey's last match against Lancashire, in place of Freddie Brown, an 18-year-old leg-spinner Bernie Constable was called up for his championship debut. With the Oval out of action, the game was moved at the last minute to Old Trafford. That left Lancashire with a long train journey north from Dover, a journey that came to a standstill at Crewe where they waited three hours for a connection. According to Cyril Washbrook, 'The station on that chilly morning looked like a recruitment centre. As cricketers we felt out of place.'

The Surrey players arrived in Manchester at 4 a.m., several sleeping the rest of the night in the Old Trafford pavilion. For two days the match was played in what Washbrook called 'an unreal atmosphere'. Then early on Friday morning, with Lancashire needing 352 for victory, the German army entered Poland and the game was abandoned. "We caught the train back to London," Constable recalled. "When we reached Euston station, it was full of kids being evacuated."

Three of the six county matches had finished inside two days, including Northamptonshire's last game at Taunton where at close of play their captain Robert Nelson slipped away quietly to join his regiment. 'He has surmounted a hard task with calm and courage,' was the *Observer*'s summary of his season's work. The game at Old Trafford was abandoned, and there was heavy rain at Leicester – so that left only one last game on that Friday morning: Sussex versus Yorkshire at Hove. It was George Cox's benefit match, and for his sake Yorkshire's skipper Brian Sellers insisted on playing it out.

In front of a small smattering of spectators Yorkshire secured a first-innings lead, then bowled Sussex out for 33. Their chief destroyer on the broken pitch was Hedley Verity, with figures of six overs, seven wickets for nine runs.

There was a ban on private motor cars south of Birmingham so the Yorkshire contingent hired a char-a-banc and made their way north in the dark through blacked-out streets and villages. 'The farther we got from Brighton,' Len Hutton wrote, 'the deeper was our conviction that we would be lucky if we ever played cricket again.'

At eleven o'clock on Sunday morning Britain was at war. It would be May 1946, six years and eight months, before another ball would be bowled in county cricket.

Many would return: Len Hutton with his left arm two inches shorter than his right; Bernie Constable as a batsman, his leg-breaks lost through inactivity; Bill Edrich after flying low-level bombing missions over Germany; Bill Bowes and Freddie Brown, weakened by years as prisoners-of-war.

Others would not come back. Among those killed were Gerry Chalk, Maurice Turnbull, Ken Farnes, Robert Nelson and Hedley Verity.

Captain Hedley Verity
Green Howards

Shot while leading his men on a night attack in Italy, 1943

Major Maurice Turnbull
Welsh Guards

Shot by a German tank in Normandy, 1944

Fl-Lt. Gerry Chalk DFC
Royal Air Force

Shot down while flying a Spitfire over France, 1943

2nd Lt. Robert Nelson
Royal Marines

Killed in a bombing raid on his barracks, 1940

1940 – 1949

Six years lost to war
A great post-war boom in attendances
Glamorgan's first championship

In every way the season of 1947 bears favourable comparison with any year within living memory. Attendances which rose beyond those known in the past clearly demonstrated the great hold the games takes on spectators once they are aware that both sides and every individual mean to expend all their energies striving for a definite result. The fine weather might have meant that, with batsmen supreme, drawn games would have predominated, but actually about three-quarters of the county championship matches were won outright.

Wisden Cricketers' Almanack 1948

No longer do the great families maintain the county clubs, so that the members in the pavilion have every comfort while the paying spectators are not even told when play has been abandoned for the day. The wealth of the clubs now comes from the folk who pay their money at the gate. Similarly inside the teams the amateurs are no longer to be respectfully "sirred" by their men, nor do they stay in lordly isolation at an hotel beyond the pockets of the professional players. County cricket clung longer than most sections of English life to the old manners, but it has rejected them now.

John Arlott, 1949

1940
Lord's Cricket Ground stages regular one-day matches, to boost morale and raise funds for good causes.
No first-class cricket is played, though some counties do play occasional matches. At Trent Bridge, over the Whit holiday, Nottinghamshire play Derbyshire in a two-day game. The teams are near full strength, but the match is an easy-going one. When Derbyshire's Bill Copson fails to arrive, one of the umpires bats in his place.
330,000 British troops are evacuated from Dunkirk as Germany tightens its control in northern France.
In September the Battle of Britain begins, with German planes launching repeated attacks on England.

1941
The *Wisden Almanack*, listing the fixtures for 1941, does not appear in print till December.
In one May night 1,400 Londoners are killed in air raids. Germany attacks Russia, ending the pact between the two countries. America enters the war after Japanese planes attack the US naval base at Pearl Harbour.

1942
The Advisory County Cricket Committee meets in December, its first gathering since the outbreak of war.
It discusses informally options for post-war cricket, hearing a proposal for two-day county games from Sussex.
Singapore falls to the Japanese. Allied troops at El Alamein in the North African desert win their first victory of the war. Germany suffers defeat, at the hands of the Russians, in Stalingrad.

1943
The West Indian cricketer Learie Constantine is refused admission to the Imperial Hotel in Russell Square.
Hotel staff call him a nigger, saying that his presence will be unacceptable to their American guests.
Italy surrenders unconditionally to the Allies.

1944
A flying bomb cuts out above a Lord's match. The players throw themselves to the ground; the bomb lands in Regent's Park. When play resumes, Jack Robertson hits a six and the crowd starts singing 'There'll always be an England'.
On 6 June, D-Day, Allied troops land in northern France. In August Paris is liberated.

1945
First-class cricket returns with five 'Victory Tests' between England and an Australian Services XI.
In the first three-day county match since 1939, Yorkshire play Lancashire at Bradford.
At Lord's, in August, England lose to a Dominions XI captained by Learie Constantine.
An MCC sub-committee considers the introduction of an inter-county knock-out competition: three-day matches, with a four-day final at Lord's. The problem of what to do in the event of a draw is the chief stumbling block, one option being to award the tie to the team higher in the championship table.
On 7 May Germany surrenders. Victory in Europe is declared.
On 6 August an atomic bomb is dropped on Hiroshima, leading Japan to surrender eight days later.
A General Election brings the Labour Party to power with a 146-seat majority.

1946
The county championship resumes. Fixtures are co-ordinated centrally for the first time; each county plays 26 matches including at least one against each of the other counties.
After the 1939 experiment with eight balls, the six-ball over returns.
As in the last three years before the war, Yorkshire are champions, with Middlesex runners-up.
In September the Football League resumes, with 950,000 spectators attending matches on the first day.

1947
For the first time since 1921 a southern county, Middlesex, wins the championship.
In worsening economic conditions, food rationing is tightened while foreign holidays and motoring for pleasure are banned.

1948
Glamorgan, who have never previously finished higher than sixth, become the ninth county to win the championship.
For the visit of the Australians, five-day Tests are introduced. Australia, under Don Bradman, wins 4-0.
The railways are nationalised, and a 'cradle to grave' National Health Service is born.
In the first Olympic Games since 1936, in London, Great Britain win only three gold medals: in rowing (two) and yachting.

1949
For the first time in its formal history the championship is shared by two counties, Middlesex and Yorkshire.
The rationing of clothes is ended.

1940

1941

SECOND WORLD WAR

338 men played in the county championship in 1939.

17 died during the six years of the war.

102 more did not return to county cricket.

1942

1943

The war made men of us. It toughened us up. After
that I was never nervous when I played cricket.

Alec Bedser

1944

1945

Championship – top three						Leading batsmen		Leading bowlers		Leading wkt-keeper	
	P	*W*	*L*	*D*	*Pts*		*Runs*		*Wickets*	Leading fielder	*Victims*
1946											
Yorkshire	26	17	1	8	216	L.B. Fishlock (Surrey)	1,963	W.E. Hollies (Warwicks)	175	W.T. Luckes (Som)	70
Middlesex	26	16	5	5	204	W.W. Keeton (Notts)	1,954	T.W.J. Goddard (Glos)	150		
Lancashire	26	15	4	7	200	D. Brookes (Northants)	1,932	J.E. Walsh (Leics)	143	J.T. Ikin (Lancs)	38
1947										L.H. Compton (Middx)	73
Middlesex	26	19	5	2	236	W.J. Edrich (Middx)	2,257	T.W.J. Goddard (Glos)	206	T.H. Wade (Essex)	73
Gloucestershire	26	17	4	5	216	J. Hardstaff (Notts)	2,230	T.P.B. Smith (Essex)	153	H. Yarnold (Worcs)	73
Lancashire	26	13	1	11	186	J.D.B. Robertson (Middx)	2,214	J.E. Walsh (Leics)	142	J.G. Langridge (Sussex)	44
Lancashire also tied one match											
1948											
Glamorgan	26	13	5	8	172	A.E. Fagg (Kent)	2,404	T.L. Pritchard (Warwicks)	163	E.A. Meads (Notts)	73
Surrey	26	13	9	4	168	L.E.G. Ames (Kent)	1,926	J.E. Walsh (Leics)	157	J.F. Parker (Surrey)	36
Middlesex	26	13	4	9	160	A.V. Avery (Essex)	1,877	B.L. Muncer (Glam)	139	A.C. Revill (Derbys)	36
1949											
Middlesex *(1=)*	26	14	3	9	192	J.G. Langridge (Sussex)	2,441	T.W.J. Goddard (Glos)	152	H. Yarnold (Worcs)	95
Yorkshire *(1=)*	26	14	2	10	192	N. Oldfield (Northants)	2,114	R.O. Jenkins (Worcs)	140		
Worcestershire	26	12	7	7	172	L. Hutton (Yorks)	2,098	W.E. Hollies (Warwicks)	128	L.F. Outschoorn (Worcs)	52

1940-1949

Leading counties

	P	W	L	D	T	%W
Middlesex	104	53	26	25	-	51.0
Yorkshire	104	50	14	40	-	48.1
Gloucestershire	104	48	24	32	-	46.2
Lancashire	104	42	14	47	1	40.4

Leading batsmen

J.D.B. Robertson (Middx)	7,589
J.G. Langridge (Sussex)	7,116
D. Brookes (Northants)	7,112
L.E.G. Ames (Kent)	7,111

Leading bowlers

T.W.J. Goddard (Glos)	630
J.E. Walsh (Leics)	569
W.E. Hollies (Warwicks)	527
C. Gladwin (Derbyshire)	438

Leading keepers & fielder

H. Yarnold (Worcs)	238
P. Corrall (Leics)	232
J.T. Ikin (Lancs)	133

Overall statistics

Runs per wicket	26.3
Runs per 100 balls	45.5
% of matches drawn	33.4

Miscellany

Playing for Somerset at Melton Mowbray in June 1946, the 46-year-old Bill Caesar notched up his first runs and wickets in first-class cricket 24 years after making his debut.

A civil servant, posted during the war to the Admiralty in Bath, he had played one game for Surrey against Scotland in 1922. Now he was playing for Bath and, with Somerset lacking two key bowlers and with no fresh supply of young talent in that most makeshift of summers, he was called up, along with a 34-year-old Yeovil detective, Richard Peters, who was playing his cricket for the Somerset Constabulary.

Peters was a little out of his depth, but Caesar had a great game, taking four wickets on the last day to help Somerset to its first post-war victory.

*

By 1949 the Trent Bridge square had grown so placid that it was almost impossible to bowl a team out on it. In June Leicestershire set Notts to score a challenging 279 in 145 minutes, and the home team got them for the loss of one wicket, a run out, with 38 minutes to spare, a scoring rate of 156 an hour. Leicestershire's young amateur captain Stuart Symington had no idea how to stem the run-flow as the mercurial left-hander Cyril Poole hit 154 in 97 minutes.

There were not many declarations at Trent Bridge after that.

At Worcester in 1949 the leg-spinner Roly Jenkins had taken two wickets in two balls when Surrey's Stuart Surridge came out to bat. In the same situation the previous year at the Oval Surridge had holed out at deep mid-on so Jenkins pushed the fielder back, tossed up the ball and Surridge obliged once more.

In the second innings Surridge managed to restrain himself, but then Jenkins was not on a hat-trick this time. In fact, he had completed one off the previous ball, emulating Albert Trott and Charlie Parker in taking two hat-tricks in a match.

*

At Taunton in 1949 Horace Hazell, Somerset's tubby slow-left-armer, was hit for 17 runs in his first three overs. Gloucestershire's Emmett and Wilson, having opted to bat first on a soft wicket, were playing their shots, but both perished to Hazell: one stumped, the other caught off a firmly struck drive.

Out came the young Tom Graveney, still on the early steps of his cricketing journey. Taking a different approach, he and Jack Crapp let Hazell bowl 15 successive maidens before lunch.

The fielders came back out. "We were all so anxious not to be guilty of breaking the sequence," one said. Eventually, after another 2.3 overs, Graveney worked a single. The spell broken, Hazell then took six for nine in eight further overs.

His 105 balls without a run remain a record in county cricket.

The championship in the 1940s

On Saturday 11 May 1946 the county championship was once more up and running, with six matches. Though there was relief that life was getting back to normal, there was also anxiety. How would the men, seven years on from their last full season of cricket, cope with the summer-long round? And would the spectators, fed on a wartime diet of one-day exhibition matches, find patience for these longer contests?

As in the years after the First War, there was a great surge in attendance. Grounds were full, gates shut on the Saturdays of county games. People were desperate to enjoy the pleasures they had been denied for too long. The players were just as keen but, as Somerset's Frank Lee wrote, 'Once the initial freshness had worn off, playing continuously for six days a week proved to be far more strenous than anticipated.'

Bill Edrich of Middlesex had not long been demobbed from the RAF: 'One of the first things I noticed,' he said, 'was that civilian rations were very different from Air Force ones; I was always hungry. It was noticeable, too, how shabby everyone looked. I had to renew a lot of cricket gear, so the coupon situation soon grew difficult for me also.'

With little serious cricket for so long, there were almost no new players. In the 12 county sides that started that Saturday in May there were 23 men in their forties and only two below the age of 25. Somerset and Glamorgan had average ages of 38, with Glamorgan's captain Johnnie Clay now in his 49th year.

There were no fast bowlers. The find of the summer was the 27-year-old medium-pacer Alec Bedser but, for the three-match Test series against India, England's selectors were reduced to partnering him with Bill Bowes, Bill Voce and Alf Gover, all men in their late thirties.

Gloucestershire took the field with nine of the team who had played the last game of 1939, but Warwickshire had a great struggle to round up any sort of eleven. Apart from the leg-spinner Eric Hollies they had little bowling, resorting to pulling players unseen out of Birmingham League sides.

One such character, a fast-bowling all-rounder, was chosen to play at Derby. On the first morning Peter Cranmer, the ever-cheerful Warwickshire captain, asked Hollies to have a quick look at him in the nets, only to receive the feedback, "Well, I don't know if he was loosening up, but he was bowling slower than I do." In the match the man, taking the new ball, bowled two gentle overs, all wide of the off stump, then Hollies took over. In the next game he was played as a batsman and bagged a pair.

Hollies, with great control of his leg-breaks, toiled away over after over, game after game, sometimes even having to take the new ball and bowl swingers. Across the season, on an average 120-over day, Hollies would bowl 52 of the 60 overs at one end. "I regularly went to sleep in the dressing room," he said. "They woke me up when it was my turn to bat."

It was a damp summer but, with such a shortage of young bowlers, a good one to be a batsman. Despite a bad back the 43-year-old Wally Hammond, who had topped the batting averages in each of the last five summers before the war, topped them again, with his best ever average, 84.90. For those who wanted the world of cricket to get back to where it had been in 1939, that was reassuring, as was the county championship table: first Yorkshire, second Middlesex, as in '37, '38 and '39.

More surprising, but appropriate in that summer of make-do-and-mend, was the name at the top of the bowling averages. In 1939 the slow-left-armer Hedley Verity had held first place, but he was now dead and replacing him at the head of the list was his successor at Yorkshire, Arthur Booth.

Booth was 43, two years older than Verity would have been. In the 1920s he had been set to take over from Wilfred Rhodes – till the old man decided to go on past fifty and Verity emerged. Through the 1930s the diminutive Booth played in the leagues and for Northumberland, one more cricketer who had not quite made it. Then, in that strange spring of 1946, Yorkshire had another look at him and, with all the canny wisdom of his years, he did not disappoint. At Bristol, while Hammond hit 143, he bowled 45 overs for 49 runs. At Edgbaston, after pulling a thigh muscle and retiring from batting, he came out to bowl 'limping badly and in obvious pain' and returned match figures of nine for 40 off 42.5 overs.

Despite the lack of young players and the miserable weather, the summer of 1946 was universally hailed a great success. In the spring Surrey had been re-laying the entire field at the Oval, Lancashire were repairing bomb damage at Old Trafford, Essex were in search of half a team and Northamptonshire were looking for a captain to replace Robert Nelson, whose promise to return after the war had been a major factor in their decision to stay in the championship. Several counties were rumoured to be close to bankruptcy, saved only by behind-the-scenes gifts from generous patrons.

Yet every county was ready to go, full of fresh hope, by May. The crowds flocked back, and the membership lists expanded as never before.

Arthur Booth

*Top of the bowling averages,
at the age of 43, in 1946.*

*A miserly bowler, who conceded runs
at just 1.40 per over, he took 111
wickets at an average of 11.61.*

*John Arlott wrote of his 'old face,
bearing the marks of strain or worry
… a man used to settling his own
problems, self-reliant and neat
with his fingers.'*

*He came close to selection for the tour
of Australia but, staying in England
in the bitterest of winters,
he developed rheumatic fever and
hardly played for Yorkshire again.*

Then came the summer of 1947. The sun shone, the pitches were hard and true, and the world of county cricket gleamed. Middlesex were the team of the year, with Denis Compton and Bill Edrich breaking batting records with carefree and exhilarating strokeplay that lifted spirits worn down by the harsh realities of austerity Britain, as Neville Cardus evocatively put it in the *Manchester Guardian*:

> Never have I been so deeply touched on a cricket ground as in this heavenly summer, when I went to Lord's to see a pale-faced crowd, existing on rations, the rocket-bomb still in the ears of most, and see the strain of anxiety and affliction passed from all hearts and shoulders at the sight of Compton in full sail, each stroke a flick of delight, a propulsion of happy, sane, healthy life. There were no rations in an innings by Compton.

Gloucestershire, inspired by the prodigious wicket-taking of their 46-year-old off-spinner Tom Goddard, challenged Middlesex hard for the title. In that best of English summers it was somehow perfect that the crucial match should be played in glorious sunshine surrounded by the splendour of Cheltenham College. With the little ground heaving with spectators, from the Cotswolds and from London, Middlesex won the tensest of contests, bringing the championship title south for the first time since they had won it in 1921.

In 1948, breaking fresh boundaries, the title went west, all the way into Wales. It was a triumph for the Glamorgan captain Wilf Wooller who three years earlier had been a prisoner of the Japanese. He had no star players, but he brought to his captaincy of the Welsh county a fierce competitiveness and a near-revolutionary emphasis on fielding.

Four points behind Glamorgan at the finish were Surrey, who were left to rue their one-wicket defeat at the Oval when, with nine Middlesex wickets down, they twice dropped Jim Sims, one of them a simple return catch put down by Jim Laker. Laker was a sensitive man, and nobody said a word, not at the time and not when the final championship table showed how his miss had cost them the title. The first person to refer to it was Laker himself when, twelve months on, in the same fixture, he dismissed Sims with a brilliant one-handed return catch. Shunning congratulation, he muttered quietly, "One year too late."

In 1948 the Australians were the centre of attention, winning the Test series 4-0 and remaining unbeaten through their 34-match programme. England, as in the years after the First War, were a long way from full recovery, the next generation of players only beginning to emerge. Yet support for the county game was stronger than it had ever been, and soon enough that would bear fruit in the Test side.

Some players of the 1940s

Relaxed concentration
129 first-class centuries

Len Hutton of Yorkshire

The greatest influence I had with my cricket was playing with and watching Sir Leonard Hutton. He was magnificent, the best batsman I ever saw.   *Brian Close*

I never experienced him being rushed or in a panic. Although in many ways he wasn't a relaxed individual, there always seemed to be a calmness.   *Richard Hutton*

Len Hutton's Moravian upbringing instilled in him values of honest craftsmanship and self-sufficiency that were always present in his batting. Learning his game in the great Yorkshire team of the 1930s, with Herbert Sutcliffe – also from Pudsey – as his opening partner and mentor, he became one of English sport's greatest stars when in 1938, at the age of 22, he hit a world record score of 364 against Australia.

A wartime gymnasium accident led to a shortening of his left arm, reducing the freedom of his strokeplay, but he remained a dependable and most attractive run-scorer. Always in a cocoon of concentration he allied gifts of light footwork and supreme timing with an exceptional ability to work out the demands of pitch, bowling and match. When conditions were easy, he brought joy with his beautiful cover drive and his deft placement of the ball, but it was when things were difficult that he was really in his element, playing many a match-winning innings for Yorkshire. His best season was in 1949 when his 3,429 first-class runs included 1,294 in June, the most ever scored by a batsman in a month, and another 1,050 in August.

The cavalier Denis Compton, with his Brylcreemed good looks, had many admirers, but for purists the greater value – and beauty – lay in the dedicated craftsmanship of Leonard Hutton.

Eric Hollies of Warwickshire

He taught me to be honest with myself. If you bowled a bad ball or something went wrong, not to look for other reasons than you. He talked about conquering yourself. Eric was always having fun on the field, but he never let it disturb his concentration.
Tom Cartwright

History remembers Eric Hollies as the man whose googly bowled Bradman in his last Test innings, a brief moment of glory in a long career, from 1932 to 1957, that brought him 2,201 wickets for Warwickshire, over 1,000 more than any other bowler – and 657 more than the runs he scored for them as the notoriously worst batsman in county cricket.

His leg-breaks and googlies did not spin prodigiously but he had, for a back-of-the-hand bowler, remarkable accuracy. So relentlessly did he probe opposing batsmen, so seldom did he offer loose balls to hit, that his captain Tom Dollery called him 'the toothache bowler'.

Hollies was the most cheerful of characters, full of quick-witted quips on the field and happy off it with a half-pint of beer, a cigarette and a chance to tell his Black Country stories of Enoch and Eli – 'Aynuk and Ayli', as he would say. For all that, he was a dedicated craftsman, willing to bowl all day, never lowering his standard. He knew what pace and flight each pitch demanded, and he remembered the weaknesses of all the batsmen. There were some, like Jack Parker of Surrey, who could not score a run against him – and knew it.

In 1956, his penultimate season, he stood in unhappily as captain, losing most of his hair with worry, but the next year, at the age of 45, he was back to his happy best with 132 wickets.

Unlike some among his county colleagues, he was a devoted husband. "Me," he would say with his lovely turn of phrase, "I'm a one-dog, one-bone man."

The toothache bowler
Across his long career he conceded runs at just 2.2 an over

Tom Goddard of Gloucestershire

> There is, about his bowling, a hostility which one would expect to feel in a fast bowler rather than a slow. He is always "at" the batsman.
> *John Arlott*

Tom Goddard started as a fast bowler with an awkward run-up. Some suggested, with his great hands, he might take up spin, but his captain would not have it and after six years in and out of the Gloucestershire team he was released. Thereupon he took himself to Lord's, got some coaching and returned in 1929 when, under the inspired captaincy of Bev Lyon, his sharply turning off-breaks took 184 wickets.

He bowled round the wicket, with fielders as close to the bat as he could coax them. A tall man, he could get the ball to lift viciously and, with a multitude of variations, he was close to unplayable on helpful pitches, taking 17 Kent wickets in a day in 1939. His loud, beseeching appeal was legendary, winning him 516 lbws, best of all the one which gained the famous tie at Bristol against the 1930 Australians.

He kept his spinning finger in service with urine and, though no conversationalist and certainly not one to show visible pleasure, he retained his great hunger for wickets. Twice in his late forties he was the season's leading wicket-taker. Then at the age of 51, having been persuaded to retire, he was summoned back and, with a pulled thigh muscle, took ten wickets in the bank-holiday match against Somerset.

"Owazeeee?"

Leading wicket-taker in 1937, 1939, 1947 and 1949

Dennis Brookes of Northamptonshire

Mister Northampton

Greatest run-scorer in the county's history

> He played in a calm and dignified manner; elegant driving was a feature of his play. He managed to make the fielding side feel that to bowl a bouncer to him was an affront against decency – not to say law and order.
> *Dickie Dodds*

There was a serenity about Dennis Brookes, as a man and as a batsman. He played his cricket without fuss or fluster, a rare point of reliability in Northamptonshire's darkest years. A Yorkshireman by birth, he had been discovered playing in rough-mown fields in the little Barkston Ash League, and after the war Yorkshire wanted him back, to open with Hutton. But he had his married home ten doors from the front gates, and he had his loyalty. So, for 15 post-war summers, the Northampton folk enjoyed the quiet elegance of his front-foot batting.

In 1954 he became the county's first professional captain, moulding a side that in 1957 were runners-up with 15 victories. Then he was asked to step down in favour of an amateur, which he did with predictable good grace, remaining an active servant of the club – as second eleven captain, Assistant Secretary, committeeman, then President – till his death in 2006.

John Langridge of Sussex

> Over the years he worked out his own particular ABC of batsmanship – all shuffle, push and dab. He mastered these movements to such an extent that he became one of the best players of quick bowling in the country, and a very dependable opening bat.
> *Trevor Bailey*

From the early 1930s through to the '50s John Langridge and older brother Jim were at the heart of the Sussex eleven. Growing up on a fruit farm in Newick, north of Lewes, they were country boys, with nothing of suavity or glamour about them. Robertson-Glasgow thought they lacked the freedom of imagination to be cricketing greats – but on the county circuit, my word, they were effective.

John was not pretty to watch as a batsman. He had an open-chested stance and no great backlift, but he remains the greatest run-scorer in Sussex history, hitting 2,000 runs in a season eleven times.

Though not athletic in build or movement, he was an outstanding first slip. In his last summer, 1955, when he was 45 years old, his huge hands held a record 66 catches in the championship. Then he turned to umpiring where his cheerful, straightforward honesty was loved and respected. Cricket was his life. Between 1928 and 1983, as player and umpire, he took the field in an unrivalled 1,131 first-class matches.

Great servant of Sussex

Most runs, 1938 and 1949
Most catches, six times

Stories of the 1940s

Number eleven hits out

Derbyshire v Essex, Chesterfield, Thursday 7 August 1947

Peter Smith was not an obvious number eleven, but then nobody was at Essex. They could all bat, and they all did. The order rarely stayed the same from one game to the next. It was part of the unpredictable fun of 'Burly' Tom Pearce's captaincy.

At the start of 1946 Dickie Dodds, fresh home from military service in India, arrived for trial as a promising leg-break bowler, only to be told to his great surprise, "You're just the man we need to open the batting." An adventurous shot-maker who thought nothing of hitting the first ball of an innings for six, he was hardly in the mould of a conventional opener – but convention did not always come into it at Essex.

Peter Smith's arrival in the team in 1929 was even odder. A 20-year-old batsman at the Chelmsford club, he did not impress when he volunteered himself for a county trial, but they taught him how to bowl leg-breaks and, always short of players, gave him five games in the first eleven. He averaged 6 with the bat and took one wicket, with a high full toss, for 233 runs. Yet they persevered.

Another who started in 1929 was Tommy Wade, who enjoyed early success as an off-spinner, then broke his arm playing soccer and finished up as the county's wicket-keeper.

After the war, with Farnes and Eastman dead and Nichols too old to return, Peter Smith and his cousin Ray, a farmer, did most of the bowling. Ray would swing the new ball, then put on his cap and bowl off-breaks, while Peter would amble in hour after hour with his dipping, sharply spinning leg-breaks and googlies. At Leicester, in May 1947, Essex got through 148 overs in the six-hour day, and the Smiths bowled 104 of them.

Peter spent much of 1946 batting at number three, hitting a hundred against Hampshire, but by August 1947, when they travelled to Chesterfield, he was down at number eleven, fresh from a pair against Worcestershire.

Derbyshire were third in the championship table, with a strong bowling side, especially on their own green pitches, and on the evening of the first day, having scored 223, they reduced Essex to 65 for six.

Next in were the young Cambridge undergraduates Trevor Bailey and Doug Insole. Bailey, who topped the Essex batting averages that summer, was at eight while Insole, who a fortnight earlier had hit three fifties in a row, was playing now as the wicket-keeper and batting at nine.

Bailey made 19, Insole 48 and at close of play Essex were 173 for eight. Next morning, when Ray Smith was out, they were 199 for nine. Frank Vigar, a steady if rather stodgy batsman, was still there on 61, and he was joined by Peter Smith for the last rites of the innings. It was just another day in the summer-long round of county cricket: a good midweek crowd at the attractive Queen's Park ground, pleasant sunshine and nothing that much at stake.

The Chesterfield pitch had bounce, the 38-year-old Bill Copson still had pace, and Peter Smith, for all his military-style moustache and his wartime years as an army captain in Egypt, was not the bravest of batsmen. "He was retreating, giving it the old wave," Doug Insole says, "and the ball would go over the slips. And in between he'd hit some very good blows."

He saw off the quicks and, when the slow-left-armer Eric Marsh came on, he despatched him for 22 in the over. "After the batsmen," the Smiths used to joke, "come the run-scorers."

Soon after lunch, despite a 61-run start, he beat Vigar to 100, reaching three figures with a copybook straight drive. After that he had a big thrash, hitting Copson for a mighty six and finishing with 163 out of a partnership of 218. It remains the highest innings ever played by a number eleven batsman.

In the second innings, when they won by five wickets, he was put up to number three – and was out for 4. Then it was down to Clacton-on-Sea, to play Leicestershire. On the first day Peter Smith bowled 50 overs, taking eight wickets; on the second Tom Pearce, demoting himself to number ten, put on 95 for the last wicket with Tommy Wade.

Of Essex's eleven at Chesterfield only Ray Smith had never made a first-class century, and he put that right the following July at Colchester – also against Derbyshire. Coming in at number nine, on a hat-trick, with Frank Vigar once more propping up the other end, he walloped 100 in 63 minutes. It was the fastest century of the summer, an achievement he repeated in both 1951 and 1955.

At Southend in 1948 the Smiths bowled 75 overs when Essex became the only team all summer to bowl out the Australians inside a day – though the tourists did score 721.

"We try to play our cricket happily," said Peter Smith, "as it is meant to be played. Essex cricket has never been sound or predictable, but it is always interesting."

Roly in his prime

What a summer Roly Jenkins had in 1949! He had spent the winter with England in South Africa, surprising everybody by topping the Test and tour bowling averages, and, with his confidence fortified, he returned home to enjoy the season of his life. With teasing, high-flighted leg-breaks he took 183 first-class wickets, including two hat-tricks in a match against Surrey; he scored 1,183 runs and, the sharpest of cover fielders, held 27 catches. For much of the summer Worcestershire, after years of mediocrity, were top of the championship table, and in almost every victory he played a vital part.

His joy was not confined to cricket. With the trip to South Africa forcing him to postpone his wedding, he was granted that rarest of privileges for a professional cricketer, a week off during the season. While the county played Cambridge University and the Royal Navy, he spent the days with his wife Olive in a guest house in North Wales. 'They say it's sunny outside,' read the postcard to his team-mates.

He grew up, the youngest of ten, in a sporting family, and he lived for his cricket. 'He loves the game as much as any man living,' the *Guardian*'s Terence Prittie wrote, 'and I do not except Captain J.W.A. Stephenson, of the Army and Essex, or even the Indian Gul Mahommed. That love is instinct in every facet of Jenkins's play.'

With the love, however, came a bundle of idiosyncrasies. He bowled with his cap on, reaching the crease with crab-like movements and exhorting the ball to "spin for Roly!" If the batsman swept him, he would throw his cap at them. "Haven't they got any proper batsmen today?" he would say or, to Somerset's Bill Alley, "I hope your chickens all die."

He was forever fretting about the finer points of his bowling technique. He could take eight wickets in an innings and be in the nets at seven the next morning, trying to sort out some fault. In later years he took to ringing Jim Laker for help: "I've lost my mechanics, Jim. I can't bowl." "What do you expect me to do, Roly?" Jim would reply. "I can't see what you're doing wrong from a hundred miles away.'

"I used to play skittles with him," Worcester's Martin Horton said. "He would still worry about his bowling for nine pins. People would say, 'We've only come for a night out, Roly,' and he'd say, 'If you got your hand here and your shoulder there …'"

In 1949, newly married and taking wickets every game, he had no such problems. At the season's end, chosen as one of *Wisden*'s Five Cricketers of the Year, he wrote a five-page article on spin bowling for an MCC book, *The Young Cricketer*.

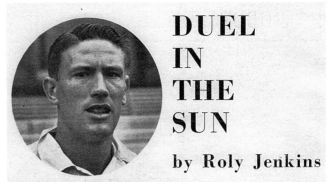

DUEL IN THE SUN

by Roly Jenkins

The well-known Worcestershire player explains why spin-bowling is a craft that can only be acquired with patience and endless practice

It is no easy task to become a first-class spin-bowler. Let me hasten to say, though, that the reward far outweighs the effort and struggle entailed. Those who achieve the skill command a fascinating and enjoyable life.

Walter Robins, former Middlesex captain and now a Test selector, a pillar of the Lord's establishment, congratulated him. "That's a very good article, Jenkins. Who wrote it for you?" And, quick as flash, in his strong Worcester accent, came the reply, "I wrote it myself, sir. Who read it for you?"

He could not resist – like the time in the war when, batting with an officer, he was told off for the way he had called a single. "Now listen here, Jenkins. You don't say 'come one'; you say 'come one, sir.'" Straight back came Roly: "And if I'm wearing a cap, sir, should I salute when we cross?"

He went off to his wedding in late June, the leading wicket-taker in the country. When he arrived back, he was glowing: "I never realised you could have so much fun without laughing," he said. Then he went out and bowled 49 overs, following that next day with an innings of 76.

That summer England played four three-day Tests against New Zealand, all of which ended in draws. England, desperate for wicket-taking bowlers, tried seven spinners. But Jenkins, their best bowler in South Africa, was not one of them.

The reason? It seems that he cracked one joke too many. On the final morning of an early-season match at Lord's, playing for MCC against Essex, he told a leading figure in the game, "I'm going to bat like an amateur today. I want to catch the early train back to Worcester." In fact, he hit a good 68 not out, but his levity led to a formal carpeting and his dropping by the selectors.

There is no evidence that it got him down. He enjoyed his summer, with Worcester and with Olive, too much for that.

Images of the 1940s

Bramall Lane, 1940

On the night of Thursday 12 December, with a clear sky and a full moon, the city of Sheffield was the target of a sustained German bombing raid. With a second raid on the Sunday night, 602 people were killed, 513 seriously injured and large parts of the city centre destroyed.

At Bramall Lane most of the stand next to the pavilion was demolished. "It was terrible," the groundsman Fred Kean recalled after the war. "There were huge craters in both pitches, and the whole area was covered with crags of cement and debris of all kinds. It was enough to break a man's heart."

It was expected to take many years to restore the ground, but with a never-say-die spirit they were staging important cricket matches there by the summer of 1943. *Wisden* reported that the wicket 'showed no sign of the damage'.

The Oval, 1945

No ground suffered more than the Oval. Requisitioned by the War Ministry, it was home to barrage balloons, an assault course and, finally, prisoner-of-war cages that were never used. By the time these men had removed nearly 2,000 posts from the field, there was nothing left of the smooth surface on which Len Hutton had hit his record-breaking 364 against Australia.

In the early months of 1946 the new groundsman Bert Lock arranged for tens of thousands of turves to be transported from Gravesend Marshes. He supervised an army of local shilling-an-hour volunteers to lay them while day after day he pulled the roller up and down.

How would the new square play? In May, when the Indian tourists batted on it, the answer became clear. For the only time in cricket history, batsmen number ten and eleven both made centuries.

1947: The summer of Edrich and Compton

Bill Edrich and Denis Compton walk to the wicket at Lord's on Whit Saturday in May 1947. The Times called them 'two batsmen entirely suited to a holiday occasion', and they did not disappoint, both scoring centuries in a partnership of 223.

After years of war the glorious summer of 1947 lifted the spirits of all cricket-lovers, none more than those who saw the batting of the Middlesex pair Bill Edrich and Denis Compton. They were free spirits: the hard-living Edrich, in the words of John Arlott, 'a personification of life and drive'; the good-looking Compton, in the words of Neville Cardus, 'eccentric and original, always young of impulse, pulling science by the beard like a cheeky schoolboy'. Between them, in all matches, they scored an extraordinary 7,355 runs, with 30 centuries.

Edrich led the way till early August but at Canterbury, in his role as fast bowler, he tore the muscles under his right shoulder. Compton, meanwhile, was carrying a bad knee, a footballing injury that flared up in the closing weeks of the summer. By the final match at the Oval, when Middlesex as Champion County beat The Rest, Compton was batting on one leg and at one stage had to retire. Yet, against some of the best bowlers in England, he managed to score 246, and Edrich hit 180.

'In the end,' Arlott wrote at the close of that summer, 'when a younger generation, who never saw Compton, ridicule our stories of him behind our backs, then we shall know that it was all a fairy story – that it was a dream that passed across English cricket in a summer of amazing sun and lit the farthest corner of every field in the land.'

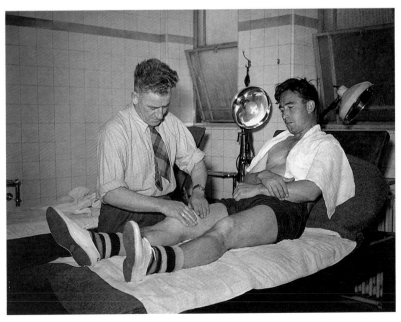

Denis Compton with the Arsenal physio, in the week after the end of the cricket season.

1946: Where can we find a captain?

The captain had to be an amateur. It is true that Leicestershire had resorted to a stopgap professional in 1935; they did the same in 1946 when they found no amateur with sufficient time or means. But that was Leicestershire. Such an option was barely possible at the grander counties.

Surrey hoped Monty Garland-Wells, their 1939 captain, would return, but his father died, he had a legal practice and he could not spare the time. Eventually, so the story goes, they decided to look for Leo Bennett, a popular man in London club cricket who had played a few games for Surrey 2nd XI before the war. He had been a major in the Worcestershire Regiment, but it was not clear where he now was.

One day there arrived at the Oval another Bennett, Nigel, who had been a major with the Royal Fusiliers in the Far East. He, too, had played a few pre-war games for the 2nd XI. Some say he was looking in to see if he could play again in 1946, others that he was renewing his membership.

"Major Bennett?" was the excited response. "We've been looking for you." And he left the office with the captaincy.

The *Cricketer* magazine was enthusiastic: 'I am told he has a pleasing personality and, when he settles down, he should make plenty of runs.'

The professionals were less impressed. He batted in the tail, and in the field he showed little understanding; he even had to be stopped from returning the new ball to the bowler by rolling it across the grass. Glad to be playing again, however, they looked on the bright side. "I reckon we can cope with him for the summer," one said. "His wife's a real cracker."

Though it has become part of cricket's folklore, some think the story of his mistaken identity was only a joke made up by the professionals. In fairness to Bennett, though *Wisden* thought his inexperience 'an unconquerable hindrance to the satisfactory acccomplishment of arduous duties', he did score 688 runs at an average of 16 and he was by no means the only such person to captain a county in the 1940s.

Lancashire appointed Tommy Higson, the chairman's son who had played a few times for the county before the war. Then, when he withdrew in April, they opted for Jack Fallows, son of the treasurer, another – like Bennett – who had never played a first-class match. The *Manchester Guardian* lamented the county's 'pious regard' for convention:

> Would it have been so very outrageous and unpopular
> if the committee had advanced boldly down the pitch
> of progress and hit that ancient ball for six?

The 39-year-old Fallows, in 23 championship matches, contributed a meagre 151 runs but, unlike Surrey who sank to 11th place, Lancashire finished a healthy third. In the words of newcomer Geoff Edrich, "Jack couldn't play, he wasn't a cricketer, but he did a good job. We had a far better season than people thought we'd have. He was good fun, a good mixer, and the senior players all helped him."

Northamptonshire turned to Peter Murray-Willis, who had done a wonderfully enthusiastic job running fund-raising matches during the war. But the day-in-day-out demands of captaining a county eleven proved beyond him. He lacked tactical acumen, and the professionals were not impressed when one day, chasing a ball to the boundary, the wind blew his cap off and he turned and ran after it. They won just one match, in his absence at Rushden, and at the end of July the committee let him go, passing the captaincy to Jack Webster, a Harrow schoolmaster on his summer holidays.

Derbyshire made do with the war-wounded greengrocer Gilbert Hodgkinson though he was only available for half the matches, while at Somerset Bunty Longrigg had to balance the rival demands of the captaincy and his solicitor's practice. When the schoolmaster Fred Castle stood in for him, Longrigg issued him with copious instructions, right down to the toss: "If the coin lands on the wicket, call heads; anywhere else, tails."

Eccentricity was par for the course at Somerset where Longrigg's successor was the Millfield headmaster Jack Meyer. He had been a good cricketer in the 1920s, but he was now 42 years old and suffering from lumbago so painful that he had to take six aspirins each morning before he could get his body moving. "He shouldn't have played," one team member, Eric Hill, said, "but everybody was too frightened to tell him."

One day at the Oval, complaining about his feet, he took his boots off, parked them behind the stumps and fielded the session in his socks. Another time, feeling hungry on a long train journey to Manchester, he pulled the communication cord and, when the train juddered to a halt, he proceeded to order meals for the whole team.

On the day before Somerset's first match of the summer he gathered them all into the large amateurs' dressing room at Taunton and, pulling out a piece of paper, proceeded like a good schoolmaster to organise them into fielding positions. "Bertie's on at this end, making 'em boom a bit ... Does everybody know where they are? ... Right. That's the end of Bertie; now it's Arthur at the other end."

Jack Meyer
Somerset, 1947

Peter Murray-Willis
Northamptonshire, 1946

Major Nigel Bennett
Surrey, 1946

Bill Sime
Nottinghamshire, 1947-50

The next day at Lord's it all went smoothly till the third wicket fell. Then Middlesex's new number five took guard, and he was a left-hander. Getting no help at all from the chuckling professionals, poor Jack Meyer took an age to sort it out.

Nottinghamshire's Bill Sime was another with his own ideas. He was brought in to provide a lighter touch than the martinet George Heane, and he certainly did that. Sime was a barrister with a lucrative practice specialising in divorce and, though Nottingham High Court tried to schedule his cases to fit with the cricket, he often missed whole sessions of play. On one occasion he left them to bat out the draw, and after an unexpected collapse they had to send for him.

"You were never quite sure what was going to happen with dear old Bill," Reg Simpson said, recalling an afternoon at Edgbaston when Sime brought himself on to bowl slow full-tosses, sending three fielders to the legside boundary. "We spent a few overs chasing the ball here and there. But the batsmen hit it on the ground so that theory went for a burton."

Then there were the third days of matches when the long afternoon session had no tea interval. Sime insisted on a short break in play during which, with a table and chair set up by the boundary, he would sit down and be served a cuppa.

As Reg Simpson put it, "Great days. Great fun."

Surrey's search to replace Nigel Bennett was resolved at the first committee meeting of 1947 when, after a long discussion, Errol Holmes, captain in the '30s, said, to gasps of astonishment, "Well, I am prepared to take on the captaincy again, as long as I am paid." A 'non-job' in the insurance business was arranged and, with generous first-class rail expenses, Holmes was able once more to be the amateur captain of Surrey.

Somerset, in desperation, appointed three captains in 1948; even then they needed two others to fill the gaps. Northamptonshire had two years of the ageing Arthur Childs-Clarke, an outgoing character who had been on the stage. The committee offered him £10 for each place the team finished above last, but no payment was required. Derbyshire turned to the 42-year-old Eddie Gothard, a fine all-round sportsman from Burton-on-Trent but another who had never played a first-class match. Under his strict leadership they played good cricket in his two years in charge. He himself offered little, but the 18 first-class victims of his gentle away-swing did include Bill Edrich, as part of a hat-trick, and Don Bradman.

Sometimes a county struck lucky. For 1947 and 1948 Lancashire were led by the all-rounder Ken Cranston, a dentist. So successful was he in his only two summers of county cricket that he played eight Tests, including the winter tour of the West Indies on which he captained England once.

Leicestershire returned to amateur ways in 1949 when they appointed a young army man, Stuart Symington, whose main credentials were topping the averages five years earlier at Canford, a minor public school in Dorset. He gave himself the role of opening bowler, but he soon realised how great a step he was taking. When Harold Gimblett smacked him round the Taunton ground, he stood in mid-pitch in despair: "If this is first-class cricket," he moaned to himself, "I've bloody well had it." By August he had slipped away.

Some of these captains, embarrassed by their failures, would never return to their counties, but in their differing ways they all did their best. It was not their fault; they were being asked to sustain a way of life that was no longer viable.

1947: 'A golden match to remember'

Gloucestershire v Middlesex, Cheltenham, 16/18 August 1947

They were queuing outside the Cheltenham College ground from half past six on Saturday morning, five hours before start of play. At eight o'clock the first motor-coach of Middlesex supporters arrived from London. By nine there were several thousand patiently waiting, winding round the pavements in a long crocodile; in one street a local singer, keen for an audience, entertained them with his repertoire of Bach motets. Then at 9.15, an hour ahead of schedule, Lieutenant-Colonel Henson, the Gloucestershire Secretary, opened the gates, and in they all swarmed. This was the game of the season: Gloucestershire, first in the championship table, versus Middlesex, four points behind in second place. They were not going to miss it.

Oh, the magic of that summer of 1947! The people were worn down by six years of war, by ration books and bombed-out city centres, by the very worst of winters, and at last the sun had come out. Cricket had the weather to show itself in its full glory, and it did not disappoint.

The Middlesex team, walking through the crowd, were amazed. "I've never been on a ground for a cricket match," Bill Edrich said, "where there was such an air of Football Cup Final excitement."

One glance at the averages in the morning papers made clear why Middlesex were strong. First in the batting, with 2,835 runs at an average of 105, was Bill Edrich; second, with 2,602 runs, was Denis Compton; while their opener Jack Robertson, with 2,389, was the only other man to have passed 2,000. They had different styles – Compton the carefree genius, Edrich the gritty fighter, Robertson the elegantly correct craftsman – but all three scored quickly, and that gave time for the bowlers to take wickets. A week earlier at the Oval, in front of 'a crowd of an immensity that would have flattered a Test match' – maybe 30,000 – they scored 537 for two in the day. Robertson made his eleventh hundred of the summer, fellow opener Syd Brown hit 98, then Compton and Edrich got to work. 'What an outlook for Surrey,' wrote *The Times*. 'Dante could have thought of no harder penance than for bowlers to be faced on a perfect Oval wicket by Edrich and Compton at four o'clock in the afternoon with 250 runs already on the board.'

Gloucestershire's success was more surprising. It was their first summer without Wally Hammond, and their batting line-up, though they had Charlie Barnett, Jack Crapp and George Emmett, was not among the strongest in the country. What they did have, however, were outstanding slow bowlers: the slow-left-armer Sam Cook and the off-spinner Tom Goddard, who had already taken 183 first-class wickets, almost 40 more than any other bowler. Crucially, they had pitches at Bristol and Gloucester that were perfect for the pair of them. Their ten home games had produced nine wins and a draw.

For many years the Bristol pitch had been a batsman's delight but, keen to stage the Test trial in 1947, Gloucestershire had been stung when Yorkshire's Brian Sellers had disparaged the idea, saying its billiard-table surface was "not worth playing on". Smarting from the rejection, they called in the Bingley Groundkeeping Research Institute, whose advice was to add large quantities of sand, as a result of which Goddard and Cook helped themselves to wickets by the dozen. Cook's finest hour, when he took nine for 42, was ironically against Sellers' Yorkshire, who were humbled inside two days.

In the August Bank Holiday match, when Goddard brought the game to a rapid conclusion with five wickets in seven balls, Somerset were bowled out for 98 and 25, a debacle that led their captain Jack Meyer to say, "It was like batting on the Weston-super-Mare beach."

Through August England sweltered in a heatwave. Each day the temperature rose to new heights, reaching 90°F during the Cheltenham match. The teams inspected the dry, dusty pitch, and both knew what they wanted: to bat first, then set the spinners to work as the pitch cracked under the hot sun. "Middlesex have won the toss and will bat," came the announcement, bringing groans around the ground.

The pitch looked made for Goddard, but the score reached 65 for one before Gloucestershire's Basil Allen brought him into the attack. Was that a mistake? In the days and years that followed, many would say so.

Compton and Robertson were with England at the Oval, but Edrich was here. Creating a stir in some papers, he had declared himself unfit for the Test but available for Middlesex. Unable to bowl or throw, he could still bat and he did so, battling to 50. 'Tom Goddard was virtually unplayable,' he wrote. 'There was no telling what he would do with the ball.'

At 12.15 the gates were closed, with a record 14,500 spectators crammed into the ground, many more than were there for the Australians in 1926. They spilled all over the grass, sitting well inside the boundary, and beyond it they stood fifteen or twenty deep, trying to glimpse what they could

RECORD-BREAKING CHELTENHAM CRICKET FESTIVAL

of the game. Everywhere, as the day grew hotter and hotter, the heads in the crowd were covered: straw hats, knotted handkerchiefs, carefully folded newspapers. One lady had a Victorian parasol while some among the demobbed soldiers in khaki-drill shorts and shirts wore topees. The First Aid men were busy all day with cases of fainting.

At the Oval, according to one reporter, 'Interest in the game at Cheltenham was so great that most of us were far more concerned about the hourly reports from the west country than we were in watching England.'

MCC had instructed county captains to 'animate their sides into enterprise', and none did this with more evangelical enthusiasm than Walter Robins. "What difference did he make as a captain?" one team member was asked, and the reply came back: "The difference between the quick and the dead."

Their approach at Cheltenham was to play shots and make what runs they could. Robins himself fell to a running catch by Colin Scott at long-on, a dismissal greeted by one supporter with a loud burst from his football rattle. Later Scott failed to hold a second catch, tripping over the boys inside the boundary. It was that sort of day.

Middlesex made 180, Gloucestershire 153, and in the last minutes of the evening Goddard with a great appeal – "Owazeeee?" – had Edrich lbw. 'I walked indoors,' the batsman wrote, 'while the ground shook with the deep-chested shouting of Gloucestershire farmers, who felt that I was but the first sheaf of a harvest.'

Edrich recalled how all weekend there was an 'atmosphere of suppressed excitement' throughout their hotel and in the streets. Robins kept them cheerful, while his fellow amateur George Mann provoked laughter at breakfast when he recounted a dream – or was it a nightmare? – in which Goddard's long spinning finger became one of the Devil's horns.

On Monday, before the effects of the heavy roller wore off, Middlesex reached 103 for two. Nightwatchman Harry Sharp,

in only his second championship match, played with patience for 46 while Robins counter-attacked, hitting 45 before falling to a catch that no one there that morning ever forgot.

There were 15,000 in the ground – more, incredibly, than had been fitted in on Saturday – and they sat 15 feet into the field in front of the scorers' tent, including a woman in her own deck chair. Spellbound they watched as Robins lifted Goddard high towards the square leg boundary on the hospital side. It looked a certain six but Cliff Monks, 'the chunky blond stonemason and Sunday organist from Coalpit Heath', ran at full tilt, stuck out a hand and plucked the ball almost off the head of a young spectator.

Many were those, Bomber Wells and Frank Keating among them, who in later life claimed to have been the spectator. Monks, never a regular, played 65 times for his county, but nothing in his career came close to the triumph of that moment. His *Wisden* obituary ran to 16 lines, and ten of them were about the catch.

Robins' dismissal left Middlesex on 103 for three, a lead of 130, but Goddard – 'striding among the wickets like a farmer scything' – soon made that 141 all out. For the third time that summer he had taken 15 wickets in a match.

The rest for the home supporters was anti-climax. Middlesex had slow-left-armer Jack Young and, in the game of his life, off-spinner Harry Sharp. The target was 169, and on the worn wicket Gloucestershire made only 100 of them.

At the Oval news of the result brought a great roar. County cricket mattered in 1947. It was certainly a game which Bill Edrich, for all the great moments of his Test career, did not forget:

> As things turned out, the match decided the championship. But it would not have mattered if it had decided the fate of the British Empire – it could not have been played more keenly by anyone on either side or, I believe, enjoyed more. It was a golden match to remember.

1948: Wooller's Welsh wizardry

'Off the field they were like a pack of happy schoolboys,' one journalist said of Wilf Wooller's Glamorgan team of 1948. He had been at the party in Hull when the Welshmen had sung *Sosban Fach* with great gusto, stirring some of the Yorkshire side to reply with the *Holmfirth Anthem*. Then he had been on the train with them to Birmingham when all journey long they had talked, laughed, played cards and argued. "It was always noisy," all-rounder Allan Watkins said. "I could be arguing with Wilf every five minutes of the day, all about cricket, all good fun. And Wilf and Haydn were always arguing. It was never quiet."

Watkins was picked for the final Test at the Oval. He had never played a first-class match for anyone but Glamorgan, and he could not get over the silence in the dressing room. "Nobody spoke to me. There was no joy in the side at all."

Wilf Wooller was the heartbeat of that Glamorgan team. A rugby three-quarter for Wales, he had spent three years of the war as a prisoner of the Japanese, years in which a fierce determination, a will to survive, had replaced the shallowness of his happy-go-lucky public-school youth.

It was his second summer as captain, and he had a master plan. With no great stars in the side, he created the best fielding unit in the country, exploiting a weakness he had spotted on the circuit: batsmen not good at playing the ball coming into their legs. Len Muncer, a leg-break bowler recruited from Middlesex, was turned into an off-spinner, 'Pete' Hever bowled in-swing, and a predatory leg trap was formed from Wooller himself, Phil Clift and, best of all, Allan Watkins. No county had ever taken fielding as seriously as this. If they ever had a bad day, Wooller would have them at the ground at 9.30 next morning for an hour of fielding practice.

He was a keen disciplinarian but not like Maurice Turnbull before the war, when the professionals had to make appointments to speak to their captain. Wooller led from the front, he was their 'Skipper', but he was always with the team; he travelled, drank, sang, argued with them.

They started the summer with a bang, winning nine of their first twelve games. Little Willie Jones, always a bag of nerves, was the first man in the country to 1,000 runs, hitting two double-centuries in a fortnight. After the first, he said, "I'll never do it again." After the second, "Dieu, people are going to expect me to do it every time." After starting to read a great pile of congratulatory telegrams, he put them away in his bag: "I think I'll open these when I get a duck."

The slow-left-armer Stan Trick, whose work in his father's garage only allowed him to play occasionally, took 22 wickets in two games at Swansea, while Len Muncer twice took 15 wickets in a match, over half of them catches in the leg trap. By mid-June their ebullient keeper Haydn Davies was saying with confidence that they would be champions. Unfancied Glamorgan, could it really happen?

Glamorgan 1948

(standing)
*Willie Jones, Phil Clift,
'Pete' Hever, Stan Trick,
Gilbert Parkhouse,
Jim Eaglestone, Jim Pleass*

(sitting)
*George Lavis, Haydn Davies,
Johnnie Clay, Wilf Wooller,
Emrys Davies, Len Muncer,
Allan Watkins*

*Eleven Welshmen – and three
from Middlesex: Len Muncer,
Jim Eaglestone and Norman Hever*

They lost their way after that, losing their place at the head of the table and reviving the pessimism of those like Emrys Davies, whose memories went back to the struggles of the 1920s when only sweepstakes, dances, whist drives and a shilling fund kept the club going. One year they had six captains and five wicket-keepers.

Then came a season-turning victory at Weston-super-Mare, when Wooller took three 'wonder-catches' as Somerset, all out for 96, lost by eight runs. Back Glamorgan went into first place, and they were still there when Surrey, one of their rivals, arrived at Cardiff in mid-August. With Watkins away at the Oval, they recalled – in a masterstroke of inspiration – the 50-year-old off-spinner Johnnie Clay.

Nobody had lived the ups and many downs of Glamorgan County Cricket Club as Clay had done. In the side from the first season in 1921, he played 31 times – 29 defeats and two rained-off draws – before he tasted victory. He captained the team through much of the '20s, kept them afloat as treasurer in the '30s, and led them again in the first year after the war.

With a quiet wit, he was a Test selector, a JP and a true gentleman. Back in the days of his captaincy, the story goes, he was too polite to ask one newcomer – a great hulk of a man, recruited from heaven knows where – whether he batted or bowled. "We'll put him in the slips," he said. "Even if he can't catch, he's a big man; something might hit him."

There he was on that never-to-be-forgotten evening at the Arms Park, his hair grey but his bowling arm still high. On a damp, drying pitch Glamorgan, thanks to a spirited 89 by Wooller, had made 239, and in the closing hour, with the ground packed, Surrey, the great Surrey, were reduced to 47 for nine. Their chief destroyer was the tall, calm figure of Johnnie Clay, at one point taking three wickets, all lbw, in an over. 'To ardent Welsh cricket followers there has never been a player like Johnnie,' wrote one reporter. 'Whenever he hits the pads, they make the welkin ring with their appeals.'

The next day Surrey lost by an innings, Clay had match figures of ten for 66 and, with Watkins still in London, receiving treatment for a shoulder injury, Clay stayed in the team as they travelled down to Bournemouth. If Glamorgan could beat Hampshire and neither Surrey nor Yorkshire won, they would be certain champions.

Rain reduced Saturday's play to ten minutes, but by mid-morning on Tuesday – with runs from Emrys Davies and Willie Jones, wickets from Len Muncer and Johnnie Clay – Hampshire were following on. At Lord's Surrey were close to defeat; at Taunton Yorkshire were struggling.

The Hampshire wickets fell: five by lunch, nine by 2.40. Then Johnnie Clay, already with five wickets in the innings, wrapped Charlie Knott, the Hampshire number eleven, on the pads, and who should be there to answer his appeal but Dai Davies, his Glamorgan companion through so many of those struggling pre-war years.

Davies always denied it, but everybody there swore that his reply was, "That's out, and we've won the championship." According to Knott, he was the first to appeal. Certainly he was prominent in the crowd that gathered in front of the pavilion, singing *Sospan Fach* and the Welsh national anthem.

Gwlad, Gwlad, pleidiol wyf i'm gwlad.

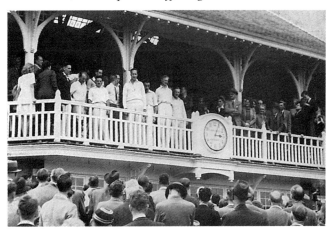

Quiet, respectable Bournemouth had never seen a scene like it. There were Welshmen everywhere, and they demanded speeches from Wooller and from Clay, whom they greeted with several choruses of *For he's a jolly good fellow*.

"This victory for Glamorgan," Clay told them, "will do a lot of good not only for cricket generally but for similar counties like Warwickshire and Hampshire. No longer is the championship the monopoly of the few."

Emrys Davies, with his ingrained pessimism, would not believe it till he had heard it on the radio. Meanwhile Allan Watkins, anxious for news in south London, studied the stop press score in each hourly edition of the evening paper.

At ten o'clock that night the team reached Cardiff railway station, where thousands of supporters were waiting for them, singing their hearts out. Wooller had gone to London, to play next day at Lord's, so it was left to Clay to make more speeches: over the station tannoy and in the street outside.

It was a triumph of teamwork and team spirit and, above all, of the great-hearted Wilf Wooller who, as John Arlott wrote, 'lived with his side, the only way to *know* cricket'.

1950 – 1959

The end of the post-war attendance boom

A decade of stability

Surrey champions seven years in a row

Our county players play too much so that, as Sir Pelham Warner says, a championship match is 'a habit, not an event'. They lose their freshness quite early in the summer, and so are disposed to jog along with an economy of effort.

No one wants to see first-class cricket become a circus. On the other hand it is not tolerable that games are simply allowed to drift into a stalemate. The dictum of A.G. Steel, written half a century ago, is even more pertinent today than it was then: "Cricket, to maintain its hold on the national character, must be eager, quick and full of action." If it fails in this, the county system must die.

E.W. Swanton, 1953

Against the increased tempo of modern life, cricket must be regarded as rather a slow-moving activity. Nevertheless I believe that cricket represents something traditional in the English way of life which will always command enough support to keep its head above water.

Harry Altham, Treasurer of MCC, 1959

In about eleven of the first-class counties I would say that, apart from the Australian year, the level of support in terms of gates and membership is insufficient. Television is a potential source of income as yet untapped, comparatively. What a great medium of entertainment Test cricket has become. Is it too much to ask the vast television public for some modest payment for the pleasure?

Wilf Wooller, May 1955

1950 All counties play 28 rather than 26 matches. Devon apply to join the championship, causing *Wisden* to propose a reorganisation into two divisions of 12, with promotion and relegation.
England, participating for the first time in football's World Cup, are beaten 1-0 by the United States of America.

1951 Tom Dollery of Warwickshire becomes the first professional cricketer to captain a championship-winning county.
The BBC reduces its radio news readers to eight, with no regional dialects or women among those chosen. "People," it explains, "do not like momentous events such as war and disaster to be read by the female voice."

1952 MCC sets up a Youth Cricket Association, with the aim of providing more cricket for 11- to 18-year-olds. A coaching scheme is created, with a first meeting in November at Lilleshall Hall in Shropshire.
Britain tests its first atomic bomb off the north coast of Australia.

1953 At the Oval in August England regain the Ashes after 19 years.
In a golden sporting summer Stanley Matthews wins his first FA Cup Final winners' medal, and Sir Gordon Richards, five days after receiving a knighthood, wins his first Derby. On the evening before Queen Elizabeth II is crowned, news arrives from Nepal that a British mountaineering expedition has reached the summit of Everest.
At Wembley in November the England football team, never beaten on home soil by a team outside the British Isles, lose 6-3 to Hungary, prompting a realisation that the national game has failed to keep pace with developments on the continent. The Times calls the game 'the twilight of the gods': 'England found themselves strangers in a strange world.'

1954 Pakistan tour England for the first time, drawing the four-Test series with a 24-run victory at the Oval.
On a windy May evening in Oxford Roger Bannister, a trainee hospital doctor, becomes the first man to run a mile in under four minutes. In 1931 the record stood at 4 minutes 10 seconds.
The Ministry of Health warns against alarmist reaction to a report linking smoking and cancer.
The last rationing ends, with the removal of restrictions on the purchase of meat.

1955 Surrey win the championship with 23 wins out of 28, the highest proportion ever. Runners-up Yorkshire win 21 out of 28, a better record than the champions in every year, bar 1955 and 1957, since 1923.
Bill Haley and the Comets top the Hit Parade with 'Rock Around The Clock', sparking teddy-boy riots.
ITV goes on air, with opponents warning that 'the lowest common denominator of taste and interest will set the standard.'

1956 Stuart Surridge, in his fifth and final year as captain, leads Surrey to a fifth consecutive title.
Jim Laker takes 19 wickets in the Old Trafford Test, giving England a third successive series victory over Australia.
British Railways undertake a programme of electrification of all its lines.

1957 Concerned by a decline in attendances, an MCC Special Committee recommends several changes, notably:
    Boundaries to be limited to a maximum of 75 yards • No more than five fielders on the leg-side • First innings to be limited to 85 overs • A knock-out competition of two-day games with each side having two 54-over innings
The counties agree to reduce boundaries and restrict leg-side fielders, but the 85-over limitation is not approved. Instead, they rework the four bonus points for first-innings lead, giving two for the lead itself, the other two only if a faster scoring rate is achieved. The introduction of a knock-out competition is deferred for further consideration.
A European Common Market is set up by France, West Germany, Italy, Belgium, Holland and Luxembourg.

1958 England beat New Zealand 4-0 in the summer's Tests. England have now gone 7½ years without a series defeat, a record that ends in Australia in the winter, amid controversy over the actions of several bowlers.
Yellow lines and parking meters are introduced in London's West End. Britain's first motorway, the Preston bypass, is opened.

1959 Yorkshire win their first outright title since 1946, ending Surrey's seven-year reign as champions.
Except for the tweak in the awarding of first-innings points, the championship in 1959 is as it was in 1950.
In a clean-up of actions, umpires no-ball seven bowlers for throwing during the summers of 1959 and 1960.
Two-thirds of the UK population now own television sets. Cinema attendances are one-third of what they were in 1950.

Championship – top three | Leading batsmen | Leading bowlers | Leading wkt-keeper / Leading fielder

1950

Team	P	W	L	D	Pts	Leading batsmen	Runs	Leading bowlers	Wickets	Leading wkt-keeper / Leading fielder	Victims
Lancashire *(1=)*	28	16	2	10	220	L.B. Fishlock (Surrey)	2,077	R. Tattersall (Lancs)	163	H. Yarnold (Worcs)	77
Surrey *(1=)*	28	17	4	7	220	A.E. Fagg (Kent)	2,019	J.H. Wardle (Yorks)	144		
Yorkshire	28	14	2	12	200	D. Kenyon (Worcs)	2,002	J.C. Laker (Surrey)	142	K.J. Grieves (Lancs)	57

1951

Team	P	W	L	D	Pts	Leading batsmen	Runs	Leading bowlers	Wickets	Leading wkt-keeper / Leading fielder	Victims
Warwickshire	28	16	2	10	216	J.D.B. Robertson (Middx)	2,452	R. Appleyard (Yorks)	169	H. Yarnold (Worcs)	85
Yorkshire	28	12	3	13	184	A.E. Fagg (Kent)	2,046	W.E. Hollies (Warwicks)	145		
Lancashire	28	8	2	18	136	M.F. Tremlett (Som)	2,018	J.A. Young (Middx)	127	J.V. Wilson (Yorks)	45

1952

Team	P	W	L	D	Pts	Leading batsmen	Runs	Leading bowlers	Wickets	Leading wkt-keeper / Leading fielder	Victims
Surrey	28	20	3	5	256	H. Gimblett (Som)	2,068	J.H. Wardle (Yorks)	158	J. Firth (Leics)	82
Yorkshire	28	17	2	9	224	H.E. Dollery (Warwicks)	2,036	C. Gladwin (Derbys)	151		
Lancashire	28	12	3	12	188	N.H. Rogers (Hants)	2,014	J.A. Young (Middx)	137	C.A. Milton (Glos)	50

Lancashire also tied one match

1953

Team	P	W	L	D	Pts	Leading batsmen	Runs	Leading bowlers	Wickets	Leading wkt-keeper / Leading fielder	Victims
Surrey	28	13	4	11	184	D. Kenyon (Worcs)	2,063	B. Dooland (Notts)	152	P.A. Gibb (Essex)	71
Sussex	28	11	3	14	168	D.S. Sheppard (Sussex)	1,982	D. Shackleton (Hants)	133	K.J. Grieves (Lancs)	45
Lancashire *(3=)*	28	10	4	14	156	H.E. Dollery (Warwicks)	1,872	R. Tattersall (Lancs)	122	W.S. Surridge (Surrey)	45
Leicestershire *(3=)*	28	10	7	11	156						

1954

Team	P	W	L	D	Pts	Leading batsmen	Runs	Leading bowlers	Wickets	Leading wkt-keeper / Leading fielder	Victims
Surrey	28	15	3	10	208	D. Kenyon (Worcs)	2,138	B. Dooland (Notts)	179	H.W. Stephenson (Som)	83
Yorkshire	28	13	3	11	186	L. Livingston (Nthnts)	1,912	G.E. Tribe (Northnts)	133	F.A. Lowson (Yorks)	36
Derbyshire	28	11	6	11	168	A.V. Wolton (Warwicks)	1,685	C. Gladwin (Derbys)	131	C.A. Milton (Glos)	36

Yorkshire also tied one match

1955

Team	P	W	L	D	Pts	Leading batsmen	Runs	Leading bowlers	Wickets	Leading wkt-keeper / Leading fielder	Victims
Surrey	28	23	5	0	284	L. Livingston (Nthnts)	1,957	G.E. Tribe (Northnts)	169	H.G. Davies (Glam)	74
Yorkshire	28	21	5	2	268	D.J. Insole (Essex)	1,907	G.A.R. Lock (Surrey)	149		
Hampshire	28	16	5	6	210	M. Tompkin (Leics)	1,865	D. Shackleton (Hants)	147	J.G. Langridge (Sussex)	66

Hampshire also tied one match

1956

Team	P	W	L	D	Pts	Leading batsmen	Runs	Leading bowlers	Wickets	Leading wkt-keeper / Leading fielder	Victims
Surrey	28	15	5	8	200	L. Livingston (Nthnts)	1,846	D.J. Shepherd (Glam)	156	J.T. Murray (Middx)	69
Lancashire	28	12	2	14	180	D. Kenyon (Worcs)	1,802	C. Cook (Glos)	139		
Gloucestershire	28	14	7	7	176	T.W. Graveney (Glos)	1,787	B. Dooland (Notts)	139	C.A. Milton (Glos)	52

1957

Team	P	W	L	D	Pts	Leading batsmen	Runs	Leading bowlers	Wickets	Leading wkt-keeper / Leading fielder	Victims
Surrey	28	21	3	4	312	J.M. Parks (Sussex)	1,861	G.A.R. Lock (Surrey)	153	J.T. Murray (Middx)	75
Northants	28	15	2	11	218	J.D.B. Robertson (Middx)	1,852	D. Shackleton (Hants)	144		
Yorkshire	28	13	4	11	190	D. Kenyon (Worcs)	1,847	B. Dooland (Notts)	129	M.J. Stewart (Surrey)	63
								H.L. Jackson (Derbys)	129		

1958

Team	P	W	L	D	Pts	Leading batsmen	Runs	Leading bowlers	Wickets	Leading wkt-keeper / Leading fielder	Victims
Surrey	28	14	5	9	212	D.M. Young (Glos)	1,755	D. Shackleton (Hants)	161	K.V. Andrew (Northants)	71
Hampshire	28	12	6	10	186	R.E. Marshall (Hants)	1,627	D.J. Halfyard (Kent)	126	J.T. Murray (Middx)	71
Somerset	28	12	9	7	174	P.B. Wight (Som)	1,506	H.L. Jackson (Derbys)	126	M.J. Stewart (Surrey)	51

1959

Team	P	W	L	D	Pts	Leading batsmen	Runs	Leading bowlers	Wickets	Leading wkt-keeper / Leading fielder	Victims
Yorkshire	28	14	7	7	204	M.J.K. Smith (Warwicks)	2,169	D. Shackleton (Hants)	126	J.M. Parks (Sussex)	85
Gloucestershire	28	12	11	4	186	H. Horton (Hants)	2,114	N.I. Thomson (Sussex)	120		
Surrey	28	12	5	11	186	D.B. Carr (Derbys)	2,092	H.L. Jackson (Derbys)	117	P.M. Walker (Glam)	57

Gloucestershire also tied one match

1950-1959

Leading counties

	P	W	L	D	T	%W
Surrey	280	157	43	80	-	56.1
Yorkshire	280	125	44	110	1	44.6
Lancashire	280	105	47	127	1	37.5
Middlesex	280	95	86	98	1	33.9

Leading batsmen

D. Kenyon (Worcs)	18,068
D.J. Insole (Essex)	15,717
D. Brookes (Northants)	15,258
J.D.B. Robertson (Middx)	14,983

Leading bowlers

D. Shackleton (Hants)	1,272
G.A.R. Lock (Surrey)	1,070
C. Gladwin (Derbyshire)	1,052
H.L. Jackson (Derbys)	1,032

Leading keepers & fielder

G.O. Dawkes (Derbys)	589
H.W. Stephenson (Som)	577
K.J. Grieves (Lancs)	351

Overall statistics

Runs per wicket	24.5
Runs per 100 balls	43.6
% of matches drawn	40.0

Miscellany

For a time in the aftermath of war Yorkshire were hoping that the Holmfirth-born Freddie Jakeman, a stocky left-hander, would be their next Maurice Leyland, but he made just one fifty in ten games and finished up with Northamptonshire.

Never the fittest of men, overweight and troubled by a bad knee, he hit ten centuries in six seasons for his adopted county – and six of them came in a great rush in 1951.

In six days in July, always playing his shots, he hit successive not-out scores of 80, 258 and 176. Then, after missing two matches with his bad knee, he returned to action, being caught for 44. The sequence of 558 runs without dismissal was a record in county cricket till broken by Graeme Hick in 1990.

*

Keeping wicket to Doug Wright, with his fast leg-breaks and great variety of deliveries, was a challenge at the best of times. Godfrey Evans was his Kent keeper, but in August 1955 he had a broken finger, his deputy Derek Ufton had returned to football, and the task fell to the young Tony Catt. At Northampton, his movement handicapped by a badly sunburnt neck, Catt established a championship record by conceding 48 byes, 44 of them in boundaries. There were also 23 leg-byes and two wides.

In time Catt became Kent's first-choice keeper – but not till some years after Wright's retirement.

Winning matches in a wet summer such as 1956 required imagination, which was not the forte of Lancashire's veteran skipper Cyril Washbrook. But when the Test selectors, of which he was one, recalled him to the England team in July, the more enterprising Geoff Edrich took over as captain.

The first day against Leicestershire at Old Trafford was lost to rain; the second ended with Lancashire, in their first innings, on 166 for no wicket, 58 runs ahead. The next morning, with rain forecast, Edrich declared. They bowled out the visitors for 122 and, amid thickening drizzle, Jack Dyson and Alan Wharton hit off the 65 runs for victory. It remains the only time a county has won a championship match without losing a wicket.

*

At Romford in May 1956 Gloucestershire were all out twice in a day for 153 and 107, of which Tom Graveney scored 100 and 67. No batsman in the championship has ever hit a higher proportion of a team's runs across two all-out innings.

At Newport that August, again with little support, Graveney hit 200 out of 298, the lowest first-class total to include a double-century. The Times called it a brilliant and masterly innings, full of firm, correct strokes, a view not shared by the Glamorgan captain Wilf Wooller who, with typical curmudgeonliness, told Graveney, "That's the worst bloody 200 I've ever seen."

The championship in the 1950s

There are many who look back on the 1950s as a golden age for English cricket. After difficult years of post-war rebuilding, England's Test team became the best in the world, not losing a series for almost eight years and winning three times in a row against Australia. In the county game the championship enjoyed a rare period of calm, undergoing no significant changes. It also threw up a Surrey team which many regard as the greatest county side of all time. They shared the title with Lancashire in 1950, then won it outright every year from 1952 to 1958.

Yet, beneath this glorious surface, there were problems developing for county cricket, problems that would lead to a plethora of changes in the years that followed. The post-war boom in attendances died away as the rival attractions of a new affluence – motor cars, television sets, foreign holidays – started to compete for people's time. By the end of the decade, several counties were back in financial distress.

Some of the smaller, less proud counties developed new ways of raising money. In 1952 Worcestershire started a county-wide football pool which was soon being copied by Leicestershire and Northamptonshire – though the latter's first efforts were not promising. Of the two men employed by their Supporters' Association to handle the venture, one quit before starting work, the other after a week, saying he did not believe in gambling. The next employee found the downstairs bar too inviting, and in desperation they asked the county's Assistant Secretary, Ken Turner, to lend a hand.

The MCC did not approve. Its Secretary called it 'easy money, which I believe to be a dangerous thing'. But, overcoming legal and religious objections, Northamptonshire's army of volunteers collected the weekly shillings down streets and in factories, and by the late 1950s the scheme had 79,000 subscribers. As Ken Turner put it, 'it was equivalent to Wembley Stadium being three-quarters full every Saturday.'

In the financial year 1958/59 Northamptonshire had expenditure of £39,536 and income of £41,854, of which well over half, £24,643, came from the Supporters' Association. At a time when greater clubs were struggling to make ends meet, the county was able to increase its playing staff to 29.

Warwickshire, so often in the forefront of progress, were another who took up the idea. With the advantage of a big city, its scheme had 650,000 supporters at its peak, the money bringing great improvements to Edgbaston, with Test cricket returning there in 1957, for the first time since the '20s.

Warwickshire were also in the vanguard when in 1949 they appointed Tom Dollery, a professional, to captain the side, and in 1951 he brought the championship to Birmingham for the first time for forty years. He was a shrewd captain, quick to spot weakness in the opposition, and his team played attractive, positive cricket, their bowling attack led by the pace of New Zealander Tom Pritchard and the leg-spin of the genial Eric Hollies.

With no great stars they were a tight-knit team, using just fifteen men, two of whom only appeared after the title had been won. Yet, while many welcomed the freshness of their success, there was disquiet that, among their twelve regulars, only two hailed from within the county's boundaries. With three from the north-east, three New Zealanders, a Cornishman and two from Berkshire, they were setting a trend that other counties would soon follow, notably Somerset who for a while were known as the League of Nations.

The Surrey side was altogether different. Of the twenty men who played most in their seven championship-winning years, only three did not grow up or attend school in Surrey: Ken Barrington from neighbouring Berkshire, Tom Clark from Bedfordshire and Jim Laker, a Yorkshireman recruited from club cricket while working for Barclays Bank in Catford.

Their batting line-up, though it contained Peter May, was not the best in the history of county cricket but, with the pitches uncovered and several of the summers wet, they consistently scored enough runs for the bowlers to do their work. And what bowlers! Alec Bedser was the leading wicket-taker in all Test history, Jim Laker the best off-spinner the game has ever seen and Tony Lock, though his action was far from pure, a deadly slow-left-armer. With Peter Loader adding pace and the close fielders holding exceptional catches, they rarely struggled to take the necessary twenty wickets.

There were summers when other counties ran them close. Yorkshire were a formidable side, finishing second four times in five years. They, too, had great bowlers: the young, fast and fiery Fred Trueman, the masterly slow-left-armer Johnny Wardle and the remarkable Bob Appleyard who, at the age of 27, took 200 wickets in his first summer in 1951. A two-in-one bowler, medium-pace with the new ball, off-spin with the old, he came out of Saturday afternoon cricket in the Bradford League to bowl an exhausting 1,313 overs, a feat all the more astonishing when it was discovered the following year that he was suffering from advanced tuberculosis and had lost the whole top half

Surrey 1957

(standing)
Herbert Strudwick
(scorer)
Bernie Constable
Ken Barrington
Tony Lock
Tom Clark
Peter Loader
Micky Stewart
Sandy Tait
(masseur)
(sitting)
Eric Bedser
Arthur McIntyre
Alec Bedser
Peter May
Jim Laker
David Fletcher

of his left lung. He underwent surgery, had eleven months in bed after which he had to learn to walk again and was given no chance of coming back. Yet come back he did, with great success, and in 1955 he topped the national bowling averages, a match-winner in a Yorkshire side that won an extraordinary 21 games out of 28 – and still came second to Surrey.

In 1953 it looked for a while as if Sussex, in their one year under the captaincy of David Sheppard, might win the championship. The future Bishop of Liverpool was in inspiring form all summer, as opening batsman and close catcher, and his leadership brought the best out of his team. "He always had time for everybody," keeper Rupert Webb says. "If you had anything on your mind, he'd walk round the ground and listen to you." "He was the first to say, 'Well caught,'" Alan Oakman recalls. "Up till then, the attitude was that you were expected to catch it." When the season was over, they each received a personal letter, thanking them for what they had done.

It did not help cricket in the 1950s that so many of the summers were cold and wet: 1954 was the worst of the century, and '56 and '58 were not much better.

Then came the glorious summer of 1959: week after week of warm sun and a championship race that involved several counties and built to a breathtaking climax.

Surrey were in decline. Alec Bedser was now 41 years old, Tony Lock was having to remodel his action, and an unwell Peter May missed much of the summer. Yet they still expected

to be champions, and in August they were one of three counties, with Yorkshire and Warwickshire, who came and went in first place. Then at Bristol Gloucestershire bowled out Yorkshire for 25 and took the lead in the final straight.

Gloucestershire's last home match, against Surrey, was at the Wagon Works ground in Gloucester and, as every older supporter remembers all too painfully, their bright idea was to take on Laker and Lock by preparing a spinners' wicket.

The Yorkshire team took advantage of their early finish at Bristol, stopping at brine baths in Droitwich where, after weeks of hot sunshine and hard grounds, they steamed the tiredness out of their muscles. Duly refreshed, they won at Worcester, then travelled to Hove for their last match. If Surrey did not win at the Oval, victory would give Yorkshire the title.

Robin Marlar, in his last week as Sussex captain, did his best to deny them, refusing to declare, and Yorkshire were left to score 215 in only 105 minutes. And, thanks to a magnificent partnership between Bryan Stott and Doug Padgett, left-hand and right-hand running Sussex ragged, they did it. With Surrey only drawing, Yorkshire were champions once more.

If anybody in England had any doubt that the county championship still mattered, they should have been in the streets and hotels of Scarborough at two o'clock that night when great crowds, waiting up, cheered the arriving Yorkshire team. "The memory of it still gets to my heart and soul," Bryan Stott says. "It will stay with me for ever."

Some players of the 1950s

Gentleman Jack
2,452 championship runs in 1951

Jack Robertson of Middlesex

> I thought he was perfect, the sort of batsman I'd have liked to have been. He scored 200 against us at Taunton one year, and he was only beaten twice. *Eric Hill*
>
> He didn't get the recognition he deserved. He played me better than anybody; he was so correct on the off-side and, if I pitched it on his leg-and-middle, he'd just flick me over square leg. I'd rather have bowled at Peter May. *Bob Appleyard*
>
> He was as near technical perfection as any player I have watched. *Denis Compton*

His fellow professionals knew how good Jack Robertson was. In the first six summers after the war he scored more runs than any other batsman, more even than Len Hutton. They were good runs, too, batting against the new ball and laying a foundation for Compton and Edrich. Alongside that pair he may have seemed sedate, but in his own unobtrusive style, light on his feet and stroking the ball with exquisite timing, he scored his runs attractively and at a good rate. At Worcester in 1949 he hit a faultless 331 in a day.

A survivor of Dunkirk, he lost prime years to the war but he returned, at 29, to hit 2,000 runs in a season nine times. He was the best of professionals: honest, dependable, smart of appearance and with a humour that bore no trace of cynicism. A wine merchant's son, he was a non-smoking teetotaller, who enjoyed reading books of history and playing with his son's model railway set. In winter he kept himself fit by gliding gracefully around dance floors.

In later life he was a kind, patient coach; he also ran a hotel in Cornwall which, to the shocked disappointment of visiting cricketers, was unlicensed.

Johnny Wardle of Yorkshire

> During the whole time he played under me, I only remember him asking for a rest on one occasion. *Norman Yardley*
>
> I wish we'd have had him at Nottinghamshire. I'd have let him bowl his chinamen all the time. He wanted to, he enjoyed it and, by gosh, he was good. He could spin it both ways, and they couldn't read it. *Reg Simpson*

Through the years much of Yorkshire's success had been built around its slow-left-arm bowlers, and that created great pressure for the young Johnny Wardle. A grammar-school boy from a mining village near Barnsley, he soon thrived in the tough environment, and in his second summer, already capped by England, he took 150 wickets. Yet it was not enough: 'He has not yet got proper Yorkshire control of length,' his captain Norman Yardley wrote.

Wardle loved his cricket. He could be an awkward cuss when it came to field placings and the end he took, but he was happy to bowl all day. In 1952 he sent down 1,857 overs, of which a record 810 were maidens. Six times he took 150 or more wickets in a season.

As an orthodox bowler he was not in the class of Rhodes or Verity, but he could also bowl chinamen and googlies which he did outstandingly for England. Wally Hammond called one of his spells in South Africa 'the finest piece of spin bowling I've ever seen'. Yorkshire, however, rarely let him bowl them, it went against the grain of their parsimony, and that frustrated him.

A thinking cricketer, he grew impatient with the amateur captains, matters coming to a head in 1958 when Ronnie Burnet, a 39-year-old engineer, was brought in to instil greater discipline. Never one to opt for diplomatic silence, Wardle spoke his mind once too often and was sacked in mid-season. It was a terrible loss for English cricket. He was at the peak of his powers.

Lost to the game too soon
Leading wicket-taker in 1952

Dickie Dodds of Essex

> The highest form of prayer I knew was to play beautiful shots for a creator who loved beautiful things. My job was to give recreation to those who came to watch. Re-creation. Lift their spirits. I believe that we can all find re-creation when we glimpse creativity. *Dickie Dodds*
>
> When he got the message, there was no bowling at the bugger. *Arthur Wellard*

Lifting their spirits
1,000 runs in each season from 1946 to 1958

Dickie Dodds was a professional cricketer like no other. Public school educated, an officer in the war, he did not smoke, did not drink, did not swear. In winter he worked for the cause of Moral Rearmament; in summer he opened the batting for Essex. 'Hit hard and enjoy it,' God told him – and he did, standing tall with his prematurely grey hair and playing shots from the first ball. With the free-spirited Doug Insole as captain, he was left to bat as he chose, and he scored plenty of entertaining and match-winning runs. 'His batting is fit for a World Eleven,' Insole wrote, 'or the madhouse.'

For his benefit match at Leyton he refused pluvius insurance, opting to pray to God. His reward was three days of sunshine, a Denis Compton century and a thrilling victory for Essex. "Wot yer going to do wiv all that money, Dick?" a boy asked him in the street, and without further thought he resolved to give it all to Moral Rearmament: "I'm going to use it to help build a new world." "Cor!"

Les Jackson of Derbyshire

Whitwell miner
143 wickets at 10.99 in 1958

> Les was the best bloody bowler in the country. He moved the ball about more than anybody. I used to finish up with bruises on the inside of both thighs. I never really felt in against him, even when I was scoring runs. *Tom Graveney*

Eddie Gothard, the Derbyshire captain, did not rate Les Jackson when he appeared for one game in 1947, but others did. They arranged for the 26-year-old to return, prepared a lively net surface and asked Gothard to face him. Black and blue, he soon changed his mind.

A quiet, uncomplaining man who had grown tough from years at the coalface, Jackson bowled through many a muscle strain and blistered foot. With a short run-up and a low arm, he offended the purists at Lord's, but he had the ability to get awkward lift and to move the ball both ways off the seam. A self-made cricketer, his only coaching came when Derbyshire sent him to Alf Gover's school, where Gover, seeing what he could do, left well alone.

He was a legend in county cricket, still taking wickets at the age of 42. How he only played two Tests, no batsman on the circuit could explain.

Bernie Constable of Surrey

> In years to come, when they recall this Surrey side, they'll talk about the bowlers and they'll talk about Peter May. But there won't be one mention of we poor batsmen who've had to score our runs on these bloody pitches. *Bernie Constable*
>
> I learned more from Bernie than from anybody else in cricket. *Micky Stewart*

Unsung hero
Surrey's top run-scorer in the 1950s

Even in that noisy Surrey team Bernie Constable chirped away so much in the covers that they called him the Cockney Sparrow, though in fact he came from a family of boatbuilders in East Molesey. His eagle eye missed nothing: "What you got a fielder there for?" "Shut up, Bernie." "Look at the way he's holding his bat. It won't go there. ... Well, give him a pack of cards then, let him play patience."

He made his debut in 1939 as a leg-spinner, but after the war he became a batsman, light on his feet and dapper, able to score crucial runs on difficult pitches. "Cricket is a game you've got to work out in your own mind," he said, "and I reckon I was good enough to do that." An outstanding fielder, he played more games than anybody in the championship years, going on till 1964. Then he worked as a joiner for Job's Dairy in Sudbury for whose cricket team he carried on chirping for many years.

Stories of the 1950s

From the back streets of Gloucester

Gloucestershire v Sussex, Bristol, Saturday 14 July 1951

Till the day he died Bryan 'Bomber' Wells never grew tired of telling the story of his debut match, embellishing the details till it became one of the great legends of English county cricket.

The tale began on Friday night in a park in Gloucester, Bomber sitting on a bench with his girlfriend. "We were having some fish and chips. It was a lovely evening, about half past nine or ten o'clock, and this huge chap came across. I thought, 'I recognise him.' It was Tom Goddard. He came up to me and he said, 'Are you Bomber Wells? Get down to Bristol tomorrow. You're playing against Sussex.'"

An apprentice compositor at a local printers, he bowled off-breaks off a two-pace run for Gloucester City on the Spa, and the next morning, with his kit in a brown paper carrier, he took the bus down to Bristol. "There must have been twenty Gloucester supporters, and we talked of nothing else but the game. But I never let on that I was playing."

No one in the Gloucestershire team had ever seen him. "He was just a boy from the sticks," Arthur Milton recalled. "He strolled in, changed, came out. Nothing fazed him."

"As far as I was concerned," Bomber said, "it was like playing for any other side I'd played for. I just wanted to go out and have a bowl."

They fielded first, and the Sussex openers put on 85. "I think they tried every bowler on the ground before they tried me. Sir Derrick even bowled himself." Sir Derrick Bailey was Gloucestershire's amateur captain, a farmer whose father had owned diamond mines in South Africa. "He used to come to matches in this Lagonda with straw in his hair and boots with cow muck on. They can, people like that, can't they?"

It was 120 for one when Bomber finally got his chance. With big hands and strong shoulders, he could spin his off-breaks at much greater pace than his two-pace run-up suggested. He also liked to bustle through his overs, preferably bowling the ball before the batsman was quite ready. That day, they say, Sir Derrick walked in from mid-off for the first ball, went back to his mark and walked in again … for the third ball.

'Wells immediately showed he could spin,' reported the *Gloucester Citizen*, 'and twice went past the left-handed Smith's bat with his off-breaks. Then he bowled a leg-break which turned so much that Smith almost played on.' "The Sussex batsmen had never seen anything like it," Tom Graveney tells. "I remember Jim Langridge batting. Very dour. Suddenly Bomber slipped a back-spinner in, and it only just missed the leg stump. George Cox at the non-striker's end was falling about with laughter." Or, as Bomber put it, "They didn't have a clue."

He bowled 25 overs and took six for 47. In the second innings he sent down another 36 overs. "I was his first county wicket," David

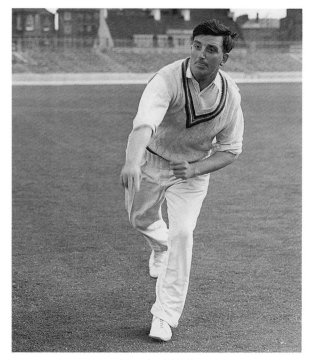

'Bomber' Wells

Sheppard recalled. "He went back into the dressing room after the match. 'Well,' he said. 'I can see, if I'm going to play for this side, I'm going to have to do a lot of bowling. I shall have to cut my run down.'"

Once, he claimed, he conspired with batsman Roly Jenkins to complete an over at Worcester during the twelve chimes of the cathedral clock. "Sir Derrick came across. 'What do you think you're doing? You're making the game look ridiculous.'"

"Sir Derrick told him to start his run further back," Tom Graveney tells. "So he sent him back about eight yards, and Bomber just took his two paces and let it go from where he was. And he pitched it right on a length."

"Sir Derrick went berserk," Bomber said. "He dropped me for two matches, but it was worth it."

He was overweight, short-sighted, couldn't bat, wasn't much of a fielder, but he was a wicket-taking bowler and, in the 1950s, that was enough.

"We've taken individuality out of the game," he would say, "and, of all games, cricket has got to have individuality. I think coaches have tried to make cricket a team game, and it isn't a team game at all, is it?"

The unlikeliest bowling spell

Leicestershire v Surrey, Leicester, Saturday 21 May 1955

Surrey were the reigning county champions, in the middle of a run of 18 outright victories, and on a damp Saturday 5,000 spectators gathered at the Grace Road ground to watch them.

For the home supporters the scoreboard at teatime had a disappointingly predictable look: Leicestershire all out for 114; Surrey 42 for one, with Peter May 28 not out. 'His firm driving,' reported *The Times*, 'looked ominous.'

"We're bowling at the wrong ends," the Leicestershire spinners told their captain Charles Palmer, a small, bespectacled man who, according to Trevor Bailey, looked more like a hen-pecked bank cashier than the Test cricketer he was.

"Fine," he replied. "I'll alter you round."

"Oh heck," he thought as he led the team back out, "I've got to get someone to bowl one over." It was a thankless task so he opted to do it himself.

Each season, bowling gentle seamers off a ten-pace run-up, he took a few wickets, but he had started that summer with a bad back and was under doctor's orders not to bowl. "Go easy on me now," he joked to Peter May. "I haven't been bowling this year." Then with his second ball he hit May's stumps.

He kept himself on, and in his second over he sent back two more batsmen. He had found a damp patch on the perfect length for his bowling, and he thought it all a great laugh. "I suppose I'd better have another over now," he kept saying.

After 12 overs he had taken eight wickets, seven of them bowled, and he had not conceded a run. If he took himself off, it would be a world record, and some of the team urged him to do so. But he carried on, and Jim Laker swung the bat, getting an inside edge down to third man for two, then hitting a two in the air through the covers.

When Terry Spencer bowled Laker, Surrey were all out for 77, and Palmer's final figures were 14 overs, 12 maidens, 7 runs, 8 wickets. Amid great cheering from the crowd, the Leicestershire team created a guard of honour as diffidently their captain walked off. His first thought was to pop his head into the Surrey dressing room: "Gentlemen, I'm so sorry," he said.

In the bar that evening he discovered – rather too quickly – how much whisky he could take. Then on Tuesday, with no twinges in his back, he bowled 13 more overs for just one run as Surrey progressed without alarm to a seven-wicket victory.

He finished with the extraordinary match figures of 8 for 8 off 27 overs. Yet, if he had had the spinners on at the right ends in the first place, he would never have bowled.

Life in the fast lane

Hampshire v Somerset, Bournemouth, Wednesday 18 June 1958

Nestled inside streets of prosperous Victorian houses, with pine trees, horse chestnuts and holme oaks, a balconied wooden pavilion and several marquees, the Dean Park ground in Bournemouth cried out for attractive cricket – and that is what it got when Hampshire won the toss and batted against Somerset. The sun blazed down and, while a loudspeaker van toured the streets, exhorting all to come to Dean Park, the freescoring Roy Marshall plundered the bowling. The previous June, at Southampton, he had won the £100 prize for the fastest century of the season, in 66 minutes, and for a while he looked as if he might be winning it for a second year.

It was mid-June. The fastest century so far, in 98 minutes, was by the new Hampshire captain Colin Ingleby-Mackenzie who, as Marshall drove ball after ball through the covers, lay fast asleep in the dressing room. Down to bat at number six, he had told them, "Wake me when I need to pad up."

Their game at Oxford the previous day had finished in the morning, and he had driven away 'at breakneck speed' to Ascot where he enjoyed, in his own words, 'a fabulous lunch and a great afternoon's racing'. He followed this by attending a cocktail party and taking dinner at the Compleat Angler in Marlow. He was staying with his predecessor Desmond Eagar in Southampton, and he finally fell into bed, fully clothed, at 7 a.m., just in time to be 'woken' by Eagar.

"You were a bit late last night, weren't you?"

"Yes, I don't think I was in bed till after midnight."

A great gambler, Ingleby-Mac had been advised by Marshall to insure his 98-minute century against its being beaten and, with the help of fellow Etonian Tom Pugh of Gloucestershire, he put down £25 at the generous odds of 4/1. It was a perfect two-way bet; either way, he would get his £100.

At lunch, with Marshall out, Hampshire were 144 for one; at tea, 232 for three. Then, three-quarters of an hour into the evening session, a fourth wicket fell, and the refreshed Hampshire captain appeared. By now the Somerset bowlers had wilted in the heat, and he 'lashed out at everything', bringing up his 50 in 32 minutes. 'I was amazed to connect repeatedly,' he said, 'and instead of declaring and leaving them half an hour's batting, I went on in a dream.'

With champagne corks popping in the marquees, the 'dream' brought Colin Ingleby-Mackenzie a 61-minute century, winning him not only the £100 prize for the fastest hundred of 1958 but also the £100 on his 4/1 bet.

Images of the 1950s

The Secretary's Rolls Royce, Brentwood, 1949

... and the attached caravan

Have caravan, will travel

Since leaving their Leyton headquarters in 1933, Essex had not owned a ground. Their summer-long programme was a series of cricket weeks: Brentwood, Ilford, Chelmsford, Westcliff, Romford, Colchester, Clacton and Southend. It came to be known as the Essex Circus. Transporting all the paraphernalia – from tubular scaffolding stands and turnstiles to the loudspeaker system – was a major enterprise.

In the late 1940s the county bought a Rolls Royce for the Secretary, Bob Paterson. Expensive to run at a time of petrol rationing, they were cheap on the second-hand market. Paterson attached a caravan to the back of it, and for each cricket week he and his wife slept on the ground. While he was busy in the pavilion and on the gate, she operated the scorecard-printing machine.

The crowds were great in those years. At Ilford in May 1949, for the visit of the new champions Glamorgan, they closed the gates on the Saturday, with more than 10,000 paying to come in. But money was always tight, especially when the crowds grew thinner in the 1950s. By 1955 the Rolls had long gone, and Trevor Bailey was doubling up as player and county secretary. The nomadic life continued, with Leyton added to the round in 1957.

In 1962, with cricket demanding more informative scoreboards than those at most of the Essex grounds, they converted a removal van and took that with them wherever they went.

Mrs Paterson, the Secretary's wife, prints the scorecards

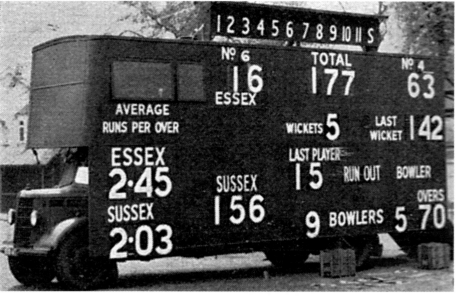

Essex's new portable scoreboard, 1962

Winter work for young fast bowlers

It was a simple idea. Alf Gover had some young fast bowlers at his cricket school in south London, and he wanted to build up their strength. Stuart Surridge owned some tree plantations where he grew willows for cricket bats, and he needed some extra labourers. What better than to send the young bowlers to fell the trees?

Among the first was Alan Moss. "It was back-bending work," he says. "We had to climb the trees and rope them. Then we'd cut the fallen trees into lengths and split them into clefts. We were out all day in all weathers. Sometimes it was pouring with rain; there were even days when we had to shake the snow off the trees."

Surrey's Peter Loader did one winter, telling the next recruit, Ken Biddulph, what to expect: "After the first three days you'll want to run away and die. Your hands will be sore and bleeding, and your back will ache more than you can imagine. But it does get better."

"The idea was to fill us out," Malcolm Heath says. "Give us an extra yard of pace."

Alan Moss (left) and Stuart Surridge
Alan Moss would play for Middlesex and England

All day they felled trees with a cross-cut saw and chopped them into rounds with axes. Hard manual work before the days of motorised tools. "In my second winter they produced a petrol-driven chain-saw," Ken Biddulph recalled, "but only the pros were allowed to use it. We had to carry it for them, and even that was hard work."

They stayed at a farmhouse where "we were fed on good home-grown food: steak every night and lashings of egg and bacon for breakfast. The perfect diet for a fast bowler. It was the best thing that ever happened to me. I never once had a back problem, not even bowling on that rock-hard surface at Taunton."

"It did me the world of good," Alan Moss says. "I must have been using every muscle in my body."

"It was so healthy, out in the fresh air," Malcolm Heath says. "The cricketers now have got these wonderful Keep Fit suites, but I don't know. I doubt if it makes them as fit as that tree felling made us."

Ken Biddulph (left) and Malcolm Heath
Ken Biddulph would play for Somerset, Malcolm Heath for Hampshire

183

Footballing cricketers of the 1950s

In the spring of 1950 Willie Watson had a dilemma. Since the war he had been playing cricket each summer, as a stylish left-handed batsman for Yorkshire, and football each winter, as an attacking wing-half for Sunderland. With the overlap of the seasons little more than the last fortnight of August, there were many others who did the same. That year, for instance, the FA Cup Final featured Denis and Leslie Compton in the winning Arsenal side, and both were playing for Middlesex in their first game the following Saturday.

The complication for Watson in 1950 was that England had entered a team into the Football World Cup in Brazil, with a pre-tournament tour of Europe. If Watson, who had played twice for England during the winter, was in the squad, he would not play cricket till late July.

After long consideration he wrote to the FA, telling them he was not available for the World Cup. They pressed him to change his mind, Yorkshire told him to put his country first, and off he went, losing £300 of earnings from Yorkshire. In fact, he did not play in any of the games in Rio and, when he got home, the FA sent him a cheque for £60, even striking out his claim for 16 shillings and three pence for a train journey to London in which, with no seats vacant, he had paid extra to sit in a first-class compartment.

There was no money in football. As late as 1957/58 the maximum weekly wage payable to a professional was £15. So it had no financial power to pull cricketers away, nor was its way of life more alluring than the four months of sunshine and comradeship offered by county cricket. The two sports had equal status: the summer and winter games of the nation.

Back from Rio, Willie Watson was short of cricket, but it did not show. He had a game in the second team and scored 168. Then, back in the county side at Taunton, he hit a fluent 122, the start of a run spree which saw him finish the summer at the head of the national batting averages. Did he benefit from playing a shorter season? 'In early September,' wrote *The Cricketer*, 'he was batting like a man in mid-June. To Watson, of course, September *was* mid-June.'

The following summer, when he was selected to play cricket for England, Watson fulfilled his long-held ambition to be a double-international, a status also achieved by Arthur Milton of Gloucestershire.

In November 1951, after only 12 games on the right wing for Arsenal, Milton won his one football cap against Austria at Wembley. Then seven years later, at Trent Bridge, he opened the England innings with Mike Smith of Warwickshire, who as an Oxford undergraduate had played one game of rugby union for England. Such combinations were possible.

Most county cricket clubs had winter footballers. During the decade Gloucestershire had five who played for Bristol City or Rovers; Kent had four with Charlton Athletic. Surrey had Ron Tindall at Chelsea and Micky Stewart at Charlton; Hampshire had Henry Horton at Southampton, Mike Barnard at Portsmouth and Bernie Harrison at Crystal Palace.

Lancashire had Jack Dyson at Manchester City. In front of a crowd of 100,000 at Wembley, he scored a goal in the 1956 Cup Final. Yet in 1960, on the final afternoon of a tense Roses match at Old Trafford, he was so overcome by nerves he was dropped from four to ten in the batting order.

Philip Neville, the Manchester United and England footballer, was said to have been the most promising cricketer Lancashire had seen for a generation; he played for their second eleven in 1992 at the age of fifteen. If he had come to maturity in the 1950s, he would probably have been a double-international, like Willie Watson and Arthur Milton, but each sport now requires all-the-year-round dedication.

Arthur Milton was a grammar-school boy who could have studied at Oxford, but he opted for a life of sport. He won the championship with Arsenal, he played for Gloucestershire for 27 summers, he even advertised Brylcreem. Yet such were the rewards in those years that at the end of it all he finished up working as a postman. On retirement he kept his Post Office bike and delivered newspapers around the Bristol Downs.

Willie Watson
Sunderland and Yorkshire

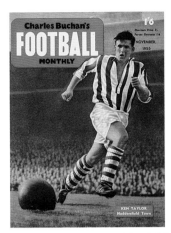

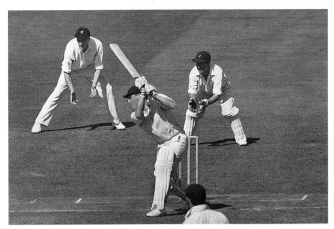

Ken Taylor: Huddersfield Town footballer, art student at The Slade and Yorkshire batsman, on his way to 200 at Edgbaston

"It's magical up there," he would say. "There's always early moisture on the grass and, when the sun comes up over the horizon, it draws it up and forms this low mist that runs all across the downs. I love it. I shall do it as long as I can."

His story is a remarkable one, but not as remarkable as that of the man who opened the batting with him in the Lord's Test of 1959, Ken Taylor. In a scenario impossible to imagine today, he was at one point in the 1950s playing cricket in the summer for Yorkshire, football in the winter for Huddersfield Town in the old First Division and, at the same time, studying art full-time, first at Huddersfield College, then at The Slade in London. One newspaper called him 'the most wanted man in England'.

He was no silver-spooned amateur. His father struggled for work in the 1930s, and the young Ken, who attended the local elementary school, shared a bed with his older brother Jeff till he was eleven. They were part of a working-class community in Huddersfield that had pride and culture, and they were brought up to make the most of themselves. "You can't play games all your life," his father told him, insisting on his going to college.

Brother Jeff, playing football for Fulham, used his earnings to study geography at London University. After that he became an opera singer, performing at Glyndebourne with Pavarotti, then Professor of Singing at Glasgow Academy of Music.

Ken only met up with his fellow footballers on Saturdays, his training consisting of lunchtime and evening runs, no ball work. He made his first-team debut at Anfield at the age of eighteen, hearing about his selection from a journalist who intercepted him when he was leaving college to attend indoor nets at Headingley.

He had a written agreement that he would report back for the start of football in August unless Yorkshire were in the running for the championship, which most years they were. It was an arrangement that did not impress Bill Shankly when he became the Huddersfield Town manager; he thought cricket was 'a lassie's game'.

Ken was not a lassie, though. He was a hard-tackling centre-half, the hardest according to the England centre-forward Tommy Taylor: "When you felt the weight of his shoulder, it was like bumping against a lump of coal." He was also a stylish opening batsman and a superb cover fielder, winning seven championships with Yorkshire. After sport he taught art for many years in Norfolk. Still working, his 2014 exhibition featured new drawings of the industrial Huddersfield of his youth.

Many believed that with greater specialisation he would have gone further. Ray Wilson, his Huddersfield contemporary, thinks Ken could have been alongside him when England won the World Cup at Wembley. Jim Swanton said that in those years he had more potential than any other cricketer outside the England Test team. And Sir William Coldstream at The Slade, a realist painter who drew his inspiration from ordinary life, was a great admirer.

So would he rather have been born forty years later and done it Philip Neville's way? "I don't have any regrets," he says. "If you took away any of the three strands of my life, it would have meant my missing out on so much pleasure."

The common thread, he believes, is concentration, the ability to 'move into another dimension': "There were times when I batted when I could feel that something else had taken over and I could play shots without thinking. It was the same in football. You lose yourself in the concentration, and unconsciously you find yourself making the right decision. It did help me in my sport that I also had to concentrate when I was drawing and painting."

1953: All over in a day

It must have seemed to Bertie Buse like a good choice for a benefit match – against Lancashire, one of the strongest counties, in his home city of Bath, on the Recreation Ground where many a time he had played at full-back for the rugby club. The Bath Cricket Festival always attracted a good crowd. With fine weather, he would have had every expectation of healthy gate takings and generous collections to set him up when he retired at the end of the season.

The weather was fine, too, but, alas, the pitch was not. The Rec was not used for club cricket so the match against Lancashire, starting on Saturday 6 June, was the first to be played there since the square had been relaid the previous October. The groundsman, employed by the council, had other duties, and he had been prevented from getting on the square by that week's Coronation celebrations. When it came to Saturday morning, the arriving Lancashire team could barely believe what they were looking at.

"You could see the squares where it had been returfed," Geoff Edrich said. "They hadn't knitted together properly. If you pushed them, they wobbled like plates of jelly."

'It was lacking in grass generally,' reported the *Manchester Guardian*, 'and what there was looked more like dried moss.'

"What do you think of it, gentlemen?" the groundsman asked, and they replied by speculating when the game would end: "Monday lunchtime at the latest."

"Oh no, the pitches always play better than they look here."

Cyril Washbrook, standing in as Lancashire captain, said afterwards they would have refused to play if it had not been a benefit match. But play they did, and the nature of the contest was clear from the first ball: Brian Statham, Lancashire's fast bowler, to Harold Gimblett.

"It pitched," Geoff Edrich recalled, "and a piece of earth came out of the wicket, half the size of the ball practically. There was the ball and this bloody place of earth coming at Harold. He looked round to us, and he said, 'It's one of those rough days, gentlemen.' He didn't last long."

Gimblett, in no mood for the battle, was run out for 0 as Somerset struggled to 55 all out. Then, with Buse taking four wickets, Lancashire sank to 46 for five. There was no point batting conventionally so the 17-year-old Peter Marner opted to hit out at everything. He struck four sixes, two in an over off Buse, and in 26 minutes he and Alan Wharton took the score from 46 to 116. With the tail also playing shots, they finished on 157.

By this time so much earth had come away that Somerset had no hope against Statham and off-spinner Roy Tattersall, both England bowlers. They were all out for 79, the game over before six o'clock.

Bertie Buse

"It's all over." Those were Buse's words to his surprised wife Elsa when he arrived home shortly afterwards. He had given ten summers of his life to the county, and he had barely taken enough money to cover his obligation to pay the costs of the away match at Old Trafford in July. He was a man who treated his money with care, and he was in despair.

In the end, it worked out well for him. Somerset let him off the away costs, and there was so much public sympathy for his misfortune that he was inundated with donations.

The county considered taking the remaining two games of the Festival elsewhere before arranging a visit to a local abbattoir. There they collected a large quantity of bull's blood and rolled it into the square. The result was a surface that lasted better, though it took prodigious turn, so much that the 17-year-old off-spinner Brian Langford, who had made his bewildered debut against Lancashire, took 25 wickets in the two matches. When the national bowling averages next appeared, he was in first place.

Excluding matches played under final-day, one-innings rules, this was the 14th time in the championship's history that a game had been completed in a single day, and Somerset had been the losing team in seven of them, four times to Lancashire. In 1894 they lost in a day twice in a week: at Old Trafford on Tuesday, then at Huddersfield on Thursday. In 1899, against Middlesex at Lord's, they lost in just three hours and five minutes, the shortest first-class match ever played.

The previous single-day match occurred at the Oval on Saturday 16 May 1953, only three weeks before Buse's benefit game, when Surrey entertained Warwickshire.

It was a wet morning, so wet that play was abandoned without a ball bowled at Lord's, but at the Oval they lost only 45 minutes. It is unlikely that modern umpires would have passed the pitch as fit for play, but in the 1950s, with wickets left open to the weather and large crowds gathered, there was a greater willingness to get out and play. The variety of surfaces was part of the challenge of playing first-class cricket.

Warwickshire opted to bat first, but against such a strong Surrey bowling side they were soon in trouble. The pitch was damp, the sun made it steam, and the cutters of Surrey's Alec Bedser, aided by the eager hands of close fielders, were too much for them. They were all out for 45. Bedser, eight for 18.

Surrey did not find it easy, either, but some tail-end hitting lifted them to 147 before Tony Lock was laid out by a ball that reared up and hit him on the head. He was taken off to hospital and, with the pitch now at its most spiteful, Warwickshire's nightmare began a second time.

A very young Tom Cartwright was opening the batting, and he put on a hard-fought 20 with Fred Gardner in Warwickshire's best stand of the match, an experience he never forgot. "You could never let the ball hit the bat," he said. "You always had to have the bat playing the ball. There is a difference. You learnt that very quickly. People say we're not competitive enough in our game now. On uncovered pitches you had to compete almost all the time. And if you survived, you learnt. County cricket on uncovered pitches was a great learning environment. I learned more in my time at the wicket in that game than I learned in any period of any other game."

He was lbw to Jim Laker for 9, and in no time, with Laker taking a hat-trick, 20 for nought became 32 for seven. There was pandemonium in the dressing room. "There wasn't a moment when people weren't putting pads on. Tom Dollery was saying to people, 'Get padded up. You're in.' And they'd say, 'No, I've been in, skipper.' It was that kind of comedy."

The ever-amiable Alan Townsend, assuming his day was over, was running himself a hot bath when he was told to pad up. He forgot to turn off the taps and rushed out to the middle, only to be run out for nought, returning to find his bath not yet full. They were all out for 51.

It was a game that no one present ever forgot. It was not the sort of cricket you would want too often but the unpredictability, the glorious uncertainty, was part of the charm in those days. Tom Cartwright certainly thought that: "I would much prefer to see people play natural cricket. Then you get a multi-faceted game. And when you take away some of the facets, which we have done, it shrinks in its artistic form, certainly in the disciplines required, and therefore the overall product is diminished."

Since those games at the Oval and Bath, only one further match has been completed in a single day: Kent versus Worcestershire at Tunbridge Wells in June 1960.

Like the Rec at Bath, the Nevill was a council ground, and that year they had left in charge a man with no knowledge of cricket. In unsettled weather he had removed all the grass, then added a layer of marl. On the day the sun came out, and the surface of rolled mud dried and broke up.

Like Brian Langford at Bath, Worcestershire's Norman Gifford, a 20-year-old slow-left-armer, was making his debut. "Even in club cricket," he says of the pitch, "I'd never seen anything like it. At first there were indentations where the ball pitched. Then the whole wicket disintegrated. It just collapsed."

Coming on at 41 for no wicket, he bowled Arthur Phebey, who returned to the pavilion to deliver his verdict on the surface: "If we get to 200 on that, we'll win by an innings."

Kent made 187, by which time, the *Worcester Chronicle* said, 'the pitch had broken up into a gravelly bed, more in keeping with a seaside beach.'

Gifford, in his naïveté, was pleased with his figures of four for 63, but he realised they were not that clever when, in under three hours, Worcestershire were all out for 25 and 61.

"Dick Richardson used to have a cigarette before batting. He put it down and said, 'Don't put that out. I'll have it when I come back.' And he did. There was that sort of feeling in the team."

They trooped across to the marquee where the Lady Mayor was hosting a drinks reception. "Here come the Worcester side," they heard her say. "Of course, they've ruined the Festival."

Gifford had been summoned from a two-day, second-eleven game at Maidstone. He had arrived at the Nevill, wondering anxiously what the step up to three-day cricket would be like.

Shadows of war

Frank Tyson was fast. At his brief peak he was unquestionably the fastest bowler in the world. Don Bradman thought him the fastest he ever saw, faster than Jeff Thomson or Harold Larwood. Doug Insole of Essex recalls batting against him and Fred Trueman in a Gentlemen/Players match, and in comparison "Fred was almost like an off-spinner." Tyson was fast. Very fast.

A bleacher's son, growing up in a council house in Middleton, he should have opened the bowling for Lancashire with Brian Statham, a combination which, with Roy Tattersall's off-spin, might have brought them the championship in the 1950s. But Lancashire rejected him – just as Essex rejected Jack Hobbs and Warwickshire Wilfred Rhodes.

They gave him one game on the second eleven in 1949, when he was just 19, on national service in the army, and it was a disaster. With the trains on strike, it took him till 5 a.m. to get home from York, and in the morning his bus to Old Trafford was held up. He arrived, breathless, as the Lancashire team were taking the field, got a ten-minute lecture on punctuality and, in a state of exhaustion, managed five wicketless overs before pulling a muscle in his back. Before he could play another game, he sprained his ankle, then broke his leg playing soccer. Lancashire concluded that he was injury-prone and lost interest.

He studied English at Durham University, played cricket in the leagues and was signed up by Northamptonshire. He was not a bowler suited to the six-day-a-week grind of county cricket, certainly not on the slow spinner's wicket at Northampton, but there were days when he was at his very fastest – never more so than in August 1953 when he went back to Old Trafford for the first time. Brian Statham said he never saw him bowl faster in England.

"The wicket was all scratched to bits," Dennis Brookes, stand-in captain of Northamptonshire, remembered. "Lancashire were running for the championship, and they deliberately got a poor wicket."

By the second morning both sides had completed an innings, with the spinners taking most of the wickets. Heavy rain drove the players into the pavilion before Lancashire could bat a second time and, when they finally resumed at 4.15, the pitch was alarmingly fast and unpredictable. Tyson, bowling with a wind behind him, got his first ball to catch the shoulder of Jack Ikin's bat, and first slip, standing way back, took the catch. Geoff Edrich, at number three, was greeted by a ball just short of a length that flew over his head and was still rising when it sailed over a jumping keeper and clattered into the sight screen.

Frank Tyson

'To bowl quick,' Frank Tyson wrote, 'is to revel in the glad animal action; to thrill in physical prowess and to enjoy a certain sneaking feeling of superiority over the other mortals who play the game. No batsman likes quick bowling, and this knowledge gives one a sense of omnipotence.'

The next lifting ball hit Geoff Edrich on the wrist, a catch going down at short leg, and Tyson soon had two more wickets. Then Tyson hit Edrich a second time on his wrist. It was terrifying stuff, especially to the next men in, watching from the sideways-on pavilion where the pace of the ball looked greater than from end on. "They were seeing these balls flying all over the place," Geoff Edrich remembered, "and they didn't fancy it. They didn't want to know really."

At the close Lancashire were 94 for seven, with Edrich on 59 not out. 'Two qualities served him,' wrote the *Manchester Guardian*. 'A courage which prevented him from taking his eyes off the ball, and the belief and determination that no match is beyond winning or saving until it is lost.'

The next day, in pain from the blows he had taken to his hand, he finished on 81 not out. Northamptonshire won by one wicket, their first ever victory at Old Trafford, and Geoff Edrich drove his Austin 8 to Cheltenham for the next match. In the morning, unable to grip his bat, he was sent across the road to the hospital, where an X-ray revealed a multiple fracture. He had scored 81 against Tyson with a badly broken wrist.

The following summer there was a tour party to Australia to be selected, and for the first time since the war England was blessed with young fast bowlers, among them Fred Trueman, Brian Statham, Peter Loader, Alan Moss and Frank Tyson. Tyson had achieved least of the five, but he did his claim no harm when, days before the final selection, he bowled against Middlesex at Lord's.

It was a fast wicket, and on the second evening, with Middlesex having only half an hour to bat, Tyson threw his all into a high-speed spell. To Bill Edrich, Geoff's older brother, he bowled a ball just short of a length. 'The ball reared upwards,' Edrich said, 'and at the time I can recall reasoning: "He can't hit the wicket at that height, I'll try a hook."' Edrich top-edged the ball into his face and, in the words of *The Times*, 'fell like a log with a sickening cry.'

He spent the night in hospital with a broken cheek-bone. But next morning, when the Middlesex team arrived, who should they find in the dressing room, smoking his pipe, but Bill Edrich, 'his face swollen and plastered'? His intention was to continue his innings, which in due course he did, coming in after Denis Compton had mis-hooked Tyson.

Tyson's first ball to the 38-year-old Edrich hit him over the heart, but 'he seemed undeterred, and he hooked at each of the four bouncers he received in his 75 minutes at the wicket.' In those moments, some say, both Tyson and Edrich booked their passages to Australia.

Nobody in county cricket had a greater reputation for bravery – to the point of madness, some thought – than Bill Edrich. In the war he had flown Blenheims on low-level, daylight bombing raids on German docks, raids that attracted anti-aircraft fire and sometimes fights with Messerschmidts.

One raid took place on the morning of a cricket match at Massingham Hall in his native Norfolk, and late replacements had to be found for the men who did not make it back.

'It was a hard and exciting game,' he wrote. 'But every now and then one's mind would flicker off to the briefing, and to joking with a pal whose broken body was now washing in the long, cold tides, and one saw again his machine cartwheeling down, flaming from nose to tail.'

Geoff Edrich and brother Bill

Brother Geoff was sent to the Far East. Captured in the jungles of Malaya, he spent three and a half years as a prisoner of the Japanese. Only six of his platoon came home.

"A lot of the boys died of a broken heart. They couldn't see the end. There was one march, when we moved camp, maybe twenty miles, when some of us were ready to pack in. And if you dropped out, that was it – you got a bayonet through you from the guards. But 'Keep going,' my friend said. You had to have one or two decent chaps with you to get through."

For the first year, in Singapore docks, it was not too hard. There was even time to play makeshift cricket matches between the English and Australian prisoners. Later, building the bridge over the River Kwai in Thailand, it was hell on earth.

"Time goes on, doesn't it? Work, sleep, bit of rice, work. It's amazing what you can put up with, really. There was fever, dysentery, cholera. It was terrible. I remember seeing this lad; he was like a skeleton. I was thinking, 'How's he walking?' It was just bones walking. You had to have a bit of luck to get through – and a bit of will power."

Down to six stone, he returned to England to find his wife on a widow's pension. Till late in his life, he rarely talked about his war, though the experience of it was inside him that day when he batted against Tyson. "Geoff was the batsman to fight hardest of all against the odds," his team-mate Ken Grieves said. "The one man who would never quit, no matter how high the odds were stacked against him."

"It all comes down to how much you want to play," was the way Geoff himself put it. "Plus you've got to have a bit of luck."

1954: Stuart Surridge's winning ways

In 1951 Surrey finished sixth, winning seven and losing six of their 28 games. In 1952 they were champions, winning 20 and losing three. Peter May, coming into the side as a young batsman, thought the great change had three main causes.

The Oval pitches became less true: 'The ball began to move about, to turn by the second innings and to have a sort of rounded bounce, not especially quick but useful to good bowlers.'

Tony Lock, after a winter coaching in a net with a low ceiling, changed from an orthodox slow-left-armer with a nice loop but little spin to a faster, flatter bowler who, on a helpful track, could get nasty turn and lift.

Finally, Stuart Surridge took over as captain. In May's opinion, 'He was simply a great and inspiring leader.'

Michael Barton, his predecessor, was of his time. A former Oxford blue, working for Dunlop, he had been plucked out of occasional club cricket, and he performed his duties as a traditional amateur, keeping a distance between himself and his team. He was a quiet and intelligent man, a good enough batsman to earn their respect, but he never quite got on top of all their moaning and groaning.

His greatest success came in 1950 when on the last day of the season they bowled out Leicestershire to share the championship title with Lancashire. But the day was not without incident. Before play Barton summoned Alec Bedser to his captain's room: "I know you've been over-bowled, Alec," he told him with caring paternalism, "but I really must ask you for one last supreme effort." And back came the gruff response: "I've never been told I'm not trying before."

In the field Leicestershire's Les Berry proved hard to remove till finally, mistiming a drive, he sent the ball in the air between mid-off and bowler, both of whom started for the catch. Barton, at first slip, called out "Laurie" for mid-off Fishlock but, alas, a substitute was on in place of Fishlock. "That's the first time you've opened your mouth all summer," Jack Parker said, "and you've just cost us the f---ing championship."

Micky Stewart joined the staff in 1953, and he knew the transformation that came with the appointment of Surridge: "Michael Barton was a very nice, popular person but, when he was captain, there was still the amateur-pro divide. The amateurs stayed in a different hotel; sometimes they'd take a dinner jacket to wear for the evening meal. Stuey totally changed the environment. He still changed in the amateur dressing room, but he had grown up in Surrey, playing with so many of the team when they were all younger."

Dickie Dodds of Essex witnessed the change:

> At one time Surrey seemed to have eleven captains, but all this ended abruptly when Stuart Surridge took over. Stuart was a large man in every way. He had a large frame, a large heart, he bowled large swingers, and he cracked the whip. Without question he was the boss. He led from the front and gave his orders, reprimands, encouragement and praise in language as spoken in the Borough Market.
>
> This is not to say that the Surrey players stopped chuntering as they batted, bowled, and especially as they fielded; it was that they now had a skipper who understood their chuntering and could orchestrate it and blend it into a harmonious, constructive whole. Through it all Stuart Surridge remained himself, and his own man, and that was perhaps his secret.

"When we went out to field under Stuey," Micky Stewart says, "it was like going over the top out of the trenches. But he led by example. As a close fielder he set the standard for everybody. He'd stand there in the field bawling orders. I remember Keith Miller saying to him, 'I wouldn't talk to my dog the way you talk to Locky.'"

To Lock, yes, but not to Jim Laker. "I swore at Jim only once," Surridge said, "and he couldn't bowl for an hour."

They won the title in 1952 and again in 1953, when Laker, Lock, Bedser and May were often away playing for England. But Surridge's greatest triumph came in 1954 when, five weeks from the end of the season, Surrey were down in eighth place, seemingly too far behind leaders Yorkshire.

It was a wretched summer, the worst the championship has ever known, and those last weeks were played out under relentlessly gloomy skies, with band after band of rain sweeping across the country. Whole days were lost to the elements, yet somehow Surrey found time to win nine of their ten matches, gaining first-innings points in the other.

The key to their success was the speed with which they bowled out sides. Whatever the state of the pitch, and in such weather it was usually treacherous, they had the right bowlers: the vicious spin of Laker and Lock, the fiendish leg-cutters of Alec Bedser, or the pace of Peter Loader, who took 14 wickets at Worcester. In 19 innings across those ten games the average total scored against them was just 105.

Five times they finished their games inside two days. On four of those occasions they sat at home on the third day while rain washed away the chances of their chief rivals, Yorkshire and Derbyshire. Were they just lucky? 'It seems that Surrey are to be chosen by the weather as champions,' wrote *The Times*. Or were they, under Surridge, making their luck?

At lunch on the final day at Cheltenham Gloucestershire, chasing 268, were 95 for two. The forecast was bad, the light was dim and there was drizzle in the air. Play did not resume, and for half an hour Surridge strode repeatedly out of the dressing room, glaring at the clouds as if to will them in another direction. Eventually, with his infectious personality, he persuaded the umpires that the south wind rustling the chestnut trees was drying the pitch, and out they all came.

He took the ball himself, came off a short run on the wet grass and in six overs took five wickets, reducing Gloucestershire to 112 all out. Ten minutes later, the heavens opened and the field turned into a lake.

By their penultimate match, at home to Worcestershire, Surrey were favourites to retain the championship, needing just one more victory to be sure. Heavy rain fell in the morning, and play did not get under way till 2 o'clock. What then unfolded was the most remarkable match ever played in the county championship, a match that more than any other encapsulated the spirit of Stuart Surridge and his Surrey side.

Worcestershire were asked to bat first and, with the sodden pitch drying awkwardly under a hot sun, Laker and Lock – with fielders clustered tightly around the bat – got turn and lift that was all but unplayable. The eleven Worcestershire batsmen lasted an hour and three quarters, faced 28.3 overs and were all out for 25. By 4.30 Surrey, with one wicket down, had taken the points for first-innings lead.

An hour later, with Peter May playing 'a little gem of an innings', they had reached 92 for three when the game took another extraordinary turn. Ken Barrington, batting with May, looked up at the balcony and saw Surridge waving them in. "He's declared!" he said with astonishment. "What are you talking about?" May replied. Then, seeing the wave for himself: "He didn't have a gin and tonic at tea, did he?"

Lasting an hour into the second day, Worcestershire were all out for 40. One batsman hit his wicket, another retired with a fractured finger, and a third was hit on the head by a rearing off-break from Jim Laker. The whole match had seen only 157 runs, fewer than any other first-class game since 1878.

Surrey were champions again. The sun broke through that morning, and the 3,000-strong cheering crowd gathered in front of the pavilion to hear Stuart Surridge make a celebratory speech from the balcony.

Stuart Surridge on the balcony

Surridge, with his burning desire to win every session, every match, every championship, brought an attitude to Surrey's cricket that had never been seen outside Yorkshire before.

The next summer, with the weather kinder, they did not draw a single game, winning 23 and losing five. Then at the end of 1956 Surridge returned to his business life, passing the captaincy to Peter May who was every bit as determined to win. His first year in charge saw the side reach its peak, winning the title with a record 94-point margin. In 14 of their 21 victories they did not lose a second-innings wicket.

The bowling was exceptional, as was the close catching – in 1957 Micky Stewart, Ken Barrington and Tony Lock between them took an extraordinary 200 catches for Surrey – but, above all, for all the moaning and groaning, they had a great team spirit. Everybody played for the side.

"For that," Peter May said, "one man was responsible, Stuart Surridge. His style of captaincy was unusual, but it worked – and we all knew it did."

191

Commonwealth immigrants

When Somerset met Northamptonshire in July 1957, there were eight overseas players taking part; it would have been nine, but for an injury to Jock Livingston in the previous match. There were five Australians, a West Indian, a New Zealander and a South African, all of whom had qualified by years of residence.

Peter Wight arrived on a cargo boat from Guyana in 1951, shivering in his tropical clothes. He planned to study engineering, but he missed his exams and, after a spell in Toronto, finished up working in a factory in Burnley. He was scoring runs in the Lancashire League so in the summer of 1953, when he visited his sister near Bridgwater, her husband offered a suggestion: "Why don't you play for Somerset? They've got no players."

Somerset were at rock bottom, not knowing where to turn for talent. After two nets and a second-eleven game, they picked him to play the Australians, and he scored a century.

His team-mate Bill Alley also reached Somerset via Lancashire. Disappointed to miss out on selection for the 1948 tour of England, he was one of several Australians whom agents persuaded to play in the Lancashire League. The money was good, better than they might make by staying in Australia and trying to break into the Test team.

Northamptonshire were the first county to spot the opportunity. With so little home-grown talent, they were always scouting the north of England, and they realised that some of the Australians had fulfilled the three-year residential qualification for overseas players.

Jock Livingston came first, followed by George Tribe and Jack Manning, a trio who did much to lift the fortunes of Northamptonshire in the 1950s. Livingston, a hard-hitting left-handed batsman, was the championship's leading run-scorer in '55 and '56 while Tribe, a back-of-the-hand left-arm bowler, was the leading wicket-taker in '56. On the county circuit of the 1950s Tribe was one of the most feared bowlers, regularly tormenting Yorkshire, with their traditional weakness against wrist spin. In one game against them he bowled 28.2 overs and took 15 wickets for 31 runs. He could also bat, doing the double in seven of his eight summers.

Keith Andrew, brought down from the Central Lancashire League to keep wicket to him, thought him "probably the best cricketer I ever played with. He had the chinaman, the googly, two or three kinds of flipper, the whole shooting match. And he studied the batsmen. His attitude was so good, too."

Nottinghamshire had the leg-spinner Bruce Dooland, the leading wicket-taker – by a long way – in '53 and '54. Trouble with one of his spinning fingers reduced him a little after that but at his peak, in the view of Reg Simpson, his Notts captain, he was "the best leg-break bowler in the history of cricket, better than Shane Warne. He had far more variety. His top spinner was an absolute devil." With Dooland in the side, Nottinghamshire leapt up the table.

Tribe and Dooland. Australia lost three series in a row to England in the 1950s, with a weakness in spin bowling, yet two of their greatest match-winners had thrown in their lot with county cricket.

Bruce Dooland
Australia to Nottinghamshire

Gamini Goonesena
Sri Lanka to Nottinghamshire

Roy Marshall
Barbados to Hampshire

Bill Alley
Australia to Somerset

Denis Foreman
South Africa to Sussex

George Tribe
Australia to Northamptonshire

Derief Taylor
Jamaica to Warwickshire

Peter Wight
Guyana to Somerset

Nottinghamshire also had Gamini Goonesena, another leg-spinner. From a wealthy background in Sri Lanka, Goonesena was a student at Cambridge University. He played his cricket as an old-fashioned amateur, turning up in vintage cars and selecting his matches: "I shan't bother to play at Ilkeston again," he said after one bruising encounter with Derbyshire's Les Jackson. In his cut-glass English accent he was forever despatching the twelfth man on errands, and he famously upset his captain on the way to one game, telling him, "Let's face it, Reg, I'm the only proper amateur in this side." English cricket was not always at ease with its immigrants.

Nor was it always easy for the immigrants to adjust to English ways. Ray Hitchcock, one of several New Zealanders who made their way to Warwickshire, was told to run a bath for an amateur – "I found that very hard to accept" – and he came close to being reported for addressing Freddie Brown, the Northants captain, by his first name. Then, when the senior professional Eric Hollies invited him round for a meal, he anxiously bought himself a new suit on credit, "only to realise that in the Black Country faggot and peas didn't warrant a suit. A cloth cap would have been better."

Denis Foreman, classified Cape Coloured in South Africa, was shocked to find he could sit where he liked on the bus. He had come to England to play football for Brighton and Hove Albion and was signed up by Sussex, just as his fellow countryman Stuart Leary, at Charlton Athletic, joined Kent.

Derief Taylor, a Jamaican, came to Warwickshire, having fought alongside Tom Dollery in the North African desert. Already 37 years old, he improved his prospects by telling the county he was born not in 1910 but 1918.

Roy Marshall, son of a wealthy plantation owner in Barbados, toured England with the West Indies in 1950, during which he scored a superb hundred at Southampton. Two years later, playing in the Lancashire League, he was asked by Hampshire to join them. He still had Test ambitions, but the English county game offered far more cricket than he could play back home so he settled here, spending two years completing his residential qualification. The biggest cultural shock for him was "the amount of swearing I heard on the pitch. We played the game hard in the West Indies. We were out to win, but dropped chances and big hits were never followed by abusive and unfriendly remarks."

Peter Wight, from Guyana, had grown up on tales of England. "I'd heard so much about county cricket," he says, "but, to tell you the truth, I thought it was just as ordinary as anything else." His wristy batting delighted the Somerset faithful, just as Roy Marshall, with his electrifying drives and cuts, thrilled the Hampshire crowds. They were special players, adding a rare spice to the English county game, and they became an integral part of it, not hired guns brought in for a season. Only Gimblett stands above Wight among Somerset's run-scorers, only Mead above Marshall for Hampshire.

Then there was Bill Alley. Already 38 when he came to Somerset in 1957, he stayed for 12 years, scoring 3,000 runs in 1961 and taking 100 wickets in 1962. With his craggy features and plain talking, his country pursuits and chicken farm, and, above all, the pugnacious way he clouted the ball when he batted, he became a true man of Somerset, loved by their cider-drinking supporters. The immigrants of the 1950s did much to enhance the English county game.

1960 – 1969

Years of great change

The arrival of one-day cricket and overseas stars

Yorkshire champions six times

Television and the family car have closed down most of the music halls and provincial repertory theatres, and many cinemas. If it is not to go the same way, cricket needs subsidising; but it always has. Of old, its deficit was underwritten by the country gentry; now that is done by the supporters' club football pools.

Cricket is a game for enthusiasts; it always has been. It would be a shame if, for the sake of the non-enthusiast's gate-money, the game were ever debased.

John Arlott, Playfair Cricket Monthly, 1962

Cricket was started for the enjoyment of the participants, only comparatively recently has spectator appeal started to exert the significant influence on law changes, and I haven't seen the good of it yet.

Knock-out cricket is a pleasantly simplified version of the real thing, but I can tell you that by comparison it is no great shakes to play, rather like playing the pitch-and-putt course on the front at Lytham St Annes, dreaming of the real thing on the championship course a few yards away.

Ted Dexter, The Observer, July 1965

The overseas players by their enterprise and natural approach brought a breath of life into the three-day match. Garfield Sobers was the outstanding personality, and his appearances with Nottinghamshire brought out the crowds.

Wisden Cricketers' Almanack 1969

1960 Counties are given the choice of playing either 28 or 32 matches, with the table decided, as before the war, by average points per match. Eight counties opt for the full 32 matches, including Yorkshire who also play Oxford and Cambridge Universities, MCC (twice) and the South Africans. Starting on Saturday 30 April, they play 37 three-day games in 18½ weeks, their first break coming on Wednesday 7 September. Then, as Champion County, they play against the Rest on Saturday 10 September. Wicket-keeper Jimmy Binks plays all 38 games.

John Kennedy, aged 43, becomes the youngest person ever to win a US Presidential election.

1961 Hampshire become the tenth county to win the championship.

The follow-on is abolished in championship matches. The new ball, previously due after 75 overs or 200 runs, does not become due till 85 overs have been bowled. Under strict qualification rules the England cricketer Tom Graveney, moving from Gloucestershire to Worcestershire, has to spend the summer playing second-eleven cricket. The Yorkshire fixture list increases to 39 games, and again keeper Jimmy Binks plays them all.

The maximum wage is abolished in football. Johnny Haynes of Fulham becomes the first £100-a-week footballer.

1962 In November the counties vote to abolish the distinction between amateur and professional cricketers.

Also in November the Beatles have their first hit record, reaching number 17 with 'Love Me Do'.

1963 The Gillette Cup, a one-day knock-out competition with a final at Lord's, is introduced.

MCC organise an experiment at Lord's, playing with the old lbw law (the ball must pitch in line) and a fourth stump. The counties revert to playing 28 matches each. It is now ten points, not twelve, for a win. The follow-on is reinstated after its two-year abolition. The no-ball law changes from the back foot to the front foot.

The Beeching Report recommends the closure of 2,128 railway stations, with the loss of 67,700 jobs.

1964 Worcestershire become the eleventh county to win the championship.

A third television channel, BBC2, is launched. Radio Caroline broadcasts non-stop music from a boat in the North Sea.

1965 For the first time two touring teams, New Zealand and South Africa, play three Tests each against England.

The administrative county of Middlesex ceases to exist on April 1.

1966 Each county plays its first 12 matches under a new experimental rule, limiting the first innings to 65 overs per side. Bowlers are not allowed to polish the ball.

For the first time there is Sunday cricket in the championship, with play allowed from 1 p.m.

Football's World Cup is held during July, with hosts England beating Germany 4-2 in the final.

1967 It is now eight points, not ten, for a victory. The 65-over first innings is abandoned after one year.

The Professional Cricketers' Association is formed.

Muhammad Ali is stripped of his heavyweight boxing title for refusing to fight in the Vietnam War.

1968 It is ten points again for a victory, and a new system of bonus points is introduced for runs scored and wickets taken during the first 85 overs: one batting point for each 25 runs over 150, one bowling point for each two wickets. Following incidents of deliberately slow play, a minimum of 20 overs in the final hour is introduced.

For the first time each county can register, without residential qualification, one overseas player. No further overseas player can be registered for three years, nor can an overseas player move county during those three years. Yorkshire, one of only four counties not to make a special signing, are champions for the seventh time in ten years. The Test and County Cricket Board is formed, taking responsibility for the county game away from MCC.

The All-England Lawn Tennis Championships at Wimbledon accept entries from professional players.

1969 A Sunday League is introduced. The counties now play 24, not 28, matches in the championship.

Rupert Murdoch from Australia gains control of the News of the World.

Championship – top three | Leading batsmen | Leading bowlers | Leading wkt-keeper / Leading fielder

	P	W	L	D	Pts	Ave	Leading batsmen	Runs	Leading bowlers	Wickets	Leading wkt-keeper / Leading fielder	Victims
1960												
Yorkshire	32	17	6	9	246	7.7	P.B. Wight (Som)	2,086	H.L. Jackson (Derbys)	146	R. Booth (Worcs)	96
Lancashire	32	13	8	11	214	6.7	R.E. Marshall (Hants)	2,062	D.J. Shepherd (Glam)	133		
Middlesex	28	12	4	12	186	6.6	H. Horton (Hants)	1,943	F.S. Trueman (Yorks)	132	P.M. Walker (Glam)	59
1961												
Hampshire	32	19	7	6	268	8.4	W.E. Alley (Som)	2,532	D. Shackleton (Hants)	153	R. Booth (Worcs)	88
Yorkshire	32	17	5	10	250	7.8	R.E. Marshall (Hants)	2,455	J.A. Flavell (Worcs)	139		
Middlesex	28	15	6	7	214	7.6	H. Horton (Hants)	2,067	L.J. Coldwell (Worcs)	135	P.M. Walker (Glam)	65
1962												
Yorkshire	32	14	4	14	224	7.0	J.R. Gray (Hants)	2,196	D. Shackleton (Hants)	161	R. Booth (Worcs)	95
Worcestershire	32	14	3	15	220	6.9	W.J. Stewart (Warwicks)	2,100	L.J. Coldwell (Worcs)	132		
Warwickshire	32	12	5	15	202	6.3	K.G. Suttle (Sussex)	2,057	O.S. Wheatley (Glam)	126	P.J. Sharpe (Yorks)	65
1963	P	W	L	D	Pts							
Yorkshire	28	13	3	12	144		P.E. Richardson (Kent)	1,798	K.E. Palmer (Som)	121	J.G. Binks (Yorks)	80
Glamorgan	28	11	8	9	124		M.E.J.C. Norman (Northants)	1,740	B.R. Knight (Essex)	116	D.G.L. Evans (Glam)	80
Somerset	28	10	6	12	118		J.B. Bolus (Notts)	1,728	D. Shackleton (Hants)	116	R. Miller (Warwicks)	42
									D.J. Shepherd (Glam)	116		
1964												
Worcestershire	28	18	3	7	191		T.W. Graveney (Worcs)	2,271	D. Shackleton (Hants)	138	R. Booth (Worcs)	95
Warwickshire	28	14	5	9	150		W.E. Russell (Middx)	2,050	T.W. Cartwright (Warwicks)	128		
Northants	28	12	4	12	130		R.C. Wilson (Kent)	1,979	A.L. Dixon (Kent)	121	D.W. Richardson (Worcs)	46
1965												
Worcestershire	28	13	4	11	144		D.M. Green (Lancs)	1,784	D. Shackleton (Hants)	133	G. Clayton (Som)	85
Northants	28	13	4	11	140		W.E. Russell (Middx)	1,724	J.A. Flavell (Worcs)	132		
Glamorgan	28	12	6	10	132		T.W. Graveney (Worcs)	1,684	J.B. Statham (Lancs)	124	P.M. Walker (Glam)	51
1966												
Yorkshire	28	15	5	8	184		A.R. Lewis (Glam)	1,960	D.L. Underwood (Kent)	143	G. Clayton (Som)	83
Worcestershire	28	13	5	10	166		J.H. Edrich (Surrey)	1,913	J.A. Flavell (Worcs)	135		
Somerset	28	13	7	8	156		P.H. Parfitt (Middx)	1,860	A. Buss (Sussex)	116	P.H. Parfitt (Middx)	42
1967												
Yorkshire	28	12	5	11	186		C.A. Milton (Glos)	1,971	T.W. Cartwright (Warwicks)	132	A.P.E. Knott (Kent)	77
Kent	28	11	3	14	176		J.B. Bolus (Notts)	1,760	G.A.R. Lock (Leics)	122		
Leicestershire	28	10	3	15	176		J.H. Edrich (Surrey)	1,658	D. Shackleton (Hants)	112	M.H. Page (Derbys)	48
1968												
Yorkshire	28	11	4	13	270		B.A. Richards (Hants)	2,039	R.M.H. Cottam (Hants)	122	D.L. Murray (Notts)	72
Kent	28	12	5	11	256		D.M. Green (Glos)	1,875	K. Higgs (Lancs)	105		
Glamorgan	28	11	6	11	237		R.M. Prideaux (Northants)	1,679	D. Wilson (Yorks)	102	P.H. Parfitt (Middx)	45
1969												
Glamorgan	24	11	0	13	250		B.W. Luckhurst (Kent)	1,593	M.J. Procter (Glos)	103	E.W. Jones (Glam)	67
Gloucestershire	24	10	6	8	219		Mushtaq Mohammad (Nthants)	1,487	R.M.H. Cottam (Hants)	100		
Surrey	24	7	1	16	210		Younis Ahmed (Surrey)	1,449	T.W. Cartwright (Warwicks)	95	M.J. Procter (Glos)	33

1960-1969

Leading counties

	P	W	L	D	%W
Yorkshire	288	122	45	121	42.4
Worcestershire	288	95	64	129	33.0
Glamorgan	288	86	81	121	29.9
Kent	276	82	63	131	29.7

Leading batsmen

K.G. Suttle (Sussex)	15,420
R.E. Marshall (Hants)	15,078
W.E. Russell (Middx)	15,056
J.H. Edrich (Surrey)	14,872

Leading bowlers

D. Shackleton (Hants)	1,161
D.J. Shepherd (Glam)	1,014
D.W. White (Hants)	927
T.W. Cartwright (Warwks)	908

Leading keepers & fielder

R. Booth (Worcs)	669
J.G. Binks (Yorks)	656
P.M. Walker (Glam)	403

Overall statistics

Runs per wicket	24.1
Runs per 100 balls	42.5
% of matches drawn	46.5

Miscellany

At Bournemouth in 1969, in the game between Hampshire and Glamorgan, Law 17 – about refusal to play – was invoked for the only time in the history of the county championship.

On the final day rain set in early, and it was still drizzling at four o'clock when the Hampshire team, misinterpreting a remark by the Glamorgan captain, packed up and went home. Then at 5.30, with the rain having cleared, the umpires led out the Glamorgan fielders. They called "Play", waited two minutes, then awarded the Welshmen the match.

For several weeks the row rumbled on, not helped by the fact that Glamorgan, with the extra points, were top of the table. Eventually they asked for the victory to be annulled, going on to win the championship without it.

*

At Trent Bridge in 1967, against Lancashire's Statham and Lever, John Howarth took part in a last-wicket stand of 21 that allowed John Parkin to reach his only first-class fifty. He also saved a game, batting out time against Essex's Robin Hobbs.

But what he never did in 13 matches for Notts, in seven innings, three of them not out, was to score a run. In his 11th match, with the game lost, he tried to hit Warwickshire's Tom Cartwright over extra cover and was stumped. No one in first-class cricket has played so many matches and remained runless.

At Clacton in 1965 the stand-in Warwickshire captain, wicket-keeper Alan Smith, was struggling. Of the county's front-line seamers Tom Cartwright was playing for England, David Brown was out injured and now Rudi Webster, their Barbadian medical student, was off the field with a sprained back. Essex, chasing 203, were 28 for no wicket, and as a last resort, with his perennial enthusiasm, AC Smith decided to have a go himself.

The fifth ball of his second over was short, and he watched in joy as Gordon Barker was caught on the square-leg boundary. Geoff Smith turned his first ball into the hands of leg slip and, off the first ball of AC's next over, Keith Fletcher skied a catch to mid-wicket. For the only time in championship history a keeper had taken off his pads and claimed a hat-trick.

*

At Swansea in 1968 the West Indies captain Garry Sobers, playing for Nottinghamshire, hit the Glamorgan left-arm pace bowler Malcolm Nash for six sixes in an over, the last of his ferocious leg-side blows sending the ball over the wall and far down the road towards the town centre.

In the dressing room afterwards, Nash took an inevitable ribbing from his team-mates. "Somebody will probably write a book about it," he said cheerfully, only to get the reply: "What will they call it? *Gone With The Wind*?"

The championship in the 1960s

The 1960s were years of crisis and change for county cricket. Some commentators counselled against excessive alarm, pointing out that paying spectators at the start of the decade were much the same in number as they had been in the 1930s and that, on top of that, the counties had almost twice as many members. But year on year, with the fading of the post-war boom, the grounds were becoming emptier. With costs rising, there was a growing consensus that, if county cricket was to survive and prosper in this new age of television and motor car, it would have to embrace change.

The weather provided little help. The summer of 1961 was a good one, but the decade as a whole – cold, gloomy and wet – was the worst in the history of the championship.

There was much tinkering with the detail of the game, all of it designed to encourage a more positive approach. For two years there was no follow-on, then there was a limitation on overs in the first innings, then bonus points for runs and wickets. There were changes to the no-ball law and the new-ball regulations, the polishing of the ball was banned, and a minimum of 20 overs was introduced for the last hour. Many of these alterations had unfortunate side-effects, and opinion divided between those looking for the next remedial change and those longing for greater stability.

In 1964 Surrey's proposal of a three-year moratorium on further change was 'well supported', but it was soon forgotten. 'The annual tampering with the game has gone past a joke,' the former Middlesex captain John Warr wrote in 1966. 'The cricket-loving public is now baffled by the stream of new regulations every spring.'

By contrast, Ossie Wheatley, then the Glamorgan captain, thinks the game has to keep refreshing itself. "The professional cricketer will always act to minimise his risk. Whatever set of rules you confront him with, he will find a way of playing within those rules. So you need to keep making him think again."

Amid all the tinkering, however, came four major changes that would have a lasting impact on the domestic game.

The first, in November 1962, was the decision to abolish the distinction between amateurs and professionals. Though many mourned the passing of the true amateur, there was an acceptance that he had faded from the scene many years earlier and that too much hypocrisy was involved in maintaining the pretence of his continued existence.

Several professionals became outstanding county captains in the 1960s: Brian Close at Yorkshire, Don Kenyon at Worcestershire, Keith Andrew at Northants, Tony Lock at Leicestershire. But others were too rooted in caution or too insecure about their own position.

At Lord's in July 1967 Roy Marshall, the Hampshire captain, was out for an exciting 153 before tea on the first day. Yet he then let his side bat well into the following day before declaring on 421, in reply to which Middlesex, under the captaincy of Fred Titmus, crawled to 371 for seven off 176 overs. It was hard to believe that the fixture, played with the amateurs Colin Ingleby-Mackenzie and Ian Bedford as captains, would have followed the same course.

The next major change was the introduction in 1963 of a one-day knock-out competition, the Gillette Cup. This was an immediate success, attracting great crowds, though the early attacking cricket did not last once captains discovered the effectiveness of negative bowling and defensive field placings.

In 1966, in a third significant change, several county clubs scheduled play on Sundays, and that too brought in the spectators. By 1969 the successes of the one-day game and Sunday play combined to produce a third competition, a 40-over Sunday League. At this point the county championship shrank from a schedule of 28 to 24 matches.

Then in 1968 came a fourth seismic change: a relaxation of the registration rules, allowing each county to employ one overseas player without any residential qualification. The West Indian Garry Sobers was the star attraction, and the wealthy Nottinghamshire won the auction for his services, offering a princely £5,000 a year plus air tickets, accommodation and car. Such was his impact, with bat, ball and captaincy, that the county rose from 15th to fourth place in the table.

In the four months of the championship, from May to August, there was no cricket elsewhere in the world so, with the exception of the touring Australians, all the best cricketers were available, and many of them came: Rohan Kanhai to Warwickshire, Barry Richards to Hampshire, Majid Khan to Glamorgan. They gave the county game a great boost.

That summer of 1968 was the 69th in which the championship had been officially contested, and for the 29th time Yorkshire were the outright winners, their seventh title in ten years. Their victory was all the more remarkable because, unlike all their main rivals, they had no overseas player, sticking proudly to their Yorkshire-born policy.

So much was changing in these years, not only in cricket but in social attitudes, and in 1967 the Professional Cricketers'

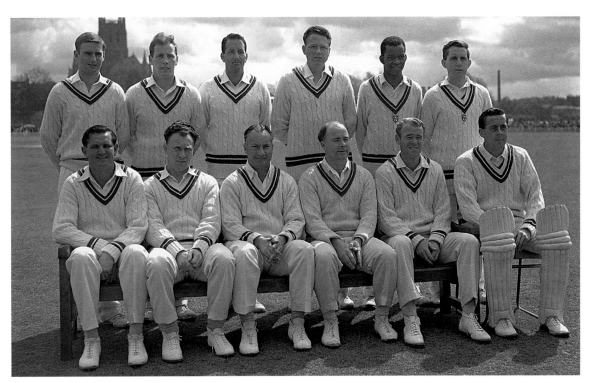

Association was formed, a trade union for first-class cricketers. Reflecting this new mood, the 36-year-old Ray Illingworth, concerned for his future at the close of 1968, asked Yorkshire for a three-year contract, not the one-year they always handed out. The response from chairman Brian Sellers was to tell him, "You can go, and take any other bugger with you." So he went, to captain Leicestershire. Within weeks of the start of the next summer, he was captain of England.

At the close of 1970 Sellers sacked Brian Close as captain, and Close departed to Somerset. Fred Trueman, Jimmy Binks, Ken Taylor all retired during this time, and Yorkshire's great years were over. Never again would they dominate the championship as they had once done. The last years of the 1960s were, in so many ways, the end of an era.

Back in 1962 Worcestershire, captained by the shrewd Don Kenyon, were almost crowned champions. They finished their programme top of the table, waiting with hope as Yorkshire travelled to Harrogate to play Glamorgan where rain washed out the whole second day. Yet Yorkshire triumphed once more, and a jubilant, 10,000-strong crowd besieged the pavilion. In the words of *The Times*, 'Yorkshiremen, though accustomed to success, are certainly not tired of it.'

Worcestershire had acquired from Gloucestershire the elegant batsman Tom Graveney, they had in Jack Flavell and Len Coldwell as potent a new-ball attack as any in England and, with men like Martin Horton and Roy Booth, they never lacked for a happy *ésprit de corps*. Sure enough, their time came in 1964 when, with 18 wins out of 28, they won their first championship, retaining it in 1965 when they added to their ranks the 'Cape Coloured' South African Basil D'Oliveira.

Theirs was a popular victory, as was that of Glamorgan in 1969. Captained by Tony Lewis, they were the first county to remain undefeated through a season since Lancashire in 1930.

The crucial moment of the Welshmen's summer came in late August at Swansea when, off the game's very last ball and with nine wickets down, Essex's John Lever attempted a second run to bring scores level. Down on the third man boundary, near the rugby stand, Glamorgan's former captain Ossie Wheatley lumbered round. Somehow he swooped and returned the ball with a once-in-a-lifetime speed and accuracy.

How the ground erupted! "The crowd surged onto the pitch," Glamorgan's Peter Walker recalls. "I've seen similar events when English counties have won, but there isn't quite the battle cry that the Welsh supporter has. At the top of the steps Wilf Wooller gave every player he could lay his hands on a great hug, which nearly broke a few ribs because he was a big fellow."

As *Wisden* put it, 'A Welsh crowd of 12,000 simply went crazy with delight.' Who said the county game was not surviving?

Some players of the 1960s

Shack
Leading wicket-taker six times

Derek Shackleton of Hampshire

> He has little to say on the field or off it. A broad grin and a slow-spoken 'Ay' or, perhaps, 'Ah, that were a good 'un' see him through most discussions. But, from time to time, he may be heard singing the song which is exclusively his own, one line of which runs something like 'I will slap thee, Billy, with a big flat fish.'   *John Arlott*

Derek Shackleton became a legend, almost a myth, in county cricket. Over after over, match after match, summer after summer, he bowled, never a hair out of place, never a long hop or a full toss, rarely even a half-volley. He was not quick, but he glided up to the crease, had a high arm and landed the ball with unfailing accuracy on its seam. "Shack will bowl till he drops dead," Somerset's Harold Gimblett said, "but he'll drop dead on a length."

Once he took his bowling partner Malcolm Heath into the nets and, with three balls, knocked down off, middle and leg stumps. "Shack, I've seen everything," exclaimed Heath. "No, you haven't," he replied and, replacing the stumps, knocked down leg, middle and off.

Born in the Yorkshire half of Todmorden, he came to Hampshire as a promising leg-spinner, but they needed a seamer and, in that role, for 20 successive years he took 100 wickets. He was never flustered, rarely showed more emotion than a 'tut-tut' when a catch went down, and was always happy to bowl. In 1962, in 17½ weeks between May 5 and September 4, he played 34 three-day matches, bowled 1,717 overs and took 172 wickets. He was a captain's dream.

A useful number eight batsman, he scored almost 10,000 runs in his career, a remarkable achievement given his admission in later life that he was blind in one eye.

Tom Graveney of Worcestershire

> I had become stale at Bristol, and the year out of the game put some steel in my soul. I came back refreshed – and determined to make Gloucestershire sorry.
>
> *Tom Graveney*

Tom Graveney in full flow was the batsman every spectator loved to watch. There was a grace, an easiness about him, his immaculate front-foot drives bearing no hint of force. With his ruddy face and his leisurely gait, his cricket spoke of fresh air and warm days in the sun.

He made his name at Bristol, though its sandy pitches did not suit his strokeplay. Some say he lacked a little in self-confidence in those early years but when, amid much intrigue, the Gloucestershire committee took the captaincy from him in the autumn of 1960, he showed his mettle, moving to Worcester rather than put up with such treatment. In a chequered Test career he had already won 48 caps but, with Gloucestershire objecting to the move, he was forced to spend a year playing in the Worcestershire second eleven.

The faster pitches at Worcester suited him, and in his first season his runs brought him a Test recall and took the county within a whisker of winning its first championship. Two years later, once more discarded by England, he had a golden year, the leading batsman in England, and the county romped away with the title, retaining it in 1965.

At first glance he looked a casual cricketer, rather as David Gower did, but in fact he was a consummate professional. He loved to play four innings each week and, though he often stayed late in the bar, he was always first in the nets in the morning. In 1966, on his 39th birthday, he resumed his start-stop Test career, and he answered all his doubters with three summers of elegant and plentiful runs, runs that remain fresh in many a memory.

Poetry in motion
Most runs in 1964

Colin Milburn of Northamptonshire

> He was a genius. Dexter had a touch of genius, but Milburn was one. All the years I played cricket, they were worth it just to see Colin at his best. *Keith Andrew*

Colin Milburn came down from the north-east in 1960, a raw, scruffy 18-year-old who chose Northants over Warwickshire because they offered an extra ten shillings a week. His great breakthrough, the innings he treasured most, came in July 1962 on a greentop at Buxton against Derbyshire's Les Jackson. In fading light, with no sight screens, he hit 102, Mick Norman 58, and nobody else got beyond 5.

At a time when audiences were dwindling, he was the tonic English cricket needed. A roly-poly figure, weighing sometimes 18 stone, he was an opening batsman who loved to take on the bowling and to do it, through triumph and disaster, with an engaging smile and a twinkle in his soft brown eyes. He might have appeared a rustic slogger, but his drives, pulls and hooks were classically played. Close to the wicket he was a good fielder, too, breaking the Northants record with 43 catches in 1964.

He made his England debut in 1966 against West Indies, averaging 52 in four Tests before being dropped for his immobility in the field. He responded at Clacton by hitting a glorious 203 before tea. A car crash deprived him of an eye in 1969, the last man the struggling English game could afford to lose.

'Ollie'
The 18-stone entertainer

Brian Statham of Lancashire

> No captain has had a more willing bowler at his command. *Cyril Washbrook*

The son of a dentist from Gorton in Greater Manchester, Brian Statham was the first real pace bowler to emerge after the war, playing for England within nine months of his Lancashire debut in 1950. He had a whippy, double-jointed action and was remarkably accurate, bringing the ball in from just short of a length to hit the top of off stump. "If you miss, I hit," he used to say. Surprisingly lacking in the fast bowler's traditional aggression, he employed his bouncer sparingly.

Unlike his England partner Fred Trueman he did not court the limelight, nor did he ever question an umpire's decision; perhaps, for all his success, he lacked a little in ambition.

He was lazy by nature. He liked his ale and his cigarettes, and he took life as it came. Yet on a cricket field he never shirked hard work. Bowling 800 and more overs each summer, he reserved his expressions of weariness for little conversations with his feet: "Come on, lads, tha's not long to go. Then tha' can have a good soak and a neet's rest." Ever willing, he captained Lancashire when they were at their lowest ebb. He was no great tactician, but he always commanded respect – and affection.

'George'
A bowling average of 15.17

Peter Walker of Glamorgan

> Peter was a great close catcher, and he never even wore a box, let alone all the armour they put on these days. *Don Shepherd*

The son of a journalist who emigrated to South Africa, Peter Walker ran away to sea on a whim when he was 16. In eighteen character-forming months he narrowly escaped being murdered in the Suez Canal, he slept rough on the streets of New York and, on a Finnish tanker crossing the Pacific, he whiled away many an hour playing catch with the ship's supply of potatoes. When they docked in Barry, he presented himself at the Glamorgan office in Cardiff's High Street.

The potatoes were the making of him, as he became the best close fielder of his age, taking 609 championship catches at a rate, over 1½ a match, unequalled in the competition's history. In 1961 he joined Percy Fender in the record books, doing 'the triple' by scoring 1,347 runs, taking 101 wickets and holding 71 catches, many of them off Glamorgan's legendary off-spinner. 'The Lord is thy Shepherd,' read his father's telegram of congratulation, 'thou shalt not want.' Intelligent, articulate and full of fun, he presented BBC's Sunday cricket for many years.

Best of the close catchers
Five times the leading fielder

Stories of the 1960s

A summer of runs for an ageing Australian

Bill Alley in 1961

Bill Alley was the last batsman to score 3,000 first-class runs in a season, the only one since the war to top 2,500 in county championship matches. And he did it, as well as taking 62 wickets and 29 catches, at the grand old age of 42.

Two crucial events took place before the season started. First, his Somerset team-mate and regular number eleven Ken Biddulph arrived in the nets on the first day with a brand new bat. Alley bowled to him and heard immediately the sweet sound it made. "Here, what's that bat you've got down there?" He banged a ball up and down on it. "That's much too good for you. I'll give you one of mine."

Then he was asked to visit a local doctor. "Bill, I want you to become a guinea pig," the man said, "and take three of these pills every day during the summer." He could not say what they were, only that they were not on the market and that "they'll help your game."

So every morning, with his team-mates joking that the pills were a youth preservative, he gulped them down, and in the evenings he drank several pints of black-and-tan, followed by a few gin-and-tonics.

He had grown up in Sydney where he did every job going, from underground driller to blacksmith's striker. He was a champion welterweight boxer, undefeated in 28 bouts, and an intimidating dance-hall bouncer. He might have been in the Australian party to England in 1948 if he had not had his jaw broken in the nets.

He came to Somerset in 1957, after years in the Lancashire Leagues. Several counties wanted him, and he chose Somerset, he claimed, because he liked "the sheer magic of the name. I couldn't have signed for Hampshire; I knew nothing of them whatsoever, but I didn't like the sound of the county. And I couldn't have played for Sussex with those ridiculous martlets plastered over their jumpers."

He was soon at home in the Quantocks, enjoying the country sports and keeping chickens, and the Somerset folk quickly took to him, as they had sixty years earlier to his compatriot Sammy Woods. Exuding a love of life, he played not stylishly but with a wily, combative spirit, and he never stopped talking, on the field or off; very little of it was appreciative of anybody else's efforts.

At Taunton in June he hit two not-out centuries, 183 and 134, to beat Surrey with minutes to spare, and later in the month, in the match he most cherished, he scored 134 and 95 against the touring Australians. Against Yorkshire he hit 155, his endless chatter even reducing Fred Trueman in mid-run-up to laughter. In all, he hit 11 centuries in his 3,017 runs, and he even found time to make a pair at Weston-super-Mare where, the story goes, the Glamorgan team unsettled him by ignoring his chatter.

"He only really had three shots," Ken Biddulph said. "The dab wide of gully, the hook – he loved to hook – and the hoik over mid-wicket. The dab, the hook and the hoik, he got 3,000 runs with those three shots."

Wisden made him one of its five cricketers of 1961, alongside four of the touring Australians, but for all the glory of his summer he was left with two regrets: that his captain had not let him bowl more, and that he never did find out what was in those pills.

The next year, now aged 43 and without the pills, he got a bookmaker to give odds of 10/1 against him doing the double. In September, with 1,915 runs and 112 wickets, he collected his £500. "You lucky bugger," the bookmaker said, but Alley was having none of that. "A bugger I might be, but lucky I'm not."

He was still going strong six years later.

"It just happened"

Worcestershire v Yorkshire, Worcester, 6 June 1961

Worcestershire had beaten the county champions Yorkshire – for the first time at Worcester since 1909, beaten them by 35 runs with 25 minutes to spare. Jack Flavell, the red-headed fast bowler, had bowled Jimmy Binks, and the crowd was on its feet, cheering the players as they started to leave the field.

Then they all stopped as out of the pavilion came another batsman, Don Wilson, with his left arm in plaster from elbow to knuckles. Suddenly there was one more wicket to take.

"You're not batting," his captain had repeatedly told him, but the ever-enthusiastic Don continued to plead. "All right. If there's just five minutes to go, you can bat."

A bone was broken at the base of his left thumb, the swelling throbbing under the plaster. He was a left-handed bat, and pain shot up his arm when he tried to grip with the fingertips of his left hand so he settled for using his top hand only. He was at best a number eight, Bob Platt at the other end a number eleven, but they survived without alarm for 15 minutes.

Ten minutes remained. Slow-left-armer Norman Gifford drifted down leg, and Don Wilson swung him away for two fours. "It's funny," he recalled years later. "When you hit a couple of fours, the pain goes completely, doesn't it?"

Down the wicket came his partner. "What the hell are you doing? We're playing for a draw." ... "We're not, Platty. We're going to win." ... "Don't be so bloody silly. The new ball's due. They've got Flavell and Coldwell."

Jack Flavell was at his peak. Day in, day out, he was as fast as anybody in the country, and in this summer of 1961 he topped the national averages with 171 wickets. With five minutes left, and 22 runs wanted, he took the new ball.

Don Wilson swung at the first delivery, and it flew through the covers for four. "I thought he'd gone completely out of his mind," Bob Platt tells, "and I don't mind that being quoted."

Don continued to hit out, and the fiery Flavell lost his cool. "I liked Jack," Bob Platt says, "but he let out more expletives in those few minutes than Fred Trueman got through in a whole season." Three fours and a two came in the over and, when Flavell did beat Don, the ball ran away for four byes. Twenty-two to win was down to four, with time for one more over.

Coldwell to Platt. "Just touch it," Don said, now the senior partner. "Let's get a one." With a push into the covers, they scampered a single. Then, with Don Wilson in a mad dream, "Coldwell ran up, and for some unknown reason it just happened that I hit him straight over his head for four."

From Dover to Middlesbrough

Yorkshire v Warwickshire, Middlesbrough, 30 August 1967

Six-day-a-week county cricket was a demanding schedule, made all the more tiring when the fixture list required overnight journeys from one end of the land to the other.

In 1962 Northamptonshire had to travel from Swansea to Dover which, with no Severn Bridge, was a 300-mile trip. Their coach arrived at the hotel at two in the morning, only for them to discover they were booked in for the following week. "Eventually," Brian Crump recalls, "they found us a place in Folkestone, and even then four or five of us had to sleep with blankets on a stage. We got to bed at four o'clock."

In August 1967 Warwickshire had to travel from Dover to Middlesbrough. On the last day at Dover they fielded in heat, losing five minutes from time. Tom Cartwright, their hard-working medium-pace bowler, was in the form of his life, his ten wickets in the match taking his tally for the season to 138. "Somebody set the showers off," he recalled, "and we just ran through them. It was like a schools day, when the kids all run through the showers. We were throwing on our shirts and ties. We got into taxis to the railway station, and they held the train up. We were half-dressed."

"It was Bank Holiday Tuesday," Alan Smith says. "There were all these people coming back from the continent. It would have been impossible to have created a worse journey for us."

"We had to go across London and up to Darlington," Tom Cartwright said. "We stayed the night there, opposite a night club that was still going strong at four in the morning. Then we had to get up early to catch the train to Middlesbrough."

Inevitably they lost the toss. And worse. They only had four bowlers and one of them, David Cook, had not arrived. "The last of the amateurs. He'd gone off from Dover on his own in his two-seater sports car. We got this message in the morning that he wasn't feeling well and had gone home."

In three weeks Cartwright, bowling first change, had got through 310 overs. He had bowled the last ball at Dover, and now on another hot day on a slow, unresponsive pitch he had to bowl the first. "Work was always evident with Tom," Middlesex's Mike Brearley says. "Effort and work. What you put in, you get out. He would fully fit any puritan's dream."

After tea Cartwright had a brief rest as Alan Smith, discarding his keeper's pads, sent down five overs. Then he resumed, bowling 44 overs in the day and taking six for 95. Throughout, *The Times* wrote, 'his length was immaculate.' In the relentless summer-long round of the county game he was the ideal cricketer.

Images of the 1960s

Coach Arthur McIntyre, in white shorts, supervises pre-season training in the Long Room

Surrey start fitness training at the Oval

Organised fitness training had never been a part of cricket. In the 1950s the great Surrey team's idea of a warm-up in the morning was a cup of tea and, in some cases, a cigarette.

The young Micky Stewart started to go in early, to do fifty minutes of interval running, till Arthur McIntyre, the senior professional, took him to task. "What's all that about? You can do that at home. If you start doing it here, we'll all be asked to do it."

Stewart, a footballer in winter, was not impressed: "People used to say, 'I can't keep running these singles if I'm looking to bat all day.' Running between the wickets was bracketed with dashing around in the field. It wasn't part of the English game."

Appointed captain in 1963, he set about changing the culture. He persuaded Arthur McIntyre, now the coach, to introduce some basic fitness work at the ground.

The players had always reported back to the Oval in early April but, with help from a major in the Army Physical Training Board, Stewart organised for them to gather two nights a week from the start of February at local school gymnasia.

It was a development not universally welcomed by the more senior players. "What's all this bloody circuit training lark?" Ken Barrington protested. "Why have we suddenly got to do this?"

Once more the game was moving on.

Essex make history with Sunday play at Valentine's Park, Ilford, 1966

'The sun shone at Ilford,' wrote *The Times*, 'the crowds poured into the tree-fringed cricket ground, and the smiles of the Essex officials grew broader and broader.'

For the first time county cricket was being played on a Sunday, starting at two o'clock so as not to clash with morning church services. Outside the ground Lord's Day Observance Society members demonstrated with placards.

Essex, prohibited by law from charging for admission, invited donations and sold scorecards at five times the normal sixpence. They collected nearly £500 from the 6,000 spectators where the previous day, with the FA Cup Final on television, the takings had been little more than £100.

It was the start of a great social change. Football followed suit, somewhat reluctantly, in 1974, the All-England Lawn Tennis Championships in 1982.

Essex versus Somerset, Sunday 15 May 1966

Here, there and everywhere

'Cricket at Stroud,' wrote John Arlott, 'is a country occasion of rare nostalgia and importance. The folk there speak of "the cricket" as did when I was a boy and the cricket sometimes came to us, seeming – like the circus elephants when they paraded through the main street – a very large matter indeed in our small country town.'

The Cotswold town of Stroud (population, 16,000) had no hotel large enough to house the visiting team. Its cricket ground, belonging to the Erinoid Plastics Company, lay in a damp valley alongside a railway embankment; it was basic in its facilities and had a low-lying square that rarely rewarded free-flowing strokeplay.

Gloucestershire, in financial difficulty, wanted to take its cricket to the people, particularly to those outside the big cities, and the Erinoid, thanks to the persistence of their cricket-mad managing director, was for eight years their choice. But the matches, staged early in the summer, were too often low-scoring, with off-spinner David Allen (career average 23, Stroud average 12) relishing the conditions. "It was a good place to give your figures a boost before the Test selectors sat down," he said.

In 1963 he took eleven for 92 in 58 overs against Glamorgan, and the county called time on the Erinoid, moving instead to Lydney (population 5,000) in the Forest of Dean. The weather was rarely kind to the annual match there – till 1969 when, in a mini-heatwave, a crowd of 5,500 packed into the ground for its first Sunday League game. The next day, alas, under a burningly hot sun, David Allen, with eight for 34, bowled out Sussex in under two hours. As a result the pitch was ruled unfit for three-day cricket.

In 1961 the championship visited 81 grounds, more than in any other summer in its history, with almost half of all fixtures played away from the main county grounds. Leading the way, in taking cricket out, were Essex, Kent and Glamorgan, all of whom staged matches at eight venues, followed by Somerset and Yorkshire at seven. Only Middlesex, guests of MCC at Lord's, stayed put for all their home games.

Essex had no choice. Since leaving Leyton in 1933, they had not owned a ground, and their summer-long programme was a series of cricket weeks: Brentwood, Ilford, Chelmsford, Westcliff, Colchester, Clacton, Leyton and Southend. It was not always ideal for the cricketers – changing in cramped rooms, adapting constantly to different playing surfaces, never having access to a practice net – but, as Trevor Bailey put it, "It was far more fun than having to play all one's home matches

in a large, ugly stadium, which more often than not was only partially filled. A crowd of 4,000 in Westcliff's Chalkwell Park was ideal but would be lost at Old Trafford." No county in those years was closer to its roots than Essex.

Yorkshire were another county without ownership of a ground. The players reported for pre-season practice to Headingley; then they hit the road, returning to Leeds only three times all summer and, unlike Essex, never staying in one place for more than a single game. Inevitably the fixture list showed little consideration – sending them overnight from Swansea to Hull, then sandwiching Taunton between Chesterfield and Bradford – but, as opening batsman Bryan Stott says, "It was a game of stamina in those days. We weren't as finely tuned as they are now."

With the most demanding schedule of the counties, and such a variety of venues, all with their own proud groundsmen, Yorkshire's success was the more remarkable. Yet their grounds were in large centres of population, each with a great cricketing tradition. Leeds, Bradford, Sheffield, Scarborough, Hull, they were not improvised small-town outposts like Stroud or Lydney, like Cowes which the players reached on "a slow and rather smelly boat" or Ashby-de-la-Zouch, where they took an extended lunch in the nearby hotel and where one of the Leicestershire team was delegated to bring a bag of six-inch nails for extra dressing-room pegs.

The heartland of Glamorgan's support lay out west, around Swansea, rather than in the cosmopolitan city of Cardiff, and in 1961 Glamorgan played five times at each. They also visited Neath, Newport, Ebbw Vale, Pontypridd, Llanelli and the steel works ground at Margam. The hospitality there was splendid, but the cricket was dire. A football pitch separated the pavilion and scoreboard from the boundary's edge, the field was open and windswept, and the works chimneys belched out sulphurous smoke that on one occasion, on a sunny day, brought the players off for bad light.

Gloucestershire travelled there in 1962. That summer there was a prize for the county who could score their first 200 runs the fastest, and on the way down, imagining a small ground, the players thought they might try to win it. Instead, they found themselves on a soft, spongy pitch, struggling to hit the ball off the square. On the final day they set Glamorgan 119 to win, and the home team were all out in the 67th over for 49. "When we came off the field," David Allen recalled, "we were all covered in this red tinge from the steel works."

*The Manor Ground,
Worthing*

*One of 81 championship
venues in 1961*

*The changing room for the
away-team professionals was
on the opposite side of the
ground from the amateurs'
room. So when Derbyshire
visited in 1961, their senior
professional Les Jackson led
his players to the boundary
edge and waited till their
captain Donald Carr
emerged on the other side.*

Gloucestershire were also the visitors when in 1948 the Ebbw Vale ground sprang an unlikely surprise. High among the hills, a mist rolled down on the first afternoon, forcing the suspension of play. Eventually it lifted to reveal a flock of sheep nibbling away at the outfield grass.

Glamorgan was not the only club whose county ground was in the wrong place. Derbyshire drew greater crowds at the pretty Queen's Park in Chesterfield than they ever did at the Racecourse Ground in Derby, once compared in the *Guardian* to the blasted heath at the opening of *Macbeth*. "Queen's Park is a lovely ground," says Derek Morgan, county captain in the 1960s, "and the crowd there is always very appreciative of what is going on. In the north of the county they're all very sports-oriented, whereas the Derby people don't really support anything. Not even the theatre or football."

Derbyshire also visited Buxton, Ilkeston and the Ind Coope brewery ground in Burton-on-Trent where in 1958 a record 39 wickets fell in a day. Such games would be a nightmare for the modern marketing teams, selling corporate hospitality packages, but they were part of the romance of cricket in those years. "You came in on the first day," says Malcolm Heath, one of Hampshire's losing team at Burton. "You took your tie off, and you stuck it on the peg. And there was this glorious uncertainty of not knowing what was going to happen."

Somerset held two cricket weeks in Bath where the crowds were always great. "The apathy in Taunton is shocking," Bill Alley, their Australian, reckoned. "I would back a move to Bath." They also played a trio of games in August in the seaside resort of Weston-super-Mare. It was there traditionally that the committee met, over a bibulous lunch, to decide the contracts for the coming year.

Hampshire always drew a good crowd of holiday-makers for their games at Bournemouth, Gloucestershire's annual visit to Cheltenham College was the highlight of their year, and there was delight for Kent supporters when the rhododendrons came into bloom at Tunbridge Wells.

Warwickshire left leafy Edgbaston for works grounds at Coventry and Nuneaton, Sussex staged weeks at Eastbourne, Hastings and Worthing, and Nottinghamshire, in the most bizarre venture of 1961, played at a little ground, owned by a brick-making company, in the village of Shireoaks. "The wicket was superb," the Notts off-spinner Bomber Wells recalled, "but there was no atmosphere at all. It was in the middle of nowhere. 'The best way of getting us here,' Jim Parks said, 'would have been to have parachuted us in.'"

County cricket was trying so hard to find a wider audience, but it did not always work. As the spotlight fell increasingly on the quality of pitches, the out-grounds dwindled in number. Then in the 1970s, as the counties went in search of commercial sponsors, it did not work to play so often away from headquarters. By 2014 there were only 14 out-grounds left on the fixture list.

1961: Hampshire play to win

Three-day cricket had its charms, but all too often the final day would begin with the best part of two innings still to be played. A good finish would then depend on the willingness of one team to make a fair declaration and the other to take up the challenge.

Judging a declaration was a fine art, and many a dressing room was the scene of argument. On one occasion the Derbyshire professionals locked their captain, Donald Carr, in the toilet to prevent him declaring. Then there was the day at Old Trafford when Lancashire's Nigel Howard talked Hampshire's Desmond Eagar into declaring; Vic Cannings was so incensed he threw his boots at Eagar. "I thought that would be the end of me with Hampshire, but Reg Dare said to him, 'You know Vic, he's got a temper.'"

Glamorgan's Wilf Wooller would never give quarter if he was up against certain captains, particularly those who were also Cambridge men. At the end of one game against Freddie Brown's Northamptonshire, when his Glamorgan batsmen, set 206 to win in 130 minutes, had ended on 60 for one, the two squared up in front of the pavilion: "Thanks for fuck all, Wilf." "Bugger off, Freddie." Len Muncer of Glamorgan turned to Northants' Dennis Brookes: "I'm glad I sent my children to elementary school," he said.

"Wilf's battles with Robin Marlar at Sussex were legendary," Peter Walker recalls. "It was a huge contest between them. The rest of us just turned up for their private battle, like the archers at Agincourt."

Yorkshire, if they are to be believed, never got a reasonable declaration from anybody. Nobody wanted to lose to them. In the five years from 1959 to 1963 they won the championship four times, and it still rankles with them that in 1961 they finished second to Hampshire, several of whose 19 victories stemmed, in the words of Ray Illingworth, from "silly declarations".

There were, in fact, only three matches in which Hampshire won after their opponents had declared. The first was at the Oval in early May, a game made bizarre by that summer's experimental abolition of the follow-on. The pitch was perfect for batting, and on the first day Edrich and Barrington hit rapid hundreds, allowing Surrey to declare before the close on 356 for four. In the remaining minutes Roy Marshall, Hampshire's Barbadian opener, batted with care. "There's a huge score for you here tomorrow, Roy," he told himself, and by way of preparation he took himself to bed at nine o'clock.

He woke at five and by breakfast had day-dreamed his way to a double-hundred. Then, in the day's second over, he was caught in the slips, and Hampshire struggled grimly to 190 all out. Surrey had no option but to bat again, closing on 107 for two, a lead of 273.

It was the benefit year of Surrey's Tony Lock, and that evening he was hosting a dance in Croydon to which he invited the

Colin Ingleby-Mackenzie

Hampshire team. Several, like Derek Shackleton and Peter Sainsbury, were not night owls, and they slipped away early. But Roy Marshall was not among them, not returning to the hotel till nearly five.

"One of his great abilities," his opening partner Jimmy Gray recalls, "was to have a lot to drink and never be drunk. My powers of recovery were terrible, but he'd sit down in the morning, eat egg and bacon and be fine."

Surrey, who had made all the running in the match, set Hampshire 308 to win in 5½ hours, and Gray, who had got to bed at 3.30, was soon back in the pavilion. But Marshall, bare-headed and bespectacled, made the declaration look far too generous with a majestic innings of 153: "He smashed them all over the place," Jimmy Gray says, "and we won with an hour to spare."

Colin Ingleby-Mackenzie was the Hampshire captain, a fun-loving Old Etonian socialite who inspired great loyalty from his team, a natural heir to his 1920s predecessor Lord Tennyson. In many ways, with his dashing middle-order batting and his good-humoured charm, he was the personification of the Brighter Cricket that Lord's was advocating – though in truth, with the medium-pacer Derek Shackleton bowling long, miserly spells, there were few sides who made it harder for batsmen to score runs.

He was popular with other captains, and that did help when a contest had to be created, as at Portsmouth against fellow title contenders Gloucestershire. After rain the last day began with Hampshire, in response to the visitors' 176, on 12 for no wicket. Should they secure the four points for first-innings lead, or should they try for 12 points for the win, gambling on an early declaration in the hope that Arthur Milton would respond in the same spirit? The captains could not collude, but after a suggestion from Ingleby-Mackenzie – "If either of us is to have a chance of catching the Tykes, one of us needs to win" – Milton set Hampshire to score 199 in 2¼ hours.

Several of the Hampshire team were opposed to the reckless strategy, and at 162 for eight, Ingleby-Mackenzie said, "I was thinking of fitting my running shoes for a quick getaway." But his gambler's luck came good as the fast bowler 'Butch' White whacked a whirlwind 33 to bring victory with two minutes to spare. 'Colin's grin was even wider than usual,' Roy Marshall wrote, 'as he chided those of us who had ridiculed his decision.'

It was a contrived result, but it made for a good day's cricket and it was widely applauded – though not by Yorkshire, whose game with Glamorgan got no further than first-innings points.

In 1960 Hampshire finished 12th; in 1962, 10th. But in that one long, hot summer of 1961 everything seemed to work out for them. When they set targets, other counties chased them all the way, never more dramatically than at Southampton when Nottinghamshire, eight wickets down, needed 19 more runs in nine minutes. The ever-jocular 'Bomber' Wells came out to bat and in a loud voice shouted down to his partner, "Are we still going for them? ... If you're not, I am." Three runs later, amid great mirth, his two partners had both been run out.

The title was won at Bournemouth when Derbyshire, set 252 to win, collapsed to 111 all out. Just as in 1948, when on the same ground Glamorgan won their first championship, there were emotional speeches from the balcony.

Hampshire's captain 'would be the last to pretend that he is a profound cricket strategist,' John Arlott wrote, 'but he has the priceless gift, denied to some more illustrious captains, of not being frightened to lose. This enables him to go on playing for a win against the odds when many another would play for a draw. This championship is a reward for his outlook and his character.'

The last declaration

Hampshire v Worcestershire, Bournemouth, Friday 27 August 1965

Ingleby-Mac captained Hampshire for four years after their triumph, but he never again hit the winning streak of 1961.

At the start of his last home match, against Worcestershire at Bournemouth, Hampshire lay in 16th place in the table. It had been a cold, wet summer, and 19 of their 25 matches had been drawn. It was not at all how he had wanted things to end.

The gambling instinct still ran strong in him. The previous year at the Oval Micky Stewart, the Surrey captain, had visited his room at lunchtime on the final day, wanting to discuss the state of the game. Instead, he found himself checking the calculations on a long bill from the Hampshire skipper's bookmaker. "What about this declaration?" Stewart asked as the five-minute bell rang. Ingleby was padded up to resume his innings. "I'll leave it to you to work out," he replied. "You tell me when to declare," which, after a few overs, Stewart duly did.

The match at Bournemouth in 1965 had much hanging on it. The little-fancied Northamptonshire side, captained shrewdly by their quiet wicket-keeper Keith Andrew, had completed their fixtures and were top of the table, on the verge of the first title in their history. Only Worcestershire, needing to win both their last two games, stood between them and a cricketing fairy tale. Imagine the joy in Northampton when they tuned their radios into the lunchtime scoreboard on the last day and heard the state of the game at Bournemouth: Worcestershire 363, Hampshire 217 for six. It was a certain draw. Surely.

Then, in a last quixotic gesture, playing the game like any other, not caring that the title was potentially at stake, Ingleby-Mackenzie declared. After one ball Don Kenyon, his opposite number, also declared, and suddenly they had a contest. Hampshire, to win, needed 147 runs in 160 minutes.

"Ingleby misread the situation completely," Worcestershire keeper Roy Booth says. "Just before lunch the pitch was wet, but the sun had come out: not brilliant but it was hot. We were in a tent at lunch, and it was getting hotter and hotter, and the pitch was literally steaming." To make matters worse, Worcestershire had two of the finest fast bowlers in the country, Flavell and Coldwell. "The ball was coming right up. Roy Marshall was fairly wild about Ingleby declaring. He had a great whack at it, and it went up in the air."

With a dangerous crust forming on the surface of the pitch, Hampshire were all out inside 17 overs for 31, and a bitterly disappointed Northamptonshire never forgave Ingleby.

But that was the man. He loved a gamble.

1962: The last amateur captains

The Conservative Party was in its eleventh year of power in the summer of 1962, with the Cabinet reflecting the importance it placed on a 'good background' for those carrying the responsibilities of leadership. Eighteen of the 21 men around the Cabinet table had been to public school, ten of them to Eton, while 16 had studied at Oxford or Cambridge.

The belief that those with such backgrounds made the best leaders was shared by most committeemen around the county cricket clubs. They wanted such men as amateur captains, set apart in social class and outlook from those who earned their living from the game.

A strong champion of this view was EW Swanton of the *Daily Telegraph*. 'English cricket,' he wrote in 1962, 'has been at its best when there has been a reasonably even balance between those who have made the game their livelihood and those who have played it basically for relaxation and enjoyment.'

In post-war Britain, however, such a distinction was proving difficult to sustain. There was no longer a class of young gentlemen with the means to spend their summers playing cricket without reward – so the counties, to attract the best of the public school and university men, had to set up indirect systems for paying them.

Some created the non-existent post of Assistant Secretary for their newly appointed captains. On this basis Andrew Corran, an Oxford graduate, took on the Nottinghamshire captaincy in 1962. Others found benefactors to provide summer-free employment. In this spirit Robin Marlar was asked by the Duke of Norfolk, Sussex President, to be his librarian at Arundel Castle. Ben Brocklehurst accepted the Somerset captaincy on condition that the county pay for a man to manage his farm, and the resulting bill was equivalent to the cost of three professional cricketers.

The most prominent amateurs were able to earn considerable sums in sponsoring products and writing books and newspaper articles. If they played for England in the winter, they earned 'broken-time payments', a system that compensated them for loss of employment. In Australia in 1958/59 Jim Laker, a professional, discovered that he was being paid £200 less than the amateur Trevor Bailey.

A joke began to circulate about a young player asked by his county whether he wished to be an amateur or a professional. "I don't mind," he replied innocently. "Whichever pays better."

Allied to the hypocrisy of all this, there was a growing sense among the post-war generation of professionals that the amateurs were not always the pure-minded Corinthians that they were supposed to be. Down in Wales Wilf Wooller was the first sledger, up to every trick in the book; Trevor Bailey saved a Test match against Australia by slowing the over rate and deliberately bowling down leg; Colin Cowdrey was suspected of not always walking when he was out; even the young David Sheppard, future Bishop of Liverpool, had to be stopped by his senior professional George Cox from clicking his fingers in the gully as the off-spinner delivered the ball.

By contrast, Yorkshire's Brian Close says, "Among the professionals there were such high moral standards. If anybody tried to cheat, like not walking when they knew they were out, their own players would set about them. The attitude of the professionals in those days was absolutely first-class."

Nevertheless, the counties preferred to appoint amateur captains if they possibly could. In the first ten summers of Conservative rule, from 1952 to 1961, eleven of the 17 counties had at some stage appointed professional captains, but by 1962 seven of those eleven had reverted to amateurs, even in some cases to men whose own cricketing abilities were well short of county standard.

One such was Ronnie Burnet, appointed Yorkshire captain in 1958. A 39-year-old chemical engineer, he had never played a game of first-class cricket, but he was a great success. Bringing through the youngsters from the second eleven, which he had captained, he moulded them into a side that won back the championship, after ten lean years, in 1959.

"He created a great atmosphere in the team," Ken Taylor says. "He didn't bowl, he hardly scored any runs and he only caught the ball when it came straight to him at mid-off, but he got an extra ten per cent out of everybody else. So it was worth having him in the side."

Across the Pennines Lancashire noted his success, and in 1962 they sought to emulate it, appointing the 34-year-old Old Reptonian Joe Blackledge, director of a family textile business in Chorley. Not only had he never played a game of first-class cricket, his days in the second eleven had ended nine years earlier. Unlike Burnet he knew none of his team.

"I am a new boy to the first-class game," he cheerfully told a reporter in April. "I shall bat number six or seven and perhaps work my way up the order on merit."

From 1954 to 1959 Lancashire had been captained by a professional, Cyril Washbrook, but his legacy was not a happy one. His mix of old-fashioned discipline and acquired snobbery alienated not only the younger generation but also such stalwarts as Alan Wharton, a staunch Labour man, and Geoff Edrich, who had had enough of being ordered about as a prisoner of the Japanese.

In 1960 the young Bob Barber, a Cambridge graduate, took over the discordant side. The committee, anxious to return to old ways, instructed him to stay in separate hotels from his team, then sacked him after two years.

Second in Barber's first year, Lancashire finished 16th under Joe Blackledge in 1962, winning only two games. "He had a hard time," Jack Bond says, "and he was a lovely fellow. You could sense that he felt everything was against him, but he never let it get him down."

There was a happier story at Middlesex where Ian Bedford was plucked out of club cricket to captain the county in 1961. Back in 1947, as a schoolboy, he had caused a sensation, his high-flighted leg-breaks taking 25 wickets in four games, but he had not played since 1950. The county, spotting his potential, had tried to get him a place at Oxford University, but he had failed his exams and was now working for a construction company.

At first the professionals were sceptical. "It's not club cricket, you know," they told him when he declared against Yorkshire, but always he seemed to proved them wrong. "He had a wonderful way with him," Don Bennett said, "and he got on so well with all the opposition captains that they all played a game of cricket with us. We didn't have many draws."

At Lord's Bennett was playing out time against Somerset when the captain joined him. Seven wickets were down, with 79 wanted in 40 minutes. "Block?" he said. "I can't block." And he thrashed a half-hour fifty that won them the match. At Gloucester they were nine wickets down, with 66 wanted in 40 minutes, and almost single-handedly he hit them off with ten minutes to spare. For Bennett, 19 years in the team, "He was top of the pops. That summer of 1961 was the best year I had at Middlesex."

Less successful was the ham-fisted attempt by the Glamorgan committee to oust the veteran Wilf Wooller. In August 1958 they imported the 34-year-old 'Tolly' Burnett, a tubby Eton schoolmaster who was immediately out of his depth in the rowdy Welsh side. As Don Shepherd so charmingly puts it, "I don't think he was ready for the hurly-burly of county cricket."

Even when counties had a good professional captain, they were not always keen to keep him. Somerset, after

Joe Blackledge of Lancashire   *Ian Bedford of Middlesex*

eight captains in ten years, appointed the professional Maurice Tremlett and, though there was an upturn in their cricket, they were soon manoeuvring behind the scenes to replace him with the 38-year-old Alan Shirreff, a retired squadron leader to whom they offered the post of Assistant Secretary. Only the intervention of the Marlborough schoolmaster Dennis Silk, playing in his summer holidays and spotting the respect the team had for Tremlett, prevented the change.

At Northampton the professional Dennis Brookes, who in time would become chairman of the local magistrates' bench, led his side to second place in 1957, only to stand down because the captaincy had been promised to the amateur Raman Subba Row when his National Service was over. Subba Row, a gifted batsman, was found an employer, whom the county duly compensated, but the team slipped backwards in his four years at the helm.

In November 1962, with a surprising suddenness, it all ended, the counties deciding by 12 votes to seven that in future there would be no professionals and amateurs, only cricketers. Swanton in the *Telegraph* called the decision deplorable. 'Will there emerge some system of non-playing managership in order to sustain the captain and impose discipline?' he asked. 'One is apprehensive of the effect of more control from the committee room.'

John Woodcock in *The Times* called it realistic: 'In principle the amateur outlook is a fine thing. It charms away routine. But the day of the genuine amateur who cultivated the game purely as a pastime has gone.'

From now on, county cricket would be a wholly professional game.

County cricket in search of new ideas

Ken Turner, the gruff Northamptonshire Secretary, called the 1960s 'years of ferment', likening cricket to 'a gently cruising boat suddenly running into rapids round a bend'. At the start of the decade Harold Macmillan had talked of 'the wind of change' blowing through the continent of Africa but, for Ken Turner reflecting on the problems besetting cricket, 'the word gale would be more appropriate.'

Turner was not a conservative, with neither a small nor a large C, but there were many in cricket who were. Wilf Wooller, the all-powerful Glamorgan Secretary, was one, and he repeatedly argued that cricket should stand its ground against 'new-fangled' ideas:

> Why should the cricket administrators pander to baser public tastes to brighten up cricket? An orgy of sixes, fours and wickets would soon pall. Would the music world hot up Bach to give him a wider bobby-soxer public? Cricket and Bach will live beyond sensationalism.

Brian Sellers, the autocratic chairman of Yorkshire, was another. His county would never employ overseas players and, when it came to Sundays, he was wholly opposed, regarding religious observance as essential to 'the fabric of the county'.

"I suppose we're wasting our time, sunshine," were Sellers' blunt words of greeting to Ken Turner as they entered the MCC Committee Room for a meeting of yet another committee of enquiry into the state of county cricket. He had seen five in thirty years, and nothing much ever came of them.

Yet Sellers and Wooller did not reflect the mainstream of thinking among cricket's administrators in the 1960s. 'A huge fallacy exists,' wrote Ken Turner, 'that cricket is run by geriatrics fifty years behind the times. In fact, the game has been in the vanguard of reform – reforms which other sports have taken up.'

In several respects cricket was proving itself to be the most progressive of the major sports in England: first to abolish amateurism, first to play on Sundays, first to experiment with new formats, first to bring overseas stars into domestic teams.

The most powerful man in English cricket in the 1960s was 'Gubby' Allen, the former England captain, now MCC treasurer. An Old Etonian stockbroker, exuding patrician authority, he lived in a house beside Lord's and held great sway behind the scenes. In the selection of this latest Committee of Enquiry, set up in September 1965, he exerted his influence.

"He was very good at bringing younger people in," says Ossie Wheatley, who as the 30-year-old captain of Glamorgan sat on the group. "So many of the counties would only think of their own interests, but Gubby was one who always put the good of the game first. He wanted to hear new ideas."

"He nominated me for the MCC committee when I was only 29," says Doug Insole, another member of the group. "I was the first non-public school bloke on it. 'Come and put a bit of life in the place,' he said to me. He liked to live by high standards, but they weren't impossible to achieve."

Then there was Mike Turner who in 1960, at the age of 25, became at Leicester the youngest Secretary of a county ever. It was he who in early 1962, spotting in the season's fixtures that Leicestershire, Northants, Notts and Derbyshire all had a three-day gap in May, organised a Midlands Knock-Out Cup,

Four members of the Special Sub-Committee: Ken Turner (Secretary of Northamptonshire), Ossie Wheatley (captain of Glamorgan),
Doug Insole (MCC Committee, Chairman of Selectors) and Mike Turner (Secretary of Leicestershire)

the success of which led to the Gillette Cup the following summer. He, too, was brought onto the committee. "When I went down to the first meeting at Lord's," he says, "I was incredibly nervous. Gubby Allen gave this great impression of superiority, but he always talked to me."

County cricket was in dire straits. The great post-war boom was over, as were the golden years of the 1950s when England went almost eight years without losing a Test series. Now, with the way of life transformed by television set, motor car and foreign holiday, attendances at matches were falling fast. At his interview for the post of Leicestershire Secretary, Mike Turner had been asked, "Do you realise that the foreseeable life of this club is only about five years?"

Survival required ancillary income, leading the young Secretary not only to develop further the county's football pool scheme but also – tapping into an important social scene – to take lessons in shooting at the home of Aubrey Sharp, a well-to-do solicitor who had played for the county before the First War. He had a man whose job was to release the clay pigeons from the roof. "Do you know Brown?" Sharp said when introducing him. "He's all right to shake hands with."

Why was cricket not attracting a greater audience? For some, the explanation lay in the changing social conditions, leading them to advocate new structures with more one-day games. For others, the explanation lay more in a lack of enterprise, a negativity that had got into the playing of the game, with the standard of the pitches held partly to blame.

The committee met twelve times between September 1965 and January 1967. It commissioned NOP, National Opinion Poll, to conduct surveys of capped players, of county members and of the general public, and it convened a meeting of all the county groundsmen. The chairman was David Clark, a farmer who had captained Kent and was the county's chairman.

The NOP survey revealed that more than six million men over the age of 16 liked cricket but that only 29% of them had been to a first-class match the previous summer. The challenge therefore was to attract some of the remaining 71%.

It was agreed that the Gillette Cup should be retained. Alongside it, their interim report floated two radical options. One was for the county championship to be made up of 16 three-day and 16 one-day matches. The other was to separate the two formats into two distinct championships. In both these proposals the one-day matches were to be played on traditional lines: win, lose or draw, with no limiting of overs.

During the summer of 1966, between the interim and the final report, county cricket took its first tentative steps into Sunday play. Despite protests and letters from the Lord's Day Observance Society – "Dear Sinner," was the standard form of address – seven counties (Derbyshire, Essex, Gloucestershire, Leicestershire, Northants, Notts and Surrey) ventured into staging Sunday play, starting after lunch, and the results were a great success. At Leicester they were instructed by the police to open the gates at 9 a.m., to get the cars off the streets.

That summer also saw an experiment in which, for 12 of each county's matches, the first innings was limited to 65 overs, allowing spectators as in one-day cricket to see both sides bat. Unfortunately this led to defensive field placings and further reduced the role of the spinner.

'Do you think there have been too many recent changes regarding the laws and playing conditions?' the *Cricketer* magazine asked its readers, and 90% responded yes.

Never before or since has county cricket asked itself more questions, and the answers were many and conflicting. Some felt that spectator appeal had to remain secondary to the maintenance of the highest possible standard of play. Even Ken Turner came to think that. 'The day of the customer paying to watch the three-day match has gone with the half-crown and elastic-sided boots,' he wrote in the 1980s. 'It would be far more sensible to eliminate all the gimmicks and use the championship as a training ground to enable England to field a side worthy of the nation.'

In the 1960s, however, there was still a hope that the crowd could be brought back – with Sunday play, one-day cricket, overseas stars, a livelier approach from the players, perhaps even fewer games to make them more special.

The Committee of Enquiry drew up its final report in January 1967, with the MCC President Sir Alec Douglas-Home in attendance. 'I never saw any member of a committee take more copious notes,' Ken Turner said. They proposed two county championships: one of 16 three-day games, played on Saturdays, Sundays and Mondays; the other of 16 one-day games during the week. Wilf Wooller in Glamorgan greeted it as "a lot of tommy-rot", and the counties, alarmed by the reduction of playing days, voted against it by 16 votes to four.

For one member of the committee – Charles Bray, the former Essex captain, now a journalist – 'a mountain of labour produced a mouse of achievement', adding that he thought the counties 'may have signed their own death warrant'.

Perhaps, as Ossie Wheatley puts it, 'it was too soon.' Before long, county cricket would make changes not dissimilar to those recommended. "We started the ball rolling," Mike Turner says. "The Clark Report was a great stimulus for fresh thinking."

Brian Close: at the heart of seven Yorkshire titles

Yorkshire were the team of the 1960s. Winning seven titles in ten years from 1959 they dominated the championship as no county has subsequently done. They had an outstanding bowling attack – Fred Trueman for pace, Ray Illingworth and Don Wilson for spin – and riches aplenty in batting, but, more than that, they knew how to win three-day matches. In that, their success owed much to the tactical acumen and courageous, if sometimes daft, spirit of Brian Close.

He burst into English cricket in the summer of 1949. A left-handed bat who also bowled both seam-up and off-spin, he was the youngest man ever to complete the season's double of 1,000 runs and 100 wickets and the youngest to play for England, leading some to talk of him with excitement as the new Frank Woolley.

But nothing in Close's life went smoothly for long. He went off to National Service and, in his only game for Yorkshire in 1950, a Roses match at Sheffield, he was batting well on the last afternoon when he slipped in mid-pitch, was run out and they lost by 14 runs. It turned out that he was not wearing spikes, and he was left to carry the blame for Yorkshire's first defeat by Lancashire since the war.

That winter he toured Australia, and he had a wretched time. He came from a loving home, he was intelligent (his grammar-school headmaster had wanted him to read mathematics at Cambridge) and he gave his all in an unselfish, enthusiastic way. But the senior players, brought up in a pre-war world in which the young knew their place, did not take to him at all. They thought him brash and conceited, though he was neither; he was just a gauche, young man unfamiliar with the ways of the world. He spent the six months in a state of miserable loneliness.

He never became another Frank Woolley. His stop-start Test career extended across 28 summers, from 1949 to 1976, during which he played just 22 Tests in 11 different series. Too often his unorthodox approach offended the purists, never more so than at Old Trafford in 1961 when, with no instructions from his captain Peter May, he tried to knock the Australian leg-spinner Richie Benaud out of the attack. It was a high-risk gamble and, when it failed, it looked bad. Jim Laker called it 'the most extraordinary innings I've ever seen by an accredited Test batsman' while on *Test Match Special* Norman Yardley, Close's first captain at Yorkshire, expressed the hope that he would never play for England again.

Briefly he became a highly successful captain of England, but that was controversially taken from him when stubbornly he refused to apologise for his part in a time-wasting episode in a county match. Behind the scenes there were many at Lord's who were relieved that he would not be in charge on the tour of the Caribbean where political sensitivities required diplomatic care.

Brian Close and Freddie Trueman
Two great characters, both born in February 1931

At Yorkshire it was a different story. He became a pivot of the side, a right-hand man to Yardley's successors, Billy Sutcliffe and Ronnie Burnet. Sutcliffe was out of his depth, unrealistically promoted by his father Herbert, but Ronnie Burnet, an older man, though he lacked first-class experience, had authority and created a good team spirit. He welcomed Brian Close's tactical suggestions, and in 1959 the championship returned after a ten-year hiatus to Yorkshire.

Their last game, the one that clinched the title, was at Hove. On the final day, knowing the championship was at stake, Sussex would not declare, and Yorkshire reached lunch still needing three wickets. "What are you going to do?" Close said to Burnet as they walked back out. "I always wanted to know what he was thinking, rather than just telling him what to do," he says. Burnet was going to bring back Fred Trueman, but Close said, "Forget Freddie, he's knackered. Get the spinners on." Would they have won without that advice? Who knows?

Burnet was keen to carry on the next year. But Brian Sellers, the autocratic chairman, had other ideas. If Burnet stayed on, he would have to release the 39-year-old Vic Wilson, an attacking left-handed batsman who that summer had lost his place in the team. If Wilson went, he would be stuck with no alternative to Close as Burnet's successor. That he did not want.

Vic Wilson had three years in charge, and they were good years, Yorkshire finishing first, second and first. But the partnership of Wilson and Close was not easy. While Burnet had been happy for Close to adjust the field between balls, the experienced Wilson tried to keep control himself.

Temperamentally they were poles apart. Close was inclined to impatience, wanting constantly to make things happen. Wilson, by contrast, preferred to think it all through. "He was a farmer," Close says, "and you know what farmers are like. They take three months to decide the grass needs cutting."

The players were all at least ten years younger than Wilson, and they saw Close as their natural leader. Fred Trueman never forgave Wilson for dropping him at Taunton when, after a previous warning, he was not present at the toss. Wilson with his old-fashioned values – "you can't have one law for one and another for the others" – also had a problem with the 21-year-old Geoff Boycott, a clerk in a pensions office who played four championship games in his last summer. Wilson advised the committee to let him go, but Close, finally inheriting the captaincy, took a different view. "Let me have him for a season," he said with characteristic optimism. "See how he is." Twelve months later Boycott was in the England team.

Close led from the front, inspirational if unconventional to the point of near-madness. At times he fielded ridiculously close to the bat, taking all manner of blows. "Pain, it's only in the mind," he would say, even believing that he could beat Muhammad Ali by standing up and taking his punches.

He once instructed openers Phil Sharpe and Ken Taylor: "I want 100 runs in 40 minutes. Don't get out, and don't make it look easy." It did nothing for their averages or their Test prospects, but it made time for the bowlers to take the wickets. "His theory," Ken Taylor says, "was that you declared on how long you needed to get the other side out, not how long they needed to get the runs. It was a different approach from most counties." As Close says, "You win championships in the field."

Where Vic Wilson had been giving Trueman plenty of bowling, thinking the fast man would be glad of the wickets (483 in three summers), Close preserved him with shorter stints. "I kept Freddie going an extra two years," he reckons.

He and Trueman had come through together, making their debut on the same day in 1949, but there was always a little Yorkshire-style friction between them. Undoubtedly Trueman would love to have been captain himself, treasuring as his proudest moment the innings victory over the Australians that he skippered in Close's absence in 1968.

Would Trueman have been a success if he had led Yorkshire? "To captain a side over a summer," Close says, "you've to look after four things, and you've to look after them in the right order. First, there's the game you're playing. Then the team. Then the individuals in the team. And lastly yourself." He laughs. "I'm not so sure Fred could have put them in that order."

The unselfish Close could. In his first six seasons in charge they won four championships, to add to the three in four years that they had won under Burnet and Wilson. With seven titles in ten years they remain one of the greatest teams in the history of the championship, and Close's input was vital throughout – or, as he puts it, "I did all bloody seven really."

He was fortunate in having at his side the brains of Ray Illingworth, a calmer character, and the keeper Jimmy Binks. Together they provided the rudder when Close's gambling instincts took the team too far off course.

But taking risks and applying pressure were what three-day cricket was all about. To be champions it was better to lose occasionally in pursuit of victory than to play out dull draws.

Four-day cricket is a different game, with less urgency, and there is still a part of Close that yearns to defy the passing of the years, to put on his whites, get out in the middle and gee them all up: "You don't want to give the batsman time to compose his thoughts. That's half the battle to getting somebody out. We're not alert now; we're too negative. Sometimes I used to move the field, stand in front of the batsman, just to make him wonder what I was doing." But not sledging: "I never went on the field to belittle the opposition. The game always came first."

His team broke up at the end of the 1960s. Illingworth, Binks, Trueman and Taylor all left, and after a disappointing summer in 1970 Brian Sellers sacked him in favour of Boycott.

Close went down to Somerset and showed his enduring worth in a triumphant seven-year swansong. In 1975, playing at Harrogate, he bumped into Sellers, and the old man was contrite. "Brian, you've done a great job at Somerset," he said. "It's the worst decision I've ever made in my life."

A brilliant tactician with a streak of child-like naïvete, combative yet generous, inspirational yet often misunderstood, Brian Close must rank among the greatest captains, and greatest characters, in the history of county cricket.

1970 – 1979

Overseas players dominate

Eight different champions in ten years

First titles for Leicestershire and Essex

A few years ago the outcome of the county championship was awaited by the cricket fraternity with bated breath. Now the enthusiasm is almost entirely confined to within the boundaries of the winning county. But if you stopped the Man in the Street on the evening of September 2, he would know that Lancashire had won the Gillette Cup alright.

Gordon Ross, Playfair Cricket Monthly, 1972

There is no need to worry about the future of cricket. People were playing cricket long before the county championship was invented; and will be doing so long after it has departed. To judge by the number of people playing the game, in this country and elsewhere, cricket is still very healthy – and that is the only sane test of any game that pretends to be a game.

Alan Gibson, The Times, 1971

Down at third man, in front of the tents, Canterbury's famous lime tree grows a good ten yards inside the boundary. When the ground was first used for cricket those old men of Kent let it be, and their successors have never dreamed of removing it, have been happy to see it reach its full nobility and height. Mr Kerry Packer, I suspect, would have chopped it down long ago, so that a few more spectators could thereby be given a view of play, a few more pounds be taken at the Canterbury gate. He would have argued that there were plenty more lime trees where that came from. But there aren't.

Geoffrey Moorhouse, 'The Best Loved Game', 1978

1970 South Africa's tour of England is cancelled and replaced by five 'Tests' between England and a Rest of the World XI. The lbw law now allows a batsman to be out if no attempt at a shot is made to a ball outside the off stump.

In Mexico England fail to retain the Football World Cup, not helped when the captain Bobby Moore is wrongly accused of stealing a gold bracelet from a jewellery shop in Bogota.

1971 Once a county championship match starts, there is no covering of the pitch at any time.

Sixty-six football supporters are crushed to death during a Rangers/Celtic match at Ibrox Park in Glasgow.

Decimal currency is introduced amid suspicions that shops are using the confusion to put up prices.

1972 A third limited-overs tournament, the Benson & Hedges Cup, is introduced. In order to accommodate this, the championship programme is reduced from 24 to 20 matches.

At the Olympic Games in Munich, Arab guerrillas launch an attack on the Israeli team.

1973 Prize money is introduced into the championship: £3,000 for the champions, £2,000 for the runners-up, £1,000 for third place, £500 for fourth place and for the sides with the season's highest run-rate and best bowling strike-rate.
The batting bonus points are altered. There is one point for a score of 75 after 25 overs, two points for 150 after 50.
Bookmakers are permitted to operate at Lord's, the Oval, Trent Bridge, Hove and the Yorkshire grounds.
Fines are introduced for slow over-rates. Lancashire and Somerset, falling below 18½ overs an hour across the season, pay £5,000 each, the money going to Derbyshire, Essex, Glamorgan and Middlesex, who exceed 19½.
Counties providing players for England receive compensation of £150 per player per match.

In a dispute over contracts the Association of Tennis Professionals boycotts the All-England Championship at Wimbledon.

1974 The two first innings are limited to a total of 200 overs, with the side batting first limited to 100 overs.
The bonus points are again altered, with a maximum of four for batting and four for bowling.

In a major reorganisation of local government Cumberland, Westmorland, Rutland and Huntingdonshire are abolished.

1975 Leicestershire become the twelfth county to win the championship.
Cricket's first World Cup, staged across two weeks in June, is won by the West Indies.

Women's rights are advanced by the passing into law of a Sex Discrimination Act and an Equal Pay Act.

1976 Middlesex become the ninth county in the nine years from 1968 to win the championship.

In the hottest summer of the century Denis Howell, Minister for Sport, is appointed Minister for Drought.

1977 Cadbury-Schweppes become the championship's first sponsors, committing to a three-year deal worth £360,000.
Prize money is increased to £4,000 for the champions, £2,500 for runners-up, £1,250 for third place. The programme increases from 20 to 22 matches. Players are permitted to wear clothes carrying a small manufacturer's emblem.
In a dispute over television rights in Australia, Kerry Packer signs up 35 cricketers, including England captain Tony Greig, to his alternative series of matches.

Red Rum becomes the first horse to win the Grand National three times, having also come second twice.

1978 Prize money for the county champions is doubled from £4,000 to £8,000.

Bjorn Borg earns £19,000 by winning Wimbledon, Jack Nicklaus £12,500 by winning the British Open Golf.

1979 Essex become the thirteenth county to win the championship.
There is a limit of one bouncer per over in county championship matches. A minimum wage is agreed for county cricketers: £4,000 for capped players; £2,500 for uncapped players over the age of 21, £1,500 under 21.

After a 'winter of discontent', the Conservative Party, led by Margaret Thatcher, is returned to power.

In six weeks in July and August Sebastian Coe sets new world records for the 800 and 1500 metres and the mile.

Championship – top three

	P	W	L	D	Pts	Leading batsmen	Runs	Leading bowlers	Wickets	Leading wkt-keeper / Leading fielder	Victims
1970											
Kent	24	9	5	10	237	G.M. Turner (Worcs)	2,346	D.J. Shepherd (Glam)	101	F.M. Engineer (Lancs)	80
Glamorgan	24	9	6	9	220	R.T. Virgin (Som)	2,233	N. Gifford (Worcs)	96	G.R.J. Roope (Surrey)	37
Lancashire	24	6	2	16	216	J.B. Bolus (Notts)	2,033	F.J. Titmus (Middx)	89	P.M. Walker (Glam)	37
1971											
Surrey	24	11	3	10	255	G. Boycott (Yorks)	2,197	L.R. Gibbs (Warwicks)	123	D.L. Bairstow (Yorks)	64
Warwickshire	24	9	9	6	255	M.J. Harris (Notts)	1,977	F.J. Titmus (Middx)	102	G.R.J. Roope (Surrey)	55
Lancashire	24	9	4	11	241	M.J. Procter (Glos)	1,762	P.J. Sainsbury (Hants)	101	*(+ 1 st while keeping)*	
1972											
Warwickshire	20	9	0	11	227	Mushtaq Mohammad (Nthnts)	1,743	T.W. Cartwright (Som)	93	G.R. Stephenson (Hants)	50
Kent	20	7	4	9	191	G.M. Turner (Worcs)	1,649	B. Stead (Notts)	93		
Gloucestershire	20	7	4	9	185	K.W.R. Fletcher (Essex)	1,644	K.D. Boyce (Essex)	80	J.F. Steele (Leics)	30
1973	P	W	L	D	Pts						
Hampshire	20	10	0	10	265	C.G. Greenidge (Hants)	1,620	P.G. Lee (Lancs)	96	G.R. Stephenson (Hants)	63
Surrey	20	9	3	8	234	J.A. Jameson (Warwicks)	1,550	T.W. Cartwright (Som)	88		
Northants	20	8	4	8	208	M.J. Smith (Middx)	1,549	B.S. Bedi (Northants)	86	C.G. Greenidge (Hants)	36
1974											
Worcestershire	20	11	3	6	227	R.T. Virgin (Northants)	1,845	A.M.E. Roberts (Hants)	111	G.R. Stephenson (Hants)	56
Hampshire	20	10	3	7	225	M.J. Harris (Notts)	1,431	V.A. Holder (Worcs)	87	G. Cook (Nthnts), J.A. Ormrod (Worcs), C.T. Radley (Middx), T.J. Yardley (Worcs)	31
Northants	20	9	2	9	203	J.A. Jameson (Warwicks)	1,420	F.J. Titmus (Middx)	85		
1975											
Leicestershire	20	12	1	7	240	G. Boycott (Yorks)	1,891	P.G. Lee (Lancs)	107	F.M. Engineer (Lancs)	70
Yorkshire	20	10	1	9	224	J.M. Brearley (Middx)	1,656	Sarfraz Nawaz (Nthnts)	94		
Hampshire	20	10	6	4	223	B.A. Richards (Hants)	1,456	J.K. Lever (Essex)	82	G.R.J. Roope (Surrey)	36
1976											
Middlesex	20	11	5	4	234	Zaheer Abbas (Glos)	2,431	Sarfraz Nawaz (Nthnts)	82	G. Sharp (Northants)	68
Northants	20	9	3	8	218	G.M. Turner (Worcs)	1,719	G.A. Cope (Yorks)	80		
Gloucestershire	20	9	5	6	210	J.A. Jameson (Warwicks)	1,692	R.D. Jackman (Surrey)	80	G.R.J. Roope (Surrey)	42
1977											
Middlesex *(1=)*	22	9	5	8	227	I.V.A. Richards (Som)	2,090	M.J. Procter (Glos)	108	G.W. Humpage (Warwks)	61
Kent *(1=)*	22	9	2	11	227	C.G. Greenidge (Hants)	1,771	J.N. Shepherd (Kent)	87		
Gloucestershire	22	9	5	8	222	Zaheer Abbas (Glos)	1,579	G. Miller (Derbys)	78	E.J. Barlow (Derbys)	34
1978											
Kent	22	13	3	6	292	D.L. Amiss (Warwicks)	2,001	D.L. Underwood (Kent)	110	D.L. Bairstow (Yorks)	65
Essex	22	12	1	9	273	C.E.B. Rice (Notts)	1,727	J.K. Lever (Essex)	97		
Middlesex	22	11	5	6	255	C.G. Greenidge (Hants)	1,711	M.W.W. Selvey (Middx)	94	C.J. Tavaré (Kent)	47
						G.M. Turner (Worcs)	1,711				
1979											
Essex	22	13	4	5	281	G.M. Turner (Worcs)	1,669	D.L. Underwood (Kent)	104	D.J. Humphries (Worcs)	56
Worcestershire	22	7	4	11	204	K.C. Wessels (Sussex)	1,619	J.K. Lever (Essex)	99		
Surrey	22	6	3	13	192	A.J. Lamb (Northants)	1,614	R.D. Jackman (Surrey)	87	G.R.J. Roope (Surrey)	40

1970s

1970-1979

Leading counties

	P	W	L	D	T	%W
Kent	214	73	45	96	-	34.1
Essex	214	72	43	98	1	33.6
Middlesex	214	68	51	94	1	31.8
Leicestershire	214	63	38	113	-	29.4

Leading batsmen

G.M. Turner (Worcs)	14,402
G. Boycott (Yorks)	12,661
M.J. Harris (Notts)	12,472
D.L. Amiss (Warwicks)	12,355

Leading bowlers

R.D. Jackman (Surrey)	731
D.L. Underwood (Kent)	654
J.K. Lever (Essex)	622
P.I. Pocock (Surrey)	618

Leading keepers & fielder

G.R. Stephenson (Hants)	531
D.L. Bairstow (Yorks)	524
G.R.J. Roope (Surrey)	326

Overall statistics

Runs per wicket	28.2
Runs per 100 balls	47.6
% of matches drawn	48.7

Miscellany

At Leicester in August 1971 Glamorgan's Don Shepherd found himself walking out to bat with the scoreboard showing 11 for eight, one run short of the lowest ever first-class total. "Shall I get out and make history, or hang about and make a couple?" he asked his partner Peter Walker. He opted for the latter, finishing on 2 not out when the last two wickets fell at 24.

*

At Swansea in 1977 Glenn Turner of Worcestershire ended the first day on 39 not out, out of 44 for two, then went off for an evening with the former New Zealand Test cricketer Bob Blair.

He ended up "having a rather heavy session of gin and tonics" and arrived next morning with a hangover. Jim Cumbes, the nightwatchman, stayed with him till the score reached 78, then a quick run of wickets reduced the innings to 93 for eight, with Turner on 72. "I couldn't understand the other batsmen," he says. "I told them there was nothing wrong with the pitch, but they didn't seem to believe me." As the last two men kept up an end, Turner took to playing extravagant shots to save the follow-on, which he did, carrying his bat for 141 out of 169.

At 83.4% it remains the highest proportion of a total a batsman has ever scored in first-class cricket. "And no," he says, "I didn't have another bottle of gin after it."

There have been five all-lbw hat-tricks in the history of the championship: by Horace Fisher of Yorkshire (1932), Jack Flavell of Worcestershire (1963), Mark Ilott of Essex (1995) and two by Mike Procter of Gloucestershire (1972 and 1979). Procter's second was against Yorkshire at Cheltenham, where one northern spectator was overheard complaining: "None of them would have been out if Dickie Bird had been umpiring."

*

No batsman has a higher average on one ground than Yorkshire's Geoffrey Boycott at the Garrison Ground in Colchester. In two visits there he was out just once for 493 runs.

He played there for the first time in 1970 when his 260 not out was the highest score made in the championship between 1959 and 1981. The following year, now captain, he returned, ending the first day on 221 not out.

Next morning he chose to bat on but, twenty-five minutes into the session, with his score on 233, he was lbw to leg-spinner Robin Hobbs, the finger raised by umpire Sam Cook.

"It was no way out," Hobbs says, recalling the conversation. "'That's out,' Sam said, and Boycott was running this leg bye. 'No, no, no, Sam,' he said. 'That can't be lbw.' 'That's out,' Sam said, and he turned to me. 'I think we've seen enough of *him*.'"

The championship in the 1970s

At last the Dodo said, '*Everybody* has won, and all
must have prizes.'

The creation of the Sunday League in 1969, followed by the
Benson & Hedges Cup in 1972, raised to four the number
of competitions, and in the 13 summers from 1969 all 17
counties won at least one trophy.

In this, county cricket was perhaps in keeping with the spirit
of the 1970s, a decade in which demands for greater equality
reduced the power of the country's traditional establishment.

The championship, historically the preserve of the few, was
won in those 13 years by ten different counties, including for
the first time Leicestershire and Essex. In both cases they had
already shaken off their long history as also-rans by winning a
one-day cup. Even the supporters of Northamptonshire and
Somerset, who had endured so many years at the bottom of
the championship pile, had days of glory in one-day finals at
Lord's. There were indeed prizes for all, and they brought a
welcome freshness to the county game.

The levelling of standard between the counties stemmed
in part from the decision in 1968 to loosen the qualification
rules for overseas players. Counties that had been struggling,
such as Nottinghamshire, Gloucestershire and Lancashire,
were lifted by the arrival of Garry Sobers, Mike Procter and
Clive Lloyd, men who not only won matches but changed the
culture of their teams.

They provided an instant boost for the county game, and
by the middle of the 1970s most counties had two, even three
such players. The qualification rules were not straightforward
– regulations about nationality and residence seldom are –
and in 1972 Warwickshire won the championship with a
team that included four West Indian Test cricketers. The
entertainment value was immense, especially from the brilliant
Rohan Kanhai, a batsman with a magical mix of orthodoxy
and improvised genius. But it did not go without comment
that early in the season, when the Pakistani Test cricketer
Billy Ibadulla was also in the Warwickshire eleven, there was
no room for Dennis Amiss, who had been in the England
team the previous summer.

At the start of the decade Glamorgan, captained by Tony
Lewis, were the reigning champions, and they looked set to
retain their title in 1970 till Kent, in last place at the start of
July, surged into the lead with a series of dynamic victories. In
the history of the championship only two men – Lord Hawke
of Yorkshire and Arthur Carr of Notts – have captained a

county for longer than the 15 years Colin Cowdrey led Kent,
and this triumph in his 14th year marked the start of a decade
in which they were the outstanding team. In the ten years they
won two championships, shared a third and were winners of
seven one-day competitions.

The following year it was the turn of another veteran
captain, Micky Stewart, the last survivor of Surrey's
great 1950s side, in whose long shadows they had played
throughout the 1960s. They made certain of the 1971 title
by gaining a second bowling point in their final match at
Southampton, the first time the championship had been
settled in this way since the introduction of such points
in 1969. Such was the Surrey joy that the afternoon's play
was briefly suspended for a celebration. 'The champagne
was brought out,' EW Swanton wrote stiffly in the *Daily
Telegraph*, 'and a lady, reputedly Mrs M.J. Stewart, broke
the long cricket custom of wifely anonymity and embraced
the triumphant captain.'

Bonus points had been introduced in 1969 to encourage
positive cricket in the first innings but, with no limit on
batting points, a high-scoring defeat could gain as many
points as a low-scoring victory. This led in 1973 to a table
in which Kent (won 4, lost 3) finished six places, and 39
points, above Somerset (won 7, lost 2). As so often before, the
counties returned to the drawing board.

The 1973 championship was the first when prize money
was at stake, and Hampshire, to the surprise of many,
collected the winners' £3,000. In Barry Richards and
Gordon Greenidge they had one of county cricket's best
ever opening partnerships, and their supposed weak link,
the new-ball attack of Middlesex cast-off Bob Herman and
young architect Tom Mottram, exceeded all expectations.
The following year Mottram gave way to the skilful Antiguan
fast bowler Andy Roberts, whose 111 wickets made him by
some distance the leading bowler in the country. He was
a true match-winner but ironically, unlike the unsung
Mottram, not a championship-winner. The weather was
cruel to Hampshire at the last, and Worcestershire pipped
them to the title.

Leicestershire, under Ray Illingworth, were champions for
the first time in 1975. Middlesex, under Mike Brearley, won
in 1976, the ninth county to win in nine years. Then in 1979
the popular Essex team rounded off county cricket's most
democratic decade with their first championship.

The dominant team of the 1960s had been Yorkshire, but they suffered a barren decade, winning nothing between the 1969 Gillette Cup, when Brian Close was still captain, and the 1983 Sunday League, when their 51-year-old manager Ray Illingworth came out of retirement to captain the team.

The lack of success, so unacceptable to Yorkshire folk, coincided with the eight-year reign of Geoffrey Boycott as captain. In each of the first seven years he was the top English batsman in the national averages, and he had a good tactical brain. But did he have the personality to get the best out of his team?

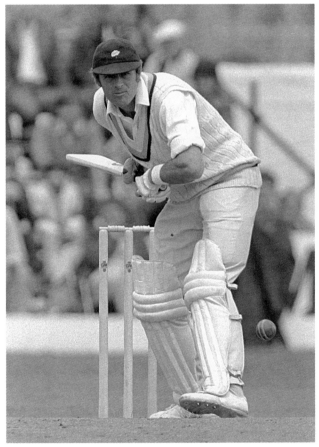

Geoffrey Boycott

The most prolific English batsman during the decade, he twice finished a season with an average above 100. Many admired the dedication with which he made the most of his talent; others found fault in his single-mindedness. 'His attitude and temperament were better suited to golf than to a team game like cricket,' wrote Trevor Bailey.

There were days when, rightly or wrongly, Boycott gave the appearance of batting primarily for himself, an issue that came to a head at Northampton in 1978. With teams limited to 100 overs in their first innings, Boycott did not hit a boundary till the 60th over, got stuck on 82 for half an hour and was finally out in the 90th over for 113. In the view of *The Times*, 'he once again scored his runs too slowly for his team's interests.'

With only ten overs left to raise the total from 267 to 300 for another batting point, John Hampshire, the only other survivor of the 1960s team, was so angry that he staged an unpremeditated protest, patting back half-volleys and making little attempt to run. Only three wickets were down, but he and Colin Johnson added just 11 runs in the ten overs, creating a furore in the press. "Why should it always have to be somebody else who plays all the strokes?" he said. The rift did not heal when at the end of the summer Hampshire replaced Boycott as captain.

In Boycott's defence he had inherited a team that had lost most of its key members, and they played with the handicap of a 'Yorkshire for the Yorkshire born' policy that put them at a major disadvantage in relation to the other 16 counties.

Yorkshire's principled stand, upholding the importance of the word county in the county championship, was in many ways admirable. But the reality was that the overseas players, along with the rise of one-day cricket, had breathed new and desperately needed life into the English game.

A better way forward was found by Somerset. For the summer of 1974 their coach Tom Cartwright persuaded the committee to abandon its policy of signing old pros from other counties. Instead, it put aside £6,000 for summer contracts for six young players. The Antiguan Viv Richards had already been identified; the other five were local lads, among them Ian Botham, Peter Roebuck, Vic Marks and Phil Slocombe. Tom Cartwright's vision was of a team drawn from the towns and villages, to which the folk would relate. "If you get these youngsters playing, coming from all over the county," he told the Secretary, "you'll have people falling over themselves to hire those marquees at Bath and Weston."

The vision became a reality. By 1979, with the free-spirited Ian Botham in his prime, Somerset's home-grown players, aided by Viv Richards and the Barbadian Joel Garner, were playing exciting cricket, drawing great crowds and winning trophies. Here, at least, the doom-mongers of the 1960s, who had wondered if county cricket could survive, were a distant memory.

The weather helped, with 1976 the hottest summer of the century. At the end of it, Tony Lewis wrote, 'I am left with the impression that cricket is more popular a spectator sport than it has been since the immediate post-war years.'

Some players of the 1970s

JK
A championship winner

John Lever of Essex

> JK was the number one bowler in county cricket, by a long way. He swung the ball both ways, and he'd run in all day every day. He just wanted to keep bowling.
>
> *Graham Gooch*

No pace bowler of the last eighty years has played as many seasons of county cricket as John Lever. From 1967 to 1989, game after game, he ran in for Essex, on his long, flowing run, never stinting, a long-spell bowler with great control, steady temperament and a love of the game that saw him playing for Essex past his 40th birthday and for the Old England XI into his 60s. Trevor Bailey called him 'the type of cricketer every captain wants in his side'.

A butcher's son, he joined Essex from the Ilford club at the age of 18, a left-arm medium-quick bowler who ran the ball away from right-handers. Soon enough, with some helpful words from Garry Sobers, he realised he needed an in-swinger and, after long hours in the nets, he developed one. Thereafter his new-ball partnership with his great friend and room-mate, Barbadian Keith Boyce, became a vital component of Essex's rise in the 1970s.

Boyce's departure at the end of 1977 placed an extra burden on Lever, and he rose to the challenge, passing 100 first-class wickets in each of the next two years, including a spell of 26 wickets in a week in the championship-winning summer of 1979. He trained hard, he enjoyed the fun of the madcap Essex dressing room, and he respected the game's best sporting traditions. Rarely missing through injury, he discovered late in his career that he had been playing with a cracked vertebra, the result of a car crash when he was sixteen.

Bob Taylor of Derbyshire

> He was the most stylish wicket-keeper in the country, the perfect model for anyone taking up a career behind the stumps. He made even the most difficult tasks look simple.
>
> *Trevor Bailey*

The initial attraction of wicket-keeping for Bob Taylor came on a cold day at his Stoke primary school when, forbidden to put his hands in his pockets, he envied the boy with the big gloves. From that accidental beginning he graduated to keeping wicket for the Bignall End club, where his captain Jack Ikin had him in the Staffordshire team at sixteen.

Inspired by a sighting of the Northamptonshire keeper Keith Andrew – "he was so easy and fluent, there was no fuss or flamboyance" – he became the best keeper of his generation, always standing right up to the stumps to medium-pacers and spinners. He had soft hands, quick reactions, great concentration and a dedication to staying fit.

Derbyshire recruited him. They were looking for a successor to George Dawkes, whose troublesome knee gave out within weeks of Taylor's arrival in 1961. Briefly in 1964 he was dropped in favour of a batsman-keeper, but a campaign in the *Derby Evening Telegraph* saw him restored and he stayed in the team till the end of 1984, by which time he had played 57 times for England and accumulated a world record of 1,649 first-class victims.

He was a useful, lower-order batsman, good enough to score six or seven hundred runs a year in his prime. Brought up in cricket's old school, he walked on 97 in a Test match at Adelaide, learning afterwards that the umpire would not have given him out, but at Abbeydale Park in Sheffield in 1981, the week after being awarded an MBE, he finally made a first-class hundred – against Derbyshire's old foes, Yorkshire.

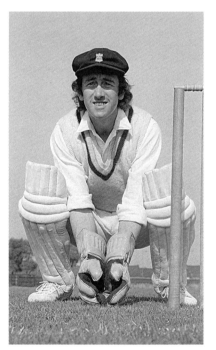

County cricket's leading keeper
1,220 championship victims

Glenn Turner of Worcestershire

> He was the best timer of the ball I've ever bowled at, and perfectly happy against the fast bowlers.
> He saw the ball so quickly from the hand, and that's the sign of a great player. *John Emburey*

300 in a day
Leading run-scorer of the 1970s

The young Glenn Turner was a slight figure with little strength, but he had great determination. In Dunedin on New Zealand's South Island he worked 18 months of nights in a bakery to afford the one-way air fare to England where Warwickshire immediately rejected him. "All he did was hit the ball back at me," David Brown recalls. "I thought he hadn't a hope of playing county cricket."

At Worcester they spotted his hardness, but his single-minded dedication – going to bed each night at nine, replaying in his mind his every dismissal – was not a recipe for success. Soon enough he came to realise that Tom Graveney's approach – in the bar till late and first in the nets in the morning – was a healthier one, and he was freed up further by the demands of the 40-over Sunday League.

In time, though never powerful, he became one of the freest scoring batsmen in the world. Only the second non-Englishman, after Don Bradman, to hit 100 first-class hundreds, he achieved the feat at Worcester, appropriately against Warwickshire, with a century before lunch and 311 in the day.

Don Shepherd of Glamorgan

Shep
Leading bowler, aged 43, in 1970

> Don Shepherd's run-up and delivery came perfectly from within: never strained, never too fast and certainly not too slow. It was as if someone had set a metronome ticking and left it running for over twenty years and for over two thousand wickets. *Tony Lewis*

Don Shepherd, from the Gower Peninsula, had played only a bare handful of matches when during National Service his natural potential as a bowler was spotted. After a summer on the Lord's ground staff he returned in 1949 to Glamorgan where for several years he opened the bowling. Keeper Haydn Davies, spotting his slightly floppy wrist, suggested he turn to off-spin, and in 1956, his first year in this new role, he took 177 wickets. From then on, for 15 years, he was one of the outstanding bowlers of county cricket, ever probing batsmen with fast and unfailingly accurate off-breaks.

With the bat he loved to give the ball a whack. It was an approach that brought him a record 156 first-class and one-day ducks, but at Swansea he did once hit a fifty in 15 minutes against the Australians.

'Shep' was at the heart of the team that won the championship in 1969, a triumph which, with his ingrained Welsh pessimism, he had difficulty in believing. "I'll wait till I've read it in the papers," he said when they began the celebrations. Glamorgan has had no more popular a player.

Peter Sainsbury of Hampshire

> When he was a boy, his grandparents took him to Beale's in Bournemouth. "What would you like, Peter?" they asked. It was a great big department store, and do you know what he said? "I'd like a ball." That's all he ever wanted. *Malcolm Heath*

Sains
An under-rated all-rounder

Peter Sainsbury was always in the game. His middle-order batting, full of artful nudges and scampered singles, calmed many a crisis; his slow-left-arm bowling, more guile than spin, dismissed many a batsman; and his brilliant fielding, hovering close at short leg, yielded many an unlikely catch. "I didn't see a better fielder," his team-mate Jimmy Gray says. "He just caught the ball and threw it back. And those people don't get publicity, do they?" The only man to play in both Hampshire's championship-winning sides, in 1961 and 1973, Sainsbury went on to coach the county for 15 years.

Beneath his quiet-spoken kindness he was a fierce competitor, determined to maintain the highest standards. In his first full summer, 1955, he took 100 wickets, including Len Hutton twice in a day on his 21st birthday, and in 1971 he took 100 again, failing by only 41 runs to achieve the by-then rare feat of the double. No Hampshire-born man has given greater service to his county.

Stories of the 1970s

One hundred years of waiting

Gloucestershire v Hampshire, Bristol, Friday 9 September 1977

It was to be the day that would banish one hundred years of disappointment. Not since 1877, when WG Grace led them to first place in the unofficial competition, had Gloucestershire been crowned champions, and now they were top of the table, just one day's good cricket away from the prize.

So often they had come close: 'robbed' by the points system in 1930; pipped by Middlesex in 1947; self-destructing with a spinners' pitch for Laker and Lock at the Wagon Works in 1959; then in 1969 frittering away a commanding lead in the table. Surely they could finish the job this time.

In July at Lord's their supporters had cheered rudely when they lifted the Benson & Hedges Cup, but this championship was the one that mattered – and they gathered at Bristol on Friday morning, more than five thousand of them, the largest crowd the ground had seen for a county match since Wally Hammond's ill-advised comeback in 1951.

It was a day laden with emotion. The players who had signed for Kerry Packer's rebel World Series Cricket were – subject to a court case – facing a ban from English cricket. At the start of play the Hampshire fielders gathered round their two Packer men, Barry Richards and Gordon Greenidge, linked hands and sang a heartfelt *Auld Lang Syne*.

Just as poignantly Gloucestershire stood to lose their new captain, the South African Mike Procter, the inspiration behind their title challenge. He had scored 115 in their first innings of 223; he had taken six wickets, with both pace and off-spin, in Hampshire's reply of 229, then hit 57 on the second evening.

"He willed us to victory with sheer force of personality," batsman Alastair Hignell says. "He never really analysed the game, he just played, and he drove us forward like a juggernaut."

"We didn't have a great side," Procter says, "but everybody worked so hard for each other that we wouldn't accept the word defeat. I was convinced we were going to win the title."

They even studied a photograph of their 1877 predecessors, noticed they all had moustaches and set about copying them. "David Shepherd got the prize for artistic merit," Hignell recalls. "He got his sideboards to meet up with his 'tache. And I think Jim Foat got the award for most pathetic effort."

Hampshire were batting before lunch, needing 271 to win. The pitch was taking turn, but Richards and Greenidge were the two great obstacles. Procter turned to the slow-left-arm of David Graveney, and in his first over he had Richards, 'at his

Mike Procter addresses the Bristol crowd

most imperious', caught at slip by Zaheer. It was 30 for one, and hopes were high. They were even higher when a minute before lunch, with the score on 59, Greenidge drove Graveney into the hands of mid-off. 'A hard but straight chance,' Alan Gibson called it in *The Times*, and it fell to earth.

In the first over after lunch, with the score still 59, the little left-hander David Turner was put down at short extra cover. And gradually, as the pair added 123 in 70 minutes, the hopes of the great crowd ebbed away. "I didn't captain very well," Procter says, determined to take the blame. "I was so convinced we were going to win, I over-attacked in the field and I bowled the spinners too long."

Hampshire won by six wickets, and the ancient Gloucestershire disappointments remained. "I just hoped that once in my lifetime we could do it," said the Cotswold forester Charlie Light. Even Alan Gibson, 'not a partisan, not a crying man, found drops stealing down my cheeks'. From the pavilion balcony Procter, fighting back his own tears, spoke. "It was very, very sad," he says now. "Emotions ran high."

"His commitment and his understanding of the occasion took away some of the sadness," Charlie Light's son John says. "He knew what it meant to us, and we knew what it meant to him. He'd let us dare to hope."

Eight years later they were hoping again, with David Graveney leading them to a 54-point lead in the table, but once more it was not to be. "We get vertigo," John Light says.

Coasting to victory

Sussex v Surrey, Eastbourne, Tuesday 15 August 1972

Sussex were having a wretched season in 1972. They arrived at Eastbourne in mid-August with one win out of 15 in the championship, one out of 11 in the Sunday League and a first-round defeat in the Gillette Cup. Morale was low.

Their match against Surrey was rain-affected, but Micky Stewart, the Surrey captain, set them 205 to win on the last afternoon and spirits were high when they reached 187 for one. There were three overs left, with off-spinner Pat Pocock to bowl the first of them. He was getting little out of the pitch and at this point had figures of 14 overs, nought for 65.

Geoff Greenidge, on 64, looked to press on, but he missed Pocock's first ball and was bowled. Two balls later Mike Buss departed in the same way. And off the last ball of the over, after scoring a two, Jim Parks was caught and bowled. It was a bizarre over but, after Sussex had taken 11 off the next one, the game was back on track. Now 200 for four, Sussex needed only five runs for victory, just one good hit.

Roger Prideaux, who had made 106 in the first innings, was on 97. "We were coasting," he says, "and I stupidly tried to go for glory and smash it over long-on for six. Robin Jackman caught me on the boundary." Mike Griffith, the captain, tried the same approach and was caught off a skier, giving 'Percy' Pocock a hat-trick. Next came Jerry Morley, who charged down the wicket to his first ball and, despite keeper Arnold Long dropping the ball, was stumped. Now it was 200 for seven.

In the middle of the mayhem the Surrey coach Arthur McIntyre rang from the Oval, wanting to know the score. Twelfth man Ian Payne took the call: "Hold on, Percy's got another one ... Blimey, he's got a hat-trick." McIntyre grew suspicious, sensing the youngster was taking the piss: "You're having me on." Then, when Morley was stumped, "I'll get you for this, Payne. Just you wait till you get back to the Oval."

John Spencer pushed a single; then Tony Buss was bowled, giving Pocock seven wickets in 11 balls, a world record. "It didn't register at all," he says. "It was all taking so long to happen, with so many batsmen coming and going."

Eight wickets were down and, with four wanted off the last ball, Udar Joshi was run out, going for a pointless second run.

Poor Sussex, it was just not their season. A fortnight later Mike Griffith announced that he was retiring as captain.

"Whenever I'm listening to a match," Micky Stewart says, "and the commentator says, 'They're coasting it now,' I always think of that day."

A watery end

The closing days of 1974

In early August 1974 Hampshire, top of the table, beat rivals Worcestershire by an innings within two days. 'Something very unexpected will have to happen,' wrote *The Times*, 'for Hampshire not to win the championship.'

With a fortnight remaining, Hampshire were almost over the line, but the next week's weather was unkind to them. They were without a game when Worcestershire beat Notts. Then Worcestershire were without a game when rain washed out a day at Southampton and Hampshire were left two wickets short of an innings victory over Glamorgan.

The advantage still lay with the southern county as they travelled to Bournemouth for their last two matches. It was here, among the pines, that they had won their two previous championships, and after two days of play against Somerset they were well on course for a third celebration. Then the rain came down: at Bournemouth but not at Worcester, where Norman Gifford's side closed the gap in the table to two points.

For the last round of matches Worcestershire were at Chelmsford where rainwater got under the covers, delaying the start. Gifford won the toss, asked Essex to bat and for a while the openers were comfortable, reaching 42 for no wicket. Then, with the sun burning down on a damp patch, Gifford set to work with his slow-left-arm bowling and in 75 minutes the Essex innings, in the words of Christopher Wordsworth in the *Observer*, 'folded like a mildewed deckchair'. They were all out for 84, Gifford taking seven for 15 in 14 overs.

At Bournemouth there was no play. Worcestershire, with four bonus points, were now two ahead of Hampshire.

On the second day there was no play at either ground as gale-force winds and torrential rain caused flooding all over the south of England. Into the night the high winds continued at Bournemouth, blowing down marquees, overturning a hut and standing the covers on their ends. But the rain abated, the wind started to dry the exposed pitch and eventually the sun came out. News arrived that the Chelmsford match had been abandoned, but the umpires at Bournemouth agreed that play could start at three o'clock.

Yorkshire were the visitors, and their captain John Hampshire won the toss. It was one-day rules now: ten for a win and no bonus points. So how was he going to play it?

He was about to announce his decision when a violent storm broke out, driving them all back into the pavilion.

Worcestershire were champions.

Images of the 1970s

The Oval, Saturday 18 September 1971
Ronnie Wood and Rod Stewart of The Faces (left), watched by a great crowd

Pop goes the Oval

For years Surrey County Cricket Club had rejected such fund-raising schemes as football pools and discotheques, the 'vulgar' initiatives that had kept the smaller counties afloat. But near-bankruptcy and a forward-looking Secretary, Geoffrey Howard, had changed their thinking by 1971.

"One of the things that attracted me to first-class cricket," Micky Stewart says, "was the crowd at the Oval when I went there as a boy. Playing there was like going on stage in front of thousands of people. If you hit a ball and it ran away for four, there would be a great cheer. But that had gone by the end of the '60s. The old dilapidated Vauxhall stand was still there, but there would be hardly anybody sitting in it. That year, 1971, we turned up on a Saturday at the end of August, with a chance of winning the championship, and the ground was almost empty. You could feel the disappointment in the dressing room."

In their financial desperation Surrey were hosting Sunday markets, Christmas funfairs, donkey derbies, anything that might bring in people and money. "There was one occasion," Micky Stewart recalls, "when I turned up in winter to have my photograph taken between two camels. I'd just bought a beautiful new overcoat, and they spat all over it."

In September 1971, on the Saturday after Surrey had won the championship, the Oval staged cricket's first pop concert. Its organiser Ricky Farr, son of the boxer Tommy, had gone bankrupt with his Isle of Wight Festival, but this time he was raising money for the Bangladesh Flood Relief Fund. Admission was £1.25, with ten per cent of the takings going to Surrey.

Outside the Hobbs Gates two thousand people queued all night; then on the day another thirty-odd thousand arrived, filling the field and terraces and providing non-stop trade for the stalls selling t-shirts, orange juice, pizzas, even the Hare Krishna magazine. Where once the cheers of the young folk of South London had been for their heroes Hobbs and Sandham, they rang out now for The Who and Rod Stewart.

The Surrey accounts for 1971 showed a rare profit of £561. In the income column was £4,210 from the pop festival.

Buxton, Monday 2 June 1975

Snow stops play in June

Snow stops play in June. Never before or since has county cricket seen the like of it. The Buxton ground, at 1,000 feet above sea level, was the highest on the circuit, and inch-deep snow lay all across it on the Monday morning. There was no other option but to abandon play for the day.

It was the first summer of Derbyshire's nomadic venture. After a dispute with the local council they had left the Racecourse Ground in Derby and were taking their games all round the county. Buxton was the most northerly of the venues, and on Saturday, with the sun weak and the air chilly, the well-wrapped spectators watched Lancashire's batsmen score 477 for five, the highest total since the first innings had been restricted to 100 overs. The West Indian Clive Lloyd's run-a-ball 167 included 11 sixes, most of them hit straight and landing in the adjoining bowling green where play was reluctantly abandoned.

Apart from a refuelling stop at Moscow airport, Lloyd had never seen snow, and on Monday morning he happily made snowballs as the players of both teams larked about.

The next day, mindful of the good crowd that had gathered, the umpires – Dickie Bird and 'Dusty' Rhodes – decided play was possible. It was only a club pitch, it had remained uncovered throughout Monday, and it was immediately apparent that batting would be nigh impossible. The ball flew off a length, taking pieces out of the surface, and the Lancashire fielders crowded around the batsmen.

Their fastest bowler was Peter Lever, but he was haunted by the memory of the Auckland Test three months earlier, when he had bowled a ball that had almost killed New Zealand's Ewan Chatfield, the batsman only brought back to life after heart massage. There was no way he was going to run in and bowl at top pace.

Even without his full menace Derbyshire sank from their starting score of 25 for two to 42 all out. One batsman, worried that he would be hit in the face, gave his false teeth to Dickie Bird and was only too happy to collect them a few balls later. It was all over before teatime, Derbyshire losing by an innings and 348 runs.

1970: Kent's remarkable rise

In the race to win the title, no champion county has come from farther back than Kent in 1970. In last place at the start of July, 13th at the start of August, they were only ninth on August 14 after three-quarters of their 24 fixtures had been played. Yet by September 4, with one match remaining, they had risen to the top.

It was a feat all the more remarkable for the fact that, through these vital weeks, they had regularly given four players to the England team: captain Colin Cowdrey, keeper Alan Knott, slow-left-armer Derek Underwood and opening batsman Brian Luckhurst. Even their other opening bat, Mike Denness, had played one Test.

Their dismal start to the summer had been a great surprise. Through the late 1960s, under the guidance of their Secretary/Manager Les Ames, they had been emerging as a team of great promise, twice finishing second in the championship, and in the spring there was real hope that they could carry off the prize in this their centenary year.

Colin Cowdrey was back, after missing most of 1969 with a ruptured Achilles tendon, but nothing clicked in the early weeks of the season, in those vital matches before they lost players to the Tests. 'Our midweek crowds were dwindling away,' Cowdrey wrote, 'disenchanted by our performances.' Indeed, so poorly were they playing that, when the great Frank Woolley, survivor from their last championship team in 1913, flew in from Canada to open a smart pavilion extension at Canterbury, he was heard to observe, "It's too good for this lot."

The crunch came after they threw away a winning position in a Gillette Cup game against Sussex. Cowdrey called it 'one of those days that happen in cricket', but Les Ames was less sanguine. After the first day of their next match at Maidstone, a day in which they had managed to take only eight Derbyshire wickets, he called a team meeting and blew his top. Nobody was spared as he castigated their lacklustre displays. Then, as they all sat in stunned silence, the Northumbrian vowels of their tall fast bowler Norman Graham were heard. "Ay, manager, you're right. Let's get cracking."

The key to it all, they resolved, was the system of bonus points: one for each two wickets and, crucially, one for each 25 runs after 150 in the first 85 overs, with no limit. With only ten points for a win, these bonus points were vital to championship success, and the batsmen had managed just 23 of them in 11 games. With the most talented of line-ups, they were barely scoring 200 in the first 85 overs.

The next day they were a team transformed. Denness and Luckhurst put on 75 at almost a run-a-minute, and the young Graham Johnson hit a bright 32. Then in a feast of glorious strokeplay Cowdrey, 'at his masterly best', and Asif Iqbal, 'powerful and exciting', rattled the score along at five an over. They had 307 on the board after 85 overs, and a declaration left them time to take a Derbyshire wicket. Rain washed away the last day but, even without their Test players, they took their new-found zest into the next match, where they won another six batting points and beat Hampshire.

The following week brought a shattering blow to Cowdrey. At the start of the previous summer he had been appointed England captain for all six Tests. He had done well in the Caribbean and in the drawn home series against Australia, and the long-held doubts about his indecisiveness seemed to have passed. But his injury allowed Ray Illingworth to step in and show his own skill as a captain, and the selectors – after intense speculation in the papers – asked Illingworth, not Cowdrey, to captain the winter's tour of Australia.

Cowdrey, for the fourth time under four captains, was invited to be vice-captain, this time under a man who had a quite different outlook from his and with whom he was not at ease. The sense of disappointment, injustice even, burned inside him, made all the worse because, as John Arlott put it, 'he has never been a better captain than he is now.' Once more he lapsed into indecision, unsure if he should accept the vice-captaincy or not.

Perhaps he lacked a little in self-belief. Born in Bangalore, the son of a tea-planter, he was separated from his parents at a young age, spending years in boarding schools and the spare rooms of relatives. Shy and nervous, he found himself lionised as the outstanding schoolboy cricketer of his generation, and he made his debut for Kent at Derby when only seventeen.

In the changing room on the first morning he sat down next to Derek Ufton, the only one of the team he knew.

"Why am I staying in a separate hotel from you?" he asked.

"Because you're an amateur and I'm a professional."

"What's the difference?"

"I'm paid to play, and you're not."

"But I've got no money."

"Don't worry. That will all be taken care of."

He was given the Kent captaincy in 1957 and, with Les Ames always at hand, he gradually raised Kent out of the trough into which it had fallen. By the middle of the 1960s it was a young side, all of whom looked up to him. "I held him in such high regard," Derek Underwood says. "He had a boyish enthusiasm for cricket that he never lost. He loved the game. He spent hours and hours talking about it. When I was young, he used to invite me to his house, and we'd work on my bowling in a net in his garden. He had this tape that he would use to look at all the angles."

Back in the now bubbling Kent dressing room Cowdrey found solace, leading them to a victory at Hove. But a draw against Worcestershire at Canterbury left them down in 13th place, too late – it seemed – to make a challenge for the championship. "What a tragedy the season isn't a week longer," Cowdrey told his batting partner Asif Iqbal as they plundered the Middlesex bowling in the next match. "We would win the title the way we are playing now."

"No, no, skipper," Asif replied. "You've got it wrong. We've got enough time. If it was any longer, we would get stale. I've already told Mike Denness. We shall win it in our last match at the Oval. You'll see." Asif did not give up. 'Not a day passed,' Cowdrey wrote, 'without his sharing his joy with the entire team.' "There's nothing to worry about," he would say. "We'll all be drinking champagne at the Oval."

Although they were low in the table, it was the tightest of races; none of the counties above them were so far ahead. With a run of victories and plenty of bonus points, Asif was right. They could quickly storm to the top.

Underwood, unusually tossing the ball up high, spun them to victory at Weston. Then they pulled off a Boy's Own win at Cheltenham, saving the follow-on by one run and chasing an improbable 340 to win at the death by one wicket. A rain-ruined draw at Northampton set them back, but they beat championship rivals Surrey at Blackheath in a game that took them up to third place.

The Blackheath match was a triumph for so many of them: for Denness and Luckhurst at the top of the order, for the young Graham Johnson's off-spin, for the Barbadian all-rounder John Shepherd, for Cowdrey himself as batsman and captain and, above all, for Asif who hit a brilliant hundred. With Kent bustling through their overs and Surrey closing in on a great victory, there was time for 22 overs in the last hour and, off the last ball of the 21st of them, Asif ran 25 yards round the boundary at long-off and held a stunning left-handed catch to seal the victory.

Two wins at Folkestone, both after losing the toss on good batting tracks, took them to first place, and now it all came down to the match at the Oval.

Celebration at the Oval
Colin Cowdrey, Stuart Leary, Les Ames, Edward Heath

With no limit on batting points, the arithmetic was troubling greater men than Cowdrey, as he discovered when he was taking his pads off after a Sunday League innings at Bournemouth. He was called to the telephone, and on the other end was the Prime Minister Edward Heath, a man of Kent who in the spring had forecast that, as in 1906, there would be a new government and a Kent championship.

"I've been trying to work out how many bonus points we need to win at the Oval. How many do you think we need?"

Hops were draped over the Oval's away team balcony, and the large crowd of Kent supporters, outnumbering their hosts, cheered with delight each bonus point as Cowdrey stroked his way to what John Arlott called 'a century of mature technique and perfect temperament'. The Prime Minister had promised to come on the final afternoon and, though hijackers were threatening to blow up four planes if Britain did not release a young Palestinian woman Leila Khaled, there he was, drinking the champagne that Asif had so joyfully predicted.

It was Kent's first championship for 57 years, but there would be two more before the decade was out – as well as seven one-day trophies. In the history of the championship, has there ever been a tirade more magnificently effective than the one delivered by Les Ames that evening at Maidstone?

The golden age of the overseas player

The county championship programme of 1967 consisted of 238 fixtures, which was much more than the total of first-class matches played in a year in all the other countries. Only in England and Wales was it possible below Test level to play full-time, professional cricket.

The rules of qualification for county cricket were complex, but essentially they required an overseas cricketer to complete a period of residence, usually two years, in a county. No county could have more than two such players on their books.

Some, such as the South African Tony Greig at Sussex and the Barbadian Keith Boyce at Essex, came by invitation. Tony Cordle, by contrast, arrived from Barbados with the intention of working for London Transport. He finished up living with his brother and sister in Cardiff, where Glamorgan recruited him from club cricket.

Roy Marshall of Hampshire, abandoning his West Indian Test career, settled permanently in England; Mushtaq Mohammad of Northamptonshire continued to play for Pakistan. The South African Basil D'Oliveira became an England cricketer; his Worcester team-mate Ron Headley might have become one, too, but he opted for the West Indies.

Such players brought freshness to the struggling county game, and in January 1967 Nottinghamshire and Somerset proposed that each county should be allowed to recruit one overseas player without any residential period. That way, they argued, the top cricketers could be brought into the English domestic game. Only six counties voted in favour, with finance the clinching argument against: 'It was feared that there might be resentment by local born players if overseas stars received higher remuneration.'

In November, after another summer of crisis for county cricket, the decision was reversed. From now on, each county could make one immediate registration, with three provisos: (i) the specially signed player could not join another county for at least three years, (ii) the county could not make another such signing for three years, even if the player had left, and (iii) the county could only ever have two overseas players.

The West Indian all-rounder Garry Sobers was everybody's number one target, and within weeks Notts had signed him, outbidding their rivals and offering him the captaincy.

That winter England were touring the Caribbean under the manager Les Ames, and Sobers confidently told Ames' wife Bunty, "I'll get them to the top four." Notts had finished out of the bottom three once in the previous eleven years so

she laughed: "I know you're good, but you're not that bloody good." Sobers, always one for a bet, got her to promise him six bottles of champagne if he succeeded.

He won the bet, securing fourth place with victory in the last match at Swansea, a game in which he rewrote the record books by hitting six sixes in an over. Sobers was the best cricketer in the world, and he played with panache and with a smile, even through the six-day-a-week routine of the county game. 'Sobers inspired his men,' *Wisden* wrote. 'Throughout a hard season, his enthusiasm remained undimmed, and he was always ready to gamble to keep a game alive.'

Another to start the season with confident talk was the 22-year-old South African Barry Richards, who told a television interviewer that he aimed to score 2,000 runs for Hampshire. He was not a star like Sobers, he had not yet played Test cricket, and his brash remark, coupled with the news that he was on a salary of £1,300, went down badly on the circuit. In his first innings of the summer he was bowled by John Snow for nought, and the Sussex fielders sent him packing with sarcasm: "Well, just another 2,000 to go, then."

Richards had the last laugh, finishing the season as the leading batsman in the county championship – in fact, the only one to score 2,000 runs.

The next year Mike Procter, also from Durban, was the championship's leading bowler, his 103 wickets taking Gloucestershire up to second place – behind Glamorgan, whose title challenge was boosted by the cultured batting of Majid Khan. In the vital game, against Worcestershire at Cardiff, he was asleep in the dressing room, his head resting on his bat handle, when it was his turn to bat. They shook him awake, and he hit a glorious 156.

In his view it was an innings that several of the overseas batsmen could have played – but not the English, too many of whom were, like Geoff Boycott, "enchained inside limited scoring arcs if the bowling is accurate". Majid's approach was freer: "I rely principally on my eyes, arms and wrists," he said.

Undoubtedly the overseas batsmen added sparkle to the county circuit, but regular exposure to English conditions also tightened their techniques. It was no coincidence that, when the West Indies emerged as one of the greatest Test teams of all time, almost all their front-line batsmen, notably Clive Lloyd, Viv Richards, Gordon Greenidge and Desmond Haynes, had played years of county cricket.

Barry Richards
Hampshire, 1968-78

Asif Iqbal
Kent, 1968-82

Mike Procter
Gloucestershire, 1968-81

Garry Sobers
Nottinghamshire, 1968-74

Lancashire recruited Farokh Engineer, the flamboyant Indian wicket-keeper, and they also had Clive Lloyd, who qualified after two years of playing in the leagues. The two of them, under the captaincy of Jack Bond, brought a new vitality to the long-underachieving county. "I would play my shots," Lloyd says, "and I think the guys realised there was no need to be cautious, to be staid. Before long we were chasing down totals, setting big scores and bowling sides out. It was a brand of cricket that people wanted to see. Old Trafford would sell out for the one-day games and the Roses matches."

Lloyd stayed at Lancashire till 1986, one of many in this first wave of overseas recruits who gave long service and became identified with their counties. In Gloucestershire Mike Procter's impact was so great – as batsman, bowler and captain – that some nicknamed the county Proctershire.

A young Greg Chappell, one of few Australians to come over, played two years for Somerset, but the three-year rule left the county unable to replace him in 1970. By contrast, Warwickshire, making the most of the small print in the regulations, won the 1972 championship with a team which included four West Indian Test cricketers – Rohan Kanhai, Alvin Kallicharran, Lance Gibbs and Deryck Murray – as well as Billy Ibadulla, who had played for Pakistan. Ironically their only difficulty came when they signed the England fast bowler Bob Willis. His former county Surrey objected to the transfer, and he was banned from playing before July.

Alec Bedser, England's chairman of selectors, blamed the ever-increasing number of overseas players for the lack of emerging home talent. He cited the case of Lancashire's Frank Hayes, of whom there were high hopes and who, because of

Lloyd, was not batting till number five. Others, such as Procter, argued that Lloyd's presence would help him: "Walking in to bat after the bowlers have been smashed around by Clive is surely an enjoyable prospect for a talented player like Hayes."

When the first three-year restriction was up, counties with only one overseas player acquired a second. For several years Hampshire had Barry Richards, probably the best batsman in the world, and Andy Roberts from Antigua, the best fast bowler, not to mention the West Indian opener Gordon Greenidge who was not classified as an overseas player as he had moved to England at the age of fourteen.

There were so many positives for county cricket. Spectators could watch such epic struggles as Barry Richards, with the championship at stake, taking on Northants' wily slow-left-armer Bishen Bedi – or Gloucestershire's elegant Zaheer Abbas scoring a double-century at Hove against his compatriot Imran Khan. There were human benefits, too, as the white South Africans played alongside black men for the first time.

Yet by 1978 Alec Bedser's reservations were widely shared, particularly as more of the overseas players were now fast bowlers who, because of their specialist role, limited opportunity for young English players more than the batsmen had.

So in March 1979 the counties set in motion a process by which in time they would all revert to one overseas player. By then the Australian tycoon Kerry Packer had revolutionised world cricket, bringing greater rewards for the top international players, and the next generation of stars was less inclined to return loyally year after year to an English county.

The heyday of the overseas player in English county cricket was over.

"Leicester's the place to go"

When Leicestershire won the championship in 1975, they became the first of only two counties – Nottinghamshire in 2005 the other – to do so without a home-grown player in their first-choice eleven.

Players who were born or grew up in the county			
Average number in each eleven in 1975			
Yorkshire	11.0		
Sussex	7.4	Warwickshire	4.3
Glamorgan	7.3	Nottinghamshire	3.8
Kent	7.3	Hampshire	3.7
Surrey	6.4	Gloucestershire	3.6
Lancashire	6.3	Somerset	3.3
Derbyshire	6.0	Worcestershire	2.0
Middlesex	5.4	Leicestershire	0.3
Essex	4.5	Northamptonshire	0.0

The county had spent most of its history among the also-rans of the championship, but their young Secretary Mike Turner had ambition and he was quick to realise how playing success and financial success could go hand in hand. He wanted a winning team and, to get that, he knew he had to attract experienced players.

In 1966 he brought Tony Lock, the former Surrey and England bowler, back from Australia and made him captain. The county prepared sandy spinners' pitches, and in his second and last summer Lock, galvanising the team with a fierce, un-Leicester-like passion, full of kissing and embracing, took them to second place.

Turner achieved a greater coup late in 1968. Ray Illingworth had fallen out with the Yorkshire chairman Brian Sellers over his contract and was on the move. Several counties wanted him – Lancashire, Nottinghamshire, Sussex and Northants – but he chose Leicestershire. Their offer was not the best financially, but it included the captaincy, which appealed to him, and he was impressed by Turner, as was his wife Shirley. "He made us both very welcome."

"Leicester's the place to go," the umpire Syd Buller told him. "You'll get a free hand there, and you can do something."

Illingworth's experience of captaincy up to this point consisted of a short spell at the age of 14 in charge of the Farsley Under-16s – "They banned me from playing because I was in the first team" – and four stand-in games for Yorkshire in 1963.

He was full of ideas, however, and he was soon making his mark at Leicester. He was greatly taken by the friendliness of the place – "In the pre-season the committee invited the players in for a drink and some food" – and he set out to make all the staff, not just the first-team players, feel part of things. "Any grievances, don't let them out of this room," he told them. "I want to look after you all."

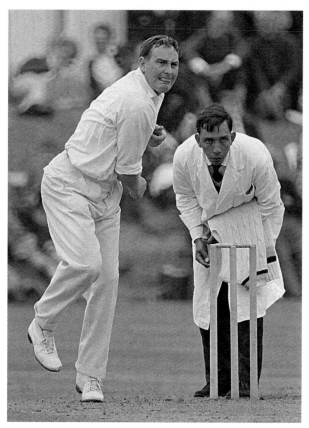

Ray Illingworth bowling, with umpire Peter Wight

Such was the immediate good impression he made that after less than four weeks of the championship season, when Colin Cowdrey tore an Achilles tendon, the selectors turned to Illingworth to lead England.

At Leicester he and Mike Turner made changes. A new groundsman Lol Spence was appointed, and he was instructed to prepare good cricket wickets, with pace and bounce, with the boundaries set back to bring the spinners into the game. Then gradually an old guard of players, jaded by long years on the circuit, were eased out in favour of younger men who were full of energy in the field and who responded to their captain's positive spirit. "Every game I played," Illingworth says, "I thought I could win it. I was hoping that would rub off on the team."

Success in one-day cricket was an important stepping stone. In 1972, in front of a full house at Lord's, they won the first Benson & Hedges Cup Final. The county had entered new territory, and Mike Turner was delighted. "Win a trophy and I can sell all the sponsorship by Christmas," he told his captain.

Membership was booming, there were new entrance gates, and the place looked good, fresh paint and flowers everywhere. "Never would I have believed Leicester would be like this," Jim Laker said when he arrived for a television commentary.

Turner continued to recruit players. For the summer of 1974, with Illingworth no longer required by England, the county's first eleven consisted of three exiled Yorkshiremen (Illingworth, Jack Birkenshaw and Chris Balderstone), an Australian (Graham McKenzie), a Rhodesian (Brian Davison), two brothers from Devon (Roger and Jeff Tolchard), John Steele from Staffordshire, Barry Dudleston from Cheshire, Norman McVicker who had been with Warwickshire, and Ken Higgs, the former England bowler whom Turner tracked down playing for Rishton in the Lancashire League.

There were no current Test cricketers, but they had a collective strength: plenty of batting and as many as eight bowlers, four of them spinners. Above all, they had a shrewd captain. "You always beat us," Worcestershire's Basil D'Oliveira told Illingworth one day, "and I'd only take two players from your side. The only difference is you." He jabbed his finger into Illingworth's chest, as was his wont. "You as captain."

It was a compliment which the Yorkshireman has treasured, along with the words of John Steele when they went out one day: "You know, it's nice to take the field knowing that other teams are frightened of us."

They won the Sunday League in 1974. Then in 1975, their annus mirabilis, they won the county championship, the Benson & Hedges Cup and the Under-25 Trophy; they were runners-up in the Second Eleven Championship, and they beat the touring Australians.

There was even the joy of a Sunday League match at Yeovil when, to his great satisfaction and not for the first time, Illingworth got the better of his Somerset counterpart, his old mate Brian Close. With two balls remaining, defeat seemed certain, but Allan Jones, never Close's favourite, bowled two half-volleys, both of which Norman McVicker hit down the ground for six. "Tell Brian cheerio," Illingworth said when Close failed to emerge from the Somerset dressing room.

How different the course of English cricket would have been if the two of them had stayed at Yorkshire. Illingworth would probably not have captained England, Close would not have inspired the young Ian Botham, and Leicestershire ... would they have won the championship?

A long day

Derbyshire v Leicestershire, Chesterfield, Monday 15 September 1975

The county championship season of 1975 ran deeper into September than ever, with the title still to be won on Monday the 15th. By this time the football clubs had played seven rounds of matches which, for Leicestershire's Chris Balderstone, a professional in both games, was a problem.

The previous summer, when his club Carlisle United were embarking on a first season in Division One, he had left cricket in mid-July. A gifted midfielder with great vision, he was in the side from the start, scoring in a 2-0 victory over Spurs that took them, after three matches, to the top of the table.

The glory did not last. After a spirited campaign Carlisle were relegated, and in July the 34-year-old Balderstone was transferred to Doncaster Rovers. Only this time, with Leicestershire challenging for the championship title, he was still playing cricket in the third week of September. Stan Anderson, the manager, was not amused.

On that Monday Leicestershire were playing Derbyshire at Chesterfield, finishing at 6.30. An hour later, thirty miles away, Doncaster were kicking off at home to Brentford. If the championship had been settled, Anderson asked, could he pick up Balderstone and drive him to the evening game?

Leicestershire had made a mess of their batting on Saturday and, even with full bowling points, had either to win at Chesterfield or to rely on Lancashire not winning with maximum points at Hove. Lancashire had bowled out Sussex for 160, and late in the morning news arrived that they were 100 for no wicket. It was a nervous time.

Leicestershire took a first innings lead of only 15, then lost early wickets. Balderstone went out to bat, his mind a whirl of thoughts: about the quick bowlers he faced, about the game at Hove and the one at Doncaster. After a while a loud cheer came from the dressing room; the championship was won.

Meanwhile Stan Anderson had arrived. According to the *Guardian*, 'he paced anxiously in front of the pavilion like an expectant father ... totally displeased as Balderstone played one glorious stroke after another.'

At the close Balderstone was on 51 not out, out of 108 for five. He had been on the field for all but eight minutes of a tense 6½-hour day, and he jumped straight into the manager's car, changing into his football kit on the high-speed journey. Doncaster drew 1-1, and in the morning Balderstone completed his century. He then took three wickets in 17 overs as Leicestershire ended their triumphant summer with victory.

1977: Schhh ... you know who

At the Oval in 1968, for the first time in a Test in England, an advertising board was displayed, an XS Insurance sign at the Vauxhall end. High in the pavilion MCC's Gubby Allen spotted it and was appalled. "What's that?" he demanded to know.

"That, Mister Allen," replied Bernie Coleman, a South London publican who had joined the Surrey committee, "is five hundred pounds, and we're broke."

At that point cricket's only significant sponsors were Gillette for the 60-over knock-out cup. It was a great success, capturing the public imagination, but for most of the counties it involved only one or two days of cricket in the summer, a bit of fun on the side.

The 40-over Sunday League arrived in 1969, sponsored by John Player, cigarette manufacturers banned since 1965 from advertising on television. They paid £65,000 a year to have the League bear their name, and at each match they set up a caravan, staffed by 'three attractive girls', that displayed their products. During the afternoon the girls would walk round the boundary, offering spectators free cigarettes.

Not only did the counties each receive £3,000, but the games attracted great crowds, the deciding match of 1970 at Old Trafford, between Lancashire and Yorkshire, playing to a full house of 33,000. They were a new audience, too, singing their hearts out as Lancashire hit their way to victory.

'Is cricket dead?' read the big, black headline in the *Sunday Times* that day. 'If it is dead,' responded one Manchester journalist, 'then round Lancashire they are making a "reet good do" of the funeral.'

Some, notably the Yorkshire captain Brian Close, thought cricket was ruining its traditional skills. Fast bowlers were hampered by restricted run-ups, spinners were marginalised, and an army of medium-pacers dominated, bowling not to take wickets but to stop run-scoring. Meanwhile batsmen, especially those in the middle order, were losing the art of building an innings. "Limited over cricket," Neville Cardus said. "It's like trying to play Beethoven on a banjo."

On the other hand the running between the wickets and the fielding developed a new dynamism – while some previously cautious batsmen discovered on Sundays that they had more shots than they realised. Two such were Glenn Turner of Worcestershire and Roy Virgin of Somerset, and in 1970 they became the two leading run-scorers in the county championship.

By 1972 there was a third one-day competition, played early in the summer. A second cigarette company, Benson &

Hedges, paid £80,000 a year to have their name on it. Their general manager, John Webb, explained the decision: "We are associating a brand of cigarette which has snob appeal with a sport that suits the image. Cricket may be played by an awful lot of people, but it remains a nice sport."

That summer also saw the start of a one-day competition, played over three matches, between England and the touring side. Prudential Assurance paid £30,000 for the naming rights, of which £26,000 went to the counties. In the West Country, Avon Tyres paid £3,000 to sponsor Somerset's match against the Australians, though only after the county agreed to switch the game from Taunton to Bath.

Sponsorship of cricket was suddenly all the rage. Esso put their name on a knock-out cup for schools, Haig on one for villages, Champagne Mercier on one for old boys' sides. There was a Watney Mann Groundsman of the Year, a Ladbrokes Man of the Match in championship games, and a Wrigley's Cricket Foundation for the young.

Television was a big selling point. With BBC providing daytime coverage of Tests, as well as a John Player match each Sunday afternoon, cricket was the number one sport on television, accounting for 20 per cent of the hours of sports broadcasting, ahead of horse racing (15½) and soccer (11½).

The county championship was not on television, and that made it less appealing to a sponsor. At the close of 1976 it had not attracted any interest, nor had the home Test matches. The task of selling them fell to Peter Lush, the sole full-time employee of the Test and County Cricket Board's Public Relations and Promotion Committee. Among those he approached were the soft drink manufacturers Schweppes. Not cigarettes or alcohol, they had a good, clean image for sport.

The chairman of Cadbury-Schweppes was Adrian Cadbury, a Cambridge rowing blue with no interest in cricket, and the managing director Basil Collins was an arts man. It was an unpromising start, but Schweppes had had a setback when their latest advertising campaign – replacing the famous "Schhh ... you know who" with "You can always tell a rotter by his total lack of Schweppes" – had been stymied by a distribution strike. So they did not reject outright the idea of sponsoring cricket. In any case, by their standards, it was not big money.

They passed the negotiations to Vernon East, their external consultant, himself a keen cricketer. He had to choose between £120,000 a year for the championship, £200,000 for the Tests or a discounted deal for the pair. By his own admission he got it "one hundred per cent wrong". He figured that the Tests, "the holy of holies", would never get called the Schweppes Tests, but the scores from the Schweppes Championship would be on the radio and in the papers every day. In fact, some newspapers, notably *The Times*, continued resolutely to call it the County Championship while the Cornhill Tests led to a massive increase in public awareness of the insurance company: from two to 17 per cent.

Vernon East visited each county to arrange the stocking of Schweppes products and the display of their banner. "Where can I put it?" he asked Wilf Wooller at Cardiff, and the reply was: "Where would you like it?" It was Glamorgan's only banner.

Early in the first summer of sponsorship the news broke that the Australian Kerry Packer was creating a rival World Series Cricket, with the TCCB proposing to ban the players who signed up for it. Vernon East recalls the panic at Schweppes: "We did wonder if it would kill off the county championship."

The crisis passed, and the Schweppes board were so delighted by the success of their venture into cricket that they immediately embarked on sponsorship of rugby. "Not football," the managing director insisted. "We don't want to be associated with hooligans."

Gillette withdrew from their cup at the end of 1980, worried that the public now associated them more with cricket than with razor blades. Such was now the appeal of sports sponsorship that the TCCB, increasing the price significantly, had three firm bids. Looking for the right image, and specifically not wanting another cigarette company, they opted for the NatWest Bank.

County cricket had come a long way in just a few years.

"The start of the Schweppes Championship"

Ford sponsors county cricket

County captains with the Ford motor cars at Lord's, 1970
Brian Langford (Som), Brian Close (Yorks), Jack Bond (Lancs),
Roy Marshall (Hants), Tony Brown (Glos), Don Bennett
(Middx coach), Brian Taylor (Essex), Ian Buxton (Derbys)

In 1970 the Ford motor company donated 21 Capris, worth £25,000, to county cricket. There was one for each of the 17 counties to raffle, Surrey raising £5,000 from theirs. There was one for each of the fastest centuries in the three competitions, and one for the first bowler to take 100 wickets in all matches.

At each ground a board listed the front-runners. On the morning of Thursday 13 August Glamorgan's off-spinner Don Shepherd reached 98 wickets, alongside Peter Lever, the Lancashire paceman who was playing for England at the Oval. Neither was in the field again that day, leaving Tony Buss of Sussex with a chance at Blackpool. He needed five wickets for cricket's greatest prize, worth far more than his £750 salary.

Ball after ball, over after over, Buss ran in 14 paces to bowl. The Lancashire openers put on 265 before he took his first wicket but, after that, they came: 96, 97, 98, 99. There was a rumour that Jack Bond, thinking of his team-mate Lever, was going to declare. But he came out to bat and, caught in the gully, was victim number 100, stopping to join in the congratulations.

In all, Buss bowled 42 overs, by far the longest stint of his career. The *Guardian* reckoned they should have driven his new car out to the pitch and given him a lift back to the pavilion. 'It certainly looked as if he could have done with it.'

1979: Essex – triumph born out of adversity

Brian 'Tonker' Taylor was a surprise choice to succeed Trevor Bailey as Essex captain in 1967. Indeed, so upset by the decision was Barry Knight, their England all-rounder, that he left Essex, spending a year in the Leicestershire second eleven while he qualified for his new county.

The 35-year-old Tonker, always spick and span, always ready to keep wicket whatever the knocks and niggles, was no master tactician, no genius of subtle man-management but, born in West Ham, he was Essex through and through – and his special brand of gruff, sergeant-major-style discipline proved perfect for the situation in which Essex cricket found itself.

No county since the war has come as close to going out of business. They had no ground to call their own, and at one stage their playing staff was down to twelve, the wages paid in the worst times by two well-to-do committeemen. Doug Insole's father Jack, a retired local government worker, supervised a scheme where spectators gave the club their Green Shield stamps, and at its peak the income from that covered the cost of more than one player. Tonker, as captain, spent his winters speaking to cricket clubs throughout the county, even undertaking a door-to-door membership drive.

Yet out of that adversity there emerged a team with as good a spirit as any county cricket has known. Tonker kept them in order as best he could but, beneath the loud bark, he was a kind man and he never crushed their youthful exuberance.

Ray East, the slow-left-armer from Suffolk, was one who pushed the limits. When Tonker imposed a curfew at their Bournemouth hotel, it was inevitable that the man out after hours would be East, whom he caught halfway up a drainpipe.

"Raymond, get your blazer on. I want a word with you outside," he would say in the dressing room, and the other nine would sit there, hearing every word of the bollocking.

East was a competitive cricketer, who would relieve the tension with clowning, so much so that Tonker took to suspecting tomfoolery even when it did not exist. There was an afternoon when East toiled for over after over, failing to get any response from the pitch, then suddenly got one to turn and lift viciously. The ball flew for four byes past Tonker, who glowered: "You did that on purpose to make me look stupid."

The young Keith Pont was another with a natural wit. In one of his first games he found himself fielding at third man at both ends, Tonker waving his hands at him in semaphore. His response at the conclusion of one over was to commandeer a child's bicycle and ride it to the other end.

"That bunch of madmen will never win anything," was Leicestershire captain Ray Illingworth's verdict on them.

Yet that was a shallow judgement. "We didn't take ourselves too seriously," Cambridge-educated off-spinner David Acfield says, "but we took the game seriously." And Tonker played a crucial part in their flowering, as East himself acknowledges. "In later life I've come to realise what he did for us."

The arrival of the Sunday League in 1969 helped. "We may not be able to bat and bowl like them," Tonker would say, "but we can field." They cottoned on early to the format, and in the first four years they were always in the top four, missing the title in 1971 by 0.003 of a run. In the view of John Lever, their left-arm swing bowler, "One-day cricket taught us how to win."

The Sunday games were popular in Essex, bringing great crowds, and in Keith Boyce they had the best all-round cricketer in the competition. Out in Barbados Trevor Bailey and Kent's Secretary Les Ames had tossed a coin for first pick of Boyce and John Shepherd, the island's two most promising young cricketers, and Ames had taken Shepherd. He did well for Kent, but no one in Essex ever regretted Ames' choice.

Essex acquired the ground at Chelmsford and, with help from the Warwickshire Supporters' Association, rich from its football pool scheme, they built a new pavilion. They stuck to a policy of equal pay for all the playing staff, with bonuses for long service, an arrangement that would only be ended when they recruited the Australian Allan Border in 1986. And they showed patience with the young ones, backing them to become good cricketers. "The committee are one hundred per cent behind you," Doug Insole told them. "But if you win by nicking the ball and not walking, then we'd rather you lost."

In 1974 the team took three crucial steps forward. Keith Fletcher became captain, the South African Kenny McEwan arrived, and a youngster from Leytonstone, Graham Gooch, established himself in the side.

"Fletch was tactically astute," Gooch says. "He knew the game inside out. And he had an incessant drive to win, which is important in county cricket because you're on a treadmill. Some county sides, they were happy for it to rain. But we weren't. 'You can't win points in the dressing room,' Fletch said. He never let things drift."

McEwan, from a farming family in the Eastern Cape, came across from Sussex where they had overseas players ahead of him, and he took to his new county immediately. "At pre-season practice we had to put up the nets ourselves and, if

somebody was moving some chairs, we had to go and help them. It was a lovely atmosphere. Every day I had a good laugh. I felt very at home."

He stayed for 12 summers, with no Test cricket to draw him away, and he hit 51 championship hundreds. "He was the cleanest striker of a ball I saw at that time," Lever says, "and he really bought into our team ethic."

The young Gooch played for England in his second summer, but there was no chance at Essex that he would become a prima donna, not that that was in his character. "He could score 300 in a Test," Acfield says, "and he'd still be back with us next day in the nets, wanting to get a hundred."

The team grew in confidence, but no trophies were won: second in the Sunday League in '76 and '77, knocked out with scores level in the Gillette semi-final in '78, when they were also runners-up in the championship. "The charm of watching you," spectators told them, "is that we know you won't win in the end."

Yet in 1979 they did win – for the first time in their history. They won the Benson & Hedges Cup at Lord's, and they won the championship by a margin of 77 points.

It helped that they had recruited Mike Denness, the former Kent and England captain, a man accustomed to winning trophies. On the first day of pre-season practice he arrived, smartly dressed, in the dressing room, only to be greeted by Keith Pont: "Excuse me, the caterers are round the back."

"He could not believe how wonderful the humour was," Acfield says. "But on the field he kept us on our toes. 'Keep working,' he used to shout." When they had a wobble in the final at Lord's, wondering if once more they were going to throw it away, Denness was calmness personified. "It's in the bag," he said, and his words spread around the field, dispelling their ingrained pessimism. At last they were winners.

Their one great sadness was that Keith Boyce, forced by a knee injury to retire in 1977, was no longer with them.

John Lever was at the heart of their championship success. In five matches in June he took 48 wickets. Then it was the turn of East and Acfield. So far that summer, Acfield says, it was not so much OB and SLA for off-breaks and slow-left-arm but LRB and SBS for 'last resort bowler' and 'seamers' ball shiner'. Yet on a wearing track at Southend they bowled Essex to a crucial victory over Notts. At Northampton, where they clinched the title, the match-winners were Stuart Turner, with ten wickets, and Brian Hardie, with a century. They all contributed.

The team stayed true to its values, a happy family with no great egos, and with that spirit the next eight years brought them a further three championships and five one-day trophies.

'The basic philosophy of the club has not changed,' wrote Doug Insole at the end of 1979, 'and the committee are determined that it will not do so. Cricket is for enjoyment and for entertainment. It must be profitable; it must be business-like; but most of all it must be cricket.'

1980 – 1989

Pitches covered during rain

Three titles each for Essex and Middlesex

Some four-day matches

There have been many times when the future of county cricket has looked bleaker than it does now. Give us a few more dry summers, by some miracle a few more leg-spinners and an assurance that the championship will remain the premier competition, and the game of county cricket, though it may change, will remain in essence, like a good book, 'the best of friends, the same today and for ever'.

Christopher Martin-Jenkins, 1981

The county championship died a death a long time ago, and an alternative should be sought immediately before more county members are driven away by rising subscriptions made necessary by poorly attended championship matches.

A letter to The Cricketer, 1987

A lot of work has been put in by our marketing department at the Oval in organising various sponsorships. You will see Surrey players this year displaying the British Airways Poundstretcher on their shirts, sweaters and track suits, and the Mazda Company has supplied us with cars. We are delighted that Nescafé have continued their sponsorship of our youth development, which also involves Poundstretcher sponsorship in the form of a youth tour to Australia. In addition Alfred Marks have again provided player-incentive sponsorship in the Britannic Assurance Championship, and George Brittain are this year's sponsors of the Player of the Month awards.

Surrey newsletter, 1985

1980 Barry Wood, leaving Lancashire immediately after receiving a benefit cheque for £62,429, is banned by the TCCB from playing for Derbyshire till July 30. Threatened with legal action, the TCCB brings the date forward to June 4. On the final day of the Centenary Test at Lord's John Arlott completes his last radio commentary.

The United States, protesting against the Soviet Union's invasion of Afghanistan, boycott the Olympic Games in Moscow. In their absence there are gold medals for several Britons, among them Daley Thompson in the Decathlon, Alan Wells in the 100 metres, Steve Ovett in the 800 metres and Sebastian Coe in the 1500 metres.

1981 Pitches are covered whenever there is rain. The 200-over limit on the two first innings, introduced in 1974, is discontinued. The number of points for a win is raised from 12 to 16.

The Lambert & Butler Cup, a seven-a-side, ten-over tournament, is played over two days in September at various floodlit football grounds. The final, at Stamford Bridge, is won by Lancashire, but the idea is not repeated.

Susan Brown, cox of the winning Oxford boat, becomes the first woman to compete in the University Boat Race.

1982 Counties can play only two overseas cricketers if both have been registered before November 1978. Otherwise there is a limit of one. Four South African-born players, ruled to be eligible for England, are exempted from this: Brian Davison (Leics), Allan Lamb (Northants), Mike Procter (Glos) and Chris Smith (Hants).

Thirty years after his death, the Olympic Committee restores the two gold medals won in 1912 by Jim Thorpe, a part-native American. He had been stripped of them when it was discovered that he had previously played semi-professional baseball.

1983 The championship programme, reduced from 24 to 20 matches in 1972 and increased to 22 in 1977, returns to 24 matches. The purpose of the change is to allow England's Test cricketers to play more often for their counties. With over-rates continuing to fall, from 19.45 an hour in 1978 to 18.62 in 1981, fines are increased.

The Derby winner Shergar is kidnapped by the IRA and never seen again.

1984 Britannic Assurance take over sponsorship of the championship from Cadbury-Schweppes.
Weather permitting, counties are obliged to bowl a minimum of 117 overs in a 6½-hour day.
South African-born Allan Lamb joins his compatriot Chris Smith in the England Test team.

After a campaign by the Daily Mail, British citizenship is fast-tracked for the South African runner Zola Budd. In the 3000-metre final in the Olympic Games in Los Angeles, she is involved in two collisions and finishes seventh.

1985 Prize money, which has risen every year since 1977, is now paid to each of the top five teams, with the champions getting £22,000. There is also prize money for the county of the month, the player of the month and the player of the season. Philip DeFreitas of Leicestershire wins £250 as the first player of the season.

English football clubs are banned from European competitions after Liverpool supporters cause 39 deaths in the Heysel stadium in Belgium. Three weeks earlier, a fire at Bradford City's Valley Parade stadium kills 56 people.
Seventeen-year-old Boris Becker becomes the youngest men's champion in Wimbledon history.

1986 The minimum number of overs to be bowled in a 6½-hour day falls: 117 in 1984, 112 in 1985, now 110. Ian Botham admits to using cannabis and is banned from playing cricket in June and July. At the end of the summer he leaves Somerset in protest against the county's decision to release Viv Richards and Joel Garner.

In football's World Cup in Mexico, Argentina's Diego Maradona scores with his hand as England are knocked out.

1987 For one year only the county game returns to leaving pitches open during rain if play has not been called off for the day.
For the first time in the competition's 60-year history the United States lose golf's Ryder Cup on home soil.

1988 The championship programme is reduced from 24 to 22 matches, with each county playing six four-day matches.
In the Olympic Games at Seoul, Canadian Ben Jonson is stripped of his 100-metres gold medal after failing a drug test.

1989 Essex and Nottinghamshire are each deducted 25 points for producing poor pitches, at Southend and Trent Bridge respectively. The penalty against Essex robs them of first place in the championship.
Ninety-six Liverpool football supporters are crushed to death at the FA Cup semi-final at Hillsborough in Sheffield.

Championship – top three						Leading batsmen		Leading bowlers		Leading wkt-keeper Leading fielder	Victims
	P	W	L	D	Pts		Runs		Wickets		

1980

Middlesex	22	10	2	10	258	P.N. Kirsten (Derbys)	1,891	R.D. Jackman (Surrey)	114	C.J. Richards (Surrey)	60
Surrey	22	10	4	8	245	G.M. Turner (Worcs)	1,755	D.R. Doshi (Warwks)	87		
Notts	22	6	5	11	178	A.J. Lamb (Northants)	1,720	V.A.P. van der Bijl (Middx)	85	Sadiq Mohammad (Glos)	27

1981

Notts	22	11	4	7	304	Zaheer Abbas (Glos)	2,230	R.J. Hadlee (Notts)	105	I.J. Gould (Sussex)	61
Sussex	22	11	3	8	302	Javed Miandad (Glam)	2,060	J. Garner (Som)	87	G.R.J. Roope (Surrey)	34
Somerset	22	10	2	10	279	G.M. Turner (Worcs)	2,043	E.E. Hemmings (Notts)	84	*(plus 8 ct + 1 st while keeping)*	

1982

Middlesex	22	12	2	8	325	A.I. Kallicharran (Warwks)	2,118	M.D. Marshall (Hants)	134	R.J. Parks (Hants)	69
Leicestershire	22	10	4	8	286	P.N. Kirsten (Derbys)	1,941	S.T. Clarke (Surrey)	85	J.W. Lloyds (Som)	28
Hampshire	22	8	6	8	250	J.G. Wright (Derbys)	1,830	N.G.B. Cook (Leics)	80	J.F. Steele (Leics)	28

1983

Essex	24	11	5	8	324	K.S. McEwan (Essex)	2,051	D.L. Underwood (Kent)	105	D.E. East (Essex)	65
Middlesex	24	11	4	9	308	G. Boycott (Yorks)	1,941	N. Gifford (Warwks)	99		
Hampshire	24	10	2	12	289	C.L. Smith (Hants)	1,831	J.K. Lever (Essex)	98	G.A. Gooch (Essex)	33

1984

Essex	24	13	3	8	355	G.A. Gooch (Essex)	2,281	R.J. Hadlee (Notts)	117	D.E. East (Essex)	74
Notts	24	12	3	9	341	D.L. Amiss (Warwks)	2,137	J.K. Lever (Essex)	106		
Middlesex	24	8	7	9	269	A.I. Kallicharran (Warwks)	2,012	E.E. Hemmings (Notts)	86	J.F. Steele (Leics)	31

1985

Middlesex	24	8	4	12	274	D.W. Randall (Notts)	1,977	N.V. Radford (Worcs)	100	G.W. Humpage (Wwks)	73
Hampshire	24	7	2	15	256	I.V.A. Richards (Som)	1,836	M.D. Marshall (Hants)	95		
Gloucestershire	24	7	3	14	241	C.L. Smith (Hants)	1,720	C.A. Walsh (Glos)	82	M.A. Lynch (Surrey)	36

1986

Essex	24	10	6	8	287	G.A. Hick (Worcs)	1,934	C.A. Walsh (Glos)	118	D.E. East (Essex)	80
Gloucestershire	24	9	3	12	259	C.G. Greenidge (Hants)	1,916	N.A. Foster (Essex)	100		
Surrey	24	8	6	10	248	J.E. Morris (Derbys)	1,654	M.D. Marshall (Hants)	100	M.A. Lynch (Surrey)	38

1987

Notts	24	9	1	14	292	G.A. Hick (Worcs)	1,868	N.V. Radford (Worcs)	109	B.J.M. Maher (Derbys)	74
Lancashire	24	10	4	10	288	G. Fowler (Lancs)	1,689	J.P. Agnew (Leics)	99		
Leicestershire	24	8	3	13	260	M.D. Crowe (Som)	1,627	R.J. Hadlee (Notts)	97	M.P. Maynard (Glam)	29

1988

Worcestershire	22	10	3	9	290	G.A. Hick (Worcs)	2,443	F.D. Stephenson (Notts)	121	S.J. Rhodes (Worcs)	77
Kent	22	10	5	7	289	G.A. Gooch (Essex)	1,631	K.E. Cooper (Notts)	99		
Essex	22	9	5	8	282	P.D. Bowler (Derbys)	1,563	J.P. Agnew (Leics)	88	C.S. Cowdrey (Kent)	31

1989

Worcestershire	22	12	3	7	319	S.J. Cook (Som)	2,173	F.D. Stephenson (Notts)	91	W.K. Hegg (Lancs)	76
Essex	22	13	2	7	313	A.J. Stewart (Surrey)	1,633	D.R. Pringle (Essex)	89		
Middlesex	22	9	2	11	266	A.P. Wells (Sussex)	1,629	S.L. Watkin (Glam)	89	G.A. Hick (Worcs)	41

1980-1989

Leading counties

	P	W	L	D	%W
Essex	230	82	39	109	35.7
Middlesex	230	80	44	106	34.8
Nottinghamshire	230	73	48	109	31.7
Surrey	230	67	52	111	29.1

Leading batsmen

W. Larkins (Northants)	13,622
G.D. Mendis (Sx/Lancs)	13,221
G.A. Gooch (Essex)	12,833
D.L. Amiss (Warwicks)	12,480

Leading bowlers

E.E. Hemmings (Notts)	648
M.D. Marshall (Hants)	630
J.K. Lever (Essex)	629
V.J. Marks (Som)	593

Leading keepers & fielder

R.J. Parks (Hants)	589
D.E. East (Essex)	488
C.S. Cowdrey (Kent)	223

Overall statistics

Runs per wicket	30.5
Runs per 100 balls	51.1
% of matches drawn	52.6

Miscellany

At Chelmsford in May 1983 Surrey, having bowled out Essex for 287, went out to bat on the second evening. The air was humid, the ball swung prodigiously and in 14.3 overs they were all out for 14, the lowest score in county cricket since 1907.

Next day, with the ball no longer swinging, Surrey captain Roger Knight hit a century, and the game was drawn. A week later Knight received a letter from a prep school headmaster. His team had recently been bowled out for totals of 23, 20 and 10; he wondered whether Surrey would like a fixture.

*

Against Yorkshire at Trent Bridge in 1988 Franklyn Stephenson, the Barbadian fast bowler, ended his Nottinghamshire season in a blaze of glory, taking 11 wickets and scoring 111 and 117.

It was one of only five occasions when a player has scored 200 runs and taken ten wickets in the same championship match. The other four – Bernard Bosanquet (Middlesex, 1905), George Hirst (Yorkshire, 1906), Ted Arnold (Worcestershire, 1909) and Johnny Douglas (Essex, 1921) – all finished on the winning side. Stephenson's efforts, however, were in vain, with Nottinghamshire losing by 127 runs.

"If only I could bat all the time," Gloucestershire's Zaheer Abbas would sometimes say, and there were games when he came close to doing just that. Only eight times in the history of the championship has a batsman hit unbeaten scores of 200 and 100 in the same match, and four of them have been by Zaheer, all in three-day games. On the final occasion, at Bath in 1981, he scored 215* and 150* at the start of a run spree that brought him seven centuries in five matches.

*

At Colchester in September 1981, chasing 325 for victory, Glamorgan were all out for 311, of which Javed Miandad hit an unbeaten 200. His eighth-wicket partner was Robin Hobbs, who was playing in his last first-class match – against his old county Essex. Together they added a vital 43 runs in 12 overs.

Hobbs' contribution was a duck, out to the first ball he had faced for six overs.

*

In September 1986 Gloucestershire keeper Jack Russell travelled directly to the Oval from his brother's funeral near Stroud. Determined to cope with his grief by immersing himself in his cricket, he hit 71 runs, his then highest score, and became only the second man in cricket history, after George Dawkes of Derbyshire, to hold a hat-trick of catches.

The championship in the 1980s

The structure of county cricket in 1989 was much the same as it had been in 1980: 17 teams, a 22-match championship and three one-day competitions. Yet, beneath this surface, there was much that was not the same.

Overseas players had brought fresh life to county cricket in the 1970s, but by 1980 their heyday was drawing to a close. The Test and County Cricket Board, concerned that they had become too dominant, were planning to reduce from two to one the number allowed in a county side, while the top players themselves, now earning much greater sums in the aftermath of Kerry Packer's World Series Cricket, were less inclined to return summer after summer to the demanding county schedule. The great days of Clive Lloyd and Mike Procter, of Garry Sobers and Asif Iqbal, were almost over.

In 1980 there were 20 overseas players whose loyalty to a single county would extend to more than 150 first-class appearances. In 1989 there were only three: Malcolm Marshall, the last survivor from 1980, at Hampshire; Courtney Walsh at Gloucestershire; and Graeme Hick, soon to become an England player, at Worcestershire.

A more profound change came when, after the wet summer of 1980, it was decided to cover pitches whenever it rained, not just when play was called off for the day. This brought county cricket into line with Test matches; it also reduced the hours of frustration, often in sunshine, which spectators had to endure.

Many traditionalists opposed the move. 'Since time began,' EW Swanton wrote in *The Cricketer*, 'variety in many forms has been the very essence and spice of English cricket, and much of the variety has derived from the ever-changing nature and behaviour of the pitch.'

The greatest concern, at a time when the West Indians were demonstrating the power of non-stop fast bowling, was the further decline that pitch-covering would cause to the art of spin bowling, an art that was already being undermined by the growth of one-day cricket.

Micky Stewart retired as a Surrey player in 1972 and, when he returned as their manager in 1979, he was shocked by the extent of the change in those years: "There were fewer spin bowlers about, and many captains didn't seem to have the same understanding of spin, the situations and conditions in which you would use it. And among the batsmen there didn't seem to be the same awareness of how to play when the ball spun. Some of it had come from playing more one-day cricket. Someone would be facing a left-arm spinner pitching middle-and-leg or middle stump, and he would try to hit it over mid-wicket. The ball would go straight up in the air, and he'd come in, saying, 'What happened there then?' The change was so marked, just in those six or seven years, and every year since it seems to have got worse."

The change to covered pitches was accompanied by an appeal to groundsman to 'prepare dry pitches, more readily responsive to spin'. Yet, whereas in 1980 there were nine spinners in the twenty leading wicket-takers in the championship, there were none in 1989.

Even Gloucestershire, with its long tradition of spinners, created a fast wicket at Bristol and, in 1985, recruited Courtney Walsh and Kevin Curran to join Syd Lawrence in a three-strong pace attack that *Wisden* called 'one of the most feared in the competition'. It took them from 17th to third place in the table, but unfortunately they bowled their overs at little more than 17 an hour, one-and-a-half below the required minimum. Consequently the county received a record fine of £8,000, £5,000 more than their prize money for finishing third.

A run of poor results by England, culminating in a 5-0 defeat by the West Indies in 1984, led to the establishment of yet another committee of enquiry into the state of English cricket, this one chaired by Charles Palmer, Chairman of the TCCB. They proposed that eight of the 24 matches in the championship be of four-day duration and that there be a return to uncovered pitches, for the three-day games at least.

A mix of three-day and four-day matches was agreed for 1988, but the return to the previous arrangement on pitch-covering lasted only for the summer of 1987. Instead, the focus turned to the penalising of sub-standard pitches. In 1989, for the first time in the history of the championship, penalty points were introduced. A county with a pitch deemed sub-standard would be deducted a draconian 25 points.

There had been mutterings of discontent around the circuit when in 1981 Nottinghamshire changed the character of their Trent Bridge pitches to suit the seam bowling of their overseas stars, Richard Hadlee and Clive Rice, especially when they won the championship on the back of their victories in home games. So perhaps there was a poetic justice to their being one of two counties to suffer the 25-point penalty in the first season, though the pitch in question was nothing more than a good old-fashioned cock-up, the result of a disastrously misjudged attempt to keep the adjoining strip dry for the preceding Test match.

More controversially Essex found themselves docked 25 points for poor pitches for their two matches at Southend, a council ground over which they had no control. The penalty cost them the championship, and it did not ease their outrage that the beneficiaries, Worcestershire, came close to a similar deduction but escaped, it was said, because they had asked for help from Harry Brind, the TCCB's Inspector of Pitches.

Essex and Middlesex were the two teams of the decade, each winning three championships and four one-day competitions. At Middlesex the captaincy passed from Mike Brearley to Mike Gatting, at Essex from Keith Fletcher to Graham Gooch, and in both cases the success continued.

Nottinghamshire won two championships, in 1981 and 1987. In both years the New Zealander Richard Hadlee was pivotal to their success. Initially an out-and-out fast bowler, he adapted to the demands of the county game by reducing his pace and run-up and concentrating on accuracy and subtle variation. The ultimate professional, never lowering his standards, he topped the championship bowling averages six times in seven years, and in 1984, in championship games alone, he did the double of 1,000 runs and 100 wickets, the only man to achieve this since the shortening of the programme in 1969.

His successor in 1988, the Barbadian fast-bowling all-rounder Franklyn Stephenson, had big boots to fill. He had not played Test cricket and had been a failure in his time with Gloucestershire, but he astonished everybody by also doing the double, though not exclusively in championship matches. His greatest weapon was a disguised slow ball, his greatest attribute a big heart. Despite missing two matches with a broken nose, he bowled more overs than anybody in the country except the Somerset off-spinner Vic Marks.

Other counties found the going tougher. In a decade which saw urban riots and a bitter, year-long miners' strike, the world of county cricket was not immune from its own outbreaks of polarising anger.

In 1983, for the first and only time in its proud history, Yorkshire finished in last place in the championship, with just one victory, and the committee's response to this was to dispense with the services of their leading batsman, the 42-year-old Geoffrey Boycott.

For some years, frustrated by the county's fall from glory, a Reform Group had been agitating, and now it sprang into action, demanding a special meeting which, amid a frenzy of plotting and intrigue, reinstated Boycott and rejected – by 3,609 votes to 3,578 – a motion of confidence in the committee. In the subsequent election some of Yorkshire

cricket's greatest names lost their seats, Fred Trueman – as he so delightfully put it – to 'some bloke with a deaf aid from Keighley'. In the midst of the mayhem Boycott emerged as the first professional cricketer to sit on his county's committee while still playing. Performances on the pitch, however, did not fulfil the hopes of the reformers; the strife continued, and Yorkshire ended the decade one place off the bottom.

"Only Yorkshire could create such bitterness and cause such self-destruction," was the response of Somerset's Vic Marks. Yet within three years Marks found himself in a packed marquee on the Bath and West Showground near Shepton Mallet, among angry supporters demanding the reinstatement of the West Indians Viv Richards and Joel Garner, whose forced departures had led to the resignation of Ian Botham.

Richards and Botham were the era's two greatest entertainers, bringing the county five one-day trophies in five years, the first in its history. Yet somehow the hoopla of their celebrity had created faultlines in the team, and the captain, Peter Roebuck, an intellectual with left-of-centre political sympathies, defied public opinion by putting team harmony before box-office glamour. Though Garner spoke movingly in the marquee, the committee won the day.

The disputes at Yorkshire and Somerset were not good for cricket, but they did at least prove that there were many in the land who remained passionate about the county game.

Ian Botham, Viv Richards and Joel Garner
Leaving the field together for the last time

Some players of the 1980s

'Deadly'
Four times leading wicket-taker

Derek Underwood of Kent

> He was a truly exceptional bowler. He bowled long spells with an action that was full of energy and effort, and he never seemed to fail, never got the nerves. He wasn't as demonstrative as some, no cursing or swearing, but inwardly he was fiercely competitive.
>
> *John Barclay*

It was said that Derek Underwood had 'the face of a choirboy, the demeanour of a civil servant and the ruthlessness of a rat-catcher'. He was certainly an innocent-looking 17-year-old when he joined the Kent team in 1963, the youngest bowler to take 100 wickets in his debut season, and he still had that deceptive look of innocence as he loped in to bowl in the late 1980s. By then he was in his 40s and the pitches were covered, but there were still days when he was unplayable, none more so than at Folkestone in 1986 when in 35.5 overs, with never a loose ball, he took seven Warwickshire wickets, Kallicharran and Amiss among them, for just 11 runs. He was not known as 'Deadly' without reason.

For a left-arm finger-spinner he was quick through the air, medium-pace even, and he knew how to adapt his flight to different pitches and batsmen. An integral part of the success of Kent in the 1970s, he was blessed with the best of keepers, Alan Knott, who, he says, "seemed to know what I was going to bowl before I did".

At all times he set himself high standards, enjoying the challenge of bowling on a flat pitch as much as the seven-wicket hauls on helpful ones. "I like your bowling," Zaheer Abbas, a supreme player of spin, once told him. "You make me concentrate."

He would have gone into his father's airgun-pellet business if he had not made it in cricket but, with his natural ability and his supreme professionalism, there was never a chance of that.

Malcolm Marshall of Hampshire

> I shall always remember the incessant chatter. If much of Malcolm characterised the calypso cricketer, much, too, epitomised the model professional.   *Mark Nicholas*
>
> He was a top performer – and a top bloke as well.   *David Lloyd*

'Maca'
134 championship wickets in 1982

Among the overseas cricketers who joined county cricket after the first wave of specially registered recruits, none gave greater value than the Barbadian Malcolm Marshall. A slightly built 21-year-old when he arrived in Southampton in the spring of 1979, he treated the county game as an opportunity to improve himself and, even at the peak of his powers, he gave his all to it, playing for Hampshire till 1993 and returning later as coach.

He was not tall and he did not have a long run-up, but for a time he was considered the fastest bowler in the world – and, with his open-chested delivery, he could move the ball late both ways. Furthermore, benefiting from a dedication to personal fitness and always wanting the ball in his hand, he could sustain his pace through long spells. The shrewdest of cricketers, with a great arsenal of deliveries, he soon knew the weaknesses of all the batsmen.

His work-rate was extraordinary. In all competitions in 1982, three-day and one-day, he bowled 1,008 overs, the hardest-worked bowler in the country, and he took 160 wickets. He also scored 891 runs, including his first Hampshire century – against a Lancashire side led by his West Indian captain Clive Lloyd, whom he dismissed in both innings. He loved his battles with Lloyd and with Viv Richards. But then he loved all his cricket. For all the menace of his run-up, his uncoiling delivery and his lethal bouncer, he played the game with a smile.

1980s

Derek Randall of Nottinghamshire

> I could always go for a record: Standing on One Leg. Give me something to do.
> *Derek Randall on Desert Island Discs, explaining his choice of the Guinness Book of Records*

'Rags'
Leading run-scorer in 1985

Derek Randall started out at Trent Bridge as Garry Sobers' favourite twelfth man, quicker to the betting shop than any of the others. They called him 'Arkle' because of his speed.

At the crease he was full of nervous mannerisms: tugging at his cap, fidgeting incessantly, talking to himself: "Come on, Rags, concentrate." He was the worst of starters, bagging eight pairs, two inside a week. But in full flow, with shots all round the wicket, there were few better sights in the county game.

He was a brilliant cover fielder, a non-stop ball of energy, with little moments of clowning to amuse the crowd. He never forget how lucky he was to be on a cricket field, not sitting all day in a draughtsman's office. Even in his late 50s he was giving his all in good club cricket, spreading his infectious joy.

For all his nervous clowning he could be meticulous in his preparations. One snowy January a visitor to his house was taken aback to find him wearing a pair of pads. "I'm breaking them in for the summer," he explained. Then they went into the front room and there was Mrs Randall in a second pair.

He was the most popular of players, with the public and with his fellow cricketers.

Graeme Hick of Worcestershire

Prolific from an early age
Leading scorer in '86, '87, '88

> Discipline is at the core of his game. Unlike lesser batsmen he never gives his wicket away, whatever his score. Watching him, you cannot tell if he is on 10 or 210. He simply carries on. It is this that frightens bowlers.
> *Peter Roebuck*

Graeme Hick arrived from Harare as a quiet, polite 17-year-old, with no trace of arrogance. He loved cricket, he loved batting and for seven summers, while he qualified for England, he broke records galore: the youngest to score 2,000 runs in a season, the youngest to hit 50 centuries.

They were golden years for Hick and for the county, whose two championships owed much to his runs: not just their volume but the unselfish speed at which he scored them. He was the best of team men, unbothered by records, and he also bowled useful off-spin and held brilliant catches in the slips.

Despite his chequered Test career, he was a towering figure in county cricket for 24 years. Only Jack Hobbs scored more centuries for one team than Hick's 140 in all formats for Worcestershire. He loved the county, so much so that he left in tears when the farewell tributes began. For all the glory of his career and the joy he had given, he had not changed. There was still no trace of arrogance.

Vintcent van der Bijl of Middlesex

> Middlesex, as a London team, had a rough edge to its humour, which could be mean. And Vintcent modified that. "I'm sorry," he'd say after we'd played badly. "I bowled two half-volleys in the first over, that set us off on the wrong foot." No one else would have said that. *Mike Brearley*

One-season wonder
85 wickets at 14.72, 49 bowled or lbw

He was a 32-year-old South African, 6'7½" tall and balding, and he had the summer of his life. A medium-quick, away-swing bowler with a long, curving run, a high arm and exceptional accuracy, he was the leading all-time wicket-taker in the Currie Cup, but his year with Middlesex in 1980 was his only serious cricket overseas. A former history teacher, whose father had played for South Africa, he was working for paper merchants who gave him the six months off. So he came with his wife and two daughters, was given a rent-free apartment in the City, saw the sights and took wickets relentlessly.

He loved the Middlesex team: from the fun-loving Barbadian Wayne Daniel to the compassionate, yet tough Mike Brearley. And they loved him: his modesty, his kindness, his effervescent optimism. With him they won both the championship and the Gillette Cup, but work prevented a second year. He returned to Natal an even better bowler, taking 54 wickets in the season at an extraordinary 9.50.

No one has played a single summer of championship cricket with greater impact.

Stories of the 1980s

A ground to remember

Sussex v Kent, Hastings, Monday 2 July 1984

For half a century, from 1924 to 1973, Sussex played neighbours Kent each year at the Central Ground in Hastings. The fixture saw its share of great batting – from Duleep's cultured 246 in 1929 to the imperious 203 scored by Ted Dexter in his first innings back from retirement in 1968 – but no cricketer enjoyed the fixture more than Derek Underwood, the Kent slow-left-arm bowler.

In 1964, only 19 years old, he set a ground record by taking nine wickets for 28 runs. Three years later he took 14 wickets in an innings victory; then in 1973, on a drying pitch, he was near to unplayable as he bowled out Sussex for 54 with figures of eight for 9. "I just kept getting wickets whenever I went there," he says, slightly bemused.

The next year Sussex switched the fixture to Hove, but they returned to Hastings in 1984, by which time Underwood was a 39-year-old veteran whose contribution on the first day, when 21 wickets fell, was two overs for 14 runs.

The next day his eight overs in the Sunday League game set another ground record with six wickets for 12 runs. Then on Monday morning, nightwatchman from Saturday, he walked out to bat. It was his 618th innings in first-class cricket, from which he had managed just two fifties, and he was up against the pace of the South African Garth le Roux.

Somehow, though the proper batsmen all got out, he survived. He had an experienced defence and some effective shots to leg but, according to the *Guardian*, 'his drives through cover invoked the image of a man batting with a crutch.'

He passed 50, 60, 70. Then in came the number ten, the Australian Terry Alderman who started to have a whack, hitting le Roux for a massive six. "I got very nervous," Derek Underwood says. "I'd made an eighty early in my career but Kevin Jarvis was our number eleven, and he really couldn't bat. So I thought I'd be left not out, short of the ton."

On 96 he gave a hard, diving chance to slip. Then two runs later Ian Greig dropped one short, and he swung it with a 'hoik' to the leg-side boundary. Only the Derbyshire wicket-keeper Bob Taylor, at the 744th attempt, has taken more innings to make a first hundred.

Then Sussex, set 193 to win, were all out for 192. It was a tie.

Five years later Underwood was back. Before a crowd of 3,000, he captained a team in an exhibition match, the last ever played on the ground before it was turned into a shopping mall.

The greatest finish of all

Somerset v Nottinghamshire, Taunton, Tuesday 11 September 1984

When the 1984 season's final round of matches started, Notts led Essex by four points. Essex travelled to Manchester, beat Lancashire in two days and were left to wait on the outcome of Notts' match at Taunton. On the fateful day they gathered in the pavilion at Chelmsford, listening to the radio bulletins.

The Somerset captain, Ian Botham, set Notts to score 297 in three hours which, with off-spinner Vic Marks and slow-left-armer Steve Booth in tandem, turned out to be 60 overs. The boundaries were not the longest on the circuit, and Notts made a good start, reaching 70 without loss.

The bulletins came through to Chelmsford. The openers were out ... 138 runs were needed in the final 20 overs ... Notts were four down, 98 to win, with their star overseas players, Clive Rice and Richard Hadlee, going well. "It was the longest day of my life," Essex captain Keith Fletcher said. "I used up more nervous energy than I ever do when playing."

Hadlee hit a ball in the air to mid-wicket where the fielder, catching it, fell onto an advertising board. Was it out? The travelling Notts supporters said no, vehemently – but yes, according to Law 32(a)(ii), it was indeed 'a fair catch'.

There were 79 needed off 10, 56 off seven, then down to 39 when Rice, after a brilliant 98, hit a full-toss from Marks towards deep square leg and was caught by the substitute fielder, Richard Ollis. With two overs left, 27 runs were wanted and the last pair were in: Andy Pick and Mike Bore, neither of them batsmen. At Chelmsford they began to relax.

Bore, 'of advancing years and girth', hit Marks for six. Then, with 14 wanted off Booth's last over, he devised a plan. "If he pitches it on the off-stump, I thought, I'll hit it straight. If it's on my legs, I'll sweep it." With 'calculated slogs', he took ten runs from the first three balls. Then he blocked the fourth.

"Picky came down. 'What did you do that for?' he asked. 'It wasn't in the right place,' I said." But the next one was pitched up on his off-stump, and Bore once more swung his bat. "As soon as I hit it, I thought, 'That's it, we've won.'"

The ball sailed high towards the old pavilion where, alas, it failed to clear the tall figure of Ollis. The cheering began in Chelmsford, and the Notts players packed their bags in silence.

"We were stunned," Bore says. "We got in the car, and I don't think we spoke a word till we were well past Gloucester."

In the last over of the last day, five months of cricket had been settled by a few inches on Taunton's long-on boundary.

The strangest of games

Lancashire v Warwickshire, Southport, 28-30 July 1982

It was a game like no other, a game in which the unexpected happened repeatedly.

The large holiday crowd at Southport spent the first day under a blazing sun, watching a glorious display of batting by Warwickshire's Alvin Kallicharran and Geoff Humpage. It was, in the words of the *Guardian*, 'a case of the rapier and the bludgeon', as the little Guyanan hooked and drove disdainfully while the former police cadet thumped 13 sixes, several of them in quick succession after the taking of the new ball. Some landed among the deckchairs in front of the pavilion, one in a nearby garden, the mightiest of them all onto the Liverpool railway line and into the record books, taking their fourth-wicket partnership past 448, the previous championship record set by Abel and Hayward in 1899.

When Humpage was finally out, the pair had put on 470 and, with the total on 523, they declared, leaving time for Gladstone Small to capture the wicket of David Lloyd before they returned to the dressing room to uncork the newly delivered champagne.

The next morning Small was no longer with them. He had been summoned to join the England team at Edgbaston, where Derek Pringle had developed a bad back in the nets. Substituting for him at Southport was the 40-year-old David Brown, Warwickshire's manager. Under a new regulation, to deal with such Test call-ups, he was permitted to bowl, which he duly did, becoming the first substitute ever to take a first-class wicket. He bowled 13 overs before giving way during the afternoon to Small, who was not needed by England and arrived at the ground after a 2½-hour drive up the M6.

Warwickshire's bowling attack was notoriously weak – the previous summer they had taken their wickets at a cost of 47 runs each, the worst average in the 100 years of three-day championship cricket – and Lancashire piled on the runs.

Their opener Graeme Fowler had pulled a thigh muscle while fielding, and he batted with David Lloyd as his runner, taking his score from an overnight 26 to 126. The ground was not large, the outfield ran gently downhill on all sides, and Lancashire, reaching 414 for six, declared 109 runs behind. They were hoping for a second Warwickshire declaration and a run chase on the final afternoon.

Then came Les McFarlane, a well-built fast bowler who three years earlier had been plucked by Northamptonshire from their Town League where, playing for a West Indian

Les McFarlane

side on rough pitches on the old racecourse, he had been running amok.

He achieved little in his games for Northants but, after an outstanding season with Bedfordshire, he was signed up by Lancashire for whom, in his first nine matches that summer, he had taken 12 wickets at the unimpressive average of 58 runs each. Yet here at Southport, on the best of batting tracks, he struck twice in two balls in the day's closing minutes. Then next morning he claimed a further four victims as Warwickshire, with five ducks, subsided to 111 all out: the Nelson total at Southport's Trafalgar Road ground. It left Lancashire to score 221 for an improbable victory.

Lloyd made an unbeaten 88 – "I didn't fancy getting out and having to run for him again," he said – while Fowler, dropped in the slips on seven, hit 128, becoming the only man ever to score 100 runs with the aid of a runner in each innings of a match. With the bowlers becoming 'progressively dispirited' under the hot sun, Fowler finished the game with a huge blow for six.

Warwickshire had lost their ten wickets for a meagre 111 runs in a match in which the other ten wickets had come at a cost of 1,163. In a season in which they failed to win a championship game, their manager David Brown sought to explain their bizarre collapse as a case of 'third-innings syndrome'.

It was Les MacFarlane's finest hour. He would play five summers of first-class cricket – for Northamptonshire, Lancashire and Glamorgan – and neither before nor after that extraordinary match at Southport, played on the easiest-paced of pitches, would he take five wickets in an innings.

Images of the 1980s

(left)
The last day of first-class cricket
at Priory Meadow, Hastings:
Sussex v Middlesex,
Tuesday 22 August 1989

(below left)
North Marine Road,
Scarborough,
during the 1985 Festival

Festival cricket no more

For much of the 20th century Scarborough and Hastings played host to end-of-season festivals. The summer-long round of the championship was over, and the players relaxed by the seaside and entertained the holidaying spectators. The touring teams stayed on to play in both festivals, and there would be such fixtures as South versus North, Gentlemen versus Players, An England XI versus A Commonwealth XI.

They were grand social occasions, especially before the last war. At Scarborough the spectators paraded across the ground during lunch, the band played throughout the day, and the players took tea on the field, served by a waiter wearing white tie and tails. Usually he had a bottle of whisky with him.

By the 1980s life had become too serious for such frolics. The glamour of the matches had faded, and the band was no more, silenced by a certain Yorkshire batsman who said they were disturbing his concentration.

Michael Parkinson raised teams to play the tourists, but by the mid-1990s the Scarborough Festival was no more than a county match or two. Hastings had gone the same way in the late 1960s, and in 1989 the historic ground was sold to developers who built a shopping mall.

Sabotage at New Road, Worcester

With one round of matches of the 1988 season left to play, leaders Worcestershire were one point ahead of Kent – and that one point was a source of grievance for Kent supporters.

At Edgbaston in June Kent bowled out Warwickshire for 107 but, because two men had been unfit to bat, they were not awarded the bowling point that came with the fall of the ninth wicket. Unsuccessfully they appealed and, in the words of *Wisden*, 'it was a point that rankled all season.' It especially rankled when it looked like being the difference between finishing second and sharing the title.

The last matches were four-day ones, and after two days Kent were well on their way to an innings victory at Canterbury. Worcestershire, at home to Glamorgan, were also winning. They had moved in the boundaries to make sure they got maximum batting points and, on 380 for six, they already had a lead of 136. Glamorgan, bottom of the table, were not the toughest of opponents, and the weather was set fair. It would take a remarkable twist for Worcestershire not to win the title now – by that one point.

But remarkable twist there was. When the groundsman pulled back the covers on the third morning, he found a large patch of engine oil close to a good length at one end. In no time the square was a hive of activity, with motor fans and industrial heaters at work. Alan Butcher, Glamorgan captain, was determined that the game would triumph, and eventually play got under way. The oily patch created no problems, certainly no more than normal on the uneven New Road pitch, and by four o'clock Worcestershire had won by an innings.

Meanwhile the police went into the crowd and led away a Kent supporter whose conversation had been decidedly suspicious but, without firm evidence, no charges were pressed.

So it fell to Worcestershire to receive the championship trophy from Prince Philip at Buckingham Palace – or it should have. The cup itself had not been collected from Trent Bridge, and after a last-minute panic the ceremony took place with a hastily acquired substitute: the Lord's Taverners Brands Hatch Motor Racing Trophy. Perhaps, after the triumph over the engine oil, it was not inappropriate.

The summer of 1981

England was not at ease with itself in the summer of 1981. Unemployment was rising towards three million, and in July riots broke out in the Toxteth district of Liverpool, spreading rapidly to cities throughout the land. The Specials reached the top of the pop chart with *Ghost Town*, a lament for the decline of their home city, Coventry, and a young protester fired blanks at the Queen during the Trooping of the Colour.

Even the genteel world of the All-England Lawn Tennis Championships at Wimbledon was not as it once had been, with the new champion, John McEnroe, fined almost a third of his £27,000 prize money for unsportsmanlike behaviour.

England's cricketers brought no comfort. Already one down in their defence of the Ashes, they stood on the verge of a humiliating innings defeat in the third Test at Headingley.

Then came Ian Botham with an astonishing innings of 149, and on Tuesday 21 July an inspired Bob Willis, bowling as if in a trance, took eight wickets as Australia, needing 130 for victory, were dismissed for 111. When Willis, driving home, turned on the six o'clock radio news and heard that their triumph was the first item, he was so overcome he had to pull off the road. The country had been desperate for some good news – and cricket, of all things, had provided it.

Meanwhile, after a wet May, an absorbing county championship race was developing. While Willis was charging in, Nottinghamshire and Sussex, who would emerge as the two front-runners, were engaged in their own struggles. At Trent Bridge Notts, thwarted for much of the day by Yorkshire's batsmen, were left to score 115 in 20 overs and managed it with only eleven balls to spare.

At Hove, where rain prevented play till after lunch, Sussex had to leave the excitement of the television to take the last five Warwickshire wickets. As they settled in their positions in the field, a shout went up from the crowd: "Border's out."

Garth le Roux, their South African fast bowler, took a hat-trick, and there was a great roar as another wicket fell at Headingley. "I felt I was playing in two matches at once," the Sussex captain John Barclay says. "The one physically, the other in spirit." In the confusion Warwickshire's last man forgot he had a runner, his dismissal allowing the Sussex players to catch the end of the Test. Then they knocked off the runs that took them to the top of the championship table.

A week later they were again trying to play cricket and watch television, this time with the sun shining on the wedding of Prince Charles and Lady Diana Spencer.

Imran Khan was the star of the Sussex side, an unpredictable force who on his day could turn a match almost single-handed, as he did in spectacular fashion at Eastbourne in August. Midway through the last afternoon Derbyshire, with five wickets down in their second innings, were leading by 231 runs. The pitch was slow and lifeless and, with David Steele and Kim Barnett batting without difficulty, they seemed content to play out the draw.

Suddenly, as if bored, Imran emerged from the deep and demanded to bowl, running off to change his footwear. He reappeared, shone up the old ball and soon got it to swing prodigiously, taking four wickets in five balls. Now Sussex needed 234 to win.

"That was clever bowling," he said imperiously to his captain as they left the field. "I feel it is my day; we must beat this lot. I think I shall bat at four. The others won't mind."

True to his word, he emerged at 74 for two and hit an 88-minute century. They won in the last over and drove off for their top-of-the-table encounter next day at Trent Bridge.

Richard Hadlee, Nottinghamshire's New Zealander, was a steadier character than Imran, a fast bowler with a consistent rhythm, metronomic accuracy and a concern for his own statistics that provided motivation even on the dull days. With South African Clive Rice, his captain, at the other end, they were as potent a new-ball force as Imran and le Roux.

This was the first summer during which pitches were covered whenever there was rain, with groundsmen encouraged to prepare dry surfaces that were more readily responsive to spin. Nottinghamshire, however, were taking a different approach, leaving plenty of grass for Hadlee and Rice. "We're going to exploit every conceivable advantage of playing at home," Rice said at the start of the summer.

Over the years county cricket has known its mutterings about pitches. Many thought the Oval in the 1950s was unfairly prepared for Laker and Lock, though the two of them took plenty of wickets in the away games. It was said that Worcester in the 1960s was spiced up for the fast bowlers Flavell and Coldwell. But no county has ever generated as much unease as Nottinghamshire in 1981. Trent Bridge was traditionally the best batting track in the country, yet that summer the average total of the team batting first was 149. And, to rub it in, it was never Notts who were batting first. In the first game, unaware of the policy, Leicestershire opted to bat; in the remaining ten games, Notts won the toss and invited their visitors to bat.

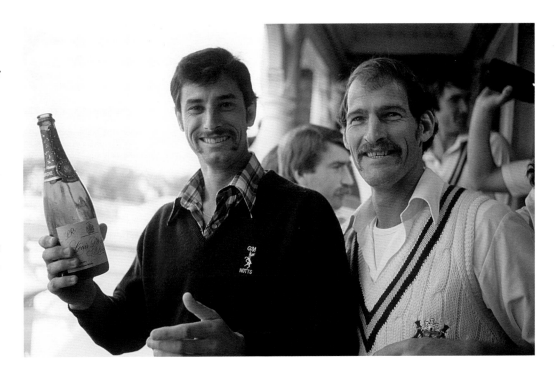

Champions

Richard Hadlee (left) and his Notts captain Clive Rice

Hadlee, from Christchurch in New Zealand, was the championship's leading bowler, with 105 wickets, and he also scored 745 runs.

Rice, from Johannesburg in South Africa, was in the top ten in both batting and bowling averages, with 1,462 runs and 65 wickets. In just three years his inspirational captaincy had transformed Nottinghamshire.

Their eleven home games produced nine wins and one defeat while away from home they won two and lost three. Such an extreme disparity created much comment – but little consensus. Mike Brearley of Middlesex scored a century at Trent Bridge and spoke glowingly of the pitch; John Woodcock in *The Times* thought Notts had 'gone too far'.

The mid-August match between Nottinghamshire and Sussex at Trent Bridge, their only meeting that summer, was billed as the championship decider, and so it proved.

For once, with Imran and le Roux among the visitors, Notts had not prepared a green pitch – rather, it was brown and worn, with some grass cuttings rolled in to make it look green. Inevitably Rice won the toss, and the Sussex batsmen soon found themselves up against the off-spin of Eddie Hemmings.

The experienced Hemmings took nine wickets in the match, but the Notts batting failed badly in the first innings, with only Basharat Hassan, their jovial Kenyan with a strange stance, preventing humiliation: 58 not out in a total of 102.

On the final day Notts needed 251 to win, and at 174 for three they looked like doing it. Then came the dramatic final hour. Wickets fell, the batsmen went off for bad light, more wickets fell, and in the gloom the last pair looked to play for the draw against Imran and le Roux. Mike Bore, the number eleven, came out wearing what the *Guardian* called 'one of those grid-iron helmets that convey no confidence whatsoever'.

When a ball from Imran struck Bore beneath the knee roll of his back pad, the whole Sussex team exploded in appeal. Peter Stevens was the umpire, in the last of his three seasons on the first-class list, and it fell to him to adjudicate the appeal which, as it turned out, settled the destination of the championship. "Not out," he said, and the match was drawn.

Meanwhile at Old Trafford England clinched the Ashes with a third victory. It was suddenly a golden summer, and next day Seb Coe broke the world record for the mile.

Notts might have slipped up in their next game at Edgbaston. At tea on the second day, on a good batting track, they declared 48 runs behind Warwickshire, hoping for a last-day declaration in response. Instead, as if to answer those who called them home-pitch specialists, Notts – with Derek Randall taking three brilliant catches – dismissed the home side for 49 and knocked off the runs before the end of the day.

Though Sussex also won their last four matches, the championship went by two points to Notts, their first trophy of any sort since 1929. Fittingly they won it at Trent Bridge, defeating Glamorgan after lunch on the second day.

As player, captain and chairman Reg Simpson had known no such success in 35 years with the club, and he was overwhelmed. "When I saw him in tears," Basharat Hassan says, "I realised just how important a day it was for Nottinghamshire cricket."

251

1982: Mike Brearley's last match at Lord's

It was the morning of Wednesday 25 August 1982. The sky was cloudy, the crowd was thin, but the moment was special for the Middlesex captain Mike Brearley. Twenty-one years on from his county debut, he was preparing for his last match at Lord's.

Back in 1961, as a first-year Cambridge student, he had been described in *The Times* as 'a budding Test match batsman in the May and Sheppard class as an undergraduate'. There were still amateurs and professionals, and the week before his first appearance for Middlesex he had kept wicket for the Gentlemen against the Players.

That social distinction had gone by the time he reported for duty at the start of 1965, his only full summer of county cricket in the 1960s. He had spent the previous winter on tour with England in South Africa, but that gave him no seniority when the Middlesex team sat down for its first meeting.

The new captain Fred Titmus, flanked by Peter Parfitt and JT Murray, addressed the squad. "If you think," Titmus said, "that now you've got a professional in charge you're going to have a democracy, you've got another think coming. Some of us have got a lot more experience of cricket, ain't we, JT?"

"You were supposed to know your place," Mike Brearley says. "You kept quiet, and you learned the game by watching other people. That was the social behaviour of everyone in the country. If you voiced an idea, they would think, 'Has he played for ten years? No. Well, what's he speaking for?'"

Six years later it was Mike Brearley himself who was addressing the squad. He was returning to cricket after a stint lecturing in philosophy at Newcastle University, and his appointment, ahead of the experienced Murray, had not gone down entirely well with one or two of the senior players.

In some respects Brearley, son of a schoolmaster who had played occasionally for Yorkshire and Middlesex, was a throwback to the gentleman amateurs who captained teams earlier in the century, an other-worldly university man full of long words and theory. But he was also a clear-thinking moderniser with a left-of-centre view of the world; he wanted to create a greater sense of democracy, a "flattened hierarchy", albeit one in which he was still in charge.

The early years of his captaincy were not easy, his unconventional decisions not to the liking of the traditionally minded professionals. "He had an irritating habit of trying to set my field for me," Fred Titmus said. "I never minded advice, so long as it coincided closely with my own views, but I thought he had some daft ideas." Titmus might well have been the unnamed

Mike Brearley in 1972

senior player who that summer complained to the chairman of cricket: "He puts people in really funny positions in the field, and the strange thing is, the ball keeps going to them."

"Jim Parks was batting at the pavilion end at Lord's against Harry Latchman's leg-breaks," Brearley recalls. "I got this feeling that, driving freely in his inside-out style, he might get a thick outside edge so I put in a deep gully. They'd think, 'That's not a proper position.' But he was caught there. That did please me."

Other ideas were less successful. "I had various faults, one of which was to be too academic. I would occasionally look through recent *Wisden*s before matches, trying to work out who'd got out to which bowlers. That was a stupid idea."

For all his soft-spoken reasonableness Brearley had an inner hardness. He knew what he wanted and gradually, as all but Fred Titmus of the old guard moved on, the team became his own. The key to success, what they had lacked, he realised, was to have a penetrative bowling attack, to which end they recruited the fast-medium Mike Selvey from Surrey, slow-left-armer Phil Edmonds from Cambridge and, at the start of 1976, Allan Jones from Somerset.

On a pre-season tour of the British Army on the Rhine, they noticed that, when the going got tough, Jones resorted to playing the fool. "Let's not laugh at him," they resolved. "Let's take him seriously, praise him when he does well." Thereafter Jones became the vital missing piece in their bowling line-up, taking the new ball with Selvey. With the dry pitches of that long, hot summer suiting the spin of Titmus, Edmonds and the South African Norman Featherstone, all five bowlers finished high in the national averages, and for the first time since the 1940s Middlesex won the championship.

In 1977 they shared the title with Kent. Titmus had by then retired, giving way to John Emburey, and they had signed the West Indian fast bowler Wayne Daniel. Meanwhile Brearley was now captain of England, beating Australia 3-0.

For the two winters before their first title Brearley had worked in a therapeutic community for disturbed adolescents, an environment in which the staff had meetings to discuss their emotional reactions to each other and to the patients. "People are more productive, more fulfilled, more likely to contribute if they feel they have a say in things." He tried to take Middlesex cricketers with him in that direction, but "the culture was very different, and I was a bit too high-minded about it, too naïve at times."

Phil Edmonds was not on a wavelength with Brearley. A strong-minded character who had grown up in Zambia, he believed that Brearley's reputation as a great captain was a myth created by his having good teams and a lot of luck.

Others found Brearley a brilliant motivator. "He made you believe in your own ability," says Roland Butcher, who came to England from Barbados at the age of 13 and in his early years at Middlesex failed to fulfil his potential as an attacking batsman. "He reminded me of my grandmother, someone who could get the best out of me in a disciplined environment."

Simon Hughes, a Durham undergraduate, came into the team in 1980. "The day he came over and asked me, aged 20, who I thought should bowl next, I felt ten feet tall, particularly when he took up my suggestion. The idea didn't work, but I was prepared to run through treacle for him for the rest of the summer."

Brearley retired from the England captaincy after India's Golden Jubilee Test in February 1980. In a garden in Bombay during an eclipse of the sun, the Middlesex chairman George Mann sprung on him that the county had signed a South African fast-medium bowler called Vintcent van der Bijl. Brearley was not at all happy: he had not been consulted, and he was suspicious of the cricketing establishment's links with white South Africa. Worse was to follow when he got home and found that, after the county's bad summer in 1979, his captaincy was under review. Before reappointing him, they wanted to know how he planned to do things differently. "I had slipped a bit," he admits, "and so had the whole team."

He organised the pre-season nets, was stricter on time-keeping and discovered that van der Bijl was a season-long match-winner. For the third time the championship was won.

England called Brearley back for a fairy-tale ending in 1981, and in his part-absence Middlesex finished fourth. Then in 1982, when at the age of 40 he played one last county season, he was determined to go out with a fourth championship.

"I found county cricket enormously enjoyable," he said, "partly because I became a good enough player at that level. With Test cricket I was always struggling so it was harder to feel I really belonged on that bigger stage. I felt I belonged on the stage of county cricket. I liked playing around the country, I liked the regularity of it, and I liked the collegiality, both within the team and between the teams. I liked the humour, too. It was very competitive, but it was friendly as well – which, to my mind, is the best form of sport."

As August drew to a close he prepared for his last match at Lord's, with the pitch dry and expected to take spin. And who should put his head round the dressing-room door, to wish him and the team 'the best of luck', but the 49-year-old Fred Titmus, calling in on his way from his sub-post office in Hertfordshire to the American Embassy where he had to collect a visa.

They had had their ups and downs over the years, but there was a deep affection at the core of the relationship, born of a shared love of cricket and of Middlesex. It was an affection that Titmus's widow expressed to Brearley when she put her arms around him after her husband's funeral. "He loved you, you know," she said, receiving the reply, "And I loved him too."

"Fred, you're just the man," Brearley said in the dressing room, and in no time a mildly protesting Titmus was standing in Clive Radley's spare flannels and Brearley's spare socks and boots. So much had changed in the world of cricket since the day at Bath in 1949 when Titmus had made his debut in the same Middlesex eleven as Brearley's father. He was even persuaded, 33 years on, to bat for the first time in a helmet.

Rain on the second day made a result unlikely, but Brearley had other ideas. With the help of Surrey's Roger Knight he set the visitors a gettable 161 in 135 minutes. The pitch, as expected, was breaking up and taking spin, and would you believe it? Phil Edmonds ricked his back, and Fred Titmus became crucial. He took three wickets, and they won with seven overs to spare.

Was that luck or genius – or, as Brearley thinks, bad planning? "We should have learned about the pitch earlier and made sure Fred was available." He even insists that the selection of Titmus was not his but Clive Radley's idea.

Whichever way, it was a special day for Mike Brearley – and also for Fred Titmus. "I came in with the father," he said, "and I went out with the son."

Middlesex were champions again.

The rise of the cricket manager

In the 1950s county cricket clubs employed few people beyond the playing and ground staff. There would be a Secretary, often a former military man still proudly carrying his title – Colonel Coldwell at Northampton, Major Bayly at Worcester, Air Vice-Marshal Taylor at Somerset – and perhaps two or three more in the office: to type, keep the books and handle membership applications. Then in the summer there would be a coach, a masseur and a scorer.

Coaching was not as we know it now. There were no training courses or qualifications before the 1950s, and the role was not seen as important. Some of the county coaches were given their positions as much in recognition of past service as for any aptitude for the role.

The wicket-keeper Keith Andrew joined Northamptonshire in 1953, and he recalled the pre-season practice that year. "Who's the old bloke behind the net with the trilby on?" he asked after about a week. "He was a smart man with a raincoat and a brown trilby. I knew he was a bit deaf because, when you spoke, he never answered." "That's the coach, Jack Mercer," came the reply. "He doesn't do much coaching, but he gives the Colonel some great tips."

Throughout the country the county first elevens would embark on four months of six-day-a-week cricket, during which the coach, if he stayed with the club, would be with the second eleven, perhaps playing in, even captaining, the side. So the first-teamers had to make their own adjustments.

"We used to rely on the senior batsmen and bowlers," Worcestershire's Martin Horton said. "Or the umpires. You'd edge one through the slips and, when you got down to the other end, there would be Jack Crapp or Emrys Davies. 'Do you realise you're lifting your head?'"

There were some fine coaches – Andrew Sandham at the Oval, Arthur Holt at Southampton, Tiger Smith at Edgbaston – but there were others less suited to the role. At Old Trafford Stan Worthington had little empathy with young cricketers while at Taunton Bill Andrews was brilliant with young boys but did little at senior level to raise standards.

The first county to break the mould was Kent. After spending most of the 1950s near the foot of the championship the morale of the players was so low that, at the start of the second day of an away match, they would be looking up the times of that evening's trains. The all-rounder Alan Dixon recalls an early game in the side: "I was having a pre-match knock, and I came back into the changing room. 'Oh, don't take your pads off,' somebody said. 'You're batting seven.' And he was right. It wasn't long before I was in."

The chaotic inefficiency of the administration did not help. Derek Ufton, the reserve wicket-keeper, remembers a game at Blackheath when, not expecting to play, he looked into the dressing room before the start. "Ah, good job you've arrived," someone said. "We've only got ten." His keeping was not needed, but he was added to the team sheet, only for them to discover too late that Stuart Leary, a promising batsman, was on the ground, thinking he had been selected.

In 1957, when the young Colin Cowdrey took over as captain, Kent appointed Les Ames as manager. He would travel with the first team, work alongside Cowdrey and find new players. Ames was ideal for the post. His playing record commanded respect: the outstanding wicket-keeper-batsman of the inter-war years, he had hit more than 100 centuries and played in 47 Tests. He was also a man with qualities that had lifted him above the normal status of the professional cricketer. In the RAF during the war he had risen to the rank of Squadron Leader, and in 1949 he was offered the Kent captaincy, turning it down because he was not prepared to play as an amateur. As part-owner of a sports shop in Gillingham and a hotel in Hastings, he could spare the time for Kent.

There was a mess to be sorted out but, according to Derek Ufton, "He didn't have to be tough because he was so efficient. Everything worked." His appointment was such a success that in 1960 he became the full-time Secretary/Manager.

Yet such were the limited finances of county cricket that it was many years before anyone returned to the Kent experiment of 1957, the appointment of a manager as a post separate from those of captain, coach and Secretary.

In late 1977 Nottinghamshire became the first county to have not a Secretary but a Chief Executive who would make all the day-to-day decisions without referring to the committee. Philip Carling, who had developed the money-spinning Trent Bridge Squash Club, was appointed, but he did not want the hiring and firing of players to fall within his remit. He asked the chairman of the cricket committee, Ken Taylor, to take on that.

Taylor, from a wealthy shipping family, had been an officer in the war, but he was a socialist and, contrary to expectations, had played for Warwickshire as a professional. By the 1970s he had a senior post with the East Midlands Electricity Board and was a stalwart of the Notts committee, where he battled quietly – though not often successfully – against the freemasons.

Ken Taylor of Nottinghamshire

He agreed to take responsibility for the playing staff but only if he could attend all the games. So, at the age of 61, he became Nottinghamshire's full-time, all-the-year-round cricket manager, complete with a secretary.

The county, though relatively wealthy, were in the doldrums, finishing last in the table in 1977, and Taylor's first summer started catastrophically when the new captain, the South African Clive Rice, signed up for Kerry Packer's World Series Cricket. The Notts committee sacked Rice, who sought legal redress and was reinstated – but not as captain. Yet, out of this turmoil, Taylor, with his background in personnel management, created harmony. "He took us by the scruff of the neck," Rice says, "and built a winning unit" – so much so that in 1981, under Rice's captaincy, Notts won the championship, their first trophy since 1929. Six years later, with Taylor and Rice still going strong, they did the double of championship and NatWest Trophy.

Within twelve months of Ken Taylor's appointment Surrey and Yorkshire were following suit, in each case turning to a distinguished former player to sort out an under-achieving team.

Surrey wooed back Micky Stewart, captain of their 1971 championship-winning side. He was about to join the board of Slazengers, the sports equipment company, where as Sales Director he had had great success, but after three months of soul-searching he followed his heart and returned to the Oval. There he divided his time between sorting out the first team and developing cricket in the county.

With the rise of one-day cricket there was now a much greater focus on results, and that suited Micky Stewart; he had learned the game in Stuart Surridge's all-conquering team. Furthermore, in his last years as captain he had experienced the growing pressures of the job so he understood the need for a manager.

He had played football for Charlton Athletic and managed Corinthian Casuals, and at times there was a little of the football manager in the way he spoke to the team. There was also a little of the sales director in the way he got out his Nobo flipchart and set them targets for the summer: "We need 8,000 runs; let's see how we're going to get those." For all that, he was a cricket man through and through; he had integrity, vision and was good with people. Surrey were soon on the up again.

The problems at the Oval were nothing compared with those Ray Illingworth faced when in 1979 he returned home from Leicester to be Yorkshire's first cricket manager. Geoff Boycott had just lost the captaincy, and a group of his supporters was fomenting dissent. Illingworth, for all his reputation and his success in generating sponsorship money, struggled to move the team forward. As a last resort in 1982 he put on his whites and took over the captaincy.

There was no improvement in Yorkshire's championship performances, but in 1983 they won the Sunday League, their first trophy for fourteen years. Illingworth, the last man born in the 1930s to take the field in a championship match (and he was born way back in 1932), was as canny a bowler as ever, topping the Sunday League's national averages.

Other counties were soon opting for managers: David Brown at Warwickshire, Jack Bond at Lancashire. In time there would be cricket development officers and academy programme directors. With advances in technology and sports science, there would be specialist coaches, fitness and conditioning experts, nutritionists, sports psychologists, even in at least one county a part-time sleep consultant.

It was another world from that of dear old Bill Andrews, the coach at Taunton in the 1960s. "We were playing a second-team game against Wiltshire," Peter Robinson recalls, "and we were getting a bit of a smacking. A few minutes after the start Bill would nip out the back and go into the Ring Of Bells. He came back just before lunch, saw the score and started having a go. John Martin was the captain. 'John, you bowled like a pr-pr-proper idiot.' He used to stutter. 'But I haven't had a bowl yet, Bill.' 'Don't you argue with me.' We saw him a bit later, and he'd nodded off."

1988: The toughest of years for Worcestershire's Phil Neale

The award of a benefit was a major event in the life of a county cricketer. It offered the chance of financial security after long years of service. But, to make the most of that opportunity, the benefit needed good organisation, and it needed hard work, with many demands throughout the year on the player's time.

Good organisation and hard work were never going to be a problem for Phil Neale. The most thorough of men, supported by the best of benefit committees, he entered January 1988 ready for action. His lavish brochure, brimming with articles and advertisements, was back from the printers, and it listed 54 events, a set of engagements that would swell to 138 by year's end. The schedule began on January 9 with a dinner at a grand Tudor house, and it ended in style with a New Year's Eve party at Worcester Racecourse. Along the way, breaking new ground, it strayed far from the corporate world, taking the team to skittles evenings in village pubs and working men's clubs.

For his first ten years as a professional cricketer, Phil Neale had played football for Lincoln City each winter. He had made his debut while still at Leeds University, completing a degree in Russian Studies; there were times when he had to read his books on the match-day coach. That could have posed a problem, but his manager Graham Taylor gave him good advice. "Be clever enough to act the peasant at times," he said. "A football dressing room is no different from a factory floor. The topics of conversation will be football, sex and television. By all means adapt to that, but never lose what's going on in your mind."

He established himself as the regular left-back in the winter of 1975/76, when they lost only four times and gained 74 points, a record in those days of two points a win. It was the making of Graham Taylor, who moved on to manage Watford, Aston Villa and England, and he left a deep impression on his young left-back, not least in the way he believed that the football club should be a part of the city. "He would organise for us to go to factories, sit down for a canteen lunch and meet the workers on the factory floor."

Dovetailing football and cricket seasons was not always easy, particularly in May 1982, at the start of his first year as Worcestershire captain. He had been offered the job by phone back in February, on the same day that his wife Chris had given birth to their second child, a boy whom they called Craig.

At the time of the call Lincoln City were hovering just above the relegation zone in Division Three, but they went on a 16-match unbeaten run that took them to the top of the table. A vital game at Chester clashed with the first Benson & Hedges match, and Lincoln won the tussle. In the morning the new captain called in at Headingley, then his drive to Chester ran into heavy traffic. Thirty-five minutes before kick-off he had to knock on a door and phone to say he was on his way.

Lincoln missed out on promotion, and his first five years as Worcestershire captain brought no great success. The committee had decided to rebuild with a younger team, and for all their potential the lack of experience led in 1985 and 1986 to three successive defeats in knock-out semi-finals.

One major step forward had been taken during 1984 when a quiet 17-year-old Zimbabwean, Graeme Hick, arrived at the County Ground. Given a net, he hit the first-team bowlers back over their heads into the next field, and they got him into the side for their last game at the Oval. Taking on the hostile Sylvester Clarke without alarm, he hit an unbeaten 82 and immediately Worcestershire signed him as their overseas player.

Another step forward came in August 1986 when they played Somerset at Weston-super-Mare. Ian Botham was returning after a two-month suspension, for admitting to the taking of cannabis, and he marked the occasion by smacking the Worcestershie bowlers around the ground for a 65-ball century. Then in the bar he confirmed the rumour that he was looking to move county, and Phil Neale showed immediate interest. They had always got on well, with football in common, and there was the added connection that the Worcestershire chairman, Duncan Fearnley, made Botham's bats.

Fearnley flew to Australia during the winter to complete the signing, and he also came back with the signature of fast bowler Graham Dilley, who wanted to leave Kent. It was a major infusion of talent, and such was the excitement that the county's membership soared, with queues all down New Road.

Botham and Dilley brought self-confidence, a belief that, whatever the state of the game, the team could win. Yes, it was all Plan A – "In a run-chase Both would always believe he was going to hit the last two balls for six" – but it lifted the team enormously. "You search for that missing ingredient," Phil Neale says, "and you never know what it is. Then suddenly you've got it, and you start winning all the close finishes."

Botham was a good team man, happy to bowl at the wrong end in an attack full of out-swingers, and he brought them into the spotlight: more matches on television and the appearance of friends such as Elton John, George Harrison and Eric Clapton. Clapton even wrote a piece in Phil Neale's benefit brochure, likening Botham to a new band member who might upset the group's chemistry and praising the captain's role in ensuring that this did not happen: 'Phil has an easy-going exterior which deceptively covers an iron will.'

They won the Sunday League in 1987, Botham's first season. Botham opened the batting with Tim Curtis, an outstanding player of quick bowling, and with Hick they were the three leading run-scorers in the competition. Neal Radford was joint leading wicket-taker, and Steve Rhodes leading keeper. It was the county's first trophy since 1974, and it brought with it a sense of expectation.

So, with a winning side to captain and a demanding benefit, 1988 was set to be the biggest year in Phil Neale's life. He had even agreed to take part in Botham's latest charity walk on behalf of research into childhood leukaemia. Between a Sportsman's Lunch at the Red Hart Inn, Inkberrow, and an Open Clay Shoot at Hadley Bowling Green Inn, he flew to Perpignon and walked the first three days of Botham's three-week, 440-mile retracing of Hannibal's march across the Alps. Botham was no slouch, either. To keep up with him, Neale, the fittest of men, found he had to jog.

His football over, Neale was in his first winter of teaching at Worcester Royal Grammar, running the football team, teaching some prep-school French and, when the headmaster was busy, brushing up his Russian for the 'O' level class.

The first two events of the benefit went well. Then came the Saturday that he has never forgotten. He got home from Villa Park, where he had stayed for a drink with Graham Taylor, to find that Craig, who had been poorly, had taken a turn for the worse: pale, shivering and coughing. They put him to bed, but he woke screaming and started to vomit uncontrollably. "Dad, am I going to die?" he asked. In hospital the nightmare continued. Then came the diagnosis: he had leukaemia.

Phil Neale rang Botham in Australia, and the big man tried to reassure him. Craig had the most common form of the illness, and the chances of survival were as high as 45 per cent.

Neale wanted to protect his family's privacy so, when he did not make it on Monday for a benefit event at Leominster Cricket Club, there were grumbles. "We're doing all this for Phil Neale, and he can't even be bothered to show up."

Craig's hair fell out; all summer his health was a concern. Once when he was rushed back to hospital his

Graeme Hick, Graham Dilley, Duncan Fearnley, Ian Botham and a soaked Phil Neale, after winning the championship

father, "knocked sideways" by the news, sat for an hour on his own on the far side of the Leicester ground. "I wasn't going to stay in the dressing room when I was so upset."

The cricket had to be played, though. On the morning of the first game Botham arrived by helicopter from Italy, but within weeks he had injured his back and missed most of the season.

Graeme Hick, however, had a magnificent summer, hitting big hundreds at a rapid pace to set up victories, never more so than at Taunton when his 405 came out of 550 while he was at the wicket. Neale was criticised for declaring when Hick needed only 20 runs to pass Archie MacLaren's record of 424, just as he had been criticised when six years earlier Glenn Turner's 311 in a day had been only 20 short of Jack Robertson's record. But the winning of the game always came first for Neale. And Hick did not mind. He was given a bowl, and before close he had taken two wickets.

For the first time the championship started with three four-day matches, and Worcestershire won them all, winning two of the three at the end of the summer too. They were the best side in England, and they carried off both championship and Sunday League. Had they won the toss on a damp morning at Lord's, they would almost certainly have won the NatWest Trophy as well.

With great fortitude, with a close family and the happiest of dressing rooms, Phil Neale got through it all, and his benefit was a great success. "I had to learn to compartmentalise," he says. "When I look back, I think, 'How did that all happen?'"

After some gruelling years Craig made a full recovery. "It did change my perspective on life. Family and things away from cricket meant much more to me afterwards."

1990 – 1999

Durham the 18th county
Programme of 17 four-day matches
New ECB forces change

Two divisions will give an edge to the county game which I think has been missing. We could not have allowed it to continue as it has done; we have been singularly unsuccessful in international cricket for far too many years. With 400 professional players, we really should have one of the best international teams in the world.

Lord MacLaurin, Chairman, England and Wales Cricket Board, 1998

Football is capturing the middle classes. We are in danger of becoming a minority spectator sport.

Tim Lamb, Chief Executive, England and Wales Cricket Board, 1997

If first-class cricket is to survive, it must attract a large audience. An emphasis on the one-day game seems quite likely to do that. Cricket has to adapt to the new audience or die – and I do not want cricket to die.

Yet one-day matches, under floodlights or by daylight, in pyjamas or white flannels, is not the same as the classic game of cricket and does not produce all the classic skills. It is halfway to baseball, a very good game but one of short-term movement aimed at excitement and quick results.

William Rees-Mogg, The Times, 1997

1990s

1990　New regulations on cricket-ball stitching are introduced to reduce the size of the seam. This increases run-scoring, as does the instruction to groundsmen to prepare better batting pitches.

Sky television broadcasts live cricket for the first time, gaining exclusive rights to England's tour of the West Indies.

Nelson Mandela is released after 27 years of captivity in South Africa.

1991　A proposal to return to uncovered pitches is supported by only Derbyshire, Kent, Northamptonshire and Yorkshire.

In a highly charged atmosphere, unprecedented in top golf, the USA regain the Ryder Cup at Kiawah Island.

1992　Durham enter the championship as the 18th county. They win two games and finish in last place.

Yorkshire, ending their long-held policy of playing only those born in the county, recruit the 19-year-old Indian batsman Sachin Tendulkar. They slip from 14th to 16th place in the table.

The regulations governing qualification are relaxed. A county may now approach any unregistered, adult cricketer. It is no longer necessary to seek permission for the approach from his county of birth or residence.

In a great year for British sport Nigel Mansell is motor racing's world champion, Nick Faldo wins the Open Golf Championship at Muirfield and Linford Christie comes first in the 100 metres at the Olympic Games in Barcelona.

The clubs in football's First Division, wanting a greater share of television revenue, break away to form a Premier League.

1993　The county championship programme is reduced to 17 matches, all of which are now of four days' duration. The bonus point system is altered to fit the four-day game.

No-balls are now worth two runs. The ball is inspected at the end of each over to prevent tampering.

The Grand National at Aintree is called off after 30 of the 39 riders fail to realise that a false start has been signalled.

1994　Warwickshire are champions, also winning the Benson & Hedges Cup and the Sunday League. They fail to gain a unique quartet of trophies when they lose to Worcestershire in the NatWest final.

Sunday trading laws are relaxed, with supermarkets permitted to open between 10 a.m. and 6 p.m.

1995　The counties vote not to give Chairman of Selectors Ray Illingworth the right to withdraw players from matches.

At the European Court of Justice Jean-Marc Bosman, a Belgian footballer, wins the right to move 'without restraint of trade' to another club on expiry of his contract. In particular, that club can be anywhere in the European Union.

1996　A proposal to create two divisions in the championship is rejected but, in order to increase the competitiveness below the leading positions, prize money is awarded to the first nine teams. The champions' prize is £65,000.

Football's European Championship is held in England, with the home team reaching the semi-finals. The resulting football fever distracts attention from England's cricketers who sink to seventh in Wisden's proposed Test rankings.

1997　The England and Wales Cricket Board is established, seeking to co-ordinate English cricket 'from the playground to the Test arena'. Its first chairman is Lord MacLaurin, retiring chairman of the supermarket chain Tesco. In August he produces a report, 'Raising the Standard', which argues for a reduction in first-class cricket in England. The counties reject its proposal for a championship with three groups of six, each playing only those not in their own group, with the three winners then competing for the title.

Prime Minister John Major, on losing the General Election, announces that he is off to the Oval to watch Surrey.

1998　Members of the Professional Cricketers' Association vote heavily in favour of two divisions. In December the counties follow suit by 15 votes to one (Glamorgan) with three abstentions (Durham, Essex and MCC).

A special general meeting of MCC extends eligibility for membership to women.

In October the contract to broadcast Test cricket in England is awarded to Channel 4.

Manchester United becomes the first football club in the world to have its own television channel.

1999　The championship starts earlier than ever, on April 13. At Old Trafford ground staff have to chip ice off the covers. It is piled behind the sight screen and is still there, unmelted, 24 hours later.

In one round of matches in October a record 26 footballers are sent off in the top four divisions.

Championship – top three

	P	W	L	D	Pts	Leading batsmen	Runs	Leading bowlers	Wickets	Leading wkt-keeper / Leading fielder	Victims
1990											
Middlesex	22	10	1	11	288	S.J. Cook (Som)	2,432	N.A. Foster (Essex)	94	S.J. Rhodes (Worcs)	67
Essex	22	8	2	12	257	G.A. Hick (Worcs)	2,273	T.A. Munton (Warwks)	75		
Hampshire	22	8	4	10	243	B.C. Broad (Notts)	2,226	M.D. Marshall (Hants)	72	D.B. D'Oliveira (Worcs)	33
1991											
Essex	22	11	5	6	312	S.J. Cook (Som)	2,370	Waqar Younis (Surrey)	113	C.P. Metson (Glam)	69
Warwickshire	22	11	4	7	299	M.W. Gatting (Middx)	2,044	N.A. Foster (Essex)	91		
Derbyshire	22	9	5	8	258	Salim Malik (Essex)	1,891	A.A. Donald (Warwks)	83	N. Hussain (Essex)	34
1992											
Essex	22	11	6	5	300	M.W. Gatting (Middx)	1,980	C.A. Walsh (Glos)	92	D. Ripley (Northants)	69
Kent	22	9	3	10	259	N.J. Speak (Sussex)	1,892	J.E. Emburey (Middx)	80		
Northants	22	8	4	10	248	P.D. Bowler (Derbys)	1,862	I.D.K. Salisbury (Sussex)	79	J.D. Carr (Middx)	39
1993											
Middlesex	17	11	1	5	272	C.W.J. Athey (Sussex)	1,432	Mushtaq Ahmed (Som)	85	R.C. Russell (Glos)	60
Worcestershire	17	9	4	3	236	D.J. Bicknell (Surrey)	1,383	S.L. Watkin (Glam)	81		
Glamorgan	17	9	5	3	231	T.S. Curtis (Worcs)	1,354	J.E. Emburey (Middx)	68	J.D. Carr (Middx)	39

Worcestershire also tied one match

	P	W	L	D	Pts	Leading batsmen	Runs	Leading bowlers	Wickets	Leading wkt-keeper / Leading fielder	Victims
1994											
Warwickshire	17	11	1	5	272	B.C. Lara (Warwks)	2,066	C.A. Walsh (Glos)	89	S.A. Marsh (Kent)	66
Leicestershire	17	8	7	2	230	C.L. Hooper (Kent)	1,579	T.A. Munton (Warwks)	81	K.J. Piper (Warwks)	66
Notts	17	8	5	4	218	R.G. Twose (Warwks)	1,395	M.M. Patel (Kent)	79	N. Hussain (Essex)	34
1995											
Warwickshire	17	14	2	1	337	M.R. Ramprakash (Middx)	2,147	A. Kumble (Northants)	105	G.J. Kersey (Surrey)	65
Middlesex	17	12	2	3	305	N. Hussain (Essex)	1,688	Mushtaq Ahmed (Som)	92		
Northants	17	12	2	3	290	P.A. de Silva (Kent)	1,661	A.A. Donald (Warwks)	88	D. Byas (Yorks)	39
1996											
Leicestershire	17	10	1	6	296	G.A. Gooch (Essex)	1,944	C.A. Walsh (Glos)	85	R.J. Turner (Som)	64
Derbyshire	17	9	3	5	269	C.J. Adams (Derbys)	1,590	M.J. McCague (Kent)	75	C.L. Hooper (Kent)	33
Surrey	17	8	2	7	262	M.A. Butcher (Surrey)	1,540	D.E. Malcolm (Derbys)	73	P.V. Simmons (Leics)	33
1997											
Glamorgan	17	8	2	7	256	S.P. James (Glam)	1,605	A.M. Smith (Glos)	78	S.A. Marsh (Kent)	56
Kent	17	8	4	5	252	D.S. Lehmann (Yorks)	1,575	Waqar Younis (Glam)	68		
Worcestershire	17	6	3	8	228	S.G. Law (Essex)	1,482	D.R. Brown (Warwks)	64	T.R. Ward (Kent)	29
1998											
Leicestershire	17	11	0	6	292	J.P. Crawley (Lancs)	1,681	C.A. Walsh (Glos)	106	R.J. Blakey (Yorks)	71
Lancashire	17	11	1	5	277	J.L. Langer (Middx)	1,393	A.R. Caddick (Som)	105		
Yorkshire	17	9	3	5	269	S.P. James (Glam)	1,268	E.S.H. Giddins (Warwks)	83	C.J. Adams (Sussex)	30
1999											
Surrey	17	12	0	5	264	S.G. Law (Essex)	1,833	A. Sheriyar (Worcs)	86	R.J. Turner (Som)	64
Lancashire	17	8	4	5	208	J. Cox (Som)	1,478	V.C. Drakes (Notts)	80		
Leicestershire	17	5	3	9	200	D.J. Sales (Northants)	1,156	M.P. Bicknell (Surrey)	71	N.V. Knight (Warwks)	30
								A.R. Caddick (Som)	71		

1990-1999

Leading counties

	P	W	L	D	%W
Warwickshire	185	79	51	55	42.7
Surrey	185	70	49	66	37.8
Essex	185	69	62	54	37.3
Middlesex	185	68	43	74	36.8

Leading batsmen

R.T. Robinson (Notts)	11,860
M.W. Gatting (Middx)	11,817
K.J. Barnett (Derbys/Glos)	11,766
M.R. Ramprakash (Middx)	11,638

Leading bowlers

S.L. Watkin (Glam)	594
M.P. Bicknell (Surrey)	549
P.C.R. Tufnell (Middx)	521
C.A. Walsh (Glos)	504

Leading keepers & fielder

S.A. Marsh (Kent)	487
R.J. Blakey (Yorks)	484
D. Byas (Yorks)	237

Overall statistics

Runs per wicket	32.6
Runs per 100 balls	53.1
% of matches drawn	36.7

Miscellany

Abergavenny's picturesque but tiny Pen-y-Pound ground, nestled among wooded hills, was no place to be a bowler.

In 1990 Glamorgan and Worcestershire set a record for a three-day championship game by scoring 1,641 runs there – for the loss of only 16 wickets. Worcestershire's Graeme Hick hit 252* and 100*, making him the youngest batsman, at the age of 24, to score 50 centuries. With scores of 171* and 69* in his previous match and 53 in the next, his 645 runs between dismissals established another championship record. Glamorgan were set 495 to win, a total only once chased successfully in the history of the championship, and they finished on 493 for six.

At the same ground in 1995 Gloucestershire's Andrew Symonds hit a record 16 sixes in an innings of 254, adding a further four in his second innings for a match tally of 20, another record. As if that were not enough for the Glamorgan bowlers, the two teams moved on to Ebbw Vale for a 40-over match next day, and Symonds hit another seven sixes.

Since its championship debut in 1983 the Abergavenny fixture had enjoyed year after year of glorious weather, but their luck ran out in 1996. Rain ruined the match and, after one further game in 1997, when play on the first morning was suspended while the wickets were realigned, county cricket said its farewell.

The Old Trafford pitch for the Lancashire/Hampshire match in 1992 was so full of runs that the TCCB's pitch inspector Harry Brind made a special journey on the final day to take an admiring look. Lancashire, chasing 344, were on 132 for no wicket, their openers batting with ease.

Then Hampshire's fast bowler Kevin Shine bowled both of them, following up with a further six wickets – five of them in nine balls, including a hat-trick. In 38 balls on the 'outstandingly good' pitch he took eight wickets for 13 runs.

*

Against Kent at Hove in 1991 Sussex, set 437 to win, were all out for 436, the highest total ever to result in a tie.

Hero for Kent was Antiguan fast bowler Tony Merrick, who toiled superbly, taking seven for 99 in what would be his last first-class game. The county had just announced his release.

*

In two innings at Luton in 1995, playing for Essex against Northamptonshire, the left-arm swing bowler Mark Ilott dismissed nine batsmen lbw, three of them in a hat-trick.

It was not his first lbw hat-trick. He had taken one ten years earlier for Watford Town Under-15s, though on that occasion he had the advantage that the umpire was his father. "I remember I kept shouting out, 'Owzat, Dad?'"

The championship in the 1990s

On a chilly, windswept day in April 1992, at the ground of Durham University, the championship welcomed its first new county for 71 years. For so long Durham's best players had had to migrate south, particularly to Northamptonshire who rarely produced cricketers of their own and whose mix of dressing-room dialects always contained its fair share of Tyne and Wear. Now at last they had a team of their own.

The Durham side that took the field for the first time was ironically rather like many Northants teams of old: recruited from far and wide. As well as the Australian Dean Jones, there were eight who had played for other counties; many of them, notably Ian Botham, were at the tail-end of their careers. It was intended as a stop-gap solution while the local players came through but, like their predecessors Glamorgan in 1921, they finished in last place. Not till 2005, their 14th year, did they win more games than they lost.

For the first four years of the 1990s the championship was won by the two outstanding teams of the 1980s, Essex and Middlesex. Their captains, Graham Gooch and Mike Gatting, were the last of a breed. Despite long Test careers they gave their all to their counties, and they retained a passion for the game that kept them playing well into their forties. They were the final survivors of the 1970s, the last batsmen to have served their apprenticeships in those distant days of uncovered pitches, and it showed in their enduring ability to score runs.

The game was moving on. In 1993 the mix of 22 three- and four-day matches gave way to a schedule of 17 four-day ones, each county playing each other once. Not since 1894, when the nine counties had all played home and away against each other, had it been that simple.

The reduction in fixtures led to the loss of more out-grounds: 39 in 1992, only 21 in 1999. Yorkshire said farewell to Middlesbrough, Harrogate, Sheffield and Bradford; Glamorgan to Pontypridd, Abergavenny and Neath.

With the rise of sports science and new technology, the role of the coach expanded. Middlesex, champions in 1993, had a captain/coach partnership in Mike Gatting and Don Bennett that operated in a way that was not so different from twenty years earlier. But in 1994 Warwickshire won the title with Dermot Reeve and Bob Woolmer, a pair of free-thinkers who were always on the lookout for new ideas. Soon most of the counties were looking for ground-breaking coaches, often from overseas.

Glamorgan appointed the Zimbabwean Duncan Fletcher in 1997, and they rose immediately from 16th to first place. Second that year were Kent under the New Zealand coach John Wright, third were Worcestershire under Zimbabwean David Houghton. The previous year Derbyshire, with the Australians Les Stillman and Dean Jones as coach and captain, had risen from 14th to second, though theirs was a short-lived triumph, their approach creating discord that saw the team tearing itself apart the following summer.

'The assumption seems to be that English coaches are useless,' wrote Vic Marks in the *Observer*. Yet, as he pointed out, amid all this foreign success there was an English coach, Jack Birkenshaw, who, at unfashionable Leicestershire and with no stars, had put together a team that won the championship twice in three years. It was one of county cricket's greatest achievements, yet when Birkenshaw was interviewed for the vacant England job, finding himself up against Duncan Fletcher, John Wright and the Australian Dav Whatmore, he had no chance. "Don't worry if you don't get the job," he was told before he even entered the room. "There'll be something for you in the future." But there never was.

English cricket was once more gripped by self-doubt. The Test team were losing not only to Australia, emphatically and repeatedly, but also to countries that once they would have beaten with second-string sides. At the end of 1999, when the *Wisden Cricket Monthly* magazine arranged the nine Test-playing countries in a table based on recent results, England were in last place – behind Sri Lanka, New Zealand and Zimbabwe.

In the summer of 1997, while England were losing once more to Australia, the debate raged, with the county game the focus of the criticism. Lord MacLaurin, chairman of the newly created England and Wales Cricket Board, thought there were too many games, leaving the players insufficient time for rest and practice. His first proposal for the championship involved a reduction from 17 to 14 matches. Nasser Hussain, a future England captain, thought there needed to be a sharper competitive edge to it all: "When the pressure point comes, English cricket crumbles. This comes from playing county cricket which is all very matey and lovey-dovey."

The counties were private clubs, concerned to provide as much cricket as possible for their members, but by the late 1990s their balance sheets were dependent on the money that came to them from the ECB. In many cases it amounted to more than half their annual income. So, if English cricket wanted the county game to be restructured, they were not in a strong position to resist.

At the end of 1998, more than a century after WG Grace had advocated it, the counties agreed to the creation of two divisions, with promotion and relegation. Then two years later they accepted that England's Test cricketers would be centrally contracted, playing for their counties only when the England team management wanted them to do so.

The pattern of overseas players was changing, too. Few stayed loyally with a county as they had done in the 1970s. The Jamaican Courtney Walsh was an exception, giving every summer from 1984 to 1998, bar West Indian tours, to Gloucestershire, and the South African Allan Donald gave almost as much service to Warwickshire. More typical, however, was the Pakistani Waqar Younis: three years at Surrey in the early 1990s, a triumphant championship-winning summer with Glamorgan in 1997, then a brief appearance for Warwickshire in 2003.

Leicestershire's overseas player in their two championship-winning years was the Trinidadian Phil Simmons. He never fulfilled his talent in Test cricket, but at Leicester he was the ideal signing: a gifted all-rounder and a great team man. In 1998, when James Whitaker and his deputy Chris Lewis were out of the side, he took over the captaincy in mid-season and stormed them to the championship with six victories in a row.

In the 1970s and 1980s the counties had often turned to the Caribbean for their overseas players. Indeed, the majority of the champion counties in the thirty years up to 1998 had West Indians in them, but Simmons was the last in that line. England was not the only Test-playing side in decline.

Amid such flux, however, there was still much to celebrate in the 1990s. It was the best decade, in terms of weather, that the county championship has ever enjoyed, with 1995 an especially glorious summer. That year the championship turned into a thrilling three-way contest between Middlesex, still captained by the evergreen Gatting, Northamptonshire, led in a last hurrah by Allan Lamb, and the reigning champions Warwickshire under Dermot Reeve.

Fewer than one in five games were drawn, for the first time since 1921, and champions Warwickshire won 14 out of 17, the highest proportion ever. Their loss to Northants, by seven runs in a fiercely competitive match at Edgbaston, was described by the two captains as the best championship game they had ever played. Whatever Nasser Hussain thought, the county game could still generate intense passion – and great cricket.

Hen Wlad Fy Nhadau

What other county can celebrate like Glamorgan? On Saturday 20 September 1997 thousands of their supporters made their way across the Severn Bridge, down the M5 to Taunton where they filled every corner of the ground in expectation of winning the title for the third time in their history. Six of their 1969 team were there among them.

They cheered as their batsmen built a first-innings lead of 275. Now they needed ten wickets and, with their match-winning paceman Waqar Younis suffering from tonsilitis, it fell to young Darren Thomas of Llanelli, only capped in the previous game, to be their hero with five of them.

It was 6.15 on an autumnal evening when the openers Steve James and Hugh Morris emerged, needing 11 runs for the title, and it was James [above] who was on strike when four were wanted. It was a moment he had dreamed of as a child; he had acted it out on his back lawn. Yet he recalls, "It was all a blur. I didn't even know how many we needed when I tickled the ball down to the fine leg boundary. I ran the first quickly and turned to find half of Wales on the field!"

1948 ... 1969 ... Every member of the team knew the dates of their championships; now 1997 had been added to them. 'Immortality in the Principality' was the team's rallying cry, invented in a light-hearted moment by batsman Adrian Dale, and they had achieved it.

The sun fell in the sky and, as the supporters sang heartily, Taunton came to seem like a town in the Welsh valleys.

Some players of the 1990s

Graham Gooch of Essex

> It was incredible how Goochie remained so passionate for Essex. He won more matches for us than any other England player did for his county.   *Keith Fletcher*
> If you're not going to do your best, then why bother?   *Graham Gooch*

'Goochie'

A record 1,058 Test runs for England in the summer of 1990 – and still time for 2,560 in all competitions for Essex

In 1968 he played his first 2nd XI match for Essex, a shy 15-year-old amazed by the grandeur of the Northampton County Ground and peeved to find himself batting at eleven, not ten. In 1997 he played his last 1st XI match for Essex, a still fit 44-year-old with more runs, first-class and one-day, than any other batsman in the history of the game.

He was not a natural athlete; he had a tendency to put on weight. But in 1978, when Essex turned him into an opener, he resolved to increase his fitness. The early-morning road runs, forcing himself out of bed at 6 a.m., paid dividends, not just physically but, in his own words, in "building self-motivation and strength of character".

He was ahead of his time in this, but in his dedication to his county he was of an earlier age. He captained Essex to three championships, never taking it easy when he returned from Test duty, always batting for the team and not himself. As late as 1996, at the age of 43, his 1,944 runs for Essex made him the leading batsman in England. "He was like a good red wine," his team-mate Ken McEwan says. "He got better as he grew older."

Success never made him swollen-headed; how could it in that Essex dressing room? Gooch may not have had the charismatic glamour of his boyhood hero Bobby Moore, but he shares with the late footballer a deep and abiding respect for the game that has given him so much.

Darren Lehmann of Yorkshire

> Darren understood what it meant to be Yorkshire's overseas player: about the history, about connecting with the spectators, about setting an example to the youngsters. And he was great fun to be around. He was a professional, he wanted to win, but most of all he wanted to enjoy his cricket. And he enjoyed other people's success as much as his own.   *David Byas*

Darren Lehmann came to Yorkshire on a one-year contract in 1997, filling in for Michael Bevan, but such was his impact that they brought him back for six more summers. As a pugnacious, left-handed batsman he scored big runs, and he scored them at a good pace, often in difficult conditions when the team most needed them. In the title-winning year of 2001 he averaged 83, with five centuries, none more vital than the magnificent 252 he hit against Lancashire at Headingley, the highest innings ever played in a Roses match.

A policeman's son from rural South Australia, Lehmann was an old-style cricketer, liking a fag and a pint of beer (though not the warm stuff served in England). But, beneath that surface, he had the best of cricket brains, he was superb with young players and he took immediately to the plain-speaking friendliness of Yorkshire. He loved the county's passion for cricket, and they loved him: not just for the runs he scored and the fight he showed on the field but for the time of day he had for everybody at the club.

The proud Yorkshire supporters took to him as one of their own, even voting him into an all-time county XI, alongside Hutton and Sutcliffe, and he signed off his time with them with an innings of 339, two runs short of the great George Hirst's county record.

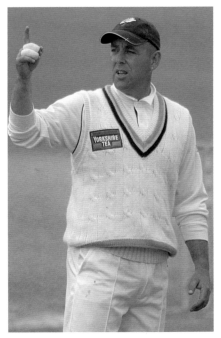

At home in Yorkshire

8,871 runs in 88 matches

Jack Russell of Gloucestershire

> He prepared so well for every game, every innings, every moment. As twelfth man you even had to get his Weetabix ready 15 minutes before the lunch break, with the right amount of milk in the bowl so that it soaked and was soft enough when he came in. *Mark Alleyne*

Stroud's finest
979 championship victims

As a boy Jack Russell always wanted to be different. At the age of twelve he even spent a night sleeping rough under a hedge, his head full of the fantasies of soldiering. Practical with his hands and happy in his own company, he might have become a draughtsman but he found his calling in wicket-keeping, and his single-minded perfectionism turned him into the best in England.

He learnt his cricket in the Stroud valley, where nobody looks out on the damp mists or breathes the Cotswold air with greater pride. As an artist he has painted its canals and railway lines, and in the car he listens to the March of the Gloucestershire Regiment.

His keeping, standing up to medium-pacers, was crucial in the county's run of one-day trophies, and his unorthodox, left-handed batting at number seven brought him two Test centuries. Indeed, it became so effective that he topped 1,000 runs – and the county's batting averages – in 1997.

Mike Gatting of Middlesex

Middlesex to the core
70 championship hundreds

> Besides his obvious talent, he has always had a tremendous enthusiasm. He has had his ups and downs in his career, but 99 times out of 100 he comes in fresh and keen to get on with it. And that's a wonderful thing. *Don Bennett*

Following Mike Brearley as captain was not an easy assignment, especially in a team of such strong-minded characters as Middlesex. But Mike Gatting was straightforward with people, he was conscientious and, in a different way from the intellectual Brearley, he had a good cricket brain. Prepared to take a risk when required, he led Middlesex to three championships and five one-day trophies in his 15 years at the helm. No one since the war has captained a county for longer.

An aircraft fitter's son, he arrived as a chirpy teenager, a bustling bundle of energy. It took him four summers to score his first century, playing for England before he did so, but he had a solid game, strong and technically correct, and he grew into the most consistent of run-scorers. Even at 41, playing one last summer in 1998, he baptised Middlesex's first visit to Southgate with his fourth double-century for the county. In later life, whether batting for Tim Rice's Heartaches or working for the ECB, he gives generously, appreciating the importance of every level of the game.

Steve Watkin of Glamorgan

> Watty had the biggest heart you could wish for in a bowler. I've seen him take his boots off at the end of a day and have blisters all over his feet and his socks caked in blood. But he was always happy to bowl. He carried the Glamorgan seam attack for years. *Hugh Morris*

A natural bowler
Leading wicket-taker in the 90s

Steve Watkin was an uncomplicated character and an uncomplicated cricketer. He was naturally fit, he took care to stay so, and he had a natural bowling action, easy to repeat, that had not changed "since I began bowling against my father on Porthcawl beach during the summer holidays". It was fine-tuned by that great coach Tom Cartwright, and for 14 summers, with rarely an injury, he ran in for Glamorgan. His arm was high, he hit the seam and he aimed relentlessly for the top of off-stump. Quicker than people expected, he could keep it tight on a flat pitch and prove dangerous on a difficult one.

For most of his Glamorgan years he was the leading seamer, his best year 1993 when in all formats, first-class and one-day, he bowled 963 overs and took 123 wickets. Then in 1997 he found himself playing the support role to the Pakistani fast bowler Waqar Younis, and their partnership was pivotal in bringing the championship title to Glamorgan.

Stories of the 1990s

Breaking all records

Brian Lara at Warwickshire, 1994

The Indian all-rounder Manoj Prabakhar was to be Warwickshire's overseas player for 1994, subject to a fitness test on an ankle that had undergone surgery. He arrived in Birmingham in early April, raring to go, but Warwickshire had their doubts – doubts that intensified when they learned that the young West Indian batsman Brian Lara was looking to try his hand at county cricket.

Lara was in the Caribbean, in the middle of a Test series against England. He signed for Warwickshire and, within days, he had hit a new record Test score of 375, creating such a surge in enquiries for membership of the Midland county that they had to hire extra office staff.

The 24-year-old was showered with gifts in his native Trinidad – a car, a house, free air travel, even the keys to an oil city – and it was much the same when he arrived at Edgbaston the day before the first game. Waiting for him was a gleaming sports car with a special number plate, L375ARA, that the DVLA later withdrew, and against all tradition he was immediately presented with his county cap.

"What's your target for the summer?" the journalists asked and, trying to keep his feet on the ground, he replied: "To get a good night's sleep and get here on time tomorrow."

The crowds packed in for the game against Glamorgan – 12,000 over the four days, twice what they would normally expect in April – and he did not disappoint them, hitting a brilliant 147. "All I want now is a massage," he said as he came off, and in the next match against Leicestershire he scored 120 and 100 not out.

Then at Taunton, in a match shortened by rain and with the handicap of a ricked neck, he led them to victory in a run chase with a dazzling 136. 'There was a certain butchery,' David Foot wrote in the *Guardian*, 'but it was carried out with delicate hands. The power came from the wrists, the dapper footwork, the eyes.'

He had hit five first-class centuries in a row, one short of the all-time record. But, on a dank morning at Lord's, with his score on 26, he fine-glanced a ball to leg and was caught behind. No one could quite believe it, though he made amends with 140 in the second innings. One six off John Emburey struck the roof of the south turret of the pavilion; a little to either side and he would have emulated Albert Trott, the only man ever to launch a ball over the Lord's pavilion.

Next came the game against Durham at Edgbaston and, with it, the chance to be the first batsman ever to hit seven centuries in eight innings. Coming out to bat on the second

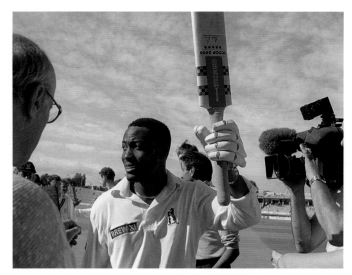

Brian Lara after scoring 501

afternoon, he mis-hit his first ball close to mid-on; on 10, he was bowled by a no-ball, and on 18 the Durham keeper Chris Scott dropped him. "I bet he gets a hundred now," Scott cursed, little guessing what was in store. By the close Lara had 111 not out.

It rained all next day, and on the last morning Durham were not interested in contriving a finish. So Lara batted on ... and on: past 300, past 400. When he took tea at 418 he knew the landmarks ahead of him: Archie MacLaren's English record of 424 and ultimately the great Hanif Mohammad's 499. Most runs in a day, most boundaries in an innings: the statisticians were in heaven.

By the time he reached 497, after almost eight hours at the wicket, he was batting with extra circumspection, determined to reach the greatest of all the records. His partner Keith Piper came down to him. "There are only two balls left, you know," he said, and Lara panicked for a moment. Then, composing himself once more, he drove the next ball to the extra cover boundary.

Now, after an extraordinary eight weeks, he held the record Test score and the record first-class score, a double only previously achieved by Bradman. But he came from a family of Seventh Day Adventists, and he was trying hard amid all the hullaballoo and the money to keep a level head. "I still don't think this makes me a great cricketer," he said. "I've so much still to learn."

After a night in which he barely slept a wink, he went down to the Oval for a vital Benson & Hedges semi-final. He left the field exhausted before Surrey's innings was over, then after a long sleep came out at number six and hit a match-winning 70. From there he headed to the airport for a brief trip home: "to see Mum".

There has never been a start like it in county cricket.

An improbable victory

Northants v Nottinghamshire, Northampton, 24-28 August 1995

The 1995 summer was one of those rare ones, like 1912, 1965 and 1976, when Northamptonshire reached the last week of August in contention for the title. Their challenge was all the more poignant for its being Allan Lamb's last season as captain. With his reputation as a hard-living maverick, eyebrows were raised when he was appointed in 1989, one journalist saying it was 'like leaving Billy Bunter in charge of the tuck shop'. But after a shaky start he settled into the job, and by 1995 he had forged a great team spirit and a dynamic style of cricket. The captaincy kept him playing into his 40s, and he wanted above all to repay Northamptonshire with their first championship.

After a week without a fixture, a week in which Lamb refreshed himself by fishing for salmon in Scotland, Northants were at home to Nottinghamshire. And the first day could hardly have gone worse. On a perfect batting track Tim Robinson, the Notts captain, won the toss, was dropped in the slips on 3 and finished the day on 204 not out, his team 353 for one. Next day they went on to 527, by which time Northants' opening bowler Paul Taylor was struggling with a groin strain and their match-winning leg-spinner Anil Kumble, weary after 50 overs, had a sore big toe. Northants ended the day on 149 for no wicket, and Lamb's only thought was to save the follow-on and hope for a fair declaration from Notts.

Lamb instructed his batsmen to be positive, and they responded magnificently. On a dry pitch the Notts spinners, Afford and Hindson, bowled badly, and in 110 overs of carnage Northants raced to 709 for seven, with centuries from Fordham, Lamb himself and the keeper Warren. Now there was another way of winning, and on the final morning Capel completed a fourth century as in nine overs they hit another 72 runs before declaring with a first-innings lead of 254.

It was a crazy summer, driven by Lamb's never-say-die spirit. Back in May and June, against Essex and Surrey, Northants had recorded the two lowest scores of the season, 46 and 59, yet won both matches. Now they were looking to win after conceding 527. Kumble bowled his fast leg-breaks for another 39 overs and, with just 17 balls to spare, they dismissed Notts for 157. It is the only time in championship history that a team has scored 500 and lost by an innings.

The Northants supporters converged on the pavilion 'almost as if the Cobblers had won the FA Cup'. In the end, to Lamb's great sadness, they did not win the championship. But my word, they played some wonderful cricket.

The divisions open up

The last matches of 1999

The championship was played in one division for the last time in 1999. All summer the table had a line drawn between ninth and tenth places, a line that grew thicker and more ominous as the season drew towards its close. When the last round of matches began, there were eleven counties, from third place to 13th, uncertain of their fate, an uncertainty made worse by the unsettled autumnal weather. Tensions were rising.

Sussex, in eighth place, travelled to Edgbaston where, opting to bat first under heavy skies, they were bowled out for 99. Warwickshire, down in eleventh place, were soon 50 for six before recovering to 207 all out. Had they deliberately prepared a result wicket? The ECB's pitch inspectors decided not but, when Sussex lost on the second evening, their captain Chris Adams accused Warwickshire of 'blatant cheating'.

The early finish at Edgbaston clarified matters at Derby. Derbyshire started the third day on 143 for three in reply to Hampshire's 362. Both counties could finish in the top nine, above Warwickshire, but Derbyshire needed to get their score to 250 for two bonus points while Hampshire, who that day announced the signing of Shane Warne, had to win outright.

Derbyshire did reach 250 but in rather odd circumstances. At 231 for eight, the crowd expected fast bowler Nixon McLean to be recalled, but Shaun Udal, standing in as Hampshire captain while Robin Smith rested a hernia in the pavilion, brought on the part-time leg spin of Giles White, and the batsmen quickly hit the 19 runs they needed. Then, amid boos and jeers, Derbyshire fed long hops and full tosses to Hampshire, even deliberately misfielding balls, to set up a declaration.

Whatever the rights and wrongs, it created a wonderful last day. Derbyshire, needing 285, slumped to 163 for seven. Then Phillip DeFreitas and Simon Lacey, veteran and novice, added 104 runs before DeFreitas holed out. Lacey battled on, his right hand broken by McLean, but on 282 for nine, three runs from victory, he chipped a catch towards the bowler and the ball somehow wedged itself between Peter Hartley's wrists.

Hampshire were euphoric, Robin Smith calling it 'one of the greatest moments of my career'. Warwickshire were furious, their mood not easing when next day they were controversially relegated from Division One of the 40-over league. They were in a winning position, ironically against Hampshire, when, five balls from the result counting, the umpires decided to abandon play.

If the ECB wanted promotion and relegation to add spice to the end-of-season matches, they had certainly been successful.

Images of the 1990s

Sachin Tendulkar

A new Yorkshireman

In the 20th century, up to 1991, Yorkshire had fielded only nine men not born within the county. All but one were amateurs, the last of whom, in 1951, was Geoffrey Keighley, an Old Etonian who was born to Yorkshire parents in France. The only professional of the nine was Cecil Parkin, and he played just once, in 1906, before somebody informed MCC that he was born twenty yards into County Durham.

In the summer of 1991 Yorkshire made the momentous decision to abandon their proud principle. After long years of cricketing disappointment and declining membership, faced with a financial crisis, they announced that in 1992 the Australian Craig McDermott would be joining them. Though Fred Trueman called the decision 'a bloody disgrace', McDermott was at least an ideal choice: a world-class fast bowler joining a team who in 1991 managed only 37 bowling bonus points, eight fewer than any other county.

A month before the season McDermott withdrew with a groin injury. The best bowler Yorkshire could find was Kenny Benjamin, a West Indian yet to make his Test debut, and he was not the calibre of player for whom they had jettisoned a century of tradition. So the Chief Executive flew to Bombay and signed the rising star of world cricket, the 18-year-old batsman Sachin Tendulkar. He was not only their first non-Yorkshire-born professional since 1906, he was their first non-white player ever.

The county shop had to throw away its 1,500 McDermott mugs, and Tendulkar scored only one championship century in another disappointing year. But membership increased by 1,500, his presence sent a fresh signal to the county's Asian communities, and the dressing room was lifted by his class.

The Yorkshire folk, rising above their reputation for hostility to outsiders, took to him from the start: his charm, his enthusiasm, his modesty. "Don't you have a go at our Sachin," one lady was heard protesting at Sheffield. "He's better than any big-headed Australian."

He was a star. Wherever they went that summer, there was an Indian restaurant offering a free meal for the whole team.

High-fives and huddles

In the years that followed the last world war, English cricket had a no-nonsense hardness about it. "Drinks?" the Warwickshire captain Tom Dollery would say. "What do you want drinks for? In the desert we had two pints of water a day – and that was for you *and* your vehicle." Or at Gloucestershire, if one of them applauded a good catch, the captain George Emmett would tell him off: "He's paid to do that. There's enough exhibitionism in cricket without your adding to it."

By the 1990s such attitudes had long gone. Sports scientists were insisting on regular rehydration while imaginative captains, keen to foster team spirit, encouraged the rituals of celebration. Warwickshire's Dermot Reeve cultivated high-fives, while at Leicester James Whitaker, an admirer of Reeve, developed a huddle. Whenever a wicket fell, his team gathered in a tight circle, sharing their joy and planning the next success.

There had been no such displays of physical intimacy when Leicestershire had won the title in 1975, as journalist Martin Johnson observed: 'The only time Raymond Illingworth was ever likely to call for a huddle was when a bit of loose change dropped out of his trouser pocket.'

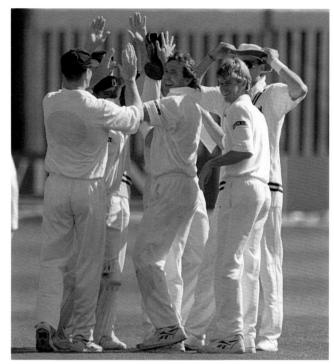

Dermot Reeve at the heart of the Warwickshire high-fives, 1995

As Leicestershire huddle, umpires Barrie Leadbeater and Peter Willey follow suit, 1996

From three days to four

County cricket had always had three-day games, right back to its beginnings in the early Victorian years. Only in 1919, in the aftermath of the First World War, was it varied, with the unsuccessful experiment with two long days.

For many years the exact hours of play in each game were left to the two counties to agree. After the Second World War there was a recommended, though not obligatory, standard: 11.30 to 6.30 on the first two days, 11.30 to 6 on the third, with an extra half hour available if either captain requested it. With 40 minutes for lunch and 15 for tea, this allowed up to 18¼ hours of playing time.

After the Second War there were few fast bowlers with long run-ups. With no drinks breaks and little changing of field positions, these hours of play allowed Essex and Leicestershire in May 1947 to bowl 420 overs in three days, a total that, under modern playing conditions, would take till the afternoon of the fifth day to reach. Two weeks later, in the First Test at Trent Bridge, it was the same story. England and South Africa bowled 587 overs in four days, a total that would now take till mid-afternoon on the seventh day.

The recommended hours could be altered by the counties, particularly if, with long journeys ahead of them, they needed to finish early on the final day. Extra time could be added to the first two days, and the total length of the match could be reduced by up to two hours.

In June 1951 Glamorgan had to travel on from Nottingham to Swansea, a tricky rail journey, so the hours of play for their Trent Bridge fixture were 11.30 to 7 on the first two days and 11 to 3 on the third. Even if they had taken the extra 30 minutes, that would have allowed only 16½ hours.

In fact, there was no question of the extra half-hour as the game was an appalling draw. Glamorgan batted first, and their captain, the single-minded Wilf Wooller, decided the pitch was 'a featherbed', of no use to bowlers. With such short hours there was nothing for it but to bat through into the second day and get four points for a draw with first-innings lead.

With 10,000 spectators in the ground on the first day, a Saturday, the Glamorgan batsmen showed no enterprise, Wooller himself the worst offender. The Notts captain Reg Simpson was a great believer in attacking cricket, and he got so annoyed by what he called 'the farce' of Wooller's tactics that he brought himself on to bowl an over of under-arm lobs. Wooller patted each one back, enflaming the crowd further after each ball by taking off his gloves and wiping his hands.

In 1955 the regulations were amended so that counties could shave only one hour off the standard time. This meant that the earliest finish on the final day was now four o'clock.

The post-war fast bowlers emerged, and there was a gradual decline in over-rates. Worse, there were games, particularly in the mid-1960s, when on the last afternoon, in a run-chase, captains deliberately slowed down the over-rate. The issue came to a head at Edgbaston in August 1967 when championship leaders Yorkshire bowled only two overs in the last 15 minutes. Brian Close's refusal to apologise cost him the England captaincy, and the next year a regulation was introduced, requiring that a minimum of 20 overs be bowled after the start of the final hour.

In 1974, for the first time, all fixtures had the same hours: 11 to 6.30 on the first two days, 11 to 6 on the third: a total of 19 hours of playing time. In 1984, with over-rates a continuing concern, it was stipulated that there would be a minimum of 117 overs on each of the first two days, 110 on the third. These figures were calculated on a rate of 18 an hour. This, however, was reduced to 17 in 1988 and 16 in 1996, when the '20 overs in the last hour' rule was altered to 16. The modern game moved at a slower pace; it could not replicate the 23 overs an hour that Essex and Leicestershire managed in 1947.

The decline in over-rates, coupled with the full covering of pitches, led to the 1980s becoming the only decade in the championship's history in which over half of all matches were drawn. The figure reached a record 63 per cent in 1985.

After England lost 5-0 to West Indies in the summer of 1984, the Test and County Cricket Board set up a working party under the chairmanship of Charles Palmer, its chairman, with a brief to look at 'the standards of play at the top level'. Twenty years earlier David Clark's committee had looked to make county cricket more attractive in itself, to bring back the missing spectators, but this time, with much of the counties' money coming from the revenue generated by Test cricket, the emphasis was on creating a better England eleven. How could the restructuring of county cricket help to achieve that?

They met nine times over the course of a year, they consulted widely and they came up with many proposals, involving all levels of cricket. For the county game they called for (i) a reduction in one-day games, (ii) a return to uncovered pitches, (iii) the introduction of some four-day games into the championship programme, and (iv) a raising of the standards of coaching.

Initially the counties, focusing on their balance sheets more than their role in producing Test cricketers, voted against all the key recommendations. But in 1987 they agreed to a return to uncovered pitches, a move that lasted only one year, and in 1988 to the introduction of six four-day games into the championship programme.

The games were scheduled at the start and end of the season and, with the weather fair, the new format made the brightest of starts. In the first round of matches Gatting, Gooch and Hick all hit double-hundreds, and the Essex/Kent match at Chelmsford reached a thrilling climax, the aggregate of 1,570 runs a new championship record.

Two summers later, to discourage the dominance of medium-pace bowling, the seam on the Reader balls was reduced from 0.9 to 0.5 millimetres, and the groundsmen, in fear of point-deductions for sub-standard pitches, all produced good batting tracks. After a warm spring, it was the driest summer since 1921, and the batsmen had a field day.

In a heatwave in early May Surrey batted for most of two days at the Oval, amassing 707 for nine. They expected the pitch to deteriorate but Lancashire, needing 558 to avoid the follow-on, ended the third day on 665 for three. 'One sometimes talks of football teams getting cricket scores,' wrote one reporter. 'Now cricket teams are getting billiard scores.'

After a 40-over Sunday match which yielded 535 runs for seven wickets, they resumed on Monday morning. The Lancashire captain David Hughes asked the scoreboard to fit a peg for the 1,000th run while Neil Fairbrother, on 311, hoped to pass Archie MacLaren's record score of 424. Exhausted from his efforts, which included a fifty in the Sunday game, he was on 366 when he pulled a ball into the hands of mid-on. "All my joints ached, my feet were sore, and for the first time I felt nervous about the prospect of breaking the record," he said. "But it was still a wonderful experience."

Lancashire were all out for 863, the two first innings adding up to a record 1,570 runs. Lancashire coach Alan Ormrod called it "the most pointless game I've ever watched", but Tim Lamb, the TCCB's Chief Executive, was not downheated: "We are seeing exactly the things we hoped for. We wanted to make life harder for the bowler."

The small seam was abandoned, and the four-day format settled down. It brought greater opportunity to middle-order batsmen, and it put an end to the contrived finishes that had come to dominate the three-day game. "Some of the counties had captains who were very good at negotiating chases on the last day," Gloucestershire's Mark Alleyne recalls. "You ended up networking, being kind to captains to try to get a good declaration. We used to be clever. Courtney Walsh would only bowl four overs in the first innings and we'd get rumours out that he was not fully fit, hoping that there would be a more generous declaration. Then in the second innings he'd come steaming in. That sort of stuff used to go on all the time."

Neil Fairbrother: the bat records details of his 366 below those of Hutton's 364 at the Oval in 1938

In 1991 the TCCB set up another committee of enquiry, this one chaired by Mike Murray, a banker and chairman of Middlesex. They recommended that the championship be all four-day matches, and this became the new format in 1993. There was a sharp fall in games that were drawn but also, with one fifth of the games finishing within three days, a significant fall in the number of days played. It was a concern to county treasurers.

Four-day cricket, unlike the one-day game, has rewarded the building of long innings, and none has been longer than the 11 hours 33 minutes Glamorgan's Steve James took to make 253 against Notts at Colwyn Bay in 1999. On the same ground the next year, after the coach had told them off for "looking to score too quickly", James hit a ten-hour 309 against Sussex. Both times his batting led to an innings victory. As in Test cricket you could now win county games by batting long and big.

Between 1950 and 1992, three-day championship cricket yielded only three triple-centuries; so far, the four-day game has seen 30. Unfortunately, for those looking to the county game to develop England's Test cricketers, 19 of them have been by batsmen who grew up overseas.

1994: Warwickshire's summer of summers

Since the introduction of one-day cricket in 1963, no county has enjoyed so successful a summer across all competitions as Warwickshire did in 1994. They won the championship with three more victories than any other side; they won both the Sunday League and the Benson & Hedges Cup; and they were runners-up in the NatWest Trophy when, losing the toss, they had conditions against them in the final.

The prize money came to more than £140,000. It was a formidable sum, though less than a group of Warwickshire committeemen, organised by former captain MJK Smith, should have received. A firm of bookmakers had offered them a yankee on the county winning the two leagues and reaching both Lord's finals, and their hastily gathered five-pound notes would have yielded £225,000 – if the bookmakers, taking fright in midsummer, had not suddenly declared it a Speciality Bet and capped their possible winnings at £100,00.

What were the key factors in Warwickshire's remarkable summer? Sitting in his cramped office as the triumphant season drew to a close, their coach Bob Woolmer named four.

First was their victory in the NatWest Final the previous September when they scored 15 off the last over to beat Sussex's record total of 321. "Winning in such spectacular fashion gave the whole club a fillip and tremendous self-belief," Woolmer said. "It showed us what is possible."

Second was the signing of the young West Indian batsman Brian Lara, whose arrival soon after scoring 375 against England brought a great buzz to Edgbaston, a buzz that only increased when in his first seven innings he hit six centuries, culminating in a record 501 against Durham. In 15 championship matches Lara hit 2,066 runs and, critically, he hit them off only 2,262 deliveries, an electrifying scoring-rate that created extra time for the bowlers to take wickets.

"His influence has rubbed off on the others," Woolmer said. Gladstone Small who had played for England and was nearing the end of his career, was as affected as any of them: "Even me, bowling with him standing there at slip, I wanted to show him that I was good, that I could play in the same team as he did. Everyone's game got raised by a huge amount.'

Third factor for Woolmer was the leadership of captain Dermot Reeve and his deputy Tim Munton. He called them "perfect foils for each other": Reeve the hyper-active innovator, creating an exuberant sense of fun, and Munton the steady professional. Reeve was at his best in the one-day games, conjuring unlikely tricks, while Munton – 'Captain Sensible' – was more in his element in the championship. With Reeve struggling all summer with niggling injuries, Munton captained nine of the 17 four-day games, and eight of their 11 victories came under him. He was a hard-working, ever-reliable medium-pacer who, in his size 12 boots, bowled more overs in the championship, 693, than anyone but the Kent slow-left-armer Min Patel, and took more wickets, 81, than anyone but Gloucestershire's Courtney Walsh. He was at the heart of their success.

It helped, Woolmer added, that not one Warwickshire player was required all summer by England, though there was anger in Birmingham when, after their glorious year, only the keeper Keith Piper was selected in either of England's two winter tour parties. Not since Nottinghamshire in 1981 had a county won the championship without a current England player, and Notts had had not one but two overseas players in the all-rounders Clive Rice and Richard Hadlee.

For Woolmer the fourth factor in their success was the emergence of several "young players of talent". Never was this more apparent than in their victory in mid-July over Surrey at Guildford, the game on which their championship success was pivoted. Reeve was out with a strained groin, Small with a strained hamstring; Lara, worn out by his early efforts, was hobbling on one knee, no longer scoring runs like clockwork; and early in the match all-rounder Paul Smith had his right hand broken while Piper suffered a badly bruised thumb.

Up against the championship leaders, they were reduced on the first day to 131 for eight. Then Dougie Brown, on his championship debut, and Graeme Welch, playing only his third game, scored fifties in a stand of 110, and that evening and the next morning Roger Twose, a part-time bowler standing in for Paul Smith, took a career-best six for 28. Andy Moles, back in the team after an appendix operation, then hit a 'workmanlike, shuffling, unfussy' 203 to set up a victory that Tim Munton's seam and Neil Smith's off-spin duly delivered. It was the best of team performances.

'Never in 17 years of professional cricket,' wrote the Hampshire captain Mark Nicholas, 'have I come across less self-centred play; never have I seen a team more tickled by each other's success; never have I seen cricketers so bent on cameos that mean nothing in averages but mean everything in victory.'

On the surface they were a highly disparate bunch: Keith Piper from a tough, uncompromising background in North London, Andy Moles from a toolmaking factory in Coventry

Warwickshire in 1994: (left) Dermot Reeve and Tim Munton with the three trophies (right) standing: Bob Woolmer, Dermot Reeve,
Michael Burns, Michael Bell, Richard Davis, Neil Smith, Dominic Ostler, Trevor Penney, Paul Smith, Stuart Nottingham (physio)
kneeling: Keith Piper, Andy Moles   sitting: Tim Munton, Roger Twose, Gladstone Small, Graeme Welch   lying: Brian Lara

and Neil Smith, son of MJK, from the prestigious Warwick School; Roger Twose with his *Financial Times* and the wild Paul Smith with his Rothman's, his can of Pepsi and his obsession with the dead rock star Jim Morrison. Yet, as fringe team member Jason Ratcliffe recalls, "When everyone walked over the white line, there was absolute unity and togetherness."

There was a period in June, after his 501, when an exhausted Lara was off the field more than he was on it – it was calculated that he excused himself from 16 hours of fielding – and that angered Dermot Reeve, with his 'team comes first' ethic. The ensuing row took some sorting out by senior figures in the club, who insisted that Lara be cut some slack, but generally they played as a unit: full of aggression, full of fun and with a sense that every team member, however junior, be included in discussions. That was Dermot Reeve's style, full of physical contact and joy. He introduced 'smile breaks', and he had them playing 'keepy-uppy' with an imaginary football while fielding.

"Fellas," he told them all at the start of the summer, "we chase a ball around a field for a job. We're not important; we don't save lives. We're entertainers. Cricket will come and go in our lives so let's enjoy it while we're here."

During the hours of play, however, the fun did not extend to exchanging pleasantries with the opposition. "We weren't choir boys, shall we say," admits Gladstone Small. "We wouldn't have won the Fair Play League."

There was a fifth factor in their success, one that Woolmer omitted to mention, and that, of course, was Woolmer himself. As a coach he was well ahead of the game, and he had in Reeve a captain receptive to new ideas. They worked on the little things: running between the wickets, slip catching, scoring their runs more quickly. They were the first team regularly to play the reverse sweep, a shot first played many years earlier by Mushtaq Mohammad at Northampton. And they made it all immensely enjoyable. "We broke records," Woolmer said, "and created expectations that inspired new levels of team camaraderie, from karaoke evenings to golf days and team songs. It was fun like I had not experienced in my whole career."

Their success, Mark Nicholas wrote, 'was a triumph for fine, detailed coaching, intelligent planning and innovative thinking that inspired a young, fit team to relish their privileged role as first-class cricketers.'

The following year Woolmer left them to be South Africa's coach, and Lara did not return, replaced by the South African fast bowler Allan Donald. Tim Munton missed several games after a back operation, and Andy Moles' Achilles tendon went in June. Yet such was their spirit, and their depth of resources, that they were champions again, winning a record 14 out of 17 matches. They also won the NatWest Trophy, and only rain in their last home match prevented them from retaining their Sunday League title. To those who had spent the summer of 1994 calling them Larashire, it was the perfect riposte.

1996: Leicestershire the 40/1 outsiders

It was easy to see the 1996 success of Leicestershire, 40/1 outsiders in the spring, in negative terms. They were an unfashionable county, playing before small crowds at an uninspiring ground. There were no stars; in fact, a good half of the side were cast-offs from other counties. 'Leicestershire were a team of modest talents,' wrote *Wisden Cricket Monthly*. 'All the more credit to them, but all the less to county cricket.'

English cricket, in low water, was looking far and wide for fresh thinking, be it from Tesco's Lord MacLaurin or the Australian coaches which more and more counties were employing. Yet here at little Leicester, almost unnoticed, a pair of Yorkshiremen were forging a revolution with simple ideas.

Jack Birkenshaw, the county's coach, came back from a winter in South Africa with one such idea. The schedule of all four-day matches, now in its fourth year, left gaps between games – so, instead of driving late at night to a distant hotel, why not set off early in the day and spend the afternoon, as away teams did in South Africa, practising at the ground, getting familiar with the field and the changing rooms? Then in the evening they could meet for a meal and a team talk.

It did not always work out. The hour and a half their Trinidadian Phil Simmons allowed to reach Swansea via Aftab Habib's house in Reading proved beyond even his driving speed. But it made a difference, as did the little "one per cent" changes that the new captain, James Whitaker, introduced: the team all taking the field together; the television on mute in the dressing room; the captain proudly wearing his blazer at the toss; the catching practice added to the end of each day in pre-season. "It was in that age when a lot of county cricketers seemed to be doing just enough to hang on," Whitaker says. "We wanted to do something different from that."

Whitaker, a Yorkshireman like Birkenshaw, albeit one – in the words of Mike Selvey in the *Guardian* – whose 'natural bombast had been polished by Uppingham School', brought modern thinking to his leadership. Nigel Briers, his predecessor, was a schoolteacher and had created a well-disciplined team. Whitaker, the son of a chocolate manufacturer, shifted the emphasis onto personal responsibility, self-belief and, above all, enjoyment. "We decided right from the start that we'd get back to the basics of why we were all professional cricketers – and that was to enjoy it."

Before the season, by letter and phone, he kept in touch with his team, wherever they were. Then at the start of each day's warm-up he would get them into a circle and lead a short exercise in visualisation. "We'd think about how we wanted the day to go," Darren Maddy, the youngster in the side, remembers. "What sort of effect we wanted to have on the day. It was all about self-belief and relaxation."

"I've always been interested in how to focus the mind," Whitaker says. "Sport is ninety per cent in the brain, isn't it?"

"It's not about if, it's about when," he would say, and he would invite the thoughts of every one of them.

"The freedom of expression was a big thing," says Phil Simmons. "Nobody felt like they couldn't say anything."

They had their share of characters, not least the trio of seamers: the left-armer Alan Mullally, dreamily playing Bob Marley songs on a guitar in the dressing room; the natty-dressing ex-miner David Millns who made it clear to Whitaker that he did not want to be "flogged to death in the morning nets" and was allowed to stroll in later than the others; and 'Bullhead' Parsons, the gnarled veteran forever moaning about bowling uphill into the wind and about the pitiful return from the benefit he had had to share with the groundsman. Yet such was the spirit in the side that, at the end of the summer, Vic Marks noted, 'Even old Gordon Parsons is playing with a hint of idealism and an absence of self-interest.'

Mullally was called up by England for the six Tests, but still they needed only 13 players all summer, fewer than any other champion county in history. "We were like the closest family you could imagine," wicket-keeper Paul Nixon says. "It's the best team environment I've ever known. Every morning we leapt out of bed and galloped into work."

Their campaign began in early May at Derby. After losing the first day to rain, Whitaker asked the home team to bat, and Kim Barnett responded with a double-century. The start was not good. "It was windy and cold," Whitaker says, "and we were a bit disconnected, as you can be when it's windy and the fielders are spread out. After a long partnership a wicket fell, and we all came together in a huddle, part out of coldness and part out of a feeling of 'Bloody hell, we've got a wicket.' Then we got another one quickly so we decided to do it again. And the more we did it, the more we found we were enjoying it."

"We were squeezing up as close as possible just to warm up," Phil Simmons recalls.

The huddle turned into a permanent feature, developing into an opportunity to talk about the way to dismiss the next batsman. "Who the hell's in charge here?" asked one umpire, and Whitaker replied: "We are. Take a look at the scoreboard."

Despite their bad start they won at Derby, and their confidence grew. The batsmen all found form: Aftab Habib, a Middlesex cast-off, hit a double-century in only his third match; Vince Wells, a bits-and-pieces player from Kent, was moved up to open the batting and in the space of seven innings hit scores of 200, 197 and 204; there were centuries from Nixon, Maddy, Ben Smith, even a maiden hundred by Millns who, in the same match against Essex, took ten wickets.

The catching benefited from the pre-season practice, and the bowling – from the workhorse Parsons to the unsung hero, off-spinner Adrian Pierson – was full of options. "The energy that swung round the team was immense," Whitaker says.

The captain himself was at the top of his game, hitting four centuries including, sweetest of all, a double-hundred in the match in late June that was the pivot of their season.

Yorkshire, top of the table, had revived their run-down Park Avenue ground in Bradford. It was the scene of so many past glories, Len Hutton's favourite ground, but the world had moved on – and, in Bradford, not for the better. The grand pavilion had been pulled down, there was razor wire on top of the roadside wall and, according to the *Guardian*, 'the players emerged from what looks like an ice-hockey sin-bin.'

It would be Yorkshire's last championship game there and, as if to rub in the sense of decline, they dropped seven catches. Whitaker, with 218, hit the highest score by a Yorkshireman against his native county, and the total of 681 for seven remains the highest ever against Yorkshire. "Declare, Leicestershire," shouted the crowd on the second afternoon. "You'll never get us out ... You're killing the game." But, thanks to the bowling of Millns, Parsons and the slow-left-armer Matthew Brimson, the Midlanders won with two sessions to spare.

Though they were a team greater than the sum of their parts, one man did stand out: Phil Simmons. He never came good in the Test arena, but he threw himself wholeheartedly into Leicestershire and he bought into Whitaker's culture. "He worshipped the game, the practice, every aspect of it," Birkenshaw says. "My god, he hit the ball hard," says Whitaker. "You would feel alive batting with him." He bowled at a brisk pace, and he stood wide at first slip and held extraordinary catches. His 1,186 runs, 56 wickets and 33 catches is the best all-round tally since the fixtures were reduced in 1993.

It was a Saturday in late September when the title was finally won, with news from the Oval that Surrey could no longer catch them. The players were at tea in the Grace Road pavilion, and the 3,000-strong crowd gathered outside. "Simmo! Simmo!" they chanted.

Meanwhile Jack Birkenshaw was anxiously ringing the Oval, to check the score. "He was the cornerstone of the whole thing," Simmons says. "He recruited so well. He didn't just know a good cricketer, he knew a good team man."

1999: The start of Surrey's third golden age

In 1999 Surrey were the last champions of the 20th century, the last winners of the old one-division championship, and in 2000 they were the first champions of the 21st century, the first winners of the new Division One. In 2002 they won a third time when, in a new era of central contracts, their four England players Alec Stewart, Graham Thorpe, Mark Butcher and Alex Tudor managed between them only 20 appearances.

With three titles in four years, their dominance of county cricket was not as enduring as the great Surrey sides of the 1890s and 1950s but, after a barren 28 years, it gave a long-overdue substance to the much-disliked Surrey Strut.

'I can live with the swagger,' wrote the former Hampshire captain Mark Nicholas, 'as it increasingly represents genuine self-confidence rather than the fabricated stuff borne of insecurity a few years ago.'

Just how long the Surrey members had waited for success was underlined at the last home game of 1999 when, with the title already won, the pavilion bar reduced the price of beer from £2 to the 20p it had been in 1971, thereby depriving their Yorkshire visitors of a good moan about London prices – though some found an outlet for their gloom in speculation about the price of beer when they were last champions.

Surrey had turned themselves into a wealthy club, and at last they were matching their commercial success with on-field performances. Unlike the teams that won the title in the mid-1990s – Warwickshire, Leicestershire and Glamorgan – Surrey were always providing players for England, five during 1999, and they needed a large squad. But it was a squad that was dominated by players who had developed their game within the county: Adam and Ben Hollioake, Darren and Martin Bicknell, Mark and Gary Butcher, Alec Stewart, Graham Thorpe, Ian Ward, Alex Tudor and Ali Brown.

The seeds of their transformation from under-achieving stars to championship winners were sown back in 1995 when a dismal season led to a major shake-up. The Australian Dave Gilbert, a friend of the new cricket committee chairman Vic Dodds, was brought in as cricket manager, and he was not slow to challenge the prevailing culture. "Surrey cricket had got itself into a terrible mess," he says. "It seemed as if all they were interested in was hanging on to their Test status and making improvements to the Oval. I kept opening my big Aussie mouth, and Vic had to keep kicking me under the table."

He ripped down the dressing-room partition that separated the capped from the uncapped players – "You almost had to ask to go in," Ali Brown recalls – and he established a code of conduct, with fierce fines for lateness: £50 up to ten minutes, £250 after that.

"David Gilbert was pivotal," says Jason Ratcliffe, an all-rounder who had come down from Warwickshire. "He joined everybody up together, made us all agree how we should behave. People actually sat and watched the cricket rather than piss about in the dressing room."

Gilbert stayed two years. In the first they won the Sunday League; in the second the Benson & Hedges Cup. He switched the captaincy from Alec Stewart, so often away on England duty, to Adam Hollioake, and he was party to the most important decision of all: the choice of overseas player for 1997. One option was to re-sign Waqar Younis, who six years earlier had taken 113 wickets in 17 championship matches.

"Winning the championship with an all-seam attack is very difficult," Adam Hollioake says. "David Gilbert and I looked at the history of the sides who had dominated the championship over a period of time, and they all had a pair of quality spinners. Surrey in the 1950s had Laker and Lock, Essex in the 1980s had Childs and Such, Middlesex had Emburey and Edmonds. And we didn't even have one."

Rather than Waqar, they recruited the 20-year-old Pakistani off-spinner Saqlain Mushtaq. Hollioake calls it "the hardest decision I ever had to make as captain" – and, when Waqar's wickets brought championship triumph to Glamorgan, it was not obvious that it was the right one. But Surrey also signed the leg-spinner Ian Salisbury from Sussex, and soon enough the spin-bowling pair, with their complementary styles, became a key element in the county's success.

In 1999 the World Cup, staged in England, kept Saqlain from Surrey till the end of June but thereafter, in only seven matches together, he and Salisbury took 88 wickets. "We had a good enough seam attack to compete in the early season," Hollioake says. "Then Saqlain became available in the dry months. If he was playing, we would pretty much put ourselves down for a win at the Oval."

Durham batsman Martin Speight remembers coming up against the Pakistani off-spinner: "Saqlain turned up with his doosra, and it was 'Christ almighty, what the bloody hell is this?' It felt like someone had invented a new game."

"When Saqlain joined," recalls Keith Medlycott, the former Surrey spinner who had succeeded Gilbert, "he was telling me about the fields he wanted for his bowling, all sorts of

(left) The match-winning spinners Ian Salisbury and Saqlain Mushtaq

(right) Surrey, the family club, in 1999: (back) brothers Darren and Martin Bicknell, Alex Tudor and father Darrel, a club steward, brothers Ben and Adam Hollioake (front) brothers Gary and Mark Butcher on either side of coach Alan, their father

Not in picture: Alec Stewart and father Micky, the President in 1999

positions around the bat that I would never have considered when I was bowling slow left-arm. But once I saw his impact, I realised that he should have whatever field he wanted."

"Medders was the best coach I played under," Hollioake says. "Mainly because of his communication skills and his man-management. He kept everybody on an even keel."

There were so many who contributed to the success, not just the England players Thorpe, Stewart, Tudor and Butcher. There was the ever-reliable seamer Martin Bicknell from Guildford: "the consummate professional, the first name on our team list," according to Medlycott.

Ali Brown, their top run-scorer in 1999: "He comes across as jovial, someone who likes to strike the ball," Hollioake says, "but he could really battle hard. He scored hundreds when we were under pressure. As captain I would turn to Mark Butcher, who had the best cricket brain in the side, for tactics; I would turn to Alec Stewart for moral and spiritual guidance; and I would turn to Alistair Brown for an alternative view. He always had an interesting way of looking at things. He was a problem solver."

And the opener Ian Ward who had fought his way back onto the staff after a spell in the wilderness when he was cleaning aircraft: "He faced a lot of testing spells against Donald, Akram, Walsh," Brown says, "and he would see us through that opening period. He was a great team man. If we had a meeting in the morning, he would bring in coffees for everyone."

At the centre of it all was Hollioake himself, a maverick who had spent his early years in Australia and who brought fresh ideas to the game. He wanted not just to win but to say to the other sides, "You're so far away from us, it's not funny."

The key game of 1999 was in July at Guildford. Hampshire, their closest rivals, were the visitors, and midway through the second day Surrey were starting their second innings with a deficit of 151 runs. "We didn't really rate Hampshire that highly," Hollioake says. "I remember saying before the second innings, 'Who here thinks we can still beat these guys by 200 runs?', and everyone was adamant we could."

Butcher and Ward opened up with a stand of 107, Thorpe hit a patient and commanding 164 and, when Hampshire were left 322 for victory on a pitch that was now taking turn, Saqlain worked his magic, taking six wickets. Hampshire, crushed by the 156-run defeat, did not win again for two months.

After Guildford the victories were emphatic. The title was won, with two matches to spare, with a two-day victory over Notts at the Oval. In the evening, after the crowds had gone, they sat together, players and staff, on the outfield.

Dale Naylor, their physio, took them through the summer game by game and, in the words of Mark Butcher, "As though round the camp fire, we recounted tales from the season and passed round the champagne-filled trophy."

Unbeaten, they won 12 of their 17 games.

2000 – 2009

Two divisions

Central contracts for England cricketers

First titles for Sussex and Durham

The time is approaching to reform the first-class county structure, as opposed to merely meddling with the cricket and the fixture list. What we have at the moment is a Victorian institution that resisted reform in the 20th century and struggled into the 21st on subsidies rather than public support.

It is easy to understand, to sympathise even, with resistance to radical reform. But if 18 counties cannot pay their way without subsidy, and if they fail the needs of the national team, do we need so many?

England in the 21st century has become an urban society, built on cities and conurbations. Why not a professional circuit based on these, rather than shires and counties, however romantically their names resonate?

Wisden Cricketers' Almanack 2001

A survey of current county cricketers

Q: Which is the most important domestic competition?

    274 chose the county championship

     17 chose the Twenty20 cup

      5 chose the Pro40 league

      5 chose the 50-over trophy

Professional Cricketers' Association, 2009

2000s

2000 The championship begins the new century with two divisions, with three teams promoted and relegated. Leading England Test cricketers are awarded central contracts, with counties compensated for their loss.

The Laws of Cricket, updated by MCC, now include a pre-amble on The Spirit of Cricket and a much-extended Law 42 on Fair and Unfair Play. A penalty of five runs is introduced for various offences.

Chelsea beat Aston Villa 1-0 in the last FA Cup Final at the old Wembley Stadium.

2001 Yorkshire win their first championship since 1968.

Slow over-rates are now penalised by point-deductions, not fines.

Sven-Goran Eriksson becomes the England football team's first non-English manager.

2002 Yorkshire, on the verge of bankruptcy, elect a four-man board to run affairs. Champions in 2001, they finish in last place. Their relegation means that in 2003, for the first time, the championship will not feature a Roses match.

More than one million people fill The Mall in London for a celebration of Queen Elizabeth's Golden Jubilee.

2003 Sussex become the 14th county to win the championship.

A player released from the England squad can return to his county in mid-match and replace a previously nominated player, even if the replaced player has already batted or bowled.

A Twenty20 competition is introduced into the county schedule, drawing large crowds. The matches are full of innovation, though a proposal for a joker over, in which runs count double, is rejected.

In the last minute of extra time in the Rugby World Cup Final, Jonny Wilkinson drops a goal to give England victory. At the European Court of Justice Maros Kolpak, a Slovak, wins the right to play in the German Handball League. Because of Slovakia's close economic ties with the European Union, he is to be treated as if he were an EU national. With South Africa, Zimbabwe and several Caribbean countries all deemed to have such economic ties with the EU, the judgment has profound consequences for county cricket, ushering in a tide of 'Kolpak' players.

2004 Warwickshire win five of their 16 matches, the lowest proportion ever by the champion county.

Parliament passes an Act that bans the hunting of foxes with hounds.

2005 After eight successive series defeats, England regain the Ashes from Australia.

Surrey are relegated as a result of an eight-point deduction for ball tampering in a match at the Oval.

Chance to Shine, a charity promoting cricket in state schools, is established. It is estimated that cricket is played in fewer than one in ten state schools. The educational background of an average county eleven in 2005 is 3.4 overseas, 2.2 private and 5.4 state. In 1965 it was 0.7 overseas, 1.3 private and 9 state.

Same-sex couples acquire new rights through civil partnerships while trans-sexuals can re-register their gender.

2006 Liverpool Victoria, an insurance company, become the championship's sixth sponsors, following Schweppes (1977-83), Britannic Assurance (1984-98), PPP Healthcare (1999-2000), Cricinfo (2001) and Frizzell (2002-05). The number of counties promoted and relegated falls from three to two.

Sky television buys exclusive rights to the broadcasting of all England's home Tests and one-day and T20 internationals.

BBC announces that it is to phase out its 48-year-old Grandstand sports programme. "It no longer punches through in this multi-channel world," the Director-General Mark Thompson says.

2007 Sussex are champions for the third time in five years.

The average rainfall in May, June and July is the highest in 310 years of record-keeping. There is widespread flooding, with no cricket played at New Road, Worcester after June 13.

Sub-prime lending in the US precipitates a financial crisis in which the world banking system comes close to collapse.

2008 Durham become the 15th county to win the championship. Their success leaves only Gloucestershire, Somerset and Northamptonshire still in search of the title.

Barack Obama, an African-American, is elected President of the United States.

2009 *Wisden chooses a woman, Claire Taylor, as one of its Five Cricketers of the Year.*

Henry Allingham dies at the age of 113. He is thought to have been the last man alive to have seen WG Grace play.

Championship – top three   Leading batsmen   Leading bowlers   Leading wkt-keeper
Leading fielder *Victims*

	P	W	L	D	Pts		*Runs*		*Wickets*		*Victims*
2000											
Surrey	16	9	2	5	213	D.S. Lehmann (Yorks)	1,477	G.D. McGrath (Worcs)	76	B.J. Hyam (Essex)	51
Lancashire	16	7	1	8	193	J.L. Langer (Middx)	1,472	S.K. Warne (Hants)	70		
Yorkshire	16	7	2	7	188	S.G. Law (Essex)	1,352	D.M. Cousins (Northants)	67	D.P. Fulton (Kent)	29
2001											
Yorkshire	16	9	3	4	219	M.E.K. Hussey (Northants)	2,055	R.J. Kirtley (Sussex)	75	N.D. Burns (Leics)	67
Somerset	16	6	2	8	203	D.P. Fulton (Kent)	1,729	M.P. Bicknell (Surrey)	72		
Kent	16	4	3	9	175	M.W. Goodwin (Sussex)	1,521	D.E. Malcolm (Leics)	68	D. Byas (Yorks)	38
2002											
Surrey	16	10	2	4	242¾	I.J. Ward (Surrey)	1,708	K.J. Dean (Derbys)	80	N.D. Burns (Leics)	63
Warwickshire	16	7	2	7	198	M.J. Di Venuto (Derbys)	1,538	M.J. Saggers (Kent)	79		
Kent	16	7	4	5	195½	N.V. Knight (Warwks)	1,520	A.J. Harris (Notts)	63	D.P. Fulton (Kent)	30
								A. Khan (Kent)	63		
2003											
Sussex	16	10	4	2	257	S.G. Law (Lancs)	1,820	Mushtaq Ahmed (Sussex)	103	R.J. Turner (Som)	65
Lancashire	16	6	2	8	223	M.E.K. Hussey (Northants)	1,697	M.S. Kasprowicz (Glam)	77		
Surrey	16	6	3	7	219	M.W. Goodwin (Sussex)	1,496	J. Lewis (Glos)	74	M.J. Powell (Northants)	29
2004											
Warwickshire	16	5	0	11	222	B.J. Hodge (Leics)	1,548	Mushtaq Ahmed (Sussex)	82	R.J. Turner (Som)	65
Kent	16	7	3	6	206	I.R. Bell (Warwks)	1,498	G. Keedy (Lancs)	72		
Surrey	16	5	5	6	195½	M.R. Ramprakash (Surrey)	1,451	Danish Kaneria (Essex)	63	G.A. Hick (Worcs)	25
2005											
Notts	16	9	3	4	236	E.C. Joyce (Middx)	1,668	Mushtaq Ahmed (Sussex)	80	C.M.W. Read (Notts)	60
Hants	16	9	3	4	233½	O.A. Shah (Essex)	1,650	G.J. Kruis (Yorks)	64		
Sussex	16	7	3	6	224	M.R. Ramprakash (Surrey)	1,568	J.M. Anderson (Lancs)	60	M.L. Love (Northants)	36
2006											
Sussex	16	9	2	5	242	M.R. Ramprakash (Surrey)	2,211	Mushtaq Ahmed (Sussex)	102	J.S. Foster (Essex)	68
Lancashire	16	6	1	9	224	H.D. Ackerman (Leics)	1,804	Zaheer Khan (Worcs)	78		
Hampshire	16	6	3	7	207	J.P. Crawley (Hants)	1,737	C.M. Willoughby (Som)	66	G.A. Hick (Worcs)	36
								R.D.B. Croft (Glam)	66	M. van Jaarsveld (Kent)	36
2007											
Sussex	16	7	3	6	202	M.R. Ramprakash (Surrey)	2,026	Mushtaq Ahmed (Sussex)	90	P. Mustard (Durham)	65
Durham	16	7	5	4	197½	D.J. Sales (Northants)	1,384	O.D. Gibson (Durham)	80		
Lancashire	16	5	2	9	190	M.J. Di Venuto (Durham)	1,329	Danish Kaneria (Essex)	74	M.E. Trescothick (Som)	33
2008											
Durham	16	6	3	7	190	M.W. Goodwin (Sussex)	1,343	J.A. Tomlinson (Hants)	67	S.M. Davies (Worcs)	68
Notts	16	5	3	8	182	H.D. Ackerman (Leics)	1,302	T.J. Murtagh (Middx)	64		
Hampshire	16	5	4	7	178	J.A. Rudolph (Yorks)	1,292	A.U. Rashid (Yorks)	62	M. van Jaarsveld (Kent)	28
2009											
Durham	16	8	0	8	240	M.E. Trescothick (Som)	1,817	Danish Kaneria (Essex)	75	P. Mustard (Durham)	62
Notts	16	4	2	10	193	M.J. Di Venuto (Durham)	1,601	J.C. Tredwell (Kent)	69	J.M. Kemp (Kent)	30
Somerset	16	3	1	12	182	M. van Jaarsveld (Kent)	1,475	S.P. Kirby (Glos)	64	M. van Jaarsveld (Kent)	30

2000s

2000-2009

Leading counties (Division One)

	P	W	L	D
Lancashire	144	45	23	76
Kent	144	45	37	62
Sussex	128	44	31	53
Surrey	128	42	25	61

Leading batsmen

M.R. Ramprakash (Mx/Sy) 14,017
M.W. Goodwin (Sussex) 11,202
M.J. Di Venuto (Derb/Dur) 11,096
S.G. Law (Esx/Lan/Derb) 10,547

Leading bowlers

Mushtaq Ahmed (Sy/Sussex) 484
R.D.B. Croft (Glam) 464
J. Lewis (Glos) 444
G. Chapple (Lancs) 441

Leading keepers & fielder

C.M.W. Read (Notts) 449
J.N. Batty (Surrey) 431

G.A. Hick (Worcs) 210

Overall statistics

Runs per wicket	33.9
Runs per 100 balls	56.5
% of matches drawn	44.4

Miscellany

In 2003 James Kirtley became the first man to be released from an England squad and to return in mid-match to his county side. A specialist bowler, he arrived on the second day of Sussex's game at Horsham to find that Kevin Innes, the bowler he would replace, was batting.

The 27-year-old Innes, an outstanding schoolboy cricketer, had never got beyond 63 before, but that day at Horsham he came off with 103 not out. A few minutes later Kirtley was bowling, and Innes was running out with the drinks.

*

Somerset's first championship match of 2007, against Middlesex, saw 1,659 runs scored for the loss of 13 wickets, with centuries scored by a record eight batsmen. During the winter the county had spent £10,000 attempting to make the square more bowler-friendly.

*

Against Leicestershire at Southgate in 2009 Middlesex used five wicket-keepers. Ben Scott started, but he fell ill on the second night. Eoin Morgan kept for most of the third morning until David Nash arrived from a second-team game at Beckenham. But the next morning Nash was injured in the warm-ups, and Neil Dexter took over until another reinforcement, John Simpson, arrived from Beckenham.

The latest date at which the championship has been decided was in 2008 when Durham's title was confirmed at 4 p.m. on 27 September, 164 days – 23½ weeks – after the start of the first round of matches. The earliest date was in 1910 when Kent won on August 12, just 102 days – 14½ weeks – after the start. Kent did not play in the first two of those weeks, either.

*

Only twice has a county won a game after following on more than 250 runs behind: Gloucestershire overcoming a deficit of 254 at Taunton in 1976 and Hampshire one of 252 against Glamorgan at the Rose Bowl in 2003.

Hampshire, in the depths of an injury crisis, had called up the Havant all-rounder Richard Hindley who at the time was painting his mother's office. His contribution on the first two days – 0/46 and 8 runs – was undistinguished, but in the second innings he hit 'several meaty blows' off Robert Croft, drove and square-cut 'an increasingly frustrated' Michael Kasprowicz and came off with a crucial 68 not out off only 70 balls.

His little finger had been broken by Kasprowicz, putting him out for a month, and to his bemused dismay he was never asked to play again. In the history of the championship only nine batsmen have a better average than his 76.

The championship in the 2000s

A new century brought major change to the county championship, with the introduction of two divisions. It was a move greeted in some quarters by scepticism. Matthew Engel, editor of *Wisden*, said that many of the counties had voted for it 'not from conviction but from a weary certainty that this was an idea that would not go away and that they would keep getting beaten over the head until they acquiesced. ... The counties have been bamboozled into a reform born of panic.'

For some it was just one more gimmick to refresh the competition, promotion and relegation bringing alive late-season matches that would otherwise have had no significance. To allay fears that an elite would develop in Division One, the counties opted for 'three up, three down' each year, and in six years of this system every county had at least one year in the top flight – and all but Kent experienced Division Two.

An elite did emerge, however, and in 2006, when six of the seven counties with Test grounds were in Division One, the system switched to 'two up, two down'. With promising players moving to the stronger teams, it became much harder for the less wealthy counties to escape from Division Two.

As with every reform of the championship, promotion and relegation had unforeseen consequences. Yes, it added spice to end-of-season matches, but all too often counties brought in ready-made players where in times past, with the season winding down, they would have given a chance to a youngster.

The change to two divisions, along with the creation of central contracts for England players, might have been expected to create a period of calm. But, if anything, criticism of the county game intensified.

England continued to lose heavily to Australia, and each defeat was followed by attacks on county cricket. There were too many teams, too many players, too many matches, too much mediocrity, too little time to rest and practise. "When you lose, you should hurt for three weeks," the England coach Duncan Fletcher said. "You should assess what happened and why. Instead, you've got the coach and the captain saying to you, 'Forget about it because we've got another game today.'"

The criticism reached a climax in September 2003, the summer when the new Twenty20 competition brought in big crowds. Lord MacLaurin, the recently retired chairman of the ECB, called for a reduction from 18 to 12 in the number of first-class counties, and he was supported by a Cricket Reform Group, made up of Bob Willis, his brother David, Mike Atherton, TV's Michael Parkinson and Saracens rugby club

chairman Nigel Wray. They also wanted to 'de-professionalise' 12 of the 18 counties and to create a streamlined board of management separate from the counties' First-Class Forum.

England captain Michael Vaughan weighed in, arguing that the counties should play only eight fixtures, not 16. Further, the games should be spaced out 'so players can rehab properly, study the opposition and prepare as if they were playing in a Test.'

The debate grew heated. Mike Soper, chairman of the First-Class Forum, accused Lord MacLaurin of changing his tune, Somerset Chief Executive Peter Anderson called Atherton and Willis 'disloyal' and 'disgraceful', and Christopher Martin-Jenkins in *The Times* argued passionately that the chief problem lay not with the county game at all but with 'the indulgent, commercially driven increase in international cricket that is messing up our domestic game'.

Amid this furore the championship responded with a climax as emotional as any in its history. Sussex, the most ancient of all the county clubs, seven times runners-up, were champions at last, and the celebrations at Hove, when the vital batting point was won, held up play for an unprecedented eight minutes.

Surrey were champions in the first year of two divisions, as they had been in the last year of one division. The promise of a dynasty to rival the 1950s was broken the following year, but they won emphatically in 2002, a campaign made poignant by the death in late March in a car crash in Australia of their young all-rounder Ben Hollioake.

His brother Adam, the captain, only returned to cricket in July, and thereafer he played as a man possessed, topping the averages with a series of scintillating innings. "The ball came down, and I was just hitting it hard. I had no emotions, no fear, no hesitancies, because I really didn't give a shit. See ball, hit ball. It was like I was having an out-of-body experience; I wasn't really there. I'd love to be able to bottle that feeling and sell it. You think, 'Wow, if only I'd known this before. All that analysing when all I had to do was not care!'"

The whole team had been galvanised by the death, as batsman Ali Brown recalls. "We put so much energy into that season that we were never the same side afterwards."

Their key bowler, as in their other title-winning years, was the Pakistani off-spinner Saqlain Mushtaq and, when he was absent for two matches in August, they called up his compatriot, the leg-spinner Mushtaq Ahmed. He impressed them but, with Saqlain returning, they did not need him. "This guy mustn't finish up with Yorkshire or Lancashire," Hollioake told the

Surrey coach Keith Medlycott. "We've got to make sure he goes somewhere where he'll never win the championship."

With Surrey's blessing Mushtaq signed for Sussex, and such was his impact that the south-coast county won their first title in his first year, adding a further two in 2006 and 2007. As a match-winner, indeed a championship-winner, he became the outstanding county bowler of the modern era.

In the midst of Sussex's three successes came titles for Warwickshire and Nottinghamshire, both of which gave some cause for concern. Warwickshire had an outstanding batting line-up – Nick Knight, Mark Wagh, Ian Bell, Jonathan Trott and the Australian Brad Hogg – and, with Knight winning 13 tosses out of 16, they piled up large totals at a good rate of scoring. But they lacked penetrative bowling, and their success, with only five wins out of 16, owed much to their ability to win maximum bonus points in drawn matches. Their bowling record, taking their wickets at 40.6 runs each, was the worst of the 18 counties.

Nottinghamshire, champions next year, had a better balanced side and, under the inspired captaincy of New Zealander Stephen Fleming, they played attacking cricket, winning nine of their 16 matches. Mick Newell, their coach, was a shrewd man who knew the characters who would create a happy team, but it did disturb some that, like Leicestershire in 1975, they won without a single Nottinghamshire man in their regular eleven.

Newell's great gift was to spot potential in players at other counties, a policy which advanced the careers of several, notably Graeme Swann. More worrying for those who saw the championship as a breeding ground for England's Test team were those counties who took maximum advantage of the European court ruling which allowed some cricketers to escape from the ECB's restriction on overseas players. This reached an extraordinary peak in a 2008 match between Leicestershire and Northamptonshire, when the two teams included ten South Africans and a West Indian, none of whom were eligible to play for England, as well as an Australian with a British passport and an Irishman who had played for his country in one-day internationals.

By this time, the England cricket team had won the 2005 Ashes and, despite a setback in Australia, were on their way to the number-one spot in the world Test rankings. So the criticism of county cricket had died down ... for now.

In 2008, to much delight, Durham won for the first time.

Yorkshire champions – with a little help from Lancashire

In 2001, after a wait of 33 years, Yorkshire were champions once more. Their captain David Byas, like his 1960s predecessor Vic Wilson, was an East Riding farmer, and his team had plenty of home-grown players. But there were also major contributions from two Australians: their star batsman Darren Lehmann and their new coach Wayne Clark, who had never set foot in England before that summer. "Forget about winning the championship," he told them when he arrived. "Trophies are the end result; it's the process that counts."

Perhaps more shocking to the Yorkshire purists, their leading wicket-taker, Steve Kirby, was a Lancastrian from Bury. For six years he had been trying to make it at Leicestershire, but injuries kept setting him back and, without a single first-team game to his name, the county gave up on him.

Not one to accept defeat, he wrote to Yorkshire, had two games in their second eleven and did well. A fiery character on the field, he had real pace and he could swing the ball.

His chance came in June when, on the second day of Yorkshire's match at home to Kent, Matthew Hoggard was called away by England. Kirby was summoned from his job as a flooring salesman in Leicester, signed a two-year contract and took Hoggard's place. Finally he was a first-class cricketer, and he celebrated when, bowling for the first time in the Kent second innings, he took seven wickets for 50 runs. "I'm not daft," he said afterwards. "I know it won't always be like this, but for the moment I'm just delirious that I've been given a second chance."

In the next home game, to rub in their loss, he took 12 for 72 against Leicestershire.

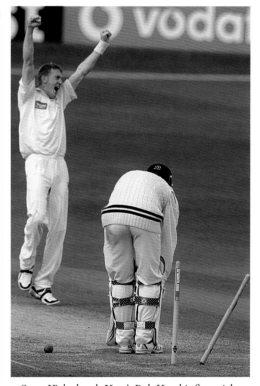

Steve Kirby bowls Kent's Rob Key, his first wicket

Some players of the 2000s

Championship winner

457 wickets in five summers

Mushtaq Ahmed of Sussex

His religion was as much a part of him as his googly. *Robin Martin-Jenkins*

I am not going to ask you if you believe in a god, but may I suggest that you pray occasionally? It will focus your mind. *Mushtaq Ahmed*

He played five full summers for Sussex, and in each of them he took many more wickets than any other bowler in the country – wickets that brought three championships to Sussex.

Yet his signing was a gamble. He had left Somerset in 1998, with doubts about both his knee and his character, and by 2002 he was bowling in the Liverpool and District League. Surrey recruited him for two games that summer and, though he went wicketless in the first at Hove, Sussex were intrigued. Could he give them that little bit of magic? When they spoke to him, they liked what they heard. He was focused and enthusiastic; he had found Allah.

He loved to bowl long spells, never worried by the odd bad ball. Like his childhood hero Abdul Qadir he was all whirling arms, and he had great variation, no ball more lethal than his hard-to-pick googly. With fielders around the bat he attacked the stumps, his frequent and impassioned lbw appeals adding hugely to the day's entertainment. He was great fun.

They left him to his prayer mat when they went to tea, and sometimes they ribbed him when his conversation returned, as it always did, to Allah. But there was deep respect – for the unfailingly positive spirit and the mental strength that his faith gave him and for his match-winning bowling. Fifteen times in those five years he took ten wickets in a match.

The Sussex members loved him, and he loved Sussex, so grateful that they had given him this second chance. Has any county in the modern age made a better signing?

Chris Read of Nottinghamshire

Taking over from Stephen Fleming, the best captain in the world, was a tough task, a bit like following Alex Ferguson, but Ready's level of personal performance was so incredible, he had the respect of the team from the outset. *Mark Wagh*

An intelligent Devonian, only 5'8" tall, Chris Read belongs in the great tradition of unshowy keepers: early anticipation, immaculate glovework, assured when standing up. In 2008, a year after England controversially discarded him, he was appointed captain of Notts and, though he would not claim that his quiet, calm leadership is in the class of his predecessor Stephen Fleming or his Devon captain Peter Roebuck, he combines a sound tactical brain with a steely, don't-mess-with-me determination. He achieved in 2010 what only one other man, Gregor MacGregor of Middlesex in 1903, has done: captain a county to the championship while keeping wicket regularly. Unlike MacGregor, who was no batsman, Read was also his team's leading run-scorer, as he was in 2009 and 2012. Among the great all-round feats in the history of the championship, Read's triumph in 2010 should not be underestimated.

His batting, playing shots from the first ball, shows a different side to his character, the side that finds delight in driving souped-up motor cars. Even after becoming a devoted family man, he bought an obscure Japanese people-carrier that could go from 0 to 60 in no time. And so it is with his middle-order batting. On many an occasion, after a poor start on the challenging Trent Bridge pitches, his Notts team-mates have been grateful for his 0 to 60 with the bat.

In the modern county game there are few who have achieved more than Chris Read.

A true all-rounder

Leading keeper in 2005 and 2010

Glen Chapple of Lancashire

> He just gets on with it; he doesn't make a great fuss about things. How he's gone 20 years at the level he has without playing Test cricket is amazing. People can't understand it. *Mike Watkinson*
>
> Other players say, "When is Chappie going to retire?" They just hate playing against him. He's such a good competitor; even a game of tiddlywinks he'd want to win. *Steven Croft*

Glen Chapple's ability to swing the ball both ways has made him a testing proposition. "When you're standing at slip," one team-mate says, "you feel you're going to get a catch every ball, even against the best batsmen." He may never have been a bowler of the highest pace, but he has kept fit, with a disciplined lifestyle, and he is proud of how he maintained his speed right through his 30s. He can also score good runs from the lower order, with six centuries and 8,440 championship runs to his name.

Even as a young lad from Earby, north of Colne, he was a good team player, reliable in the best way, with plenty of heart and spirit. Quiet and not especially outgoing by nature, he has matured into a captain highly respected by his team and by opponents alike. Approachable, hard-working, loyal to Lancashire, no one deserved more to lift the trophy when in 2011 the county finally won the championship again.

Wholehearted Lancastrian
920 championship wickets

Robert Croft of Glamorgan

> Crofty had a real passion for playing for Glamorgan, a passion for representing Wales. He's always said that his Tests for England were like playing for the British Lions. *Mark Wallace*
>
> I'm not Murali. I'm not coming here with a bag of tricks. I'm just coming here made up of one hundred per cent effort and a big heart. *Robert Croft*

From the west Wales village of Hendy, from where he has never moved, Robert Croft is a Welshman to his core. He speaks the language, he fly-fishes the rivers; he has even been honoured by the Gorsedd of Bards. At the National Eisteddfod at Bala they dressed him in a long, green robe, named him Robert o'r Hendy, then flew him in a helicopter to his match at Colwyn Bay.

A thinking off-spinner, growing cannier with each passing summer of his 24-year career, he was capable of patient, defensive spells and of match-winning ones when he spun the ball sharply, then deceived batsmen with a non-turning 'skidder'. Never frightened of hard work, never short of inner steel, he was always amongst the busiest bowlers each year, and he scored vital runs, too. In the championship-winning summer of 1997, his contribution of 577 runs and 54 wickets was crucial.

A throwback to another age, he played with pride for Glamorgan till he was 42.

Proud Welshman
500 runs & 50 wickets ten times

Marcus Trescothick of Somerset

> That feeling you get when the ball meets the middle of the bat and you see it fly to the boundary, I get the same buzz from it today as I did in schoolboy cricket. There is nothing like it. *Marcus Trescothick*
>
> Even as a young kid he'd be hitting thousands and thousands of cricket balls with his dad, going to every training session. You almost had to fight the bat out of his hands. *Peter Trego*

At the age of 15, playing at the local Keynsham club and anywhere else he could get a game, he scored an incredible 4,000 runs. At 18, hitting his first two hundreds for Somerset and a double for England Under-19s, he looked destined for greatness, a tall left-handed batsman with a rare gift of timing.

There followed five years when his progress was fitful, then a surprise England call-up and 76 Tests before in late 2006 he turned his back on the long months away from home. An autobiography revealed inner turmoil, but his team-mates at Taunton decided not to worry about that. "Let's just be normal and take the piss out of him," one suggested, and in that atmosphere he turned into the most consistent run-scorer in the country. Serious-minded about the game, abundantly respected and Somerset through and through, he took on the captaincy in 2010 and so nearly led the county to its first championship.

'Banger'
7,460 runs in five years

Stories of the 2000s

Farewell to Northlands Road

Hampshire v Yorkshire, Southampton, Saturday 16 September 2000

The championship said farewell to the County Ground, Southampton in September 2000. Yorkshire were the visitors and on a dry pitch, which took 'an abnormal amount of spin' from the start, they set Hampshire 272 to win. At 113 for one the home supporters were full of hope.

The roars could be heard from down the road at the Dell where Southampton's footballers, with a 2-0 win over Newcastle United, were lifting themselves out of the Premiership's relegation zone. But there was no such prospect for the cricketers. In this first summer of two divisions their last hope of avoiding the drop had passed, their fate cruelly rubbed in when in this last game they suffered an eight-point deduction for a sub-standard pitch. It was a sad ending for the old ground.

Remorselessly the Yorkshire spinners Fisher, Middlebrook and Lehmann worked their way through the Hampshire batting line-up, taking the ninth wicket off the last ball of an over as the pavilion clock moved its minute hand towards the 5.30 close. The required overs had been bowled, and the Hampshire number eleven Peter Hartley lingered on the boundary, hoping the umpires were going to remove the bails. They did not. So he stood at the non-striker's end and watched as his fellow Yorkshire exile Alex Morris set out to survive six balls from slow-left-armer Ian Fisher.

With every Yorkshire fielder clustered expectantly around the bat, Morris negotiated the first five without alarm. Then came the last ball that the championship would ever see at Northlands Road, and he edged it into the hands of second slip.

The next day, at the end of a Sunday League match, a lone Royal Marine bugle accompanied the lowering of the pavilion flag, leaving the ground to the bulldozers and the demolition men. The following summer the Dell would go the same way.

The groundsman tops the averages

Warwickshire's Tony Frost in the summer of 2008

On a cold morning in January 2008, in his second winter on the ground staff, Tony Frost was verti-draining the outfield at Edgbaston. His days as a professional cricketer were over, and he was enjoying his new life, soaking up so much new knowledge.

His career as a wicket-keeper/batsman had had its highs, none greater than winning the championship in 2004, but it had come to a premature end in 2006 when curvature of the spine had forced his retirement at the age of only 30.

The end was particulary sad because the coach Mark Greatbatch had given him a book to read, *Golf is a Game of Confidence* by Bob Rotella, and it had changed his whole approach to cricket. 'Stay in the present. Pre-determined and negative thoughts only slow your reaction times.' He played six matches early in that summer of 2006, and he topped the county's batting averages.

Two years later he broke away from verti-draining as the new coach Ashley Giles approached him. Tim Ambrose, their keeper, had just been called up by England. Was there any way Tony could help by filling in during the summer?

He practised hard, and in the first match he saved the game by batting out the draw on the last afternoon. Then, with Ambrose back, he returned to his duties on the ground. "On a beautiful day, preparing a pitch or cutting the outfield with my music in," he says, "it's very soothing."

From mid-May to August Ambrose was with England, and in his place Tony Frost hit the form of his life: 90 against Middlesex, a career-best 144 at Gloucester, his first two fifties in 50-over cricket, even a Twenty20 fifty. His back made keeping hard work, but the combination of Rotella's positive thinking and the knowledge that he had a career to fall back on gave him a relaxed confidence when batting. "I didn't feel the pressure as much as I used to," he says.

When Ambrose returned, he stayed in the team as a batsman, and at Chelmsford he hit 242 not out. As he waited to bat for the last time that summer, team-mate Neil Carter told him he needed 59 runs for his 1,000. "But I blocked it out. To think about that, it would have gone against everything I'd tred to do all summer." He scored 62, finishing the season with an average of 83.58, the highest in the land.

In a table in *Wisden*, listing the leading batsman of each summer, he sits beside Ramprakash, Bell and Dravid.

Back from the Ashes

Hampshire's Shane Warne in the summer of 2005

The Ashes series of 2005 was as draining, physically and emotionally, as any in modern history. After five epic battles, all crowded into eight weeks, England held on for a draw at the Oval that won back the Ashes after 16 years of defeat. The following day, amid great cheering crowds, the team were paraded on an open-top bus through the streets of London, then entertained at Downing Street. By the end of it all, most of them were visibly the worse for wear.

Paul Collingwood, who had played only the last Test, returned to Durham for their final match, and the next week Ian Bell appeared for Warwickshire. But that was all the county championship saw of the England team in its last two rounds of matches. They were centrally contracted, and they had earned a rest.

The Australian Shane Warne had certainly earned a rest. Till the second week of July he had thrown his all into captaining Hampshire, taking them to the top of the Division One table. Then in the five Tests he bowled 253 overs, almost 60 more than anybody else on either side, and he scored vital runs. Yet the day after the Oval Test he got into his car and drove to Cardiff to join up again with Hampshire. Simon Katich, their other Australian, did the same.

Warne was fulfilling an ambition to lead that had been denied him by Australia, and he had transformed the culture of the South Coast county. "The brand of cricket we played was totally different," his vice-captain Shaun Udal says. "It was aggressive, and we were led by someone with the power and the presence to back his chat up with performances. He made you believe in yourself."

Not for Warne the game that drifted into the cul-de-sac of a draw. Everything was focused on winning and, in the field, on taking wickets. "He came up to me once," the fast-medium seamer Dimi Mascarenhas recalls, "and he said, 'How are you trying to get this guy out?' And I was like 'Um'. I wasn't. I was just bowling. Just that question made me think about bowling in a different way."

Warne played a tough game, in the Australian style, and they finished last in the Spirit of Cricket table. But there was much more to him than his combativeness. "He's got a very sensitive side to him which is never portrayed in the press," Udal says. "I know if I've got any troubles I can always speak to him. He would remember people's names. He was very big on manners and politeness, like he always shook the gateman's hand. He used to say, 'Manners are free.'"

Rod Bransgrove, the chairman, concurs: "I once heard him telling his players to be sure to thank the dinner ladies."

Udal captained the five matches during the Ashes series. "There was never a day that went by when Warney wouldn't ring and see how things were going. He'd ask about particular players. 'I see he

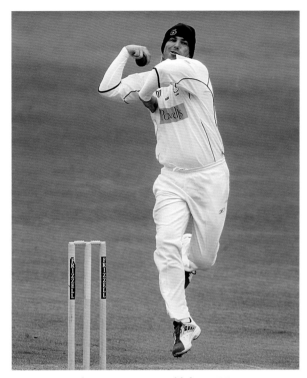

Shane Warne on a cold day in May

didn't get any runs – what happened?' His input was there, even when he wasn't with us."

It was all boiling up to a last-round encounter at the Rose Bowl between Hampshire and championship leaders Notts, captained by New Zealander Stephen Fleming. Their earlier game at Trent Bridge had ended with Warne's Hampshire snatching a victory when Notts, with six wickets in hand, only needed 26 to win.

"Within three days of the Ashes being lost," Udal says, "he and Simon Katich were playing for us at Cardiff. They wanted to. But you could see in Warnie's eyes he was tired. His body was tired."

Warne, the hardest-worked bowler in England that year, took five wickets as they beat Glamorgan. Then they thrashed Notts by an innings. But by then, thanks to a contrived finish at Canterbury, where Kent had tried to keep alive their own slim hope of the title, Notts were champions. Warne was furious, calling the Canterbury finish "one of the dumbest things I've ever seen".

He had fought hard and in vain to keep the Ashes with Australia, and he had been every bit as determined to bring the championship to Hampshire.

Images of the 2000s

Hot, Hot, Hot

The summer of 2006 saw Surrey's Mark Ramprakash break several records. He was the first batsman to hit 150 in five successive matches; his first-class average of 103 was the highest ever by an Englishman, and he passed 2,000 runs for the season in only 20 innings.

Yet still the Test selectors, seeing him as a man unable to handle pressure, did not return to him. So, while England were going down to a 5-0 defeat in Australia, he was winning over Saturday night's television audience on *Strictly Come Dancing*. He was nicknamed 'Mister Sex in Sequins', with one judge, Arlene Phillips, calling him "a beautiful man in a beautiful body". In the final he and Karen Hardy danced a salsa, to the calypso *Hot, Hot, Hot*, and it brought a standing ovation and a perfect score of four tens from the judges.

It was the second year running, following the success of Yorkshire's Darren Gough, that a cricketer had won, and it revived a link between cricket and dancing that had lain dormant for many years. Jack Hobbs, CB Fry and Johnny Tyldesley had all been accomplished ballroom dancers, recommending it as a way of keeping fit in winter.

In the 1950s the Hampshire batsman Alan Rayment and his wife, qualified ballroom teachers, ran a dance studio in the Hamtun House Hotel next to the Southampton ground. He had taken lessons as a teenager when the president of his cricket club, Finchley, told him that dancing would speed up his footwork when batting.

"Sports people are fit," he says. "They have a trained ability to concentrate and receive instruction, and Mark had a wonderful teacher in Karen Hardy. But he was coming out of cricket, with its all-male banter, and he had first to overcome his embarrassment at the overtly sexual environment of the show. Once he adjusted to the way professional dancers neutralise all that, he could focus on attaining a high level of performance."

"I've never been more nervous in my life," Ramprakash says of the moment when he stood behind the curtain and for the first time heard his name called. "But as a cricketer I was used to performing in the moment, and I felt prepared for the mental side of the show from the work I had done with the England psychologist."

It was fourteen weeks of relentlessly hard work, under the gaze of the cameras, and his performance in the final dance, he said, "was as important to me as anything I have ever done in my life".

Without him England were already 3-0 down in Australia, but live on television, in front of 12 million viewers, he rose to the occasion magnificently.

"He showed me what being a true competitor is all about," Karen Hardy says. "Respect for your teammates, and a lot of hard work, heart and determination."

'He displayed the kind of footwork that would have been useful Down Under,' *The Times* suggested.

The 38-year-old Ramprakash returned to cricket, hitting ten centuries in 15 games for Surrey in 2007. He became the first batsman to score more than 30 per cent of a county's total runs in a season and the first to average 100 two years running.

"Dancing does speed up your reflexes," Alan Rayment says. "I expect his footwork was even quicker that year."

Mark Ramprakash and Karen Hardy,
Strictly Come Dancing, November 2006

Flooding at Worcester

June 2007 was a wet month, very wet, and the heavy rain that fell in the final week – a month's worth in a day – flooded Worcestershire's New Road ground. It was the eighth time in the club's history that the field had gone under water during the cricket season, and it wreaked havoc with their Twenty20 programme. They relocated to Kidderminster for the game against Northamptonshire but, unable to get into the store room, they had to ask their opponents to bring the stumps.

The water receded and, on the weekend before the next championship match, a 'Marigold Army' of 250 volunteers, young and old, all armed with yellow rubber gloves and squeegees, cleaned every single seat and railing. It was a great community effort, encapsulating the best of Worcestershire as a family club, but it was all to no avail. The outfield did not drain, there was more rain and – to the great annoyance of Kent who had wanted to play at Kidderminster – not a ball was bowled.

A Twenty20 game was moved to Derby, where it rained, and a match against Sri Lanka A to a local school ground where spectators were asked to bring their own seating and drinks. Finally they got the New Road ground back to normal for the championship match against Lancashire on July 20.

It was fit for play at nine in the morning. But, alas, the rain came back. Torrential rain. In nearby Pershore 5.6 inches were recorded in the day. The Severn and Teme rivers burst their banks, and the next day the M5 was closed, with thousands of travellers spending the night in their vehicles or in service stations. In Worcester the water rose to nearly 17 feet above normal, close to its all-time record in March 1947.

The director of cricket Steve Rhodes swam through the deep water to retrieve a laptop from his office in a flooded portakabin, and that was it for cricket that summer at New Road. They played the last two championship matches at Kidderminster, and they won the Pro40 League after 'home games' at Derby, Edgbaston and Taunton.

The cost to the club was in excess of one million pounds. To their relief, however, to the tune of £375,000, they discovered that an insurance policy, taken out the previous year when they staged an Elton John concert, had no exclusion for flood damage.

Ground developments

The Rose Bowl

Hampshire's old County Ground at Northlands Road in Southampton was cramped and rundown, with no room to expand. So in the 1990s they decided to move. A site was identified, open fields to the east of the city, and they tried their luck with an application to the recently created National Lottery.

By the time the Lottery said yes, with its first major sporting grant, the scheme had grown greatly. Now it was to be 'a landmark site for domestic and international cricket', also serving as 'a sporting hub for the local community'.

A golf course, squash courts, a top architect to design a pavilion for the future: some of the decision-makers were chartered accountants, but in the excitement generated by the successful bid – which, along with the ground sale, gave them £15m – they lost control of the budget.

In the autumn of 2000, with the old ground under demolition and the new one only part-constructed, they stood on the verge of bankruptcy.

Their saviour was a local businessman, Rod Bransgrove, who had sold his pharmaceutical company. He was passionate about cricket, right back to the days when as a boy he had collected autographs at the Oval. "Haven't I signed for you before?" Micky Stewart once asked him. "Yes," he replied without inhibition. "But I can swap six of yours for a Peter Parfitt."

Disappointed that his Surrey trials came to nothing, he migrated in time to Hampshire where he played for 15 years for a team of friends, The Staggerers, and got to know many of the county's players, helping to organise their benefits. So in 2000, with money in the bank, he relished the prospect of helping out. He injected capital, and the club was restructured as a public limited company. Hampshire, first to abandon the traditional members' club, were striking into new territory.

The summer of 2001 brought first-class cricket to the Rose Bowl. The pitches were unpredictable and the players had to change in marquees but, according to Rod Bransgrove, "It was great fun. Morale was very high." Why, the dressing rooms were even going to have jacuzzis.

If Rod Bransgrove had been involved from the start, he would have argued for a more modest scheme, but he is proud of the customer feedback after their first Test in 2011 – and proud of their community work. The boxing club, which started with six members, now has 500; the golf course is being expanded to 18 holes; and the new Cage Cricket is appealing to youngsters. There is a Learning Centre and work with the young unemployed. "We need more multi-generational activities, teaching respect and standards, making youngsters into good people," he says. "Cricket can provide that."

This most modern of grounds now has a capacity of 25,000.

Hove

How wonderfully fitting that the fortunes of Sussex, the county of Ranjitsinhji and his nephew Duleep, of the Nawab of Pataudi and Imran Khan, should be revived by a substantial legacy from the son of an Indian trader.

Spen Cama's father brought Indian carpets to North London to sell. He contracted a serious chest disease and died in hospital, but not before he had fallen in love with a Welsh nurse who, after his death, gave birth to his child. Mother and boy moved down to Brighton where the young Spen fell in love with cricket. At the age of 19, in 1927, he founded with friends a wandering team which they called the Preston Nomads.

Ten years later, while studying for the Bar, Spen Cama bought several plots of land at Fulking, using them to create a ground for the Nomads. Inheriting his father's entrepreneurial spirit, he acquired changing rooms from the Hove Tennis Club and converted an old railway store shed into a pavilion.

He never practised as a barrister, opting instead to build up an extensive property portfolio, but his passion for cricket remained constant. A left-arm bowler, he captained the Nomads for many years, playing till the age of 60. From 1981 to 1983 he was President of Sussex.

He died without family in 2001, leaving one-third of his money to the county club. It was thought that this might amount to as much as £4 million but, by the time the assets had been realised, a boom in property prices had taken the sum to well over £10 million.

Sussex resolved early to spend the legacy on capital improvements. Should they follow Hampshire's example: sell up and move out of town, create a brand new ground capable of staging Test matches? No, it was better to stay in their Hove heartland and look after their existing members.

The Sussex captain Mike Yardy was consulted. "We want to play in front of big crowds," he said. But did he mean big crowds or full houses? "Full houses." It was not going to be another Rose Bowl.

The first plan featured a five-storey stand, offices, flats, a restaurant and a conference centre, but local residents objected. So they settled for a scheme that blended better with the surrounding streets and retained more sympathetically the traditional ambience of Sussex cricket.

"We are building a seaside county cricket ground, not a stadium," the new chief executive Dave Brooks said in 2009.

The pavilion was enhanced, a 1,500-seat stand was built, and the tired, old Gilligan Stand gave way to a smart, new building that includes a press box, physiotherapy rooms and a gym, with seats for spectators on top. But it was not all change. The ground capacity has stayed at 7,000, and at the Cromwell Road end the grass bank and deckchairs remain.

The players come and go

Right up to his death in 1932, Lord Harris was all-powerful in his role as MCC Treasurer, and he exercised his power, as a ferocious stickler for detail, in enforcing the regulations that governed the registration of county cricketers. He was determined that counties would only select those properly qualified by birth or residence and that the movement of players between counties would be fiercely discouraged.

In August 1923 Worcestershire, bottom of the table as they had been the previous summer, enjoyed a little run of three victories that owed much to the batting of Leonard Crawley, a Cambridge undergraduate on vacation, and Victor Fox, a professional footballer with Middlesbrough. Against Northamptonshire they shared a partnership of 304 runs.

Their success brought them to the attention of Lord Harris, who discovered that neither man was properly qualified for Worcestershire. This led to a spectacular scene in the Long Room at Lord's in which Lord Deerhurst, the county's President, took on Lord Harris: "May I congratulate your Lordship on having buggered the career of another young cricketer?" The argument became so heated that, behind their backs, the Essex captain Johnny Douglas mimed the role of a boxing match referee. Neither Crawley nor Fox was allowed to play county cricket in the following two summers.

The regulations were loosened a little in 1939, allowing cricketers unwanted by one county to move more easily to another. Through the 1950s several Yorkshiremen, unable to get into their own side, found their way to other counties. There were also a few instances of cricketers moving, with permission, to captain another county: Mike Smith to Warwickshire, Willie Watson to Leicestershire, Raman Subba Row to Northamptonshire, Ossie Wheatley to Glamorgan.

In the 1964 championship there were 27 players on their second county, and in all but two cases they had moved without fuss. The exceptions were Tom Graveney who, on losing the Gloucestershire captaincy in the autumn of 1960, moved to Worcestershire, and Peter Richardson, who moved from Worcestershire to Kent two years earlier. Graveney had played 48 Tests, Richardson 25, yet – because their counties objected to the moves – both were forced to spend a year playing second-eleven cricket. It was a fate that also befell the England cricketer Barry Knight who, upset at being passed over for the Essex captaincy, signed for Leicestershire in 1967.

The ground shifted in 1970 when Tom Cartwright, against the wishes of Warwickshire, signed for Somerset. Like Graveney, Richardson and Knight, he faced a year out of the game, but unlike them he was a strong trade unionist and he had the support of the recently formed Professional Cricketers' Association. "I was angry," he said. "I was married with kids, and all I was looking to do was to pursue my profession, to build a future. I had no freedom of movement. It was an appalling situation. I thought it was quite unacceptable for them to try to block me like that."

With his case argued by Jack Bannister of the PCA, he triumphed. Though Bob Willis missed the first half of 1972 when after a pay dispute he moved from Surrey to Warwickshire, the regulations were never so strictly enforced again.

The movement of players increased. Before the Second War there was only one cricketer who appeared for three counties, and he was an amateur of no great distinction, Jack Gentry. In 1919, serving in the county's regiment, he played once for Hampshire. In 1922 and 1923, he played eight times for Surrey where he was living. Then in 1925 he played once for Essex, his county of birth.

In 1959 Bob Berry, a professional, became the first man to be capped by three counties, moving when no longer required from Lancashire to Worcestershire, then to Derbyshire. Then in 1980 Allan Arthur Jones broke new ground, signing for Glamorgan after spells with Sussex, Somerset and Middlesex.

Jones' four counties were matched in 1982 by Jim Cumbes, then in 1999 by Jason de la Pêna, a fast-medium bowler who never quite made it. Despite appearing for four counties, he played only eight championship matches in his nine summers as a professional cricketer. After that he became a successful sports presenter on Sky television.

With the 21st century came two divisions and a further increase in the movement of players. By 2014 there were 29 men who had represented four counties in the championship. Three of them – AJ Harris, Simon Katich and Damien Wright – have played for five while one, Marcus North, has reached six.

In part this has been the result of changes in employment law. In part it reflects a wider world in which people are less inclined to stay put through their working lives. It also stems from the changing pattern of overseas players. With other countries staging cricket throughout the year, the top players are rarely available for a whole English summer. So counties, under pressure to achieve success, often find themselves bringing in a succession of overseas stars, each staying for only part of the season.

Kyle Hogg

The only cricketer to have played for three counties in a championship season.

In 2007 he played once for Lancashire, twice on loan for Worcestershire and twice on loan for Warwickshire.

Marcus North

The only cricketer to have played for six counties in the championship.

Durham (2004)
Lancashire (2005)
Derbyshire (2006, 2014)
Gloucestershire (2007-08)
Hampshire (2009)
Glamorgan (2012-13)

An outstandingly successful player of this type was Muttiah Muralitharan, the Sri Lankan spinner whom Lancashire brought in for five part-seasons in nine years. A popular character, he took 236 wickets in 33 matches, the only bowler in championship history to average seven wickets a game.

At present a county can have two overseas players registered at any one time. The registrations must be for a minimum of 21 days, and only one can play in any championship match.

In 2004, when two were allowed per match, Durham started with the Australian batsman Marcus North, in the first of his six engagements, and the Pakistani fast bowler Shoaib Akhtar, the 'Rawalpindi Express' whose 34 wickets in seven games for Durham the previous summer had put him at the top of the national averages. An unfit Shoaib managed only two games, and in his place Durham tried several replacements: Reon King from Guyana, Tahore Mughal from Pakistan, Pallav Kumar from India, Andy Blignaut from Zimbabwe and finally Shaun Tait, the Young Bradman Cricketer of the Year from South Australia. All were disappointing, with Tait unable to establish a run-up and finishing his two matches with figures of 18 overs, no wickets for 176 runs. After that, Durham settled for the 21-year-old Graham Onions from Gateshead.

Four years later Shoaib reappeared as a potential saviour for Surrey who, with three matches left, were threatened with relegation. He arrived in England without the correct visa and was sent back. Before returning, he stopped off for an appearance on Indian television. Then, when he did turn up for the last two games, it became clear that the seven months since he had last bowled left him short of pace. Described by *Wisden* as 'more Thomas the Tank Engine than Rawalpindi Express', he took one wicket for 117 runs.

In the fast-moving world of global cricket, checking overseas scores is not simple, as Worcestershire discovered when in 2011 they offered a two-year contract to a 26-year-old Cambridge graduate Adrian Shankar on the back of a series of outstanding innings in Sri Lanka during the winter. After a poor start to the season, it emerged that he was, in fact, 29 years old, that he had never been in the Arsenal Football Academy as he claimed and that the elaborate website containing all his Sri Lankan scores was a fiction which he himself had created.

Those registered as overseas cricketers can only play for one county in a summer, a restriction that otherwise no longer applies. Steven Crook, in 2005, was the first cricketer to appear for two counties in the same championship season. Under a regulation that allows a mid-season transfer, provided the new county offers a contract that extends to the next summer, he played once for Lancashire, then moved to Northamptonshire for whom he played three times in September.

The regulations also allow a home player to be loaned out, even if he has already played for his own county. Under this arrangement Kyle Hogg played for three counties in 2007, while in 2012 Sajid Mahmood, for Lancashire and Somerset, finished up playing four times against Sussex, having a hand in Murray Goodwin's dismissal in all four games.

In 2014 James Tredwell, kept out of the Kent side by the promising off-spinner Adam Riley, ten years his junior, was loaned to Sussex for championship fixtures only. Tredwell, a member of England's one-day team, played his first four-day game for Sussex against Yorkshire at Arundel. Then on the fifth day, when the Sussex team were at Canterbury for a T20 match, Tredwell bowled for Kent against them.

County cricket has come a long way since Lord Harris's day.

2003: Good old Sussex by the sea

As the 21st century began, Surrey were the strongest county side, winning three championships in four years. Each time they won a match they rubbed in their superiority by returning to their dressing room and belting out their own victory song. "Much to our annoyance," Sussex all-rounder Robin Martin-Jenkins recalls. "We would be on the other side of a thin wall, trying to have a team talk, and we could hardly hear ourselves for their singing – and the banging of the bats on the floor as they sang."

Sussex resolved to do the same, choosing the song that from time to time during their matches at Hove would ring out from an operatic voice in the crowd: *Good old Sussex by the sea*.

Composed in the 1900s, it became during the First World War a popular marching song:

> *You may tell them all that we stand or fall*
> *For Sussex by the sea.*

But in time it metamorphosed into the anthem of the football terraces at Brighton and Hove Albion, and that was the version the cricketers sang:

> *Oh we're going up and we'll win the Cup*
> *For Sussex by the sea.*

They heightened the emotion with a ritual in which captain Chris Adams would nominate a man of the match whose task it was to start them off by singing the first line.

Seven times in the 20th century, from Ranji's side of 1902 to John Barclay's of 1981, Sussex finished as runners-up in the championship, and in July 2003 their supporters were in the same familiar territory, in the slipstream of the mighty Surrey, expecting once more to come close and to be disappointed.

But not the team itself. Under the passionate Adams, in his sixth year down from Derbyshire, and with the Pakistani Mushtaq Ahmed and the Zimbabwean Murray Goodwin, they carried none of the historic baggage of the county's failures.

Surrey, with their team of Test stars, came to Hove at the end of July, and Adams, with a first-innings lead of 74, delayed his declaration on the last day. The crowd slow-handclapped in frustration, the press was full of criticism, but back in the dressing room they did not mind. "We thought we'd done the right thing," Robin Martin-Jenkins says. "We'd gone head to head with Surrey, and we'd held our own. That was a major game for us. After that the confidence grew and grew."

What a long way the county had come in six years, since the meeting in March 1997 when 900 members had packed into Brighton's Grand Hotel and, amid much un-Sussex-like anger, had thrown out the whole committee.

What a long way they had come in just three years, since the autumn of 2000 when the new regime, surveying a season in which the county had finished last in the newly formed Division Two, thought long and hard before renewing the contract of coach Peter Moores. Adams had been captain for three years, and with typical emotion he promised to resign if the summer of 2001 did not bring major improvement.

Michael Bevan, their Australian, decided not to return, and in his place came Murray Goodwin, who proved to be, in the words of Robin Martin-Jenkins, "a real breath of fresh air. We didn't have a star dominating the team talks but a solid player who got a lot of runs and who was great in the dressing room."

Away from cricket Goodwin knew how to enjoy himself, but his dedication to the cause was absolute. "He lived and watched every ball," says Mark Robinson, a team-mate who joined the coaching staff in 2002. "He had a great desire to score runs every day of the week: Lord's on a sunny day or Derby on a wet one. He helped the young players, too."

Pressed into opening the batting, Goodwin scored runs in all formats, bringing the best out of his fellow opener Richard Montgomerie. Robinson had his finest season with the ball, in support of James Kirtley and the left-arm Jason Lewry, two of the best new-ball bowlers on the circuit, and they were energised by an influx of fresh, young talent: batsman Michael Yardy, wicket-keeper Matt Prior and spin-bowling all-rounders Mark Davis and Umer Rashid. They put the woes of 2000 behind them by winning the Division Two title.

Peter Moores was establishing himself as English cricket's most innovative coach, introducing ice baths, healthy diets, imaginative practice drills and computer-generated analysis. "County cricket is changing," he said, "and players are waking up. They don't just work, they work with a clear plan."

"He changed the whole culture of the club," Robinson says.

That summer their former President Spen Cama, owner of a large portfolio of properties, died, leaving one third of his fortune to the county. Earmarked for ground development, it gave the club a financial security it had never known.

Of greater immediate impact on the team was the death on a pre-season tour of Grenada in April 2002 of Umer Rashid, drowned while attempting to rescue his brother below the Concord Waterfalls. "He was the most well-liked cricketer of everybody at the club," Robin Martin-Jenkins says, "and a burgeoning talent, too. It was a real shock. A lot of us grew up a lot in that year; it put cricket into perspective for us.

We were a very tight squad after Umer's death. It helped us to become a good team, to take the rough with the smooth."

They ended their first season in Division One in sixth place, their best for 18 years. "A magnificent achievement," Adams called it, and it even included a victory over Surrey, who had recruited Mushtaq Ahmed for their last games. He failed to take a wicket, but Sussex were intrigued. The death of Rashid had left a gap. Perhaps Mushtaq could fill it.

Opinions were divided on the leg-spinner. His earlier stint at Somerset had left doubts about his character, but now he had found religion. "It was obvious when you met him that he was in a good place to do well," Mark Robinson says.

In a long discussion in committee John Barclay, chairman of cricket, recalled the words of Spen Cama when Barclay's team lost out in 1981: "I would give anything for dear old Sussex to win the county championship." "Who knows?" Barclay said. "Mushy might just give us a chance."

The summer of 2003 began well. The dressing rooms had been freshly painted, and each player had on his locker his squad number and the Sussex martlets. Early results were patchy, including a bad defeat at the Oval, but they grew in self-belief as Goodwin, Prior and the Welshman Tony Cottey hit form with the bat, Lewry and Kirtley with the ball – and Mushtaq took wickets galore. "He could open up a game that was going nowhere," Robinson says.

Mushtaq's ambition was to take 100 wickets in the 16-game summer, a feat he achieved, and the Sussex members took him to their hearts. "He loves playing cricket," John Barclay said. "It shows, and it rubs off on everybody else."

The pivotal day was Saturday 6 September. While Surrey were going down to a shock innings defeat at Canterbury, Sussex, 107 for six in reply to Middlesex's 392, added 430 for the last four wickets. Matt Prior, still young and free of shot, hit his fourth century of the campaign, and in the innings of his life Mark Davis, watched for the first time by his two brothers, over from South Africa, hit a patient and vital 168. To add piquancy to it all, the game had begun with the opening of a new scoreboard, dedicated to the memory of Umer Rashid.

They came down to earth with a bump at Old Trafford, losing by an innings. That, however, set up the best possible ending, the winning of the championship in front of their long-suffering Hove supporters. On the crucial day the queues were forming from eight o'clock, the ground full of excited expectancy. "I don't mean to be selfish," Murray Goodwin said as he went out, "but I really hope I'm the one to hit the run that wins the title."

At lunch 15 runs were wanted for the vital batting point, with only two wickets down, and Jim Parks, Sussex President, spoke to the umpires. Would it be possible to suspend play to allow the team to do a lap of honour? There were 3,000 in the ground, and more flocked in during the interval.

Goodwin pulled a ball to the mid-wicket boundary, and the greatest mid-match celebration in championship history began. It was a full eight minutes before the game resumed.

The papers had been full of negative comment about county cricket from all and sundry, from Lord MacLaurin to Michael Parkinson, but the crowd at Hove had no thought for that. They cheered, they wept and, above all, they sang.

'Good old Sussex by the sea,' they sang.

Celebrations stop play

In front:
Mushtaq Ahmed
Standing:
Robin Martin-Jenkins
Tim Ambrose
Matt Prior
Murray Goodwin
Tony Cottey
Kevin Innes
Chris Adams
Mark Davis
Richard Montgomerie
and
Shaun Rashid
(12th man)

The rise of Durham

It was always an anomaly that the north-east, with its passion for cricket, should not have a team in the county championship. For years their best players had to travel south to take part in the first-class game, many to Northamptonshire which maintained close scouting links with Northumberland and Durham.

Geoff Cook, a grammar-school boy from Middlesbrough, was one such. Spotted while playing for Durham Under-15s, he forsook the chance to study English at Hull University in favour of a place in a Northamptonshire side which at one point in the early 1970s was taking the field with six north-easterners in its eleven.

Cook spent twenty years in the Northants team, eight of them as captain, and his retirement in 1990 coincided with another bid by Durham to enter the county championship, this one led by Don Robson, a formidable Labour politician who was both leader of the Durham County Council and chairman of the National Cricket Association at Lord's. To add weight to the application, Cook was invited back north – on the understanding that, if the county was successful, he would be its director of cricket, assembling the necessary team and identifying the grounds on which they would play.

In those heady first days, when they bowled over the TCCB with their mix of passion and professionalism, they quickly met the requirement to raise one million pounds, the athlete Brendan Foster squeezing every penny of goodwill out of local businesses. And, with Robson's political clout, they acquired a field in Chester-le-Street, close to the A1(M), and set about creating a ground. There was plenty of scepticism – the young Mike Atherton at a dinner in Jesmond in July 1991 said it was a bad move, there were already too many counties – but, in the words of Cook, "The whole area was abuzz with the prospect of first-class cricket."

A team had to be in place for the start of 1992. The minor-county side was not outstanding; their best local talent had already gone south, and there were restrictions on the transfer of players. So they recruited several men nearing the ends of their careers, notably Ian Botham whose signing added great kudos to the enterprise. Led by the former Gloucestershire captain David Graveney, they won only two matches, finishing in last place just as the previous newcomers Glamorgan had done in 1921. But the sense of adventure never deserted them – nor did the great enthusiasm of the region dampen. In its season's round-up *The Times* voted Durham 'the most hospitable county'.

The brand-new Riverside ground at Chester-le-Street opened on schedule in 1995, but the team was struggling. Simon Brown, a left-arm fast-medium bowler who had come home from Northamptonshire, turned in sterling performances, but they lacked the firepower to capitalise on the lively new pitch and in 1996 they failed to win a game.

Simon Hughes, one of the original recruits, likened the thoughtful Geoff Cook to Mao Tse-Tung with his Five-Year Plan, but Cook had none of the dictator's powers. "We were living hand to mouth, season to season, with the players we were recruiting," he says. "It was difficult to plan ahead."

Norman Gifford was employed to coach the first team while Cook took a leaf out of Yorkshire's book, establishing an academy for young players. They persuaded the Durham Senior League to let them enter a team into its top division, providing vital match experience, and six of the first intake went on to play in the first-class game, notably the batsman Michael Gough and the fast bowler Steve Harmison.

The following years brought only fleeting moments of success, and in 2002 they were back at the bottom of the championship pile, as they were again in 2004. Yet this was not the full story. In 2003 the Riverside staged its first Test match, and the academy was creating a healthy flow of cricketers, so much so that in 2005 the England Test team included three of them: Steve Harmison, Paul Collingwood and Liam Plunkett.

With a good crop of locally produced players, they made two inspired signings for 2005: the Australian Michael Hussey, to captain the side, and the South African Dale Benkenstein, who was playing league cricket in Cumbria and who had circulated many of the counties with his details.

They won promotion from Division Two, but the next summer, with Hussey not returning and with their England trio absent, they struggled once more. Relegated in the 40-over league, bottom of their Twenty20 group, they only survived in Division One by some freak results in the last round of matches.

"Cricket can be a fickle game," Geoff Cook says, "but in sport you have to be good enough to capitalise on whatever luck goes your way."

The following March their coach Martyn Moxon decided to return to his native Yorkshire. With so little time to find a replacement, the county accepted an offer from Cook to stand in.

The championship had come a long way since his debut for Northants in 1971. "In those days, with uncovered pitches, it was a more rounded game in terms of technique, but it was a

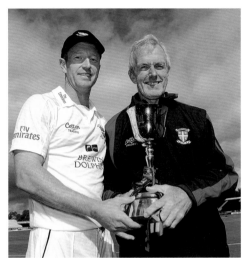

Three championship titles in six years
2008: Steve Harmison and Dale Benkenstein   2009: Will Smith   2013: Paul Collingwood and Geoff Cook

treadmill. If you lost a game on Tuesday, it wasn't a disaster. You drove off in the car and started again on Wednesday morning. Now the county championship is like 16 mini-Test matches. There is a lot more preparation for each game, time to get your skills in order and analyse the opposition, and if you can't win it's important not to lose. By 2007 the championship was as strong as it had been for a long, long time."

Cook could not have taken on the first team at a better time. They had a captain in Benkenstein who led from the front with the bat and kept calm: "He had a great ability to undramatise things. He knew that, as long as everybody was putting in the effort, the game would look after itself." They had the 39-year-old Barbadian Ottis Gibson, wanting to prove himself in a last hurrah with Durham: "He brought a real passion for cricket and an overt competitiveness." They had the Tasmanian batsman Michael Di Venuto: "He was outrageously good for us." And they now had a whole phallanx of talented local players, among them Graham Onions, Phil Mustard, Gary Muchall, Ben Harmison and Mark Davies.

They won the 50-over trophy and the second division of the 40-over league and were runners-up in the championship. "We had some wonderful games here, and the local people started to get the feel of quality cricket. Out of the blue, they had a winning team to follow. And there was no reason for it, apart from having brilliant people led by a brilliant captain."

The next year, with self-belief coursing through their veins, they won the championship. On the last morning, with hundreds of supporters making the long early-morning journey down to Canterbury, Steve Harmison – an inspiring embodiment of the north-easterners' rise – took the field with a broken bone in his left wrist and grabbed three wickets in four balls to seal the triumph.

Benkenstein stood down, believing that English counties should have English captains, and his successor Will Smith led them to a second triumph in 2009, a season in which – with Harmison available regularly, Di Venuto again in outstanding form and Ian Blackwell adding quality slow bowling – they remained unbeaten. Their closest rivals Nottinghamshire lost both times against them by an innings.

"They were the best championship side I ever played against," the Notts batsman Alistair Brown says. "They had Harmison from one end, getting balls up past your chin, and at the other end really skilful bowlers where you needed to get on the front foot. It was a proper seam attack. I never played Test cricket, but playing against that Durham side felt as close to Test standard as possible."

The rise of Durham is one of the great stories of modern English cricket, and it shows no sign of being temporary. In 2013, led by the veteran Paul Collingwood, whose great Durham spirit had been forged back in the hard years of the 1990s, they won the championship for a third time in six years.

It was a success all the more poignant because in June Geoff Cook, out running, had a heart attack and lay lifeless for several minutes. The applause when Collingwood dedicated the trophy to him was moving, even by the warmest Durham standards.

"I've been extraordinarily lucky," Cook says.

2010 – 2014

A widening gap between the divisions

Lancashire champions again at last

The season is now 24 weeks long

The virtual absence of England players has robbed the County Championship of what remained of its glamour, and the days when top-drawer overseas stars returned time and again to the same club have fallen victim to the international treadmill.

We can never go back to a time when England cricketers sped off down the motorway to join their counties as soon as a Test was over. But there is an uncomfortable feeling that England have prospered despite the domestic system; that it is performances in Lions matches which mean more; and that the County Championship is now tolerated – to paraphrase David Cameron on Gordon Brown – as analogue cricket in a digital age. The picture is getting fuzzy.

Wisden Cricketers' Almanack 2012

Two current players take a test of cricket knowledge

Q: How many county championships have Yorkshire and Lancashire won between them?

Lancashire player: Three?

Yorkshire player: No, it's got to be more than that. I reckon seven.

Lancashire player: Never.

The Cricketer, September 2011

2010 The points system for the championship changes again. Instead of 14 for a win and 4 for a draw, it is now 16 and 3. The proportion of matches ending in a draw falls to its lowest, 34 per cent, since the creation of two divisions. The traditional start-of-season match between MCC and the champion county is played not at Lord's but at the Sheikh Zayed Stadium in Abu Dhabi, starting on 29 March. Floodlights and pink balls are used, but the crowd consists only of a party of 60 Durham supporters, a few relatives of the players and several resident cats.

At Wimbledon the first-round match between the six-foot-nine-tall American John Isner and the Frenchman Nicholas Mahout is on court for 11 hours and five minutes, spread across three days. Isner, who serves a record 113 aces, wins the final set by 70 games to 68, but it is a different story when he returns next day for the second round. Blistered and exhausted, he serves not one ace in a crushing 74-minute defeat. "My shoulder, it's just kinda dead," he says.

2011 Lancashire are outright winners of the championship for the first time since 1934. With Old Trafford out of action, while the square is turned ninety degrees, the county plays all its home matches at out-grounds: six at Liverpool, one each at Blackpool and Southport.

Following revelations of phone hacking, the News of the World is closed by its owner Rupert Murdoch after 168 years of publication. Its last contribution to cricket reporting is to reproduce a tweet from England spinner Graeme Swann: 'Lost at Lords, drug tester staring at my manhood after the game, worlds worst drivers all on the M1 together.'

2012 Lancashire become the third county, after Yorkshire in 2002 and Nottinghamshire in 2006, to be relegated in the season after being crowned champions.

With floodlights now allowed in championship matches, the programme gets under way on Thursday 5 April, its earliest start ever, allowing Derbyshire's Dan Redfern to hit the earliest championship hundred of all time. England has enjoyed a mini-heatwave the previous week, but the first-day temperature at Leicester is 6°C. At Taunton Vernon Philander, newly arrived from South Africa, says he has never played cricket in such cold.

London becomes the first city to stage the modern Olympic Games three times.

The Great Britain team, with a best-ever 29 golds, finish third in the medals table. Among the first to win gold is the cyclist Bradley Wiggins, who only ten days earlier became the first Briton to win the Tour de France.

Lord's Cricket Ground stages the archery where on the first day the partially blind Im Dong-hyun from South Korea, only identifying his target by colour perception, sets a new world record with a score of 699 out of 720. Britain's leading competitor, fourth-placed Larry Godfrey, is inspired by the venue: "I know WG Grace will be with me when I walk down the stairs," he says. After each of his victories he entertains the full house of 6,500 with a flamboyantly mimed cricket shot. Middlesex members, meanwhile, have no county cricket at Lord's between June 9 and August 26.

2013 *The Cricketer's 'secret county professional', in his season's preview, tips Surrey to win the championship, with Durham to finish last in the division. Surrey, in fact, finish last, and Durham are champions.*

England beat Australia for the third series running, a feat last achieved in the 1950s, but less than three months passes before the two teams are contesting the Ashes in Australia. This time Australia win all five Tests emphatically.

At Wimbledon Andy Murray becomes the first British man to win the singles title since Fred Perry in 1936.

2014 Yorkshire win the championship outright for the 31st time. When the county last won in 2001, the prize money was £105,000. Now it is £583,000, of which £425,000 is shared by the players.

T20 cricket is rescheduled: from a block of matches in mid-summer to a regular Friday evening slot. County championship matches move predominantly to Sunday starts. Three weeks in July and August are kept free for a 50-over tournament. As a result Middlesex find they have completed half their championship fixtures by June 4.

The Church of England votes in favour of the ordination of women bishops.

Rory McIlroy wins the British Open Golf Championship. Ladbrokes, the bookmakers, pay out £180,000 to his father Gerry who had bet in 2004 that his boy would win within ten years. The odds of 500-1 were longer than the 175-1 paid out to 167 people who bet that the footballer Luis Suarez would bite an opponent during the World Cup in Brazil.

Championship – top three

Leading batsmen		Leading bowlers		Leading wkt-keeper	

2010

	P	W	L	D	Pts	Leading batsmen	Runs	Leading bowlers	Wickets	Leading wkt-keeper / fielder	Victims
Notts	16	7	5	4	214	M.R. Ramprakash (Surrey)	1,595	A.R. Adams (Notts)	68	C.M.W. Read (Notts)	63
Somerset	16	6	2	8	214	A. Lyth (Yorks)	1,509	G.M. Hussain (Glos)	67		
Yorkshire	16	6	2	8	203	J.C. Hildreth (Som)	1,440	J.A.R. Harris (Glam)	63	M. van Jaarsveld (Kent)	35

2011

	P	W	L	D	Pts	Leading batsmen	Runs	Leading bowlers	Wickets	Leading wkt-keeper / fielder	Victims
Lancashire	16	10	4	2	246	M.E. Trescothick (Som)	1,673	D.D. Masters (Essex)	93	J.A. Simpson (Middx)	65
Warwickshire	16	9	4	3	235	Z. de Bruyn (Surrey)	1,383	T.J. Murtagh (Middx)	80		
Durham	16	8	4	4	232	M.W. Goodwin (Sussex)	1,372	T.E. Linley (Surrey)	73	R. Clarke (Warwks)	39
								A. Richardson (Worcs)	73		

2012

	P	W	L	D	Pts	Leading batsmen	Runs	Leading bowlers	Wickets	Leading wkt-keeper / fielder	Victims
Warwickshire	16	6	1	9	211	N.R.D. Compton (Som)	1,191	G. Onions (Durham)	70	M.D. Bates (Hants)	52
Somerset	16	5	1	10	187	C.J.L. Rogers (Middx)	1,086	C.J.C. Wright (Warwicks)	62	G.O. Jones (Kent)	52
Middlesex	16	5	4	7	172	V. Chopra (Warwks)	1,028	T.S. Roland-Jones (Middx)	61	L.A. Dawson (Hants)	35

2013

	P	W	L	D	Pts	Leading batsmen	Runs	Leading bowlers	Wickets	Leading wkt-keeper / fielder	Victims
Durham	16	10	4	2	245½	M.M. Ali (Worcs)	1,375	G. Onions (Durham)	70	P. Mustard (Durham)	65
Yorkshire	16	7	2	7	221	E.J.H. Eckersley (Leics)	1,275	A. Richardson (Worcs)	69	M.E. Trescothick (Som)	30
Sussex	16	5	3	8	188	D.I. Stevens (Kent)	1,268	M.G. Hogan (Glam)	67		

2014

	P	W	L	D	Pts	Leading batsmen	Runs	Leading bowlers	Wickets	Leading wkt-keeper / fielder	Victims
Yorkshire	16	8	1	7	255	J.M. Vince (Hants)	1,525	M.H.A. Footitt (Derbys)	82	M.A. Wallace (Glam)	68
Warwickshire	16	8	4	4	238	A. Lyth (Yorks)	1,489	S.J. Magoffin (Sussex)	72		
Sussex	16	6	4	6	210	E.C. Joyce (Sussex)	1,398	J.A. Brooks (Yorks)	68	A. Lyth (Yorks)	35

Relegation and Promotion 2000-2014

	Relegation from Division One	Promotion from Division Two
2000	Hampshire, Durham, Derbyshire	Northamptonshire, Essex, Glamorgan
2001	Northamptonshire, Glamorgan, Essex	Sussex, Hampshire, Warwickshire
2002	Hampshire, Somerset, Yorkshire	Essex, Middlesex, Nottinghamshire
2003	Essex, Nottinghamshire, Leicestershire	Worcestershire, Northamptonshire, Gloucestershire
2004	Worcestershire, Lancashire, Northamptonshire	Nottinghamshire, Hampshire, Glamorgan
2005	Surrey, Gloucestershire, Glamorgan	Lancashire, Durham, Yorkshire
2006	Nottinghamshire, Middlesex	Surrey, Worcestershire
2007	Warwickshire, Worcestershire	Somerset, Nottinghamshire
2008	Kent, Surrey	Warwickshire, Worcestershire
2009	Sussex, Worcestershire	Kent, Essex
2010	Kent, Essex	Sussex, Worcestershire
2011	Yorkshire, Hampshire	Middlesex, Surrey
2012	Lancashire, Worcestershire	Derbyshire, Yorkshire
2013	Derbyshire, Surrey	Lancashire, Northamptonshire
2014	Lancashire, Northamptonshire	Hampshire, Worcestershire

2010-2014

Leading counties (Division One)

	P	W	L	D
Warwickshire	80	34	20	26
Durham	80	33	20	27
Yorkshire	64	24	11	29
Somerset	80	24	17	39

Leading batsmen

C.J.L. Rogers (Derb/Mdx)	6,058
M.E. Trescothick (Som)	5,429
J.H.K. Adams (Hants)	5,321
E.C. Joyce (Sussex)	5,204

Leading bowlers

T.J. Murtagh (Middx)	295
D.D. Masters (Essex)	280
A.R. Adams (Notts)	256
A. Richardson (Worcs)	254

Leading keepers & fielder

C.M.W. Read (Notts)	268
J.A. Simpson (Middx)	255
D.H.K. Mitchell (Worcs)	136

Overall statistics

Runs per wicket	31.4
Runs per 100 balls	55.6
% of matches drawn	40.0

Miscellany

Question: Who holds the record for having had a hand in most dismissals in a championship match?

In September 2013, faced with relegation, Surrey prepared a dry, turning track for their penultimate home match, but in blistering heat it was Middlesex's 6'5" off-spinner Ollie Rayner who made best use of it, taking 15 wickets for 118 runs. He also held three catches, at mid-on and slip, and thus equalled the record set by the Notts fast bowler Frank Matthews, who in 1923 took 17 wickets and a catch against Northants.

Asked if he expected his performance to lead to greater things, Rayner said he hoped so; it was the best day of his career. "But I might just end up the answer to a trivia question."

*

At Chester-le-Street on 18 September 2014 Northants were all out twice in three hours – for 83 and, following on, 90.

Chief destroyer was Durham's seamer Chris Rushworth who, bowling a good length in overcast conditions, found movement off the pitch. He took nine wickets in the first innings; then in the second, expecting only a short spell, he took six of the first seven before being rested. From first wicket to last he needed just 80 balls to take his 15 wickets.

It called for a celebratory drink – except that, raising money for Save The Children, he had given up alcohol for the year.

At the Oval in September 2013, taking time off from his A-level studies at Whitgift School, Surrey's Dominic Sibley hit 242 against Yorkshire, becoming at the age of 18 years 19 days the youngest double-centurion in championship history.

The youngest centurion, at 17 years 245 days, remains Godfrey Bryan who, between leaving Wellington College and joining the Army, hit 124 on debut for Kent in 1920.

*

At the Oval in September 2014 Harvey Hosein, an 18-year-old wicket-keeper, made his debut for Derbyshire. "Do the basics well," he told himself as they walked out, and he did just that, leading them off before tea with seven catches.

He added four more in the second innings to equal the championship record for a wicket-keeper.

*

The day/night match at Sharjah, between Pakistan and Australia, ended at 2.09 a.m. on 4 September 2012. Abdur Rehman then flew to Gatwick and was driven to Hove where he took the field for Somerset shortly before lunch.

A slow-left-arm bowler, he took three wickets, bringing to four his tally since midnight. He is thought to be the only professional cricketer to have played on two continents on the same day.

The championship in the 2010s

The two-division championship entered its second decade in the 2010s, and with each passing year it becomes clearer that the gap has widened between the stronger counties in Division One and the weaker ones in Division Two.

From 2007 to 2014 seven counties were in Division One for at least seven of the eight summers: Durham, Lancashire, Nottinghamshire, Somerset, Sussex, Warwickshire and Yorkshire. With the exception of Somerset, they all won the title during those years. They are the current elite.

Five counties – Hampshire, Kent, Middlesex, Surrey and Worcestershire – have oscillated between the divisions, none more so than Worcestershire, with four promotions and three relegations in nine years.

Six counties have spent at least seven of the eight summers in Division Two: Derbyshire, Essex, Glamorgan, Gloucestershire, Leicestershire and Northamptonshire.

Perhaps in the next eight years Sussex and Somerset, well-run smaller counties with loyal supporters, will not maintain their status as Division One regulars. Perhaps wealthy Surrey will regain its historic place among the elite and Glamorgan, drawing on its Welsh pride, will move up into the middle group, enjoying some summers in Division One. Such changes of fortune are possible, even likely. But, given the financial realities of modern county cricket, it is harder to imagine Warwickshire becoming an also-ran as they were in the 1980s or Leicestershire rising to the top as they did in the 1990s.

The levelling out of the counties, so much a feature of the last third of the 20th century, has been reversed. We are back to the great gulf in standard that existed in earlier times, albeit with two divisions to institutionalise the gulf and four-day cricket on covered pitches to reduce the likelihood of surprise results.

It was not what many of the counties had in mind when they voted for promotion and relegation. Their main aim was to create some extra interest in the end-of-season matches. But now the widening gap between the divisions is largely accepted as a good thing, a raising of the standard for those playing in Division One.

With players having much greater freedom of movement than in former times, the two-division structure has made it harder for the lesser counties to retain their best players. They cannot match the pay on offer at the wealthier clubs nor is success in their Division Two cricket as likely to lead to selection for England.

The 32-mile journey north from Leicester to Nottingham has brought international selection for Stuart Broad, James Taylor and Harry Gurney, and at the end of 2014 Greg Smith followed them in the hope of similarly advancing his career. He will be joined by Will Gidman from Gloucestershire, another keen to test himself in Division One.

Nottinghamshire, a well-run county club with a Test match ground, have become masters at recruiting and developing players from other counties. When they won the championship in 2010 the majority of the squad were with their second county, including three men who had been regular members of other title-winning sides: Mark Wagh (Warwickshire), Alistair Brown (Surrey) and Ryan Sidebottom (Yorkshire).

Once such a feat would have been remarkable. Indeed, only Albert Hallam – a slow bowler for Lancashire in 1897, then for Nottinghamshire, the county of his birth, in 1907 – did it in the first 85 years of the championship. Yet here were three in one team, and the story was repeated two years later when Warwickshire's winning side included Rikki Clarke (Surrey), Darren Maddy (Leicestershire) and Tim Ambrose (Sussex). When Ian Blackwell (Durham) joined them on loan in late August, they took the field with four men who had won the championship with other counties, as well as another four who had played elsewhere: Vikram Chopra (Essex), William Porterfield (Gloucestershire), Chris Wright (Middlesex & Essex) and Boyd Rankin (Middlesex & Derbyshire).

Masterminding the assembly of the team was director of cricket Ashley Giles, an astute judge of a player. But not every county was happy with the way the transfer system was taking hold, a discontent that bubbled to the surface in 2008 when Giles attempted to recruit Steve Kirby and Alex Gidman from Gloucestershire. John Light, the Gloucestershire chairman, called the approach to the players 'a hand grenade in our dressing room', complaining that Giles, as an England selector, had a conflict of interest when he sought to persuade them that a move to Warwickshire would be in their interests.

"All I am doing is working to make England cricket better," Giles responded, and the row blew over with neither player leaving Gloucestershire – though both in time would sign for Division One teams. Such transfers have now become an accepted part of the county game, with no one raising an eyebrow when in 2014 two directors of cricket were appointed England selectors: Mick Newell of Nottinghamshire and Angus Fraser of Middlesex.

If this increasing movement of players has weakened the traditional link between a county eleven and the population it represents, the establishment at each county of academy programmes, developing the most talented local youngsters, has had the opposite effect.

Yorkshire were the first to undertake such a scheme, the brainchild of their former player Bob Appleyard who brought the idea back from Australia in 1988. Never one to accept defeat, he battled his vision through a fractured Yorkshire committee, even persuading them to situate the academy at the run-down Park Avenue ground at Bradford, and he raised so much money in donations that the county only had to find £15,000 a year towards the first four-year budget of £260,000. He also developed a link with Bradford University that saw the development of a specialist course in Cricket Management and Coaching.

In time the other counties established academies, though few have been on the same scale or achieved the same success. In September 2014, when Yorkshire won the championship at Trent Bridge, they were fielding an eleven, ten of whom had been through their academy, nine of them county-born. Only the fast bowler Jack Brooks, signed from Northamptonshire, had come in from outside.

Among their number was Huddersfield-born Ryan Sidebottom, whose father Arnie had played for Yorkshire in the 1970s and '80s. The only survivor of their last title in 2001, Ryan was a Yorkshire cricketer through and through, yet between the two triumphs for his home county he had won the championship with Nottinghamshire in 2005 and 2010, the first man to be a regular member of two title-winning sides for two counties.

Andrew Gale and Jason Gillespie, captain and coach
For all the celebration of Yorkshire's home-grown success, there were many – President Dickie Bird among them – who thought the crucial factor was the winning mentality injected into the team by the Australian Gillespie.

Chris Rogers – one triple and eight double hundreds in the championship

From county success to Test cricket at the age of 35

Once upon a time a cricketer in his 30s, if he did well in the county game, could force his way into the England side. It happened in 1975 to the grey-haired, bespectacled David Steele of Northamptonshire, a journeyman pro who was selected to take on the Australians Lillee and Thomson and was so successful he was voted the BBC Sports Personality of the Year.

It has not worked like that in recent years. The linkage between county and Test cricket is not the same, with at least one recent England coach having such a poor opinion of the championship that he paid little regard to performances in it.

Yet in 2013 a veteran county batsman did get called up to play Test cricket, and in ten Ashes matches he scored 830 runs at an average of 43. Only he was an Australian, the 35-year-old Chris Rogers who had been playing in the championship for ten summers: for Derbyshire, Leicestershire, Northamptonshire and Middlesex.

"I remember speaking about my future to John Inverarity, our chairman of selectors," he says, "and he said to me that he wanted me to play in the county championship, because he had a great respect for it. If a young player wants to develop his long-form game, I would advise him to play county cricket and to expose himself to the great variety of conditions. The standard of it is really good. I wouldn't have been the Test batsman I am without it."

Stories of the 2010s

One hundred years on from Alletson

Surrey v Essex, Whitgift School, 18/19 May 2011

It was dark overhead at the Whitgift School, and the new ball was nipping about off the seam. "It's not an easy pitch," the Essex opener Alastair Cook told Graham Napier as he left the dressing room. "See out the day."

The previous June the 31-year-old Napier had suffered a double-stress fracture of the back, leaving him wondering if he would ever play again. "You have this feeling of letting down the team," he reflects. "It all moves on so quickly, and you're left behind." Through the long winter months he battled hard to get fit, and his attitude to the game changed. "I realised how much I loved playing cricket. I told myself that, if I played again, I was going to enjoy every single moment, the bad days as well as the good. It's just a game."

The good days were plenty as the new season unfolded: a hat-trick in a second-eleven game, another hat-trick in a 40-over game and now at last he was back in the championship team. He went out to bat at number seven, a place higher than he liked, and he played watchfully till the close, finishing on 25 not out.

The next morning the sky was blue, the pitch no longer had devils in it, and he resolved to enjoy himself. For three overs he played with care. Then, when the tall, pacy Chris Tremlett dropped one short, he instinctively hooked it, sending the ball flying over square leg out of the ground. "That got me going," he says with a smile, and soon he was cutting Tremlett for a six over the short off-side boundary.

Wickets fell and, when Chris Wright came in at 350 for eight, Napier gave free rein to his hitting. Back in 2008 he had captured the headlines by hitting 16 sixes in a T20 game at Chelmsford; now in the four-day game he was free to play the same way.

A Colchester lad, with his trusty local bat from Warsop Stebbing, he reached 83 in good time. It was a hundred years less one day since Ted Alletson at Hove had hit his way from 47 to 189 in 52 balls, and now came a blaze of boundaries that rivalled even that. He took 18 off an over from paceman Tim Linley, reaching his hundred with a magnificently struck six, his fifth, over extra cover.

Linley was replaced by the off-spinner Gareth Batty, and he should have had Napier caught on the long-off boundary for 118. The chance went down, and the next Batty over went for 28 runs.

Ball after ball flew out of the ground, several into the busy Brighton Road. Cars were hit, a bus was struck, and the box of replacement balls appeared so often the umpires resorted to taking two at a time. "I was trying to hit every ball," he says, "but also trying to keep control of the emotion."

He took lunch on 150, then resumed where he had left off. Batty continued to bowl but, even with eight men on the boundary, Napier

Graham Napier
"I'm a bowler first, not a batsman."

hit him for three sixes in his first over. At the other end Wright played sensibly for 34 runs, their partnership of 190 only ending when he was run out. At that stage Napier was on 196, his 16 sixes equalling the world record set by the Australian Andrew Symonds at Abergavenny in 1995.

The Whitgift ground was a small one, but almost all of Napier's hits would still have been sixes on much bigger fields. "I was hitting it cleanly," he says.

Full of the joy of playing cricket once more, and true to the style of his innings, Napier looked to complete his 200 with a record 17th six. He pulled a short ball from Meaker, then watched with disappointment as it flew high in the air, falling down near gully into the keeper's gloves. "One shot too many," he said philosophically as the Surrey fielders congratulated him.

His last 113 runs had come off just 33 balls.

Retired hot

Gloucestershire v Kent, Cheltenham College, 13 July 2013

The temperature was touching 32°C, the hottest July day for seven years, and the Met Office, warning of 'dangerous weather', issued a Level 3 heatwave alert, one short of an emergency. On the Brecon Beacons two Territorial Army soldiers died of heat exhaustion. Everywhere it was stiflingly hot.

At Cheltenham, Kent, chasing 411 for victory, had reached 390 for seven, thanks largely to brilliant batting by Brendan Nash. Brought up in Brisbane, playing his Test cricket for the West Indies, he was well accustomed to such heat.

Yet, after five hours in the middle, he too was struggling. He had slept badly in a furnace-like hotel room with no air-conditioning and a window that barely opened; he was tired from long hours of fielding on the hard ground, and the tension of the game was taking its toll. With hindsight he might have done better to have paced his innings, not started out "running like a madman, hustling twos and threes" on the small ground.

A bouncer whizzed past his grille, and he sensed things were not right. He peered across at the scoreboard, and it was just a blur; he did not even know he was on 199. His partner James Tredwell met him in mid-pitch to discuss the state of the game and, with his head down, he barely responded. "He probably thought I was focused." He was at the non-striker's end when, sensing a problem, the umpire called for a drink.

Before it arrived, he collapsed onto the ground, breathing in heavy gasps. After a ten-minute break, they helped him off, lying him down in a dark corridor with a wet towel over his face. There the noises drifted in: a roar as Tredwell was out, then another roar which turned out to be an Australian wicket on the television. In the dark the noises swam around his head.

"Can you bat? Can you bat?" he heard the coach Jimmy Adams asking. His pads still on, he sat up in hope. "I did want to, and for a while I thought I would if we only needed a few." But the second time Adams appeared, he heard the physio's voice: "He's done. He's not batting." When the last pair won the game, he was too far gone to recognise the cheers.

The heatwave went on relentlessly. A team-mate drove him home to Canterbury and, after a day off, rehydrating, he was back in action, fielding energetically at point for a day and a half in the next championship match. "I was thinking, 'I shouldn't have played'," he says.

Then he went out and hit another century.

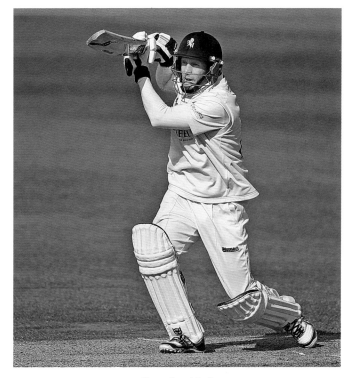

Brendan Nash
One run short of his first double century in England

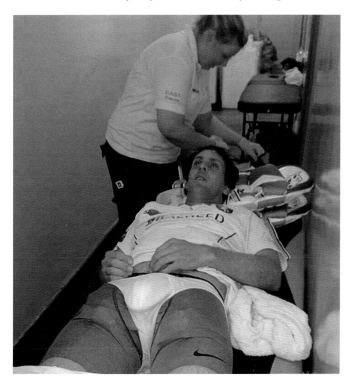

Images of the 2010s

Kent versus Glamorgan, Canterbury, Monday 12 September 2011

Pink balls and floodlights

Would the county championship attract a larger audience if it moved its hours of play into the evening? In September 2011 there was nothing riding on Kent's last home game, against Glamorgan, so the two counties agreed to give it a try.

Unfortunately the weather was distinctly autumnal, with a bitter crosswind, and the nine o'clock finish proved unpopular with spectators. Pink balls were used but Tiflex, suppliers for Division Two matches, could supply only twelve of them so the umpires were instructed not to replace them if at all possible. They did not swing, the stitching on the first one split, and the players complained that they were hard to pick up in the twilight. In the second innings Kookaburra balls, with a different pink, were used.

John Stephenson of the ECB, however, was optimistic. "From what I've seen, this form of the game is viable," he said. "There are different nuances that you have to get used to, but it's worth trying."

The pink ball is yet to reappear in the championship.

Umpires Nigel Cowley and Martin Bodenham with Kent captain Geraint Jones, who inspects the pink ball suspiciously

Middlesex versus Sussex, Lord's, May Bank Holiday Monday, 2012

Away from Lord's

No county has made less use of out-grounds than Middlesex. For many years, with Lord's at their disposal, the attitude was, "Why would you choose to play elsewhere?"

Yet, while other counties have abandoned out-grounds, the schedule of cricket at Lord's has forced Middlesex to increase their use of them. In recent years they have visited Southgate, Uxbridge and in 2014 the Merchant Taylor's School at Northwood, the championship's first new venue since Essex went to Garon Park, Southend in 2005.

Middlesex played a full T20 game at Merchant Taylor's on Sunday, but by the next morning, when the championship match was due to start, a band of heavy rain had arrived and it did not let up. Hard as the ground staff worked to clear the water, the rain persisted. The game was abandoned on the third day.

Middlesex will try again in 2015.

Middlesex versus Sussex, Northwood, May Bank Holiday Monday, 2014

2010: A dramatic last day

Poor Nottinghamshire. They won the first four matches of 2010 and, for most of the summer, were clear favourites to be crowned champions. In September, however, everything went wrong. Disappointing performances in their two penultimate matches allowed Somerset and Yorkshire to draw close to them at the top of the table. Then, when the final round of fixtures started, Fate – or, rather, the Manchester weather – turned cruelly against them.

The Yorkshire team were only fifty miles away across the Pennines, Somerset at Chester-le-Street, but in the first three days they both managed enough play to take their matches into a third innings, each with a chance of victory.

Meanwhile, in a wet Manchester, Nottinghamshire, who had opted to bat first, had reached just 89 for two. They had batted for one over on the first day, 27 on the second and none at all on the third. Even when the outfield dried enough to allow play on the second evening, the glare of the sun coming off the media centre drove them back into the pavilion. "I don't know whether to laugh or to cry," Notts captain Chris Read said after the third-day wash-out. "I'm feeling in a state of resignation."

The team met for a meal that evening. The forecast for the final day was good. Was there any way that, in 96 overs of cricket, they could get enough points to win the championship? Somerset were now six ahead of them so, if they won, they would be champions. Durham, two wickets down in their second innings, were only 31 runs ahead.

But if Somerset did not win? They did the calculations, and two options emerged. One was to persuade Lancashire to play a contrived game, each forfeiting an innings. Notts would be fed some easy runs, then Lancashire would go for the agreed target and Notts would have to bowl them out. But that depended on Lancashire's co-operation.

The other option was to get nine points – three for a draw and six bonus points – and hope Yorkshire did not win. At Headingley Yorkshire were 51 for one, 10 runs ahead of Kent. There was a good chance they would only draw.

Six bonus points? That was a score of 400, followed by three wickets. It was a tall order in only 96 overs, but the majority went for it. "Bash out the runs and get the wickets," they said. "We can do it."

Their coach Mick Newell, a man keen to examine every last detail, sat up late in the bar, talking to all and sundry as he went over the possibilities again and again.

Next morning their calculations were thrown into disarray when the umpires, concerned about wet patches on the edge of the square, delayed the start for an hour. With only 80 overs now available, to score 311 runs and take three wickets, Chris Read explored the other option with Lancashire. What sort of target would be acceptable to them?

"160 in two sessions," they replied, and Read walked away.

"From the look on their faces," he says, "I'm not sure they realised we could win the championship the other way."

What a day it was! By the time the Notts batsmen finally made their way out at Old Trafford, Yorkshire's innings was in ruins. The Kent off-spinner James Tredwell had taken a hat-trick, and Yorkshire's overnight score of 51 for one would soon be 130 all out. Barring an extraordinary collapse by Kent, the title was now a two-horse race.

Giles Clarke, chairman of the ECB and a Somerset man, knew which of the two counties were favourites, and he arrived at Chester-le-Street with the trophy. Somerset were one of only three counties, with Northamptonshire and Gloucestershire, who had never won the crown, so this promised to be a special day in his life – as it did for all Somerset supporters. Some of them had made the 350-mile trip to the Riverside ground to be there and, as the news filtered through of Yorkshire's collapse and Notts' late start, their jubilant sense of destiny grew.

Somerset were the team of the year. Captained for the first time by Marcus Trescothick, not only were they leading the championship table on the last day but they had won their way in style to the finals of both the 20-over and 40-over cups.

The 40-over game at Lord's was two days away, but the T20 final at the Rose Bowl was the one blot on their summer. Hampshire won off the last ball only because none of the Somerset fielders realised that the batsman completing the leg-bye had a runner and could have been run out. But that would be quickly forgotten if they now won their first championship.

As lunch drew close at Chester-le-Street, they captured the crucial wickets of Michael Di Venuto and Ian Blackwell. Durham, five wickets down, were only 115 runs ahead, and the new ball was soon due. With the news that Notts were lunching on 172 for four, still short of the first of their six bonus points, the Somerset supporters dared to hope.

By two o'clock Yorkshire had lost. "We got ahead of ourselves," their captain Andrew Gale said ruefully. "We were thinking how many to set them before putting in the work and getting the runs on the board."

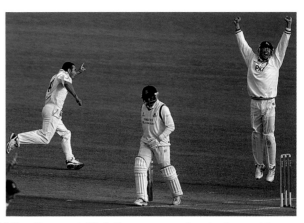

Losers and winners: Yorkshire's captain Andrew Gale in the moment of defeat, Somerset's Nick Compton agreeing the draw with Durham's Michael Di Venuto, and Nottinghamshire's Andre Adams and Mark Wagh celebrating the wicket of Shivnarine Chanderpaul

The out-of-form Samit Patel went in at number six. His team-mates hoped that his quick-scoring approach would come good in front of the television cameras, and it did. He hit 96 in 91 balls and, with the Australian Adam Voges, he took the score past 300 with still only four wickets down. "It was the best Samit played all year," Mick Newell says, "and it says a lot about him that he did it when it really mattered."

At Chester-le-Street, with the pitch dry and flat, the Durham batsmen were proving hard to dismiss, and a brief shower did not help. Trescothick, 'distracted by every murmur in the crowd', tried everything as the prospect of victory began to dim.

At Old Trafford Patel lofted slow-left-armer Kerrigan into the hands of long-on and on the stroke of tea, with Voges still in and the score on 350, Chris Read fell the same way. "I was kicking myself," he says. "Adam was playing the innings of his life, and I was thinking, 'The sooner we get to 400, the better.'"

Durham were finally all out, leaving Somerset to score an improbable 181 in 17 overs. Their batsmen had a go, but the boundaries were long and, with 133 wanted off only five overs, they shook hands on a draw and retreated to the pavilion to watch the end of the Notts game on the dressing-room television.

On 386 Voges was caught in the deep, and the ninth wicket fell at 390. That left the last pair, Darren Pattinson and Ryan Sidebottom, to score ten runs, and with steady nerves they opted to get them in singles. One mistake now, and they would need six, not three, wickets to win the title.

For twenty minutes it went on, with their Notts team-mates in agonies of suspense. "Paul Franks didn't see a ball of it," Mick Newell says. "He watched the footage of it for the first time in mid-October."

Sidebottom pushed the ball into space, and barely had the two of them grounded their bats for the 400th run than they were sprinting towards the dressing room. The harder task lay ahead, taking three wickets in 17 overs, but the belief surged through them all. "I don't know why," Chris Read says. "I felt that, if we got to 400, we'd get the three wickets."

Lancashire's top order was not the strongest in Division One, but they had at number four the West Indian Shivnarine Chanderpaul, the last batsman on earth you would want to see when you needed to take a wicket quickly. The sun had come out, too, raising fears among some that the glare off the media centre might thwart them again. Every moment was precious.

After three overs nothing had happened, creating a surge of hope for the watching Somerset side. Then Sidebottom had Karl Brown caught at first slip by Alex Hales, and in the next over Andre Adams, the leading wicket-taker in England, bowled a beauty to have Mark Chilton caught by Read.

In came Chanderpaul. The field crowded around him, and three balls later Adams, surprisingly bowling over the wicket to the left-hander, had Chanderpaul caught by Patel at third slip. The ecstatic bowler raced off in celebration, so fast that it was a while before anybody caught up with him. In the final hour of their long summer, against all the odds of the last four days, they had won county cricket's greatest prize.

The Chester-le-Street ground had been prepared for Giles Clarke to present the trophy to his beloved Somerset so at Old Trafford Chris Read had to make do with a replica cup, but he did not mind: "It was the best day of my cricketing career."

Poor Somerset. Two days later they ended their might-have-been summer with defeat at Lord's.

2011: Lancashire triumph away from Old Trafford

The summer of 2011 might have been the worst in the history of Lancashire County Cricket Club, perhaps even the last. With their Old Trafford ground deprived of Test match status, they had been given planning permission by Trafford Borough Council for a major redevelopment, involving the sale of some land to the supermarket Tesco, but the council's decision was being challenged.

If the High Court ruled against Lancashire in July, the club would be left with catastrophic debts and no clear future. There were times in the run-up to the hearing when they came close to being unable to pay the wages of their staff.

There was no pre-season trip abroad, and their overseas player, the Sri Lankan Farveez Maharoof, was being offered so little money they were worried whether he and his family would have enough to live on.

Work was already under way at Old Trafford, with the square – unusually sideways on to the pavilion – being rotated ninety degrees. As a result their championship matches were relocated to out-grounds at Liverpool, Southport and Blackpool. For the only time in their history they were not a Manchester-based club.

Lancashire, the most heavily populated of the English counties and with a rich tradition of league cricket, had not won the championship since 1950. Even that was only a title shared with Surrey; their last outright victory went back 77 years to 1934, beyond the living memory of all but a few. Five times in nine years, between 1998 and 2006, they had been

runners-up and in 2007, when they finished third, they fell only 24 runs short of championship glory in their last match at the Oval. "I've never seen a changing room like it in my life," captain Mark Chilton said. "The lads are just broken."

Back then they had the money for a succession of top-quality overseas players, including Muttiah Muralitharan and VVS Laxman. They also had the experience of Stuart Law and Dominic Cork. By contrast, their squad for 2011 had only one star, the England pace bowler Jimmy Anderson, and his contribution was limited to five wickets in two games. Perhaps Andrew Gale, the Yorkshire captain, was just stirring the pot when on television he tipped Lancashire for relegation, but there were few outside the county who saw them as title contenders.

Yet all the negatives turned into positives. The majority of the team were young, local lads who had come through together, and they played for each other with great spirit. "We're just a group of mates playing cricket," all-rounder Tom Smith said.

In the first match the 22-year-old Karl Brown from Atherton hit a maiden century; in the second there were career-best scores by 22-year-old Luke Procter from Oldham and the 26-year-old keeper Gareth Cross from Bury; in the fourth the 21-year-old slow-left-armer Simon Kerrigan from Preston won the game with a spell of five wickets for seven runs.

The move from Old Trafford worked well for them. In the previous five summers they had played 32 times there, and all but nine of the games had ended in draws. "It was a hard slog

The match at Southport, where one six landed in the gutter of a house

to push for results," Mike Watkinson, their director of cricket, says. "Often you expended a lot of energy in not quite winning, then you went into the next game carrying injuries and a bit of fatigue."

The out-ground wickets had more life in them, and they produced results in seven of the eight fixtures, helped in part by being away from Manchester's damp micro-climate. The county had always suffered more lost days than most – an annual average of 77 hours in the last eleven years, equivalent to nearly five hours a game – but in 2011 they lost just 15 hours. Only Sussex fared better.

The players enjoyed the out-grounds. "Four thousand at Liverpool is going to have more atmosphere than four thousand at Old Trafford," batsman Steven Croft says. "You are playing in front of a packed house, and you're closer to the supporters. We definitely felt that."

Croft learned his cricket at the Blackpool club, and he hit a century in the county's match there. "I walked to the ground, and I was totally relaxed when I went out to bat. It almost felt like I was playing in a club game."

Though born in Australia, Paul Horton had been to school down the road from Liverpool's Aigburth ground, and he too felt the link with his community. "When we played there, I didn't have enough complimentary tickets to go round all my family and friends."

Even the lunches were different from Old Trafford. "At Liverpool," Croft says, "you get chips on some days, curry on another. I think that might have been a factor in our success – the opposition tucking in a bit too much."

They won five of the first six matches, but Durham beat them twice. They won two nail-biters against Yorkshire, but they lost badly in early September at Worcester, and that put Warwickshire ahead of them.

Maharoof had been called away by Sri Lanka after only four appearances, but he returned in August. And such was the spirit in the team that, when he found himself left out of the last games, he threw himself wholeheartedly into twelfth-man duties. "He was the poorest paid player on the team," Mike Watkinson says, "and he gave his heart and soul to us. He was carrying the drinks, doing all the menial tasks that a young kid would normally do. It just epitomised what we were about that year. Everybody got stuck in."

Their coach Peter Moores had brought the championship for the first time to Sussex. Could he repeat his success with Lancashire?

Gary Keedy celebrates the direct hit that ended Somerset's innings

Victory over Hampshire at Liverpool, won minutes from time by Simon Kerrigan's 9/51, kept them in the hunt, and it all came down to the last day of their last match. Warwickshire could clinch the title with victory at Southampton, but their hopes evaporated as Hampshire's batsmen thwarted them. That left the door open for Lancashire at Taunton, but they too struggled to take wickets.

Somerset had started the day five runs ahead with five wickets down in their second innings, and Lancashire's captain, the old warrior Glen Chapple, bowling with a heavily bandaged hamstring and drugged up with painkillers, summoned a burst of real pace to reduce them to the equivalent of 15 for seven. Then the Somerset lower order, led by a century by Peter Trego, blocked their progress.

The lead passed 200, time was running short, and still there was one wicket to take. "We're screwed," Glen Chapple thought. Then, in a moment that encapsulated their summer of surprise, the veteran Gary Keedy threw down the wicket, the first direct hit of his 17-year career. "We'd been throwing at a stump all winter and all summer," Moores says, "and you say to people, 'There'll be a moment when this could win the championship.' And there it was."

"At that instant I thought, 'We've won it'," Chapple says. "It was still a hell of a chase, but in the dressing room there was hope and belief again." They needed 211 in 34 overs, and in the first 17 Paul Horton and Stephen Moore hit 117. Then Steven Croft and Karl Brown, the best of friends, saw them home with almost five overs to spare.

How they celebrated that night and for weeks afterwards all across Lancashire. They had won their High Court appeal, they had won the championship again at last, and they had proved Yorkshire wrong. They had not been relegated. In fact, Yorkshire had.

Some new players in 2014

A hundred on championship debut – Uncle Chris at Kent took 40 innings

Will Tavaré of Gloucestershire

> When I came to the ground as an Under-11, Courtney Walsh was playing for the county.
> To be on the other side of it now, to be playing for the same team as him, it's cool.

It came as a surprise to Will Tavaré to be selected for the first championship match. "I wasn't expecting it," he says. "I was nervous for two days beforehand." On a cloudy morning at Bristol, Hampshire opted to bowl, and an early wicket brought him to the crease. Watched by his father, a biochemistry professor who had played for the county seconds and by other family and friends, he lost his nervousness in the middle, getting to 32 without mishap. Then he pushed at a ball outside off-stump – "a nothing shot" – and in the slips Sean Ervine, of all people, dropped the catch. "That moment," he reflects, "could have changed my life."

A well-organised batsman, he proceeded calmly to 95. Then he hit a full-toss from Liam Dawson to long-on for six, emulating a childhood hero, Chris Taylor, with a century on championship debut. It was all much harder than in the second eleven – "There was never a bad bowler; I didn't find a single moment easy all summer" – but, with the confidence of that first innings, he scored a further three hundreds, topping 1,000 runs in all first-class games.

It had been a long journey from the back garden where his grandfather had taught him to block, from his game at the age of eight for his club's 3rd XI, and from his first-class debut for Loughborough University against Kent when "I was shocked how big a step-up it was. It made me realise where I was at." Some of his friends gave up, and he might have done, too – but he stuck to his long-held ambition. Two winters in Melbourne club cricket helped, and a summer captaining the Gloucestershire second eleven. Then that happy arrival in the county game.

Charlie Morris of Worcestershire

> Chanderpaul was one of my favourite scalps. It was a bit surreal. I remember bowling to him but not really thinking that it was Chanderpaul. He was there batting, but I didn't really believe it. I bowled a good-length ball, it just nipped away from him, and Tom Kohler-Cadmore caught it at slip. I was absolutely ecstatic.

Charlie Morris's one objective for 2014 was to make his championship debut: to get a Worcestershire number and wear the green cap. That would be "the real deal", the moment he had dreamed of since the age of eight when down in Devon he had first seen cricket on television and his Royal Marine father had driven him to Toys'R'Us to buy a set. It was the dream that looked like it would not happen when in 2010, at the age of 18, he underwent surgery on his back. It was a dark time, especially for one with such an outdoor life: rock climbing, sailing, mountain biking.

Alan Richardson's retirement had left a space at Worcestershire for a reliable seam bowler, and Charlie Morris was given the first chance to fill it. And fill it he did, not yet to the standard of Richardson but well enough to play all 16 games and to take 52 wickets. Not since 1992, when the counties each played 22 games, has a home-grown bowler claimed as many championship victims in his debut season.

He loves the four-day game: the way it swings back and forth, the way the pitch changes, the mental side of it all. "It's brilliant. As a bowler you build pressure over longer periods, but then there are times when the game accelerates and your one-day skills come in. So the championship encompasses all forms of cricket. That's why I hold it in such regard."

52 championship wickets in 500 overs

Sam Hain of Warwickshire

I had so many emotions going out to the middle. But I actually felt quite calm. I thought, 'Whatever happens, you just enjoy it.' A few of the Middlesex guys knew it was my debut but, once I got off the mark, they did their own thing and that was that. It didn't feel too different, just that the bowlers were more skilful and it moved along at a higher pace.

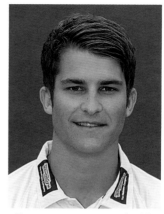

The 18-year-old Sam Hain made a patient 42 on debut. Then three games later, with 134 against Northants, he became the county's youngest century-maker, and by September he had added a further three. No batsman in championship history has hit his fourth hundred by a younger age.

He relished the challenge. He scored 63 in a run-chase against Notts and, when the fielders crowded round him chirping away, he thought, "Wow, this is first-class cricket." Then at Lord's, where he hit a hundred, he thought, "Just to play here is a dream come true." And he loved the four-day format, with its ups and downs and its chance to bat all day: "That's cricket at its best, I reckon."

The son of English parents, he grew up on Queensland's Gold Coast, so he's had more than the cricket to adapt to. "Birmingham is a couple of hours from any beach so I've started playing golf."

Four centuries, one a double, in only 12 matches

Jake Libby of Nottinghamshire

I was gutted to get out. But then to see everyone on their feet and understand what I'd achieved was a special moment. I sat down in the changing room, and I took ten minutes to myself. I just sat there. I had to calm down, take a breath, because it was all a bit overwhelming.

Jake Libby was not thought good enough for the university side in his first two years at Cardiff. But, when his course ended, his coach in Cornwall, recognising his patience and inner toughness, got him a trial at Nottingham, where in his first innings for the 2nd XI he hit 225. Further hundreds followed, and to his great surprise he was in the Notts team for the last match against Sussex at Trent Bridge.

Quiet by nature, he had much to handle: the big-name team-mates he had only met in pre-match training, the large crowd, the big stadium with its floodlights and TV screens, then the bowling of Steve Magoffin and Chris Jordan, swinging the ball at pace. "I just tried to back my ability, to play the ball rather than the occasion. It was a bit daunting, but I sort of settled into it."

The second Notts batsman, after Freddie Stocks in 1946, to score a century on championship debut

At one stage they came hard at him with short balls – "It got my heart racing a bit" – but he survived to score a five-hour century. "If I'd been batting that long," joked one T20-loving mate, "I'd have scored 400." "I prefer the longer format," Libby says. "It's more a test of character, of mental strength."

Aneurin Donald of Glamorgan

T20 might have a bigger crowd and be more exciting, but it's what you do in first-class cricket that you're judged on. That's the real test of your technique and your mental game.

"He's got a head plenty old enough for his age," Don Shepherd, the great bowler of the 1960s, says of Nye Donald, the A-level student who made his debut in Glamorgan's last match of 2014.

It was a big step for him – bowlers swinging the ball both ways, South African leg-spinner Imran Tahir to face – but he had played adult cricket from the age of 12 and he was not intimidated. "He's a compulsive hooker," Tom Alsop, a fellow England Under-19, told his Hampshire team-mates, so they peppered him with short balls, and he top-edged a hook in the first innings. But in the second, with the game almost lost, his free-scoring strokeplay came good. One cut off Matt Coles nearly went for six, his favourite moment, and he used his feet to hit Tahir for two straight sixes, one out of the ground.

He has come a long way from the nine-year-old who, spotting friends playing cricket at Gorseinon, was fascinated by all their equipment. But he knows he has a long way still to go. "I like to be an entertainer, but I've got to learn how to make 100s, not 40s and 50s. That's the challenge of four-day cricket."

59 on debut against Division Two champions Hampshire

1890-2015: 125 Not Out

How the world has changed since that Monday morning in May 1890 when WG Grace and his brother EM, the Doctor and the Coroner, walked out to bat against Yorkshire at the new Ashley Down ground north of Bristol. For them it was just another inter-county match; they had no sense that historians of the future would come to consider it the first fixture of the County Championship proper, the beginning of the journey for a competition that is still with us 125 years later.

In 1890 Grace called the county contests 'the most exciting of all ... the backbone of the game', and through to the 1920s there were plenty of summers when there were no Test matches and the championship held centre stage.

In 1890 there were only eight first-class counties. They started on Monday 12 May, and they finished on Saturday 30 August, a span of 16 weeks in which each county undertook either 14 or 16 three-day games. It was a schedule that allowed the best amateurs to play most of the matches.

The championship grew and grew. New counties joined, many of them starting out without satisfactory finances, and the competition did its best to accommodate them all, allowing each county to play however many matches it chose.

The championship's high-water mark, in terms of its schedule, came in the early 1960s, just before the rise of one-day cricket, when the county game, once more in financial difficulty, crowded as much as possible into its four-month season. The 17 teams played 28 or 32 three-day matches each, which – with further matches against the tourists and the universities – committed the players, now almost all full-time professionals, to a remorseless, summer-long round of six-day-a-week cricket all over England. A competition of 54 games in 1890 had grown to one of 254 games.

Many have been the changes since then: one-day cricket, Sunday play, overseas players, covered pitches, four-day matches, two divisions, central contracts, 'Kolpak' migrants. In spite of its reputation for tradition the championship has rarely stood still for long, and now the summer schedule is almost unrecognisable from what it was fifty years ago.

The counties still play around 90 days a year. But now a quarter of them are limited-overs games, and they are the greater money-spinners. So the championship of 16 four-day matches fits in as best it can. In 2015 it starts on Sunday 12 April, three weeks earlier than it started in 1962, and it ends on Friday 25 September, almost three weeks later than in 1962. The 16 matches are spread over 24 weeks.

For some years the T20 games were held in a mid-summer cluster, designed to attract star overseas players, but the crowds turned out in greater numbers when they were spread out. So now it is the 50-over competition which has its fixtures condensed into a three-week period. Once more the championship goes into a long break just as it approaches its climax.

In 2015 Lancashire play one four-day match, away at Colwyn Bay, between July 10 and August 20, Hampshire and Essex one each between July 23 and September 1.

"How is a spinner supposed to come through in April and May when it's wet and it's seaming all over the place, and then in September when it's raining again?" asks Shaun Udal, the former Hampshire and England off-spinner. "We're never going to produce match-winning spinners with that scheduling. When I started, we were playing championship cricket all through the summer."

For much of its history the championship enforced strict rules of qualification, seeking to preserve the connection between county sides and the populations they represented. But now, with the best players migrating to the top Division One sides, the emphasis has switched towards creating a greater intensity of competition, a higher standard of play at the level just below Test cricket. The development of England players is paramount.

County cricket clubs are pulled in every direction: trying to provide entertaining and successful cricket for their members, trying to produce high-quality players for the England team, trying to balance their books with off-the-field initiatives and to be at the heart of their communities.

There is no ideal structure, no ideal solution. There never has been in county cricket. It has never paid its way for long, and it has never come up with a format that is wholly satisfactory. It is blamed when the England team has a run of poor results, and it is blamed when the absence of the England players lowers its standard.

Yet, 125 years on from the brothers Grace at Bristol, it is still with us. And it has a wonderful history, a history to celebrate.

On Sunday 12 April 2015 the men who walk out at Taunton and Northampton, Leicester and Lord's will be following in the footsteps of Grace and Hirst, Woolley and Larwood, Graveney and Laker, Gooch and Hadlee, Trescothick and Mushtaq. Great players all. May county cricket see many more such men in the years to come!

The Appendix

The championship's evolving format

How has the game changed?

Champion counties and their captains

Which are the greatest sides?

Is batting or bowling more important?

Unusual dismissals

The grounds

The players

The umpires

Behind the scenes

Some facts and figures

Some county championship records

One-day tournaments

Minor counties and second elevens

The championship's evolving format

Number of teams

1890	1891	1895	1899	1905	1919	1920	1921	1992
8	9	14	15	16	15	16	17	18

Number of days for each match

1890-1918	1919	1920-87	1988-91	1992-2014
3	2	3	3 or 4	4

Number of matches each county plays

1890-91	1892-94	1895-1928	1929-32	1933-39	1946-49	1950-59	1960-62
variable	16	variable	28	variable	26	28	28 or 32

1963-68	1969-71	1972-76	1977-82	1983-87	1988-92	1993-99	2000-14
28	24	20	22	24	22	17	16

Point scoring system

Except from 1890 to 1895, percentages (or average points per game) were used when counties played different numbers of games.
Not included in this list are details about ties, games where scores finish level and games where play is possible only on the final day.

1890   1 for win, -1 for loss. Champions have most points.

1896   1 for win, -1 for loss. Points are divided by games won and lost.

1910   1 for win. Points are divided by all games, including draws.

1911   5 for win, 3 or 1 for draw, depending on first-innings lead.

1919   1 for win. Points are divided by all games, including draws.

1920   5 for win, 2 for draw.

1924   5 for win, 3 or 1 for draw, depending on first-innings lead.

1928   8 for win, 5 or 3 for draw, depending on first-innings lead.

1931   15 for win, 5 or 3 for draw, depending on first-innings lead.

1938   12 for win, 4 for first-innings lead in a draw or loss.

1957   12 for win, 2 for first-innings lead in a draw or loss, 2 for faster scoring-rate in first innings.

1958   If points are equal, county with more wins are champions. Team batting second only get faster scoring points if ahead at time of passing first team's total.

1963   10 for win, 2 for first-innings lead in a draw or loss.

1966   10 for win, 2 for first-innings lead whatever the result.

1967   8 for win, 2 for draw, 4 for first-innings lead whatever the result.

1968   10 for win, 0 for draw. Bonus points for first 85 overs in first innings: 1 for each two wickets, 1 for each 25 runs above 150.

1973   Two new batting bonus points added: 1 for 75 runs in first 25 overs, 1 for 150 runs in first 50 overs.

1974   Bonus points for first 100 overs, limited to 4 batting, 4 bowling: batting at 150, 200, 250, 300 runs; bowling at 3, 5, 7, 9 wickets.

1977   12 for win plus bonus points.

1981   16 for win plus bonus points.

1989   Penalty points for sub-standard pitch.

1993   Bonus points for first 120 overs. Batting points now at 200, 250, 300, 350 runs.

1996   16 for win, 3 for draw, plus bonus points.

1999   12 for win, 4 for draw, plus bonus points.

2000   Two divisions created, with promotion and relegation. Bonus points for first 130 overs: batting points, now five, at 200, 250, 300, 350, 400 runs; bowling points, now three, at 3, 6, 9 wickets. Penalty points for slow over-rates.

2003   14 for win, 4 for draw, plus bonus points.

2010   16 for win, 3 for draw, plus bonus points. Bonus points for first 110 overs.

2014   16 for win, 5 for draw, plus bonus points.

Playing regulations on declaration, follow-on and length of innings

1890   Declaration allowed on last day only. Follow-on compulsory if first-innings deficit 80 or more runs.

1894   Follow-on deficit now 120 runs.

1900   Declaration allowed from lunchtime on second day.

1900   Follow-on deficit raised to 150 runs and no longer compulsory.

1910   Declaration allowed at any time on second day.

1946   Declaration allowed on first day if 300 runs scored.

1951   Declaration allowed at any time.

1961   Follow-on abolished *(two years only)*.

1966   First innings restricted to 65 overs in some matches *(one year only)*.

1974   The two first innings are limited to a total of 200 overs.

1981   No limitation on first innings.

How has the game changed?

Overs and no-balls

1890	Five-ball overs.
1900	Six-ball overs.
1939	Eight-ball overs *(one year only)*.
1968	A minimum of 20 overs to be bowled in final hour.
1984	A minimum number of overs to be bowled in a day.
1996	Minimum overs in final hour reduced to 16.
1997	Two runs for no-balls and wides, in addition to runs scored off them.
2003	Wides now one run.

These tables relate to the laws and regulations in the county championship.

The runs increase

The figures vary from year to year, influenced by the weather and by adjustments to the laws. But the long-term trend, particularly since 1970, has been for higher scores and faster run rates.

There was little change in runs per wicket between 1900 and 1969, but thereafter, with covering of pitches, advances in bat manufacture and the introduction of four-day cricket, the numbers have risen significantly.

The best summer for batsmen remains 1990, the year in which groundsmen were instructed to prepare better batting pitches and when the seam on the ball was reduced. Runs that year were scored at a record 38.7 per wicket.

The rate of scoring before the First World War was not matched till the 1980s. In the dry summer of 1911 it reached 53.7 runs per 100 balls, a record till 1990. The highest rate to date is 58.7 in 2007.

Runs per wicket		Runs per 100 balls	
1890-99	22.1	1890-99	45.7
1900-14	24.1	1900-14	49.5
1919-39	25.1	1919-39	48.1
1946-59	25.0	1946-59	44.2
1960-69	24.1	1960-69	42.5
1970-79	28.2	1970-79	47.6
1980-89	30.5	1980-89	51.1
1990-99	32.6	1990-99	53.1
2000-14	33.0	2000-14	56.2

The overs decrease

When Yorkshire were all out for 887 at Edgbaston in 1896, they received 274.3 five-ball overs in 10 hours 50 minutes. Even with more changing of ends, that works out at the equivalent of 21.1 six-ball overs per hour.

An inspection of the Nottinghamshire scorebook for the summer of 1954 reveals that the overs in their games that year were bowled at an average of 20.5 an hour.

In the 1960s, with concern that over-rates were declining, figures were published each year in *Wisden*. In 1966 the rate was 19.2 an hour; by 1972 it had fallen to 18.0. This prompted the introduction of fines for counties averaging less than 18.5 across the summer. At this point the method of calculation was altered, with time deducted for the fall of wickets.

From 1984 counties had to bowl a minimum number of overs in a day. Initially the figure was based on 18 an hour,

but by 1996 it was down to 16. With extra minutes allowed for the fall of each wicket, the day's play often ran beyond the allotted time. In 2001 fines were replaced by the deduction of points in the championship table.

Recent scorebooks suggest that, by the old system of calculation, where time was not allowed for the fall of wickets, overs are now bowled at approximately 15.3 an hour.

Run-rates have risen, over-rates have fallen. Combining the two, it is possible to compare the average number of runs scored in a day.

In 1954, with a typical hour yielding 52.8 runs off 20.5 overs, a spectator would have seen 316 runs in six hours of cricket.

In 2013, with a typical hour yielding 50.9 runs off 15.3 overs, a spectator would have seen 315 runs, much as in 1954, but he or she would have stayed longer than six hours to see those runs.

Leg before wicket

1890 For the batsman to be lbw, the ball must both pitch in line with the wickets and hit the batsman in line with the wickets.

1929 An lbw can follow slight contact of bat on ball *(five years only)*.

1935 The ball can also pitch on the off-side of the wicket but must hit the batsman in line with the wickets.

1970 An lbw can follow a ball pitched on the off-side only if the ball hits the batsman in line with the wickets *and* he has made no genuine attempt to play the ball.

1972 An lbw can follow a ball pitched on the off-side if the ball hits the batsman in line with the wickets *or* if it strikes him on the off-side and he has made no genuine attempt to play the ball.

Boundaries

1890 Four runs if the ball reaches the boundary. Six runs if the ball is hit out of the ground.

1910 Six runs if the ball is hit over the boundary.

1957 Boundaries to be no more than 75 yards from pitch *(till 1965)*.

Covering of pitches

Up to 1954, once a match has begun, the only covering of the pitch that is allowed is for a rest day, i.e. from Saturday night till Monday morning.

1955 A pitch can be covered if both captains and umpires agree that any further rain will considerably delay a restart.

1959 Covering can take place overnight or after play has been called off for the day *(one year only)*.

1965 The bowlers' ends, up to a distance four feet in front of the popping crease, can be covered at any time.

1981 Full covering of pitches during rain *(except in 1987)*.

Limitations on fielding positions

Up to 1956 there is no restriction on the positions of the fielders.

1957 There may be no more than five fielders on the leg-side, of whom no more than two may be behind square.

1966 The restriction to five fielders on the leg-side is dropped, but there can still be only two behind square on the leg-side.

Spin bowling

The proportion of wickets taken by spin bowlers has varied from year to year, affected by the weather and by the many changes in laws and playing conditions. Yet, across the decades, there is the clearest of patterns. Spin bowling has been in decline for more than fifty years.

Between the wars spinners took almost 40% of the wickets, with a peak above 45% in the early 1930s. In nine of the first 11 summers after the war the figure was above 50%, reaching an all-time high of 56% in 1950. Then spin bowling began its decline.

The full covering of pitches from 1981 saw the proportion of spinners' wickets fall further, a trend that was not reversed by the full introduction of four-day cricket in 1993.

In the 2000s, led by Sussex's Mushtaq Ahmed, there was a brief upturn, with a proportion of close to 30% in 2007. In that year seven of the 13 bowlers to take 50 championship wickets were spinners, though only Robert Croft among them was not an overseas player.

In the last four summers spinners have taken fewer than 20% of the wickets.

Percentage of wickets taken by spinners	
1919-1939	39
1946-1959	50
1960-1980	36
1981-1992	27
1993-2010	24
2011-2014	19

Bowling styles before 1914 are not always clear

Modes of dismissal

When the county championship began in the 1890s, almost ten times as many batsmen were bowled as were given out lbw.

This changed as batsmen increasingly used their pads as part of their defensive technique; then the lbw law was extended to counteract this excessive pad play; and, more recently, the development of Hawk-Eye has given umpires the confidence to award more lbws. As a result, more batsmen are now being given out lbw than are bowled.

With a decline in spin bowling, the number of stumpings has fallen to 1.4%, barely one third of the number between the wars. In 2013 the 18 counties managed 40 stumpings between them in the whole summer, 12 fewer than Kent's Les Ames alone took in the championship in 1932.

Percentages of all dismissals					
	b	*lbw*	*ct*	*st*	*run out*
1890-99	40.0	4.1	49.2	3.3	3.2
1900-14	36.3	6.9	50.6	3.4	2.7
1919-39	33.0	12.5	47.4	4.0	2.7
1946-59	29.8	11.6	51.9	3.3	3.1
1960-79	24.2	12.1	58.7	1.9	3.0
1980-99	20.6	15.9	59.1	1.8	2.4
2000-14	18.0	19.3	59.3	1.4	2.0

Champion counties and their captains

Year	County	Captain	Year	County	Captain
1890	Surrey	John Shuter	1903	Middlesex	Gregor MacGregor
1891	Surrey	John Shuter	1904	Lancashire	Archie MacLaren
1892	Surrey	John Shuter	1905	Yorkshire	Lord Hawke
1893	Yorkshire	Lord Hawke	1906	Kent	Cloudesley Marsham
1894	Surrey	Kingsmill Key	1907	Nottinghamshire	Arthur Jones
1895	Surrey	Kingsmill Key	1908	Yorkshire	Lord Hawke
1896	Yorkshire	Lord Hawke	1909	Kent	Edward Dillon
1897	Lancashire	Albert Hornby	1910	Kent	Edward Dillon
1898	Yorkshire	Lord Hawke	1911	Warwickshire	Frank Foster
1899	Surrey	Kingsmill Key	1912	Yorkshire	Sir Archibald White
1900	Yorkshire	Lord Hawke	1913	Kent	Edward Dillon
1901	Yorkshire	Lord Hawke	1914	Surrey	Cyril Wilkinson
1902	Yorkshire	Lord Hawke			

Year	County	Captain	Year	County	Captain
1919	Yorkshire	David Burton	1930	Lancashire	Peter Eckersley
1920	Middlesex	Pelham Warner	1931	Yorkshire	Frank Greenwood
1921	Middlesex	Frank Mann	1932	Yorkshire	Frank Greenwood
1922	Yorkshire	Geoffrey Wilson	1933	Yorkshire	Brian Sellers
1923	Yorkshire	Geoffrey Wilson	1934	Lancashire	Peter Eckersley
1924	Yorkshire	Geoffrey Wilson	1935	Yorkshire	Brian Sellers
1925	Yorkshire	Arthur Lupton	1936	Derbyshire	Arthur Richardson
1926	Lancashire	Leonard Green	1937	Yorkshire	Brian Sellers
1927	Lancashire	Leonard Green	1938	Yorkshire	Brian Sellers
1928	Lancashire	Leonard Green	1939	Yorkshire	Brian Sellers
1929	Nottinghamshire	Arthur Carr			

Year	County	Captain	Year	County	Captain
1946	Yorkshire	Brian Sellers	1957	Surrey	Peter May
1947	Middlesex	Walter Robins	1958	Surrey	Peter May
1948	Glamorgan	Wilf Wooller	1959	Yorkshire	Ronnie Burnet
1949 *(joint)*	Middlesex	George Mann	1960	Yorkshire	Vic Wilson
	Yorkshire	Norman Yardley	1961	Hampshire	Colin Ingleby-Mackenzie
1950 *(joint)*	Lancashire	Nigel Howard	1962	Yorkshire	Vic Wilson
	Surrey	Michael Barton	1963	Yorkshire	Brian Close
1951	Warwickshire	Tom Dollery	1964	Worcestershire	Don Kenyon
1952	Surrey	Stuart Surridge	1965	Worcestershire	Don Kenyon
1953	Surrey	Stuart Surridge	1966	Yorkshire	Brian Close
1954	Surrey	Stuart Surridge	1967	Yorkshire	Brian Close
1955	Surrey	Stuart Surridge	1968	Yorkshire	Brian Close
1956	Surrey	Stuart Surridge			

1969-1992

Between the introduction of the Sunday League and the full introduction of four-day matches

1969	Glamorgan	Tony Lewis	1981	Nottinghamshire	Clive Rice
1970	Kent	Colin Cowdrey	1982	Middlesex	Mike Brearley
1971	Surrey	Micky Stewart	1983	Essex	Keith Fletcher
1972	Warwickshire	Alan Smith	1984	Essex	Keith Fletcher
1973	Hampshire	Richard Gilliat	1985	Middlesex	Mike Gatting
1974	Worcestershire	Norman Gifford	1986	Essex	Graham Gooch
1975	Leicestershire	Ray Illingworth	1987	Nottinghamshire	Clive Rice
1976	Middlesex	Mike Brearley	1988	Worcestershire	Phil Neale
1977 *(joint)*	Kent	Asif Iqbal	1989	Worcestershire	Phil Neale
	Middlesex	Mike Brearley	1990	Middlesex	Mike Gatting
1978	Kent	Alan Ealham	1991	Essex	Graham Gooch
1979	Essex	Keith Fletcher	1992	Essex	Graham Gooch
1980	Middlesex	Mike Brearley			

1993-2014

Since the full introduction of four-day matches

1993	Middlesex	Mike Gatting	2004	Warwickshire	Nick Knight
1994	Warwickshire	Dermot Reeve	2005	Nottinghamshire	Stephen Fleming
1995	Warwickshire	Dermot Reeve	2006	Sussex	Chris Adams
1996	Leicestershire	James Whitaker	2007	Sussex	Chris Adams
1997	Glamorgan	Matthew Maynard	2008	Durham	Dale Benkenstein
1998	Leicestershire	James Whitaker	2009	Durham	Will Smith
1999	Surrey	Adam Hollioake	2010	Nottinghamshire	Chris Read
2000	Surrey	Adam Hollioake	2011	Lancashire	Glen Chapple
2001	Yorkshire	David Byas	2012	Warwickshire	Jim Troughton
2002	Surrey	Adam Hollioake	2013	Durham	Paul Collingwood
2003	Sussex	Chris Adams	2014	Yorkshire	Andrew Gale

Winning counties

Yorkshire	31 + *one shared*
Surrey	18 + *one shared*
Middlesex	10 + *two shared*
Lancashire	8 + *one shared*
Warwickshire	7
Kent	6 + *one shared*
Essex	6
Nottinghamshire	6
Worcestershire	5
Durham	3
Glamorgan	3
Leicestershire	3
Sussex	3
Hampshire	2
Derbyshire	1

Most successful captains

Lord Hawke	8
Brian Sellers	6
Stuart Surridge	5
Brian Close	4
Mike Brearley	3 + *one shared*
Chris Adams	3
Edward Dillon	3
Keith Fletcher	3
Mike Gatting	3
Graham Gooch	3
Leonard Green	3
Adam Hollioake	3
Kingsmill Key	3
John Shuter	3
Geoffrey Wilson	3

Which are the greatest sides?

The best season

Unbeaten

There are 18 instances of counties remaining unbeaten in a season. In three cases this was in Division Two; in two others (Yorkshire 1926, 1928) the county did not win the championship.

Of the 13 champion counties who remained unbeaten, Yorkshire 1925 won most games (21 out of 32) while Notts 1907 won the highest proportion (15 out of 20 – or 15 out of 19, if you exclude a game abandoned without a ball bowled).

Most wins

There are four instances of counties winning more than 20 games in a season, with Yorkshire's 25 in 1923 the greatest. Two of the four instances occurred in 1955, when in a programme of 28 matches Surrey won 23 and runners-up Yorkshire 21. No other county has won three-quarters of its games and not won the championship.

The highest proportion of wins was by Warwickshire, who won 14 and lost two of their 17 games in 1995.

The best run of seasons

Consecutive championships

Surrey stand supreme, with seven successive championships between 1952 and 1958. On two other occasions a county has won four championships in a row: both times Yorkshire.

Since the shortening of the programme in 1969, no county has won more than two consecutively.

Yorkshire won eight titles in ten years from 1931, but since 1969 no county has done better than Essex who won five in ten years between 1983 and 1992. It would have been six if they had not incurred a penalty for a sub-standard pitch in 1989.

Much is often made of Yorkshire's improvement from 1959, when they won seven championships in ten years after only one shared title in the previous ten years. Yet a comparison of their playing record in the two periods suggests that Surrey's extraordinary dominance might have been more significant than any great upturn in Yorkshire's own results:

1949-58   Won 45.0% Lost 14.0%   One shared title
1959-68   Won 45.5% Lost 15.8%   Seven titles

In their seven consecutive championships Surrey won 61.7% of their games, including a record 15 in a row in 1954/55. This gives their team in those years a strong claim to the title of greatest championship side ever.

Unbeaten champion counties			
Yorkshire	1900	Glamorgan	1969
Lancashire	1904	Warwickshire	1972
Nottinghamshire	1907	Hampshire	1973
Yorkshire	1908	Leicestershire	1998
Yorkshire	1925	Surrey	1999
Lancashire	1928	Durham	2009
Lancashire	1930		

Most wins			
Yorkshire	1923	25	*L1 D6*
Surrey	1955	23	*L5 D0*
Yorkshire	1925	21	*L0 D11*
Yorkshire	1955	21	*L5 D2*

Highest proportion of wins			
Warwickshire	1995	14/17	82.3%
Surrey	1955	23/28	82.1%
Surrey	1892	13/16	81.2%
Surrey	1894	13/16	81.2%

Most consecutive titles		
Surrey	1952-58	7
Yorkshire	1922-25	4
Yorkshire	1937-46	4

Interrupted runs of titles		
Yorkshire	1931-46	8 in 10
Surrey	1950-58	7½ in 9
Yorkshire	1959-68	7 in 10
Surrey	1890-95	5 in 6

Proportion of matches won		
Surrey	1952-58	61.7%
Surrey	1890-95	61.2%
Yorkshire	1931-46	59.4%
Yorkshire	1959-68	45.5%

The best across the history of the championship

Across the 125 years of the county championship – 115 seasons, with ten lost to war – Yorkshire are the county with much the best record. They have won the title 31 times, sharing it on a 32nd occasion.

They have won a higher proportion of their matches than any other county, and they are the only county to win more than twice as many as they have lost.

Only six counties have won more matches than they have lost, and they are the ones known in the early days of the competition as the Big Six: Yorkshire, Surrey, Middlesex, Kent, Lancashire and Nottinghamshire.

In the table below, ranking counties by their percentage of wins, Essex in sixth are the best placed of the counties to enter the championship after 1890, while Gloucestershire in seventh are highest of those who have never won the title.

Durham have drawn fewest of their matches (31.7%), followed by Gloucestershire (34.3%) and Kent (36.1%); Lancashire the most (44.4%).

Full match records 1890-2014							
	Played	*Won*	*Lost*	*Drawn*	*Tied*	*%Won*	*%Lost*
Yorkshire	2,756	1,183	447	1,124	2	42.9	16.2
Surrey	2,285	1,031	544	1,108	2	38.4	20.3
Middlesex	2,473	901	607	962	3	36.4	24.5
Kent	2,631	936	741	949	5	35.6	28.2
Lancashire	2,723	968	543	1,209	3	35.5	19.9
Essex	2,478	719	719	1,034	6	29.0	29.0
Gloucestershire	2,563	738	944	879	2	28.8	36.8
Sussex	2,696	767	861	1,062	6	28.4	31.9
Nottinghamshire	2,531	711	705	1,114	1	28.1	27.9
Warwickshire	2,458	688	695	1,073	2	28.0	28.3
Hampshire	2,524	668	823	1,029	4	26.5	32.6
Durham	378	100	158	120	0	26.5	41.8
Worcestershire	2,296	615	831	948	2	25.7	34.7
Northamptonshire	2,212	551	758	900	3	24.9	34.3
Derbyshire	2,404	591	852	960	1	24.6	35.4
Somerset	2,462	594	943	922	3	24.1	38.3
Leicestershire	2,443	547	888	1,007	1	22.4	36.3
Glamorgan	2,003	440	689	874	0	22.0	34.4

Abandoned and cancelled matches have not been included in this table.

Is batting or bowling more important?

To some extent it is a silly question; you need both. But how often is the championship won by the team with the best bowling and how often by the one with the best batting?

Each year in *Wisden* a table lists for each county the average runs per wicket it has scored, i.e. its batting average, and the runs per wicket its opponents have scored, i.e. its bowling average.

Averages are imperfect things. They take no account of the context of those runs and wickets, nor the speed of them, and both are vital factors in the winning of a game. For instance, there have been teams whose batsmen have been prepared to sacrifice their wickets in pursuit of quick runs, giving their bowlers time to take 20 wickets, and their average of runs per wicket will not look good.

Nevertheless the averages do provide some clues.

Strong in both batting and bowling

On 15 occasions a county has had the best average for both batting and bowling. On 14 of these occasions the county were champions. The exception was in 1926 when Yorkshire (won 14, lost 0) finished second to Lancashire (won 17, lost 2).

Best average for both batting and bowling	
Yorkshire	1902, 1925, 1926, 1931, 1932, 1935, 2014*
Surrey	1890, 1954, 1957, 2000
Kent	1910, 1913
Essex	1991
Middlesex	1993
* Yorkshire 2014 among Division One teams only	

There have been six years when a county has had a batting average twice its bowling average. Yorkshire, between the wars, provide five of these. Surrey in 1957 are the only post-war team to achieve this.

In two-division cricket, where Division One teams do not play the weaker counties, it should be harder to achieve such dominance, but Durham in 2009 averaged 41.76 with the bat and 25.01 with the ball, while Yorkshire in 2014 averaged 44.78 with the bat and 27.67 with the ball.

At the other end of the scale there have been seven occasions, none later than 1922, when a county has had a batting average less than half its bowling average. Worst of all were Worcestershire in 1920; they averaged 14.75 with the bat and 40.88 with the ball.

In 2013 Leicestershire, in Division Two, came close to joining this group.

Stronger in bowling than batting

In more than half of the seasons the championship has been won by the county with the best bowling average, and in most of the other years the champions have finished among the best three or four for bowling.

Up to the Second World War, when there was such a gulf between strong and weak counties, there was only one year when the champion county was not also relatively strong in batting. Derbyshire, champions in 1936, had the best bowling average but were only 11th in the batting.

Since the war, however, there have been 19 occasions when the champions have been in eighth place or lower in the batting.

Champions with notably better bowling averages		
Essex 1979	15th batting	1st bowling
Nottinghamshire 1981	12th batting	1st bowling
Essex 1986	16th batting	1st bowling
Durham 2008	14th batting *	1st bowling
* Durham 2008 were 7th in Division One, 14th overall		

Stronger in batting than bowling

By contrast it has been rare for a county significantly stronger in batting to win the title. In only 24 of the 105 championship seasons since 1900 has the team with the best batting average won, and in 13 of these they were also the best bowling team.

Warwickshire in 2004 have been the most extreme case, with a batting average of 47.74, the best in the country, and a bowling average of 40.60, the worst. By pursuing a strategy of gaining maximum bonus points and not losing games, they won the title with only five wins in 16 matches.

Champions with notably better batting averages		
Middlesex 1920	1st batting	7th bowling
Warwickshire 1972	2nd batting	9th bowling
Leicestershire 1975	1st batting	8th bowling
Warwickshire 2004	1st batting	18th bowling *
* Warwickshire 2004 were 9th in Division One, 18th overall		

The conclusion?

What does it all add up to? Probably no more than that it is hard to win the championship without an outstanding bowling attack. I suspect we all knew that already.

Unusual dismissals

A total of 619,690 wickets have been taken in the county championship.
Of these, 21 have involved cricket's more obscure laws.

Handled the ball			
C.W. Wright	Notts v Glos	Bristol	1893
K. Ibadulla	Wwks v Hants	Coventry	1963
A. Rees	Glam v Middx	Lord's	1965
C.A. Pujara	Derbys v Leics	Derby	2014

Cheteshwar Pujara was given out when he instinctively swatted away a ball that was falling on his wicket. Alan Rees went the same way in 1965, though in his case he had slipped over and was stopping the ball from rolling onto his stumps.

Till 1899 a ball lodging in a batsman's clothing was deemed to be still live, and in 1893 Charles Wright was given out for removing a ball that had settled in the knee roll of his pad. Some have suggested that the bowler, WG Grace, had mischievously invited him to do this.

Hit the ball twice			
G.B. Nichols	Som v Glos	Bristol	1896
A.F.A. Lilley	Wwks v Yorks	Edgbaston	1897
J.H. King	Leics v Surrey	Oval	1906

The only circumstance in which a batsman can be given out 'hit the ball twice' is if he attempts to run after making the second hit. Dick Lilley always insisted that his dismissal was wrong; he was only tapping the ball away.

It is said that in pre-championship days one Sussex batsman was given out for hitting the ball twice because his partner, ignorant of the law, had set off for a run.

Obstructing the field			
T. Straw	Worcs v Wwks	Worcester	1899
J.P. Whiteside	Leics v Lancs	Leicester	1901
T. Straw	Worcs v Wwks	Edgbaston	1901
M.R. Ramprakash	Surrey v Glos	Cheltenham	2011

Mark Ramprakash was given out when the umpires judged that he had altered the course of a second run to impede a fielder's attempt to run him out.

The other three instances were more blatant. John Whiteside stopped a possible run-out by intercepting the ball with his bat while Tom Straw, the Worcestershire keeper, was twice given out for interfering with a fielder taking a catch.

Run out before the ball is bowled			
E.J. Tyler	Som v Kent	Taunton	1894
G. Barker	Essex v Glam	Cardiff	1956
A.W.R. Barrow	Som v Surrey	Taunton	2012

Surrey's Murali Kartik created a storm of booing when he ran out Alex Barrow who, as non-striker, was out of his crease before the ball was bowled.

It was 56 years since the championship had seen such a dismissal. Then it was the ever-combative Glamorgan captain Wilf Wooller who ran out Essex's Gordon Barker.

Retired out			
C.J.M. Fox	Kent v Sussex	Hove	1891
F. Davidson	Derbys v Yorks	Chesterfield	1898
W. Bestwick	Derbys v Leics	Chesterfield	1899
F.H. Bateman-Champain	Glos v Worcs	Worcester	1904
P.F. Warner	Middx v Essex	Leyton	1920
T.E. Sidwell	Leics v Surrey	Oval	1921
K. Howard	Lancs v Derbys	Liverpool	1963

Pelham Warner had to depart in mid-innings for a selectors' meeting at Lord's. Charles Fox was nowhere to be seen at the end of the lunch interval. The other five were all not out overnight and absent when play resumed in the morning.

Francis Bateman-Champain had most reason to be upset by his dismissal. On 82 not out, he was hoping to make his first century for five years, but his train from Cheltenham to Worcester was delayed.

Frank Davidson was reported as absent on account of a 'prior league engagement'. With the Derbyshire team having followed on 544 runs behind, he may have felt that it was not worth his returning.

The only instance of 'retired out' to occur since 1921 was in 1963 when Ken Howard missed his train from Manchester to Liverpool. On the same morning, down in Tunbridge Wells, Ron Hooker did not arrive in time to resume his innings for Middlesex. He was spared Howard's fate, however, as none of the six batsmen due to come in after him had arrived either. Driving from north London, they were caught in heavy traffic. So the whole Middlesex innings was declared closed.

The grounds

The county championship, starting at Ashley Down in Bristol
on 12 May 1890, has been played on 168 grounds.
It would have become 169 if a ball had been bowled in Middlesex's
match at Merchant Taylor's School in Northwood in May 2014.

Austin Walter 'Bosser' Martin supervises the pulling of the Oval's heavy roller.
Between 1924 and 1940 'Bosser' produced the best batting pitches in the country.
The Oval has staged 1,257 championship matches, more than any other ground.

Lost grounds

The following 28 grounds, on which county championship games have been played, are no longer used for cricket:

Essex
Chelmsford – Hoffman's Social Club
Harlow – Sports Centre

Glamorgan
Cardiff – Arms Park
Newport – Rodney Parade

Gloucestershire
Stroud – Erinoid

Hampshire
Southampton – Northlands Road

Kent
Dover – Crabble
Gillingham – Garrison Ground
Tonbridge – Angel

Leicestershire
Coalville – Fox and Goose
Coalville – Town Ground
Hinckley – Coventry Road
Loughborough – Brush Ground
Loughborough – College

Northamptonshire
Peterborough – Baker Perkins

Somerset
Bristol – Imperial Ground
Yeovil – Johnson Park
Yeovil – West Hendford

Sussex
Hastings – Central Recreation Ground

Warwickshire
Coventry – Butts Ground
Coventry – Courtaulds
Coventry – Morris Motors

Worcestershire
Dudley – Tipton Road

Yorkshire
Dewsbury – Savile Town
Huddersfield – Fartown
Hull – The Circle
Sheffield – Bramall Lane
York – Wigginton Road

They came only once

There have been 14 grounds on which championship cricket has been played on only one occasion.

Wigginton Road, York   1890

The Yorkshire Gentlemen, owners of the ground, were the prime movers and, with the help of extra local trains, they raised a crowd of 5,000. But the game, played in poor light, was all over by 3.45 on the second day. Kent proved feeble opponents, not helped on the first day when three of their team, 'due to a discrepancy in regard to the telegraphic summons which had been forwarded to them', arrived too late to bat.

Old County Ground, Town Malling   1890

Kent's attempt to revive county cricket at the historic ground was a financial disaster. Its location, north-west of Maidstone, was hard to reach, the pitch was poor, and the match ended on the second afternoon. The players had to crawl up the steps of an oast house to reach their changing area.

Thrum Hall, Halifax   1897

As at York, Kent were the visitors when the championship was played for the only time in Halifax, and again they had lost by the second afternoon. The exposed ground was 800 feet above sea level, and the Yorkshire committeemen decided against returning to 'the chill air of the neighbourhood'.

Batsford Road, Moreton-in-Marsh   1914

Arthur Conway of Worcestershire never forgot the little Cotswold ground. A 'swerve' bowler, he took only 39 wickets in his 22 championship appearances, but 15 of them were in the two-day victory at Moreton. One hundred years on, his 15/87 remain the best bowling figures for Worcestershire.

Lune Road, Lancaster   1914

The local silk spinners were given a holiday to swell the crowd for Lancashire's venture north, and the cricket lasted three days. But opinions differed on the surroundings. The *Manchester Guardian* waxed lyrical about the sunshine on the hilltop castle, but the *Evening Chronicle* was unimpressed by the constant shunting of trains on the adjoining railway line.

Downside School, Stratton-on-the-Fosse   1934

Glamorgan captain Maurice Turnbull persuaded Somerset to play them at his old school. His reward was a duck and a game spoilt by rain. For the only time in the championship, play was suspended at noon and 6pm while an angelus sounded.

Town Ground, Coalville   1950

Charles Palmer, newly appointed Secretary and captain, scored his first Leicestershire century at Coalville's Town Ground, but his abiding memory was of the profuse apologies he kept making to Warwickshire for the lack of basic facilities.

Sports Club, Evesham   1951

Worcestershire invited Gloucestershire just across the boundary, but the Evesham pitch, growing dusty and worn, did not stand up to three days of use.

Tivoli Road, Hornsey   1959

MCC were playing Cambridge University at Lord's so, for the first time, Middlesex had to find another ground in the county.

Steetley Company Ground, Shireoaks   1961

The Steetley Company, makers of furnace bricks, had a managing director with a passion for cricket, and he persuaded Notts to play at his ground in the mining village of Shireoaks. The pitch was superb, the boundaries short, and the two first innings produced 701 runs for the loss of seven wickets.

Millfield School, Street   1961

It was a last-minute replacement for Glastonbury, where the pitch was unfit. Warwickshire's Jim Stewart had a field day with the short boundaries, hitting 11 sixes in the match.

Sports Centre, Harlow   1970

Harlow replaced Brentwood, where Essex had been bowled out for 34 in 1969, but the county had bought the ground at Chelmsford and in 1971 opted to play more games there.

Chain Wire Club, Stourport-on-Severn   1980

Worcestershire's venture into the north started well, with a good Saturday crowd and a score of 387 against Lancashire. Then heavy rain fell on the uncovered pitch and, when play resumed on Tuesday, Norman Gifford, with vicious spin, returned match figures of 10/40. The next year the company owning the ground hit hard times and withdrew their sponsorship.

Town Ground, Heanor   1987

The playing area of 118 by 106 yards, perhaps the smallest ever in the championship, made for good six-hitting fun in the Sunday League but it was simply too cramped for the longer game – and the pronounced slope did nothing to help the humour of the visiting bowlers. Malcolm Marshall was warned for bombarding Derbyshire's Kim Barnett with bouncers.

The players

6,821* cricketers have appeared in the county championship:
from the Victorian hero WG Grace who faced the first ball at Bristol in 1890
to 17-year-old Aneurin Donald who made his debut in the last match of 2014.
803 men played only once; 99 failed to score a run, take a wicket or hold a catch.

* This includes Samuel Jackson who, on the second day of the Roses match in 1891, was summoned to Old Trafford when one of the Yorkshire team was taken ill. He did not arrive in time to field but, unusually for a substitute, was permitted to bat. With Yorkshire following on, he scored 9 and 0.

It does not include Mr EF Mathews who appeared on a Middlesex scorecard in 1892. He was, in fact, the barrister Evan Nepean, who had 45 games for the county. Why he should have been playing that match under an alias is not known.

Averaging 100 with the bat

Six batsmen have averages of 100 or more in the county championship. Three are modern overseas players: the Australian Damien Martyn (two matches for Yorkshire, out twice for 342 runs), the South African Con de Lange (four matches for Northants, out once for 156 runs) and the Australian Ricky Ponting (seven matches for Somerset and Surrey, out seven times for 790 runs). The other three go back to the 1920s.

Cec Tyson (Yorkshire, 1921)
Two matches and a batting average of 101.5

Picked for Yorkshire's first game of 1921 at Southampton, Cec Tyson, a grafting left-handed batsman, captured the headlines with unbeaten scores of 100 and 80.

Already 32 years old, he had taken full-time employment, as player and groundsman, at the Whitwood Colliery's Cricket and Athletics Club, and they expected him to be there. So, after scoring 0 and 23 in the Roses match at Old Trafford, he became unavailable for further Yorkshire games.

It caused a great to-do. At the next Yorkshire Cricket Council meeting the Whitwood Club was accused of breaking established club-county agreements. Tyson himself was present at the meeting, but a proposal that he be heard was ruled out of order.

A record crowd gathered for Whitwood's next Saturday game, against Featherstone, and Tyson hit 107, receiving almost three pounds from a collection. Meanwhile the place he had vacated in the county side was filled by a young left-hander from the Harrogate club, Maurice Leyland.

Horace Bloomfield (Surrey, 1921)
Two matches and a batting average of 169

The bespectacled 'Blum', a wristy, attacking batsman who played in plimsolls, hit 107 not out against Northamptonshire and 9 and 53 not out against Leicestershire.

The next summer, picked to play against Oxford and Cambridge Universities, he failed in all four innings. After that, he returned to scoring his runs for Lloyds Bank.

Joe O'Gorman (Surrey, 1927 and 1928)
Three matches and a batting average of 106

Joe O'Gorman was a small man, lithe and athletic, an acrobatic dancer. With his brother Dave they were the O'Gorman Brothers, a song, dance and cross-talk comedy act that played around the variety halls of England. In the 1930s they became popular in the United States and earned a fortune, many times more than what professional cricketers earned.

They played their cricket as amateurs, though always with great seriousness and dedication. They started before the First War with the Vaudevillians on Clapham Common, then via the Honor Oak and Richmond clubs they rose to the Surrey second eleven where Joe in particular had great success. In one match in 1926 he hit a hundred and took 12 wickets.

At the Oval the following May he played two games for the Surrey first team. A leg-spinner with a great repertoire of deliveries, he took four wickets, including one with his first ball in county cricket, and, batting at nine, he hit not-out scores of 31, 20 and 42. But he could not go up to Headingley for the next game as he had a week-long booking at the Victoria Palace Theatre. Nevertheless he contrived to play for the seconds at the Oval, making it in time for his slot in the 6.15 performance.

Even after a week of shows in Newcastle or Manchester he would catch an overnight sleeper for a Sunday game with the Thespids, a show-business side that played at Wimbledon.

He made one further appearance for Surrey, at Leicester, where he was bowled for 13. His grandson, Tim, played for Derbyshire from 1987 to 1996.

They played only once

S.E. Ellis (Somerset, 1902)

Of SE Ellis, who played for Somerset at Old Trafford in June 1902, we know almost nothing: not his date of birth or death, not his other cricket, not even his first names. Most unusually for a cricketer who has played in the championship, he leaves no more trace than an entry in a scorebook.

That summer Somerset were always looking for players. For the game at Old Trafford, the *Taunton Courier* paid tribute to the efforts of the captain Sammy Woods and the Secretary: 'The final constitution of the team showed to what straits they were reduced in getting players together to represent the county.'

Ellis's first day as a county cricketer was rained off. Maybe he spent it in the pavilion, playing cards with his new team-mates.

Woods, in later life, told a story of an unspecified game when they boarded the train to the north of England with only ten men. Could it have been this match? And could the eleventh man of his story have been SE Ellis?

> On the way I got talking to a fellow who said he'd made hundreds and hundreds in club cricket. So I made him our eleventh man. He made nought and nought, and it turned out he hadn't played since he was ten, but wanted to get a close view of the game for nothing. He was a very good whist-player.

If it was indeed Ellis, Woods did him a disservice. The poor man scored 5 and 0 and took part in a famous nine-run victory, Somerset's first win in Lancashire.

Geoff Hurst (Essex, 1962)

Which cricketer never took a wicket for his county but got a hat-trick for England? For three summers from 1962 Hurst, a Chelmsford lad, played for the Essex second eleven. His only first-team game was at Liverpool where, taking the place of his fellow West Ham footballer Eddie Presland, he scored 0* and 0.

Fred Hyland (Hampshire, 1924)

No cricketer, with a single first-class appearance, has played in a shorter match. A bowler at the Ringwood club, 'stockily built and with powerful, hairy arms', Hyland took the field at Northampton at 5.45 on a wet first day. Then, after two overs, the rain returned, washing out the rest of the game.

'By his ten wet minutes on the first-class field,' wrote Ronald Mason in *Sing All A Great Willow*, 'he had as irrevocably joined the ranks as WG.' In later life, *Wisden* recorded, 'he earned a reputation as a nurseryman in Cheshire.'

Captain Percy Ashton (1924)

Ashton lost an eye in the First World War and played in glasses, but he was good enough to hit 31 and 21 in his only match for Essex. Out of practice after a spell abroad, he batted, wrote *The Times*, 'with much more freedom than anyone else'.

His cavalier approach, however, led to one of county cricket's more eccentric dismissals. Attempting to sweep a ball to leg from a position so low that he was almost prone on the turf, he was hit on the head and given out lbw.

Peter Pickering (Northamptonshire, 1953)

Pickering, a former Chelsea goalkeeper, was at his desk at the British Timken works outside Northampton when the announcement came on the tannoy: "Would Peter Pickering report to the Chairman's office immediately?"

"Ah, Pickering, you're required at Old Trafford. Freddie Brown has hurt his hand. There is a car being made ready. Get up there as fast you can."

The Northants team were back in the field after lunch when he arrived, and he took several minutes to convince the gateman that he was playing in the match.

The pitch was poor and the scores low, but he made crucial runs, 22 and 37. "He played as if they were schoolboys," his captain Dennis Brookes said. "He wasn't waiting to see if the ball turned or popped; he just hit it." As a result they won by one wicket, the county's first victory at Old Trafford.

Mark Patterson (Surrey, 1999)

Called up in an injury crisis, the Ulsterman Mark Patterson played only one championship game for Surrey, against Notts at the Oval, but what a game it turned out to be! On the first morning his pace bowling took three top-order wickets; on the second evening he found himself in the middle of great celebrations as Surrey secured their first title for 28 years.

Plagued by back problems, he never got a second call-up, becoming a teacher in Ipswich and a football referee.

Josiah Coulthurst (Lancashire, 1919)

Jos Coulthurst, a fast-medium bowler from Blackburn, was picked by Lancashire for their last game of 1919, at Old Trafford, but the two-day match was ruined by rain. On the first day, when Lancashire made 198 for six, he did not bat; on the second day, there was no play. Never again selected, he remains the only county championship cricketer never to set foot on the field of play.

The umpires

'Buddy' Oldfield was a gifted batsman, but he was the most nervous of men. Next in to bat, he would sit by the window, smoking cigarette after cigarette and blinking furiously. He played for Northants to the age of 42 but, after three games at the start of 1954, despite a century against the mighty Surrey, he decided his eyesight had gone and retired. Within a month, however, he was back on the county circuit as an umpire.

There was no training, no apprenticeship in minor cricket. Old players were assumed to know the game, there was none of the paperwork or regulations of today's various competitions, and batsmen helped the umpires by walking when they were out.

The transition could be hard. Jack Board, the Gloucestershire keeper, found himself bellowing an appeal the first time there was a caught-behind, and Eddie Paynter, the Lancashire batsman, gave up because he spent too much money in the bar, meeting up with old friends.

It was not always predictable which players would take to the umpire's life. Dickie Bird, a bag of nerves as a player, was allocated to the Oval for his second match and so concerned was he to be in good time that he turned up at six in the morning, 90 minutes before the groundsman arrived. But he gained good marks from the outset and stood in 66 Tests – while Derek Shackleton, the calmest of men in his long career, was so anxious that he would practise the signals in the umpires' room. Once, when a catch was taken on the boundary, he raised his arms for a six, only to be told the fielder was inside the rope. "I'm sorry," he said in a fluster and signalled a four.

Some umpires gave lbws more freely than others. Eddie Phillipson, the former Lancashire paceman, was one who counted his victims through the season, and bowlers queued up to come on at his end.

"If I ever become an umpire," the Gloucestershire slow-left-armer Sam Cook used to curse when batsmen swept him to leg, "I shall have the sharpest finger in the country." And he was true to his word, sending batsmen on their way when they played across the line. There was a school of thought that umpires should do that. "They looked after the game," Cook's team-mate 'Bomber' Wells used to say. "They didn't let you play shots like that."

Research has shown that, of the 100 umpires who have stood in most games in the county championship, the three greatest not-outers were Frank Chester, Syd Buller and Dickie Bird, all of whom were considered the best umpires of their day. By comparison with them, Cook and Phillipson gave more than two and a half times as many lbws. Yet modern technology takes the side of those who raised the finger more readily.

Frank Chester was destined to be a great Test cricketer. He is the only man in the history of the championship to score three centuries before the age of 19, and he took wickets, too. But he lost an arm in the First War, and he became an umpire. In his first match he gave both captains out – one lbw, one stumped – and he was told, "You won't last long. If you give skippers out, you sign your own death warrant."

The captains assessed the umpires. Between the wars an umpire lost his livelihood if Lord's received three bad reports on him. It did happen, at least once, and the man in question, a long-established umpire, was not even allowed to know which the matches were. According to recent research, captains up to the 1980s were 15% less likely to be given lbw when batting – and 25% more likely to win an lbw appeal when bowling.

Before the Second War an umpire was not allowed to stand in a game involving his former county. This might have created difficulties in the summer of 2000, when ten of the 26 umpires on the first-class list were former Somerset players.

Surrey's Harry Baldwin had a reputation for being anti-Surrey when he umpired them, though it is thought that this was not so much down to an excess of fair play as to an ancient grudge. "He does us twice every year," the Surrey skipper Stuart Surridge once complained to his opposite number.

But no one took the matter further. That was just life.

Some facts

More than 400 umpires have stood in county championship matches, as well as an unknown number of others who have deputised when an umpire has been absent or ill – or, in at least one case, enjoyed a little too much liquid refreshment at lunch.

121 umpires have stood in ten or more summers, of whom 26 played in Tests and 12 never played a first-class game.

The youngest man to umpire a county championship match was the 24-year-old Thomas Shoubridge, a Liverpool club cricketer who played once for Sussex and who stood in one game at Liverpool in 1893. The oldest was Bob Thoms, the Middlesex cricketer who was still standing in 1900 at the age of 74.

Bill Reeves

Bill Reeves was, to quote Dudley Carew, 'the Sam Weller of umpires, quick of retort, ingenious of smile, unfailing in friendliness'. 'If silence or dullness fell upon the game,' wrote Robertson-Glasgow, 'there was Bill Reeves to put it right.'

The son of a railwayman, he played the last of his 271 games for Essex a week before his 46th birthday. As he departed the match at Leyton, he was staggering under the weight of two large bags perched upon his shoulders. "That's my benefit," he explained. "One's silver, one's copper. They've collected round the ground for me."

"Are you taking them to the bank?" "Bank? No bloody fear. *I'm* the bank around here."

A month later, at Ashby-de-la-Zouch, he was back as an umpire, becoming a good enough one to stand in five Tests.

He stood in the first match the 18-year-old Denis Compton played for Middlesex, a bank-holiday game at Lord's in 1936. Compton, batting at number eleven, had scored 14 when he was given out by Reeves. As they left the field

Compton's partner, Gubby Allen, protested: "He was never lbw." "Don't you worry about that boy, Mr Allen," said Reeves cheerfully. "He'll be all right. But I'm dying for a pee."

He got into hot water in 1931 when, in a rain-affected match at Cowbridge in the Vale of Glamorgan, he allowed the two captains to contrive a finish with a pair of freak declarations. It turned out that Law 54 had been broken, and the captains and umpires were summoned to Lord's. Reeves was determined to make light of the matter. "That rule doesn't apply, sir," he said chirpily. "We were in a foreign country."

On another occasion he gave an lbw against a batsman who was rather full of himself. "I hit that, Bill," the man protested. "Go on, you're out," was the gruff reply. Then, when the man had departed, Reeves asked a nearby fielder, "What do you think, Harry?" "Oh, he hit it right enough."

Quick as a flash, and with great satisfaction, Reeves turned to the non-striker. "I've been waiting for years to make a mistake against that bugger."

Player 1897 to 1921
Umpire 1921 to 1939

Alec Skelding

A distinctive figure with his white hair, craggy face and thick spectacles, the first English umpire to wear Australian-style white boots, Alec Skelding was one of the great characters of county cricket, standing from 1931 to 1958 when he was 72 years old.

In only his second summer he gave the first all lbw hat-trick, accompanying his third decision with the words, "As God's my witness, that's out, too."

Though a fast bowler in his youth, he was not always that quick to raise his finger. Once, at the start of play, he admitted to the non-striker Joe Hardstaff, "There'll be no lbws this morning. I've put my reading glasses on by mistake."

He had been a boxer and could handle himself physically, once wading into the crowd in the football stand at Bramall Lane to "sort that lot out". He was also a well-read man, fond of quoting snatches of Shakespeare in a loud, gravelly voice.

There was always a touch of theatre about him. He even wrote his own poem, *The Umpire's Lament*, composed on a wet day at Lord's. Bordering on doggerel, it reflected on the 'trials and troubles' of county cricket's umpires:

A-worrying over rumours of lbw bloomers
And departure times of home-returning trains.

In one game, growing frustrated by the constant muddle on the scoreboard, he walked across to the boundary and gave a man three halfpence. "Do us a favour, old cock," he said. "Buy a paper, will you, and tell us all the score."

On a bitterly cold, windy day at Leicester, he walked from the pitch to a man sitting beside the open pavilion gate. "Excuse me," he said. "Do you mind closing that door, 'cos there's a hell of a bloody draft coming out."

"And that, gentlemen," he would always say as he took off the bails at close of play, "concludes the entertainment for the day."

Player 1912 to 1929
Umpire 1931 to 1958

Behind the scenes

Scorers

The longest serving of county cricket's current scorers is Tony Kingston, who completed his 25th year with Northamptonshire in 2014. But, as he is 75 years old, he is unlikely to stay in position for longer than George 'Chicko' Austin who scored for 52 years for Warwickshire – or a predecessor of Kingston at Northampton, Leo Bullimer, who did 51.

'Chicko' Austin joined the office staff at Edgbaston as a 14-year-old in 1904. With neat handwriting, he was given the scorer's duties in 1911 after the players complained that his predecessor was forever cadging money off them. It is said that he never missed a ball of a Warwickshire game till he was taken ill during a match in May 1963. He died a week later.

Leo Bullimer, whose real name was Leon Boullemier, was the grandson of Emperor Napoleon III's physician, and the son of a ceramic artist who came to England during the Franco-Prussian War. He kept goal for Lincoln City, became a football referee and not only scored for Northamptonshire but worked tirelessly to raise money for the county. He started scoring in 1900, when he was 25, five years before the county joined the championship, and he was still scoring in 1950. Even in the darkest days of the 1930s, when the county went four years without winning a game, he remained cheerful. "Bully was a great enthusiast," Dennis Brookes remembered. "He used to come in the dressing room every morning. 'This is the one,' he'd say. 'We're going to win this.'" Alas, when the day finally came and they beat Leicestershire, 'Bully' was not there. He had broken his kneecap while alighting from a train.

Often the position of scorer was given to a former player. At Surrey Andrew Sandham, scorer of 107 first-class hundreds, retired as coach at the age of 68, only to do 12 years as scorer. When they introduced fielder identification lights, it became clear that he could not see to the middle, and the Secretary Geoffrey Howard had to relieve him of the

'Chicko' Austin

job: "His wife had died. Surrey County Cricket Club was his life. And I was pensioning him off. 'You can't do that,' people told me. 'It will kill him.' But when I told him, he looked so relieved. 'Thank goodness,' he said. 'I didn't know how to tell you myself.'"

Jack Mercer, the old Glamorgan all-rounder, was still scoring for Northants in 1981 when he was 88 years old, often relying on his fellow scorer when he got too caught up in telling a story or if he had a little nap. "It's all approximate," he used to say when he read out the scores.

The Trent Bridge library supervised by Peter Wynne-Thomas

The cakes in the Ladies' Pavilion at Worcester

Secretaries

In 1902 the first England-Australia Test of the summer was played at Edgbaston. Warwickshire were in their eighth year as a first-class county, and they had never previously staged a match on this scale. New stands were erected, thousands of seats brought in, and staff were hired specially for the three days: 60 gatemen, 60 police and almost 200 caterers. Then on the first day, adding to the pressure at the gates, hundreds of members arrived with their unpaid annual subscriptions.

In charge was the young Secretary, Rowland Ryder. There were no other clerical staff, he had no typewriter or telephone, and at the end of the day he sat on his own in the pavilion counting out the money and balancing the books. When the groundsman John Bates finished his day's work, he came in and helped. They left for home at three in the morning.

That winter, after the county had made an annual loss, he walked the streets of Birmingham and its suburbs, knocking on several thousand doors to recruit 600 new members.

Many were his duties in those days. There was an annual trip to Lord's to arrange the fixtures: 'where the silk hat and the frock coat were *de rigueur*'. There was the purchase of a horse to pull the roller, a task for which he had no qualification and which, alas, ended badly when the horse dropped dead.

Then there was the team to be assembled: 'Matches started on Mondays, and I often spent Sunday in a hansom cab trying to find someone to complete the team.' Once, when most of the amateurs were on a shooting trip, the committee instructed Ryder himself to go down to the Oval as captain, but he persuaded a friend, in his only appearance for Warwickshire, to go in his place. They lost by an innings.

Ryder remained Secretary till 1944, an increasingly autocratic figure who perched his glasses on the end of his nose and who was said to wear a hat at all times, even in the office. He was devoted to Warwickshire, turning down the chance to be the Secretary of the Royal & Ancient Golf Club and, in one financial crisis, he volunteered a cut of £100 to his annual pay. He passed his position as Secretary to his assistant Leslie Deakins, who remained in office till 1976 through years that saw Warwickshire become a wealthy club.

The same long service, with little in the way of support staff, was the story at Yorkshire where three Secretaries spanned the years from 1864 to 1971. The first, JB Wostinholm, was 'a hard-headed Yorkshireman ... a perfect Tartar', and in 1889 he doubled up as secretary/manager of the newly formed Sheffield United football club, where he raised the teams. Perhaps not a manager in the modern sense, he nevertheless took United to the League title in 1898, with Yorkshire winning the championship later in the year.

His successor, Frederick Toone, moved Yorkshire County Cricket Club from Sheffield to Leeds. He came from Leicestershire, where he had raised the membership from 500 to 1,800, and he soon boosted Yorkshire's. He was an 'organiser supreme', and he did much to look after the professionals, especially with their benefits. With a membership of 6,000, he ran the office calmly and efficiently with the aid of just one assistant. When he died in office in 1930, the committee thought long before promoting the assistant, but the 25-year-old John Nash did not disappoint them, serving for 40 years.

At Kent, in 1885, AJ Lancaster took over, at the age of 26, from his father and stayed for 50 years, but the longest-serving of all was Will Taylor, Secretary of Derbyshire from 1908 to 1959. He began in office in the leisurely 'Golden Age' of Edwardian cricket when he was often called upon to travel to away games as scorer or twelfth man; he guided the club through many a financial crisis, cultivating an annual donation from the Duke of Devonshire; he got the club going again after two world wars, his duties expanding to include the Secretaryship of the local Conservative Association; and he was still on the Derbyshire committtee as Honorary Secretary in 1972 when one-day cricket and overseas players were the new panaceas.

After the war Glamorgan and Hampshire opted for Secretary/Captains in Wilf Wooller and Desmond Eagar. Each stayed as Secretary for 30 years, long after their playing days, becoming masters rather than servants of their committees.

Mike Turner, Secretary at Leicester from 1960 to 1993, was a pioneer, guiding the small club through 20 successive years of profit in the 1970s and '80s. Increasingly, with the need for fresh sources of income, county clubs became businesses with large administrative staffs, and the Secretaries – as in the case of Mike Turner – were turned into Chief Executives.

Mike Vockins began at Worcester in 1971, back in the days when Wooller and Eagar, cricket men to the bone, held forth at the Lord's meetings, and he left in 2001, the last Secretary to serve for 30 years. At the close of 2014 only three of the current crop have been in post for even five years. The elder statesman is Middlesex's Vinny Codrington, appointed in 1997.

At the end of his last day, Mike Vockins took home with him the sign beside his parking space: 'Reserved for Secretary'.

County cricket had moved on.

Some facts and figures of county championship matches

Batting

Most runs in career	
C.P. Mead (Hants, 1906-36)	46,268
F.E. Woolley (Kent, 1906-38)	43,703
J.B. Hobbs (Surrey, 1905-34)	38,737
E.H. Hendren (Middx, 1907-37)	37,418
H. Sutcliffe (Yorks, 1919-39)	32,814
E. Tyldesley (Lancs, 1909-36)	31,903
D.L. Amiss (Wwks, 1960-87)	31,617
W.G. Quaife (Wwks, 1895-1928)	31,467
D. Kenyon (Worcs, 1946-67)	31,375
W.R. Hammond (Glos, 1920-51)	31,344
T.W. Hayward (Surrey, 1893-1914)	30,967
J.T. Tyldesley (Lancs, 1895-1923)	30,865

Highest batting average in career	
D.S. Lehmann (Yorks, 1997-2006)	68.76
K.S. Ranjitsinhji (Sussex, 1895-1920)	62.04
G. Boycott (Yorks, 1962-86)	58.27
M.R. Ramprakash (Mdx, Sy, 1987-2012)	58.18
C.B. Fry (Hants, Sussex, 1894-1921)	56.77
W.R. Hammond (Glos, 1920-51)	56.67
S.G. Law (Esx, Lancs, Derb, 1996-2009)	56.52
C.J.L. Rogers (De, Le, Nr, M, 2004-14)	54.38
G.A. Hick (Worcs, 1984-2008)	54.19
Javed Miandad (Sussex, Glam, 1976-85)	54.19
A.J. Lamb (Northants, 1978-95)	53.79
K.S. Duleepsinhji (Sussex, 1926-32)	53.09

Qualification: 8,000 runs

Most runs in a season	
C.P. Mead (Hants, 1928)	2,843
T.W. Hayward (Surrey, 1906)	2,814
H. Sutcliffe (Yorks, 1932)	2,624
J.T. Tyldesley (Lancs, 1901)	2,605
F.E. Woolley (Kent, 1928)	2,582
W.R. Hammond (Glos, 1933)	2,578
J.H. Parks (Sussex, 1937)	2,578
K.S. Ranjitsinhji (Sussex,1900)	2,563
W.E. Alley (Somerset, 1961)	2,532
W.R. Hammond (Glos, 1927)	2,522
J.B. Hobbs (Surrey, 1914)	2,499
E.H. Hendren (Middx, 1933)	2,479

Bowling

Most wickets in career	
A.P. Freeman (Kent, 1914-36)	3,151
W. Rhodes (Yorks, 1898-1930)	3,112
C.W.L. Parker (Glos, 1905-35)	3,022
T.W.J. Goddard (Glos, 1922-52)	2,678
D. Shackleton (Hants, 1948-69)	2,542
A.S. Kennedy (Hants, 1907-36)	2,418
F.J. Titmus (Mdx, Sy, 1949-82)	2,171
W.E. Hollies (Wwks, 1932-57)	2,105
G.H. Hirst (Yorks, 1891-1921)	2,095
J.C. White (Som, 1909-37)	2,080
J.T. Hearne (Middx, 1890-1914)	2,032
C. Blythe (Kent, 1899-1914)	2,032

Lowest bowling average in career	
G.A. Lohmann (Surrey, 1890-96)	12.94
H. Verity (Yorks, 1930-39)	13.20
R.J. Hadlee (Notts, 1978-87)	14.50
J.B. Statham (Lancs, 1950-68)	15.17
W.E. Bowes (Yorks, 1929-47)	15.31
A. Mold (Lancs, 1890-1901)	15.34
R. Appleyard (Yorks, 1950-58)	15.40
R. Peel (Yorks, 1890-97)	15.54
W. Rhodes (Yorks, 1898-1930)	15.71
S. Haigh (Yorks, 1895-1913)	15.71
C.H. Parkin (Yorks, Lancs, 1906-26)	15.93
H. Larwood (Notts, 1924-38)	16.29

Qualification: 400 wickets

Most wickets in a season	
A.P. Freeman (Kent, 1933)	252
A.P. Freeman (Kent, 1930)	249
A.P. Freeman (Kent, 1931)	241
T. Richardson (Surrey, 1895)	239
T. Richardson (Surrey, 1897)	238
A.P. Freeman (Kent, 1928)	216
W.C. Smith (Surrey, 1910)	215
T.W.J. Goddard (Glos,1937)	215
A.P. Freeman (Kent, 1932)	209
W. Rhodes (Yorks, 1900)	206
T.W.J. Goddard (Glos, 1947)	206
C.W.L. Parker (Glos, 1931)	205

All-round play

Most runs and wickets in career		
W. Rhodes (Yorks, 1898-1930)	26,859	3,112
G.H. Hirst (Yorks, 1891-1921)	27,314	2,095
F.E. Woolley (Kent, 1906-38)	43,703	1,578
J.W. Hearne (Middx, 1909-36)	25,819	1,356
J. Langridge (Sussex, 1924-53)	25,893	1,257
V.W.C. Jupp (Sx, Wwks, 1909-38)	20,139	1,349
J.R. Gunn (Notts, 1896-1925)	21,588	1,061
J.H. King (Leics, 1895-1925)	21,333	1,008
W.G. Quaife (Wwks, 1895-1928)	31,467	840
D.B. Close (Yorks, Som, 1949-77)	25,376	886
D.E. Davies (Glam, 1924-54)	24,831	810

Qualification: 20,000 runs and 800 wickets

Most runs and wickets in a season		
G.H. Hirst (Yorks, 1906)	1,771	182
F.E. Woolley (Kent, 1922)	1,868	142
F.E. Woolley (Kent, 1920)	1,548	164
F.E. Woolley (Kent, 1914)	1,933	112
F.E. Woolley (Kent, 1921)	1,621	123
F.J. Titmus (Middx, 1961)	1,501	123
J.W. Hearne (Middx, 1920)	1,552	119
G.H. Hirst (Yorks, 1911)	1,540	119
A.E. Relf (Sussex, 1913)	1,560	116
F.A. Tarrant (Middx, 1914)	1,524	112
J.L. Hopwood (Lancs, 1934)	1,583	110

Qualification: 1,500 runs and 110 wickets

Fielding

Most catches in career	
F.E. Woolley (Kent, 1906-38)	712
J.G. Langridge (Sussex, 1928-55)	707
C.A. Milton (Glos, 1948-74)	642
D.B. Close (Yorks, Som, 1949-77)	625
P.M. Walker (Glam, 1956-72)	609
C.P. Mead (Hants, 1906-36)	603
J. Seymour (Kent, 1902-26)	599
J. Tunnicliffe (Yorks, 1891-1907)	580
P.J. Sainsbury (Hants, 1954-76)	566
W.R. Hammond (Glos, 1920-51)	531
M.J. Stewart (Surrey, 1954-72)	524
D.C. Morgan (Derbys, 1950-69)	523

Highest catches per match in career	
P.M. Walker (Glam, 1956-72)	1.515
G.R.J. Roope (Surrey, 1964-82)	1.511
J. Tunnicliffe (Yorks, 1891-1907)	1.503
M.E. Trescothick (Som, 1993-2014)	1.493
W.S. Surridge (Surrey, 1947-56)	1.466
G.A. Hick (Worcs, 1984-2008)	1.417
W.R. Hammond (Glos, 1920-51)	1.408
M.J. Di Venuto (Sus, De, Du, 1999-2012)	1.404
J.G. Langridge (Sussex, 1928-55)	1.400
B.A. Richards (Hants, 1968-78)	1.354
G.A.R. Lock (Surrey, Leics, 1946-67)	1.337
D. Byas (Yorks, Lancs, 1986-2002)	1.309

Qualification: 250 catches

Most catches in a season	
J.G. Langridge (Sussex, 1955)	66
P.M. Walker (Glam, 1961)	65
P.J. Sharpe (Yorks, 1962)	65
M.J. Stewart (Surrey, 1957)	63
J. Tunnicliffe (Yorks, 1901)	62
J.G. Langridge (Sussex, 1933)	59
P.M. Walker (Glam, 1960)	59
D.W. Richardson (Worcs, 1961)	59
W.R. Hammond (Glos, 1928)	58
J. Tunnicliffe (Yorks, 1904)	57
K.J. Grieves (Lancs, 1950)	57
P.M. Walker (Glam, 1959)	57

Wicket-keeping

Most victims in career	
R.W. Taylor (Derbys, 1961-84)	1,220
H. Strudwick (Surrey, 1902-27)	1,131
F.H. Huish (Kent, 1895-1914)	1,128
B. Taylor (Essex, 1950-73)	1,127
H. Elliott (Derbys, 1920-47)	1,124
J.T. Murray (Middx, 1952-75)	1,123
H.R. Butt (Sussex, 1890-1912)	1,042
R. Booth (Yorks,Worcs, 1951-70)	1,040
S.J. Rhodes (Yorks,Worcs, 1984-2004)	1,014
J.H. Board (Glos, 1891-1914)	983
R.C. Russell (Glos, 1982-2004)	979
D.L. Bairstow (Yorks, 1970-90)	967

Highest victims per match in career	
P. Mustard (Durham, 2003-14)	3.464
R.J. Turner (Som, 1992-2005)	3.245
C.M.W. Read (Notts, 1998-2014)	3.228
J.N. Batty (Sy, Glos, Nthnts, 1997-2013)	3.183
G.O. Jones (Kent, 2001-14)	3.174
J.S. Foster (Essex, 2000-14)	3.112
M.A. Wallace (Glam, 1999-2014)	2.882
D.E. East (Essex, 1981-89)	2.837
R.C. Russell (Glos, 1982-2004)	2.821
L.D. Sutton (Som, De, La, 1998-2011)	2.801
R.J. Parks (Hants, Kent, 1980-93)	2.792
S.J. Rhodes (Yorks, Worcs, 1984-2004)	2.786

Qualification: 400 victims

Most victims in a season	
L.E.G. Ames (Kent, 1929)	102
L.E.G. Ames (Kent, 1928)	100
R. Booth (Worcs, 1960)	96
H. Yarnold (Worcs, 1949)	95
R. Booth (Worcs, 1962)	95
R. Booth (Worcs, 1964)	95
F.H. Huish (Kent, 1911)	91
G. Duckworth (Lancs, 1928)	91
J.T. Murray (Middx, 1960)	91
J.G. Binks (Yorks, 1960)	90
H. Elliott (Derbys, 1935)	88
R. Booth (Worcs, 1961)	88

Long service

Most matches as player	
W. Rhodes (Yorks, 1898-1930)	762
F.E. Woolley (Kent, 1906-38)	707
C.P. Mead (Hants, 1906-36)	668
N. Gifford (Worcs, Wwks, 1960-88)	617
W.G. Quaife (Wwks, 1895-1928)	611
G.H. Hirst (Yorks, 1891-1921)	600
F.J. Titmus (Middx, Surrey, 1949-82)	598
W.E. Astill (Leics, 1906-39)	591
D.J. Shepherd (Glam, 1950-72)	590
D.B. Close (Yorks, Som, 1949-77)	580
D. Denton (Yorks, 1894-1920)	575
R. Illingworth (Yorks, Leics, 1951-83)	572

Most matches as umpire	
T.W. Spencer (1950-80)	571
F.R. Chester (1922-55)	531
D.J. Constant (1969-2006)	523
H.G. Baldwin (1932-62)	517
A.G.T. Whitehead (1970-2005)	511
P.B. Wight (1966-95)	483
J. Moss (1899-1929)	462
A. Skelding (1931-58)	453
R. Julian (1972-2001)	447
A.E. Street (1909-34)	446
W.A.J. West (1896-1925)	433
W.E. Phillipson (1956-78)	427

Most matches as player or umpire	
J.G. Langridge (1928-83)	921
A. Jepson (1938-84)	794
P.B. Wight (1954-95)	785
W. Rhodes (1898-1930)	762
J.F. Crapp (1936-78)	755
J.H. Hampshire (1961-2005)	732
W.F.F. Price (1926-67)	723
C. Cook (1946-86)	711
B.J. Meyer (1957-97)	710
H. Elliott (1920-60)	707
F.E. Woolley (1906-38)	707
D. Denton (1894-1930)	704

Some county championship records

Team scores

Totals of 800 or more						
887	Yorkshire v Warwickshire	Edgbaston	1896
863	Lancashire v Surrey	The Oval	1990
850-7	Somerset v Middlesex	Taunton	2007
811	Surrey v Somerset	The Oval	1899
810-4	Warwickshire v Durham	Edgbaston	1994
803-4	Kent v Essex	Brentwood	1934
801-8	Derbyshire v Somerset	Taunton	2007
801	Lancashire v Somerset	Taunton	1895

Totals of 20 or less			
12	Northamptonshire v Gloucestershire	Gloucester	1907
13	Nottinghamshire v Yorkshire	Trent Bridge	1901
14	Surrey v Essex	Chelmsford	1983
15	Northamptonshire v Yorkshire	Northampton	1908
15	Hampshire v Warwickshire	Edgbaston	1922
16	Warwickshire v Kent	Tonbridge	1913
20	Sussex v Yorkshire	Hull	1922
20	Derbyshire v Yorkshire	Sheffield	1939
20	Essex v Lancashire	Chelmsford	2013

Individual scores

Scores of 340 or more				
501*	B.C. Lara	Warwickshire v Durham	Edgbaston	1994
424	A.C. MacLaren	Lancashire v Somerset	Taunton	1895
405*	G.A. Hick	Worcestershire v Somerset	Taunton	1988
366	N.H. Fairbrother	Lancashire v Surrey	The Oval	1990
357*	R. Abel	Surrey v Somerset	The Oval	1899
344*	M.W. Goodwin	Sussex v Somerset	Taunton	2009
343*	P.A. Perrin	Essex v Derbyshire	Chesterfield	1904
342	J.L. Langer	Somerset v Surrey	Guildford	2006
341	G.H. Hirst	Yorkshire v Leicestershire	Leicester	1905
341	C.M. Spearman	Gloucestershire v Middlesex	Gloucester	2004

All-round performances

Two centuries and 10 wickets in the same match							
103	100*	3-75	8-53	B.J.T. Bosanquet	Middlesex v Sussex	Lord's	1905
111	117*	6-70	5-45	G.H. Hirst	Yorkshire v Somerset	Bath	1906
111	117	4-105	7-117	F.D. Stephenson	Nottinghamshire v Yorkshire	Trent Bridge	1988

Batting partnerships

Highest partnerships for each wicket					
1	555	P. Holmes, H. Sutcliffe	Yorkshire v Essex	Leyton	1932
2	465*	J.A. Jameson, R.B. Kanhai	Warwickshire v Gloucestershire	Edgbaston	1974
3	523	M.A. Carberry, N.D. McKenzie	Hampshire v Yorkshire	Southampton	2011
4	470	A.I. Kallicharran, G.W. Humpage	Warwickshire v Lancashire	Southport	1982
5	401	M.B. Loye, D. Ripley	Northamptonshire v Glamorgan	Northampton	1998
6	411	R.M. Poore, E.G. Wynyard	Hampshire v Somerset	Taunton	1899
7	344	K.S. Ranjitsinhji, W. Newham	Sussex v Essex	Leyton	1902
8	292	R. Peel, Lord Hawke	Yorkshire v Warwickshire	Edgbaston	1896
9	283	A. Warren, J. Chapman	Derbyshire v Warwickshire	Blackwell	1910
10	235	F.E. Woolley, A. Fielder	Kent v Worcestershire	Amblecote	1909

Bowling

Best bowling figures in an innings

10-10	H. Verity	Yorkshire v Nottinghamshire	Headingley	1932
10-18	G. Geary	Leicestershire v Glamorgan	Pontypridd	1929
10-30	C. Blythe	Kent v Northamptonshire	Northampton	1907
10-32	H. Pickett	Essex v Leicestershire	Leyton	1895
10-35	A. Drake	Yorkshire v Somerset	Weston-super-Mare	1914
10-36	H. Verity	Yorkshire v Warwickshire	Headingley	1931

Best bowling figures in a match

17-48	C. Blythe	Kent v Northamptonshire	Northampton	1907
17-56	C.W.L. Parker	Gloucestershire v Essex	Gloucester	1925
17-67	A.P. Freeman	Kent v Sussex	Hove	1922
17-89	F.C. Matthews	Nottinghamshire v Northamptonshire	Trent Bridge	1923
17-91	H. Verity	Yorkshire v Essex	Leyton	1933
17-92	A.P. Freeman	Kent v Warwickshire	Folkestone	1932

Wicket-keeping

Most victims in an innings

8 ct	D.E. East	Essex v Somerset	Taunton	1985
8 ct	S.A. Marsh	Kent v Middlesex	Lord's	1991
8 ct	J.N. Batty	Surrey v Kent	The Oval	2004

Most victims in a match

11 ct	A. Long	Surrey v Sussex	Hove	1964
11 ct	D.L. Bairstow	Yorkshire v Derbyshire	Scarborough	1982
11 ct	W.K. Hegg	Lancashire v Derbyshire	Chesterfield	1989
11 ct	A.J. Stewart	Surrey v Leicestershire	Leicester	1989
10 ct, 1 st	K.J. Piper	Warwickshire v Derbyshire	Chesterfield	1994
7 ct, 4 st	J.N. Batty	Surrey v Lancashire	Old Trafford	2004
11 ct	H.R. Hosein	Derbyshire v Surrey	The Oval	2014

The record for most stumpings is 9 by F.E. Huish
for Kent v Surrey, The Oval, 1911 – he also held one catch

Fielding

Most catches in an innings

7	M.J. Stewart	Surrey v Northamptonshire	Northampton	1957
7	A.S. Brown	Gloucestershire v Nottinghamshire	Trent Bridge	1966
7	R. Clarke	Warwickshire v Lancashire	Liverpool	2011

Most catches in a match

10	W.R. Hammond	Gloucestershire v Surrey	Cheltenham	1928

One-day tournaments

1962   The first inter-county one-day tournament takes place in early May: the Midlands Knock-Out Competition, brainchild of Leicestershire Secretary Mike Turner. Four counties participate: Derbyshire, Leicestershire, Northamptonshire and Nottinghamshire. Each innings is limited to 65 overs. In the semi-finals there is a maximum of 15 overs per bowler; in the final there is no restriction. Northamptonshire are the winners.

1963   The first-class counties take part in a 65-over knock-out competition. Gillette, the sponsors, contribute a total of £6,500. In the final at Lord's the winners Sussex score 168 in 60.2 overs; in reply Worcestershire are all out for 154 in 63.2 overs. The following year the matches are reduced to 60 overs. Leading minor counties take part from 1964, their first success against a first-class county coming when Durham beat Yorkshire in 1973.

1969   The 40-over Sunday League begins. The sponsors are cigarette manufacturers John Player. The BBC, who broadcast a game each Sunday afternoon, offer a prize of £250 for the fastest televised fifty. Keith Boyce, Essex's West Indian, is the first winner with a 23-minute fifty against Lancashire. More memorably, at Yeovil, he is at the non-striker's end for most of the bowling spell of the Somerset off-spinner Brian Langford who in eight overs does not concede a run. During the summer the average 40-over total is just over 150.

1972   A third competition, the 55-over Benson & Hedges Cup, begins. Twenty teams take part: the 17 first-class counties plus Cambridge University, Minor Counties (North) and Minor Counties (South). They play in four groups to establish quarter-finalists. The Lord's final, won by Leicestershire, takes place in July. The next summer it is Oxford University's turn, and in their first match, with a young Imran Khan, they beat Northamptonshire.

1977   BMW offers £50,000 for an end-of-season knock-out cup between the summer's four competition winners. After objections from the existing sponsors, the Test and County Cricket Board turns down the offer.

1981   In September a 10-over, seven-a-side tournament, sponsored by Lambert & Butler, is played under floodlights at five leading football grounds. Lancashire win the final on an artificial pitch with 37-yard boundaries at Stamford Bridge. Only 2,564 spectators attend, and the tournament is dropped. 'The cricket lacked conviction,' the TCCB says.

1993   Sponsors change, their money increases, but the main formats are unaltered till 1993 when the B&H Cup loses its group stage and the Sunday League becomes a 50-over contest with 12 o'clock starts and coloured clothing. The League reverts to 40 overs in 1994, the B&H to group stages in 1995. From 1996 the B&H games are 50 overs.

1999   In a major shake-up the League is increased to 45 overs, leaves its regular Sunday slot and is split into two divisions. Both the knock-out cups are 50 overs, with participation in the B&H Super Cup limited to the eight top teams in the previous year's championship. The next year the old B&H, with its group stages, returns.

2003   The Twenty20 Cup arrives. The 18 counties, in three groups, play five games each. Then the semi-finals and final are played in a day at Trent Bridge, with Surrey the first winners. Space is cleared for these games by the abolition of the Benson & Hedges Cup. The success of Twenty20, soon rebranded T20, sees a rapid expansion of the group-stage games: from five to eight to ten to a massive 16 in 2011. Meanwhile the other two tournaments undergo further changes before in 2010 they coalesce into the CB40, a 40-over tournament with group stages leading to an end-of-season Lord's final. For four summers the 50-over game, as played internationally, does not feature in the schedule. Then in 2014 the CB40 turns into the 50-over Royal London One-Day Cup.

Winners   In 52 years there have been 136 inter-county one-day tournaments. The winners are listed opposite.
Lancashire have won 16, Warwickshire 12, Hampshire and Kent 11, Essex 10, Gloucestershire and Sussex 9.
The captain leading his team to most trophies has been Mark Alleyne (Gloucestershire, 1997-2004) with seven, including all three in 2000. He is followed by Mike Denness (Kent, 1971-76) with six. Jack Bond (Lancashire, 1968-72) has arguably the best record, winning five out of ten one-day competitions during his time in charge. Graham Gooch of Essex has scored most runs (16,296); John Lever of Essex has taken most wickets (609).

	Gillette, etc	Sunday League, etc	Benson & Hedges	T20
1963	Sussex			
1964	Sussex			
1965	Yorkshire			
1966	Warwickshire			
1967	Kent			
1968	Warwickshire			
1969	Yorkshire	Lancashire		
1970	Lancashire	Lancashire		
1971	Lancashire	Worcestershire		
1972	Lancashire	Kent	Leicestershire	
1973	Gloucestershire	Kent	Kent	
1974	Kent	Leicestershire	Surrey	
1975	Lancashire	Hampshire	Leicestershire	
1976	Northamptonshire	Kent	Kent	
1977	Middlesex	Leicestershire	Gloucestershire	
1978	Sussex	Hampshire	Kent	
1979	Somerset	Somerset	Essex	
1980	Middlesex	Warwickshire	Northamptonshire	
1981	Derbyshire	Essex	Somerset	
1982	Surrey	Sussex	Somerset	
1983	Somerset	Yorkshire	Middlesex	
1984	Middlesex	Essex	Lancashire	
1985	Essex	Essex	Leicestershire	
1986	Sussex	Hampshire	Middlesex	
1987	Nottinghamshire	Worcestershire	Yorkshire	
1988	Middlesex	Worcestershire	Hampshire	
1989	Warwickshire	Lancashire	Nottinghamshire	
1990	Lancashire	Derbyshire	Lancashire	
1991	Hampshire	Nottinghamshire	Worcestershire	
1992	Northamptonshire	Middlesex	Hampshire	
1993	Warwickshire	Glamorgan	Derbyshire	
1994	Worcestershire	Warwickshire	Warwickshire	
1995	Warwickshire	Kent	Lancashire	
1996	Lancashire	Surrey	Lancashire	
1997	Essex	Warwickshire	Surrey	
1998	Lancashire	Lancashire	Essex	
1999	Gloucestershire	Lancashire	Gloucestershire	
2000	Gloucestershire	Gloucestershire	Gloucestershire	
2001	Somerset	Kent	Surrey	
2002	Yorkshire	Glamorgan	Warwickshire	
2003	Gloucestershire	Surrey		Surrey
2004	Gloucestershire	Glamorgan		Leicestershire
2005	Hampshire	Essex		Somerset
2006	Sussex	Essex		Leicestershire
2007	Durham	Worcestershire		Kent
2008	Essex	Sussex		Middlesex
2009	Hampshire	Sussex		Sussex
2010		Warwickshire		Hampshire
2011		Surrey		Leicestershire
2012		Hampshire		Hampshire
2013		Nottinghamshire		Northamptonshire
2014		Durham		Warwickshire

Minor counties and second elevens

1895 Organised by the Worcestershire Secretary Paul Foley, an unofficial Second Class Counties Championship is set up. The final table lists seven counties – Bedfordshire, Durham, Hertfordshire, Norfolk, Oxfordshire, Staffordshire and Worcestershire – each of whom has played a minimum of eight matches, though these include games against other second-class counties. The joint winners are Norfolk and Durham; Worcestershire will later be bracketed with them.

1899 Worcestershire, after three outright victories, join the first-class counties.
The counties reaching the minimum of eight matches vary from year to year. Surrey become the first county to enter a second eleven in the Second Class Counties Championship.

1901 The competition is officially recognised by MCC. There are now 17 participating counties, including second elevens from Surrey and Yorkshire. Now only matches between these 17 teams count in the final table.

1902 The competition is used for an experimental lbw law, which does not require the ball to pitch in line with the wickets. It is pronounced a failure and abandoned after one summer.

1906 Staffordshire are champions for the first time, with Sydney Barnes taking 119 wickets in 12 matches. He will still be topping the competition's bowling averages in 1931, at the age of 58.

1907 The competition is regionalised, with North, Midlands, East and West sections, each containing five or six counties. The four winners then enter a knock-out tournament. Lancashire are the first second eleven to be champions.

1912 After two summers in which there are only two regions, it is back to one division. If the two top teams have not met, the second can challenge the first for the title. Staffordshire, unbeaten in second place, challenge Norfolk, who find that several of their best men have gone away. They cannot raise 'a representative side' so the title is put in abeyance.

1914 With war declared in early August, many fixtures are cancelled; Hertfordshire forfeit their challenge match against Staffordshire. It will be the summer of 1920 before the competition resumes.

1933 Yorkshire Second XI, in second place, challenge and beat Norfolk to win the title. Seven weeks later, when *Wisden* editors check the table, it is discovered that an error has occurred in the allocation of points. Wiltshire, not Yorkshire, should have been in second place. The competition is declared 'undecided'.

1959 A new second-eleven competition is won by Gloucestershire, for whom 'Bomber' Wells takes 87 wickets in 12 games. Nine county second elevens play in both competitions. Sometimes the games between them count towards the Minor Counties Championship, sometimes towards the Second Eleven Championship and in six cases towards both.

1964 Worcestershire are denied a hat-trick of second-eleven championships by Lancashire whose final victory over Derbyshire is largely due to slow-left-armer Peter Robinson, who takes 12 wickets for 67 runs. Robinson is, in fact, a Worcestershire player, on a one-match trial with Lancashire. Next day he signs for Somerset.

1969 In late August Buckinghamshire are certain of first place in the Minor Counties table. If they beat Bedfordshire, Cornwall in second place will challenge them for the title. But if they lose, it is Bedfordshire who will finish second and there will be no such match; the teams have already met. Buckinghamshire duly lose and become champions.

1983 The Minor Counties Championship is split into East and West divisions, with a final between the two teams. Only Somerset still enter a second eleven, and they will withdraw after 1987, to be replaced by a Wales Minor Counties XI.

1997 Devon, led by the former Somerset captain Peter Roebuck, become the first team to win the Minor Counties Championship four years in a row. *Wisden* calls Roebuck 'an inspirational leader', but the real surprise, after a first-class career as a specialist batsman, is his emergence as the competition's leading bowler.

2010 The Second Eleven Championship is split into North and South divisions, with a play-off final. MCC uses the competition for developing young players, entering two teams: MCC Universities and MCC Young Cricketers.

Minor Counties champions

1895	Durham *	1924	Berkshire	1959	Warwickshire II	1989	Oxfordshire
(joint)	Norfolk	1925	Buckinghamshire	1960	Lancashire II	1990	Hertfordshire
1896	Worcestershire	1926	Durham	1961	Somerset II	1991	Staffordshire
1897	Worcestershire	1927	Staffordshire	1962	Warwickshire II	1992	Staffordshire
1898	Worcestershire	1928	Berkshire	1963	Cambridgeshire	1993	Staffordshire
1899	Buckinghamshire	1929	Oxfordshire	1964	Lancashire II	1994	Devon
(joint)	Northamptonshire	1930	Durham	1965	Somerset II	1995	Devon
1900	Durham	1931	Leicestershire II	1966	Lincolnshire	1996	Devon
(joint)	Glamorgan	1932	Buckinghamshire	1967	Cheshire	1997	Devon
	Northamptonshire	1933	*undecided*	1968	Yorkshire II	1998	Staffordshire
1901	Durham	1934	Lancashire II	1969	Buckinghamshire	1999	Cumberland
1902	Wiltshire	1935	Middlesex II	1970	Bedfordshire	2000	Dorset
1903	Northamptonshire	1936	Hertfordshire	1971	Yorkshire II	2001	Cheshire
1904	Northamptonshire	1937	Lancashire II	1972	Bedfordshire	*(joint)*	Lincolnshire
1905	Norfolk	1938	Buckinghamshire	1973	Shropshire	2002	Herefordshire
1906	Staffordshire	1939	Surrey II	1974	Oxfordshire	*(joint)*	Norfolk
1907	Lancashire II			1975	Hertfordshire	2003	Lincolnshire
1908	Staffordshire	1946	Suffolk	1976	Durham	2004	Bedfordshire
1909	Wiltshire	1947	Yorkshire II	1977	Suffolk	*(joint)*	Devon
1910	Norfolk	1948	Lancashire II	1978	Devon	2005	Cheshire
1911	Staffordshire	1949	Lancashire II	1979	Suffolk	*(joint)*	Suffolk
1912	*in abeyance*	1950	Surrey II	1980	Durham	2006	Devon
1913	Norfolk	1951	Kent II	1981	Durham	2007	Cheshire
1914	Staffordshire	1952	Buckinghamshire	1982	Oxfordshire	2008	Berkshire
		1953	Berkshire	1983	Hertfordshire	2009	Buckinghamshire
1919	*no contest*	1954	Surrey II	1984	Durham	2010	Dorset
1920	Staffordshire	1955	Surrey II	1985	Cheshire	2011	Devon
1921	Staffordshire	1956	Kent II	1986	Cumberland	2012	Cornwall
1922	Buckinghamshire	1957	Yorkshire II	1987	Buckinghamshire	2013	Cheshire
1923	Buckinghamshire	1958	Yorkshire II	1988	Cheshire	2014	Staffordshire

Most frequent winners: Staffordshire 12, Buckinghamshire 9 + 1 shared, Durham 7 + 2 shared, Devon 7 + 1 shared, Lancashire II 7

* Wisden, contrary to its original judgement, now regards the 1895 championship as also shared by Worcestershire.

Second Eleven champions

1959	Gloucestershire	1973	Essex	1987	Kent & Yorkshire	2001	Hampshire
1960	Northamptonshire	1974	Middlesex	1988	Surrey	2002	Kent
1961	Kent	1975	Surrey	1989	Middlesex	2003	Yorkshire
1962	Worcestershire	1976	Kent	1990	Sussex	2004	Somerset
1963	Worcestershire	1977	Yorkshire	1991	Yorkshire	2005	Kent
1964	Lancashire	1978	Sussex	1992	Surrey	2006	Kent
1965	Glamorgan	1979	Warwickshire	1993	Middlesex	2007	Sussex
1966	Surrey	1980	Glamorgan	1994	Somerset	2008	Durham
1967	Hampshire	1981	Hampshire	1995	Hampshire	2009	Surrey
1968	Surrey	1982	Worcestershire	1996	Warwickshire	2010	Surrey
1969	Kent	1983	Leicestershire	1997	Lancashire	2011	Warwickshire
1970	Kent	1984	Yorkshire	1998	Northamptonshire	2012	Kent
1971	Hampshire	1985	Nottinghamshire	1999	Middlesex	2013	Lancashire
1972	Nottinghamshire	1986	Lancashire	2000	Middlesex	2014	Leicestershire

Most frequent winners: Kent 8 + 1 shared, Surrey 7, Hampshire 5, Middlesex 5, Yorkshire 4 + 1 shared, Lancashire 4

Bibliography

In writing this book, I have drawn on many written sources: books, newspapers and magazines.

The newspapers I have consulted have been:
The Times, Guardian, Daily Telegraph and many of the local newspapers available from the British Newspaper Archive.

The magazines have been:
Cricket, Cricket Field, The Cricketer, Playfair Cricket Monthly, Wisden Cricket Monthly and *The Wisden Cricketer*.

The books are as follows:

Reference books

Wisden Cricketers' Almanack
Playfair Cricket Annual
Philip Bailey, Philip Thorn & Peter Wynne-Thomas,
   Who's Who of Cricketers (Hamlyn, 1993)
Robert Brooke, *A History of the County Cricket Championship*
   (Guinness, 1991)
Bill Frindall, *The Wisden Book of Cricket Records*
   (Macdonald Queen Anne Press, 1986)
E.W. Swanton, George Plumptre & John Woodcock,
   Barclays World of Cricket (Collins, 1986)

General histories

H.S. Altham, *A History of Cricket* (George Allen & Unwin, 1962)
W.G. Grace, *Cricket* (JW Arrowsmith, 1891)
Benny Green, *A History of Cricket* (Barrie & Jenkins, 1988)
Eric Parker, *The History of Cricket* (Seeley Service, 1950)
Roy Webber, *The County Cricket Championship* (Phoenix, 1957)

County histories

The series published by Christopher Helm (1988-1993)
Derbyshire, by John Shawcroft
Glamorgan, by Andrew Hignell
Gloucestershire, by David Green
Hampshire, by Peter Wynne-Thomas
Kent, by Dudley Moore
Lancashire, by Peter Wynne-Thomas
Leicestershire, by Dennis Lambert
Middlesex, by David Lemmon
Northamptonshire, by Matthew Engel and Andrew Radd
Nottinghamshire, by Peter Wynne-Thomas
Surrey, by David Lemmon
Warwickshire, by Jack Bannister
Worcestershire, by David Lemmon
Yorkshire, by Anthony Whitehouse

Other county histories
David Allen, *Hampshire CCC 1946-2006* (Phillimore, 2007)
Brian Bearshaw, *From the Stretford End* (Partridge, 1990)
Charles Bray, *Essex County Cricket* (Convoy, 1950)
Leslie Duckworth, *The Story of Warwickshire Cricket*
   (Stanley Paul, 1974)
David Foot, *Sunshine, Sixes and Cider* (David Charles, 1986)
Lord Harris, *A History of Kent County Cricket*
   (Eyre & Spottiswoode, 1907)
J.M. Kilburn, *A History of Yorkshire Cricket* (Stanley Paul, 1970)
Grahame Parker, *Gloucestershire Road* (Pelham, 1983)
A.W. Pullin, *A History of Yorkshire County Cricket 1903-1923*
   (Chorley & Pickersgill, 1924)
Peter Roebuck, *From Sammy to Jimmy* (Partridge, 1991)
M.D. Vockins, *Worcestershire – A Pictorial History* (Severn, 1980)
Wilfred Wooller, *A History of Glamorgan* (Arthur Barker, 1971)

Cricket grounds

published by the Association of Cricket Statisticians & Historians
Derbyshire, by John Shawcroft
Durham, by Steven Draper
Essex, by Bob Harragan
Glamorgan, by Andrew Hignell
Gloucestershire, by Douglas Miller
Hampshire, by various
Kent, by Howard Milton
Lancashire, by Malcolm Lorimer and Don Ambrose
Leicestershire, by Eric Snow
Middlesex, by William A. Powell
Nottinghamshire, by Peter Wynne-Thomas
Somerset, by Bob Harragan
Warwickshire, by Robert Brooke
Worcestershire, by Les Hatton
Yorkshire, by Steven Draper

Biographies and autobiographies

Bill Alley, *My Incredible Innings* (Pelham, 1969)

Bill Alley, *Standing the Test of Time* (Empire, 1999)

Leslie Ames, *Close of Play* (Stanley Paul, 1953)

John Arlott, *Jack Hobbs* (John Murray, 1981)

Mike Atherton, *Opening Up* (Hodder & Stoughton, 2002)

Simon Barnes, *Phil Edmonds: A Singular Man* (Kingswood, 1986)

Keith Booth, *The Father of Modern Sport* (Parrs Wood Press, 2002)

Paddy Briggs, *John Shepherd* (ACS, 2009)

Gerald Brodribb, *The Croucher* (Constable, 1985)

Robert Brooke, *F.R. Foster* (ACS, 2011)

Roland Butcher, *Rising to the Challenge* (Pelham, 1989)

Ray Cairns, *Glenn Turner's Century of Centuries* (Hodder, 1983)

Mike Carey, *Les Jackson* (Tranters, 1997)

A.W. Carr, *Cricket With The Lid Off* (Hutchinson, 1935)

Frank Chester, *How's That!* (Hutchinson, 1956)

Brian Close, *Close to Cricket* (Stanley Paul, 1968)

James P. Coldham, *Lord Hawke* (Crowood, 1990)

Colin Cowdrey, *M.C.C.* (Hodder & Stoughton, 1976)

Mike Denness, *I Declare* (Arthur Barker, 1977)

Leslie Duckworth, *S.F. Barnes – Master Bowler* (Hutchinson, 1967)

Ray East, *A Funny Turn* (George Allen & Unwin, 1983)

W.J. Edrich, *Cricket Heritage* (Stanley Paul, 1949)

Keith Fletcher, *Captain's Innings* (Stanley Paul, 1983)

David Foot, *Harold Gimblett* (Fairfield Books, 2003)

Cyril P. Foley, *Autumn Foliage* (Methuen, 1935)

Mike Gatting, *Leading from the Front* (Queen Anne Press, 1988)

A.E.R. Gilligan, *Sussex Cricket* (Chapman & Hall, 1933)

M.A. Green, *Sporting Campaigner* (Stanley Paul, 1956)

Tony Greig, *My Story* (Stanley Paul, 1980)

Walter Hammond, *Cricket My Destiny* (Stanley Paul, 1939)

John Hampshire, *Family Argument* (George Allen & Unwin, 1983)

Basharat Hassan, *Basher (*Notts CCC, 2004)

Lord Hawke, *Recollections and Reminiscences* (Williams, 1924)

Patsy Hendren, *Big Cricket* (Hodder & Stoughton, 1934)

Andrew Hignell, *The Skipper* (Limlow, 1995)

Andrew Hignell, *Turnbull* (Tempus, 2001)

Alan Hill, *Herbert Sutcliffe* (Simon & Schuster, 1991)

Alan Hill, *Johnny Wardle* (David & Charles, 1988)

Alan Hill, *Les Ames* (Christopher Helm, 1990)

Alan Hill, *Peter May* (Andre Deutsch, 1996)

J.B. Hobbs, *My Cricket Memories* (Heinemann, 1924)

Eric Hollies, *I'll Spin You A Tale* (Museum Press, 1955)

E.R.T. Holmes, *Flannelled Foolishness* (Hollis & Carter, 1957)

W.E. Howard, *Fifty Years' Cricket Reminiscences of a Non-Player* (Lancashire CCC, 1928)

Gerald Howat, *Plum Warner* (Unwin Hyman, 1987)

Martin Howe, *Rockley Wilson* (ACS, 2008)

Simon Hughes, *A Lot of Hard Yakka* (Headline, 1997)

Colin Ingleby-Mackenzie, *Many A Slip* (Oldbourne, 1962)

Steve James, *Third Man to Fatty's Legs* (First Stone, 2004)

Gilbert Jessop, *A Cricketer's Log* (Hodder & Stoughton, 1922)

David Kynaston, *Bobby Abel* (Secker & Warburg, 1982)

Allan Lamb, *My Autobiography* (Coloins Willow, 1996)

Tony Laughton, *Captain of the Crowd* (Boundary Books, 2010)

Frank Lee, *Cricket, Lovely Cricket* (Stanley Paul, 1960)

H.W. Lee, *Forty Years of English Cricket* (Henrry Richardson, 1948)

David Lemmon, *Percy Chapman* (Queen Anne Press, 1985)

David Lemmon, *'Tich' Freeman* (George Allen & Unwin, 1982)

J.K. Lever, *A Cricketer's Cricketer* (Unwin Hyman, 1989)

Brian Luckhurst, *Boot Boy to President* (KOS Media, 2004)

Roy Marshall, *Test Outcast* (Pelham, 1970)

David Matthews, *Derek Shackleton* (Blackberry Downs, 1998)

Colin Milburn, *Largely Cricket* (Stanley Paul, 1968)

Douglas Miller, *Born to Bowl* (Fairfield Books, 2004)

Douglas Miller, *Jack Bond* (ACS, 2010)

Douglas Miller, *M.J.K. Smith* (ACS, 2013)

Don Mosey, *Boycott* (Methuen, 1985)

Patrick Murphy, *'Tiger' Smith* (Readers Union, 1981)

Phil Neale, *A Double Life* (Ringpress, 1990)

Paul Nixon, *Keeping Quiet* (History Press, 2012)

Ian Peebles, *'Patsy' Hendren* (Macmillan, 1969)

Barry Phillips, *Arthur Wellard* (Mayfield, 1996)

Mike Procter, *Mike Procter and Cricket* (Pelham, 1981)

Mark Ramprakash, *Strictly Me* (Mainstream, 2009)

Derek Randall, *The Sun Has Got His Hat On* (Willow, 1984)

Derek Randall, *Rags* (Sport-in-Print, 1992)

Dermot Reeve, *Winning Ways* (Boxtree, 1996)

Brian Rendell, *Walter Robins* (ACS, 2013)

Barry Richards, *The Barry Richards Story* (Faber & Faber, 1978)

Norman Rogers, *Eric Hollies* (Warwickshire, 2002)

Fred Root, *A Cricket Pro's Lot* (Edward Arnold, 1937)

Alan Ross, *Ranji* (Harvill Press, 1983)

Jack Russell, *Unleashed* (Collins Willow, 1997)

Christopher Scoble, *Colin Blythe* (Sports Books, 2005)

Garry Sobers, *My Autobiography* (Headline, 2002)

Richard Streeton, *P.G.H. Fender* (Faber & Faber, 1981)

Maurice Tate, *My Cricketing Reminiscences* (Stanley Paul, 1935)

Fred Titmus, *My Life in Cricket* (John Blake, 2005)

Derek Underwood, *Beating the Bat* (Stanley Paul, 1975)

Peter Walker, *It's Not Just Cricket* (Fairfield Books, 2006)

Johnny Wardle, *Happy Go Johnny* (Robert Hale, 1957)

P.F. Warner, *My Cricketing Life* (Hodder & Stoughton, 1920)

Willie Watson, *Double International* (Stanley Paul, 1956)

S.M.J. Woods, *My Reminiscences* (Chapman & Hall, 1925)

Frank Woolley, *The King of Games* (Stanley Paul, 1935)

Norman Yardley, *Cricket Campaigns* (Stanley Paul, 1950)

Bibliography (2)

Other books

Vernon Addison & Brian Bearshaw,
   Lancashire Cricket at the Top (Stanley Paul, 1971)
John Arlott, *Alletson's Innings* (Epworth Press, 1957)
John Arlott, *Australian Challenge* (Heinemann, 1961)
John Arlott, *John Arlott's Book of Cricketers* (Lutterworth, 1979)
John Arlott, *Cricket in the Counties* (Saturn Press, 1950)
John Arlott, *Gone to the Cricket* (Longmans Green, 1948)
John Arlott, *Gone to the Test Match* (Longmans Green, 1949)
John Arlott, *Vintage Summer* (Eyre & Spottiswoode, 1967)
Trevor Bailey, *Championship Cricket* (Frederick Muller, 1961)
Trevor Bailey, *The Greatest Since My Time* (Hodder, 1989)
John Barclay, *The Appeal of the Championship*
   (Fairfield Books, 2002)
Ralph Barker, *Ten Great Bowlers* (Chatto & Windus, 1967)
Mihir Bose, *Cricket Voices* (Kingswood, 1990)
Dave Bracegirdle, *What Do Points Make?* (Notts CCC, 2010)
Mike Brearley, *The Art of Captaincy* (Hodder & Stoughton, 1985)
Gerald Brodribb, *Hit for Six* (Heinemann, 1960)
Gerald Brodribb, *Next Man In* (Putnam, 1952)
Neville Cardus, *Cricket* (Longmans, Green & Co, 1930)
Neville Cardus, *Days in the Sun* (Grant Richards, 1924)
Neville Cardus, *The Playfair Cardus* (Dickens Press, 1963)
Dudley Carew, *To The Wicket* (Chapman & Hall, 1946)
Peter Cox, *Sixty Summers* (Labatie, 2006)
Keith Farnsworth, *Bramall Lane* (Farnsworth, 1988)
David Foot, *Beyond Bat and Ball* (Good Books, 1993)
David Foot, *Cricket's Unholy Trinity* (Stanley Paul, 1985)
David Foot, *Fragments of Idolatry* (Fairfield Books, 2001)
David Foot & Ivan Ponting, *Sixty Summers* (Fairfield Books, 2006)
David Frith, *By His Own Hand* (Stanley Paul, 1990)
Roy Genders, *League Cricket in England* (Werner Laurie, 1952)
Anthony Gibson, *Of Didcot and the Demon* (Fairfield Books, 2009)
Home Gordon, *Background of Cricket* (Arthur Barker, 1939)
Graham Hardcastle & Chris Ostick,
   Champions – about bloomin' time (Max Books, 2011)
Simon Hughes, *From Minor to Major* (Hodder & Stoughton, 1992)
Neil Jenkinson, *Cricket's Greatest Comeback* (JW McKenzie, 1998)
J.M. Kilburn, *Overthrows* (Stanley Paul, 1975)

David Lemmon, *For the Love of the Game* (Michael Joseph, 1993)
Jeremy Malies, *Great Characters from Cricket's Golden Age*
   (Robson Books, 2000)
Michael Marshall, *Gentlemen and Players* (Grafton, 1987)
Ronald Mason, *Plum Warner's Last Season* (Epworth, 1970)
Ronald Mason, *Sing All A Green Willow* (Epworth, 1967)
Anthony Meredith, *The Demon and the Lobster* (Kingswood, 1987)
Patrick Murphy, *Fifty Incredible Cricket Matches*
   (Stanley Paul, 1987)
Patrick Murphy, *The Centurions* (Fairfield Books, 2009)
Patrick Murphy, *The Spinner's Turn* (J.M. Dent, 1982)
Bruce Murray & Goolam Vahed, *Empire & Cricket*
   (University of South Africa, 2009)
Ian Peebles, *Straight from the Shoulder* (Hutchinson, 1968)
Ian Peebles, *Talking of Cricket* (Museum Press, 1953)
George Plumptre, *Homes of Cricket* (Macdonald, 1988)
Clive Porter, *Kent Cricket Champions* 1906 (Limlow, 2000)
T.C.F. Prittie, *Lancashire Hot-Pot* (Hutchinson, 1949)
T.C.F. Prittie, *Mainly Middlesex* (Hutchinson, 1939)
R.C. Robertson-Glasgow, *Cricket Prints* (Werner Laurie, 1943)
R.C. Robertson-Glasgow, *More Cricket Prints* (Werner Laurie, 1948)
Rowland Ryder, *Cricket Calling* (Faber, 1995)
John Shawcroft, *Golden Mondays* (ACS, 2011)
John Shawcroft, *Local Heroes* (SportsBooks, 2006)
Grenville Simons, *Lillywhite's Legacy* (Wisteria Books, 2004)
E.W. Swanton, *As I Said At The Time* (Collins Willow, 1983)
Peter Thomas, *Yorkshire Cricketers 1839-1939* (Hodgson, 1973)
Gavin Turner, *A Century at Bath* (Broadcast Books, 2001)
Peter Walker, *Cricket Conversations* (Pelham, 1978)
Keith Walmsley, *Brief Candles* (ACS, 2012)
Tony Ward, *Typhoon Tyson to Twenty/20* (Fasirfield Books, 2011)
Tim Wellock, *Summers with Durham* (Caboodle, 2009)
Chris Westcott, *Class of '59* (Mainstream, 2000)
Peter Wynne-Thomas, *Nottinghamshire: Cricket's Double Champions*
   (Heinemann, 1988)
N.W.D. Yardley & J.M. Kilburn, *Homes of Sport – Cricket*
   (Peter Garnett, 1952)
Various authors, *County Champions* (Heinemann, 1982)

I have also had access to the following unpublished works:
Ann Beeching, *Sponsorship in County Cricket* (1972)
David Pracy, *Gentlemen and Players of Essex* (2007)
H.E. Roslyn, *Memories of Gloucestershire Cricket* (1939)
Ken Turner, *My Years at Northamptonshire*
Mike Vockins, *A Ramble Through Cricket*

Acknowledgements

This book could not have been written without a great deal of help from many, many people, and I would like to thank them all. The cricket community is a most generous one, and I hope that I will have the opportunity to repay some of the kindnesses I have received.

I would especially like to thank:

Benj Moorehead, for the great help he has given in researching the county cricket of the last twenty years and for his perceptive feedback on my text;

Rob Taylor, for his skilful work in fine-tuning the images, designing the jacket and advising me on the page layout;

Scyld Berry, for his support and for the crucial role he played in ensuring the financial viability of this book;

Paul Coupar, for his most helpful reading of the manuscript;

John Barclay, for his regular encouragement and guidance;

David Smith, for use of his library and for his always good advice;

Chris Saunders, for allowing me free access to his warehouse of old books and for producing the special limited editions of the book;

Robert Brooke and Peter Wynne-Thomas, two cricket historians who are always generous with their great knowledge;

Ron Deaton, for his ever helpful support;

Roger Mann, for his help with the early photographs;

Graham and Diana Morris, for their help with recent photographs;

Matt Buxton, for help in the sourcing of other photographs;

Peter Griffiths, for supplying such comprehensive statistics;

Douglas Miller, for talking through with me those statistics;

the late Ken Biddulph, for the inspiration he gave me to start down this road of cricket writing back in the 1990s;

and, most of all, Susanna Kendall, design consultant, editor-in-chief and long-suffering supporter.

This book draws on interviews and help which I have received from many, many people, both in the year of its writing and in the years in which I have been exploring cricket history.

In addition to those listed above, I would like to thank all those, living and dead, who have given their time to help me or Benj Moorehead. They include:

David Acfield, Dave Allen, David Allen, Mark Alleyne, Keith Andrew, Bob Appleyard, Trevor Bailey, Bob Barber, Derek Barnard, Michael Barton, Alec Bedser, Don Bennett, Dickie Bird, Jack Birkenshaw, Jack Bond, Roy Booth, David Bowden, Geoffrey Boycott, Rod Bransgrove, Mike Brearley, Vince Broderick, Robin Brodhurst, Dennis Brookes, Alistair Brown, David Byas, Vic Cannings, Tom Cartwright, Alan Castell, Brian Close, Bernie Coleman, Bernie Constable, Geoff Cook, Geoff Cope, Chris Cowdrey, Steven Croft, Brian Crump, Mark Davis, Tony Debenham, Alan Dixon, George Dobell, Dickie Dodds, Aneurin Donald, John Dye, Mike Eagar, Ray East, Vernon East, Geoff Edrich, David Foot, Tony Frost, Mike Gatting, Roger Gibbons, Peter Gibbs, Anthony Gibson, Norman Gifford, Richard Gilliat, Graham Gooch, Tom Graveney, Jimmy Gray, Paul Grayson, Tommy Greenhough, Sam Hain, David Hall, Maurice Hallam, Meriel Harris, Malcolm Heath, Andrew Hignell, Amanda Hill, Eric Hill, Ray Hitchcock, Robin Hobbs, Richard Holdridge, Adam Hollioake, Dick Holste, Martin Horton, Geoffrey Howard, John Howarth, Richard Hutton, Ray Illingworth, Doug Insole, Olive Jenkins, Frank Keating, Roger Knight, Allan Lamb, Brian Langford, Clive Leach, David Leatherdale, John Lever, Tony Lewis, Jake Libby, Charlie Light, John Light, Simon Lister, Malcolm Lorimer, Peter Lush, Ken McEwan, Darren Maddy, Vic Marks, Robin Marlar, Robin Martin-Jenkins, Keith Medlycott, David Millns, Arthur Milton, Howard Milton, Derek Morgan, Charlie Morris, Hugh Morris, John Mortimore, Alan Moss, Tim Munton, Graham Napier, Brendan Nash, Phil Neale, Mick Newell, Derek Newton, Alan Oakman, Brian O'Gorman, Dominic Ostler, Charles Palmer, Jim Parks, Frank Parr, Cyril Perkins, Steve Pittard, Bob Platt, Pat Pocock, David Pracy, Jason Ratcliffe, Alan Rayment, Chris Read, Harold Rhodes, Mark Robinson, Peter Robinson, Peter Roebuck, Chris Rogers, Fred Rumsey, David Ryder, Peter Sainsbury, Nicholas Sharp, Don Shepherd, David Sheppard, Phil Simmons, Reg Simpson, Gladstone Small, Alan Smith, Mike Smith, Martin Speight, Terry Spencer, John Stern, Jim Stewart, Micky Stewart, Bryan Stott, Raman Subba Row, Will Tavaré, Bob Taylor, Ken Taylor, Alan Townsend, Peter Trego, Mike Turner, Shaun Udal, Derek Ufton, Derek Underwood, Doug Verity, Mike Vockins, Mark Wagh, Peter Walker, Mark Wallace, Chris Waters, Allan Watkins, Mike Watkinson, Rupert Webb, Bomber Wells, Vince Wells, Ossie Wheatley, James Whitaker, Peter Wight, Don Wilson, Vic Wilson, Merv Winfield and John Woodcock.

Index

347